BY THE SAME AUTHORS

O Jerusalem!

Is Paris Burning?

Or I'll Dress You in Mourning

Freedom at Midnight

Larry Collins
and
Dominique Lapierre

TARANG PAPERBACKS

TARANG PAPERBACKS
a division of
Vikas Publishing House Pvt Ltd
Regd. Office: 5 Ansari Road, New Delhi 110002
Head Office: **Vikas House, 20/4 Industrial Area, Sahibabad 201010**
Distt. Ghaziabad, U.P. (India)

First published in India, 1976

ISBN 0-7069-2511-4

First edition, 1978
Fiftheenth edition, 1984

Printed at Vikas Publishing House Pvt Ltd (Printing Division)
Sahibabad, U.P. (India)

Contents

Maps

'The responsibility for governing India has been placed by the inscrutable decree of providence upon the shoulders of the British race.'

RUDYARD KIPLING

'The loss of India would be final and fatal to us. It could not fail to be part of a process that would reduce us to the scab of a minor power.'

WINSTON CHURCHILL
to the House of Commons
February 1931

'Long years ago we made a tryst with destiny, and now the time comes when we shall redeem our pledge . . . At the stroke of the midnight hour, while the world sleeps, India will awake to life and freedom. A moment comes, which comes but rarely in history, when we step out from the old to the new, when an age ends, and when the soul of a nation, long suppressed, finds utterance . . .'

JAWAHARLAL NEHRU
to the Indian Constituent Assembly
New Delhi, August 14, 1947

Prologue

The rude arch of yellow basalt thrusts its haughty form into the city's skyline just above a little promontory lapped by the waters of the Bay of Bombay. The Bay's gentle waves barely stir the sullen green sludge of debris and garbage that encircles the concrete apron sloping down from the arch to the water's edge. A strange world mingles there in the shadows cast by its soaring span: snake charmers and fortune tellers, beggars and tourists, dishevelled hippies lost in a torpor of sloth and drug, the destitute and dying of a cluttered metropolis. Barely a head is raised to contemplate the inscription, still clearly legible, stretched along the summit: 'Erected to commemorate the landing in India of their imperial majesties, George V and Queen Mary on the second of December MCMXI.'

Yet, once, that vaulting Gateway of India was the Arch of Triumph of the greatest empire the world has ever known. To generations of Britons, its massive form was the first glimpse, caught from a steamer's deck, of the storied shores for which they had abandoned their Midlands villages and Scottish hills. Soldiers and adventurers, businessmen and administrators, they had passed through its portals, come to keep the *Pax Britannica* in the empire's proudest possession, to exploit a conquered continent, to take up the White Man's burden with the unshakeable conviction that theirs was a race born to rule, and their empire an entity destined to endure.

All that seems so distant now. Today, the Gateway of India is just another pile of stone, at one with Nineveh and Tyre, a forgotten monument to an era that ended in its shadows barely a quarter of a century ago.

1

'A Race Destined to Govern and Subdue'

London, New Year's Day, 1947

It was the winter of a great nation's discontent. An air of melancholia hung like a chill fog over London. Rarely, if ever, had Britain's capital ushered in a New Year in a mood so bleak, so morose. Hardly a home in the city that festive morning could furnish enough hot water to allow a man to shave or a woman to cover the bottom of her wash-basin. Londoners had greeted the New Year in bedrooms so cold their breath had drifted on the air like puffs of smoke. Precious few of them had greeted it with a hangover. Whisky, in the places where it had been available the night before for New Year's Eve celebrations, had cost £8 a bottle.

The streets were almost deserted. The passers-by hurrying down their pavements were grim, joyless creatures, threadbare in old uniforms or clothes barely holding together after eight years of make-do and mend. What few cars there were darted about like fugitive phantoms guiltily consuming Britain's rare and rationed petrol. A special stench, the odour of post-war London, permeated the streets. It was the rancid smell of charred ruins drifting up like an autumn mist from thousands of bombed-out buildings.

And yet, that sad, joyless city was the capital of a conquering nation. Only seventeen months before, the British had emerged victorious from mankind's most terrible conflict. Their achievements, their courage in adversity then, had inspired an admiration such as the world had never before accorded them.

The cost of their victory, however, had almost vanquished the British. Britain's industry was crippled, her exchequer bankrupt, her once haughty pound sterling surviving only on injections of American and Canadian dollars, her Treasury unable to pay the staggering debt she'd run up to finance the war. Foundries and factories were closing everywhere. Over two million Britons were unemployed. Coal production was lower than it had been a decade earlier and, as a result, every day, some part of Britain was without electric power for hours.

For Londoners, the New Year beginning would be the eighth consecutive year they'd lived under severe rationing of almost every product they consumed: food, fuel, drinks, energy, shoes, clothing. 'Starve and shiver,' had become the byword of a people who'd defeated Hitler proclaiming 'V for Victory' and 'Thumbs Up'.

Only one family in fifteen had been able to find and afford a Christmas turkey for the holiday season just past. Many a child's stocking had been empty that Christmas eve. The treasury had slapped a 100% purchase tax on toys. The word most frequently scrawled on the windows of London's shops was 'No': 'No potatoes', 'No logs', 'No coal', 'No cigarettes', 'No meat'. Indeed, the reality confronting Britain that New Year's morning had been captured in one cruel sentence by her greatest economist. 'We are a poor nation,' John Maynard Keynes had told his countrymen the year before, 'and we must learn to live accordingly.'

Yet, if Londoners did not have enough hot water that morning to make a cup of tea with which to welcome the New Year, they had something else. They could, because they were English, lay claim to a blue and gold document which would guarantee their entry to almost a quarter of the earth's surface, a British passport. No other people in the world enjoyed such a privilege. That most extraordinary assemblage of dominions, territories, protectorates, associated states and colonies which was the British Empire, remained on this New Year's Day 1947, largely intact. The lives of 560 million people, Tamils and Chinese, Bushmen and Hottentots, pre-Dravidian aborigines and Melanesians, Australians and Canadians, were still influenced by the actions of those Englishmen shivering in their unheated London homes. They could, that morning, claim domain over almost three hundred pieces of the earth's surface from entities as small and as unknown as Bird Island, Bramble Cay and Wreck Reef to great, populous stretches of Africa and Asia. Britain's proudest boast was still true: every time Big Ben's chimes tolled out over the ruins of Central London that New Year's Day, at sunrise, somewhere in the British Empire, a Union Jack was riding up a flagstaff.

No Caesar or Charlemagne ever presided over a comparable realm. For three centuries its scarlet stains spreading over the maps of the world had prompted the dreams of schoolboys, the avarice of her merchants, the ambitions of her adventurers. Its raw materials had fuelled the factories of the Industrial Revolution, and its territories furnished a protected market for their goods. 'Heavy with gold, black with industrial soot, red with the blood of conquest,' the Empire had made in its time a little island kingdom of less than 50 million people the most powerful nation on earth, and London the capital of the world.

Now, almost furtively, a black Austin Princess slipped down the deserted streets of that capital towards the heart of the city. As it passed Buckingham Palace and turned on to the Mall, its sole passenger stared moodily out at the imperial boulevard passing before his eyes. How often, he reflected, had Britain celebrated the triumphs of empire along its course. Half a century earlier, on 22 June 1897, Queen Victoria's carriage had come clattering down its length for the festival that had marked its zenith, her Diamond Jubilee. Gurkhas, Sikhs, Pathans, Hausas from Africa's Gold Coast, the Fuzzy Wuzzies of the Sudan, Cypriots, Jamaicans, Malaysians, Hong Kong Chinese, Borneo headhunters, Australians and New Zealanders, South Africans and Canadians had all in their turn marched down the Mall to the plaudits of that energetic race to whose empire they'd belonged. All that had represented an extraordinary dream for those Englishmen and the generations that had succeeded them along the Mall. Now even that was to be snatched away from them. The age of imperialism was dead and it was in recognition of that historic inevitability that the black Austin Princess was running its lonely course down the avenue which had witnessed so many of its grandiose ceremonies.

Its passenger sank back in his seat. His eyes, this holiday morning, should have been gazing on a different sight, a sun-drenched Swiss ski slope. An urgent summons, however, had interrupted his Christmas vacation and sent him to Zurich where he'd boarded the RAF aircraft which had just deposited him at Northolt Airport.

His car passed Parliament Street and drove down a narrow lane up to what was probably the most photographed doorway in the world, Number 10 Downing Street. For six years, the world had associated its simple wooden frame with the image of a man in a black homburg, a cigar in his mouth, a cane in his hands, fingers upthrust in a 'V' for Victory. Winston Churchill had fought two great battles while he'd lived in that house, one to defeat the Axis, the other to defend the British Empire.

Now, however, a new Prime Minister waited inside 10 Downing Street, a Socialist don whom Churchill had disparaged as 'a modest man with much to be modest about'.

Clement Attlee and his Labour Party had come to office publicly committed to begin the dismemberment of the Empire. For Attlee, for England, that historic process had inevitably to begin by extending freedom to the vast, densely populated land Britain still ruled from the Khyber Pass to Cape Comorin – India. That superb and shameful institution, the British Raj, was the cornerstone and justification of the Empire, its most remarkable accomplishment and its most constant care. India with its Bengal Lancers and its silk-robed Maharajas, its tiger hunts and its polo maidans, its pugree helmets and its chota pegs of whisky, its royal elephants caparisoned in gold and its starving *sadhus*, its mulligatawny soups and haughty *mem-sahibs*, had incarnated the imperial dream. The handsome rear-admiral stepping from his car had been called to 10 Downing Street to end that dream.

Louis Francis Albert Victor Nicholas Mountbatten, Viscount Mountbatten of Burma was, at 46, one of the most noted figures in England. He was a big man, over six feet tall, but not a trace of flab hung from his zealously exercised waist line. Despite the terrible burdens he'd carried in the past six years, the face, familiar to millions of the readers of his country's penny press, was remarkably free of the scars of strain and tension. His features, so astonishingly regular that they seemed, almost, to have been conceived as a prototype of facial design, his undiminished shock of dark hair setting off his hazel eyes, conspired to make him seem a good five years younger than he was this January morning.

Mountbatten knew well why he'd been summoned to London. Since his return from his post as Supreme Allied Commander South-East Asia, he'd been a frequent visitor to Downing Street as a consultant on the affairs of the nations which had fallen under SEAC's command. On his last visit, however, the Prime Minister's questions had quickly focused on a nation that had not been part of his theatre of operations, India. The young admiral had suddenly had a 'very nasty, very uneasy feeling'. His premonition had been justified. Attlee intended to name him Viceroy of India. The Viceroy's was the most important post in the empire, the office from which a long succession of Englishmen had held domain over the destinies of a fifth of mankind. Mountbatten's task, however, would not be to rule India from that office. His assignment would be one of the most painful an Englishman could be asked to undertake, to give it up.

Mountbatten wanted no part of the job. He entirely endorsed the idea that the time had come for Britain to leave India. His heart, however, rebelled at the thought that it would be he who would be called on to sever the ancient links binding Britain and the bulwark of her empire. To discourage Attlee he had thrown up a whole series of demands, major and minor, from the number of secretaries he'd be allowed to take with him to the aircraft, the York MW102 he'd employed in Southeast Asia, which would be placed at his disposal. Attlee, to his dismay, had agreed them all. Now, entering the Cabinet Room, the admiral still hoped somehow to resist Attlee's efforts to force the Indian assignment on him.

With his sallow complexion, his indifferently trimmed moustache, his shapeless tweed suits which seemed blissfully ignorant of a pressing iron's caress, the man waiting for Mountbatten exuded in his demeanour something of that grey and dreary city through which the admiral's car had just passed. That he, a Labour Prime Minister, should want a glamorous, polo-playing member of the royal family to fill the most critical position in the empire that Labour was pledged to dismantle, seemed, at first sight, an incongruous idea.

There was much more to Mountbatten, however, than his public image indicated. The decorations on his naval uniform were proof of that. The public might consider him a pillar of the Establishment; the Establishment themselves tended to regard Mountbatten and his wife as dangerous radicals. His command in Southeast Asia had given him a knowledge of Asian nationalist movements few in England could match. He had dealt with the supporters of Ho Chi Minh in Indo-China, Sukarno in Indonesia, Aung San in Burma, Chinese Communists in Malaya, unruly trade unionists in Singapore. Realizing they represented Asia's future, he had sought accommodations with them rather than, as his staff and Allies had urged, trying to suppress them. The nationalist movement with which he would have to deal if he went to India was the oldest and most unusual of them all. In a quarter of a century of inspired agitation and protest, its leadership had forced history's greatest empire to the decision Attlee's Party had taken: let Britain leave India in good time rather than be driven out by the forces of history and armed rebellion.

The Prime Minister began by reviewing the Indian scene. The Indian situation, he said, was deteriorating with every passing day and the time for urgent decision was at hand. It was one of the paradoxes of history that at this critical juncture, when Britain was at last ready to give India her freedom, she could not find a way to do so. What should have been Britain's finest hour in India seemed destined to become a nightmare of unsurpassable horror. She had conquered and ruled India with what was, by colonial standards, relatively little bloodshed. Her leaving it threatened to produce an explosion of violence that would dwarf in scale and magnitude anything India had experienced in three and a half centuries.

The root of the problem was the age old antagonism between India's 300 million Hindus and 100 million Moslems. Sustained by tradition, by antipathetic religions, by economic differences, subtly exacerbated through the years by Britain's own policy of Divide and Rule, their conflict had reached boiling point. The Moslem leaders now demanded that Britain rip apart the unity she had so painstakingly erected to give them an Islamic state of their own. The cost of denying them their state, they warned, would be the bloodiest civil war in Asian history.

Just as determined to resist their demands were the leaders of the Congress Party representing most of India's 300 million Hindus. To them, the division of the sub-continent would be a mutilation of their historic homeland almost sacrilegious in its nature.

Britain was trapped between those two apparently irreconcilable positions, sinking slowly into a quagmire from which she seemed unable to extricate herself. Time and again British efforts to resolve the problem had failed. So desperate had the situation become, that the present Viceroy, an honest, forthright soldier, Field-Marshal Sir Archibald Wavell, had just submitted to the Attlee government his last-ditch recommendations. Should all else fail, he suggested the British announce 'we propose to withdraw from India in our own method and in our own time and with due regard to our own interests; and that we will regard any attempt to interfere with our programme as an act of war which we will meet with all the resources at our command.'

Britain and India, Attlee told Mountbatten, were heading towards a major disaster. The situation could not be allowed to go on. Wavell was a man of painfully few words, and, Attlee said, he'd been unable to establish any real contact with his loquacious Indian interlocutors.

A fresh face, a fresh approach was desperately needed if a crisis were to be averted. Each morning, Attlee revealed, brought its batch of cables to the India Office announcing an outburst of wanton savagery in some new corner of India. It was, he indicated, Mountbatten's solemn duty to take the post he'd been offered.*

A sense of foreboding had been filling Mountbatten as he listened to the Prime Minister's words. He still thought India was 'an absolutely hopeless proposition'. He liked and admired Wavell with whom he'd often discussed India's problems during his regular

* Although Mountbatten didn't know it, the idea of sending him to India had been suggested to Attlee by the man at the Prime Minister's side, his Chancellor of the Exchequer, Sir Stafford Cripps. It had come up at a secret conversation in London in December, between Cripps and Krishna Menon, an outspoken Indian left-winger and intimate of the Congress leader Jawaharlal Nehru. Menon had suggested to Cripps and Nehru that Congress saw little hope of progress in India so long as Wavell was Viceroy. In response to a query from the British leader, he had advanced the name of a man Nehru held in the highest regard, Louis Mountbatten. Aware that Mountbatten's usefulness would be destroyed if India's Moslem leaders learned of the genesis of his appointment the two men had agreed to reveal the details of their talk to no one. Menon revealed the details of his conversation with Cripps in a series of conversations with one of the authors in New Delhi in February 1973, a year before his death.

visits to Delhi as Supreme Allied Commander in Southeast Asia.

Wavell had all the right ideas, Mountbatten thought. If he couldn't do it, what's the point of my trying to take it on? Yet he was beginning to understand there was no escape. He was going to be forced to accept a job in which the risk of failure was enormous and in which he could easily shatter the brilliant reputation he'd brought out of the war.

If Attlee was going to force it on him, however, Mountbatten was determined to impose on the Prime Minister the political conditions that would give him at least some hopes of success. His talks with Wavell had given him an idea what they were.

He would not accept, he told the Prime Minister, unless the government agreed to make an unequivocal public announcement of the precise date on which British rule in India would terminate. Only that, Mountbatten felt, would convince India's sceptical intelligentsia that Britain was really leaving and infuse her leaders with the sense of urgency needed to get them into realistic negotiations.*

Second, he demanded something no other Viceroy had ever dreamed of asking, full powers to carry out his assignment without reference to London and, above all, without constant interference from London. The Attlee government could give the young admiral his final destination but he, and he alone, was going to set his course and run the ship along the way.

'Surely,' Attlee asked, 'you're not asking for plenipotentiary powers above His Majesty's Government, are you?'

'I am afraid, Sir,' answered Mountbatten, 'that that is exactly what I am asking. How can I possibly negotiate with the Cabinet constantly breathing down my neck?'

A stunned silence followed his words. Mountbatten watched with satisfaction as the nature of his breathtaking demand registered on the Prime Minister's face, hoping, as he did, that it would prompt Attlee to withdraw his offer.

Instead, the Prime Minister indicated with a sigh his willingness to accept even that. An hour later, shoulders sagging, Mountbatten emerged from the portal of Downing Street. He knew he was condemned to become India's last Viceroy, the executioner, in a sense, of his countrymen's fondest imperial dream.

Getting back into his car, a strange thought struck him. It was exactly seventy years, almost to the hour, from the moment his own great-grandmother had been proclaimed Empress of India on a plain

* Wavell too had recommended a time limit to Attlee during a London visit in December 1946.

outside Delhi. India's princes, assembled for the occasion, had begged the heavens that day that Queen Victoria's 'power and sovereignty' might 'remain steadfast forever'.

Now, on this New Year's morning one of her great-grandsons had initiated the process which would fix the date on which 'forever' would come to an end.

* * *

History's most grandiose accomplishments can sometimes have the most banal of origins. Great Britain was set on the road to the great colonial adventure for five miserable shillings. They represented the increase in the price of a pound of pepper proclaimed by the Dutch privateers who controlled the spice trade.

Incensed at what they considered a wholly unwarranted gesture, twenty-four merchants of the City of London gathered on the afternoon of 24 September 1599, in a decrepit building on Leadenhall Street. Their purpose was to found a modest trading firm with an initial capital of £72,000 subscribed by 125 shareholders. Only the simplest of concerns, profit, inspired their enterprise which, expanded and transformed, would ultimately become the most noteworthy creation of the age of imperialism, the British Raj.

The Company received its official sanction on 31 December 1599, when Queen Elizabeth I signed a royal charter assigning it exclusive trading rights with all countries beyond the Cape of Good Hope for an initial period of fifteen years. Eight months later, a 500-ton galleon named the *Hector* dropped anchor in the little port of Surat, north of Bombay. It was 24 August 1600. The British had arrived in India. Their initial landing was a modest one. It came in the solitary figure of William Hawkins, Captain of the *Hector*, a dour old seaman who was more pirate than explorer. Hawkins marched off into the interior, prepared to find rubies as big as pigeons' eggs; endless stands of pepper, ginger, indigo, cinnamon; trees whose leaves were so enormous that the shade they cast could cover an entire family, potions derived from elephants' testicles to give him eternal youth.

There was little of that India along the Captain's march to Agra. There, however, his encounter with the great Moghul compensated for the hardships of his journey. He found himself face to face with a sovereign beside whom Queen Elizabeth appeared the ruler of a provincial hamlet. Reigning over 70 million subjects, the Emperor Jehangir was the world's richest and most powerful monarch, the fourth and last of India's great Moghul rulers.

The first Englishman to reach his court was greeted with a gesture which might have disconcerted the 125 worthy shareholders of the

East India Trading Company. The Moghul made him a member of the Royal Household and offered him as a welcoming gift the most beautiful girl in his harem, an Armenian Christian.

Fortunately, benefits of a nature more likely to inspire his employer's esteem than the enrichment of his sex life, also grew out of Captain Hawkins' arrival in Agra. Jehangir signed an imperial firman authorizing the East India Company to open trading depots north of Bombay. Its success was rapid and impressive. Soon, two ships a month were unloading mountains of spices, gum, sugar, raw silk and Muslin cotton on the docks along the Thames and sailing off with holds full of English manufactures. A deluge of dividends, some of them as high as 200%, came pouring down on the firm's fortunate shareholders.

The British, generally, were welcomed by the native rulers and population. Unlike the zealous Spaniards who were conquering South America in the name of a redeeming God, the British stressed that it was in the name of another God, Mammon, that they had come to India. 'Trade not territory', the Company's officers never ceased repeating, was their policy.

Inevitably, however, as their trading activities grew, the Company's officers became enmeshed in local politics and forced, in order to protect their expanding commerce, to intervene in the squabbles of the petty sovereigns on whose territories they operated. Thus began the irreversible process which would lead England to conquer India almost by inadvertence. On 23 June 1757, marching through a drenching rainfall at the head of 900 Englishmen of the 39th Foot and 2000 Indian sepoys, an audacious general named Robert Clive routed the army of a troublesome Nawab in the rice paddies outside a Bengali village called Plassey.

Clive's victory opened the gates of northern India. With it, the British conquest of India truly started. Their merchants gave way to the builders of empire; and territory, not trade, became the primary concern of the British in India.

The century that followed was one of conquest. Although they were specifically instructed by London to avoid 'schemes of conquest and territorial expansion', a succession of ambitious governor generals relentlessly embraced the opposite policy. In less than a century a company of traders was metamorphosed into a sovereign power, its accountants and traders into generals and governors, its race for dividends into a struggle for imperial authority. Without having set out to do so, Britain had become the successor to the Moghul Emperors.

From the outset, her intent was always one day to relinquish the possessions she had so inadvertently acquired. As early as 1818, the Marquess of Hastings noted: 'A time, not very remote, will arrive when England will, on sound principles of policy, wish to relinquish the domination which she has gradually and unintentionally assumed over this country.' Empires, however, were more naturally acquired than disposed of and the moment foreseen by Hastings was to be considerably more remote than the Marquess might have imagined.

British rule nonetheless brought India benefits of considerable magnitude, *Pax Britannica* and reasonable facsimiles of Britain's own legal, administrative and educational institutions. Above all, it gave India the magnificent gift which was to become the common bond of its diverse peoples and the conduit of their revolutionary aspirations, the English language.

The first manifestation of those aspirations came in the savage Mutiny in 1857. Its most important result was an abrupt change in the manner in which Britain governed India. After 258 years of fruitful activities, the Honourable East India Company's existence was terminated. Responsibility for the destiny of 300 million Indians was transferred to the hands of a 39-year-old woman whose tubby figure would incarnate the vocation of the British race to dominate the world, Queen Victoria. Henceforth, Britain's authority was to be exercised by the crown, represented in India by a kind of nominated king ruling a fifth of humanity, the Viceroy.

With that change began the period the world would most often associate with the British Indian experience, the Victorian era. Its predominant philosophy was a concept frequently enunciated by the man who was its self-appointed poet laureate – Rudyard Kipling – that white Englishmen were uniquely fitted to rule 'lesser breeds without the law'. The responsibility for governing India, Kipling proclaimed, had been 'placed by the inscrutable decree of providence upon the shoulders of the British race'.

Ultimately, responsibility was exercised at any given time by a little band of brothers, 2000 members of the Indian Civil Service, the ICS, and 10,000 British officers of the Indian Army. Their authority over 300 million people was sustained by 60,000 British soldiers and 200,000 men of the Indian Army. No statistics could measure better than those the nature of Britain's rule in India after 1857 or the manner in which the Indian masses were long prepared to accept it.

The India of those men was that picturesque, romantic India of Kipling's tales. Theirs was the India of gentlemen officers in plumed shakos riding at the head of their turbaned sepoys; of district magistrates lost in the torrid wastes of the Deccan; of sumptuous imperial balls in the Himalayan summer capital of Simla; cricket matches on the manicured lawns of Calcutta's Bengal Club; polo games on the sunburnt plains of Rajasthan; tiger hunts in Assam; young men sitting down to dinner in black ties in a tent in the middle of the jungle, solemnly proposing their toast in port to the King Emperor while jackals howled in the darkness around them; officers in scarlet tunics pursuing rebellious Pathan tribesmen in the sleet or unbearable heat of the Frontier; the India of a caste unassailably certain of its superiority, sipping whiskies and soda on the veranda of its Europeans Only Clubs. Those men were, generally, the products of families of impeccable breeding but less certain wealth; the offspring of good Anglican country churchmen; talented second sons of the landed aristocracy; sons of schoolmasters, classics professors and above all of the previous generation of the British in India. They mastered on the playing fields and in the classrooms of Eton, Harrow, Charterhouse, Haileybury, the disciplines that would fit them to rule an empire: excellence at 'games', a delight in 'manly pursuits', the ability to absorb the whack of a headmaster's cane or declaim the Odes of Horace and the verses of Homer. 'India', noted James S. Mill, 'was a vast system of outdoor relief for Britain's upper classes.'

It represented challenge and adventure, and its boundless spaces an arena in which England's young men could find a fulfilment their island's more restricted shores might deny them. They arrived on the docks of Bombay at nineteen or twenty, barely able to raise a stubble on their chins. They went home thirty-five or forty years later, their bodies scarred by bullets, by disease, a panther's claws or a fall on the polo field, their faces ravaged by too much sun and too much whisky, but proud of having lived their part of a romantic legend.

A young man's adventure usually began in the theatrical confusion of Bombay's Victoria Station. There, under its red brick neo-Gothic arches, he discovered for the first time the face of the country in which he'd chosen to spend his life. It was usually a shock, a whirlpool of frantically scurrying, shoving, shouting human beings, darting in and out among jumbles of cases, valises, bundles, sacks, bales all scattered in the halls of the station without any apparent regard for order. The heat, the crisp smell of spices and urine evaporating in the sun were overwhelming. Men in sagging *dhotis* and flapping night shirts, women in saris, bare arms and feet jangling with the gold bracelets on their wrists and ankles, Sikh soldiers in scarlet turbans, emaciated *sadhus* in orange and yellow loincloths, deformed children and beggars thrusting out their stunted limbs for baksheesh, all assailed him. The relief of a young lieutenant or newly-appointed officer of the ICS on boarding the dark green cars of the Frontier Mail or the Hyderabad Express was usually enormous. Inside, behind the curtains of the first-class carriages, a familiar world waited, a world of deep brown upholstered seats and a dining-car with fresh white linen and champagne chilling in silver buckets; above all, a world in which the only Indian face he was likely to encounter was that of the conductor collecting his tickets. That was the first lesson a young officer learned. England ran India, but the English dwelt apart.

A harsh schooling awaited the empire's young servants at the end of their first passage to India. They were sent to remote posts, covered by primitive roads and jungle tracks, inhabited, if at all, by only a few Europeans. By the time they were twenty-four or twenty-five, they often found themselves with sole responsibility for handing down justice to and administering the lives of a million or more human beings, in areas sometimes larger than Scotland.

His apprenticeship in those remote districts eventually qualified a young officer to take his privileged place in one of those green and pleasant islands from which the aristocracy of the Raj ran India, 'cantonments', golden ghettos of British rule appended like foreign bodies to India's major cities.

Inevitably, each enclave included its green expanse of garden, its slaughterhouse, its bank, its shops and a squat stone church, a proud little replica of those in Dorset or Surrey. Its heart was always the same: an institution that seemed to grow up wherever more than two Englishmen gathered, a club. There, in the cool of the afternoon, the British of the cantonment could gather to play tennis on their well-kept grass courts, or slip into white flannels for a cricket match. At the sacred hour of sundown, they sat out on their cool lawns or on their rambling verandas while white-robed servants glided past with their 'sundowners', the first whisky of the evening.

The parties and receptions in imperial India's principal cities – Bombay, Calcutta, Lahore, Delhi, Simla – were lavish affairs. 'Everyone with any standing had a ballroom and a drawing-room at least eighty feet long,' wrote one *grande dame* who lived in Victorian India. 'In those days, there were none of those horrible buffets where people go to a table with a plate and stand around eating with whomsoever they choose. The average private dinner was for thirty-five or forty with a servant for each guest. Shopkeepers and commercial people were never invited nor, of course, did one ever see an Indian socially, anywhere.

'Nothing was as important as precedence and the deadly sin was to ignore it. Ah, the sudden arctic air that could sweep over a dinner party if the wife of an ICS joint secretary should find herself seated below an army officer of rank inferior to that of her husband.'

Much of the tone of Victorian India was set by the '*memsahibs*', the British wives. To a large extent, the social separation of the English and the Indians was their doing. Their purpose, perhaps, was to shield their men from the exotic temptations of their Indian sisters, a temptation to which the first generations of Englishmen in India had succumbed with zest, leaving behind a new Anglo-Indian society suspended between two worlds.

The great pastime of the British in India was sport. A love of cricket, tennis, squash and hockey would be, with the English language, the most enduring heritage they would leave behind. Golf was introduced in Calcutta in 1829, 30 years before it reached New York, and the world's highest course laid out in the Himalayas at 11,000 feet. No golf bag was considered more chic on those courses than one made of an elephant's penis – provided, of course, its owner had shot the beast himself.

The British played in India but they died there, too, in very great numbers, often young. Every cantonment church had its adjacent graveyard to which the little community might carry its regular flow of dead, victims of India's cruel climate, her peculiar hazards, her epidemics of malaria, cholera, jungle fever. No more poignant account of the British in India was ever written than that inscribed upon the tombstones of those cemeteries.

Even in death India was faithful to its legends. Lt St John Shawe, of the Royal Horse Artillery, 'died of wounds received from a panther on 12 May 1866, at Chindwara'. Maj. Archibald Hibbert, died 15 June 1902, near Raipur after 'being gored by a bison', and Harris McQuaid was 'trampled by an elephant' at Saugh, 6 June 1902. Thomas Henry Butler, an Accountant in the Public Works Department, Jubbulpore, had the misfortune in 1897 to be 'eaten by a tiger in Tilman Forest'.

Indian service had its bizarre hazards. Sister Mary of the Church of England Foreign Missionary Services died at the age of 33, 'Killed while teaching at the Mission School Sinka when a beam eaten through by white ants fell on her head'. Major General Henry Marion Durand of the Royal Engineers, met his death on New Year's Day 1871 'in consequence of injuries received from a fall from a Howdah while passing his elephant through Durand Gate, Tonk'. Despite his engineering background, the general had failed that morning to reach a just appreciation of the difference in height between the archway and his elephant. There proved to be room under it for the elephant, but none for him.

No sight those graveyards offered was sadder, nor more poignantly revealing of the human price the British paid for their Indian adventure, than their rows upon rows of undersized graves. They crowded every cemetery in India in appalling numbers. They were the graves of children, children and infants killed in a climate for which they had not been bred, by diseases they would never have known in their native England.

Sometimes a lone tomb, sometimes three or four in a row, those of an entire family wiped out by cholera or jungle fever, the epitaphs upon those graves were a parents' heartbreak frozen in stone: 'In memory of poor little Willy, the beloved and only child of Bomber William Talbot and Margaret Adelaide Talbot, the Royal Horse Brigade, Born Delhi 14 December 1862. Died Delhi 17 July 1863.'

In Asigarh, two stones side by side offer for eternity the measure of what England's glorious imperial adventure meant to many an ordinary Englishman. '19 April 1845. Alexander, 7-month-old son of Conductor Johnson and Martha Scott. Died of cholera,' reads the first. The second, beside it, reads: '30 April 1845, William John, 4-year-old son of Conductor Johnson and Martha Scott. Died of cholera.' Under them, on a larger stone, their grieving parents chiselled a last farewell:

> One blessing, one sire, one womb
> Their being gave.
> They had one mortal sickness
> And share one grave
> Far from an England they never knew.

Obscure clerks or dashing blades, those generations of Britons policed and administered India as no one before them had.

Their rule was paternalistic, that of the old public schoolmaster disciplining an unruly band of boys, forcing on them the education he was sure was good for them. With an occasional exception they were able and incorruptible, determined to administer India in its own best interests – but it was always they who decided what those interests were, not the Indians they governed.

Their great weakness was the distance from which they exercised their authority, the terrible smugness setting them apart from those they ruled. Never was that attitude of racial superiority summed up more succinctly than by a former officer of the Indian Civil Service in a parliamentary debate at the turn of the century. There was, he said, 'a cherished conviction shared by every Englishman in India, from the highest to the lowest, by the planter's assistant in his lonely bungalow and by the editor in the full light of his presidency town, from the Chief Commissioner in charge of an important province to the Viceroy upon his throne – the conviction in every man that he belongs to a race which God has destined to govern and subdue'.

The massacre of 680,000 members of that race in the trenches of World War I wrote an end to the legend of a certain India. A whole generation of young men who might have patrolled the Frontier, administered the lonely districts or galloped their polo ponies down the long maidans was left behind in Flanders fields. From 1918 recruiting for the Indian Civil Service became increasingly difficult. Increasingly, Indians were accepted into the ranks both of the civil service and the officer corps.

On New Year's Day 1947, barely a thousand British members of the Indian Civil Service remained in India, still somehow holding 400 million people in their administrative grasp. They were the last standard bearers of an elite that had outlived its time, condemned at last by a secret conversation in London and the inexorable currents of history.

2

'Walk Alone, Walk Alone'

Srirampur, Noakhali, New Year's Day, 1947

Six thousand miles from Downing Street, in a village of the Gangetic Delta above the Bay of Bengal, an elderly man stretched out on the dirt floor of a peasant's hut. It was exactly twelve noon. As he did every day at that hour, he reached up for the dripping wet cotton sack that an assistant offered him. Dark splotches of the mud packed inside it oozed through the bag's porous folds. The man carefully patted the sack on to his abdomen. Then he took a second, smaller bag and stuck it on his bald head.

He seemed, lying there on the floor, a fragile little creature. The appearance was deceptive. That wizened 77-year-old man beaming out from under his mudpack had done more to topple the British Empire than any man alive. It was because of him that a British Prime Minister had finally been obliged to send Queen Victoria's great-grandson to New Delhi to find a way to give India her freedom.

Mohandas Karamchand Gandhi was an unlikely revolutionary, the gentle prophet of the world's most extraordinary liberation movement. Beside him, carefully polished, were the dentures he wore only when eating and the steel-rimmed glasses through which he usually peered out at the world. He was a tiny man, barely five feet tall, weighing 114 pounds; all arms and legs like an adolescent whose trunk has yet to rival the growth of his limbs. Nature had meant Gandhi's face to be ugly. His ears flared out from his oversized head like the handles of a sugar bowl. His nose buttressed by squat, flaring nostrils thrust its heavy beak over a sparse white moustache. Without his dentures, his full lips collapsed over his toothless gums. Yet Gandhi's face radiated a peculiar beauty because it was constantly animated, reflecting with the quickly shifting patterns of a magic lantern his changing moods and his impish humour.

To a century fraught with violence, Gandhi had offered an alternative, his doctrine of *ahimsa* – non-violence. He had used it to mobilize the masses of India to drive England from the sub-continent with a moral crusade instead of an armed rebellion, prayers instead of machine-gun fire, disdainful silence instead of the fracas of terrorists' bombs.

While Western Europe had echoed to the harangues of ranting

demagogues and shrieking dictators, Gandhi had stirred the multitudes of the world's most populous area without raising his voice. It was not with the promise of power or fortune that he had summoned his followers to his banner, but with a warning: 'Those who are in my company must be ready to sleep upon the bare floor, wear coarse clothes, get up at unearthly hours, subsist on uninviting, simple food, even clean their own toilets.' Instead of gaudy uniforms and jangling medals, he had dressed his followers in clothes of coarse, homespun cotton. That costume, however, had been as instantly identifiable, as psychologically effective in welding together those who wore it, as the brown or black shirts of Europe's dictators.

His means of communicating with his followers were primitive. He wrote much of his correspondence himself in longhand, and he talked: to his disciples, to prayer meetings, to the caucuses of his Congress party. He employed none of the techniques for conditioning the masses to the dictates of a demagogue or a clique of ideologues. Yet, his message had penetrated a nation bereft of modern communications because Gandhi had a genius for the simple gesture that spoke to India's soul. Those gestures were all unorthodox. Paradoxically, in a land ravaged by cyclical famine, where hunger had been a malediction for centuries, the most devastating tactic Gandhi had devised was the simple act of depriving himself of food – a fast. He had humbled Great Britain by sipping water and bicarbonate of soda.

God-obsessed India had recognized in his frail silhouette, in the instinctive brilliance of his acts, the promise of a Mahatma – a Great Soul – and followed where he'd led. He was indisputably one of the galvanic figures of his century. To his followers, he was a saint. To the British bureaucrats whose hour of departure he'd hastened, he was a conniving politician, a bogus Messiah whose non-violent crusade always ended in violence and whose fasts unto death always stopped short of death's door. Even a man as kind-hearted as Wavell, detested him as a 'malevolent old politician . . . Shrewd, obstinate, domineering, double-tongued', with 'little true saintliness in him'.

Few of the English who'd negotiated with Gandhi had liked him; fewer still had understood him. Their puzzlement was understandable. He was a strange blend of great moral principles and quirky obsessions. He was quite capable of interrupting their serious political discussions with a discourse on the benefits of sexual continence or a daily salt and water enema.

Wherever Gandhi went, it was said, there was the capital of India. Its capital this New Year's Day was the tiny Bengali village of Srirampur where the Mahatma lay under his mudpacks, exercising his authority over an enormous continent without the benefit of radio, electricity or running water, thirty miles by foot from the nearest telephone or telegraph line.

The region of Noakhali in which Srirampur was set, was one of the most inaccessible in India, a jigsaw of tiny islands in the water-logged delta formed by the Ganges and the Brahmaputra rivers. Barely forty miles square, it was a dense thicket of two and a half million human beings, 80% of them Moslems. They lived crammed into villages divided by canals, creeks and streams, reached by rowing-boat, by hand-poled ferries, by rope, log or bamboo bridges swaying dangerously over the rushing waters which poured through the region.

New Year's Day 1947 in Srirampur should have been an occasion of intense satisfaction for Gandhi. He stood that day on the brink of achieving the goal he'd fought for most of his life: India's freedom.

Yet, as he approached the glorious climax of his struggle, Gandhi was a desperately unhappy man. The reasons for his unhappiness were everywhere manifest in the little village in which he'd made his camp. Srirampur had been one of the unpronounceable names figuring on the reports arriving almost daily on Clement Attlee's desk from India. Inflamed by fanatical leaders, by reports of Hindus killing their co-religionists in Calcutta, its Moslems, like Moslems all across Noakhali, had suddenly turned on the Hindu minority that shared the village with them. They had slaughtered, raped, pillaged, and burned, forcing their neighbours to eat the flesh of their Sacred Cows, sending others fleeing for safety across the rice paddies. Half the huts in Srirampur were blackened ruins. Even the shack in which Gandhi lay had been partially destroyed by fire.

The Noakhali outbursts were isolated sparks but the passions which had ignited them could easily become a firestorm to set the whole sub-continent ablaze. Those horrors, the outbursts which had preceded them in Calcutta and those which had followed to the north-west in Bihar where, with equal brutality, a Hindu majority had turned on a Moslem minority, explained the anxiety in Attlee's conversation with the man he urgently wanted to dispatch to New Delhi as Viceroy.

They also explained Gandhi's presence in Srirampur. The fact that, as their hour of triumph approached, his countrymen should have turned on each other in communal frenzy, broke Gandhi's heart. They had followed him on the road to independence, but they had not understood the great doctrine he had enunciated to get them there, non-violence. Gandhi had a profound belief in his non-violent creed. The holocaust the world had just lived, the spectre of nuclear destruction now threatening it, were to Gandhi the conclusive proof that only non-violence could save mankind. It was his desperate desire that a new India should show Asia and the world this way out of man's dilemma. If his own people turned on the doctrines he'd lived by and used to lead them to freedom, what would remain of Gandhi's hopes? It would be a tragedy that would turn independence into a worthless triumph.

Another tragedy, too, threatened Gandhi. To tear India apart on religious lines would be to fly in the face of everything for which Gandhi stood. Every fibre of his being cried out against the division of his beloved country demanded by India's Moslem politicians, and which many of its English rulers were now ready to accept. India's people and faiths were, for Gandhi, as inextricably interwoven as the intricate patterns of an oriental carpet.

'You shall have to divide my body before you divide India,' he had proclaimed again and again.

He had come to the devastated village of Srirampur in search of his own faith and to find a way to prevent the disease from engulfing all India. 'I see no light through the impenetrable darkness,' he had cried in anguish as the first communal killings had opened an abyss between India's Hindu and Moslem communities. 'Truth and non-violence to which I swear, and which have sustained me for fifty years, seem to fail to show the attributes I have ascribed to them.'

'I have come here,' he told his followers, 'to discover a new technique and test the soundness of the doctrine which has sustained me and made my life worth living.'

For days, Gandhi wandered the village, talking to its inhabitants, meditating, waiting for the counsel of the 'Inner Voice' which had so often illuminated the way for him in times of crisis. Recently, his acolytes had noticed he was spending more and more time on a curious occupation: practising crossing the slippery, rickety, log bridges surrounding the village.

That day, when he had finished with his mudpack, he called his followers to his hut. His 'Inner Voice' had spoken at last. As once ancient Hindu holy men had crossed their continent in barefoot pilgrimage to its sacred shrines, so he was going to set out on a Pilgrimage of Penance to the hate-wasted villages of Noakhali. In the next seven weeks, walking barefoot as a sign of his penitence, he would cover 116 miles, visiting 47 of Noakhali's villages.

He, a Hindu, would go among those enraged Moslems, moving from village to village, from hut to hut, seeking to restore with the poultice of his presence Noakhali's shattered peace.

Because this was a pilgrimage of penance, he decreed he wanted no other companion but God. Only four of his followers would accompany him. They would live on whatever charity the inhabitants of the villages they visited were ready to offer them. Let the politicians of his Congress Party and the Moslem League wrangle over India's future in their endless Delhi debates, he said. It was, as it always had been, in India's villages that the answers to her problems would have to be found. 'This,' he said, 'would be his "last and greatest experiment." If he could "rekindle the lamp of neighbourliness", in those villages cursed by blood and bitterness, their example might inspire the whole nation.' Here in Noakhali, he prayed, he could set alight again the torch of non-violence and conjure away the spectre of communal warfare which was haunting India.

His party set out at dawn. Gandhi's pretty nineteen-year-old great-niece Manu had put together his spartan kit: a pen and paper, a needle and thread, an earthen bowl and a wooden spoon, his spinning-wheel and his three gurus, a little ivory representation of the three monkeys who 'hear no evil, see no evil, speak no evil'. She also packed in a sack the books that reflected the eclecticism of the man marching into the jungle: the *Bhagavad-Gîtâ*, a Koran, the *Practice and Precepts of Jesus*, and a book of Jewish thoughts.

With Gandhi at their head, the little band marched over the dirt paths, past the ponds and groves of betel and coconut palms to the rice paddies beyond. The villagers of Srirampur rushed for a last glimpse of this bent 77-year-old man striding off with his bamboo stave in search of a lost dream.

As Gandhi's party began to move out of sight across the harvested paddies, the villagers heard him singing one of Rabindranath Tagore's great poems set to music. It was one of the old leader's favourites and as he disappeared they followed the sound of his high-pitched, uneven voice drifting back across the paddies.

'If they answer not your call,' he sang, 'walk alone, walk alone.'

* * *

The fraternal bloodshed Gandhi hoped to check had for centuries rivalled hunger as India's sternest curse. The great epic poem of Hinduism, the *Mahabharata*, celebrated an appalling civil slaughter on the plains of Kurukshetra, north-west of Delhi, 2500 years before Christ. Hinduism itself had been brought to India by the Indo-European hordes descending from the north to wrest the subcontinent from its semi-aboriginal Dravidian inhabitants. Its sages had written their sacred vedas on the banks of the Indus centuries before Christ's birth.

The faith of the Prophet had come much later, after the cohorts of Genghis Khan and Tamerlane had battered their way down the Khyber Pass to weaken the Hindu hold on the great Gangetic plain. For two centuries, the Moslem Moghul emperors had imposed their sumptuous and implacable rule over most of India, spreading in the wake of their legions the message of Allah, the One, the Merciful.

The two great faiths thus planted on the sub-continent were as different as could be found among the manifestations of man's eternal vocation to believe. Where Islam reposed on a man, the Prophet, and a precise text, the Koran, Hinduism was a religion without a founder, a revealed truth, a dogma, a structured liturgy or a churchly establishment. For Islam, the Creator stood apart from his creation, ordering and presiding over his work. To the Hindu, the Creator and his creation were one and indivisible, and God a kind of all pervading cosmic spirit to whose manifestations there would be no limit.

The Hindu, as a result, worshipped God in almost any form he chose: in animals, ancestors, sages, spirits, natural forces, divine incarnations, the Absolute. He could find God manifested in snakes, phalli, water, fire, the planets and the stars.

To the Moslem, on the contrary, there was but one God, Allah, and the Koran forbade the Faithful to represent him in any shape or form. Idols and idolatry to the Moslem were abhorrent; paintings and statues blasphemous. A mosque was a spare, solemn place in which the only decorations permitted were abstract designs and the repeated representations of the 99 names of God.

Idolatry was Hinduism's natural form of expression and a Hindu temple was the exact opposite of a mosque. It was a kind of spiritual shopping centre, a clutter of Goddesses with snakes coiling from their heads, six-armed Gods with fiery tongues, elephants with wings talking to the clouds, jovial little monkeys, dancing maidens and squat phallic symbols.

Moslems worshipped in a body, prostrating themselves on the floor of the mosque in the direction of Mecca, chanting in unison their Koranic verses. A Hindu worshipped alone with only his thoughts linking him and the God he could select from a bewildering pantheon of three to three and a half million divinities. It was a jungle so complex that only a handful of humans who'd devoted their lives to its study could find their way through it. At its core was a central trinity: Brahma, the Creator; Shiva, the Destroyer; Vishnu, the Preserver – positive, negative, neutral forces, eternally in search, as their worshippers were supposed to be, of the perfect equilibrium, the attainment of the Absolute. Behind them were

Gods and Goddesses for the seasons, the weather, the crops, and the ailments of man like Maryamma, the smallpox Goddess revered each year in a ritual strikingly similar to the Jewish Passover.

The greatest barrier to Hindu-Moslem understanding, however, was not metaphysical, but social. It was the system which ordered Hindu society, caste. According to Vedic scripture, caste originated with Brahma, the Creator. Brahmins, the highest caste, sprang from his mouth; Kshatriyas, warriors and rulers, from his biceps; Vaishyas; traders and businessmen, from his thigh; Sudras, artisans and craftsmen, from his feet. Below them, were the outcasts, the Untouchables who had not sprung from divine soil.

The origins of the caste system, however, were notably less divine than those suggested by the Vedas. It had been a scheme employed by Hinduism's Aryan founders, to perpetuate the enslavement of India's dark, Dravidian populations. The word for caste, *varna*, meant colour, and centuries later, the dark skins of India's Untouchables gave graphic proof of the system's real origins.

The five original divisions had multiplied like cancer cells into almost 5000 sub-castes, 1886 for the Brahmins alone. Every occupation had its caste, splitting society into a myriad of closed guilds into which a man was condemned by his birth to work, live, marry and die. So precise were their definitions that an iron smelter was in a different caste to an ironsmith.

Linked to the caste system was the second concept basic to Hinduism, reincarnation. A Hindu believed his body was just a temporary garment for his soul. Each life was only one of his soul's many incarnations in its journey through eternity, a chain beginning and ending in some nebulous merger with the cosmos. The *Karma*, the accumulated good and evil of each mortal lifetime, was a soul's continuing burden. It determined whether, in its next incarnation, that soul would move up or down in the hierarchy of caste. Caste had been a superb device to perpetuate India's social inequities by giving them divine sanction. As the Church had counselled the peasants of the Middle Ages to forget the misery of their lives in the contemplation of the hereafter, so Hinduism had for centuries counselled the miserable of India to accept their lot in humble resignation as the best assurance of a better destiny in their next incarnation.

To the Moslems to whom Islam was a kind of brotherhood of the Faithful, that whole system was anathema. A generous, welcoming faith, Islam's fraternal embrace drew millions of converts to the mosques of India's Moghul rulers. Inevitably, the vast majority of them were Untouchables, seeking in the brotherhood of Islam an acceptance their own faith could offer them only in some distant incarnation.

With the collapse of the Moghul Empire at the beginning of the eighteenth century, a martial Hindu renaissance spread across India, bringing with it a wave of Hindu-Moslem bloodshed. Britain's conquering presence had forced its *Pax Britannica* on the warring sub-continent, but the mistrust and suspicion in which the two communities dwelt remained. The Hindus did not forget that the mass of Moslems were the descendants of Untouchables who'd fled Hinduism to escape their misery. Caste Hindus would not touch food in the presence of a Moslem. A Moslem entering a Hindu kitchen would pollute it. The touch of a Moslem's hand could send a Brahmin shrieking off to purify himself with hours of ritual ablutions.

Hindus and Moslems shared the villages awaiting Gandhi's visit in Noakhali, just as they shared the thousands of villages all through the northern tier of India in Bihar, the United Provinces, the Punjab. They dwelt, however, in geographically distinct neighbourhoods. The frontier was a road or path, frequently called the Middle Way. No Moslem would live on one side of it, no Hindu on the other.

The two communities mixed socially, attending each other's feasts, sharing the poor implements with which they worked. Their intermingling tended to end there. Intermarriage was almost unknown. The communities drew their water from separate wells and a caste Hindu would choke before sipping water from the Moslem well perhaps yards from his own. In the Punjab, what few scraps of knowledge Hindu children acquired came from the village Pandit who taught them to write a few words in Punjabi in mud with wheat stalks. The same village's Moslem children would get their bare education from a sheikh in the mosque reciting the Koran in a different language, Urdu. Even the primitive drugs of cow's urine and herbs with which they struggled against the same diseases, were based on different systems of natural medicine.

To those social and religious differences, had been added an even more divisive, more insidious distinction, economic. The Hindus had been far swifter than the Moslems to seize the opportunities British education and Western thought had placed before India. As a result, while the British had been socially more at ease with the Moslems, it was the Hindus who had administered India for them.* They were India's businessmen, financiers, administrators, professional men. With the Parsees, the descendants of ancient Persia's

* The Moslems had also been subtly penalized in the two or three decades after 1857 for the role their community had played in the Indian Army Mutiny.

fire-worshipping Zoroastrians, they monopolized insurance, banking, big business and India's few industries.

In the towns and small cities, the Hindus were the dominant commercial community. The ubiquitous role of the moneylender was almost everywhere discharged by Hindus, partly because of their aptitude for the task, partly because of the Koranic proscription preventing Moslems from practising usury.

The Moslem upper classes, many of whom descended from the Moghul invaders, had tended to remain landlords and soldiers. The Moslem masses, because of the deeply engrained patterns of Indian society, rarely escaped in the faith of Mohammed the roles that caste had assigned their forebears in the faith of Shiva. They were usually landless peasants in the service of Hindus or Moslems in the country, labourers and petty craftsmen in the service of Hindu employers in the city.

That economic rivalry accentuated the social and religious barriers between the two communities and made communal slaughters such as that which had shattered the peace of Srirampur a regular occurrence. Each community had its pet provocations with which it would launch them.

For the Hindus it was music. Music never accompanied the austere service of the mosque and its strains mingling with the mumble of the Faithfuls' prayers was a blasphemy. There was no surer way for the Hindus to incite their Moslem neighbours than to set up a band outside a mosque during Friday prayers.

For the Moslem, the favourite provocation involved an animal, one of the grey, skeletal beasts lowing down the streets of every city, town and village in India, aimlessly wandering her fields, the object of the most perplexing of Hinduism's cults, the Sacred Cow.

The veneration of the cow dated back to Biblical times, when the fortunes of the pastoral Indo-European peoples migrating on to the sub-continent depended on the vitality of their herds. As the rabbis of ancient Judea had forbidden pig's flesh to their people to save them from the ravages of trichinosis, so the *sadhus* of ancient India proclaimed the cow sacred so as to save from slaughter in times of famine the herds on which their peoples' existence depended.

As a result, India had in 1947 the largest bovine herd in the world, 200 million beasts, one for every two Indians, an animal population larger than the human population of the United States. 40 million cows produced a meagre trickle of milk averaging barely one pint per animal per day. 40 or 50 million more were beasts of burden, tugging their bullock carts and ploughs. The rest, 100-odd million, were sterile, useless animals roaming free through the fields, villages and cities of India. Every day their restless jaws chomped through the food that could have fed ten million Indians living on the edge of starvation.

The instinct for survival alone should have condemned those useless beasts. Yet, so tenacious had the superstition become, that cow slaughter remained an abomination for those very Indians who were starving to death so that the beasts could continue their futile existence. Even Gandhi maintained that in protecting the cow it was all God's work that man protected.

To the Moslems, the thought that a man could so degrade himself as to worship a dumb animal was repugnant. They took a perverse delight in driving a lowing, protesting herd of cows past the front door of a Hindu Temple *en route* to the slaughter house. Over the centuries, thousands of human beings had accompanied those animals to their death in the riots which often followed each such gesture.

While the British ruled India, they managed to keep a fragile balance between the two communities, at the same time using their antagonism as an instrument to ease the burden of their rule. Initially, the drive for Indian independence was confined to an intellectual elite in which Hindus and Moslems ignored communal differences to work side by side towards a common goal. Ironically, it was Gandhi who had disrupted that accord.

In the most spiritual area on earth, it was inevitable that the freedom struggle should take on the guise of a religious crusade, and Gandhi had made it one. No man was ever more tolerant, more genuinely free of any taint of religious prejudice than Gandhi. He desperately wanted to associate the Moslems with every phase of his movement. But he was a Hindu, and a deep belief in God was the very essence of his being. Inevitably, unintentionally, Gandhi's Congress Party movement began to take on a Hindu tone and colour that aroused Moslem suspicions.

Their suspicions were strengthened as narrow-minded local Congress leaders persistently refused to share with their Moslem rivals whatever electoral spoils British rule allowed. A spectre grew in Moslem minds: in an independent India they would be drowned by Hindu majority rule, condemned to the existence of a powerless minority in the land their Moghul forebears had once ruled.

One perspective seemed to offer an escape from that fate, the creation of a separate Islamic nation on the sub-continent. The idea that India's Moslems should set up a state of their own was formally articulated for the first time on four and a half pages of typing paper in a nondescript English cottage at 3 Humberstone Road in Cambridge. Its author was a forty-year-old Indian Moslem graduate student named Rahmat Ali, and the date at the head of his proposal was 28 January 1933. The idea that India formed a single nation, Ali wrote, was 'a preposterous falsehood'. He called for a Moslem nation carved from the provinces of north-west India where the Moslems were predominant, the Punjab, Kashmir, Sind, the Frontier, Baluchistan. He even had a name to propose for his new state. Based on the names of the provinces that would compose it, it was 'Pakistan – land of the pure'.

'We will not crucify ourselves,' he concluded in a fiery, if inept metaphor, 'on a cross of Hindu nationalism.'

Adopted by the body that was the focal point of Moslem nationalist aspirations, the Moslem League, Rahmat Ali's proposal gradually took hold of the imagination of India's Moslem masses. Its progress was nurtured by the chauvinistic attitude of the predominantly Hindu leaders of Congress who remained determined to make no concession to their Moslem foes.

The event which served to catalyse into violence the rivalry of India's Hindu and Moslem communities took place on 16 August 1946, just five months before Gandhi set out on his penitent's march. The site was the second city of the British Empire, a metropolis whose reputation for violence and savagery was unrivalled, Calcutta. Calcutta, with the legend of its Black Hole, had been a synonym for Indian cruelty to generations of Englishmen.

Hell, a Calcutta resident had once remarked, was being born an Untouchable in Calcutta's slums. Those slums contained the densest concentration of human beings in the world, foetid pools of unrivalled misery, Hindu and Moslem neighbourhoods interlaced without pattern or reason.

At dawn on 16 August, howling in a quasi-religious fervour, Moslem mobs had come bursting from their slums, waving clubs, iron bars, shovels, any instrument capable of smashing in a human skull. They came in answer to a call issued by the Moslem League, proclaiming 16 August 'Direct Action Day', to prove to Britain and the Congress Party that India's Moslems were prepared 'to get Pakistan for themselves by "Direct Action" if necessary'.

They savagely beat to a sodden pulp any Hindu in their path and stuffed their remains in the city's open gutters. The terrified police simply disappeared. Soon tall pillars of black smoke stretched up from a score of spots in the city, Hindu bazaars in full blaze.

Later, the Hindu mobs came storming out of their neighbourhoods looking for defenceless Moslems to slaughter. Never, in all its violent history, had Calcutta known 24 hours as savage, as packed with human viciousness. Like water-soaked logs, scores of bloated corpses bobbed down the Hooghly river towards the sea. Others, savagely mutilated, littered the city's streets. Everywhere, the weak and helpless suffered most. At one crossroads, a line of Moslem coolies lay beaten to death where a Hindu mob had found them, between the poles of their rickshaws. By the time the slaughter was over, Calcutta belonged to the vultures. In filthy grey packs they scudded across the sky, tumbling down to gorge themselves on the bodies of the city's 6000 dead.

The Great Calcutta Killings, as they became known, triggered bloodshed in Noakhali, where Gandhi was; in Bihar; and on the other side of the sub-continent in Bombay.

They changed the course of India's history. The threat the Moslems had been uttering for years, their warnings of a cataclysm which would overtake India if they were denied their own state, took on a terrifying reality. Suddenly, India was confronted by the awful vision that had sickened Gandhi and sent him into the jungles of Noakhali: civil war.

To another man, to the cold and brilliant lawyer who had been Gandhi's chief Moslem foe for a quarter of a century, that prospect now became the tool with which to pry India apart. History, beyond that written by his own people, would never accord Mohammed Ali Jinnah the high place his achievements merited. Yet, it was he, more than Gandhi or anyone else, who held the key to India's future. It was with that stern and uncompromising Moslem Messiah, leading his people to another man's Promised Land, that Queen Victoria's great-grandson would have to contend when he reached India.

In a tent outside Bombay in August 1946, he had evaluated for his followers in the Moslem League the meaning of Direct Action Day. If Congress wanted war, he declared, then India's Moslems would 'accept their offer unhesitatingly'.

Pale lips pressed into a grim smile, his piercing eyes alight with repressed passion, Jinnah had that day flung down the gauntlet to Congress, to the British.

'We shall have India divided,' he vowed, 'or we shall have India destroyed.'

3
'Leave India to God'

London, January 1947

'Look,' said Louis Mountbatten, 'a terrible thing has happened.'

Two men were alone in the intimacy of a Buckingham Palace sitting-room. At times like this, there was never any formality between them. They sat side by side like a couple of old school friends chatting as they sipped their tea. Today, however, a special nuance enlivened Mountbatten's conversational tone. His cousin King George VI represented his court of last appeal, the last faint hope that he might somehow avoid the stigma of becoming the man to cut Britain's ties with India. The King was after all Emperor of India and entitled to the final word on his appointment as Viceroy. It was not to be the word the young admiral wished to hear.

'I know,' replied the King with his shy smile, 'the Prime Minister's already been to see me and I've agreed.'

'You've agreed?' asked Mountbatten. 'Have you really thought it over?'

'Oh, yes,' replied the King quite cheerfully. 'I've thought it over carefully.'

'Look,' said Mountbatten. 'This is very dangerous. Nobody can foresee any way of finding an agreement out there. It's almost impossible to find one. I'm your cousin. If I go out there and make the most deplorable mess, it will reflect very badly on you.'

'Ah,' said the sovereign, 'but think how well it will reflect on the monarchy if you succeed.'

'Well,' sighed Mountbatten, sinking back into his chair, 'that's very optimistic of you.'

He could never sit there in that little salon without remembering another figure who used to sit in the chair across from his, another cousin, his closest friend, who had stood beside him on his wedding day at St Margaret's, Westminster, the man who should have been King, David, Prince of Wales. From early boyhood, they had been close. When in 1936, as Edward VIII, David had abdicated the throne for which he had been trained because he was not prepared to rule without the woman he loved, 'Dickie' Mountbatten had haunted the corridors of his palace, the King's constant solace and companion.

How ironic, Mountbatten thought. It was as David's ADC that he had first set foot on the land he was now to liberate. It was

17 November 1921. India, the young Mountbatten had noted in his diary that night, 'is the country one had always heard about, dreamt about, read about.' Nothing on that extraordinary royal tour would disappoint his youthful expectations. The Raj was at its zenith then, and no attention was too lavish, no occasion too grand for the heir to the imperial throne, the Shahzada Sahib, and his party. They travelled in the white and gold viceregal train, their journey a round of parades, polo games, tiger hunts, moonlit rides on elephants, banquets and receptions of unsurpassed elegance proffered by the crown's staunchest allies, the Indian princes. Leaving, Mountbatten thought, 'India is the most marvellous country and the Viceroy has the most marvellous job in the world.'

Now, with the confirming nod of another cousin, that 'marvellous job' was his.

A brief silence filled the Buckingham Palace sitting-room. With it, Louis Mountbatten sensed a shift in his cousin's mood.

'It's too bad,' the King said, a melancholy undertone to his voice, 'I always wanted to come out to see you in Southeast Asia when you were fighting there, and then go to India, but Winston stopped it. I'd hoped at least to go out to India after the war. Now I'm afraid I shan't be able to.'

'It's sad,' he continued, 'I've been crowned Emperor of India without ever having gone to India and now I shall lose the title from here in this palace in London.'

Indeed, George VI would die without ever setting foot on that fabulous land. There would never be a tiger hunt for him, no parade of elephants jangling past in silver and gold, no line of bejewelled maharajas bowing to his person.

His had been the crumbs of the Victorian table, a reign unexpected in its origins, conceived and matured in the shadows of war, now to be accomplished in the austerity of a post-war, Socialist England. On the May morning in 1937 when the Archbishop of Canterbury had pronounced Prince Albert, Duke of York, George the Sixth, by the Grace of God, King of Great Britain, Ireland and the British Dominions beyond the seas, Defender of the Faith, Emperor of India, 16 million of the 52 million square miles of land surface of the globe had been linked by one tie or another to his crown.

The central historic achievement of George VI's reign would be the melancholy task foretold by the presence of his cousin in his sitting-room. He would be remembered by history as the monarch who had reigned over the dismemberment of the British Empire. Crowned King Emperor of an Empire that exceeded the most extravagant designs of Rome, Alexander the Great, Genghis Khan, the Caliphs or Napoleon, he would die the sovereign of an island kingdom on its way to becoming just another European nation.

'I know I've got to take the "I" out of GRI. I've got to give up being King Emperor,' the monarch noted, 'but I would be profoundly saddened if all the links with India were severed.'

George VI knew perfectly well that the great imperial dream had faded. But if it had to disappear, how sad it would be if some of its achievements and glories could not survive it, if what it had represented could not find an expression in some new form more compatible with a modern age.

'It would be a pity,' he observed, 'if an independent India were to turn its back on the Commonwealth.'

The Commonwealth could indeed provide a framework in which George VI's hopes might be realized. It could become a multi-racial assembly of independent nations with Britain, *prima inter pares*, at its core. Bound by common traditions, a common past, common symbolic ties to his crown, the Commonwealth could exercise great influence in world affairs. Britain, at the hub of such a body, would still speak in the councils of the world with an echo of that imperial voice that had once been hers. London might still be London; cultural, spiritual, financial and mercantile centre for much of the world. The imperial substance would have disappeared, but a shadow would remain to differentiate George VI's island kingdom from those other nations across the English Channel.

If that ideal was to be realized, it was essential India remain within the Commonwealth. If India refused to join, the Afro-Asian nations which in their turn would accede to independence in the years to come would almost certainly follow her example. That would condemn the Commonwealth to become just a grouping of the Empire's white dominions.

Influenced by a long anti-imperial tradition however, George VI's Prime Minister and the Labour Party, did not share the King's inspiration. Attlee had not even told Mountbatten he was to make an effort to keep India in the Commonwealth.

George VI, as a constitutional monarch, could do virtually nothing to further his hopes. His cousin, however, could and Louis Mountbatten ardently shared the King's aspirations. No member of the royal family had travelled as extensively in the old Empire as he had. His intellect had understood and accepted its imminent demise; his heart ached at the thought.

Sitting there in the Buckingham Palace sitting-room, Victoria's two great-grandsons reached a private decision. Louis Mountbatten would become the agent of their common aspiration for the Commonwealth's future.

In a few days, Mountbatten would insist that Attlee include in his terms of reference a specific injunction to maintain an independent India, united or divided, inside the Commonwealth if at all possible. In the weeks ahead, there could be no task to which India's new Viceroy would devote more thought, more persuasiveness, more cunning than that of maintaining a link between India and his cousin's crown.

*

In a sense, no one might seem more naturally destined to occupy the majestic office of Viceroy of India than Louis Mountbatten. His first public gesture had occurred during his christening when, with a wave of his infant fist, he had knocked the spectacles from the bridge of his great-grandmother's imperial nose.

His family's lineage, with one passage through the female line, went back to the Emperor Charlemagne. He was, or had been, related by blood or marriage to Kaiser Wilhelm II, Tsar Nicholas II, Alfonso XIII of Spain, Ferdinand I of Rumania, Gustav VI of Sweden, Constantine I of Greece, Haakon VII of Norway and Alexander I of Yugoslavia. For Louis Mountbatten, the crises of Europe had been family problems.

Thrones, however, had been in increasingly short supply by the time Mountbatten was eighteen at the end of the First World War. The fourth child of Victoria's favourite grand-daughter, Princess Victoria of Hesse, and Prince Louis of Battenberg, her cousin, had had to savour the royal existence at second hand, playing out the summers of his youth in the palaces of his more favoured cousins. The memories of those idyllic summers remained deeply etched in his memory: tea parties on the lawns of Windsor Castle at which every guest might have worn a crown; cruises on the yacht of the Tsar; rides through the forests around Saint Petersburg with his haemophiliac cousin, the Tsarevitch, and the Tsarevitch's sister, the Grand Duchess Marie, with whom he fell in love.

With that background, Mountbatten could have enjoyed a modest income, token service under the crown; the pleasant existence of a handsome embellishment to the ceremonials of a declining caste. He had chosen quite a different course, however, and he stood this winter morning at the pinnacle of a remarkable career.

Mountbatten had just become 43 when, in the autumn of 1943, Winston Churchill searching for 'a young and vigorous mind', had appointed him Supreme Allied Commander Southeast Asia. The authority and responsibility that command placed on his youthful shoulders had only one counterpart, the Supreme Allied Command of Dwight Eisenhower. One hundred and twenty-eight million people across a vast sweep of Asia fell under his charge. It was a command which at the time it was formed, he would later recall, had had 'no victories and no priorities, only terrible morale, a terrible climate, a terrible foe and terrible defeats'.

Many of his subordinates were twenty years and three or four ranks his senior. Some tended to look on him as a playboy who used his royal connection to slip out of his dinner jacket into a naval uniform and temporarily abandon the dance floor of the Café de Paris for the battlefield.

He restored his men's morale with personal tours to the front; asserted his authority over his generals by forcing them to fight through Burma's terrible monsoon rains; cajoled, bullied and charmed every ounce of supplies he could get from his superiors in London and Washington.

By 1945, his once disorganized and demoralized command had won the greatest land victory ever wrought over a Japanese Army. Only the dropping of the atomic bomb prevented him from carrying out his grand design, 'Operation Zipper', the landing of 250,000 men from ports 2000 miles away on the Malay Peninsula, an amphibious operation surpassed in size only by the Normandy landing.

As a boy, Mountbatten had chosen a naval officer's career to emulate his father who had left his native Germany at fourteen and risen to the post of First Sea Lord of the Royal Navy. Mountbatten had barely begun his studies as a cadet, however, when tragedy shattered his adored father's career. He was forced to resign by the wave of anti-German hysteria which swept Britain after the outbreak of World War I. His heartbroken father changed his family name from Battenberg to Mountbatten at King George V's request and was created Marquess of Milford Haven. The First Sea Lord's equally affected son vowed to fill one day the post from which an unjust outcry had driven his father.

During the long years between the wars, however, his career had followed the slow, unspectacular path of a peacetime officer. It was in other, less martial fields that the young Mountbatten had made his impression on the public. With his charm, his remarkable good looks, his infectious gaiety, he was one of the darlings of Britain's penny press, catering to a world desperate for glamour after the horrors of war. His marriage to Edwina Ashley, a beautiful and wealthy heiress, with the Prince of Wales as his best man, was the social event of 1922.

Rare were the Sunday papers over the next years that did not contain a photograph or some mention of Louis and Edwina Mountbatten, the Mountbattens at the theatre with Noel Coward, the Mountbattens at the Royal Enclosure at Ascot, dashing young Lord Louis water-skiing in the Mediterranean or receiving a trophy won playing polo.

They constituted an image Mountbatten never denied; he revelled in every dance, party and polo match. But beneath that public image there was another figure of which the public was unaware. It emerged when the dancing was over.

The glamorous young man had not forgotten his boyhood vow. Mountbatten was an intensely serious, ambitious, and dedicated naval officer. He possessed an awesome capacity for work, a trait which would leave his subordinates gasping all his life. Convinced that future warfare would be patterned by the dictates of science and won by superior communications, Mountbatten eschewed the more social career of a deck officer to study signals.

He came out top of the Navy Higher Wireless Course in 1927, then sat down to write the first comprehensive manual for all the wireless sets used by the Navy. He was fascinated by the fast-expanding horizons of technology and plunged himself into the study of physics, electricity and communications in every form. New techniques, new ideas, were his passions and his playthings.

He obtained for the Royal Navy the works of a brilliant French rocketry expert, Robert Esnault Pelterie. Their pages gave Britain an eerily accurate forecast of the V-bomb, guided missiles and even man's first flight to the moon. In Switzerland, he ferreted out a fast-firing anti-aircraft gun designed to stop the Stuka dive bomber; then spent months forcing the reluctant Royal Navy to adopt it.

He had followed the rise of Hitler and German rearmament with growing apprehension. He had also watched with pained but perceptive eyes the evolution of the society that had driven his beloved uncle Nicholas II from the throne of the Tsars. Increasingly, as the thirties wore on, Mountbatten and his wife spent less and less time on the dance floor, and more and more in a crusade to awaken friends and politicians to the conflict both saw was coming.

On 25 August 1939, a proud Mountbatten took command of a newly commissioned destroyer, HMS *Kelly*. A few hours later the radio announced Hitler and Stalin had signed a non-aggression pact. The *Kelly*'s captain understood the import of the announcement immediately. Mountbatten ordered his crew to work day and night to reduce the three weeks needed to ready the ship for sea.

Nine days later, when war broke out, the captain of the *Kelly* was slung over the ship's side in a pair of dirty overalls, sloshing paint on her hull along with his able seamen. The next day, however, the *Kelly* was in action against a German submarine.

'I will never give the order "Abandon ship",' Mountbatten promised his crew. 'The only way we will ever leave this ship is if she sinks under our feet.'

The *Kelly* escorted convoys through the channel, hunted U-boats in the North Sea, dashed through fog and German bombers to help rescue six thousand survivors of the Narvik expedition at the head of the Namsos Fiord in Norway. Her stern was damaged at the mouth of the Tyne and her boiler room devastated by a torpedo in the North Sea. Ordered to scuttle, Mountbatten refused, spent a night alone on the drifting wreck, then, with eighteen volunteers, brought her home under tow.

A year later, in May 1941 off Crete, the *Kelly*'s luck ran out. She took a bomb in her magazine and went down in minutes. Faithful to his vow, Mountbatten stayed on her bridge until she rolled over, then fought his way to the surface. For hours, he held the oil-spattered survivors around a single life raft, leading them in singing 'Roll Out the Barrel' while German planes strafed them. Mountbatten won the DSO for his exploits on the *Kelly* and the ship a bit of immortality in the film *In Which We Serve*, made by Mountbatten's friend Noel Coward.

Five months later, Churchill, searching for a bold young officer to head Combined Operations, the commando force created to develop the tactics and technology that would eventually bring the Allies back to the continent, called on Mountbatten. The assignment proved ideal for his blend of dash and scientific curiosity. Vowing he was a man who would never say no to an idea, he opened his command to a parade of inventors, scientists, technicians, geniuses and mountebanks. Some of their schemes, like an iceberg composed of frozen sea water mixed with five per cent wood pulp to serve as a floating and unsinkable airfield, were wild fantasies. But they also produced Pluto, the underwater trans-channel pipeline, the Mulberry artificial harbours and the landing and rocket craft designs that made the Normandy invasion possible. For their leader, they ultimately produced his extraordinary elevation to Supreme Command of South-East Asia at the age of 43.

Now preparing to take on the most challenging task of his career, Mountbatten was at the peak of his physical and intellectual powers. The war at sea and high command had given him a capacity for quick decision and brought out his natural talent for leadership. He was not a philosopher or an abstract thinker, but he possessed an incisive, analytical mind honed by a lifetime of hard work. He had none of the Anglo-Saxon affection for the role of the good loser. He believed in winning. As a young officer, his crews had once swept the field in a navy regatta because he had taught them an improved rowing technique. Criticized later for the style he'd introduced, he had acidly observed that he thought the important thing was 'crossing the finishing line first'.

His youthful gaiety had matured into an extraordinary charm and a remarkable facility for bringing people together. 'Mountbatten,' remarked a man who was not one of his admirers, 'could charm a vulture off a corpse if he set his mind to it.'

Above all, Mountbatten was endowed with an endless reservoir of self-confidence, a quality his detractors preferred to label conceit. When Churchill had offered him his Asian command, he had asked for 24 hours to ponder the offer.

'Why,' snarled Churchill, 'don't you think you can do it?'

'Sir,' replied Mountbatten, 'I suffer from the congenital weakness of believing I can do anything.'

Victoria's great-grandson would need every bit of that self-confidence in the weeks ahead.

Penitent's Progress I

At every village, his routine was the same. As soon as he arrived, the most famous Asian alive would go up to a hut, preferably a Moslem's hut, and beg for shelter. If he was turned away, and sometimes he was, Gandhi would go to another door. 'If there is no one to receive me,' he had said, 'I shall be happy to rest under the hospitable shade of a tree.'

Once installed, he lived on whatever food his hosts could offer: mangoes, vegetables, goat's curds, green coconut milk. Every hour of his day in each village was rigorously programmed. Time was one of Gandhi's obsessions. Each minute, he held, was a gift of God to be used in the service of man. His own days were ordered by one of his few possessions, a sixteen-year-old, eight-shilling Ingersoll watch that was always tied to his waist with a piece of string. He got up at two o'clock in the morning to read his *Gita* and say his morning prayers. From then until dawn he squatted in his hut, patiently answering his correspondence himself in longhand by pencil. He used each pencil right down to an ungrippable stub because, he held, it represented the work of a fellow human being and to waste it would indicate indifference to his labours. Every morning at a rigidly appointed hour, he gave himself a salt and water enema. A devout believer in nature cures, Gandhi was convinced that was the way to flush the toxins from his bowels. For years, the final sign a man had been accepted in his company, came when the Mahatma himself offered to give him a salt and water enema.

At sun-up, Gandhi began to wander the village, talking and praying incessantly with its inhabitants. Soon he developed a tactic to implement his drive to return peace and security to Noakhali. It was a typically Gandhian ploy. In each village he would search until he'd found a Hindu and a Moslem leader who'd responded to his appeal. Then he'd persuade them to move in together under one roof. They would become the joint guarantors of the village's peace. If his fellow Moslems assailed the village's Hindus, the Moslem promised to undertake a fast to death. The Hindu made a similar pledge.

But on those blood-spattered byways of Noakhali, Gandhi did not limit himself to trying to exorcise the hatred poisoning the villages through which he passed. Once he sensed a village was beginning to understand his message of fraternal love, he broadened the dimension of his appeal. India for Gandhi was its lost and inaccessible villages, like those hamlets along his route in Noakhali. He knew them better than any man alive. He wanted his independent India built on the foundation of her re-invigorated villages, and he had his own ideas on how to re-order the patterns of their existence.

'The lessons which I propose to give you during my tour are how you can keep the village water and yourselves clean,' he would tell the villagers; 'what use you can make of the earth, of which your bodies are made; how you can obtain the life force from the infinite sky over your heads; how you can reinforce your vital energy from the air which surrounds you; how you can make proper use of sunlight.'

The ageing leader did not satisfy himself with words. Gandhi had a tenacious belief in the value of actions. To the despair of many of his followers, who thought a different set of priorities should order his time, Gandhi would devote the same meticulous care and attention to making a mudpack for a leper as preparing for an interview with a Viceroy. So, in each village he would go with its inhabitants to their wells. Frequently he would help them find a better location for them. He would inspect their communal latrines, or if, as was most often the case, they didn't have any, he would teach them how to build one, often joining in the digging himself. Convinced bad hygiene was the basic cause of India's terrible mortality rate, he'd inveighed for years against such habits as public defecation, spitting, and blowing out nostrils on the paths where most of the village poor walked barefoot.

'If we Indians spat in unison,' he had once sighed, 'we would form a puddle large enough to drown three hundred thousand Englishmen.' Every time he saw a villager spitting or blowing his nose on a footpath, he would gently reprimand him. He went into homes to show people how to build a simple filter of charcoal and sand to help purify their drinking water. 'The difference between what we do and what we could do,' he constantly repeated, 'would suffice to solve most of the world's problems.'

Every evening he held an open prayer meeting, inviting Moslems to join in, being careful to recite as part of each day's service, verses from the Koran. Anyone could question him on anything at those meetings. One day a villager remonstrated with him for wasting his time in Noakhali when he should have been in New Delhi negotiating with Jinnah and the Moslem League.

'A leader,' Gandhi replied, 'is only a reflection of the people he leads.' The people had first to be led to make peace among themselves. Then, he said, 'their desire to live together in peaceful neighbourliness will be reflected by their leaders.'

When he felt a village had begun to understand his message, when its Moslem community had agreed to let its frightened Hindus return to their homes, he set out for the next hamlet, five, ten, fifteen miles away. Inevitably, his departure took place at precisely 7.30. As at Srirampur, the little party would march off, Gandhi at its head, through the mango orchards, the green scum-slicked ponds where ducks and wild geese went honking skywards at their approach. Their paths were narrow, winding their way through palm groves and the underbush. They were littered with stones, pebbles, protruding roots. Sometimes the little procession had to struggle through ankle-deep mud. By the time they reached their next stop, the 77-year-old Mahatma's bare feet were often aching with chilblains, or disfigured by bleeding sores and blisters. Before taking up his task again, he soaked them in hot water. Then, Gandhi indulged in the one luxury of his penitent's tour. His great-niece and constant companion, Manu, massaged his martyred feet – with a stone.

*

For thirty years those battered feet had led the famished hordes of a continent in prayer towards their liberty. They had carried Gandhi into the most remote corners of India, to thousands of villages like those he now visited, to lepers' wading pools, to the worst slums of his nation, to palaces and prisons, in quest of his cherished goal, India's freedom.

Mohandas Gandhi had been an eight-year-old schoolboy when the great-grandmother of the two cousins sipping their tea in Buckingham Palace had been proclaimed Empress of India on a plain near Delhi. For Gandhi, that grandiose ceremony was always associated with a jingle he and his playmates had chanted to mark the event in his home town of Porbandar, 700 miles from Delhi on the Arabian Sea:

Behold the mighty Englishman!
He rules the Indian small
Because being a meat eater
He is five cubits tall.

The boy whose spiritual force would one day humble those five-cubit Englishmen and their enormous empire could not resist the challenge in the jingle. With a friend, he cooked and ate a forbidden piece of goat's meat. The experiment was disastrous. The eight-year-old Gandhi promptly vomited up the goat and spent the night dreaming the animal was cavorting in his stomach.

Gandhi's father was the hereditary *diwan*, prime minister, of a tiny state on the Kathiawar peninsula near Bombay and his mother an intensely devout woman given to long religious fasts.

Curiously, Gandhi, destined to become India's greatest spiritual leader of modern times, was not born into the Brahmin caste that was supposed to provide Hinduism with its hereditary philosophical and religious elite. His father was a member of the *vaishyas*, the caste of shopkeepers and petty tradesmen which stood halfway up the Hindu social scale, above Untouchable and *sudras*, artisans, but below Brahmins and *kshatriyas*, warriors.

At thirteen, Gandhi, following the Indian tradition of the day, was married to an illiterate stranger named Kasturba. The youth who was later to offer the world a symbol of ascetic purity revelled in the consequent discovery of sex.

Four years later, Gandhi and his wife were in the midst of enjoying its pleasures when a rap on the door interrupted their love-making. It was a servant. Gandhi's father, he announced, had just died.

Gandhi was horrified. He was devoted to his father. Moments before he'd been by the bed on which his father lay dying, patiently massaging his legs. An urgent burst of sexual desire had seized him and he'd tiptoed from his father's room to wake up his pregnant wife. The joy of sex began to fade for Gandhi. An indelible stamp had been left on his psyche.

As a result of his father's death, Gandhi was sent to England to study law so he might become prime minister of a princely state. It was an enormous undertaking for a devout Hindu family. No member of Gandhi's family had ever gone abroad before. Gandhi was solemnly pronounced an outcast from his shopkeepers' caste, because, to his Hindu elders, his voyage across the seas would leave him contaminated.

Gandhi was wretchedly unhappy in London. He was so desperately shy that to address a single word to a stranger was a painful ordeal; to produce a full sentence agony. Physically, at nineteen he was a pathetic little creature in the sophisticated world of the Inns of Court. His cheap, badly-cut Bombay clothes flopped over his undersized body like loose sails on a becalmed ship. Indeed, he was so small, so unremarkable, his fellow students sometimes took him for an errand boy.

The lonely, miserable Gandhi decided the only way out of his agony was to become an English gentleman. He threw away his Bombay clothes and got a new wardrobe. It included a silk top-hat, an evening suit, patent-leather boots, white gloves and even a silver-tipped walking stick. He bought hair lotion to plaster his unwilling black hair on to his skull. He spent hours in front of a mirror contemplating his appearance and learning to tie a tie. To win the social acceptance he longed for, he bought a violin, joined a dancing class, hired a French tutor and an elocution teacher.

The results of that poignant little charade were as disastrous as his earlier encounter with goat's meat. The only sound he learned to coax from his violin was a dissonant wail. His feet refused to acknowledge three-quarter time, his tongue the French language, and no amount of elocution lessons were going to free the spirit struggling to escape from under his crippling shyness. Even a visit to a brothel was a failure. Gandhi couldn't get past the parlour.

He gave up his efforts to become an Englishman and went back to being himself. When finally he was called to the bar, Gandhi rushed back to India with undisguised relief.

His homecoming was less than triumphant. For months, he hung around the Bombay courts looking for a case to plead. The young man whose voice would one day inspire 300 million Indians proved incapable of articulating the phrases necessary to impress a single Indian magistrate.

That failure led to the first great turning point in Gandhi's life. His frustrated family sent him to South Africa to unravel the legal problems of a distant kinsman. His trip was to have lasted a few months; he stayed a quarter of a century. There, in that bleak and hostile land, Gandhi found the philosophical principles that transformed his life and Indian history.

Nothing about the young Gandhi walking down a gangplank in Durban harbour in May 1893, however, indicated a vocation for asceticism or saintliness. The future prophet of poverty made his formal entry on to the soil of South Africa in a high white collar and the fashionable frock coat of a London Inner Temple barrister, his brief case crammed with documents on the rich Indian businessman whose interests he'd come to defend.

Gandhi's real introduction to South Africa came a week after his arrival on an overnight train ride from Durban to Pretoria. Four decades later Gandhi would still remember that trip as the most formative experience of his life. Halfway to Pretoria a white man stalked into his first-class compartment and ordered him into the baggage car. Gandhi, who held a first-class ticket, refused. At the next stop the white called a policeman and Gandhi with his luggage was unceremoniously thrown off the train in the middle of the night.

All alone, shivering in the cold because he was too shy to ask the station master for the overcoat locked in his luggage, Gandhi passed the night huddled in the unlit railroad station, pondering his first brutal confrontation with racial prejudice. Like a medieval youth during the vigil of his knighthood, Gandhi sat praying to the God of the *Gita* for courage and guidance. When dawn finally broke on the little station of Maritzburg, the timid, withdrawn youth was a changed person. The little lawyer had reached the most important decision of his life. Mohandas Gandhi was going to say 'no'.

A week later, Gandhi delivered his first public speech to Pretoria's Indians. The advocate who'd been so painfully shy in the courtrooms of Bombay had begun to find his tongue. He urged the Indians to unite to defend their interests and, as a first step, to learn how to do it in their oppressors' English tongue. The following evening, without realizing it, Gandhi began the work that would ultimately bring India freedom by teaching English grammar to a barber, a clerk and a shopkeeper. Soon he had also won the first of the successes which would be his over the next half-century. He wrung from the railway authorities the right for well-dressed Indians to travel first- or second-class on South Africa's railways.

Gandhi decided to stay on in South Africa when the case which had sent him there had been resolved. He became both the champion of South Africa's Indian community and a highly successful lawyer. Loyal to the British Empire despite its racial injustice, he even led an ambulance corps in the Boer War.

Ten years after his arrival in South Africa, another long train ride provoked the second great turning point in Gandhi's life. As he boarded the Johannesburg-Durban train one evening in 1904, an English friend passed Gandhi a book to read on the long trip, John Ruskin's *Unto This Last*.

All night Gandhi sat up reading as his train rolled through the South African veldt. It was his revelation on the road to Damascus. By the time his train reached Durban the following morning, Gandhi had made an epic vow: he was going to renounce all his material possessions and live his life according to Ruskin's ideals.

Riches, Ruskin wrote, were just a tool to secure power over men. A labourer with a spade served society as truly as a lawyer with a brief, and the life of labour, of the tiller of the soil, is the life worth living.

Gandhi's decision was all the more remarkable because he was, at that moment, a wealthy man earning over £5000 a year from his law practice, an enormous sum in the South Africa of the time.

For two years, however, doubts had been fermenting in Gandhi's mind. He was haunted by the *Bhagavad Gita*'s doctrine of renunciation of desire and attachment to material possessions as the essential stepping-stone to a spiritual awakening. He had already made experiments of his own: he had started to cut his own hair, do his laundry, clean his own toilet. He had even delivered his last child. His doubts found their confirmation in Ruskin's pages.

Barely a week later, Gandhi settled his family and a group of friends on a hundred-acre farm near Phoenix, fourteen miles from Durban. There, on a sad, scrubby site consisting of a ruined shack, a well, some orange, mulberry and mango trees, and a horde of snakes, Gandhi's life took on the pattern that would rule it until his death: a renunciation of material possessions and a striving to satisfy human needs in the simplest manner, coupled with a communal existence in which all labour was equally valuable and all goods were shared.

One last, painful renunciation remained, however, to be made. It was the vow of *Brahmacharya*, the pledge of sexual continence and it had haunted Gandhi for years.

The scar left by his father's death, a desire to have no more children, his rising religious consciousness all drove him towards his decision. One summer evening in 1906 Gandhi solemnly announced to his wife, Kasturba, that he had taken the vow of *Brahmacharya*. Begun in a joyous frenzy at the age of thirteen, the sexual life of Mohandas Gandhi had reached its conclusion at the age of 37.

To Gandhi, however, *Brahmacharya* meant more than just the curbing of sexual desires. It was the control of all the senses. It meant restraint in emotion, diet, and speech, the suppression of anger, violence and hate, the attainment of a desireless state close to the *Gita*'s ideal of non-possession. It was his definitive engagement on the ascetic's path, the ultimate act of self-transformation. None of the vows Gandhi took in his life would force upon him such intense internal struggle as his vow of chastity. It was a struggle which, in one form or another, would be with him for the rest of his life.

It was, however, in the racial struggle he'd undertaken during his first week in South Africa that Gandhi enunciated the two doctrines which would make him world-famous: non-violence and civil disobedience.

It was a passage from the Bible which had first set Gandhi meditating on non-violence. He had been overwhelmed by Christ's admonition to his followers to turn the other cheek to their aggressors. The little man had already applied the doctrine himself, stoically submitting to the beatings of numerous white aggressors. The philosophy of an eye for an eye led only to a world of the blind, he reasoned. You don't change a man's convictions by chopping off his head or infuse his heart with a new spirit by putting a bullet through it. Violence only brutalizes the violent and embitters its victims. Gandhi sought a doctrine that would force change by the example of the good, reconcile men with the strength of God instead of dividing them by the strength of man.

The South African government furnished him an opportunity to test his still half-formulated theories in the autumn of 1906. The occasion was a law which would have forced all Indians over the age of eight to register with the government, be fingerprinted and carry special identity cards. On 11 September, before a gathering of angry Indians in the Empire Theatre in Johannesburg, Gandhi took the stand to protest against the law.

To obey it, he said, would lead to the destruction of their community. 'There is only one course open to me,' he declared, 'to die but not to submit to the law.' For the first time in his life he led a public assembly in a solemn vow before God to resist an unjust law, whatever the consequences. Gandhi did not explain to his audience how they would resist the law. Probably he himself did not know. Only one thing was clear; it would be resisted without violence.

The new principle of political and social struggle born in the Empire Theatre soon had a name, *Satyagraha*, Truth Force. Gandhi organized a boycott of the registration procedures and peaceful picketing of the registration centres. His actions earned him the first of his life's numerous jail sentences.

While in jail, Gandhi encountered the second of the secular works which would deeply influence his thought, Henry Thoreau's essay *On Civil Disobedience*'* Protesting against a US government that

* The third was Leo Tolstoy's *The Kingdom of God is Within You.* He admired Tolstoy's insistence on applying his moral principles in his daily life.

condoned slavery and was fighting an unjust war in Mexico, Thoreau asserted the individual's right to ignore unjust laws and refuse his allegiance to a government whose tyranny had become unbearable. To be right, he said, was more honourable than to be law-abiding.

Thoreau's essay was a catalyst to thoughts already stirring in Gandhi. Released from jail, he decided to apply them in protest against a decision of the Transvaal to close its borders to Indians. On 6 November 1913, 2037 men, 127 women, and 57 children, Gandhi at their head, staged a non-violent march on the Transvaal's frontiers. Their certain destiny was jail, their only sure reward a frightful beating.

Watching that pathetic, bedraggled troop walking confidently along behind him, Gandhi experienced another illuminating revelation. Those wretches had nothing to look forward to but pain. Armed white vigilantes waited at the border, perhaps to kill them. Yet fired by faith in him and the cause to which he'd called them, they marched in his footsteps, ready, in Gandhi's words, to 'melt their enemies' hearts by self-suffering'.

Gandhi suddenly sensed in their quiet resolution what mass, non-violent action might become. There on the borders of the Transvaal he realized the enormous possibilities inherent in the movement he'd provoked. The few hundreds behind him that November day could become hundreds of thousands, a tide rendered irresistible by an unshakeable faith in the non-violent ideal.

Persecution, flogging, jailing, economic sanctions followed their action, but they could not break the movement. His African crusade ended in almost total victory in 1914. He could go home at last.

*

The Gandhi who left South Africa in July 1914 was a totally different person from the timid young lawyer who'd landed in Durban. He had discovered on its inhospitable soil his three teachers, Ruskin, Tolstoy and Thoreau. From his experience he had evolved the two doctrines, non-violence and civil disobedience, with which, over the next thirty years, he would humble the most powerful empire in the world.

An enormous crowd gave Gandhi a hero's welcome when his diminutive figure passed under the spans of Bombay's Gateway of India on 9 January 1915. The spare suitcase of the leader passing under that imperial archway contained one significant item. It was a thick bundle of paper covered with Gandhi's handwritten prose. Its title *Hind Swaraj* – 'Indian Home Rule', made one thing clear.

The two men held remarkably similar views on non-violence, education, diet, industrialization, and corresponded briefly before Tolstoy's death.

Africa, for Gandhi, had been only a training ground for the real battle of his life.

Gandhi settled near the industrial city of Ahmedabad on the banks of the Sabarmati River where he founded an ashram, a communal farm similar to those he'd founded in South Africa. As always, Gandhi's first concern was for the poor. He organized the indigo farmers of Bihar against the oppressive exactions of their British landlords, the peasants of the drought-stricken province of Bombay against their taxes, the workers in Ahmedabad's textile mills against the employers whose contributions sustained his ashram. For the first time, an Indian leader was addressing himself to the miseries of India's masses. Soon Rabindranath Tagore, India's Nobel Prizewinner, conferred on Gandhi the appellation he would carry for the rest of his life, 'Mahatma'. 'The Great Soul in Beggar's Garb,' he called him.

Like most Indians, Gandhi was loyal to Britain in World War I, convinced Britain in return would give a sympathetic hearing to India's nationalist aspirations. Gandhi was wrong. Britain instead passed the Rowlatt Act in 1919, to repress agitation for Indian freedom. For weeks Gandhi meditated, seeking a tactic with which to respond to Britain's rejection of India's hopes. The idea for a reply came to him in a dream. It was brilliantly, stunningly simple. India would protest, he decreed, with silence, a special eerie silence. He would do something no one had ever dreamed of doing before; he would immobilize all India in the quiet chill of a day of mourning, a *hartal*.

Like so many of Gandhi's political ideas, the plan reflected his instinctive genius for tactics that could be enunciated in few words, understood by the simplest minds, put into practice with the most ordinary gestures. To follow him, his supporters did not have to break the law or brave police clubs. They had only to do nothing. By closing their shops, leaving their classrooms, going to their temples to pray or just staying at home, Indians could demonstrate their solidarity with his protest call. He chose 7 April 1919 as the day of his *hartal*. It was his first overt act against the Government of India. Let India stand still, he urged, and let India's oppressors listen to the unspoken message of her silent masses.

Unfortunately, those masses were not everywhere silent. Riots erupted. The most serious were in Amritsar in the Punjab. To protest against the restrictions clamped on their city as a result, thousands of Indians gathered on 13 April, for a peaceful but illegal meeting in a stone- and debris-littered compound called Jallianwalla Bagh.

There was only one entrance to the compound down a narrow alley between two buildings. Through it, just after the meeting had begun, marched Amritsar's Martial Law Commander, Brigadier R. E. Dyer, at the head of fifty soldiers. He stationed his men on either side of the entry and, without warning, opened fire with machine-guns on the defenceless Indians. For ten full minutes, while the trapped Indians screamed for mercy, the soldiers fired. They fired 1650 rounds. Their bullets killed or wounded 1516 people. Convinced he'd 'done a jolly good thing', Dyer marched his men back out of the Bagh.

His 'jolly good thing' was a turning point in the history of Anglo-Indian relations, more decisive even than the Indian Mutiny 63 years before.* For Gandhi it was the final breach of faith by the empire for which he had compromised his pacifist principles. He turned all his efforts to taking control of the organization which had become synonymous with India's nationalist aspirations.

The idea that the Congress Party might one day become the focal point of mass agitation against British rule in India would surely have horrified the dignified English civil servant who had founded the party in 1885. Acting with the blessings of the Viceroy, Octavian Hume had sought to create an organization which would canalize the protests of India's slowly growing educated classes into a moderate, responsible body prepared to engage in gentlemanly dialogue with India's English rulers.

That was exactly what Congress was when Gandhi arrived on the political scene. Determined to convert it into a mass movement attuned to his non-violent creed, Gandhi presented the party with a plan of action in Calcutta in 1920. It was adopted by an overwhelming majority. From that moment until his death, whether he held rank in the party or not, Gandhi was Congress's conscience and its guide, the unquestioned leader of the independence struggle.

Like his earlier call for a national *hartal*, Gandhi's new tactic was electrifyingly simple, a one word programme for political revolution: non-co-operation. Indians, he decreed, would boycott whatever was British: students would boycott British schools; lawyers, British courts; employees, British jobs; soldiers, British honours. Gandhi himself gave the lead by returning to the Viceroy the two medals he'd earned with his ambulance brigade in the Boer War.

* Dyer was reprimanded for his actions and asked to resign from the army. He was, however, allowed to retain full pension benefits and other rights due him. His demonstration was applauded by most of the British in India. In clubs all across the country his admiring countrymen took up a collection on his behalf, amassing the then prodigious sum of £26,000 to ease the rigours of his premature retirement.

Above all, his aim was to weaken the edifice of British power in India by attacking the economic pillar upon which it reposed. Britain purchased raw Indian cotton for derisory prices, shipped it to the mills of Lancashire to be woven into textiles, then shipped the finished products back to India to be sold at a substantial profit in a market which virtually excluded non-British textiles. It was the classic cycle of imperialist exploitation and the arm with which Gandhi proposed to fight it was the very antithesis of the great mills of the Industrial Revolution that had sired that exploitation. It was a primitive wooden spinning-wheel.

For the next quarter of a century Gandhi struggled with tenacious energy to force all India to forsake foreign textiles for the rough cotton *khadi* spun by millions of spinning-wheels. Convinced the misery of India's countryside was due above all to the decline in village crafts, he saw in a renaissance of cottage industry heralded by the spinning-wheel the key to the revival of India's impoverished countryside. For the urban masses, spinning would be a kind of spiritual redemption by manual labour, a constant, daily reminder of their link to the real India, the India of half a million villages.

The wheel became the medium through which he enunciated a whole range of doctrines close to his heart. To it, he tied a crusade to get villagers to use latrines instead of the open fields, to improve hygiene and health by practising cleanliness, to fight malaria, to set up simple village schools for their offspring, to preach Hindu-Moslem harmony: in short an entire programme to regenerate India's rural life.

Gandhi himself gave the example by regularly consecrating half an hour a day to spinning and forcing his followers to do likewise. The spinning ritual became a quasi-religious ceremony; the time devoted to it, an interlude of prayer and contemplation. The Mahatma began to murmur: '*Rama, Rama, Rama*' (God) in rhythm to the click – click – click of the spinning-wheel.

In September 1921, Gandhi gave a final impetus to his campaign by solemnly renouncing for the rest of his life any clothing except a homespun loincloth and a shawl. The product of the wheel, cotton *khadi*, became the uniform of the independence movement, wrapping rich and poor, great and small, in a common swathe of rough white cloth. Gradually Gandhi's little wooden wheel became the symbol of his peaceful revolution, of an awakening continent's challenge to Western imperialism.

Splashing through ankle-deep mud and water, on precarious, rock-strewn paths, sleeping endless nights on the wooden planks of India's third-class railway carriages, Gandhi travelled to the most remote corners of India preaching his message. Speaking five or six times a day, he visited thousands of villages.

It was an extraordinary spectacle. Gandhi would lead the march, barefoot, wrapped in his loincloth, spectacles sliding from his nose, clomping along with the aid of a bamboo stave. Behind him came his followers in identical white loincloths. Closing the march, hoist like some triumphant trophy over a follower's head, rode the Mahatma's portable toilet, a graphic reminder of the importance he attached to sound sanitation.

His crusade was an extraordinary success. The crowds rushed to see the man already known as a 'Great Soul'. His voluntary poverty, his simplicity, his humility, his saintly air made him a kind of Holy Man, marching out of some distant Indian past to liberate a new India.

In the towns he told the crowds that, if India was to win self-rule, she would have to renounce foreign clothing. He asked for volunteers to take off their clothes and throw them in a heap at his feet. Shoes, socks, trousers, shirts, hats, coats cascaded into the pile until some men stood stark naked before Gandhi. With a delighted smile Gandhi then set the pile ablaze, a bizarre bonfire of 'Made in England' clothing.

The British were quick to react. If they hesitated to arrest Gandhi for fear of making him a martyr, they struck hard at his followers. Thirty thousand people were arrested, meetings and parades broken up by force, Congress offices ransacked. On 1 February 1922, Gandhi courteously wrote to the Viceroy to inform him he was intensifying his action. Non-co-operation was to be escalated to civil disobedience. He counselled peasants to refuse to pay taxes, city dwellers to ignore British laws and soldiers to stop serving the crown. It was Gandhi's non-violent declaration of war on India's colonial government.

'The British want us to put the struggle on the plane of machine-guns where they have the weapons and we do not,' he warned. 'Our only assurance of beating them is putting the struggle on a plane where we have the weapons and they have not.'

Thousands of Indians followed his call and thousands more went off to jail. The beleaguered governor of Bombay called it 'the most colossal experiment in world history and one which came within an inch of succeeding'.

It failed because of an outburst of bloody violence in a little village of United Provinces. Against the wishes of almost his entire Congress hierarchy Gandhi called off the movement because he felt his followers did not yet fully understand non-violence.

Sensing that his change of attitude had rendered him less dangerous, the British arrested him. Gandhi pleaded guilty to the charge of sedition, and in a moving appeal to his judge, asked for the maximum penalty. He was sentenced to six years in Yeravda prison near Poona. He had no regrets. 'Freedom,' he wrote, 'is often to be found inside a prison's walls, even on a gallows; never in council chambers, courts and classrooms.'

Gandhi was released before the end of his sentence because of ill-health. For three years, he travelled and wrote, patiently training his followers, inculcating the principles of non-violence to avoid a recurrence of the outburst that had shocked him before his arrest.

By the end of 1929, he was ready for another move forward. In Lahore, at the stroke of midnight, as the decade expired, he led his Congress in a vow for *swaraj*, nothing less than complete independence. Twenty-six days later, in gatherings all across India, millions of Congressmen repeated the pledge.

A new confrontation between Gandhi and the British was inevitable. Gandhi pondered for days waiting for his 'Inner Voice' to counsel him on the proper form of that confrontation. The answer proposed by his 'Inner Voice' was the finest fruit of his creative genius. So simple was the thought, so dramatic its execution, it made Gandhi world-famous overnight. Paradoxically, it was based on a staple the Mahatma had given up years before in his efforts to repress his sexual desires as part of his vow of chastity: salt.

If Gandhi spurned it, in India's hot climate it was an essential ingredient in every man's diet. It lay in great white sheets along the shore-lines, the gift of the eternal mother, the sea. Its manufacture and sale, however, was the exclusive monopoly of the state, which built a tax into its selling price. It was a small tax, but for a poor peasant it represented, each year, two weeks' income.

On 12 March 1930, at 6.30 in the morning, his bamboo stave in his hand, his back slightly bent, his familiar loincloth around his hips, Gandhi marched out of his ashram at the head of a cortege of 79 disciples and headed for the sea, 241 miles away. Thousands of supporters from Ahmedabad lined the way and strewed the route with green leaves.

Newsmen rushed from all over the world to follow the progress of his strange caravan. From village to village the crowds knelt by the roadside as Gandhi passed. His pace was a deliberately tantalizing approach to his climax. To the British, it was infuriatingly slow. The weird, almost Chaplinesque image of a little, old, half-naked man clutching a bamboo pole, marching down to the sea to challenge the British Empire, dominated the newsreels and press of the world day after day.

On 5 April, at six o'clock in the evening, Gandhi and his party finally reached the banks of the Indian Ocean near the town of Dandi. At dawn the next morning, after a night of prayer, the group marched into the sea for a ritual bath. Then Gandhi waded ashore and, before thousands of spectators, reached down to scoop up a piece of caked salt. With a grave and stern mien, he held his fist to the crowd, then opened it to expose in his palms the white crystals, the forbidden gift of the sea, the newest symbol in the struggle for Indian independence.

Within a week all India was in turmoil. All over the continent Gandhi's followers began to collect and distribute salt. The country was flooded with pamphlets explaining how to make salt from sea water. From one end of India to another, bonfires of British cloth and exports sparkled in the streets.

The British replied with the most massive round-up in Indian history, sweeping people to jail by the thousands. Gandhi was among them. Before returning to the confines of Yeravda prison, however, he managed to send a last message to his followers.

'The honour of India,' he said, 'has been symbolized by a fistful of salt in the hand of a man of non-violence. The fist which held the salt may be broken, but it will not yield up its salt.'

London, 18 February 1947

For three centuries, the walls of the House of Commons had echoed to the declarations of the handful of men who had assembled and guided the British Empire. Their debates and decisions had fixed the destiny of half a billion human beings scattered around the globe and helped impose the domination of a white, Christian, European elite on over a third of the earth's inhabitable land surface.

Now, tensely expectant, the members of the House of Commons shivered in the melancholy shadows stretching out in dark pools from the corners of their unheated hall to hear their leader pronounce a funeral oration for the British Empire. His bulky figure swathed in a black overcoat, Winston Churchill slumped despondently on the Opposition benches. For four decades, since he had joined the Commons, his voice had given utterance in that hall to Britain's imperial dream, just as, for the past decade, it had been the goad of England's conscience, the catalyst of her courage.

He was a man of rare clairvoyance but inflexible in many of his convictions. He gloried in every corner of the realm but for none of them did he have sentiments comparable to those with which he regarded India. Churchill loved India with a violent and unreal affection. He had gone out there as a young subaltern with his regiment, the 4th Queen's Own Hussars; played polo on the dusty maidans, gone pig-sticking and tiger hunting. He had climbed the Khyber Pass and fought the Pathans on the North-west Frontier. He was, forty-one years after his departure, still sending two pounds every month to the Indian who'd been his bearer for two years when he was a young subaltern. His gesture revealed much of his sentiments about India. He loved it first of all as a reflection of his own experience there and he loved the idea of doughty, upright Englishmen running the place with a firm, paternalistic hand.

His faith in the imperial dream was unshakeable. He had always maintained that Britain's position in the world was determined by the Empire. He sincerely believed in the Victorian dogma that those 'lesser breeds, without the law' were better off under European rule than they would have been under the tyranny of local despots. Despite the perception he had displayed on so many world issues, India was a blind spot for Churchill. Nothing could shake his passionately-held conviction that British rule in India had been just and exercised in India's best interests; that her masses looked on their rulers with gratitude and affection; that the politicians agitating for independence were a petty-minded, half-educated elite, unreflective of the desires or interests of the masses. Churchill understood India, his own Secretary of State for India had noted acidly, 'about as well as George III understood the American colonies.'

Since 1910 he had stubbornly resisted every effort to bring India towards independence. He contemptuously dismissed Gandhi and his Congress followers as 'men of straw'. More than any other man in that chamber, Churchill was torn by the knowledge that his successor at 10 Downing Street was undertaking the task he had refused to contemplate, dismembering the Empire. If he and his Conservative Party had been defeated in 1945, however, they still commanded an absolute majority in the House of Lords. That gave him the power, if he chose to exercise it, to delay Indian independence by two full years. Distaste spreading like a rash over his glowering face, he watched the spare Socialist who'd succeeded him as Prime Minister rise to speak.

The brief text in Clement Attlee's hand had been largely written by the young admiral he was sending to New Delhi to negotiate Britain's departure from India and whose name he was about to reveal. Louis Mountbatten had, with characteristic boldness, proposed it as a substitute for the lengthy document Attlee himself had drafted. It defined the new Viceroy's task in simple terms. Above all, it contained the new and salient point Mountbatten had maintained was essential if there was to be any hope of breaking the Indian log-jam. He had wrestled with Attlee for six weeks to nail it down with the precision he wanted.

The chilly assembly stirred as Attlee began to read the historic announcement. 'His Majesty's Government wishes to make it clear,' he began, 'that it is their definite intention to take the necessary steps to effect the transference of power into responsible Indian hands by a date not later than June 1948.'

A stunned silence followed as his words struck home to the men in the Commons. That they were the inevitable result of history and Britain's own avowed course in India did not mitigate the sadness produced by the realization that barely fourteen months remained to the British Raj. An era in British life was ending. What the *Manchester Guardian* would call the following morning 'the greatest disengagement in history' was about to begin.

The bulky figure slumped on his bench rose when his turn came to protest, to hurl out one last eloquent plea for empire. Shaking slightly from cold and emotion, Churchill declared that the whole business was 'an attempt by the government to make use of brilliant war figures in order to cover up a melancholy and disastrous transaction'.

By fixing a date for independence Attlee was adopting one of Gandhi's 'most scatter-brained observations – "Leave India to God".'

'It is with deep grief,' Churchill lamented, 'that I watch the clattering down of the British Empire with all its glories and all the services it has rendered mankind. Many have defended Britain against her foes. None can defend her against herself . . . let us not add by shameful flight, by a premature, hurried scuttle – at least let us not add to the pangs of sorrow so many of us feel, the taint and sneer of shame.'

They were the words of a master orator, but they were also a futile railing against the setting of a sun. When the division bell rang, the Commons acknowledged the dictate of history. By an overwhelming majority, it voted to end British rule in India no later than June 1948.

Penitent's Progress II

The deeper his little party penetrated into Noakhali's bayous, the more difficult Gandhi's mission became. The success he'd enjoyed with the Moslems in the first villages through which he'd passed had alerted the leaders in those that lay ahead. Sensing in it a challenge to their own authority, they had begun to stir the populace's hostility to the Mahatma and his mission.

This morning, his pilgrim's route took him past a Moslem school where seven- and eight-year-old children sat around their sheikh in an open-air classroom. Beaming like an excited grandfather rushing to embrace his favourite grandchildren, Gandhi hurried over to speak to the youngsters. The sheikh leapt up at his approach. With quick and angry gestures, he shooed his pupils into his hut, as though the old man approaching was a bogeyman come to cast some evil spell over them. Deeply pained by their flight, Gandhi stood before the doorway of the sheikh's hut, making sad little waves of his hand to the children whose faces he could make out in the shadows. Dark eyes wide with curiosity and incomprehension, they stared back at him. Finally Gandhi touched his hand to his heart and sent them the Moslem greeting '*salaam*'. Not a single childish hand answered his pathetic sign. Gandhi turned away and resumed his march.

There had been other incidents. Four days before someone had sabotaged a bamboo support holding up a rickety bridge of bamboo poles over which Gandhi was due to cross. Fortunately, it had been discovered before the bridge could collapse and send Gandhi and his party tumbling into the muddy waters ten feet below. On another morning, his route had taken him through a grove of bamboo and coconut trees. Every tree seemed to be festooned with a banner proclaiming slogans like 'Leave, you have been warned', 'Accept Pakistan', or 'Go for your own good'.

Those signs had no effect on Gandhi. Physical courage, the courage to accept without protest a beating, to face danger with quiet resolution was, Gandhi maintained, the prime characteristic required of a non-violent man. Since the first beating he'd received in South Africa, physical courage had been an attribute the frail Gandhi had displayed in abundance.

Muffling the inner sorrow the hostile signs and the children's rejection had provoked, Gandhi trudged serenely towards his next stop. It had been a damp, humid night and the alluvial soil on the narrow path along which his party walked was slick and slippery under the heavy dew. Suddenly, the little procession came to a halt. At its head, Gandhi laid aside his bamboo stave and bent down. Some unknown Moslem hands had littered the track on which he was to walk barefoot with shards of glass and lumps of human excrement. Tranquilly, Gandhi broke off the branch of a stubby palm. With it, he stooped and humbly undertook the most defiling act a Hindu can perform. Using his branch as a broom, the 77-year-old penitent began to sweep that human excrement from his path.

*

For decades, the most persistent English foe of the elderly man patiently cleaning the faeces from his way had been the master orator of the House of Commons. Winston Churchill had uttered in his long career enough memorable phrases to fill a volume of prose, but few of them had imprinted themselves as firmly on the public's imagination as those with which he had described Gandhi just sixteen years earlier, in February 1931: 'half-naked fakir'.

The occasion that prompted Churchill's outburst occurred on 17 February 1931. One hand holding his bamboo stave, the other clutching the edges of his white shawl, Mahatma Gandhi had that morning shuffled up the red sandstone steps to Viceroy's House, New Delhi. He was still wan from his weeks in a British prison but the man who had organized the Salt March did not come to that house as a suppliant for the Viceroy's favours. He came as India.

With his fistful of salt and his bamboo stave, Gandhi had rent the veil of the temple. So widespread had support for his movement become, that the Viceroy, Lord Irwin, had felt obliged to release him from prison and invite him to Delhi to treat with him as the acknowledged leader of the Indian masses. He was the first and the greatest in a line of Arab, African and Asian leaders who in the decades to come would follow his route from a British prison to a British conference chamber.

Winston Churchill had correctly read the portents of the meeting. He had assailed 'the nauseating and humiliating spectacle of this one-time Inner Temple lawyer, now seditious fakir, striding half-naked up the steps of the Viceroy's palace, there to negotiate and parley on equal terms with the representative of the King Emperor'.

'The loss of India,' he said with a clairvoyance that foreshadowed his speech sixteen years later, 'would be final and fatal to us. It could not fail to be part of a process that would reduce us to the scale of a minor power.'

His words, however, had no impact on the negotiations in New Delhi. These covered eight meetings over three weeks and produced what became known as the Gandhi-Irwin pact. Its text read like a treaty between two sovereign powers, and that was the measure of Gandhi's triumph. Under it, Irwin agreed to release from jail the thousands of Gandhi's followers who'd followed their leader to prison.* Gandhi for his part agreed to call off his movement and

* There would be no more immediate beneficiary of the pact than a young Sikh student named Gurcharan Singh. Arms bound behind his back, Gurcharan

attend a round table conference in London to discuss India's future.

Six months later, to the astonishment of a watching British nation, Mahatma Gandhi walked into Buckingham Palace to take tea with the King Emperor dressed in a loincloth and sandals, a living portrayal of Kipling's Gunga Din with 'nothing much before and rather less than 'arf o' that behind'. Later, when questioned on the appropriateness of his apparel, Gandhi replied with a smile 'the king was wearing enough for both of us'.

The publicity surrounding their meeting was in a sense the measure of the real impact of Gandhi's London visit. The round table conference he'd come to attend was a failure. London was not yet ready to contemplate Indian independence.

The real work Gandhi proclaimed lay 'outside the conference . . . The seed which is being sown now may result in a softening of the British spirit.' No one did more to soften it than Gandhi. The British press and public were fascinated by this man who wanted to overthrow their empire by turning the other cheek.

He had walked off his steamer in his loincloth carrying his bamboo stave. Behind him there were no aides-de-camp, no servants, only a handful of disciples and a goat, who tottered down the gangplank after Gandhi, an Indian goat to supply the Mahatma's daily bowl of milk. He ignored the hotels of the mighty to live in a settlement house in London's East End slums.

The man who had first come to London as an inarticulate tongue-tied student almost never stopped talking. He met Charlie Chaplin, Jan Smuts, George Bernard Shaw, the Archbishop of Canterbury, Harold Laski, Maria Montessori, coal miners, children, Lancashire textile workers thrown out of work by his campaigns in India; virtually everyone of importance except Winston Churchill who adamantly refused to see him.

Singh was walking that morning down a long corridor in Lahore prison towards a courtyard where a hangman waited to put an end to his life.

As Gurcharan Singh came within sight of the gallows tree, he heard footsteps running down the corridor behind him. He glanced back and saw his English jailer, a major named Martin, running after his party waving a blue piece of paper.

'Congratulations!' Martin shouted.

Gurcharan Singh almost fainted. 'You British are impossible,' he gasped, 'you're hanging me and you want to congratulate me on it.'

'No', the flustered Martin explained, 'all executions had been suspended because of the pact just signed in Delhi'. Several weeks later, Gurcharan Singh was freed. His first, grateful gesture was a pilgrimage to Gandhi's ashram. There the ardent student revolutionary fell under the Mahatma's spell and vowed to follow in Gandhi's footsteps. Ironically it was he who one day would hold in his arms the dying figure of the leader who had saved his life.

The impression Gandhi made was profound. The newsreels of the Salt March had already made him famous. To the masses of a Britain beset by industrial unrest, unemployment and grave social injustice, this messenger from the East in his Christ-like cotton sheet with his even more Christ-like message of love, was a fascinating and vaguely disturbing figure. Gandhi himself, perhaps, put his finger on the roots of much of that fascination in a radio broadcast to the USA.

World attention had been drawn to India's freedom struggle, he said, 'because the means adopted by us for attaining that liberty are unique . . . the world is sick unto death of blood-spilling. The world is seeking a way out and I flatter myself with the belief that perhaps it will be the privilege of the ancient land of India to show the way out to a hungering world.'

The western world Gandhi was visiting was not yet ready for the way out proposed by this revolutionary who travelled with a goat instead of a machine-gun. Already Europe's streets echoed to the stomp of jackboots and the shrieks of impassioned ideologues. Nonetheless, when he left, thousands of French, Swiss and Italians flocked to the railroad stations on his route to the Italian port of Brindisi to gape at the frail, toothless man leaning from the window of his third-class compartment.

In Paris, so many people swarmed to the station that Gandhi had to climb on a baggage cart to address them. In Switzerland, where he visited his friend, the author Romain Rolland, the dairymen of Léman clamoured for the privilege of serving the 'king of India'. In Rome, he warned Mussolini fascism would 'collapse like a house of cards', watched a football game and wept at the sight of the statue of Christ on the Cross in the Sistine Chapel.

Despite that triumphant progress across Europe, Gandhi suffered much on the voyage home. 'I have come back empty-handed,' he told the thousands who greeted him in Bombay. India would have to return to civil disobedience. Less than a week later the man who had been the King Emperor's tea-time guest in London was once again His Imperial Majesty's guest – this time back in Yeravda prison.

For the next three years, Gandhi was in and out of prison while in London Churchill thundered, 'Gandhi and all he stands for must be crushed'. Despite Churchill's opposition, however, the British produced a basic reform for India offering her provinces some local autonomy, the Government of India Act of 1935. Finally released from jail, Gandhi turned from his political combat to devote three years to two projects particularly close to him, the plight of India's millions of Untouchables and the situation in her villages.

With the approach of World War II, Gandhi became more convinced than ever that the non-violence which had been the guiding principle of India's domestic struggle was the only philosophy capable of saving man from self-destruction.

When Mussolini overran Ethiopia, he urged the Ethiopians to 'allow themselves to be slaughtered'. The result, he said, would be more effective than resistance since 'after all, Mussolini didn't want a desert'. Sickened by the Nazis' persecution of the Jews, he declared: 'If ever there could be justifiable war in the name of and for humanity, war against Germany to prevent the wanton persecution of a whole race would be completely justified.'

'Still,' he said, 'I do not believe in war.' He proposed 'a calm and determined stand offered by unarmed men and women possessing the strength of suffering given to them by Jehovah.' 'That,' he said, 'would convert [the Germans] to an appreciation of human dignity.'

Not even the atrocities which were perpetrated in the concentration camps of Europe were to make him doubt the essential correctness of his attitude.

When war finally broke out, Gandhi prayed that the holocaust might at least produce, like some sudden burst of sunshine after the storm, the heroic gesture, the non-violent sacrifice, that would illuminate for mankind the path away from a tightening cycle of self-destruction.

While Churchill summoned his countrymen to 'blood, toil, tears and sweat', Gandhi, hoping to find in the English a people brave enough to put his theory to the ultimate test, proposed another course. 'Invite Hitler and Mussolini to take what they want of the countries you call your possessions,' he wrote to the English at the height of the blitz. 'Let them take possession of your beautiful island with its many beautiful buildings. You will give all this, but neither your minds nor your souls.'

That course would have been a logical application of Gandhi's doctrine. To the British, and above all to their indomitable leader, his words rang out like the gibberish of an irrelevant old fool.

Gandhi could not even convince the leadership of his own Congress movement that pacifism was the right course. Most of his followers were dedicated anti-fascists and anxious to take India into the fight if they could do so as free men. For the first time, but not the last, Gandhi and his disciples parted company.

It took Churchill to drive them back together. His position on India remained as rigid as ever. He refused to consider any of the compromises which would have allowed India's Nationalists to join the war effort. When he held his first meeting with Franklin Roosevelt to frame the Atlantic Charter, he made it clear that, as far as he was concerned, India was not to fall under its generous provisions. His American partner was stunned by his sensitivity on the subject. Soon, another of his phrases was being repeated in the Allies' councils: 'I have not become His Majesty's First Minister to preside over the dissolution of the British Empire.'

It was not until March 1942, when the Japanese Imperial Army was at India's gates, that Churchill, under pressure from Washington and his own colleagues, sent a serious offer to New Delhi. To deliver it, he selected a particularly sympathetic courier, Sir Stafford Cripps, a vegetarian and austere Socialist with long, friendly relations with the Congress leadership. Considering its author the proposal Cripps carried was remarkably generous. It offered the Indians the most Britain could be expected to concede in the midst of a war, a solemn pledge of what amounted to independence, dominion status, after Japan's defeat. It contained, however, in recognition of the Moslem League's increasingly strident calls for an Islamic state, a provision which could eventually accommodate their demand.

Forty-eight hours after his arrival, Gandhi told Cripps that the offer was unacceptable because it contemplated the 'perpetual vivisection of India'. Besides, the British were offering India future independence to secure immediate Indian co-operation in the violent defence of Indian soil. That was not an agreement calculated to sway the apostle of non-violence. If the Japanese were to be resisted, it could be only in one way for Gandhi, non-violently.

The Mahatma cherished a secret dream. He was not opposed to the spilling of oceans of blood, provided it was done in a just cause. He saw rank on serried rank of disciplined, non-violent Indians marching out to die on the bayonets of the Japanese until that catalytic instant when the enormity of their sacrifice would overwhelm their foes, vindicate non-violence, and change the course of human history.

Churchill's plan, he decreed, was 'a post-dated cheque on a failing bank'. If he had nothing else to offer, Gandhi told Cripps, he might as well 'take the next plane home'.*

The day after Cripps' departure was a Monday, Gandhi's 'day of silence', a ritual he had observed once a week for years to conserve his vocal chords and promote a sense of harmony in his being.

* Cripps did not leave immediately. He nearly succeeded in getting the Congress leadership to break with the Mahatma. The issue was the degree to which they would be allowed to supervise India's war efforts. Once again, it was Churchill who prevented an agreement being reached.

Unhappily for Gandhi and for India, his 'Inner Voice', the voice of his conscience, was not observing a similar vigil. It spoke to Gandhi and the advice it uttered proved disastrous.

It came down to two words, the two words which became the slogan of Gandhi's next struggle: 'Quit India'. The British should drop the reins of power in India immediately, Gandhi proposed. Let them 'leave India to God or even anarchy'. If the British left India to its fate the Japanese would have no reason to attack.

Just after midnight, 8 August 1942, in a stifling hot Bombay meeting hall, Gandhi, naked to the waist, sent out a call to arms to his followers of the All India Congress Committee. His voice was quiet and composed, but the words he uttered carried a passion and fervour uncharacteristic of Gandhi.

'I want freedom immediately,' he said, 'this very night, before dawn if it can be had.'

'Here is a *mantra*, a short one I give you,' he told his followers. ' "Do or die". We shall either free India or die in the attempt; we shall not live to see the perpetuation of our slavery.'

What Gandhi got before dawn was not freedom but another invitation to a British jail. In a carefully prepared move the British swept Gandhi and the entire Congress leadership into prison for the duration of the war. A brief outburst of violence followed their arrest but, within three weeks, the British had the situation under control.

Gandhi's tactic played into the hands of the Moslem League by sweeping his Congress leaders from the political scene at a crucial moment. While they languished in jail, their Moslem rivals supported Britain's war effort, earning by their attitude a considerable debt of gratitude. Not only had Gandhi's plan failed to get the English to quit India; it had gone a long way to making sure that, before leaving the country, they would feel compelled to divide it.

This would be Gandhi's last sojourn in a British prison. By the time it ended the old man would have spent a total of 2338 days in jail, 249 in South Africa, 2089 in India. Gandhi's keepers confined him not to the familiar grounds of the Yeravda jail where he had already spent so much time but in the nearby palace of the Aga Khan. Five months after his prison term began, Gandhi announced he was going to undertake a 21-day fast. The reasons behind it were obscure, but the British were in no mood to compromise. Churchill informed New Delhi that, if Gandhi wanted to starve himself to death, he was free to go ahead and do so.

Midway through the fast, Gandhi began to sink. Unyielding, the British started discreet preparations for his death. Two Brahmin priests were brought to the prison and held in readiness to officiate at the cremation. Under the cover of darkness the sandalwood for his funeral pyre was secretly taken into the palace. Everyone was ready for his death except the 74-year-old Gandhi. He had weighed less than 110 pounds when the fast began. Yet 21 days on a diet of water mixed with salt and an occasional drop of lemon and moosambi juice couldn't kill his towering spirit. He survived his self-imposed ordeal.

Another one awaited him, however. The sandalwood that had been destined for his cremation would feed the flames of another funeral pyre, his wife's. On 22 February 1944 the woman he had married as an illiterate, thirteen-year-old child died, her head resting in Gandhi's lap. Gandhi had not been prepared to disavow a principle to save her life. He believed in nature cures and he also believed that to administer medicine by hypodermic needle performed a violent action upon the human body. Aware that his wife was dying from acute bronchitis, the British flew a supply of rare and precious penicillin to the prison. But at the last minute, when Gandhi learned the drug which could have saved his dying wife would have to be administered intravenously, he had refused her doctors permission to give it to her.

After her death, Gandhi's own health failed rapidly. He contracted malaria, hookworm and amoebic dysentery. In his weakened and depressed state, it was clear he would not survive long. A reluctant Churchill was finally prevailed on to release him so he would not die in a British jail.

He was not going to die in a British India, either. Ensconced in a hut on the beachfront estate of a wealthy supporter near Bombay, Gandhi slowly recovered his health. As he did so, Churchill, who had not bothered to reply to his Viceroy's urgent cables on India's growing famine, sent New Delhi a petulant cable. Why, he asked, hadn't Gandhi died yet?

A few days later, Gandhi's host entered his hut to find one of the Mahatma's followers standing on his head, another in transcendental meditation, a third asleep on the floor and the Mahatma himself on his open toilet staring raptly into space.

He burst into gales of laughter. Why, Gandhi asked as he emerged from his toilet, was he laughing?

'Ah *Bapu*,' laughed his host, 'look at this room: one man standing on his head, another meditating, a third sleeping, you on your toilet – and these are the people who are going to make India free!'

* * *

Northolt Airport, 20 March 1947

The aircraft waited in the early morning light on the runway of Northolt airport where, two and a half months earlier, Louis Mountbatten had landed on New Year's Day. Charles Smith, his valet, had already stowed on board the Mountbattens' personal luggage, 66 pieces, a collection so complete it included a set of silver ashtrays with the new Viceroy's family crest. His wife had casually placed in the overhead rack an old shoe-box. Finding it would cause a moment of panic on the flight out. Packed inside was a family heirloom, a diamond tiara Lady Mountbatten would wear when she was proclaimed Vicereine.

Stowed away also were all the documents, the briefs, the position papers the new Viceroy and his staff would have to guide them in the months ahead. The most important among them covered only two pages and was signed by Clement Attlee. It set out the terms of Mountbatten's mission. No Viceroy had ever received a mandate like it. Mountbatten had, for all practical purposes, written it himself. Its terms were clear and simple. He was to make every effort to arrange for the transfer of British sovereignty in India to a single, independent nation within the Commonwealth by 30 June 1948. As a guide he was to follow as far as possible a plan formulated eight months earlier by a cabinet mission sent to New Delhi under the chairmanship of Sir Stafford Cripps. It proposed, as a compromise with the Moslem demand for Pakistan, a federated India with a weak central government. There was, however, no question of forcing an agreement out of India's warring politicians. If by 1 October, six months after taking power, Mountbatten saw no way of getting them to agree on a plan for a united India, then he was to recommend his alternative solution to India's dilemma.

As his York MW102* went through its final checks, Mount-

* Mountbatten was particularly attached to the converted Lancaster bomber. It had flown him on countless missions during his days as Supreme Commander South-East Asia. He had fitted it out with bunks for a relief crew which would shorten the time required for the London-Delhi journey by eliminating crews rest stops on the ground.

The plane, in fact very nearly kept him from going to India at all. One day, Mountbatten happened to be in his London office when an RAF Group Captain called his ADC, Lt-Col Peter Howes, to advise him that the York MW 102 would not be available for use by the new Viceroy. Mountbatten took the phone from his ADC's hands.

'Group Captain,' he said, 'I wish to thank you.'

'Thank me?' said the perplexed officer.

'Yes,' continued Mountbatten. 'You see when I accepted this appointment, I

batten paced the tarmac alongside with two of his old wartime comrades who were going off to India with him. Capt. Ronald Brockman, head of his personal staff, and Lt-Commander Peter Howes, his senior ADC. On how many trips, Brockman thought, had that converted Lancaster bomber carried Mountbatten to front-line posts in the jungles of Burma, to the great conferences of the war. Beside him, the usually ebullient Admiral was moody and introspective. The crewman announced the flight was ready.

'Well,' sighed Mountbatten, 'we're off to India. I don't want to go. They don't want me out there. We'll probably come home with bullets in our backs.'

The three men mounted the aircraft. The engines came to life. The York fled down the runway, cut across the sun and pointed east to India to close the great adventure Capt. Hawkins had begun by sailing east in his galleon the *Hector*, three and a half centuries earlier.

stipulated as one of my conditions that I should be allowed to take the York to Delhi with me. You tell me I cannot have this aircraft and I am most grateful to you. I did not want to be Viceroy of India and now you've saved me from the job.'

A stunned silence settled over the room as he hung up. Within minutes he had his plane.

4

A Last Tattoo for the Dying Raj

Penitent's Progress III

Nothing could stop him. Fired by his unquenchable spirit, the old man drove his bare and aching feet from village to village, applying the balm of his love to India's sores. Slowly, the wounds began to heal. In the wake of Gandhi's wan and bent silhouette, the passions cooled. Timidly, uncertainly, peace spread its mantle over the blood-drenched marshes of Noakhali.

Its return did not end Gandhi's suffering, however. A private drama had accompanied him on his march along those hate-filled footpaths, a drama whose dimensions would eventually scandalize some of his oldest associates, alarm millions of Indians, and baffle the historians who would one day attempt to comprehend all the facets of Mohandas Gandhi's complex character. It would also produce one of the gravest personal crises in the life of the 77-year-old man who was the conscience of India.

Yet its roots were in no way sunk in the great political struggle of which he'd been the principal figure for a quarter of a century. They lay in that force which Gandhi had struggled to sublimate and control for forty years, sex. Its locus was a nineteen-year-old girl, Gandhi's great-niece, Manu. Manu had been raised by Gandhi and his wife as their own granddaughter. She had nursed Kasturbai Gandhi on her deathbed and, before dying, Kasturba had confided her to her husband's care.

'I've been a father to many,' Gandhi promised the girl, 'to you I am a mother.' He fussed over her like a mother, supervising her dress, her diet, her education, her religious training. The problem which arose in Noakhali had begun in a conversation between them just before Gandhi set out on his pilgrimage. With the shyness of a young girl confessing something to her mother, Manu had admitted to Gandhi she had never felt the sexual impulses normal in a girl of her age.

To Gandhi, with his convoluted philosophy of sex, her words had special importance. Since he had sworn his own vow of chastity, Gandhi had maintained that sexual continence was the most important discipline his truly non-violent followers, male and female, had to master. His ideal non-violent army would be composed of sexless soldiers because otherwise, Gandhi feared, their moral strength would desert them at a critical moment.

Gandhi saw in Manu's words the chance to make of her the perfect female votary. 'If out of India's millions of daughters, I can train even one into an ideal woman by becoming an ideal mother to you,' he told her, 'I shall have rendered a unique service to womankind.' But first, he felt he had to be sure she was telling the truth. Only his closest collaborators were accompanying him in Noakhali, he informed her, but she would be welcome provided she submitted to his discipline and went through the test to which he meant to subject her.

They would, he decreed, share each night the crude straw pallet which passed for his bed. He regarded himself as a mother; she had said she found nothing but a mother's love in him. If they were both truthful, if he remained firm in his ancient vow of chastity and she had never known sexual arousal, then they would be able to lie together in the innocence of a mother and daughter. If one of them was not being truthful, they would soon discover it.

If, however, Manu was being truthful then, Gandhi believed, she would flourish under his close and constant supervision. His own sexless state would stifle any residual desire still lurking in her. Pygmalion-like, a transformation would come over her. She would develop clarity of thought and firmness of speech. A new spirit would suffuse the girl, giving her a pure, crystalline devotion to the great task which awaited her.

Manu had accepted and her lithe figure had followed Gandhi's traces across the swamp-lands of Noakhali. As Gandhi had known it would, his decision had immediately provoked the consternation of his little party.

They think all this is a sign of infatuation on my part,' he told Manu after a few nights together. 'I laugh at their ignorance. They do not understand.'

Very few people would. Only the purest of Gandhi's followers would be able to follow the complex reasoning behind this latest manifestation of a great spiritual struggle, which for Gandhi, went all the way back to that evening in South Africa in 1906 when he had announced to his wife his decision to take the vow of *Brahmacharya*, chastity. In swearing that pledge,* Gandhi was setting out on a path almost as old as Hinduism itself. For countless centuries, a Hindu's route to self-realization had passed by the sublimation of that vital

* The impulses thrusting Gandhi to take his vow were not Hindu alone. As Christ's dictum of turning the other cheek had been vital in helping him formulate his non-violent ideal, so Jesus's words referring to 'those who become eunuchs for my sake . . . for love of the Kingdom of Heaven', had inspired him in taking his ancient Hindu pledge.

force responsible for the creation of life. Only by forcing his sexual energy inward to fuel the furnace of his spiritual force, the Hindu ancients maintained, could a man achieve the spiritual intensity necessary to self-realization.

To aid men sworn to lead the chaste life, those Hindu sages had laid down a code of conduct for *Brahmacharya* called the nine-fold wall of protection. A true *Brahmachari* was not supposed to live among women, animals or eunuchs. He was not allowed to sit on the same mat with a woman or even gaze upon any part of a woman's body. He was counselled to avoid the sensual blandishments of a hot bath, an oily massage or the alleged aphrodisiac properties of milk, curds, *ghee* or fatty foods.

Gandhi had not become chaste so as to live in a Himalayan cave, however. That kind of chastity involved little self-discipline or moral merit, he maintained. He had taken his vow because he firmly believed the sublimation of his sexual energies would give him the moral and spiritual power to accomplish his mission. His kind of *Brahmachari* was a man who had so suppressed his sexual urge that he could move normally in the society of women without feeling any sexual desire in himself or arousing it in them. A *Brahmachari*, he wrote, 'does not flee the company of women,' because for him 'the distinction between man and woman almost disappears'.

The real *Brahmachari*'s 'sexual organs will begin to look different', Gandhi declared. 'They remain as mere symbols of his sex and his sexual secretions are sublimated into a vital force pervading his whole being.' The perfect *Brahmachari* in Gandhi's mind was a man who could 'lie by the side even of a Venus in all her naked beauty, without being physically or mentally disturbed'.

It was an extraordinary ideal and Gandhi's fight to attain it was doubly difficult because the sex drive he was struggling to suppress had been strongly and deeply rooted. For years after taking his vow, Gandhi experimented with different diets, looking for one which would have the slightest possible impact on his sexual organs. While thousands of Indians sought out exotic foods to stimulate their desires, Gandhi spurned in turn, spices, green vegetables, certain fruits, in his efforts to stifle his.

Thirty years of discipline, prayer and spiritual exercise were needed before Gandhi reached the point at which he felt he had rooted out all sexual desire from his mind and body. His confidence in his achievement was shattered one night in Bombay in 1936, in what he referred to as 'my darkest hour'. That night, at the age of 67, thirty years after he'd sworn his *Brahmachari*'s vow, Gandhi awoke from a dream with what would have been to most men of that age a source of some satisfaction, but was to Gandhi a calamity, an erection. There, quivering between his loins, was proof he had still not reached the ideal towards which he'd been striving for three decades. Gandhi was so overwhelmed by anguish at 'this frightful experience', that he swore a vow of total silence for six weeks.

He pondered for months over the meaning of his weakness, debating whether he should retreat into a kind of Himalayan cave of his own making. He finally concluded his horrible nightmare was a challenge to his spiritual force thrown up by the forces of evil. He decided to accept the challenge, to press on to his goal of extirpating the last traces of sexuality from his being.

As his confidence in the mastery of his desires came back, he gradually extended the range of physical contact he allowed himself with women. He nursed them when they were ill and allowed them to nurse him. He took his bath in full view of his fellow ashramites, male and female. He had his daily massage virtually naked, with young girls most frequently serving as his masseuses. He often gave interviews or consulted the leaders of his Congress Party while the girls massaged him. He wore few clothes and urged his disciples, male and female, to do likewise because clothes he said, only encouraged a false sense of modesty. The only time he ever addressed himself directly to Winston Churchill was in reply to his famous phrase 'half-naked fakir'. He was trying to be both, Gandhi said, because the naked state represented the true innocence for which he was striving. Finally, he decreed that there would be no problem in men and women who were faithful to their vow of chastity sleeping in the same room at night, if they happened, in the performance of their duties, to find themselves together at nightfall.

The decision to have Manu share his pallet so he could guide more totally her spiritual growth was, to Gandhi, a natural outgrowth of that philosophy. During the agonizing days of his penitent's pilgrimage, her delicate figure was rarely out of his sight. From village to village, she shared the crude shelters offered him by the peasants of Noakhali. She massaged him, prepared his mudbaths, cared for him when he was striken with diarrhoea. She slept and rose with him, prayed by his side, shared the contents of his beggar's bowl. One bitter February night she awoke to find the old man shaking violently by her side. She massaged him, heaped on his shivering frame whatever scraps of cloth she could find in the hut. Finally, Gandhi dozed off and, she later noted, 'we slept cosily in each other's warmth until prayer time'.

For Gandhi, secure in his own conscience, there was nothing improper or even remotely sexual in his relations with Manu.

Indeed, it is almost inconceivable that the faintest tremor of sexual arousal passed between them. To the Mahatma, the reasoning which had led him to perform what was, for him, a duty to Manu, was sufficient justification for his action. Perhaps, however, deep in his subconscious, other forces he ignored helped propel him to it.

In the twilight of his life, Gandhi was a lonely man. He had lost his wife and closest friend in wartime prison. He was losing the support of some of his oldest followers. He risked losing the dream he'd pursued for decades. He had never had a daughter and, perhaps, the one failure in his life had been in his role as a father. His eldest son, embittered because he'd felt his father's devotion to others had deprived him of his share of paternal affection, was a hopeless alcoholic who had staggered drunk to his dying mother's bedside. Two of his other sons were in South Africa and rarely in contact with Gandhi. Only with his youngest son did he enjoy a normal father-son relation. In any event, whatever the explanation, a deep, spiritual bond was destined to link the Mahatma and the shy, devoted girl so anxious to share his misery during the closing months of his life.

As word of what was happening spread beyond his entourage, a campaign of calumnies, spread by the leaders of the Moslem League, grew up about Gandhi. The news reached Delhi, spreading intense shock among the leaders of Congress waiting to begin their critical talks with India's new Viceroy.

Gandhi finally confronted the rumours in an evening prayer meeting. Assailing the 'small talk, whispers and innuendo around him', he told the crowd that his great-niece Manu shared his bed with him each night and explained why she was there. His words calmed his immediate circle, but when he sent them to his newspaper *Harijan* to be published, the storm broke again. Two of the editors quit in protest. Its trustees, fearful of a scandal, did something they had never dreamed of doing before. They refused to publish a text written by the Mahatma.

The crisis reached its climax in Haimchar, the last stop on Gandhi's tour. There, Gandhi revealed his intention to carry his mission to the province of Bihar where, this time, he would work with his fellow Hindus who had killed the members of a Moslem minority in their midst.

His words alarmed the Congress leadership in Delhi who feared the effect his relationship with Manu could have on Bihar's orthodox Hindu community. A series of emissaries discreetly asked him to abandon it before leaving for Bihar. He refused.

Finally, it was Manu herself, perhaps prodded by one of those emissaries, who gently suggested to the elderly Mahatma that they suspend their practice. She remained absolutely at one with him, she promised. She was renouncing nothing of what they were trying to achieve. The concession she proposed was only temporary, a concession to the smaller minds around them who could not understand the goals he sought. She would stay behind when he left for Bihar. Saddened, Gandhi agreed.

New Delhi, March–April 1947

In his immaculate white naval uniform, 'he looked like a film star' to the 23-year-old captain of the Grenadier Guards just appointed one of his ADCs. Serene and smiling, his wife at his side, Louis Mountbatten rode up to Viceroy's House in a gilded landau built half a century before for the royal progress through Delhi of his uncle, George V. At the instant his escort reached the palace's grand staircase, the bagpipes of the Royal Scots Fusiliers skirled out a plaintive welcome to India's last Viceroy.

A faint, sad smile on his face, the outgoing Viceroy, Lord Wavell, waited at the head of the staircase. The very presence in New Delhi of those two men represented a break with tradition. Normally, an outgoing Viceroy sailed with due pomp from the Gateway of India while the next steamer bore his successor towards its spans, thus sparing India the embarrassment of having two Gods upon its soil at the same time. Mountbatten himself had insisted on this breach of custom so he could talk with the man to whom he formally bowed his head as he reached the top of the stairs.

For a moment, in the intermittent glare of flashbulbs, the two men stood chatting. They were a poignantly contrasting pair: Mountbatten the glamorous war hero, exuding confidence and vitality; Wavell, the one-eyed old soldier, adored by his subordinates, brusquely sacked by the politicians, a man who had sadly noted in his diary not long before that, for the past half decade, his had been the unhappy fate 'to conduct withdrawals and mitigate defeats'.*

Wavell escorted Mountbatten through the heavy teak doors to the Viceroy's study and his first direct confrontation with the awesome problems awaiting him.

* The Attlee government had treated Wavell in particularly brutal fashion. He had been in London when Mountbatten was asked to replace him, but given no hint he was about to be sacked. He learned the news only hours before Attlee made it public. It was only on Mountbatten's insistence that Attlee accorded him the elevation in his rank in the peerage which traditionally was offered a departing Viceroy.

'I am sorry indeed that you've been sent out here in my place,' Wavell began.

'Well,' said Mountbatten, somewhat taken aback, 'that's being candid. Why? Don't you think I'm up to it?'

'No, it's not that,' replied Wavell, 'indeed, I'm very fond of you, but you've been given an impossible task. I've tried everything I know to solve this problem and I can see no light. There is just no way of dealing with it. Not only have we had absolutely no help from Whitehall, but we've now reached a complete impasse here.'

Patiently, Wavell reviewed his efforts to reach a solution. Then he stood up and opened his safe. Locked inside were the only two items he could bequeath his successor. The first sparkled on dark velvet folds inside a wooden box. It was the diamond-encrusted badge of the Grand Master of the Order of the Star of India, the emblem of Mountbatten's new office, which, forty-eight hours hence, he would hang around his neck for the ceremonial which would officially install him as Viceroy.

The second was a manilla file on which was written the words 'Operation Madhouse'. It contained the only solution the able soldier had to propose to India's dilemma. Sadly, he took it out of the safe and laid it on his desk.

'This is called "Madhouse",' he explained, 'because it is a problem for a madhouse. Alas, I can see no other way out.'

It called for the British evacuation of India, province by province, women and children first, then civilians, then soldiers, a move likely, in Gandhi's words, to 'leave India to chaos'.

'It's a terrible solution, but it's the only one I can see,' Wavell sighed. He picked up the file from his desk and offered it to his stunned successor.

'I am very, very, very sorry,' he concluded, 'but this is all I can bequeath you.'

As the new Viceroy concluded that sad introduction to his new functions, his wife on the floor above Wavell's study was receiving a more piquant introduction to her new life. On reaching their quarters, Edwina Mountbatten had asked a servant for a few scraps for the two sealyhams, Mizzen and Jib, which the Mountbattens had brought out from London. To her amazement, thirty minutes later, a pair of turbaned servants solemnly marched into her bedroom, each bearing a silver tray set with a china plate on which was laid several slices of freshly-roasted chicken breast.

Eyes wide with wonder, Edwina contemplated that chicken. She had not seen food like it in the austerity of England for weeks. She glanced at the sealyhams, barking at her feet, then back at the chicken. Her disciplined conscience would not allow her to give pet such nourishment.

'Give me that,' she ordered.

Firmly grasping the two plates of chicken, she marched into the bathroom and locked the door. There, the woman who would offer in the next months the hospitality of Viceroy's House to 25,000 people, gleefully began to devour the chicken intended for her pets.

* * *

The closing chapter in a great story was about to begin. In a few minutes on this morning of 24 March 1947, the last Englishman to govern India would mount his gold and crimson viceregal throne. Installed upon that throne, Louis Mountbatten would become the twentieth and final representative of a prestigious dynasty, his would be the last hands to clasp the sceptre that had passed from Hastings to Wellesley, Cornwallis and Curzon.

The site of his official consecration was the ceremonial Durbar Hall of a palace whose awesome dimensions were rivalled only by those of Versailles and the Peterhof of the Tsars. Ponderous, solemn, unabashedly imperial, Viceroy's House, New Delhi, was the last such palace men would ever build for a single ruler. Indeed, only in India with its famished hordes desperate for work would a palace like Viceroy's House have been built and maintained in the twentieth century.

Its façades were covered with the red and white stone of Barauli, the building blocks of the Moghuls whose monuments it had succeeded. White, yellow, green, black marble quarried from the veins that had furnished the glistening mosaics of the Taj Mahal, embellished its floors and walls. So long were its corridors that in its basement servants rode from one end of the building to the other on bicycles.

This morning, those servants were giving a last polish to the marble, the woodwork, the brass of its 37 salons and its 340 rooms. Outside, in the formal Moghul gardens, 418 gardeners, more than Louis XIV had employed at Versailles, laboured to provide a perfect trim to its intricate maze of grass squares, rectangular flower beds and vaulted water-ways. 50 of them were boys hired just to scare away the birds. In their stables, the 500 Punjabi horsemen of the Viceroy's bodyguard adjusted their white and gold tunics as they prepared to mount their superb black horses. Throughout the house, gold and scarlet turbans flaring above their foreheads, their white tunics already embroidered with the new Viceroy's coat of arms, other servants scurried down the corridors on a final errand. For the last time, they all, gardeners, chamberlains, cooks, stewards, bearers, horsemen, all the retainers of that feudal fortress lost in the twentieth century, joined in preparing the enthronement of one of that select company of men for whom it had been built, a Viceroy of India.

In one of the private chambers of the great house, a man contemplated the white full-dress admiral's uniform his employer would wear to take possession of Viceroy's House's majestic precincts. No flaring turban graced his head. Charles Smith was not a product of the Punjab or Rajasthan, but of a country village in the south of England.

With a meticulous regard for detail acquired over a quarter of a century of service in Mountbatten's employ, Smith slipped the cornflower-blue silk sash of the world's most exclusive company, the Order of the Garter, through the right epaulette and stretched it taut across the uniform's breast. Then he looped the gold aiguillettes which marked the uniform's owner as a personal ADC to King George VI through the right epaulette.

Finally, Smith took his employer's medal bar and the four major stars he would wear this morning from their velvet boxes. With respect and care he gave a last polish to their gleaming gold and silver enamel forms: the Order of the Garter, the Order of the Star of India, the Order of the Indian Empire, the Grand Cross of the Victorian Order.

Those rows of ribbons and crosses marking the milestones of Louis Mountbatten's career were, in their special fashion, the milestones along the course of Charles Smith's life as well. Since he had joined Mountbatten's service as third footman at the age of eighteen, Smith had walked in another man's shadow. In the great country houses of England, in the naval stations of empire, in the capitals of Europe, his employer's joys had been his, his triumphs, his victories, his sorrows, his griefs. During the war, he had joined the service and eventually followed Mountbatten to South-East Asia. There, from a spectator's seat in the City Hall of Singapore, Charles Smith had watched with tears of pride filling his eyes as Mountbatten, in another uniform he'd prepared, had effaced the worst humiliation Britain had ever endured by taking the surrender of almost three-quarters of a million Japanese soldiers, sailors and airmen.

Smith stepped back to contemplate his work. No one in the world was more demanding when it came to dressing a uniform than Mountbatten, and this was not a morning to make a mistake. Smith unbuttoned the jacket and sash, and gingerly lifted it from the dress dummy on which it rested. He eased it over his own shoulders and turned to a mirror for a final check. There, for a brief and poignant moment before that mirror, he was out of the shadows. For just a second, Charles Smith, too, could dream he was the Viceroy of India.

Slipping his tunic heavy with its load of orders and decorations, over his torso, Louis Mountbatten could not help thinking of those magic weeks a quarter of a century earlier when he'd discovered India by the side of his cousin, the Prince of Wales. Both of them had been dazzled by the majestic air surrounding the Viceroy of India as he presided over his empire. So much pomp, so much luxury, such homage seemed to accompany his slightest gesture that the Prince of Wales himself had remarked, 'I never understood how a king should live until I saw the Viceroy of India.'

Mountbatten remembered his own youthful amazement at the panoply of imperial power that focused on the person of one Englishman the allegiance of the world's densest masses. He recalled his awe at the manner in which the viceregal establishment had blended the glitter of a European court, and the faintly decadent aura of the feasts of the Orient. Now, against his will, that viceregal throne with all its pomp and splendour was about to be his. His Viceroyalty, alas, would bear little resemblance to that gay round of ceremonies and hunting that had stirred his youthful dreamings. His youthful ambitions were to be fulfilled, but in the real world, not the fairy-tale world of 1921.

A knock on the door interrupted his meditation. He turned. The rigorously unemotional Mountbatten started at the sight framed in the doorway of his bedroom. It was his wife, a diamond tiara glittering in her brown hair, her white silk gown clinging to the curves of a figure as slim and supple as it had been that day she had walked out of St Margaret's, Westminster, on his arm.

*

Like her husband, Edwina Mountbatten seemed to have been sought out for the blessings of a capricious Providence. She had beauty. She possessed a fine intellect, more penetrating some thought than her husband's. She had inherited great wealth from her maternal grandfather, Sir Ernest Cassel, and social position from her father's family whose forebears included England's great nineteenth-century Prime Minister, Lord Palmerston, and the famous philanthropic politician, the seventh Earl of Shaftesbury. There had been clouds in her paradise. An intensely unhappy childhood after her mother's early death had left her with an introverted nature. She was easily hurt and kept the pain of those hurts locked inside her where they corroded the linings of her being. Small things pained her.

Unlike her ebullient husband who never hesitated to criticize anything that displeased him and accepted criticism with lofty aplomb, Edwina Mountbatten took offence easily. 'You could tell Lord Mountbatten what you wanted, any way you wanted to,' recalled one of their senior aides. 'With Lady Louis, you had to proceed with the utmost care.'

She had locked her shyness, her introverted nature into the strait-jacket of an unyielding will. By that will, she made herself into something which nature had not intended her to be: an outgoing woman, seemingly extroverted. But the price was always there to be paid. She had been speaking in public for a decade, sometimes two or three times a week, yet, before making a major speech, her hands shook almost uncontrollably. Her health was as fragile as a porcelain vase. She suffered almost daily from the cruel thrusts of a migraine headache, but no one outside her family knew, because physical weakness was not something she was prepared to indulge. Unlike her self-confident husband who could boast he 'never, never worried', Edwina worried constantly. While he slept immediately and soundly, sleep's solace came to her only as a pill-induced torpor.

Two distinctly separate periods had marked the Mountbattens' quarter of a century together. During the first fourteen years of their marriage, while Louis Mountbatten was slowly moving up the naval ladder, he had insisted they exclude her wealth and their social position from the naval environment in which they spent much of their time. Away from the naval stations, however, in London, Paris and on the Riviera, Edwina became, her daughter recalled, 'the perfect social butterfly', a zealous party-giver and party-goer, blazing through the twenties with the intensity of a Fitzgerald heroine. When she was not dancing, she sought the stimulation of adventure: chartering a copra schooner in the South Pacific, flying on the first flight from Sydney to London, being the first European woman up the Burma Road.

That carefree, innocent period in their life had ended with Mussolini's invasion of Ethiopia. By Munich, the transformation was complete. From then on, her life was dominated by the conviction that it was immoral not to be fully occupied by the pursuit of some social or political good. The giddy heiress became a social reformer, the social butterfly a concerned activist with a liberal outlook little appreciated by her peers.

During the war, she led the St John Ambulance Brigade with its 60,000 members. When Japan surrendered, her husband urgently requested her to tour the Japanese prisoner-of-war camps so as to organize the care and evacuation of their most desperate inmates.

Before the first soldiers of his command had set foot on the Malayan Peninsula, Edwina Mountbatten, armed only with a letter from her husband, her only escort a secretary, three of her husband's staff officers and an Indian ADC, plunged into territory still under Japanese control. She continued all the way to Balikpan, Manila and Hong Kong, fearlessly berating the Japanese, forcing them to provide food and medicine for their prisoners until Allied help could arrive. Thousands of starving, wretchedly-ill men were saved by her actions.

Like her husband, she ended the war with a chestful of well-earned decorations. Now she was to play at his side a vital role in New Delhi. She would be his first and most trusted confidante, his discreet and private emissary in moments of crisis, his most effective ambassador to the Indian leaders with whom he would have to deal.

Like her husband, she, too, would leave behind in India the imprint of her style and character. A woman of extraordinary versatility, Edwina Mountbatten would be able in an evening to preside over a formal banquet for 100 in a silk evening dress, a diamond tiara glittering in her hair, and, the following morning, in a simple uniform, walk through mud up to her ankles to cradle in her lap the head of a child dying of cholera in the filth of an Indian hovel. She would display in those moments a human compassion some found lacking in her husband. Hers was not the condescending gesture of a great lady perfunctorily acknowledging the misery of the poor, but a heartfelt sorrow for India's sufferings. The Indians would see the sincerity of Edwina Mountbatten's feelings and respond in turn to her as they had never responded before to an Englishwoman.

*

As his wife advanced across the room towards him, Mountbatten could not help thinking what a strange resolution this day was to their destinies. Less than a mile separated the bedroom in which they stood contemplating each other and the spot on which he had asked Edwina Ashley to marry him a quarter of a century before. It was 14 February 1922, and they had been sitting out the fifth dance of a Viceroy's ball in honour of the Prince of Wales. Their hostess that evening, the Vicereine, Lady Reading, had not been overjoyed at the news. The young Mountbatten, she had written to his new fiancee's aunt, did not have much of a career before him.

Mountbatten remembered her words now. Unable to suppress a smile, he took his wife's arm and set out to install her on Lady Reading's gold and crimson throne.

India was always a land of ceremonial splendour and on that March morning, when Louis Mountbatten was to be made Viceroy, the blend of Victorian pomp and Moghul munificence that had stamped the rites of the Raj was still intact. Spread before the broad staircase leading to the Durbar Hall, the heart of Viceroy's House, were honour guards from the Indian Army, Navy and Air Force. Sabres glittering in the morning sunlight, Mountbatten's bodyguard, in scarlet and gold tunics, white breeches and glistening black leather jackboots lined his march to the hall.

Inside, under its white marble dome, the elite of India waited: high court judges, their black robes and curling wigs as British as the law they administered; the Romans of the Raj, senior officers of the Indian Civil Service, the pale purity of their Anglo-Saxon profiles leavened by a smattering of more sombre Indian faces; a delegation of maharajas gleaming like gilded peacocks in their satin and jewels; and, above all, Jawaharlal Nehru and his colleagues in Gandhi's Congress, their rough homespun cotton *khadi* harbingers of the onrushing future.

When the first members of Mountbatten's cortege stepped into the hall, four trumpeters concealed in niches around the base of the dome began a muted fanfare, their notes rising as the procession moved forward. The lights of the great hall, dimmed at first, rose in rhythm to the trumpets' gathering crescendo. At the instant India's new Viceroy and Vicereine passed through the great doorway, they blazed to an incandescent glare, and the trumpets sent a triumphant swirl of sound reverberating around the vaulted dome. Solemn and unsmiling, the Mountbattens slow-marched down the carpeted aisles towards their waiting thrones.

A kind of apprehension, a rising tension not unlike that he had once known on the bridge of the *Kelly* in the uncertain moments before battle, crowded in on Mountbatten. Each gesture measured to the grandeur of the moment, he and his wife moved under the crimson velvet canopy spread over their gilded thrones and turned to face the assembly. The Chief Justice stepped forward and, his right hand raised, Mountbatten solemnly pronounced the oath that made him India's last Viceroy.

As he pronounced its concluding words, the rumble of the cannon of the Royal Horse Artillery outside rolled through the hall. At that same instant all across the sub-continent, other cannons took up the ponderous 31-gun salute. At Landi Kotal at the head of the Khyber Pass; Fort William in Calcutta where Clive had set Britain on the road to her Indian Empire; the Lucknow Residence where the Union Jack was never struck in honour of the men and women who had defended it in the Mutiny of 1857; Cape Comorin, past whose monazite sands the galleons of Queen Elizabeth I had sailed; Fort St. George in Madras where the East India Company had its first land grant inscribed on a plate of gold; in Poona, Peshawar and Simla; everywhere there was a military garrison in India, troops on parade presented arms as the first gun exploded in Delhi. Frontier Force Rifles, the Guides Cavalry, Hodson's and Skinner's Horse, Sikhs and Dogras, Jats and Pathans, Gurkhas and Madrasis poised while the cannon thundered out their last tattoo for the British Raj.

As the sound of the last report faded through the dome of Durbar Hall, the new Viceroy stepped to the microphone. The situation he faced was so serious that, against the advice of his staff, Mountbatten had decided to break with tradition by addressing the gathering before him.

'I am under no illusion about the difficulty of my task,' he said. 'I shall need the greatest goodwill of the greatest possible number, and I am asking India today for that goodwill.'

As he finished the guards threw open the massive Assam teak doors of the Hall. Before Mountbatten was the breath-taking vista of Kingsway and its glistening pools, plunging down the heart of New Delhi. Overhead the trumpets sent out another strident call. Suddenly, walking back down the aisle, Mountbatten felt his apprehension slip away. That brief ceremony, he realized, had turned him into one of the most powerful men on earth.

Forty-five minutes later, back in civilian clothes, Mountbatten settled at his desk. As he did, his *jamadar chaprasis*, his office footman, walked in in his gold turban bearing a green leather despatch box which he ceremoniously set in front of the Viceroy. Mountbatten opened it and pulled out the document inside. It was a stark confirmation of the power which he had just inherited, the final appeal for mercy of a man condemned to death. Fascinated and horrified, Mountbatten read his way through each detail. The case involved a man who had savagely beaten his wife to death in front of a crowd of witnesses. It had been so thoroughly combed, passed through so many appeals, that there were no extenuating circumstances to be found. Mountbatten hesitated for a long minute. Then, sadly, he took a pen and performed the first official act of his Viceroyalty.

'There are no grounds for the exercise of the Royal prerogative of mercy,' he noted on the cover.

Before setting out to impose his ideas on India's political leaders, Louis Mountbatten sensed he had first to impose his own personality on India. India's last Viceroy might, as he had glumly predicted at Northolt Airport, come home with a bullet in his back, but he would be a Viceroy unlike any other India had seen. Mountbatten firmly believed, 'it was impossible to be Viceroy without putting up a great, brilliant show.' He had been sent to New Delhi to get the British out of India, but he was determined they would go in a shimmer of scarlet and gold, all the old glories of the Raj honed to the highest pitch one last time.

He ordered all the ceremonial trappings suppressed during the war to be restored: ADCs in dazzling full-dress, guard-mounting ceremonies, bands playing, sabres flashing, 'the lot'. He loved every splendid moment of it, but a far shrewder concern than his own delight in pageantry underlay it.

The pomp and panoply was designed to give him a viceregal aura of glamour and power, to provide him a framework which would give his actions an added dimension. He intended to replace the 'Operation Madhouse' of his predecessor by an 'Operation Seduction' of his own, a mini-revolution in style directed as much towards India's masses as the leaders with whom he would have to negotiate. It would be a shrewd blend of contrasting values, of patrician pomp and common touch, of the old spectacles of the dying Raj and new initiatives pre-figuring the India of tomorrow.

Strangely, Mountbatten began his revolution with the stroke of a paint brush. To the horror of his aides, he ordered the gloomy wooden panels of the viceregal study in which so many negotiations had failed, to be covered with a light, cheerful coat of paint more apt to relax the Indian leaders with whom he'd be dealing. He shook Viceroy's House out of the leisurely routine it had developed, turning it into a humming, quasi-military headquarters. He instituted staff meetings, soon known as 'morning prayers', as the first official activity of each day.

Mountbatten astonished his new ICS subordinates with the agility of his mind, his capacity to get at the root of a problem and, above all, his almost obsessive capacity for work. He put an end to the parade of *chaprasis* who traditionally bore the Viceroy his papers for his private contemplation in green leather despatch boxes. He did not propose to waste his time locking and unlocking boxes and penning handwritten notes on the margins of papers in the solemn isolation of his study. He preferred taut, verbal briefings.

'When you wrote "may I speak?" on a paper he was to read,' one of his staff recalled, 'you could be sure you'd speak, and you'd better be ready to say what was on your mind at any time, because the call could come at two o'clock in the morning.'

It was above all the public image Mountbatten was trying to create for himself and his office that represented a radical change. For over a century, the Viceroy of India, locked in the ceremonial splendours of his office, had rivalled the Dalai Lama as the most remote God in Asia's pantheon. Two unsuccessful assassination attempts had left him enrobed in a cocoon of security, isolating him from all contact with the masses he ruled. Whenever the Viceroy's white and gold train moved across the vast spaces of India, guards were posted every 100 yards along its route 24 hours in advance of its arrival. Hundreds of bodyguards, police and security men followed each of his moves. If he played golf, the fairways were cleared and police posted along them behind almost every tree. If he went riding, a squadron of the Viceroy's bodyguard and security police jogged along after him.

Mountbatten was determined to shatter that screen. First, he announced he and his wife or daughter would take their morning rides unescorted. His words sent a wave of horror through the house, and it took him some time to get his way. But he did, and suddenly the Indian villagers along the route of their morning rides began to witness a spectacle so unbelievable as to seem a mirage: the Viceroy and Vicereine of India trotting past them, waving graciously, alone and unprotected.

Then, he and his wife made an even more revolutionary gesture. He did something no Viceroy had deigned to do in two hundred years: visit the home of an Indian who was not one of a handful of privileged princes. To the astonishment of all India, the viceregal couple walked into a garden party at the simple New Delhi residence of Jawaharlal Nehru. While Nehru's aides looked on dumb with disbelief, Mountbatten took Nehru by the elbow and strolled off among the guests, casually chatting and shaking hands.

The gesture had a stunning impact. 'Thank God,' Nehru told his sister that evening, 'we've finally got a human being for a Viceroy and not a stuffed shirt.'

Anxious to demonstrate that a new esteem for the Indian people now reigned in Viceroy's House, Mountbatten accorded the Indian military, two million of whom had served under him in South-East Asia, a long overdue honour. He had three Indian officers attached to his staff as ADCs. Next, he ordered the doors of Viceroy's House to be opened to Indians, only a handful of whom had been invited into its precincts before his arrival. He instructed his staff that there were to be no dinner parties in the Viceroy's House without Indian guests. Not just a few token guests; henceforth, he ordered, at least half the faces around his table were to be Indian.

His wife brought an even more dramatic revolution to the viceregal dining table. Out of respect for the culinary traditions of her Indian guests, she ordered the house's kitchens to start preparing dishes which, in a century of imperial hospitality, had never been offered in Viceroy's House, Indian vegetarian food. Not only that, she ordered the food to be served on flat Indian trays and servants with the traditional wash basins, jugs and towels to stand behind her guests so they could, if they chose, eat with their fingers at the Viceroy's table, then wash their throats with a ritual gargle.

That barrage of gestures large and small, the evident and genuine affection the Mountbattens displayed for the country in which their own love affair had had its beginnings, the knowledge that the new Viceroy was a deliverer and not a conqueror, the respect of the men who'd served under him in Asia; all combined to produce a remarkable aura about the couple.

Not long after their arrival the *New York Times* noted, 'no Viceroy in history has so completely won the confidence, respect and liking of the Indian people.' Indeed, within a few weeks, the success of 'Operation Seduction' would be so remarkable that Nehru himself would tell the new Viceroy only half jokingly that he was becoming a difficult man to negotiate with, because he was 'drawing larger crowds than anybody in India'.

The words were so terrifying that Louis Mountbatten at first did not believe them. They made even the dramatic sketch of the Indian scene Clement Attlee had painted him on New Year's Day seem like a description of some tranquil countryside. Yet the man uttering them in the privacy of his study had a reputation for brilliance and an understanding of India unsurpassed in the viceregal establishment. A triple blue and a first at Oxford, George Abell had been the most intimate collaborator of Mountbatten's predecessor.

India, he told Mountbatten with stark simplicity, was heading for a civil war. Only by finding the rapidest of resolutions to her problems was he going to save her. The great administrative machine governing India was collapsing. The shortage of British officers caused by the decision to stop recruiting during the war and the rising antagonism between its Hindu and Moslem members, meant that the rule of that vaunted institution, the Indian Civil Service, could not survive the year. The time for discussion and debate was past. Speed, not deliberation, was needed to avoid a catastrophe.

Coming from a man of Abell's stature, those words gave the new Viceroy a dismal shock. Yet they were only the first in a stream of reports which engulfed him during his first fortnight in India. He received an equally grim analysis from the man he'd picked to come with him as his Chief of Staff, General Lord Ismay, Winston Churchill's Chief of Staff from 1940 to 1945. A veteran of the sub-continent as officer in the Indian Army and military secretary to an earlier Viceroy, Ismay concluded, 'India was a ship on fire in mid-ocean with ammunition in her hold.' The question, he told Mountbatten, was: could they get the fire out before it reached the ammunition?

The first report Mountbatten received from the British Governor of the Punjab warned him 'there is a civil war atmosphere throughout the province'. One insignificant paragraph of that report offered a startling illustration of the accuracy of the Governor's words. It mentioned a recent tragedy in a rural district near Rawalpindi. A Moslem's water buffalo had wandered on to the property of his Sikh neighbour. When its owner sought to reclaim it, a fight, then a riot, erupted. Two hours later, a hundred human beings lay in the surrounding fields, hacked to death with scythes and knives because of the vagrant humours of a water buffalo.

Five days after the new Viceroy's arrival incidents between Hindus and Moslems took 99 lives in Calcutta. Two days later, a similar conflict broke out in Bombay leaving 41 mutilated bodies on its pavements.

Confronted by these outbursts of violence, Mountbatten called India's senior police officer to his study and asked if the police were capable of maintaining law and order in India.

'No, Your Excellency,' was the reply, 'we cannot.' Shaken, Mountbatten put the same question to Field-Marshal Sir Claude Auchinleck, Commander-in-Chief of the Indian Army. He got the same answer.

Mountbatten quickly discovered that the government with which he was supposed to govern India, a coalition of the Congress Party and the Moslem League put together with enormous effort by his predecessor, was in fact an assembly of enemies so bitterly divided that its members barely spoke to one another. It was clearly going to fall apart, and when it did, Mountbatten would have to assume the appalling responsibility of exercising direct rule himself with the administrative machine required for the task collapsing underneath him.

Confronted by that grim prospect, assailed on every side by reports of violence, by the warnings of his most seasoned advisers, Mountbatten reached what was perhaps the most important decision he would make in his first ten days in India. It was to condition every other decision of his Viceroyalty. The date of June 1948 established in London for the Transfer of Power, the date he himself had urged on Attlee, had been wildly optimistic. Whatever solution he was to reach for India's future, he was going to have to reach it in weeks, not months.

'The scene here,' he wrote in his first report to the Attlee government on 2 April 1947, 'is one of unrelieved gloom . . . I can see little ground on which to build any agreed solution for the future of India.'

After describing the country's unsettled state, the young admiral issued an anguished warning to the man who had sent him to India. 'The only conclusion I have been able to come to,' he wrote, 'is that unless I act quickly, I will find the beginnings of a civil war on my hands.'

5

An Old Man and his Shattered Dream

New Delhi, April 1947

There was no one else in the room. Not even a secretary unobtrusively taking notes disturbed the two men. Convinced of the urgency of the situation facing him, Mountbatten had decided to employ a revolutionary tactic for his negotiations with India's leaders. For the first time in its modern history, India's destiny was not being decided around a conference table, but in the intimacy of private conversation. The tête-à-tête just beginning in the Viceroy's freshly painted study was the first in a series. Those conversations would determine whether India would be spared the horror of civil war foreseen in Louis Mountbatten's first report to London. Five men would participate in them, Louis Mountbatten and four Indian leaders.

Those four Indians had spent the better part of their lives agitating against the British and arguing with each other. All of them were past middle age. All of them were lawyers who had first honed their forensic skills in London's Inns of Court. For each of them, their coming conversations with India's new Viceroy would be the greatest argument of their lifetimes, the debate for which each of them had, in a sense, been preparing for a quarter of a century.

In Mountbatten's mind, there was no question what the outcome of that debate should be. Like many Englishmen, he looked on India's unity as the greatest single legacy Britain could leave behind. He had a deep, almost evangelical desire to maintain it. To respond to the Moslem appeal to divide the country was, he believed, to sow the seeds of tragedy.

Every effort to get India's leaders to agree to a solution to their country's problems in the quasi-public glare of a formal meeting had ended in a hopeless deadlock. But here, in the privacy of his study, reasoning with them one by one, Mountbatten hoped he might bring them to agreement in the brief time at his disposal. Supremely confident of his own powers of persuasion, confident, above all of the compelling logic of his case, he was going to try to achieve in weeks what his predecessors had been unable to achieve in years; to get India's leaders to agree on some form of unity.

With his white Congress cap fixed on his balding head, a fresh rose twisted through the third buttonhole of his vest, the man before him was one of the familiar figures on India's political landscape. In his own slightly feline way, Jawaharlal Nehru was as impressively striking a figure as India's new Viceroy. The sensual features of a face whose expression could change in an instant from angelic softness to daemonic wrath were often tinged with a glimmer of sadness. While Mountbatten's features were almost always composed, Nehru's rarely were. His moods and humours slipped across his face like shadows passing across the waters of a lake.

He was the only one of the Indian leaders that Mountbatten already knew. The two men had met after the war when Nehru was on a visit to Singapore, where Mountbatten had his SEAC headquarters. Ignoring his advisers, who'd counselled him to have nothing to do with a rebel whose shoes still bore the dust of a British prison yard, Mountbatten had met the Indian leader.* The two immediately sympathized with each other. Nehru rediscovered in the company of Mountbatten and his wife an England he had not known for forty years, the England his years in British jail had almost eradicated from his memory, that open and welcoming England he had known as a schoolboy. The Mountbattens delighted in Nehru's charm, his culture, his quick humour. To the horror of his staff, Mountbatten had even spontaneously decided to ride through Singapore's streets in his open car with Nehru at his side. His action, his advisers had warned, would only dignify an anti-British rebel.

'Dignify him?' Mountbatten had retorted. 'It's he who will dignify me. One day this man will be Prime Minister of India.'

Now, his prophecy had been realized. It was to his position as Prime Minister of India's interim government that Nehru owed the honour of being the first of India's four leaders to enter Mountbatten's study.

*

For Jawaharlal Nehru, the conversation beginning in the Viceroy's study was just the latest episode in a continuing dialogue with his country's colonizers that had occupied most of his life. Nehru had been a pampered guest in the best country houses in England. He had dined off the gold service of Buckingham Palace and the tin plates of a British prison. His interlocutors had included Cambridge dons, Prime Ministers, Viceroys, the King Emperor – and jail-keepers.

Born into an eastern aristocracy as old and as proud as any produced by India's British rulers, that of the Kashmiri Brahmins,

* On 22 January 1944, while visiting his 33rd Army Corps in Ahmednagar, Mountbatten had learned Nehru was detained in the city. Noting he had over a million Indian soldiers under his command, he requested permission to visit the Indian leader. His request was denied.

Nehru had been sent to England at sixteen to finish his education. He spent seven gloriously happy years there, learning Latin verbs and cricket at Harrow, studying science, Nietzsche and Chaucer at Cambridge, admiring the reasoning of Blackstone at the Inns of Court. With his gentle charm, elegant manners, rapidly expanding culture, he had enjoyed an extraordinary social success wherever he went. He moved easily through the drawing-rooms of English society absorbing with the sponge of his still malleable personality the values and mannerisms he found there. So complete was the transformation wreaked by those seven years in England that, on his return to Allahabad, his family and friends found him completely de-Indianized.

The young Nehru soon discovered, however, the limits of his de-Indianization. He was blackballed when he applied for membership in the local British Club. He might have been a product of Harrow and Cambridge, but to the all white, all British – and devotedly middle-class – membership of the Club, he was still a black Indian.

The bitterness caused by that rejection haunted Nehru for years and hastened him towards the cause which became his life's work, the struggle for Indian independence. He joined the Congress Party, and his agitation on its behalf soon qualified him for admission to the finest political training school in the British Empire, British jails, where Nehru spent nine years of his life. In the solitude of his cell, in prison courtyards with his fellow Congress leaders, he had shaped his vision of the India of tomorrow. An idealist immersed in the doctrines of social revolution, Nehru dreamed of reconciling on the soil of India his two political passions: the parliamentary democracy of England and the economic socialism of Karl Marx. He dreamed of an India freed alike of the shackles of poverty and of superstition, unburdened of capitalism, an India in which the smoke stacks of factories reached out from her cities, an India enjoying the plenitude of that Industrial Revolution to which her colonizers had denied her access.

No one might have seemed a more unlikely candidate to lead India towards that vision than Jawaharlal Nehru. Under the cotton *khadi* he wore in deference to the dictates of Congress, he remained the quintessential English gentleman. In a land of mystics, he was a cool rationalist. The mind that had exulted in the discovery of science at Cambridge never ceased to be appalled by his fellow Indians who refused to stir from their homes on days proclaimed inauspicious by their favourite astrologers. He was a publicly declared agnostic in the most intensely spiritual area in the world, and he never ceased to proclaim the horror the word 'religion' inspired in him. Nehru despised India's priests, her *sadhus*, her chanting monks and pious sheikhs. They had only served, he felt, to impede her progress, deepen her divisions and ease the task of her foreign rulers.

And yet, the India of those *sadhus* and the superstition-haunted masses had accepted Nehru. For thirty years he had travelled across India haranguing the multitudes. Clinging to the roofs and sides of tramways to escape the slums of India's cities, on foot and by bullock cart in the countrysides, his countrymen had come by the hundreds of thousands to see and hear him. Many in those crowds could not hear his words nor understand them when they did. For them, it had been enough however just to see, over the ocean of heads around them, his frail and gesticulating silhouette. They had taken *darshan*, a kind of spiritual communion received from being in the presence of a great man and that had sufficed.

He was a superb orator and writer, a man who treasured words as a courtesan jewels. Anointed early by Gandhi, he had advanced steadily through the ranks of Congress eventually to preside over it three times. The Mahatma had made it clear that it was on his shoulders that he wished his mantle to fall.

For Nehru, Gandhi was a genius. Nehru's cool, pragmatic mind had rejected almost all of Gandhi's great moves: civil disobedience, the Salt March, Quit India. But his heart had told him to follow the Mahatma and his heart, he would later admit, had been right.

Gandhi had been, in a sense, Nehru's *guru*. It was he who had re-Indianized Nehru, sending him into the villages to find the real face of his homeland, to let the fingers of his soul touch India's sufferings. Whenever the two men were in the same place, Nehru would spend at least half an hour sitting at 'Bapuji's' feet, sometimes talking, sometimes listening, sometimes just looking and thinking. Those were, for Nehru, moments of intense spiritual satisfaction, perhaps the closest brush his atheist's heart would ever have with religion.

Yet, so much separated them: Nehru, the religion-hating atheist; Gandhi, to whom an unshakeable belief in God was the very essence of being: Nehru, whose hot temper had made him a notably imperfect soldier of non-violence, a man who adored literature and painting, science and technology, the very things Gandhi ignored or detested as being responsible for much of mankind's misery.

Between them a fascinating father-son relation grew up, animated by all the tensions, affections and repressed guilt such a relationship implied. All his life, Nehru had had an instinctive need for a dominant personality near him, some steadying influence to whom he could turn in the crises engendered by his volatile nature. His father, a bluff, jovial barrister with a penchant for good Scotch and Bordeaux, had first filled that role. Since his death, it had been Gandhi.

Nehru's devotion to Gandhi remained total, but a subtle change was overtaking their relationship. A phase in Nehru's life was drawing to a close. The son was ready to leave his father's house for the new world he saw beyond its gates. In that new world, he would need a new *guru*, a *guru* more sensitive to the complex problems that would assail him there. Although he was perhaps unaware of it as he sat in the Viceroy's study that March afternoon, a vacuum had opened in the psyche of Jawaharlal Nehru.

*

Much had changed in the world and in their own lives since Nehru and Mountbatten had met for the first time, but the undercurrent of mutual sympathy which had warmed their earlier encounter soon made itself felt in the Viceroy's study. It was not surprising that it should. Although Mountbatten, of course, did not know it, Nehru was partially responsible for his being there.

Besides, there was a great deal to bind the scion of a 3000-year-old line of Kashmiri Brahmins and the man who claimed descent from the oldest ruling family in Protestantism. They both loved to talk and expanded in each other's company. Nehru, the abstract thinker, admired Mountbatten's practical dynamism, the capacity for decisive action that wartime command had given him. Mountbatten was stimulated by Nehru's culture, the subtlety of his thought. He quickly understood that the only Indian politician who would share and understand his desire to maintain a link between Britain and a new India was Jawaharlal Nehru.

With his usual candour, the Admiral told him that he had been given an appalling responsibility and he intended to approach the Indian problem in a mood of stark realism. As they talked, the two men rapidly agreed on two major points: a quick decision was essential to avoid a bloodbath; the division of India would be a tragedy.

Then Nehru turned to the actions of the next Indian leader who would enter Mountbatten's study, the penitent marching his lonely path through Noakhali and Bihar. The man to whom he'd been so long devoted was, Nehru said, 'going around with ointment trying to heal one sore spot after another on the body of India instead of diagnosing the cause of the eruption of the sores and participating in the treatment of the body as a whole.'

In offering a glimpse into the growing gulf separating the Liberator of India and his closest companions, Nehru's words provided Mountbatten with a vital insight into the form his actions in Delhi should take. If he could not persuade India's leaders to keep their country united, he was going to have to persuade them to divide it. Gandhi's unremitting hostility to partition could place an insurmountable barrier in his path. His only hope in that event would be to persuade the leaders of Congress to break with their leader and agree to divide India as the only solution to their country's dilemma. Nehru would be the key if that happened. He was the one ally Mountbatten had to have. Only he, Mountbatten thought, might have the authority to stand out against the Mahatma.

Now his words had revealed the discord between Gandhi and his party chiefs. Mountbatten might be forced to widen and exploit that gap. He spared no effort to win Nehru's support. On none of India's leaders would Operation Seduction have more impact than the realistic Kashmiri Brahmin. A friendship that would prove decisive in the months to come was beginning that afternoon.

Taking Nehru to the door Mountbatten told him: 'Mr Nehru, I want you to regard me not as the last British Viceroy winding up the Raj, but as the first to lead the way to a new India.' Nehru turned and looked at the man he had wanted to see on the viceregal throne. 'Ah,' he said, a faint smile creasing his face, 'now, I know what they mean when they speak of your charm as being so dangerous.'

* * *

Once again, Churchill's half-naked fakir was sitting in the viceregal study, there 'to negotiate and parley on equal terms with the representative of the King Emperor'.

'He's rather like a little bird,' Louis Mountbatten thought, as he contemplated that famous figure at his side, 'a kind of sweet, sad sparrow perched on my armchair.'*

They made an odd couple: the royal sailor who loved to dress up in uniformed splendour and the elderly Indian who refused to cover his nakedness with anything more than a sheet of rough cotton. Mountbatten, handsome, the vitality surging from his muscled athlete's body; Gandhi, whose little frame almost disappeared into his armchair; the advocate of non-violence and the professional warrior; the aristocrat and the man who had chosen to live his life immersed in the poverty of the most destitute masses on the globe; Mountbatten, the wartime master of the technology of communica-

* As a young man accompanying his cousin the Prince of Wales on his royal tour of India in 1921, Mountbatten had tried, unsuccessfully, to arrange a meeting between Gandhi and the heir to the imperial crown. He had no difficulty convincing his adventurous cousin; Gandhi, however, had organized a boycott of the royal visit and the Viceroy, Lord Reading, had no intention of allowing a meeting between the two to take place. Nor would he allow Mountbatten to see him alone.

tions, forever searching for some new electronic gadget to enhance the complex signal net that linked him to the millions of his command; Gandhi, the fragile Messiah who mistrusted all that paraphernalia and yet still communicated with his public as few figures in this century had been able to.

All of those elements, almost everything in their backgrounds, seemed to destine the two men to disagreement. And yet, in the months ahead, Gandhi the pacifist would, according to one of his intimates, find in the soul of the professional warrior 'the echo of certain of the moral values that stirred in his own soul'. For his part, Mountbatten would become so attached to Gandhi that on his death he would predict that 'Mahatma Gandhi will go down in history on a par with Christ and Buddha'.

So important had Mountbatten considered this first meeting with Gandhi that he had written to the Mahatma inviting him to Delhi even before the ceremony enthroning him as Viceroy. Gandhi had drafted his reply immediately, then with a chuckle, told an aide, 'wait a couple of days before putting it in the mail. I don't want that young man to think I'm dying for his invitation.'

That 'young man' had accompanied his invitation with one of those gestures for which he was becoming noted and which sometimes infuriated his fellow Englishmen. He had offered to send his personal aircraft to Bihar to fly Gandhi to Delhi. Gandhi, however, had declined the offer. He had insisted on travelling, as he always did, in a third-class railway carriage.

To underline the importance he attached to their first contact and to give their meeting a special cordiality, Mountbatten had asked his wife to be present. Now, contemplating the famous figure opposite them, worry and concern swept over the viceregal couple. The Mahatma, they both immediately sensed, was profoundly unhappy, trapped in the grip of some mysterious remorse. Had they done something wrong? Neglected some arcane law of protocol?

Mountbatten gave his wife an anxious glance. 'God,' he thought, 'what a terrible way to start things off!' As politely as he could, he asked Gandhi if something was troubling him.

A slow, sorrowful sigh escaped the Indian leader. 'You know,' he replied, 'all my life, since I was in South Africa, I've renounced physical possessions.' He owned virtually nothing, he explained: his *Gita*, the tin utensils from which he ate, mementoes of his stay in Yeravda prison, his three '*gurus*'. And his watch, his old eight-shilling Ingersoll he hung from a string around his waist because, if he was going to devote every minute of his day to God's work, he had to know what time it was.

'Do you know what?' he asked sadly. 'They stole it. Someone in my railway compartment coming down to Delhi stole the watch.' As the frail figure lost in his armchair spoke those words, Mountbatten saw tears shining in his eyes. In an instant, the Viceroy understood. It was not the loss of his watch that so pained Gandhi. What hurt was that they had not understood. It was not an eight-shilling watch an unknown hand had plucked from him in that congested railway car, but a particle of his faith.*

Finally, after a long silence, Gandhi began to talk of India's current dilemma. Mountbatten interrupted with a friendly wave of his hand. 'Mr Gandhi,' he said, 'first, I want to know who you are.'

The Viceroy's words reflected a deliberate tactic. He was determined to get to know those Indian leaders before allowing them to begin assailing him with their minimum demands and final conditions. By putting them at ease, by getting them to confide in him, he hoped to create an atmosphere of mutual confidence and sympathy in which his own dynamic personality could have greater impact.

The Mahatma was delighted by the ploy. He loved to talk about himself and in the Mountbattens he had a pair of people genuinely interested in what he had to say. He rambled on about South Africa, his days as a stretcher bearer in the Boer War, civil disobedience, the Salt March. Once he said, the West had received its inspiration from the East in the messages of Zoroaster, Buddha, Moses, Jesus, Mohammed, Rama. For centuries, however, the East had been conquered culturally by the West. Now the West, haunted by spectres like the atomic bomb, had need to look eastwards once again. There, he hoped, it might find the message of love and fraternal understanding he sought to preach.

Their conversation went on for two hours. It was punctuated by a simple, yet extraordinary gesture, a gesture which provided a clue as to how successful Mountbatten's overtures had been, how responsive a chord they were striking in Gandhi.

Halfway through their talks, the trio strolled into the Moghul Gardens for photographs. When they finished, they turned to re-

* Almost six months later, in September 1947, when Gandhi was staying in Birla House, New Delhi, a stranger appeared one afternoon asking to see the Mahatma. At first he refused to give his name or tell Gandhi's secretary why he wanted to see him. Finally he admitted he had stolen Gandhi's watch. He had come to return it and ask his forgiveness. 'Forgive you?' exclaimed the secretary. 'He will embrace you.' He took the man to Gandhi. He squatted before the Mahatma, changing a few words the secretary could not hear. Then Gandhi embraced him and, giggling like a child who had recovered a lost toy, he called his followers to see the watch and meet the prodigal son who'd returned it.

enter the house. The 77-year-old leader loved to walk with his hands resting upon the shoulders of two young girls, to whom he fondly referred as his 'crutches'. Now, the revolutionary who'd spent a lifetime struggling with the British, instinctively laid his hand upon the shoulder of Britain's last Vicereine and, as tranquilly as if he were strolling off to his evening prayer meeting, re-entered the Viceroy's study.

By the time Gandhi returned to the Viceroy's study for their second meeting, Delhi was already gasping in the first searing blast of India's hot season. Under the sun's white glare the bright dhak trees in the Moghul Gardens seemed to emit sparks, and an orange rind shrivelled into a crisp parchment minutes after it was peeled. The only fresh glade in the city was Louis Mountbatten's study. The reverence for detail which had led him to paint the study had also led him to make sure it was equipped with the best air-conditioner in Delhi, a machine that allowed him to work in a refreshing 75 degrees.

Its presence was nearly responsible for a catastrophe. Passing with brutal abruptness from Delhi's furnace heat into the chilly study, Gandhi, the implacable foe of technology, got an unhappy introduction to the blessings of air-conditioning. Seeing his half-naked guest trembling, Mountbatten rang for his ADC who arrived with his wife.

'My God,' exclaimed Edwina Mountbatten, 'you'll give the poor man pneumonia!'

She rushed to the machine, snapped it off, threw open the window, then hurried off to get one of her husband's old Royal Navy sweaters to cover Gandhi's shaking shoulders.

When Gandhi was finally warm again, Mountbatten took his guest on to the terrace for tea. A brace of servants brought Mountbatten his in a bonewhite china service stamped with the viceregal crest. Manu, who had accompanied Gandhi, laid out the spare meal she'd brought along for him: lemon soup, goat's curds and dates. Gandhi ate it with a spoon whose handle had been broken above the ladle and replaced by a piece of bamboo lashed to its stub with a string. The battered tin plates in which it was served, however, were as English as the Sheffield sterling of the viceregal service. They came from Yeravda prison.

Smiling, Gandhi proffered his goat's curds to Mountbatten. 'It's rather good,' he said, 'do try this.'

Mountbatten looked at the yellow, porridge-like sludge with something less than unalloyed delight. 'I don't think really I ever have,' he murmured, hoping that those words might somehow discourage his guest's effort at generosity. Gandhi was not, however, to be so easily dissuaded.

'Never mind,' he replied, laughing, 'there's always a first time for everything. Try it now.'

Trapped, Mountbatten dutifully accepted a spoonful. It was, he thought, 'ghastly'.

The preliminaries of their conversations ended there on the lawn and Mountbatten got down to a process that had invariably taxed his predecessors' patience and good temper, negotiating with Gandhi.

The Mahatma had, indeed, been a difficult person for the British to deal with. Truth, to Gandhi, was the ultimate reality. Gandhi's truth, however, had two faces, the absolute and the relative. Man, as long as he was in the flesh, had only fleeting intimations of absolute truth. He had to deal with relative truth in his daily existence. Gandhi liked to employ a parable to illustrate the difference between his two truths. Put your left hand in a bowl of ice-cold water, then in a bowl of lukewarm water, he would say. The lukewarm water feels hot. Then put the right hand in a bowl of hot water and into the same bowl of lukewarm water. Now the lukewarm water feels cold; yet its temperature is constant. The absolute truth is the water's constant temperature, he would observe, but the relative truth, perceived by the human hand, varied. As that parable indicated, Gandhi's relative truth was not a rigid thing. It could vary as his perceptions of a problem changed. That made him flexible but it also, to his British interlocutors, sometimes made him appear a two-faced, cunning Asiatic. Even one of his disciples once exclaimed to him in exasperation: 'Gandhiji, I don't understand you. How can you say one thing last week, and something quite different this week?'

'Ah,' Gandhi replied, 'because I have learned something since last week.'

India's new Viceroy moved, therefore, into serious talk with Gandhi with trepidation. He was not persuaded that the little figure 'chirping like a sparrow' at his side could help him elaborate a solution to the Indian crisis, but he knew he could destroy his efforts to find one. The hopes of many another English mediator had foundered on the turns of his unpredictable personality. It was Gandhi who had sent Cripps back to London empty-handed in 1942. His refusal to budge on a principle had helped thwart Wavell's efforts to untie the Indian knot. His tactics had done much to frustrate the most recent British attempts to solve the problem, that of the Cabinet Mission whose plan was supposed to serve as Mountbatten's point of departure. Only the evening before, Gandhi had reiterated to his prayer meeting that India would be divided, 'over my dead body. So long as I am alive, I will never agree to the partition of India.'

If a reluctant Mountbatten was driven to the decision to partition India, he would find himself in the distasteful position of having to impose his will on Gandhi. It was not the elderly Mahatma's body he would have to break, but his heart.

It had always been British policy not to yield to force, he told Gandhi, to open their talks on the right note, but his non-violent crusade had won and, come what may, Britain was going to leave India. Only one thing mattered in that coming departure, Gandhi replied. 'Don't partition India,' he begged. Don't divide India, the prophet of non-violence pleaded, even if refusing to do so meant shedding 'rivers of blood'.

Dividing India, Mountbatten assured Gandhi, was the last solution he wished to adopt. But what alternatives were open to him?

Gandhi had one. So desperate was he to avoid partition that he was prepared for a Solomonic judgment. Give the Moslems the baby instead of cutting it in half. Place three hundred million Hindus under Moslem rule by asking his rival Jinnah and his Moslem League to form a government. Then hand over power to that government. Give Jinnah all India instead of just the part he wanted.

Mountbatten was ready to grasp at any straw to avoid partition. The suggestion had an *Alice in Wonderland* ring to it, but then so had some of Gandhi's other ideas and they had worked.

'Whatever makes you think your own Congress Party will accept?' he asked Gandhi.

'Congress,' Gandhi replied, 'wants above all else to avoid partition. They will do anything to prevent it.'

What, Mountbatten asked, would Jinnah's reaction be?

'If you tell him I am its author his reply will be: "Wily Gandhi",' the Mahatma said, laughing.

Mountbatten was silent for a moment. There was much in Gandhi's proposal that seemed unworkable. He was not prepared to commit his own prestige to it at this early juncture. But neither was he going lightly to dismiss any idea that might hold India together.

'Look,' he said, 'if you can bring me formal assurance that Congress will accept your scheme, that they'll try sincerely to make it work, then I'm prepared to entertain the idea.'

Gandhi fairly flew out of his chair at his words. 'I am entirely sincere,' he assured Mountbatten. 'I will tour the length and breadth of India to get the people to accept if that is your decision.'

A few hours later, an Indian journalist spoke to Gandhi as he walked towards his evening prayer meeting. The Mahatma, he thought, seemed 'to bubble with happiness'. As they approached the prayer ground, he suddenly turned to the newsman. With a gleeful smile, he whispered: 'I think I've turned the tide.'

* * *

'Why, this man is trying to bully me!' an unbelieving Louis Mountbatten thought. Operation Seduction had come to a sudden halt at the rock-like figure planted opposite him. With his *khadi* dhoti whirled about his shoulders like a toga, his bald head glowing, his scowling demeanour, the man jammed into that chair looked to the Viceroy more like a Roman senator than an Indian politician.

Vallabhbhai Patel, however, was India's quintessential politician. He was an Oriental Tammany Hall boss who ran the machinery of the Congress Party with a firm and ruthless hand. He should have been the easiest member of the Indian quartet for Mountbatten to deal with. Like the Viceroy, he was a practical, pragmatic man, a hard but realistic bargainer. Yet the tension between them was so real, so palpable, that it seemed to Mountbatten he could reach out and touch it.

Its cause was in no way related to the great issues facing India. It was a slip of paper, a routine government minute issued by Patel's Home Ministry, dealing with an appointment. Mountbatten, however, had read in its tone, in the way Patel had put it out, a calculated challenge to his authority.

Patel had a well-earned reputation for toughness. He had an instinctive need to take the measure of a new interlocutor, to see how far he could push him. That piece of paper on his desk, Mountbatten was convinced, was a test, a little examination he had to go through with Patel before he could get down to serious matters.

*

Vallabhbhai Patel was passed a cable announcing his wife's death as he was pacing the floor of a Bombay court-room summing up his case for the jury. He glanced at it, thrust it into his pocket, and continued his peroration without breaking off his sentence.

That incident formed part of the legend of Vallabhbhai Patel and was a measure of the man. Emotion, one of his associates once observed, formed no part of his character. The remark was not wholly exact. Patel was an emotional man but he never let those emotions break through the composed façade he turned to the world. If he gave off one salient impression it was that of a man wholly in control of himself.

In a land in which men threw their words around like sailors their money after three months at sea, Patel hoarded his phrases the way a miser hoards coins. His daughter, who had been his constant companion since his wife's death, rarely exchanged ten sentences with him a day. When Patel did talk, however, people listened.

Patel was Indian from the uppermost lump of his bald head to the calluses on the soles of his feet. His Delhi home was filled with books but every one of them was written by an Indian author about India. He was the only Indian leader who sprang from the soil of India. His father had been a peasant farmer in Gujerat province near Bombay and Patel still lived his life at a peasant's rhythm. He rose faithfully at 4 a.m. and was in bed just as regularly each night at 9.30. The first waking hours of each day Patel spent on his toilet, doing the bulk of his reading, 30 newspapers sent to him daily from every part of India. His life was watched over with jealous vigilance by his daughter and eldest child, Maniben. For two decades, she had been his secretary, his ADC, his confidante, the mistress of his household. So close was their relationship they even shared the same bedroom.

Patel's vocation for Indian nationalism had come from his father who'd gone off to fight the British at the side of a local warlord in the 1857 Mutiny. He'd spent the winter nights of his boyhood around the dung fire of their peasants' hut, listening to his old soldier's tales. Soon after, he left the land for good to work in the great textile mills of Ahmedabad where Gandhi was to found his first Indian ashram. He studied at night, saved almost every rupee he earned until, at 33, he was able to send himself to London to study the law.

He never saw the London of the Mayfair drawing-rooms where Nehru had been an admired guest. The London he knew best was the library of the Inns of Court. He walked twice a day the ten miles separating the courts from his lodging to save the bus fare. The day he was called to the bar, he took another walk, to the docks, to book a passage home. Once he returned, he never left India again.

He settled in Ahmedabad, practising law with brilliant effect for the mill owners whose wage slave he'd once been. Patel had not even looked up from his nightly bridge game the first time he'd heard Gandhi speak in the Ahmedabad Club. Someone, however, brought him a text of the Mahatma's speech and as he read its lines a vision rose from its pages: the vision his father had inspired around a dung fire in the winter nights of his boyhood.

He sought Gandhi out and offered him his services. In 1922 Gandhi, anxious to see what civil disobedience might achieve, asked Patel to organize an experimental campaign among 87,000 people in

137 villages in the county of Bardoli north of Bombay. His organization was so comprehensive, so complete, that the campaign succeeded beyond even Gandhi's hopes. From that moment on, Patel had shared with Nehru the place just below Gandhi's in the independence movement. Employing his special genius he had assembled the Congress Party's machine, thrusting its tentacles into the remotest corners of India.

Patel had always been profoundly wary of his brother in Congress *khadi*, Nehru. The two men were natural rivals and their ideas of what independent India should be were markedly different. Patel had no use for Nehru's Utopian dream of building a new society. He dismissed his visions of a brave new Socialist world as 'this parrot cry of Socialism'. Capitalist society worked, he maintained, the problem was to Indianize it, to make it work better, not jettison it for an impracticable ideal.

'Patel,' one of his aides noted, 'came from an industrial town, a centre for machines, factories and textiles. Nehru came from a place where they grew flowers and fruit.'

He scorned Nehru's fascination with foreign affairs, the great debates of the world. He knew where power was to be found and that was where he was, in the Home Ministry, developing the loyalty of what would be independent India's police, security, and information services, as he had developed the loyalty of the Congress machine. Nehru might wear Gandhi's mantle but he walked with an uneasy tread, because he knew the legions behind him longed for another Caesar. Like Jinnah, with whom his relations were cordial, Patel was underestimated, his importance undervalued by a world whose regards were riveted on Gandhi and Nehru. It was an error. Patel, one of his aides said, 'was India's last Moghul'.

*

The Viceroy looked at the note which had offended him, then passed it across his desk to Patel. Quietly he asked him to withdraw it. Patel brusquely refused.

Mountbatten studied the Indian leader. He was going to need the support of this man and the machinery he represented. But he was sure he would never get it if he did not face him down now.

'Very well,' said Mountbatten, 'I'll tell you what I'm going to do. I'm going to order my plane.'

'Oh,' said Patel, 'why?'

'Because I'm leaving,' Mountbatten replied. 'I didn't want this job in the first place. I've just been looking for someone like you to give me an excuse to throw it up and get out of an impossible situation.'

'You don't mean it!' exclaimed Patel.

'Mean it?' replied Mountbatten. 'You don't think I am going to stay here and be bullied by a chap like you, do you? If you think you can be rude to me and push me around, you're wrong. You'll either withdraw that minute or one of us is going to resign. And let me tell you that if I go, I shall first explain to your Prime Minister and to Mr Jinnah why I am leaving. The breakdown in India which will follow, the blood that will be shed, will be on your shoulders and no one else's.'

Patel stared at Mountbatten in disbelief.

Come, come, he declared, Mountbatten wasn't going to throw over the Viceroyalty after only a month on the job.

'Mr Patel,' Mountbatten answered, 'you evidently don't know me. Either you withdraw your minute here and now, or I shall summon the Prime Minister and announce my resignation.'

A long silence followed. 'You know,' Patel finally sighed, 'the awful part is I think you mean it.'

'You're damned right I do,' answered Mountbatten.

Patel reached out, took the offending minute off Mountbatten's desk and slowly tore it up.

* * *

A lone light bulb, its contours speckled with carbonized insects, hung from the hut's ceiling. Naked to the waist, Gandhi squatted on a straw mattress on the cement floor. The others, talking excitedly, were gathered around him. Dark eyes sparkling with awe and glee, the urchins of the Bhangi sweepers' colony, the foetid slum of the Untouchables who swept Delhi's streets and cleaned out her toilets, stared through the window at their prophet.

The men crowded about Gandhi would be the leaders of a free India. They were there in that blighted slum, its air reeking from the stench of the human excrement rotting in its open sewers, its inhabitants' faces crusted with the sores of a hundred diseases, because Gandhi had decided to pass his Delhi sojourn there. The struggle for the oppressed of Hindu society, its Untouchables whom he called *harijans* – Children of God – had rivalled the struggle for national freedom in Gandhi's heart.

Untouchables constituted a sixth of India's population. Supposedly condemned by their sins in a previous incarnation to a casteless existence, they were readily identifiable by the darkness of their skin, their cringing submissiveness, their ragged dress. Their name expressed the contamination which stained a caste Hindu at the slightest contact with them, a stain which had to be removed by a ritual, purifying bath. Even their footprints in the soil could defile some Brahmin neighbourhoods. An Untouchable was obliged to shrink from the path of an approaching caste Hindu lest his shadow fall across his route and soil him. In some parts of India, Untouchables were allowed to leave their shacks only at night. There, they were known as Invisibles.

No Hindu could eat in the presence of an Untouchable, drink water drawn from a well by his hands, use utensils he'd soiled by his touch. Many Hindu temples were closed to them. Their children were not accepted in schools. Even in death they remained pariahs. Untouchables were not allowed to use the common cremation ground. Invariably too poor to buy logs for their own funeral pyres, their corpses were usually consumed by vultures rather than flames.

In some parts of India they were still bought and sold like serfs along with the estates they worked. A young Untouchable was generally assigned the same value as an ox. In a country of social progress, they enjoyed only one privilege. Whenever an epidemic struck down a sacred cow, the Untouchable who carted off the rotten carcass was allowed to sell the meat to his fellow outcasts.

Since his return from South Africa, Gandhi had made their cause his. His first Indian ashram had nearly failed because he had welcomed them into its folds. He massaged them, nursed them. He had even insisted on publicly performing the most demeaning act a caste Hindu could accomplish to demonstrate his loathing of Untouchability; he had cleaned out an Untouchable's toilet. In 1932, he had nearly died for them, fasting to thwart a political reform which he feared would institutionalize their separation from Indian society. By always moving around India as they did, when they were able to travel, in third-class railway carriages, by living in their slums, Gandhi was trying to force them to remain conscious of their misery.*

In a few months, weeks even, most of the men around Gandhi would be government ministers occupying the enormous offices

* His effort was not without its disadvantages for his Congress colleagues. Shortly after his arrival in Delhi, Lord Mountbatten asked one of Gandhi's closest associates, the poetess Sarojini Naidu, whether, in view of the determined poverty in which Gandhi chose to live, the Congress Party could really protect him. 'Ah', she laughed, 'you and Gandhi may imagine that when he walks down that Calcutta station platform looking for a suitably crowded third class carriage that he's alone. Or, when he's in his hut in the Untouchables' Colony, he's unprotected. What he doesn't know is that there are a dozen of our people dressed as Untouchables walking behind him, crowding into that carriage.' When he moved into the Bhangi Colony in Delhi, she explained, a score of Congress workers, again scrupulously clothed as *harijans* were sent in to live in the hovels around his. 'My dear Lord Louis,' she concluded, 'you will never know how much it has cost the Congress Party to keep that old man in poverty.'

from which the British had run India, crossing Delhi in chauffeur-driven American cars. He had deliberately obliged them to make this pilgrimage to one of India's worst slums to give them a Gandhian reminder of the realities of the nation they would soon govern.

It was India's political realities, however, that occupied those men this evening. It was suffocatingly hot and to ease its miseries Gandhi was using his air-conditioner, a wet towel wrapped like a turban around his bald head. To his distress, the tempers of his followers were as warm as the night around them.

When, a few days earlier, Gandhi had fervently assured Mountbatten that the Congress Party was prepared to do anything to prevent partition, he had been wrong. His error was the measure of the slowly widening gulf between the ageing Mahatma and the men around him, the men he had developed as the leaders of the Congress Party.

For a quarter of a century, those men had followed Gandhi. They had thrown off their western suits for his *khadi*, moved their fingers to the unfamiliar rhythms of the spinning-wheel. In his name they had marched into the flailing *lathis* of the police and the gates of British jails. Quelling occasional doubts, they had followed him on his improbable crusades to the improbable triumph now beckoning: independence wrested from the British by Gandhian non-violence.

They had followed him for many reasons, but above all because they saw that his unique genius for communicating with the soul of India could draw mass support to their banner. The potential differences between them had been submerged in the common struggle with the British. Now, in that hot Delhi night, those differences began to emerge as they debated Gandhi's plan to make Jinnah Prime Minister. If they refused to endorse his scheme, Gandhi argued, the new Viceroy might find himself driven into a corner from which the only escape would be partition. Walking from village to village in Noakhali and later Bihar, applying his 'ointment' to India's sore spots, Gandhi had understood infinitely better than those political leaders in Delhi the tragedy partition might produce. He had seen in the huts and swamps of Noakhali what havoc communal fury, once unleashed, could wreak. Partition, he argued, risked unleashing those passions, not dampening them. Desperately he begged his followers to accept his idea as perhaps their last chance to keep India united and to prevent that tragedy.

He could not budge Nehru and Patel. There was a limit to the price they were prepared to pay to keep India united and handing over power to their foe, Jinnah, transgressed it. They did not share Gandhi's conviction that partition would inevitably lead to terrible violence. Broken-hearted, Gandhi would have to report to the Viceroy that he had not been able to carry his colleagues with him. The real break was still some distance ahead, but Gandhi and those men he'd so patiently groomed were fast approaching a parting of the ways. The culmination of Gandhi's crusade was now drawing near, and it would end as it had begun, in the stillness of his soul.

* * *

There was no need for the air-conditioner whirring in the viceregal study that April afternoon. The chill emanating from the austere and distant leader of the Moslem League was quite sufficient to cool its atmosphere. From the instant he'd arrived, Mountbatten had found Mohammed Ali Jinnah in a most frigid, haughty and disdainful frame of mind.

The key member of the Indian quartet, the man who would ultimately hold the solution to the sub-continent's dilemma in his hands, had been the last of the Indian leaders to enter the Viceroy's study. A quarter of a century later, an echo of his distant anguish still haunting his voice, Louis Mountbatten would recall, 'I did not realize how utterly impossible my task in India was going to be until I met Mohammed Ali Jinnah for the first time.'

Their meeting had begun with an unhappy gaffe, a gaffe poignantly revealing of the meticulous, calculating Jinnah to whom no gesture could be spontaneous. Realizing he would be photographed with the Mountbattens, Jinnah had carefully memorized a pleasant little line to flatter Edwina Mountbatten, who he was sure would be posed between the Viceroy and himself.

Alas, poor Jinnah! It was he and not Edwina who wound up in the middle. But he couldn't help himself. He was programmed like a computer, and his carefully rehearsed line just had to come out. 'Ah,' he beamed, 'a rose between two thorns.'

Inside the study, he began by informing Mountbatten he had come to tell him exactly what he was prepared to accept. As he had with Gandhi, Mountbatten interrupted with a wave of his hand. 'Mr Jinnah,' he said, 'I am not prepared to discuss conditions at this stage. First, let's make each other's acquaintance.'

Then, with his legendary charm and verve, Mountbatten turned the focus of Operation Seduction on the Moslem leader. Jinnah froze. To that aloof and reserved man who never unbent with even his closest associates, the very idea of revealing the details of his life and personality to a perfect stranger must have seemed appalling.

Gamely Mountbatten struggled on, summoning up all the reserves of his gregarious, engaging personality. For what seemed to him like hours, his only reward was a series of monosyllabic grunts from the man beside him. Finally, after almost two hours, Jinnah began to soften. As the Moslem leader left his study, Mountbatten sighed to Alan Campbell-Johnson, his press attaché: 'My God, he was cold! It took most of the interview to unfreeze him.'

*

The man who would one day be hailed as the father of Pakistan had first been exposed to the idea at a black-tie dinner at London's Waldorf Hotel in the spring of 1933. His host was Rahmat Ali, the graduate student who had set the idea on paper. Rahmat Ali had arranged the banquet with its oysters and un-Islamic Chablis at his own expense hoping to persuade Jinnah, India's leading Moslem politician, to take over his movement. He received a chilly rebuff. Pakistan, Jinnah told him, was 'an impossible dream'.

The man whom the unfortunate graduate student had sought to make into the leader of a Moslem separatist movement had, in fact, begun his political career by preaching Hindu-Moslem unity. His family came from Gandhi's Kathiawar peninsula. Indeed, had not Jinnah's grandfather for some obscure reason become a convert to Islam, the two political foes would have been born into the same caste. Like Gandhi, Jinnah had gone to London to dine in the Inns of Court and be called to the bar. Unlike Gandhi however, he had come back from London an Englishman.

He wore a monocle and superbly cut linen suits which he changed three or four times a day so as to remain cool and unruffled in the soggy Bombay climate. He loved oysters and caviare, champagne, brandy and good claret. A man of unassailable personal honesty and financial integrity, his canons were sound law and sound procedure. He was, according to one intimate, 'the last of the Victorians, a parliamentarian in the mode of Gladstone or Disraeli.'

A brilliantly successful lawyer, Jinnah moved naturally to politics and for a decade worked to keep the Hindus and Moslems of Congress united in a common front against the British. His disenchantment with Congress dated from Gandhi's accession to power. The impeccably dressed Jinnah was not going to be bundled off to some squalid British jail half naked in a *dhoti* wearing a silly little white cap. Civil disobedience, he told Gandhi, was for 'the ignorant and the illiterate'.

The turning point in Jinnah's career came after the 1937 elections when Congress refused to share with him and his Moslem League the spoils of office in those Indian provinces where there was a substantial Moslem minority. Jinnah was a man of towering vanity and he took Congress's action as a personal rebuke. It convinced him he and the Moslem League would never get a fair deal from a Congress-run India. The former apostle of Hindu-Moslem unity became the unyielding advocate of Pakistan, the project he had labelled an 'impossible dream' barely four years earlier.

A more improbable leader of India's Moslem masses could hardly be imagined. The only thing Moslem about Mohammed Ali Jinnah was his parents' religion. He drank, ate pork, religiously shaved his beard each morning and just as religiously avoided the mosque each Friday. God and the Koran had no place in Jinnah's vision of the world. His political foe, Gandhi, knew more verses of the Moslem Holy Book than he did. He had been able to achieve the remarkable feat of securing the allegiance of the vast majority of India's Moslems without being able to articulate more than a few sentences in their traditional tongue, Urdu.

Jinnah despised India's masses. He detested the dirt, the heat, the crowds of India. Gandhi travelled India in filthy third-class railway carriages to be with the people. Jinnah rode first-class to avoid them.

Where his rival made a fetish of simplicity, Jinnah revelled in pomp. He delighted in touring India's Moslem cities in princely processions, riding under victory arches on a kind of Rosebowl style float, preceded by silver-harnessed elephants and a band booming out 'God Save The King' because, Jinnah observed, it was the only tune the crowd knew.

His life was a model of order and discipline. Even the phlox and petunias of his gardens marched out from his mansion in straight, disciplined lines and when the master of the house paused there it was not to contemplate the beauty of his plants but to verify the precision of their alignment. Law books and newspapers were his only reading. Indeed, newspapers seemed to be this strange man's passion. He had them mailed to him from all over the world. He cut them up, scrawled notes in their margins, meticulously pasted them into scrapbooks that grew in dusty piles in his office cupboards.

Jinnah had only scorn for his Hindu rivals. He labelled Nehru 'a Peter Pan', a 'literary figure' who 'should have been an English professor, not a politician', 'an arrogant Brahmin who covers his Hindu trickiness under a veneer of Western education'. Gandhi, to Jinnah, was 'a cunning fox', 'a Hindu rivalist'.

The sight of the Mahatma, during an interval in a conversation in Jinnah's mansion, stretched out on one of his priceless Persian carpets, his mudpack on his belly, was something Jinnah had never forgotten – or forgiven.

Among his Moslems Jinnah had no friends, only followers. He had associates, not disciples and, with the exception of his sister, ignored his family. He lived alone with his dream of Pakistan. He was almost six feet tall but weighed barely one hundred and twenty pounds. The skin on his face was stretched so fine that his prominent cheekbones below seemed to emit a translucent glow. He had thick, silver-grey hair, and – curiously enough for a man whose sole companion for seventeen years had been a dentist, his sister – a mouthful of rotting yellow teeth. So stern, so rigorously composed was Jinnah's appearance he gave off an aura of steely, spartan strength. It was an illusion. He was a frail, sick man who already, in the words of his physician, had been living for three years on 'will-power, whisky and cigarettes'.

It was the first of those that was the key to the character and achievements of Jinnah. His rivals accused him of many a sin, his friends of many a slight. But no one, friend or foe, would ever accuse Mohammed Ali Jinnah of a lack of will-power.

*

Mountbatten and Jinnah held six critical meetings during the first fortnight of April 1947. They were the vital conversations – not quite ten hours in length – which ultimately determined the resolution of the Indian dilemma. Mountbatten went into them armed with 'the most enormous conceit in my ability to persuade people to do the right thing, not because I am persuasive so much as because I have the knack of being able to present the facts in their most favourable light'. As he would later recall, he 'tried every trick I could play, used every appeal I could imagine', to shake Jinnah's resolve to have partition. Nothing would. There was no argument that could move him from his consuming determination to realize the impossible dream of Pakistan.

Jinnah owed his commanding position to two things. He had made himself absolute dictator of the Moslem League. There were men below him who might have been prepared to negotiate a compromise but, so long as Mohammed Ali Jinnah was alive, they would hold their silence. Second, more important, was the memory of the blood spilled in the streets of Calcutta a year before.

Mountbatten and Jinnah did agree on one point at the outset – the need for speed. India, Jinnah declared, had gone beyond the stage at which a compromise solution was possible. There was only one solution, a speedy 'surgical operation'. Otherwise, he warned, India would perish.

When Mountbatten expressed concern lest partition might produce bloodshed and violence, Jinnah reassured him. Once his 'surgical operation' had taken place, all troubles would cease and India's two halves would live in harmony and happiness. It was,

Jinnah told Mountbatten, like a court case he'd handled between two brothers embittered by the shares assigned them under their father's will. Yet, two years after the court had adjudicated their dispute, they were the greatest friends. That, he promised the Viceroy, would be the case in India.

The Moslems of India, Jinnah insisted, were a nation with a 'distinctive culture and civilization, language and literature, art and architecture, laws and moral codes, customs and calendar, history and traditions'.

'India has never been a true nation,' Jinnah asserted. 'It only looks that way on the map. The cows I want to eat, the Hindu stops me from killing. Every time a Hindu shakes hands with me he has to wash his hands. The only thing the Moslem has in common with the Hindu is his slavery to the British.'

Their arguments became, the Viceroy would later recall, an 'amusing and rather tragic game of round and round the mulberry bush'; Jinnah, the March Hare of *Alice in Wonderland*, never conceding a point; Mountbatten, the determined advocate of unity, driving at Jinnah from every angle, until he was afraid lest, as he noted at the time, 'I drove the old gentleman quite mad.'

For Jinnah, the division he proposed was the natural course. That division, however, would have to produce a viable state and that, Jinnah argued, meant that two of India's great provinces, the Punjab and Bengal, would have to go into his Pakistan, despite the fact that each contained enormous Hindu populations.

Mountbatten could not agree. The basis of Jinnah's argument for Pakistan was that India's Moslem minority should not be ruled by its Hindu majority. How then justify taking the Hindu minorities of Bengal and the Punjab into a Moslem state? If Jinnah insisted on dividing India to get his Islamic state, then the very logic he'd used to get it would compel Mountbatten to divide the Punjab and Bengal as part of the bargain.

Jinnah protested. That would give him an economically unviable, 'moth-eaten Pakistan'. Mountbatten, who didn't want to give him any Pakistan at all, told the Moslem leader, that if he felt the nation he was to receive was as 'moth-eaten' as all that, he'd prefer he didn't take it.

'Ah,' Jinnah would counter, 'Your Excellency doesn't understand. A man is a Punjabi or a Bengali before he is Hindu or Moslem. They share a common history, language, culture and economy. You must not divide them. You will cause endless bloodshed and trouble.'

'Mr Jinnah, I entirely agree.'

'You do?'

'Of course,' Mountbatten would continue. 'A man is not only a Punjabi or Bengali before he is a Hindu or a Moslem, he is an Indian before all else. You have presented the unanswerable argument for Indian unity.'

'But you don't understand at all,' Jinnah would counter, and the discussions would start around the mulberry bush again.

Mountbatten was stunned by the rigidity of Jinnah's position. 'I never would have believed,' he later recalled, 'that an intelligent man, well-educated, trained in the Inns of Court was capable of simply closing his mind as Jinnah did. It wasn't that he didn't see the point. He did, but a kind of shutter came down. He was the evil genius in the whole thing. The others could be persuaded, but not Jinnah. While he was alive nothing could be done.'

The climax to their talks came on 10 April, less than three weeks after Mountbatten's arrival in India. For two hours he begged, cajoled, argued, and pleaded with Jinnah to keep India united. With all the eloquence he could command, he painted a picture of the greatness India could achieve, 400 million people of different races and creeds, bound together by a Central Union Government, with all the economic strength that would accrue to them from increased industrialization, playing a great part in world affairs as the most progressive, single entity in the Far East. Surely, Mr Jinnah did not want to destroy all that, to condemn the sub-continent to the existence of a third-rate power?

Jinnah remained unmoved. He was, Mountbatten sadly concluded, 'a psychopathic case, hell bent on this Pakistan.'

Meditating alone in his study after Jinnah's departure, Mountbatten realized he was probably going to have to give him what he wanted. His first obligation in New Delhi was to the nation that had sent him there, Britain. He longed to preserve India's unity, but not at the expense of his country becoming hopelessly entrapped in an India collapsing in chaos and violence.

He had to have a solution, he had to have it fast, and he could not impose it by force. Military command had given Mountbatten a penchant for rapid, decisive actions, such as the one he now took. In future years, his critics would assail him for having reached it too quickly, for acting like an impetuous sailor and not a statesman. Mountbatten, however, was not going to waste any more time on what he was certain would be futile arguments. He could argue with Jinnah, he concluded, until hell froze over, and hell in India would be the only consequence.

He was prepared to acknowledge with blunt realism that Operation Seduction had failed to make an impact on the Moslem leader. The partition of India seemed increasingly the only escape. It now remained for Mountbatten to get Nehru and Patel to accept the principle and to find a plan for it which could win their support.

The following morning he reviewed his talk with Jinnah for his staff. Then, sadly, he turned to his Chief of Staff, Lord Ismay. The time had come, he said, to begin drawing up a plan for the partition of India.

* * *

Inevitably, Mountbatten's decision would lead to one of the great dramas of modern history. Whatever the manner in which it was executed, it was bound to end in the mutilation of a great nation whose unity was the most imposing result of three and a half centuries of British colonization. To satisfy the exigent demands of Mohammed Ali Jinnah, two of India's most distinctive entities, the Punjab and Bengal, would have to be carved up. The result would make Pakistan a geographic aberration, a nation of two heads separated by 970 miles of Himalayan peaks and Indian territory. Twenty days, more time than was required to sail from Karachi to Marseilles, would be needed to make the sea trip around the subcontinent from one half of Pakistan to the other. A non-stop flight between its two parts would require a four-engined aircraft, machines which would prove expensive luxuries for the new state.

If the geographical distance dividing the two halves of Pakistan would be great, however, the psychological distance between the two peoples inhabiting them would be staggering. Apart from a common faith in Allah the One, the Merciful, Punjabis and Bengalis shared nothing. They were as different as Finns and Greeks. The Bengalis were short, dark and agile, racially a part of the masses of Asia. The Punjabis, in whose veins flowed the blood of thirty centuries of conquerors, were scions of the steppes of Central Asia, and their Aryan features bore the traces of Turkestan, Russia, Persia, the deserts of Arabia. Neither history nor language nor culture offered a bridge by which those two peoples might communicate. Their marriage in the common state of Pakistan would be a union created against all the dictates of logic.

The Punjab was the crown jewel of India. Half the size of France, it ran from the Indus River in the north-west all the way to the outskirts of Delhi. It was a land of sparkling rivers and golden fields of wheat, great rich fields rolling down to a distant blue horizon, an oasis blessed by the Gods in the midst of India's arid face. Its name meant 'Country of Five Rivers', after the five torrents to whose waters the Punjab owed its natural fertility. The most famous of them was one of the great rivers of the globe, the Indus, which had given its name to the Indian sub-continent.

Five thousand years of tumultuous history had fashioned the Punjab's character and given it its identity. Its plains had resounded to the galloping hooves of Asia's conquering hordes. It was in the Punjab that the celestial song of Hinduism's sacred book, the *Bhagavad Gita*, had been inspired by a mystic dialogue between Lord Krishna and the warrior king Arjuna. The Persian legions of Darius and Cyrus, the Macedonians of Alexander the Great had camped on its plains. Mauryas, Scythians, Parthians had occupied them before being dispersed by waves of Huns and the Caliphs of Islam bringing their monotheistic faith to India's polytheistic Hindu millions. Three centuries of Moghul domination brought India to the apogee of its power and, sprinkled it with its priceless heritage of monuments. Finally the Punjab's indigenous Sikhs, with their rolled beards and their uncut hair packed in their multi-coloured turbans, conquered the province in their turn before succumbing to its latest occupants, the British.

The Punjab was a blend as subtle and complex as the mosaics decorating the monuments of its glorious Moghul past. To divide it would force an irreparable wound upon its population. Fifteen million Hindus, sixteen million Moslems and five million Sikhs shared its 17,932 towns and villages. Although divided by religion, they spoke a common language, clung to common traditions, and an equal pride in their distinctive Punjabi personality. Their economic co-existence was fashioned even more intricately. The area's prosperity rested upon a man-made miracle which, by its very nature, could not be divided, the immense network of irrigation canals built by the British which had made the Punjab the granary of India. Running from east to west across the entire province, their nourishing fingers had brought vast stretches of arid desert under cultivation and enriched the existence of millions of Punjabis. The province's proud network of railways and roads designed to deliver the Punjab's products to the rest of India, followed the same pattern. Wherever it went, the frontier of a partitioned Punjab would have to run from north to south, slicing the province's vascular system in two. Nor could any frontier be drawn that would not cut the proud and bellicose Sikh community in half, leaving at least two million Sikhs, with the rich lands they had reclaimed from the desert and some of their most sacred sites, inside a Moslem state.

Indeed, wherever the boundary line went, the result was certain to be nightmare for millions of human beings. Only an interchange of populations on a scale never realized before in history could sort out the havoc it would wreak. From the Indus to the bridges of Delhi, for over 500 miles, there was not a single town, not a single village, cotton grove or wheat field which would not somehow be threatened if the partition plan Lord Ismay had been ordered to prepare was carried out.

The division of Bengal at the other end of the sub-continent held out the possibilities of another tragedy. Harbouring more people than Great Britain and Ireland combined, Bengal contained 35 million Moslems and 30 million Hindus in an expanse of land running from tiger-stalked jungles at the foot of the Himalayas to the steaming marshes through which the thousand fingers of the Ganges and Brahmaputra rivers drained into the Bay of Bengal. Despite its division into two religious communities, Bengal, even more than the Punjab, was a distinct entity of its own. Whether Hindus or Moslems, Bengalis sprang from the same racial stock, spoke the same language, shared the same culture. They sat on the floor in a certain Bengali manner, ordered the sentences they spoke in a peculiar Bengali cadence, each rising to a final crescendo, celebrated their own Bengali New Year on 15 April. Its poets, like Tagore, were regarded with pride by all Bengalis.

They were the descendants of a culture whose roots went back in time to the pre-Christian era when a Buddhist civilization flourished in Bengal. Obliged to renounce their Buddhist faith by a Hindu dynasty in the first centuries after Christ, the Bengalis of the east greeted the arrival of Mohummed's warriors along their frontier as a release from Hindu oppression and eagerly embraced Islam. Since then, Bengal had been divided into religious halves, Moslems to the east, Hindus to the west.

In 1905, Lord Curzon, one of the most able Viceroys to rule India, tried to take advantage of that religious split to divide Bengal into two administratively more manageable halves. His efforts ended in failure six years later when a bloody revolt proved the Bengalis more prone to nationalist sentiments than religious passions.

If the Punjab seemed singled out for the blessings of the Divine, Bengal appeared the object of its malediction. A land seared by droughts alternating with frightening typhoon floods, Bengal was a kind of immense, steaming swamp in whose humid atmosphere flourished the two crops to which it owed a precarious prosperity, rice and jute. The cultivation of those two crops followed the province's religious frontiers, rice to the Hindu west, jute to the Moslem east.

The key to Bengal's existence, however, lay not in its crops. It was a city, the city which had been the springboard for Britain's conquest of India, the second city, after London, of the Empire, and first port of Asia, Calcutta, site of the terrible killings of August 1946.

Everything in Bengal, roads, railways, raw materials, industry, funnelled into Calcutta. If Bengal was split into its eastern and western halves, Calcutta, because of its physical location, seemed certain to wind up in the Hindu west, which would condemn the Moslem east to slow but inexorable asphyxiation. If almost all of the world's jute grew in East Bengal, all the factories which transformed it into rope, sacks, and cloth were clustered around Calcutta in West Bengal. The Moslem east which produced the jute grew almost no food at all, and its millions survived on the rice grown in the Hindu west.

In April 1947, Bengal's last British Governor, Sir Frederick Burrows, an ex-sergeant in the Grenadier Guards and railways trade union leader, predicted that East Bengal, destined to become one day Bangladesh, was condemned, in the event of India's partition, to turn into 'the greatest rural slum in history'.

No aspect of partition, however, was more illogical than the fact that, even if Jinnah's Pakistan was fully realized, it would still deliver barely half of India's Moslems from the alleged inequities of Hindu majority rule which justified the state in the first place. The remaining Moslems were so scattered throughout the rest of India that it was humanly impossible to separate them. Islands in a Hindu sea, they would be the first victims of a conflict between the countries, India's Moslem hostages to Pakistan's good behaviour. Indeed, even after the amputation, India would still harbour almost 50 million Moslems, a figure which would make her the third largest Moslem nation in the world, after Indonesia and the new state drawn from her own womb.

* * *

If Louis Mountbatten, Jawaharlal Nehru, or Mahatma Gandhi had been aware in April 1947 of one extraordinary secret, the division threatening India might have been avoided. That secret was frozen on to the grey surface of a piece of film, a film which could have upset the Indian political equation and would almost certainly have changed the course of Asian history. Yet so precious was the secret that even the British CID, one of the most effective investigative agencies in the world, was ignorant of its existence.

The heart of the film was two dark circles no bigger than a pair of ping-pong balls. Each was ringed by an irregular white border like the corona of the sun eclipsed by the moon. Above them, a galaxy of little white spots stretched up the film's grey surface towards the top of the thoracic cage. That film was an X-ray, the X-ray of a pair of human lungs. The black circles were pulmonary cavities, gaping holes in which the lung's vital tissues no longer existed. The little chain of white dots indicated areas where more pulmonary or pleural tissue was already hardening and confirmed the diagnosis: tuberculosis was devouring the lungs. The damage was already so extensive that the human being whose lungs were on that film could have barely two or three years to live.

Sealed in an unmarked envelope, those X-rays were locked in the office safe of Dr Jal R. Patel, a Bombay physician. The lungs depicted on them belonged to the rigid and inflexible man who had frustrated Louis Mountbatten's efforts to preserve India's unity. Mohammed Ali Jinnah, the one unmovable obstacle between the Viceroy and Indian unity, was living under a sentence of death.

In June 1946, nine months before Mountbatten's arrival, Dr Patel had lifted those X-rays from their developing bath and discovered the terrible disease that threatened to put a rapid end to Jinnah's life. Tuberculosis, the cruel scourge which annually took the lives of millions of undernourished Indians, had invaded the lungs of the prophet of Pakistan at the age of seventy.

All his life, Jinnah had suffered from delicate health due to his weak pulmonary system. Long before the war, he'd been treated in Berlin for complications arising out of an attack of pleurisy. Frequent bronchitis since then had diminished his strength and weakened his respiratory system to the point at which the effort demanded by a major speech would leave him panting for hours.

In Simla in late May 1946, bronchitis had again struck the Moslem League leader. Jinnah's devoted sister Fatima got him on a train to Bombay, but *en route* his condition worsened. So alarming did his state become that she sent an urgent call to Dr Patel. Patel boarded his train outside Bombay. His distinguished patient's condition, he quickly discovered, was 'desperately bad'. Warning Jinnah he would collapse if he tried to get through the reception waiting for him at Bombay's Grand Railroad Station, Patel bundled him off the train at a suburban station and into a hospital. It was while he was there, slowly regaining his strength, that Patel discovered what would become the most closely guarded secret in India.

If Jinnah had been just any unfortunate victim of tuberculosis, he would have been confined in a sanatorium for the rest of his life. Jinnah, however, was not a normal patient. When he was discharged from hospital, Patel brought him to his office. Sadly, he revealed to his friend and patient the fatal illness which was stalking him. He was, he told Jinnah, reaching the end of his physical resources Unless he severely reduced his work load, rested much more frequently, gave up cigarettes and alcohol, and eased the pressures on his system he did not have more than one or two years to live.

Jinnah received that harsh news impassively. Not the slightest expression crossed his pale face. There was no question, he told Dr Patel, of abandoning his life's crusade for a sanatorium bed. Nothing except the grave was going to turn him from the task to which he'd appointed himself of leading India's Moslems at this critical juncture in their history. He would follow the doctor's advice and reduce his work load only in so far as it was compatible with that great duty. Jinnah knew that if his Hindu enemies learned he was dying, their whole political outlook could change. Thcy might wait until he was in his grave, then unravel his dream with the more malleable men underneath him in the hierarchy of the Moslem League.*

Fortified every two weeks by injections given him in secret by Dr Patel, Jinnah returned to work. He made no effort whatsoever to follow his doctor's advice. He was not going to let his rendezvous with death cheat him of his other rendezvous with history. With extraordinary courage, with an intense and consuming zeal that sent his life's candle guttering out in a last harsh burst of flame, Jinnah lunged for his lifetime's goal. 'Speed,' Jinnah had told Mountbatten in their first discussions of India's future, was 'the essence of the contract'. And so, too, had it become the essence of Mohammed Ali Jinnah's own contract with destiny.

*

The eleven men seated around the oval table in the conference chamber solemnly waited for Lord Mountbatten to begin their proceedings. They were, in a sense, the descendants of the 24 founding fathers of the East India Company, the men whose mercantile appetites had sent Britain along the sea-lanes to India three and a half centuries earlier. They were the pillars of the empire born of their avarice, the governors of the eleven provinces of British

* Mountbatten's predecessor, Lord Wavell, noted in his diary on 10 January and 28 February 1947, reports that Jinnah was 'a sick man'. They did not, however, indicate whether the Viceroy was aware of how grave the Moslem leader's illness really was. In any event, Mountbatten himself was never given in any of his briefings any hint that Jinnah was a dying man, information which, if available, he noted a quarter of a century after Jinnah's death, would have had a vital bearing on his actions in India. There are indications Jinnah's second in command, Liaqat Ali Khan, was aware of his illness in the last six months of his life. His daughter Wadia told the authors of this book in an interview in Bombay in December 1973, that she only became aware her father had tuberculosis after his death. She herself is personally persuaded Jinnah confided his secret to his sister Fatima, but he probably would not let her reveal it to anyone else or seek help for him.

India. They stood at the pinnacle of careers of service to the Indian Empire, savouring that high authority of which they might have dreamed as young men in the remote and lonely postings of their youth. Only two of them were Indians.

Capable and dedicated men, they offered India the responsible exercise of authority acquired by a lifetime of service. India, in its turn, offered them an opportunity to live in a splendour almost regal in its dimension. The official residences in which they dwelled were palaces staffed by scores of retainers. Their writ ran over territories as vast and as populous as the largest nations of Europe. They crossed their territories in the comfort of their private railway cars, their cities in Rolls-Royces with turbaned escorts, their jungles on elephant back.

Ranged around the table in order of precedence came first the heads of the three great Presidencies; Bombay, Madras and Bengal. The other provinces followed: the Punjab first, then Sind with its port of Karachi, United Provinces, Bihar, Orissa, Assam, site of the famous tea plantations on the Burmese frontier, the Central Province and finally the North-west Frontier Province guarding the Khyber Pass and the Afghan Frontier.

Their meeting was an awkward confrontation for Mountbatten. At 46, he was the youngest man at the table. He had brought to Delhi none of the usual qualifications for his office, a brilliant parliamentary career or a background of administrative achievement. He was a comparative stranger in the India to which most of the eleven governors had devoted an entire career, mastering its complex history, learning its dialects, becoming as some of them had, world-renowned experts on phases of its existence. They were proud men, certain to be sceptical of any plan put before them by the neophyte in their midst.

Yet Mountbatten was personally convinced his lack of expertise was not the disadvantage it seemed. They, the experts, had not found a solution because, he suspected, 'they were too steeped in the old British Raj school and were always trying to find a solution which would do the least possible violence to the system as it existed.' Mountbatten began by asking each governor to describe the situation in his province. Eight of them painted a picture of dangerous, troubled areas, but provinces in which the situation still remained under control. It was the portrait offered by the governors of the three critical provinces, the Punjab, Bengal, and the North-west Frontier (the NWFP), that sobered the gathering.

His features drawn, his eyes heavy with fatigue, Sir Olaf Caroe, Cerberus at the passes through which invaders had poured into

India for thirty centuries, spoke first. He had been kept awake all night by a stream of cables detailing fresh outbursts of trouble in his province. Almost all Caroe's career had been spent on that edge of the Empire. No westerner alive could rival his knowledge of its unruly Pathan tribesmen, their culture and language. His capital of Peshawar still harboured one of the world's most picturesque bazaars and once a week a camel caravan from Kabul came down the Khyber Pass to nourish it with skins, fruit, wool, crockery, watches, sugar, some of those goods smuggled out of the USSR. The labyrinthine grottoes of his mountainous province sheltered scores of secret arms factories from which flowed a profusion of ornate and deadly weapons to arm Masudis, Afridis, Wazirs, the legendary warrior tribes of the Pathans.

The province was close to disintegration, he warned, and if this happened, the old British nightmare of invading hordes from the north-west forcing the gates of the empire might be realized. The Pathan tribes of Afghanistan were poised to come pouring down the Khyber Pass to Peshawar and the banks of the Indus in pursuit of land they'd claimed as theirs for a century. 'If we're not jolly careful,' he said, 'we are going to have an international crisis on our hands.'

The portrait drawn by Sir Evan Jenkins, the taciturn governor of the Punjab, was even grimmer. A Welshman, Jenkins had given himself to the Punjab with a passion equal to Caroe's for the Frontier. So total was his devotion that the old bachelor was accused by his critics of having married his Punjab 'to the point where he forgot the rest of India existed'. Whatever solution was chosen for India's problems, he declared, it was certain to bring violence to the Punjab. At least four divisions would be needed to keep order if partition were decided upon. Even if it were not, they would still face a demand by the Sikhs for an area of their own. 'It's absurd to predict the Punjab will go up in flames if it's partitioned,' he said, 'it's already in flames.'

The third governor, Sir Frederick Burrows of Bengal, was ill in Calcutta, but the briefing on the province's situation as offered by his deputy was every bit as disquieting as the reports from the NWFP and the Punjab.

When those reports were finally finished, Mountbatten's staff passed out a set of papers to each governor. They carried the details, Mountbatten announced, 'of one of the possible plans under examination.' It was called, 'for easy reference,' Plan Balkan and it was the first draft of the partition plan Mountbatten had ordered his Chief of Staff Lord Ismay to prepare a week earlier.

A shock ran through the assembled governors as they began to turn its pages. They were apostles and architects of Indian unity. Most of them had spent their lives reinforcing the ties they now learned a departing Britain might decide to dismantle.

The plan, aptly named after the Balkanization of the States of Central Europe after World War I, would allow each of India's eleven provinces to choose whether it wished to join Pakistan or remain in India; or, if a majority of both its Hindus and Moslems agreed, become independent. Mountbatten told his assembled governors he was not going 'lightly to abandon hope for a united India'. He wanted the world to know the British had made every effort possible to keep India united. If Britain failed it was of the utmost importance that the world know it was, 'Indian opinion rather than a British decision that had made partition the choice.' He himself thought a future Pakistan was so inherently unviable that it should 'be given a chance to fail on its own demerits', so that later 'the Moslem League could revert to a unified India with honour'.

Those eleven men displayed no enthusiasm for partition. Nor, however, did they oppose it. The fact was that even they did not have any other solution to propose.

That evening, in the state dining-room of Viceroy's House, with the oil portraits of India's first nineteen Viceroys looking down upon them like ghostly judges from the past, the governors and their wives closed their last conference with a formal banquet presided over by Lord and Lady Mountbatten. At the end of the dinner, the servants brought out decanters of port. When the glasses were filled, Louis Mountbatten stood and raised his glass to their company. None of them realized it, but a tradition was ending with his gesture. Never again would a Viceroy of India propose to his assembled governors the traditional toast Mountbatten now offered to his cousin more than 4,000 miles away: 'Ladies and Gentlemen, the King Emperor!'

The Frontier and the Punjab, Late April 1947

The awesome white cone of Nanga Parbat filled the round windows of the viceregal York. It thrust its sculpted peak 25,000 feet into the air a hundred miles north of the aircraft. From one end of the horizon to another, the plane's passengers could follow the dark snow-capped walls of the great mountain range to which it belonged, the Hindu Kush, the barrier to those desolate, frozen reaches known as the Roof of the World. The York twisted south, flew above the serpentine coils of the Indus and began its approach over the mud-walled, fortress-like compounds of Peshawar, storied capital of the North-west Frontier Province.

As the plane swept towards the airport, its passengers suddenly caught a glimpse of an enormous, milling mob barely restrained by a beleaguered line of police. Louis Mountbatten had decided to suspend temporarily the conversations in his air-conditioned office so as personally to take the political temperature of his two most troubled provinces, the Punjab and the NWFP.

The news he was coming had swept over the Frontier. In 24 hours, summoned by the leaders of Jinnah's Moslem League, tens of thousands of men from every corner of the province had been converging on Peshawar. Overflowing their trucks, in buses, cars, on special trains, chanting and waving their arms, they had spilled into the capital for the greatest popular demonstration in its history.

Now, those tall, pale-skinned Pathans prepared to offer the Viceroy a welcome of an unexpected sort. Tired, their tempers rising in the heat and dirt, barely responsive to their leaders' commands, they were working themselves towards a dangerous frenzy. The police had confined them in an enormous low-walled enclosure running between a railroad embankment and the sloping walls of Peshawar's old Moghul fortress. Irritated and unruly, they threatened to mar the conciliatory tones of Operation Seduction with the discordant rattle of gunfire.

They were there because of the anomalous political situation of a province whose population was 93% Moslem, but which was governed by a Congress party ministry. The Congress leader was a tribal chieftain named Abdul Ghaffar Khan, a bearded giant who resembled an Old Testament prophet and had devoted his life to carrying Gandhi's message of love and passive resistance to Pathan tribesmen for whom the blood feud and the vendetta were an integral part of existence. This incongruous figure had won their support until, faithful to Gandhi, he'd opposed Jinnah's call for an Islamic state. Since then, stirred by Jinnah's agents, the population had turned against Ghaffar Khan and the government he'd installed in Peshawar. The huge, howling crowd greeting Mountbatten, his wife and 17-year-old daughter Pamela was meant to give final proof that it was the Moslem League and not the 'Frontier Gandhi' which now commanded the province's support. The worried governor, Sir Olaf Caroe, bundled the party into a well-escorted car for the trip to his residence. The crowd, growing more unruly by the hour, threatened to burst out of the area in which the police had herded them and start a headlong rush on the governor's residence. If they did, the vastly outnumbered military guarding the house would have no choice but to open fire. The resulting slaughter would be appalling. It would destroy Mountbatten, his hopes of finding a solution, and his Viceroyalty in a sickening bloodbath.

The worried governor suggested there was only one way out, an idea condemned by his police and army commander as sheer madness. Mountbatten might expose himself to the crowds, hoping a glimpse of him would somehow mollify them.

Mountbatten pondered a few moments. 'All right,' he said, 'I'll take a chance and see them.' To the despair of Caroe and his security officers, his wife Edwina insisted on coming with him.

A few minutes later, a jeep deposited the viceregal couple and the governor at the foot of the railway embankment. On the other side of that precarious dyke, 100,000 hot, dirty, angry people were shouting their frustration. Mountbatten took his wife by the hand and clambered up the embankment. As they reached the top, they discovered themselves only fifteen feet away from the surging waves of a sea of turbans. The ground under their feet shook with the impact of the gigantic crowd stampeding forward in front of them. Before that terrifying ocean of human beings, incarnating in their shrieks and gesticulations the enormity and the passions of the masses of India, the Mountbattens for an instant were dizzy. Whirling spirals of dust stirred by thousands of rushing feet clotted the air. The noise of the crowd was an almost tangible layer of air crushing down on them. It was a decisive instant in Operation Seduction, an instant when anything was possible.

Watching their silhouettes as they stared uncertainly out at the crowd, Sir Olaf Caroe felt an apprehensive shudder. In that crowd were twenty, thirty, forty thousand rifles. Any madman, any bloodthirsty fool, could shoot the Mountbattens 'like ducks on a pond'. For the first seconds they stood there, Caroe sensed the crowd was in an ugly mood. 'It's going to go wrong,' he thought for a fleeting instant.

Mountbatten did not know what to do. He couldn't articulate a syllable of Pushtu, the crowd's tongue. As he pondered, an unexpected phenomenon began to still the mob as if hypnotized; stopping perhaps with its strange vibrations an assassin's hand. For this entirely unplanned meeting with the Empire's most renowned warriors, Mountbatten happened to be wearing the short-sleeved, loose-fitting bush jacket he had worn as Supreme Allied Commander in Burma. One aspect of it struck the crowd. It was its colour, green. Green was the colour of Islam, the blessed green of the *Hajis*, the holy men who had made the pilgrimage to Mecca. Instinctively, those tens of thousands read in that green uniform a gesture of solidarity with them, a subtle compliment to their great religion.

His hand still clutching her but his eyes straight ahead, Mountbatten hissed to his wife: 'Wave to them.' Slowly, graciously, the frail Edwina raised her arm to the crowd, with his. India's fate seemed for an instant suspended on those hands climbing above the crowd's head. A questioning silence had briefly drifted over the unruly crowd. Suddenly, as Edwina's pale arm began to stroke the sky, a cry, then a roaring ocean of noise burst from the crowd. From tens of thousands of throats came an interminable, constantly repeated shout, a triumphant litany marking the successful passing of the most dangerous seconds of 'Operation Seduction'.

'*Mountbatten Zindabad*!' those embittered Pathan warriors screamed, '*Mountbatten Zindabad* – Long Live Mountbatten!'

Forty-eight hours after his confrontation with the Pathans, Mountbatten and his wife landed in the Punjab. Sir Evan Jenkins, immediately led the viceregal pair to a little village 25 miles from Rawalpindi. There a shocked Mountbatten was able to verify the accuracy of the governor's warning issued fourteen days earlier that his province was in flames and get his first, direct contact with the horrors sweeping India.

The young naval captain who had seen most of his shipmates die in the wreck of his destroyer off Crete, the leader who'd led millions through the savage jungle war in Burma, was overwhelmed by the spectacle in that little hamlet of 3500 people, which had once been typical of India's half million villages.

For centuries, Kahuta's dirt alleys had been shared in peace by 2000 Hindus and Sikhs and 1500 Moslems. That day, side by side in the village centre, the stone minaret of its mosque and the rounded dome of the Sikhs' *gurudwara* were the only identifiable remnants of Kahuta left on the skyline of the Punjab.

Just before Mountbatten's visit, a patrol of the British Norfolk Regiment on a routine reconnaissance mission passed through the village. Kahuta's citizens, as they had for generations, were sleeping side by side in mutual confidence and tranquillity. By dawn, Kahuta had for all practical purposes ceased to exist and its Sikhs and Hindus were all dead or had fled in terror into the night.

A Moslem horde had descended on the village like a wolf pack, setting fire to the houses in its Sikh and Hindu quarters with buckets of gasoline. In minutes, the area was engulfed in fire and entire families, screaming pitifully for help, were consumed by the flames. Those who escaped were caught, tied together, soaked with gasoline and burned alive like torches. Totally out of control, the fire swept into the Moslem quarter and completed the destruction of Kahuta. A few Hindu women, hauled from their beds to be raped and converted to Islam, survived; others had broken away from their captors and hurled themselves back into the fire to perish with their families.

'Until I went to Kahuta,' Mountbatten reported back to London, 'I had not appreciated the magnitude of the horrors that are going on.'

His confrontation with the crowd in Peshawar, the atrocious spectacle of one devastated Punjabi village, were the last proofs Mountbatten needed. The judgment he'd made after ten days of meetings in his air-conditioned New Delhi study was sound. Speed was the one overwhelming imperative, if India was to be saved. If he did not move immediately, India was going to collapse and the British Raj and his Viceroyalty would collapse in disarray along with her. And if speed was essential, then there was only one way out of the impasse, the solution from which he personally recoiled, but which India's political situation dictated – partition.

* * *

The last, painful phase in the pilgrimage of Mahatma Gandhi began on the evening of 1 May 1947, in the same spare hut in New Delhi's sweepers' colony in which a fortnight before he had unsuccessfully urged his colleagues to accept his plan to hold India together. Cross-legged on the floor, a water-soaked towel plastered once again to his bald head, Gandhi followed with sorrow the debate of the men around him, the high command of the Congress Party. The final parting of the ways between Gandhi and those men, foreshadowed in their earlier meeting, had been reached. All Gandhi's long years in jail, his painful fasts, his *hartals* and his boycotts, had been paving stones on the road to this meeting. He had changed the face of India and enunciated one of the original philosophies of his century to bring his countrymen to independence through non-violence; and now his sublime triumph threatened to become a terrible tragedy. His followers, their tempers worn, their patience exhausted, were ready to accept the division of India as the last, inescapable step to independence.

Gandhi did not oppose partition simply out of some mystical devotion to Indian unity. His years in the villages of India had given him an intuitive feeling for the soul of his country. Partition, that intuition told him, was not going to be the 'surgical operation' Jinnah had promised Mountbatten. It would be a sickening slaughter that would turn friend on friend, neighbour on neighbour, stranger on stranger, in thousands of those villages he knew so well. Their blood would be shed to achieve an abhorrent, useless end, the division of the sub-continent into two antagonistic parts condemned to gnaw at each other's entrails. Generations of Indians for decades to come, Gandhi believed, would pay the price of the error they were preparing to commit.

Gandhi's tragedy was that he had that evening no real alternative to propose beyond his instinct, the instinct those men had so often followed before. This night, however, he was no longer a prophet. 'They call me a Mahatma,' he bitterly told a friend later, 'but I tell you I am not even treated by them as a sweeper.'

Like Mountbatten, Nehru, Patel and the others all felt a catastrophe menaced India and partition, however painful it might be, was the only way to save the country. Gandhi believed with all his heart and soul that they were wrong. Even if they were right, he would have preferred chaos to partition.

Jinnah, he told his followers, will never get Pakistan unless the British give it to him. The British would never do that in the face of the Congress majority's unyielding opposition. They had a veto over any action Mountbatten proposed. Tell the British to go, he begged, no matter what the consequences of their departure might be. Tell them to leave India 'to God, to chaos, to anarchy, if you wish, but leave'.

'We will go through fire,' he believed, 'but the fire will purify us.'

He was a voice crying in the wilderness. Even his two hand-picked deputies were not ready to heed one last time the voice that had so often given utterance to their joint aspirations.

Patel had been prepared to concede partition even before Mountbatten's arrival. He was ageing, he'd suffered two heart attacks, and he wanted to get on with it, to end these ceaseless debates and get down to the task of building an independent India. Give Jinnah his state, he argued, it wouldn't survive anyway. In five years, the Moslem League would be knocking at their door begging for India's reunification.

Nehru was a torn and anguished man, caught between his deep love for Gandhi and his new admiration and friendship for the Mountbattens. Gandhi spoke to his heart, Mountbatten to his mind. Instinctively, Nehru detested partition, yet his rational spirit told him it was the only answer. Since reaching his own conclusion that there was no other choice, Mountbatten had been employing all the charm and persuasiveness of Operation Seduction to bring Nehru to his viewpoint. One argument was vital. With Jinnah gone. Hindu India could have the strong central government Nehru would need if he was going to build the socialist state of his dreams. Ultimately, he, too, stood out against the man he'd followed so long.

With these two voices in favour, the rest of the high command quickly fell into line. Nehru was authorized to inform the Viceroy that, while Congress remained 'passionately attached to the idea of a United India', it would accept partition provided the two great provinces of Punjab and Bengal were divided. The man who had led them to their triumph was left alone with his tarnished victory and his broken dream.

At 18.00 the following day, 2 May, exactly 40 days after it had landed in New Delhi, the viceregal York MW102 took off from Palam airport for London. This time, its most important passenger was Mountbatten's Chief of Staff Lord Ismay and he carried with him for submission to His Majesty's Government a plan for the division of India.

All Mountbatten's hopes had foundered, finally, on the rock of Jinnah's intransigence. He was ignorant of the one factor in the equation which might have changed things, Jinnah's illness. For the rest of his life, Mountbatten would look back on his failure to move Jinnah as the single great disappointment of his career. His personal anguish at the prospect of going down in history as the man who divided India could be measured by a document flying back to London with Ismay, Mountbatten's fifth personal report to the Attlee government.

Partition, Mountbatten wrote, 'is sheer madness,' and 'no one would ever induce me to agree to it were it not for this fantastic communal madness that has seized everybody and leaves no other course open'.

'The responsibility for this mad decision,' he wrote, must be placed 'squarely on Indian shoulders in the eyes of the world, for one day they will bitterly regret the decision they are about to make.'

6

A Precious Little Place

Simla, May 1947

Louis Mountbatten had no need for air-conditioning now. The view from his study's window alone was enough to cool him: the snow-tipped crests of the world's highest mountain chain, the Himalayas, the glacial wall dividing India from Tibet and China. No longer did his eyes recoil at bleak landscapes withering in India's remorseless heat. The vision before him now was one of unremitting green; emerald lawns, soaring stands of fir, delicate clumps of mountain fern. Exhausted by weeks of unceasing strain, Mountbatten had followed a tradition laid down by his predecessors. On Ismay's departure for London, he had abandoned Delhi for the most bizarre product of the British Raj, a strangely anomalous, consummately English creation planted in the Himalayan foothills, the little town of Simla.

Five months out of every year for over a century that miniature Sussex hamlet 7300 feet high tucked just below the roof of the world, had become a great imperial capital, the site from which the British ruled their Indian Empire and its associated satellites from the Red Sea to Burma. It was a precious little place, with its octagonal bandstand rimmed with blue and white striped pillars, its broad esplanades, immaculate gardens, the Tudor belfry of Christ Church Cathedral, its bells cast, in the muscular tradition of Victorian Christianity, from the brass of cannons captured during the Sikh wars. A thousand miles from the sea, served by one narrow-gauge railway, a gruelling journey by car, Simla poised disdainfully above the scorched and over-populated plains of India, cool, green and unmistakably English.

Each year in mid-April when the warm weather arrived, the Viceroy's departure for Simla in his white and gold viceregal train signalled that the mountain capital's season had begun. The Raj followed: bodyguards, secretaries, ADCs, generals, ambassadors and their staffs, every major ICS functionary of India's central administration. Behind came a cohort of tailors, hairdressers, boot and saddle makers, silversmiths by appointment to HE the Viceroy, wine and spirit merchants, *memsahibs* with their mounds of luggage, their flocks of domestics and their turbulent progeny. Until 1903, the railroad line ended 42 miles away at Kalka and there that whole incredible cohort transferred to two-horse tongas for the eight-hour trip, up the hills to Simla. Baggage followed by bullock cart and the backs of men. Long lines of coolies bore upon their work-bent spines an interminable flow of cases full of potted shrimps, *foie gras*, sausages, Bordeaux, champagne to supply the banquets which gave Simla's season an elegance unparalleled in India.

The coolies were necessary because, in Simla, the clap of hooves and the bark of the internal combustion engine was replaced by the soft pit-pat of human feet. An old tradition insisted that only three carriages, and later cars, were allowed in Simla, those of the Viceroy, the Commander-in-Chief of the Indian Army and the Governor of the Punjab. God, said a local joke, had applied for permission to have a car in Simla but was refused. Simla's standard conveyance until the British left India was the rickshaw. They were good-sized, recalled one owner, 'not those wretched little things that stick in your ribs', and four men were required to pull each one up and down Simla's precipitous slopes. A fifth ran alongside to relieve the others.

By tradition they did not wear shoes. Their employers compensated them, however, by the sumptuousness of their uniforms. Families competed to have the most elegantly turned-out coolies. The Viceroy's had the exclusive right to scarlet. One Scot put his in kilts. Another resident had two sets of uniforms for his, one for daytime, one for the evening. All usually wore on the breast of their uniforms the cyphers or the coat of arms of the family in whose service they were expending their lungs. Almost without exception those coolies of Simla suffered from tuberculosis.

The feasts towards which they bore their employers were brilliant and the most brilliant of all took place in Viceregal Lodge. The rickshaws of the town's aristocracy bore red rosettes which entitled them to use the Viceroy's private entry for grand balls and garden parties. The others bore white rosettes and used the public entrance. Whatever the colour of their rosettes, the rickshaw's occupants could feel sure of one thing: once inside, with the exception of a maharaja or two, they would not have to rub shoulders with any citizens of the country they governed.

'You simply cannot imagine the brilliance of a ball at Viceregal Lodge in the old days,' mused one woman, 'the long lines of the rickshaws in the night moving slowly up the hill, each with its little oil lamp glittering in the darkness and the only sound the soft patter of hundreds of bare feet.'

The other centre of Simla's social life was Cecil's Hotel, a hostelry whose hospitality was as lavish as any in the world. Each evening at 8.15 a turbaned butler marched down its carpeted corridors tolling a dinner gong as though it was a P & O steamer. The guests, in black tie and evening dresses, came down to dine at tables covered with Irish linen, Mappin and Webb silverware, Doulton porcelain and German Bohemian crystal, glasses for champagne, whisky, wine, port and water at each place.

Simla's heart was the Mall, a broad avenue running from one end of the ridge in which the town was set to the other, an exclusively English presence of tea shops, banks and stores, its surface as cleanly scrubbed as the Viceroy's porcelain. At one end stood Christ Church Cathedral into which the Commander-in-Chief, in full uniform, led the colony every Sunday, there to listen to 'a proper choir – all English voices'. Until World War One, Indians were not allowed to walk on the Mall.

That prohibition had represented the essence of Simla. The annual move to its heights was more than just a seasonal escape from the heat. It was a subtle reaffirmation of Britain's racial superiority, of the solidity of those virtues which set the British apart from the pullulating brown millions sweltering at their feet on the parched reaches of India.

Much of that old Simla was already gone by the time Louis Mountbatten arrived in early May 1947. Now an Indian could even walk down the Mall – providing he was not wearing the national dress of his country.*

Mountbatten may have been exhausted by his intensive negotiations, but he was also in an exuberant, confident mood. He had, after all, achieved in six weeks what his predecessors had failed to accomplish in years. He had delivered to 10 Downing Street a plan that offered Britain an honourable exit from India and to the Indians a solution, however painful, to their impasse.

Because he had been able to wring plenipotentiary powers out of Attlee before leaving London, he had not been obliged to secure the

* Simla changed with an easily foreseen rapidity after independence. The Indians, because of its connotations, abandoned it as their summer capital. 'The only thing which remains of the old Simla,' M. S. Oberoi, owner of Cecil's Hotel and chairman of Oberoi's Hotels Ltd, lamented in 1973, 'is the climate.' One English survivor of Simla's grand days still lives in the town, an 87-year-old widow named Mrs Henry Penn Montague. She lives alone now in the dark and melancholy Victorian mansion of her maternal uncle, the Finance Member of Lord Curzon's Viceregal Council, surrounded by six dogs, five cats, four servants and a house full of memorabilia. Mrs Penn Montague, who speaks six languages, rises every day at four in the afternoon. Breakfast is followed by high tea at sunset after which Mrs Montague retires to a room she has equipped with a Zenith Transoceanic radio. There, while Simla sleeps, Mrs Penn Montague listens to her radio until dawn, eavesdropping on the world. At 4.00 a.m., hers is perhaps the only light burning between Simla and Tibet.

formal agreement of the Indian leaders to his plan before sending it back to England. He had only to assure the Attlee government that they would accept it when it was put before them.

His plan was a distillation of what Mountbatten had learned in the privacy of his study. It represented his careful evaluation, based on his knowledge of each leader's intimate sentiments and convictions, of what they would accept when the chips were down. So confident was he of his judgment that just before leaving for Simla he had formally announced his intention to present it to them on his return on 17 May.

Simla's brisk climate, its Olympian calm, however, inspired reflection and uncharacteristic doubts began to gnaw at the Viceroy. Since the plan had reached London, he had been inundated by a stream of cables from the Attlee government proposing textual modifications which, while they would not alter its substance, would change its tone.

More serious, however, was the real concern which underlay his growing apprehension. If the implications in the plan he had sent to London were fully realized, it was not into two independent nations that the great Indian sub-continent would be divided, but three.

Mountbatten had inserted in the plan a clause which would allow an Indian province to become independent if a majority of both its communities wished to. That clause was intended to provide that the sixty-five million Hindus and Moslems of Bengal could join into one viable country with the great seaport of Calcutta as their capital.

The idea had been placed before Mountbatten by Calcutta's Moslem leader, Shaheed Suhrawardy, a nightclub- and champagne-loving politician who, ten months earlier, had unleashed the terrors of Direct Action Day on his city. The Viceroy liked it. Contrasted to Jinnah's aberrant, two-headed state, it seemed an entity likely to endure. To his surprise, he had discovered Bengal's Congress Hindu leaders intrigued by the project. He had quietly encouraged their interest. He had even discovered Jinnah would not oppose the idea. He had not, however, exposed it to Nehru and Patel, and it was this oversight that disturbed him now. Would they, in fact, accept a plan that might cost them the great port of Calcutta with its belt of textile mills owned by the industrialists who provided their party's principal financial support? If they didn't, Mountbatten, after all the assurances he'd given London, was going to look a bloody fool in the eyes of India, Britain and the world.

A sudden inspiration struck him. He would reassure himself by private discussions with the Indian leader, whom, to the distress of his staff, he'd invited to spend a holiday with him in Simla. More than ever, Mountbatten saw his relationship with the gracious and elegant Jawaharlal Nehru as the prime support of his own policies in India, and the prime hope of a warm understanding between Britain and her old Indian Empire in the years to come.

His wife's friendship with the Indian Prime Minister had grown too. Women like Edwina Mountbatten were rare in the world and rarer still in the India of 1947. No one had been better able to draw Nehru from his shell when doubts and depression gripped him than the attractive aristocrat who radiated so much compassion, intelligence and warmth. Often, over tea, a stroll in the Moghul Gardens, or a swim in the viceregal pool, she had been able to charm Nehru out of his gloom, redress a situation and subtly encourage her husband's efforts.

Determined to follow his instinct, Mountbatten called the members of his staff to his study and explained his idea to them. They were horrified. To show the plan to Nehru without exposing it to Jinnah would be a complete breach of faith with the Moslem leader, they pointed out. If he discovered it, Mountbatten's whole position would be destroyed.

For a long time, Mountbatten sat silently drumming the tabletop with his fingertips.

'I'm sorry,' he finally announced. 'Your arguments are absolutely sound. But I have a hunch that I must show it to Nehru, and I'm going to follow my hunch.'*

That night, Mountbatten invited Nehru to his study for a glass of port. Casually, he passed the Congress leader a copy of the plan as it had been amended by London, asking him to take it to his bedroom

* It was not the first time Mountbatten had gone against the combined advice of his staff. In February 1941, leading four of his flotilla of K-class destroyers through the Bay of Biscay en route to Gibraltar, he received a flash from the First Sea Lord informing him that the German pocket battleships *Scharnhorst* and *Gneisenau* had just been sighted steering for Saint-Nazaire, and ordering him to proceed to intercept them. It was sunset. Mountbatten ordered his flotilla to steer a course for Brest. His staff rushed to the bridge protesting that they'd been ordered to make for Saint-Nazaire, not Brest. No, Mountbatten said, they'd been ordered to intercept the two German ships and he had a hunch. If he were the Admiral commanding those two ships, he said, he would not be steering on his true course at sunset when the last reconnaissance planes of the day were out. The fact they were spotted heading for Saint-Nazaire meant their real destination was Brest. They would stay on the course he'd assigned them. Mountbatten's hunch turned out to be correct. The two ships were indeed heading for Brest. Unfortunately, although his destroyers raced for Brest at 32 knots, the Germans' headstart was too great. They reached the French port safely.

and read it. Then, perhaps, Nehru might let him know informally what reception it was likely to get from Congress. Flattered and happy, Nehru agreed.

A few hours later, while Mountbatten devoted himself to his regular evening relaxation, constructing his family's genealogical table, Jawaharlal Nehru began to scrutinize the text designed to chart his country's future. He was horrified by what he read. The vision of the India that emerged from the plan's pages was a nightmare, an India divided, not into two parts, but fragmented into a dozen pieces. The door Mountbatten had left open for Bengal would become, Nehru foresaw, a wound through which the best blood of India would pour. He saw India deprived of its lungs, the port of Calcutta along with its mills, factories, steel works; Kashmir, his beloved Kashmir, an independent state ruled by a despot he despised; Hyderabad become an enormous, indigestible Moslem body planted in the belly of India; half a dozen other princely states clamouring to go off on their own. The plan, he believed, would exacerbate all India's fissiparous tendencies – dialect, culture, race – to the point at which the sub-continent would risk exploding into a mosaic of weak, hostile states. The British had run India for three centuries with the byword 'Divide and Rule'. They proposed to leave it on a new one: 'Fragment and Quit'. White-faced, shaking with rage, Nehru stalked into the bedroom of his confidant Krishna Menon who'd accompanied him to Simla. With a furious gesture, he hurled the plan on to his bed.

'It's all over!' he shouted.

Mountbatten got his first intimation of his friend's violent reaction in a letter early the following morning. For the confident Viceroy, it was 'a bombshell'. As he read it, the whole structure he had so carefully erected during the past six weeks came tumbling down like a house of cards. The impression his plan left, Nehru wrote, was one of 'fragmentation and conflict and disorder'. It frightened him and was certain to be 'resented and bitterly disliked by the Congress Party'.

Reading Nehru's words, the poised, self-assured Viceroy who'd proudly announced to the world that he was going to present a solution to India's dilemma in ten days time, suddenly realized he had no solution at all. The plan the British Cabinet was discussing that very day, the plan he'd assured Attlee would win Indian acceptance, would never get past the one element in India that had to accept it, the Congress Party.

Mountbatten's critics might accuse him of over-confidence, but he was not a man to brood over setbacks. Instead of desponding at Nehru's reaction, Mountbatten congratulated himself on showing him the plan, and set out to repair the damage. Fortunately for the Viceroy, his friendship with Nehru would survive the shock. At Mountbatten's behest, Nehru agreed to stay on another night to give him time to draft a revised plan which might be acceptable to Congress. It would have to close the loopholes that had so distressed Nehru. The new plan would offer India's provinces and princes only one choice – India or Pakistan.

The dream of an independent Bengal was gone. Mountbatten remained convinced, however, that Jinnah's two-headed state could not survive. Some time later, he predicted to the man who would succeed him in Viceroy's House, C. R. Rajagopalachari, that East Bengal would be out of Pakistan in a quarter of a century. The Bangladesh war of 1971 was to confirm his prediction with just one year to spare.

To redraft his plan, Mountbatten called into his study the highest ranking Indian in his viceregal establishment. It was a supreme irony that at that critical juncture the Indian to whom Mountbatten turned had not even entered that vaunted administrative elite, the Indian Civil Service. No degree from Oxford or Cambridge graced his office walls. No family ties had hastened his rise. V. P. Menon was an incongruous oddity in the rarified air of Viceroy's House, a self-made man.

Eldest son in a family of twelve, Menon had quit school at 13 to work successively as a construction worker, coal miner, factory hand, stoker on the Southern Indian Railways, unsuccessful cotton broker and schoolteacher. Finally, having taught himself to type with two fingers, he talked his way into a job as a clerk in the Indian administration in Simla in 1929.*

What followed was probably the most meteoric rise in that administration's history. By 1947, it had carried Menon to one of the most senior posts on the Viceroy's staff, where he had quickly won Mountbatten's confidence and later affection.

Mountbatten informed Menon that, by that evening, he would have to redraft the charter that would give India her independence.

* When Menon arrived in Delhi en route to Simla, he discovered every rupee he owned had been stolen. Despairing, he finally approached an elderly, distinguished Sikh, explained his plight and asked for a loan of 15 rupees, to cover his fare to Simla. The Sikh gave him the money. When Menon asked for his address so he could pay it back, the Sikh said: 'No, until the day you die, you will always give that sum to any honest man who asks your help.' Six weeks before his death, his daughter recalls, a beggar came to the family home in Bangalore. Menon sent his daughter for his wallet, took out fifteen rupees, and gave it to the man. He was still repaying his debt.

Its essential option, partition, had to remain and it must above all continue to place the responsibility for making the choice upon the Indians themselves through the vote of their provincial assemblies.

Menon finished his task in accordance with Mountbatten's instructions. Between lunch and dinner, he had performed a *tour de force*. The man who had begun his career as a two-finger typist culminated it by redrafting, in barely six hours on an office porch looking out on the Himalayas, a plan which was going to re-order the sub-continent and alter the map of the world.

* * *

Stricken with a violent attack of appendicitis, Manu's slender figure shook under the blankets her great-uncle had heaped over her. Her eyes were dulled by a racking fever. Her body was hunched into a foetal position in an instinctive effort to minimize the terrible pain in her abdomen. Silent and worried, Gandhi hovered at her side.

Once again he faced a challenge to his faith. Gandhi had had a deep-rooted belief in nature cures. He denounced modern medicine for its emphasis on the body's physical aspects at the expense of the spirit, for counselling pills and drugs when what was needed was restraint and self-discipline, for being too concerned with money. The fields of India, he maintained, were filled with natural, medicinal herbs placed there by God to cure the nation's ill. To Gandhi, nature cure was an extension of his non-violent philosophy. It was for that reason he had refused to allow his wife's body to be subjected to the violence of a hypodermic needle as she lay dying in the Aga Khan's palace.

When Manu had begun to complain of a pain in her abdomen, Gandhi prescribed the treatment nature cure dictated: mudpacks, a strict diet and enemas.

Her condition worsened. Now, 36 hours later, a crisis was at hand. For all his faith in nature cures, Gandhi had also studied medicine at great length. He knew very well what malady was gripping his great-niece.

As it had been in Noakhali, her faith in him was total. She had confided herself entirely to his hands, ready to do whatever he wanted. Gandhi was in agony. His nature treatment had failed. To him its failure, Manu's illness, were manifestations of their spiritual imperfections. But, as he would later note, he did not 'have the courage to let a girl entrusted to me die like that'. He broke down and admitted defeat. 'With the utmost reluctance,' the man who had denied his dying wife the violent therapy of a hypodermic needle decided to allow his dying great-niece the violence of the surgeon's

The Gentle Prophet of a Nonviolent Revolution

To a century fraught with violence, Gandhi offered an alternative—nonviolence and civil disobedience. In Churchill's famous phrase, a "half-naked fakir", Gandhi crisscrossed his nation on foot and in third-class railway cars to stress his identity with the impoverished masses. He took tea at Buckingham Palace with the King-Emperor, dressed in the homespun cotton sheet that was his uniform, and practiced a life of spartan simplicity. The symbol of his challenge to the Age of Imperialism was the primitive wooden spinning wheel on which he labored religiously every day.

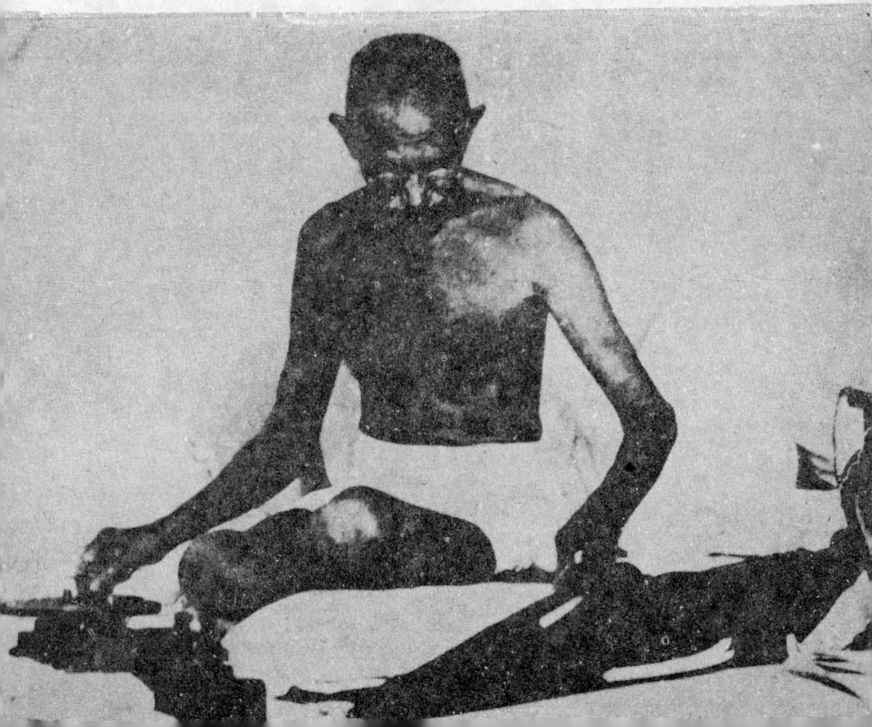

"A Race Destined to Govern and Subdue"

Whether exercised by a district officer like the young man in his bungalow (below), circa 1875, or Lord Mountbatten, among a few of his servants (top opposite), British rule in India in the Victorian Age was characterized by its panache, its rigor, its honesty and the enormous social gap which set India's rulers apart from the masses they ruled. Attended by scores of turbaned servants, the officers of the Indian Army (opposite bottom) "dined in" in solemn splendor at least once a month

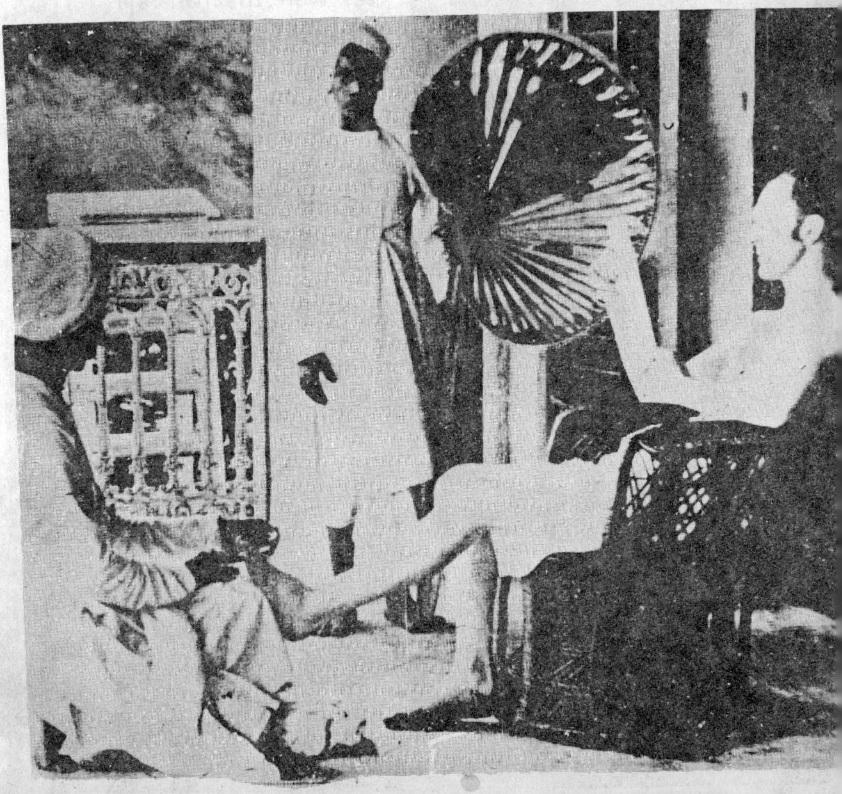

The Maharajas: Last of a Fabled Breed

Providence. Kipling wrote, created the maharajas to offer mankind a spectacle. Theirs was a world of marble palaces and scented harems, tigers and elephants, fabulous jewels and hoards of gold. In 1947, India's 565 maharajas, nawabs, princes and rajas still ruled over a third of India's land surface and 100 million Indians. Sport and sex were the maharajas' preferred pastimes. Even legs crippled at birth couldn't keep the Maharaja of Udaipur (right) from hunting tiger. His colleague, Maharaja of Patiala, parades under a golden canopy (below).

India's Last Viceroy and Vicereine

Lord and Lady Mountbatten arrived in Delhi on March 22, 1947 to preside over the coming Independence of India. After long and difficult negotiations with Mahatma Gandhi (opposite top) and other Indian leaders, Mountbatten secured on June 3, 1947 the agreement of his partners to the plan that would divide India into two separate nations (opposite bottom). Present, at Mountbatten's left, were Mohammed Ali Jinnah, Liaquat Ali Khan and Rab Nishtar for the Moslem League, and at his right, Jawaharlal Nehru, Vallabhbhai Patel and Acharya Kripalani for Congress and Baldev Singh for the Sikhs.

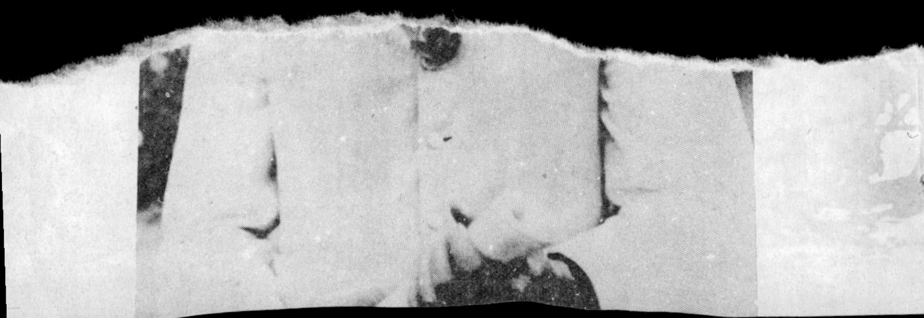

The Last Crusade of the Liberator of India

His hands resting upon the shoulders of his "walking sticks", his great-nieces Abha (left) and Manu (right), Gandhi sets off for the last crusade of his life: to restore peace and love in the villages of Bengal torn by hate and murder.

The Day an Age Ended

New Delhi, August 15, 1947 : Engulfed in a hysterical, happy throng, the Mountbattens' gilded carriage becomes a kind of life raft tossed upon the sea of humans celebrating India's independence (top). Two days earlier, the Mountbattens were in Karachi (bottom) to celebrate Pakistan's independence.

"With No Joy in My Heart"

His personal emblem, a freshly plucked rose, in the button-hole of his tunic, a pensive Jawaharlal Nehru poses for a moment in the garden of the Viceroy's house (below). Anxious to reconcile on Indian soil the parliamentary democracy of Britain and the economic socialism of Karl Marx, Nehru agreed with Mountbatten that the only alternative to dividing India was civil war. Reluctantly he turned his back on his old leader, Gandhi, and "with no joy in my heart" commended the Viceroy's plan to partition India, to his countrymen.

But India's freedom was won at a terrible price. Partition hurled ten million wretched people onto the roads, the railways and the unharvested fields of the Punjab in the greatest migration in human history (opposite).

The Inadvertent Architect of a Tragedy and Some of His Victims

Surrounded by four of the Indian assessors who were supposed to aid him, Sir Cyril Radcliffe (white suit, below) poses in the Punjab, one of the two Indian provinces it was his unhappy lot to divide. Born in India of a Sikh father and an abducted Moslem woman, Tanvier Boota Singh (bottom left) was one of the 10 million Indians to loose her home. Sikh journalist K.S. Duggal (bottom right) and Muslim medical student Aisha Ali, also lost their home. But found love. They married and are today living in New Delhi.

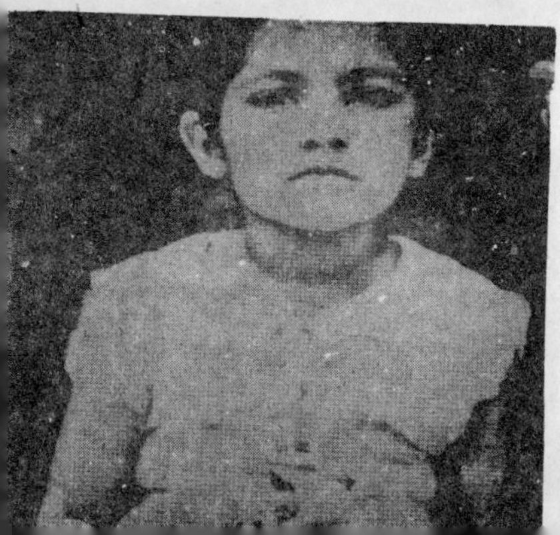

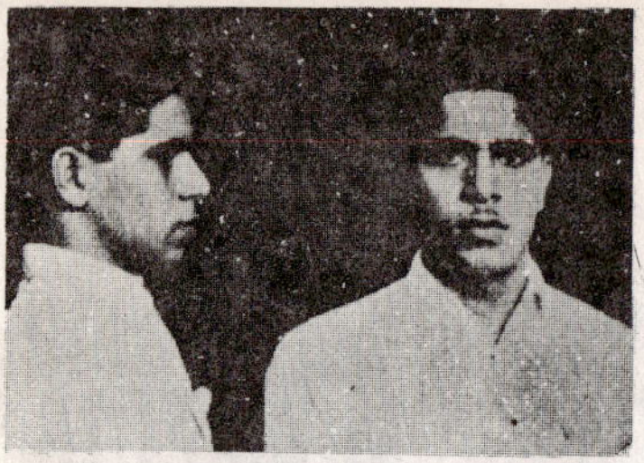

The Men who Killed Gandhi

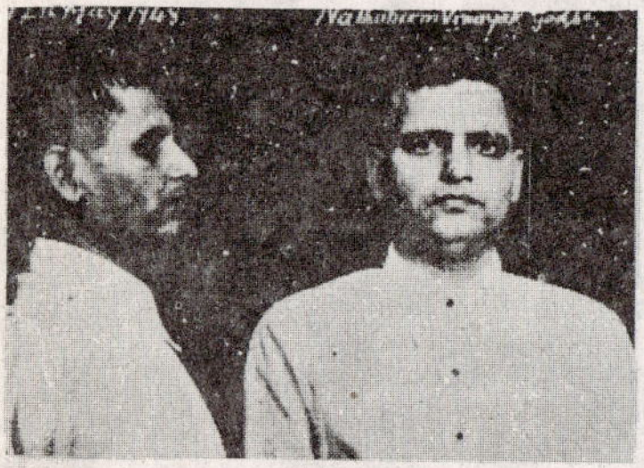

Seated, left to right, Narayan Apte, 34 —hanged; Veer Savarkar —acquitted; Nathuram Godse, 39, the killer, a fanatic newspaperman—hanged; Vishnu Karkare, 34, anti-Moslem proprietor of a tawdry travellers' hotel—life imprisonment. Standing, Shanker Kistaya, Badge's servant—convicted, but acquitted on appeal; Gopal Godse, 29, the killer's brother—life imprisonment; Madanlal Pahwa, 20, a Punjabi refugee who'd sworn to avenge his mutilated father—life imprisonment; Digamber Badge, 37, the arms peddler who disguised himself as a holy man—turned state's witness, released. (Opposite) police photos

India's Holy Man Died Pronouncing the Name of God

As he had hoped he would, Gandhi died crying "He Ram" ("Oh God !") with his last breath. Face frozen in the still serenity of death, India's murdered Mahatma offers his visage to his countrymen for an ultimate and pathetic darshan. His followers' parting tribute, a shower of rose petals, litters his winding sheet, made of cotton he had spun himself on his wooden spinning wheel.

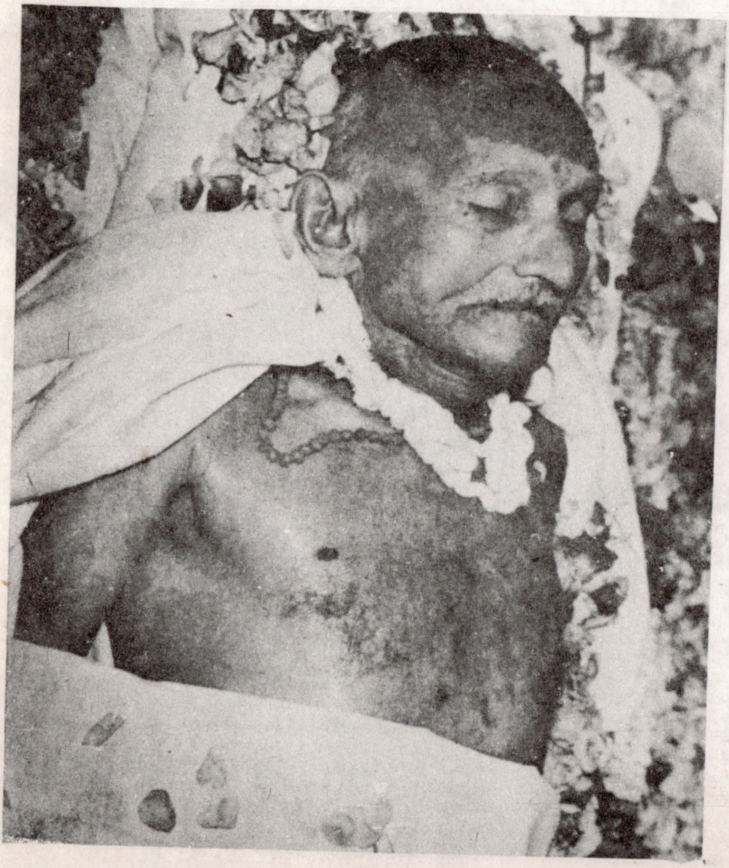

scalpel. Manu was rushed to the hospital for an emergency appendectomy.

As she slipped under the anaesthetic, Gandhi gently placed his palm on her brow. 'Hold on to Ramanama,' he told her, 'and all will be well.'

Hours later, one of her doctors, shocked at Gandhi's haggard regard, took the Mahatma aside. Rest, he begged Gandhi, ease the strain on his being. 'The people need your services more than ever.'

Gandhi looked at him with disconsolate eyes. 'Neither the people nor those in power have any use for me,' he sadly replied. 'My only wish is to die in harness, taking the name of God with my last breath.'

7

Palaces and Tigers, Elephants and Jewels

New Delhi, May 1947

The turbaned servant advanced in reverent silence towards the mammoth figure of his master. Caressing with his bare feet the tiger, panther and antelope skins that littered his long march across the room, he bore to his employer's bedside a silver tray ordered in London in 1921 to mark the tour of India of His Royal Highness the Prince of Wales. The vermeil teapot set upon it gave off the delicious fragrance of the special blend simmering inside, a mixture flown twice a month from London along with the biscuits accompanying it, by the firm of Fortnum and Mason. On the walls of the bedroom, in its shadowy corners, were the stuffed animal heads and a host of silver trophies garnered by its occupant with his long-bore rifle, his polo stick or his cricket bat, all of which he wielded with a gentleman's skill.

The servant set the tray on a bedside table and bent down to his master. The man was a Sikh and his black beard, tightly rolled in a silk net, circled his sleeping face like an ebony collar.

'Bed tea,' the servant whispered with obsequious softness.

The six-foot-four-inch figure below him stretched with a long and feline gesture. As he swung to his feet, another servant emerged from the shadows to cover his muscular shoulders with a silk robe. Shaking the sleep from his eyes, His Most Gracious Highness Yadavindrah Singh, the eighth Maharaja of the Indian State of Patiala, gazed out on another day.

Yadavindrah Singh presided over the most remarkable body in the world, an assembly unlike any other man had ever spawned or was likely to spawn in the future. He was the Chancellor of the Chamber of Indian Princes. On this May morning, almost two years after the cyclone of Hiroshima and the end of a war that had shaken the world's foundations, the 565 maharajas, nawabs, rajas and rulers composing that chamber still reigned as absolute, hereditary sovereigns over one third of India's land surface and a quarter of her population. They reflected the fact that under the British there had been two Indias, the India of its provinces, administered by the central government in Delhi, and the separate India of her princes.

The princes' anachronistic situation dated from Britain's haphazard conquest of India when rulers who received the English with open arms or proved worthy foes on the battlefield, were allowed to remain on their thrones provided they acknowledged Britain as the paramount power. The system was formalized in a series of treaties between the individual rulers and the British crown. The princes had recognized the 'Paramountcy' of the King Emperor as represented in New Delhi by the Viceroy and ceded to him control of their foreign affairs and defence. They received in return Britain's guarantee of their continuing autonomy inside their states.

Certain princes like the Nizam of Hyderabad or the Maharaja of Kashmir ruled over states which rivalled in size or population the nations of Western Europe. Others like those in the Kathiawar peninsula near Bombay lived in stables and governed domains no larger than London's Richmond Park. Their fraternity embraced the richest man in the world and princes so poor that their entire kingdom was a cow pasture. Over four hundred princes ruled states smaller than twenty square miles. A good number of them offered their subjects an administration far better than that the British provided. A few were petty despots more concerned with squandering their state's revenues to slake their own extravagant desires than with improving the lot of their peoples.

Whatever their political proclivities, however, the future of India's ruling princes, with their average of 11 titles, 5·8 wives, 12·6 children, 9·2 elephants, 2·8 private railway cars, 3·4 Rolls-Royces and 22·9 tigers killed, posed a grave problem in the spring of 1947. No solution to the Indian equation would work if it failed to deal with their peculiar situation.

For Gandhi, Nehru and the Congress the answer was evident. The princes' reign should be terminated and their states merged into an independent India. That was hardly a solution designed to appeal to Yadavindrah Singh and men like him. His state of Patiala in the heart of the Punjab was one of the richest in India and he had an army the size of an infantry division, bulwarked by Centurion tanks, to defend it if necessary.

An atmosphere of concern and tension hung about the Chancellor of the Chamber of Indian Princes as he sipped his tea. He knew something on this May morning that the Viceroy of India did not know. He knew that, 6000 miles from his Punjabi state, in London, a man was making a desperate plea so that his future and that of his fellow princes would not be that to which Nehru and the Socialists of Congress wished to condemn them.

* * *

The man who was to make that plea was not a maharaja but an Englishman. He was in London without the Viceroy's knowledge or approval. Sir Conrad Corfield was a missionary's son, who represented one of the great strengths and at the same time great weaknesses of the British who had run India. Corfield had spent most of his career in the service of India's princely states and as a result those states were his India. His judgment of what was good for India was what was good for her princes. He loathed their enemies, Nehru and Congress, with a fervour at least equal to theirs.

Corfield was, in May 1947, the Viceroy's Political Secretary, his deputy responsible for exercising the authority that the princes had ceded to the King Emperor. Absorbed since arriving in Delhi by the task of finding a solution to the conflict between Congress and the Moslem League, Mountbatten had had little time to wrestle with the problem of Corfield and the princes. That had not disturbed Corfield. Deeply suspicious of his superior's ripening friendship with Nehru, Corfield had flown to London to secure his princes a better deal than he thought Mountbatten would be prepared to give them. Corfield was making his plea in a room rendered unique in deference to the princes of India. The octagonal London office of the Secretary of State for India, known since the days of John Morley as the 'gilded cage', could be entered by either of two doors opposite the secretary's desk, exactly alike in every detail. Thus two maharajas of equal rank could enter the secretary's presence at precisely the same instant, so that neither would suffer a loss of face or precedence.

Corfield set his argument before the occupant of that office, the Earl of Listowel, with force and vigour. India's princes had surrendered their powers to the British crown and only to the British crown, he argued. At the moment India became independent those powers should revert to them. They would then be free to work out whatever new arrangement they could with India or Pakistan, or if they chose, and it were practicable, they could become independent. Anything less would be a violation of the treaties that linked Britain to the states.

Corfield's interpretation was in the strict legal sense right. Its practical consequences, however, would be appalling to contemplate. If the implications in Corfield's impassioned plea were realized, an independent India would be menaced with Balkanization on a scale even Nehru in Simla had not contemplated.

* * *

It had once seemed to Rudyard Kipling that Providence had created the maharajas just to offer mankind a spectacle, a dazzling vision of marble palaces, tigers, elephants and jewels. Powerful or humble, rich or poor, theirs was an extraordinary breed, whose members had fuelled those legends of an India now on the brink of extinction. The accounts of their vices and virtues, their extravagances and prodigalities, their follies and their eccentricities, had enriched folklore and entranced a world hungry for exotic dreams. Their day was ending, but when the maharajas of India were gone, the world would be a duller place.

The legend that surrounded India's princes was the work of a relatively small number of their company, those rulers with the wealth, the time and the appetite to indulge their most imaginative fantasies. A series of consuming passions united those extravagant gentlemen and they pursued them with rare devotion. Hunting, cars, sport, their palaces and harems all figured among them, but most often jewels were a maharaja's best friends.

The Maharaja of Baroda practically worshipped gold and precious stones. His court tunic was of spun gold and only one family in his state was allowed to weave its threads. The fingernails of each member of the family were grown to extraordinary length, then cut and notched like the teeth of a comb so they could caress the gold threads into perpendicular perfection.

His collection of historic diamonds included the Star of the South, the seventh biggest diamond in the world, and the diamond offered by Napoleon III to Eugénie. The most precious bauble in his treasure chest was a collection of tapestries made entirely of pearls into which had been woven ornate designs of rubies and emeralds.

The Maharaja of Bharatpur had an even more remarkable collection. His masterpieces were made of ivory. Each represented years of labour for an entire family. Their work demanded an extraordinary exactitude, peeling down the ivory of elephants' tusks. The largest topaz in the world gleamed like a Cyclopean eye from the turban of the Sikh Maharaja of Kapurtala, its apricot brilliance set off by a field of 3000 diamonds and pearls. The fabulous treasure of the Maharaja of Jaipur was buried in a Rajasthan hillside, the site guarded from generation to generation by a particularly bellicose Rajput tribe. Each Maharaja was allowed to visit the site once in his lifetime to select the stones which would embellish his reign. Among its marvels was a necklace composed of three tiers of rubies each the size of a pigeon's egg and three enormous emeralds, the largest of which weighed 90 carats.

Centrepiece of the great Sikh Maharaja of Patiala's collection was a pearl necklace insured by Lloyds for one million dollars. The most intriguing item, however, was a diamond breastplate, its luminous surface composed of 1001 brilliantly matched blue-white diamonds. Until the turn of the century it had been the custom of the Maharaja of Patiala to appear once a year before his subjects naked except for that diamond breastplate, his organ in full and glorious erection. His performance was adjudged a kind of temporal manifestation of the Shivaling, the phallic representation of Lord Shiva's organ. As the Maharaja walked about, his subjects gleefully applauded, their cheers acknowledging both the dimensions of the princely organ and the fact that it was supposed to be radiating magic powers to drive evil spirits from the land.

An early Maharaja of Mysore was informed by a Chinese sage that the most efficacious aphrodisiacs in the world were made of crushed diamonds. That unfortunate discovery led to the rapid impoverishment of the state treasury as hundreds of precious stones were ground to dust in the princely mills. The dancing girls, whom the resulting potions were meant, in a sense, to benefit, were paraded through the state on elephants whose trunks were studded with rubies and whose ears were decorated with elephant ear-rings composed of the prince's surviving diamonds.

The Maharaja of Baroda went about on an elephant even more gaudily arrayed. The animal was a 100-year-old monster whose great tusks had skewered twenty rivals in as many combats. All his equipment was in gold: the howdah in which the prince rode, his harness, the great saddle-cloth, or *shabrack*, covering his back. Like pendants, ten gold chains hung from each of the pachyderm's ears. Each chain was worth £25,000 and each represented one of his victories.

In both practice and folklore, the elephant had been for generations the princes' preferred means of locomotion. Symbols of the cosmic order, born from the hand of Rama, they were in Hindu mythology the pillars of the universe, the supports of the sky and the clouds. Once a year, Mysore prostrated himself in veneration before the largest bull elephant in his herd, thus rekindling his alliance with nature's forces.

A prince's standing might be measured in the number, the age and the size of the animals filling his elephant stables. Not probably since Hannibal had marched across the Alps, had the world seen a collection of elephants to rival those put on display once a year in Mysore for the Hindu festival of the Dussehra. One thousand animals draped in elaborately woven blankets of flowers, their foreheads studded with jewels and gold, paraded through the streets of the city. To the strongest bull elephant went the honour of carrying the throne of the Maharaja, a pedestal of massive gold draped in gold-brocaded velvet and surmounted by an umbrella, the symbol of princely power. Behind that animal came two more decorated in comparable splendour and bearing empty howdahs. As they came into sight, a respectful silence settled upon the crowds along their path. These empty howdahs were supposed to contain the spirits of the Maharaja's forebears.

In Baroda, the princely *fêtes* were inevitably highlighted by elephant fights. Their combats were terrifying spectacles. Two enormous bull elephants driven mad with fury by lances thrust into their flanks like a picador's jab at a fighting bull were unleashed on each other. Shaking the ground with their enormous weight and the sky with their frightened trumpetings, they fought until one of them was killed.

The Raja of Dhenkanal, a state in eastern India, provided thousands of guests each year with an opportunity to witness an equally impressive but less bloody exhibition by his elephants, the public copulation of two of the most select denizens of his stables.

A Maharaja of Gwalior decided before the turn of the century to ornament his palace with a chandelier carefully calculated to surpass in dimension the largest chandelier in Buckingham Palace. Once he'd ordered it in Venice, however, someone pointed out to the Maharaja that the roof of his palace might not support its weight. He resolved the problem by having his heaviest pachyderm hoisted to the palace roof with a specially constructed crane. When the roof failed to collapse under the animal's weight, the Maharaja announced – correctly, it would turn out – that it would support his new chandelier.

The coming of the motor car inevitably confined the royal elephants to ceremonial, rather than functional tasks. The first automobile imported into India in 1892, a French-made De Dion Bouton, was destined for the garage of the Maharaja of Patiala. Its pride of place was recorded for posterity by the number on its licence plate – 'O'. The Nizam of Hyderabad acquired his automobiles with a technique worthy of his legendary reputation for economy. Whenever his royal eyes fell on an interesting car inside the walls of his capital, he sent word to its owner that His Exalted Highness would be pleased to receive it as a gift. By 1947, the Nizam's garage overflowed with hundreds of cars he never used.

Inevitably, the favoured automotive plaything of India's princes was the Rolls-Royce. They imported them in all forms and sizes, limousines, coupés, station wagons and even trucks. The Maharaja of Patiala's tiny Dion was eventually dwarfed in his garages by his mechanical elephants, twenty-seven enormous Rolls. The most exotic Rolls in India was a silver-plated convertible belonging to the Maharaja of Bharatpur. Rumour had it that mysterious, sexually stimulating waves emanated from its silver frame and the most gracious gesture the Maharaja could accomplish was to loan it to a princely colleague for his wedding. Bharatpur had also ordered a Rolls done up as a shooting brake for his hunts. One day in 1921, he took the Prince of Wales and his young ADC, Lord Louis Mountbatten, out in it after black buck. 'The car,' the future Viceroy of India noted in his diary that night, 'went over wild, open country, smashing through holes and over boulders, heaving and rocking like a boat at sea.'

The most extraordinary princely vehicle in India, however, was a Lancaster styled to the bizarre design of the Maharaja of Alwar. It was gold-plated inside and out. The chauffeur, manipulating a steering wheel in sculptured ivory, reposed on gold-brocaded cushion. Behind him, the body of the car was a perfectly reproduced replica of the coronation coach of the kings of England. By some mechanical miracle its engine was still able to hurl that weighty vehicle along the road at 70 mph.

With all the revenue, duties and taxes amassed in their states at their disposal, the princes of India were uniquely equipped to indulge their personal eccentricities.

The passion of the Maharaja of Gwalior, who ruled over one of the best run states in India, was electric trains. Even in his wildest pre-Christmas fantasies, a young boy could not conjure up an electric train set to rival the Maharaja's. It was laid out over 250 feet of solid silver rails set on a mammoth iron table at the centre of the palace banquet hall. Special tunnels cut in the palace walls prolonged the tracks into the royal kitchen. The Maharaja's guests were placed around the table and the ruler sat at its head, presiding over a mammoth control panel that bristled with levers, accelerators, switches and alarm signals. These controlled the trains that delivered dinner to the prince's guests. By manipulating his control panel, the prince could pass the vegetables, send the potatoes shuttling through the banquet hall, or order an express to the kitchens for a second helping for a hungry guest. He could also, with the flick of a switch, deprive a guest of his dessert by sending the dessert trains speeding past his waiting plate.

One evening, in the midst of a formal banquet in honour of the Viceroy, the prince's control panel short-circuited. While their Excellencies looked on aghast, his electric trains ran amok, racing from one end of the banquet hall to the other, indifferently sloshing gravy, roast beef and a *purée* of peas over the Maharaja's guests. It was a catastrophe without parallel in the annals of the railway.

Dogs were the peculiar passion of the Nawab of Junagadh, a principality north of Bombay. His favourite pets were assigned to apartments equipped with telephones, electricity and domestic servants, habitations of a style and comfort vastly superior to that of all but a tiny handful of his subjects. They were borne off to marble mausoleums in a canine graveyard to the strains of Chopin's funeral march.

He marked the 'wedding' of his favourite bitch Roshana to a Labrador named Bobby with a ceremony so grandiose that he invited every prince, celebrity and dignitary in India, including the Viceroy, to attend. To his chagrin, the Viceroy declined. Still, 150,000 people crowded the route of the nuptial cortege which was led by the prince's bodyguard and the royal elephants in full regalia. After the parade, the Nawab offered a lavish banquet in the canine couple's honour before they were led off to their beautifully appointed bridal suite. Those proceedings cost the Nawab £60,000, a sum which could have financed the basic human needs of 12,000 of his 620,000 impoverished subjects for an entire year.

The palaces of India's great maharajas were monuments which rivalled the Taj Mahal in size and opulence, although not necessarily taste. Mysore's 600-room palace surpassed the dimensions of Viceroy's House itself. Twenty of those rooms were devoted exclusively to housing the collection of tigers, panthers, elephants and bisons killed by three generations of princes in the jungles of the state. At night, with its roofs and windows outlined by thousands of light bulbs, it looked like some monstrous ocean liner decked out for a gala, landlocked by error in the middle of India. Nine hundred and fifty-three windows, each set in its hand-carved marble frame, covered one façade of Jaipur's marble Palaçe of the Wind. Udaipur's white marble palace rose ghost-like from the mists of a shimmering lake.

Having decided during a visit to the Palace of Versailles that he could be a reincarnation of the great Louis XIV, the very able Maharaja of Kapurthala determined to reproduce the glories of the Sun King in his tiny state. Importing a horde of French architects and decorators, he built himself a replica of Versailles at the foot of the Himalayas. He filled it with Sèvres vases, Gobelin tapestries, French antiques, proclaimed French the language of his court, and dolled up his turbaned Sikh retainers in the powdered wigs, silk waistcoats, knickers and silver-buckled slippers of the Sun King's courtiers.

The thrones in some of those palaces were the most elaborate and luxurious objects ever designed as receptacles for human posteriors.

Mysore's was made from a ton of solid gold, reached by nine steps equally in gold representing the nine steps of the God Vishnu in his ascent to truth. Orissa's throne was an enormous bed. He had bought it from an antique dealer in London and studded it with an appropriate number of jewels. Its particular charm stemmed from the fact it was an exact copy of Queen Victoria's wedding bed.

The throne of the Nawab of Rampur was placed in a hall the size of a cathedral. The columns which surrounded the podium on which it reposed were white marble representations of nude women. The originality of his throne owed its inspiration to another idea provided by the Sun King. Cut into the rich gold brocade of its cushion was a hole providing direct access to a chamber pot. With an appropriately princely rumble, the ruler was thus able to relieve his royal person without interrupting the flow of the affairs of state.

Time often hung heavy on the hands of the indolent gentlemen who inhabited those palaces. To fill it, they devoted themselves to two pastimes, sex and sport. Whether he was Hindu or Moslem, the harem was an integral part of a real ruler's palace, the prince's private preserve kept regularly stocked with dancing girls and concubines.

Usually, the jungles of his state were equally a ruler's private preserve; their fauna, and above all, their tigers, of which 20,000 still existed in India in 1947, the protected prey of his rifle. Bharatpur bagged his first tiger at eight. By the time he was 35, the skins of the tigers he'd killed, stitched together, provided the reception rooms of his palace with what amounted to wall to wall carpeting. His territory also witnessed what was surely a record duck slaughter, 4482 birds in three hours during a shoot in honour of a Viceroy, Lord Hardinge. The Maharaja of Gwalior killed over 1400 tigers in his lifetime and was the author of a work destined for a limited if select audience, *A Guide to Tiger Shooting*.

The acknowledged master of his generation in both fields was the Sikh Sir Bhupinder Singh, the Magnificent, the seventh Maharaja of Patiala and father of the Chancellor of the Chamber of Princes. Indeed, for the world between two wars, Sir Bhupinder incarnated the Maharajas of India. With his six-foot-four-inch frame, his 300 pounds, his sensual lips and arrogant eyes, his black moustache swept up into perfectly waxed needle points, his carefully rolled black beard, he seemed to have stepped into the twentieth century off the ivory of some Moghul miniature.

His appetite was such that he could consume twenty pounds of food in the course of a strenuous day or a couple of chickens as a tea-time snack. He adored polo and galloping across the polo fields of the world at the head of his Tigers of Patiala, he accumulated a roomful of silver trophies. To sustain those efforts, his stables harboured 500 of the world's finest polo ponies.

From his earliest adolescence, Bhupinder Singh demonstrated a remarkably refined aptitude for an equally worthy princely pastime, sex. As he came to maturity his devotion to his harem eventually surpassed even his passions for polo and hunting. He personally supervised the steady accumulation of its inmates, selecting new recruits with a connoisseur's appreciation of variety in appearance and accomplishment in action. By the time the institution reached its fullest fruition, it contained 350 ladies.

During the torrid Punjab summers, the harem moved out of doors in the evening to Bhupinder's pool. The prince stationed a score of bare-breasted girls like nymphs at intervals around its rim. Chunks of ice bobbing in the pool's water gave the hot air a delicious chill while the Maharaja floated idly about, coming to port from time to time to caress a breast or sip a whisky. The walls and ceilings of Bhupinder's private quarters were covered with representations of the erotic temple sculptures for which India is justly famous, a catalogue of copulative possibilities to exhaust the most inventive mind and athletic body. A wide silk hammock slung in one corner of the room allowed Bhupinder Singh, in a sense, to suspend the laws of gravity while attempting to perform in that state some of the more complex manœuvres suggested by his ceiling.

To satisfy his insatiable habits, the imaginative Maharaja embarked on a programme which would allow him to remodel the charms of his concubines as his own taste changed. Sir Bhupinder opened his harem doors to a parade of perfumers, jewellers, hairdressers, beauticians and dressmakers. He even kept a team of French, British and Indian plastic surgeons on standby to alter the physiognomies of his favourites according to his fluctuating tastes or the dictates of the London fashion magazines. Further to stimulate his princely ardours, he converted one wing of the harem into a laboratory whose test tubes and vials produced an exotic blend of scents, cosmetics, lotions and philtres.

All those piquant refinements ultimately only served to screen the fatal weakness in the Maharaja's oriental pleasure dome. What man, even a Sikh as handsomely endowed by nature as Sir Bhupinder was, could satisfy the 350 highly trained and motivated ladies lurking behind the harem's grilles? Recourse to aphrodisiacs was inevitable. His Indian doctors worked up a number of savoury concoctions based on gold, pearls, spices, silver, herbs and iron. For a while, their most efficacious potion was based on a mixture of shredded carrots and the crushed brains of a sparrow.

When its benefits began to wane, Sir Bhupinder called in a group of French technicians whom he naturally assumed would enjoy special expertise in the matter. Alas, even the effects of their treatment based on radium proved ephemeral because they, like their predecessors, had no cure for the real illness from which the Maharaja suffered. It was not lack of virility that afflicted the jaded and sated prince. His was a malady that plagued not a few of his surfeited fellow rulers. It was boredom. He died of it.

Inevitably, in God-obsessed India, legend and folklore ascribed divine descent to some princes. The Maharajas of Mysore traced their ancestry to the moon. Once a year, at the autumnal equinox, the Maharaja became in the eyes of his people a living God. For nine days like a sadhu in a Himalayan cave, he secluded himself in a darkened room of his palace. He didn't shave or wash. No human hand was allowed to touch him, no eye to glimpse him during those days when his body was supposedly inhabited by a God. The ninth day he emerged. An elephant draped in gold tapestries, its forehead covered with an emerald-studded shield, waited at the palace gate to bear him amidst an escort of lancers on camel and horseback to an un-God-like destination, the Mysore race track. There, before the multitudes of his subjects jammed into the stands, Brahmin priests chanting *mantras* bathed, shaved and fed him. As the sunset and darkness shrouded the track, a jet black horse was brought to the prince. At the instant he mounted it, thousands of torches around the perimeter of the track were lit. In their flickering roseate glare, the prince galloped around the track on his black horse to the applause of his subjects, most of them grateful because the Son of the Moon was back amongst his people, some more mundanely thankful for the picturesque pageant their ruler had offered them.

The Maharajas of Udaipur traced their descent from an even more impressive celestial body, the sun. Theirs was the most ancient throne in India, a rule that had run uninterrupted for at least 2000 years. Once a year Udaipur, too, became a kind of living God. Erect in the prow of a galley resembling Cleopatra's barge, he was borne back across the crocodile-infested waters of the lake surrounding his palace for a symbolic re-installation in its premises. On the deck behind him the nobles of his court in long white muslin robes stood ranged in grateful veneration.

Less grandiose in their pretentions, but no less pious were the rulers of Benares, the sacred city on the banks of the Ganges. By tradition the eyes of the Maharaja of those blessed precincts had to open each day on a sole and unique vision, the Hindu symbol of cosmic eternity, a Sacred Cow. Each dawn a cow was led to the window of the princely bedchamber and jabbed in the ribs so that her mooing would stir the pious Maharaja from his slumber. Once, during a visit to his colleague the Nawab of Rampur, fulfilling that morning ritual posed a grave problem because the Maharaja's quarters were located on the second floor of his host's palace. The Nawab finally resorted to an ingenious tactic to maintain the integrity of his guest's dawns. He bought a crane which each morning hoisted a cow in a sling up to the Maharaja's bedroom window. Terrified by her unnatural voyage, the poor animal emitted a series of moos so piercing that they not only woke up the pious Maharaja, but most of the rest of the palace as well.

Pious or atheist, Hindu or Moslem, rich or poor, decadent or saintly, the maharajas had been for almost two centuries the surest pillars of British rule in India. It was in their relations with the states that the British had applied to greatest effect the 'Divide and Rule' doctrine with which they were accused of governing India. In theory, the British could remove a ruler from his throne for misrule. In fact, a ruler could get away with almost any kind of outrageous behaviour down to and including a few discreet murders without the British disturbing him – provided his loyalty had remained intact. The inevitable result was a series of grateful and generally reactionary princely enclaves studded like anchors against a revolutionary wind throughout those parts of India ruled directly by the British.

The princes' loyalty took more tangible forms as well. The Maharaja of Jodhpur's Lancers led the charge that took Haifa from the Turks in Allenby's Palestine campaign on 23 September 1917.* Bikaner's Camel Corps fought at Britain's side in two wars in China, Palestine, Egypt, France and under Louis Mountbatten's orders in Burma. Gwalior sent the beleaguered British three battalions of infantry and a hospital ship in 1917. All those forces were raised, equipped, paid for and maintained by the rulers themselves, not the government of India. The Maharaja of Jaipur, a major in the Lifeguards, led his First Jaipur Infantry up the slopes of Italy's

* In a more peaceful sphere, the same Maharaja had introduced Western society to the tapered riding breeches 'jodhpurs' favoured in his state during Queen Victoria's Diamond Jubilee celebrations in London. On arriving for the festivities, the unfortunate prince discovered that the ship carrying his luggage had gone down at sea. To save the situation he was forced to divulge to a London tailor the secret of how his favourite trousers were made.

Monte Cassino in 1943. The Maharaja of Bundi won the Military Cross in action with his battalion in Burma.

The grateful British acknowledged their debt to their faithful and generous vassals by showering them with honours and the baubles they loved best of all, jewel-studded decorations. Gwalior, Cooch Bihar and Patiala were accorded the honour of riding as honorary ADCs beside the royal carriage of Edward VII at his coronation. Oxford and Cambridge conferred their degrees, honorary and earned, on the rulers and their progeny. The bejewelled chests of the crown's most loyal princes were embellished by the glittering stars of the Order of the Star of India or the Order of the Indian Empire.

It was above all by the subtle gradations of a particularly ingenious form of award that the esteem of the paramount power for its vassals was to be measured. The number of guns in the salute accorded a ruler provided the final and definitive proof of his place in the princely hierarchy. It was within the Viceroy's power to increase the number of guns in a salute so as to reward a ruler for exceptional services, or to reduce the salute as a punishment. Size and population were not the sole factors determining a man's salute. Fidelity to the paramount power and the blood and treasure expended in its defence were equally important. Five rulers – Hyderabad, Gwalior, Kashmir, Mysore and Baroda – were entitled to the supreme accolade, 21 guns. Nineteen, seventeen, fifteen, thirteen eleven and nine gun states were ranged behind them. For 425 unfortunate rajas and nawabs, rulers of insignificant little principalities, there was no salute at all. They were India's forgotten rulers, the men for whom the guns never tolled.

The India of the maharajas was often noted for substantial achievements as well. Where the rulers were enlightened men, often Western-educated, the state's subjects enjoyed benefits and privileges unknown in those areas administered directly by the British. Baroda had banned polygamy and made education free and universal before the turn of the century. He had campaigned for the Untouchables with a zeal less well known, but no less sincere than Gandhi's. He created institutions to house and educate them and personally financed the education of the man who became their leader, Dr Bhimrao Ambedkar, at Columbia University in New York. Bikaner had turned parts of his Rajasthan desert kingdom into a paradise of artificial lakes and gardens for his subjects' use. Bhopal offered women an equality of status and position unequalled in India. Mysore harboured Asia's best science faculty and a chain of hydroelectric dams and industries. The descendant of one of history's greatest astronomers, a man who had translated Euclid's *Principles of Geometry* into Sanskrit, the Maharaja of Jaipur, maintained in his capital one of the world's outstanding observatories. With the Second World War, a new generation of rulers had begun to ascend the thrones, men usually less flamboyant, less self-indulgent than their fathers, more conscious of the need for change and the reformation of their states. One of the first acts of the eighth Maharaja of Patiala was to close the harem of his father Sir Bhupinder Singh the Magnificent. The Maharaja of Gwalior married a commoner, the brilliant daughter of a civil servant, and moved out of his father's vast palace. Unhappily for those men and many others like them who ruled their states responsibly and ably, the public would always associate the maharajas of India with the excess and extravagances of a handful among them.

For two of India's states, for two princes enjoying the supreme honour of 21 guns, the initiative undertaken in London by Sir Conrad Corfield had profound significance. Both states were enormous. Both were landlocked. Both had rulers whose religion differed from that of the vast majority of their subjects. Both rulers caressed the same dream: to convert their states into wholly independent, sovereign nations.

Of all the bizarre and exotic rulers in India, Rustum-i-Dauran, Arastu-e-Zaman, Wal Mamalik, Asif Jah, Nawab Mir Osman, Alikhan Bahadur, Muzaffar-ul-Mulk Nizam-al-Mud, Sipah Salaar, Fateh Jang, His Exalted Highness, Most Faithful Ally of the British Crown, the seventh Nizam of Hyderabad was surely the most bizarre. A devout and learned Moslem, he and an Islamic ruling caste presided over the largest and most populous state in India, an entity of 20 million Hindus and only 3 million Moslems set in the heart of the sub-continent. He was a frail, little, old man of five foot three weighing barely 90 pounds. Years of devoted chewing of betel nut had reduced his teeth to a line of rotting reddish-brown fangs. He lived in constant dread of being poisoned by some jealous courtier and was followed everywhere by a food taster whom he obliged to share his unvarying diet of cream, sweets, fruits, betel nuts and a nightly bowl of opium. The Nizam was the only ruler in India entitled to the appellation 'Exalted Highness', a distinction conferred on him by a grateful Britain in recognition of his £25 m. contribution to their war-chest in World War I.

In 1947, the Nizam was reputed to be the richest man in the world and the legends of his wealth were surpassed only by the legends of the avarice with which he sought to hold it intact. He dressed in rumpled cotton pyjamas and ill-formed grey slippers bought in the local market place for a few rupees. For 35 years he'd worn the same soiled, dandruff-encrusted fez. Although he owned a gold service for 100 places, he ate off a tin plate, squatting on a mat in his bedroom. So stingy was he, he smoked the cigarette stubs left behind by his guests. When a state occasion forced him to put champagne on the princely table, he saw to it the single bottle he reluctantly set out never got more than three or four places from him. In 1944 when Wavell was arriving for a viceregal visit, the Nizam cabled Delhi enquiring whether, in view of its high wartime cost, the Viceroy really insisted on being served champagne. Once a week, after Sunday service, the English Resident came to call. Faithfully a retainer appeared with a tray containing a cup of tea, a biscuit and a cigarette for the Nizam and his guest. One Sunday, the Resident arrived unannounced with a particularly distinguished visitor. The Nizam whispered to his servant who returned to offer the visitor a second tray on which had been set one cup of tea, one biscuit and one cigarette.

In most states, it was the custom once a year for the nobles to make their prince a symbolic offering of a gold piece which the ruler touched, then returned to its owner. In Hyderabad, there was nothing symbolic about the offering. The Nizam grabbed each gold piece and dropped it into a paper bag beside his throne. On one occasion when one fell, he was on his hands and knees like a shot, racing its owner along the floor to the rolling coin.

Indeed, so miserly was the Nizam that when his doctor arrived from Bombay to give him an electro-cardiogram, he couldn't make his machine work. The doctor finally discovered why. In order to save on his electricity bill, the Nizam had cut back the palace's current: no machine could function properly on it.

The Nizam's bedroom looked like a slum hut, its furnishings consisting of a battered bed and table, three kitchen chairs, overflowing ashtrays and waste-paper baskets emptied once a year on the Nizam's birthday. His office was littered with stacks of dusty state archives, its ceiling a forest of cobwebs.

Yet, tucked into the corners of that palace was a fortune beyond counting. In one drawer of the Nizam's desk, wrapped in an old newspaper, was the Jacob diamond, a bauble the size of a lime: 280 sparkling, precious carats. The Nizam used it as a paper-weight. In the overgrown garden was a convoy of dozens of trucks mired in mud up to their axles from the weight of their loads, solid gold ingots. The Nizam's jewels, a collection so enormous it was said the pearls alone would cover all the pavements of Piccadilly Circus, were spilled like coals in a scuttle on the floors of his cellars; sapphires, emeralds, rubies, diamonds mingled in indiscriminate heaps. He had well over two million pounds in cash – sterling, rupees – wrapped in old newspapers, stuck in dusty corners of the palace's basement and attic. There they earned a kind of negative interest from the jaws of the rats who annually gnawed their way through thousands of pounds of the Nizam's fortune.

The Nizam had a sizeable army equipped with heavy artillery and aircraft. Indeed, he had every possible requirement for independence except two – a seaport and the support of his people.

His overwhelmingly Hindu population detested the Moslem minority which ruled them. Nonetheless, there was no question about the future that the miserly, slightly demented ruler of a state half the size of France foresaw for himself.

'At last,' he shouted, leaping from his chair when Sir Conrad Corfield had informed him of Britain's decision to leave India by June 1948, 'I shall be free.'

A similar ambition burned in the breast of another powerful prince at the other end of India. Reigning over the enchanted valley that cradled one of the world's most beautiful sites, the Vale of Kashmir, Hari Singh, Maharaja of Kashmir was a Hindu of a high Brahmin sub-caste whose 4 million subjects were overwhelmingly Moslem. His state, set against the awesome crests of the Himalayas, was the attic to the Roof of the World, the remote, wind-swept spaces of Ladakh, Tibet and Sinkiang, a vital crossroads where India, a future Pakistan, China and Afghanistan were certain to meet.

Hari Singh was a weak, vacillating, indecisive man who divided his time between opulent feasts in his winter capital in Jammu and the beautiful, flower-choked lagoons of his summer capital, Srinagar, the Venice of the Orient. He had begun his reign with a few timid aims at reform, quickly abandoned for an authoritarian rule which kept his jails filled with political foes. Their most recent occupant had been none other than Jawaharlal Nehru. The prince had ordered Nehru arrested when he'd tried to visit the state of his ancestors. Hari Singh too, had an army to defend the frontiers of his state and give his claims to independence a menacing emphasis.

8

A Day Cursed by the Stars

London, May 1947

The man riding up to 10 Downing Street should have been contrite or, at the least, apprehensive. Louis Mountbatten was neither. He had flown to London in response to a request from Attlee for a personal explanation of what had gone wrong in Simla. Lord Ismay, his Chief of Staff, had warned him at the airport that the government was, 'hopping mad. They don't know what you're doing and they're not sure you do, either'.

Mountbatten, however, had in his briefcase the new draft of his plan prepared by V. P. Menon after Nehru had vigorously rejected his earlier text. He was confident it held the key to the Indian dilemma. Before leaving Simla he'd received Nehru's assurance that Congress would accept it. Mountbatten did not propose 'to do any explaining away'. He intended, instead, to substitute this plan for the old one and tell Attlee and his Cabinet 'how lucky they were I'd had my hunch'.

Poised and smiling, Mountbatten got out of his car and walked past the popping flash-bulbs into the building in which, just six months earlier, he'd been given his terrible charge.

Waiting for him were Attlee, Sir Stafford Cripps, and the other key members of the Labour government involved with India. Their greetings were cordial but restrained. Undaunted, Mountbatten sat down and set to work. 'I gave them no apology,' he later recalled, 'nor any explanations. I had the most frightful, not quite conceit, but complete and absolute belief that it all depended on me and they really had to do what I said.'

As a result of the changes in his original draft cabled to Delhi he had, he said, played a hunch and shown it to Nehru. That had revealed certain fundamental Congress objections which would have produced a disaster had the plan been formally submitted to Congress. They had been met in his new draft and he was confident he had now placed before them a plan all concerned would accept. Beyond that, he told Attlee, he could now reveal a remarkable piece of news.

He had been able to honour the pledge he'd made the King before leaving London. He could now assure the Attlee government that an independent India and Pakistan would remain linked to Britain in the British Commonwealth. Jinnah had always wanted to keep an independent Pakistan in the Commonwealth, but to Congress maintaining a tie to the Crown, the symbolic link binding the Commonwealth's members, had been a difficult concept to accept. The British Crown had been, after all, the symbol against which their struggle had been directed.

Patiently, persistently, almost secretively, Mountbatten had stressed the advantages of a Commonwealth tie, pointing out that it was the only way India could secure the loan of the officers she would need to complete the development of her armed forces. While he was in Simla, he'd received a message from Vallabhbhai Patel. The shrewd Congress leader knew Mountbatten was in a hurry to see power transferred to Indian hands. So was he. Patel suggested Mountbatten employ a time-saving device for the actual transfer of power; simply to proclaim India and Pakistan independent dominions like Canada inside the British Commonwealth. That way all concerned, Patel pointed out, could avoid the lengthy process of drawing up constitutions and electing bodies to which Britain would formally hand over. If Mountbatten acted quickly, long before the old deadline of 30 June 1948, then a grateful Congress would not sever the Commonwealth ties that automatically went with dominion status.

Mountbatten was delighted. Patel's proposal was in fact what he'd been secretly lobbying for weeks. He had eagerly ordered V. P. Menon to incorporate the idea into the redrafted plan he was submitting to Attlee.

The key to the situation now, he said, was speed. He had put before them a plan for the Transfer of Power which he could assure them was acceptable to the Indians. It would keep both nations in the British Commonwealth. Delay now would risk immersing Britain in the situation against which he'd been warning them since his arrival in India, a sub-continent sinking into civil war. The burden was on them. How quickly could they drive through Parliament the legislation necessary to realize his plan?

It was an awesome demonstration of Mountbatten at his dynamic, persuasive best. By the time he'd finished the 'hopping mad' Attlee government was eating out of his hand. They accepted his new draft plan without the alteration of so much as a comma.

'My God,' exclaimed Ismay, the veteran of so many stormy scenes in Downing Street, as they left the meeting, 'I've seen some performances in my lifetime, but what you just did to the people in there beats them all!'

The familiar figure in the bed, a quilted dressing-gown falling from his shoulders, half-rim spectacles poised on the bridge of his nose, his constant trade mark, a cigar, clamped in his mouth, had been one of the fixtures on the horizon of Louis Mountbatten's life.

Among Mountbatten's early memories was the image of Churchill, the young, flamboyant First Lord of the Admiralty, chatting with his father, then First Sea Lord. Mountbatten's mother had once warned him light-heartedly that the man who would one day be the symbol of European resistance to Hitler, was 'unreliable'. He had committed what was, in her eyes, an unpardonable sin. He had failed to return a book he'd borrowed.

The young naval officer and the unheeded politician calling for Britain's rearmament had become friendly in the months after Munich. Later, after Churchill had given him his first major wartime command at Combined Operations, a close relationship had grown up between the two men. Mountbatten had been a frequent visitor to Churchill's wartime command post at 10 Downing Street.*

Churchill, Mountbatten knew, was very fond of him, but, he thought, 'for all the wrong reasons. He thought I was a swashbuckler, a warrior. He had no idea what my political outlook was.'

* Mountbatten had, in fact, been Churchill's luncheon guest along with Max Beaverbrook, the newspaper publisher, on Saturday, June 21, 1941. The Prime Minister announced when he joined his guests, 'I've got some very exciting news. Hitler is going to attack Russia tomorrow. We've spent all morning trying to evaluate what it means.'

'I'll tell you what'll happen,' Beaverbrook said. 'They'll go through the Russians like a dose of salts. God, they'll wipe them up! They'll be through in a month or six weeks.' 'Well,' said Churchill, 'the Americans think it will take more like two months and our own chiefs think at least that. I myself think they may last as long as three months, but then they'll fold up and we'll be back where we started with our backs to the wall.'

Mountbatten was forgotten for some time until Churchill turned to him and said, almost apologetically, 'Ah, Dickie, do tell us about your battle in Crete.'

'It's past history,' Mountbatten replied, 'but may I be allowed to give an opinion about what's going to happen in Russia?'

Somewhat reluctantly Churchill agreed.

'I disagree with Max,' said Mountbatten, 'I disagree with the Americans, our chiefs and, quite honestly, I disagree with you, Prime Minister. I don't think the Russians are going to fold up. I don't think they're going to be defeated. This is the end of Hitler. It's the turning point of the war.'

'Well, now Dickie,' said Churchill, 'why should your views be so different?'

'First,' answered Mountbatten, 'because Stalin's purge trials have eliminated much potential internal opposition to which the Nazis might have appealed. Second, and it's painful for me to say this because my family ruled there for so long, but the people now feel they have a stake in the country. This time they'll fight. They feel they have something to lose.'

Churchill was not impressed. 'Well, Dickie,' he said, 'it's very nice to hear a young, enthusiastic voice like yours. But we'll see.'

The young admiral was certain he would 'have been dropped like a shot' for his views on South-East Asia's future had Churchill been re-elected in 1945.

Now he had come at Attlee's request, to get Churchill to perform what would be one of the most painful acts of the old Tory's political career. He wanted his personal blessing on the plan which would begin the dismemberment of Churchill's beloved empire.

'Winston,' Attlee had told Mountbatten when asking him to see Churchill, 'holds the key in England. Neither I nor any of my government could possibly persuade him, but he's fond of you. He trusts you. You have a chance.'

Their meeting began on a difficult note. Churchill, Mountbatten knew, thought the very idea the Indians should ever be allowed to try to run themselves was madness. 'He was absolutely sincere,' Mountbatten remembered, 'in his belief that the worst thing which could happen to India would be to have its efficient British administration of proven integrity removed and replaced by a whole lot of 'inexperienced, theoretical and probably corrupt Indians'.

As he reviewed his efforts in India, Mountbatten kept his eyes on the great bald head glaring at him from the bed. For half a century, Churchill had said 'no' to every move to bring India along the road to independence. One last Churchillian 'no' now would be a devastating blow to all Mountbatten's hopes. With the Tory majority in the House of Lords, Churchill had the power to delay passage of India's independence bill for two full years.

That, the ambitious young Viceroy knew, 'would be absolutely fatal.' Congress's agreement to his plan was conditional on dominion status being offered immediately. His government, his administration, a sub-continent seething with communal passions, could not survive two years' delay.

Eyes half-closed, Churchill listened to Mountbatten's arguments with the inscrutable air of a Buddha lost in transcendental meditation. Nothing, the perspective of India's collapse, chaos, civil disorder, awakened his impassive features.

Mountbatten had, however, brought back from Simla one argument that could arouse the old leader's emotions. It was Congress's promise to accept dominion status if it was offered immediately. As he skilfully opened the vista of the Raj's most implacable foes agreeing to remain within the ranks of the British Commonwealth, Churchill's attitude altered perceptibly: his beloved empire might be dying, but here, at least, was the hope something of it would remain. There would be something left of that old India where he'd burned out his romantic youth. Much more important, some of those

British links Churchill sincerely believed indispensable to India's future well-being could now be maintained.

Suspiciously, he eyed Mountbatten. Did he have anything in writing? he asked. Mountbatten said he had a letter from Nehru, now with Attlee, indicating Congress would accept, providing dominion status was conferred without delay.

And what about his old foe, Gandhi?

Gandhi, Mountbatten admitted, was unpredictable. He was the one potentially grave danger. But with the help of Nehru and Patel, he hoped he could contain him in a crisis.

Churchill glowered on his bed, thinking, his cigar clutched between his teeth.

Finally, he declared that, if Mountbatten really could deliver the formal, public acceptance of all the Indian parties to his plan, then, 'the whole country' would be behind him. He and his Conservative Party would join Labour in cramming through Parliament the historic legislation Mountbatten needed before its summer recess. India could become independent not in years or months, but in weeks, even days.

New Delhi, May–June 1947

Dark, velvet pillars, the smoke of a series of funeral pyres crept into the Indian skies at points scattered across the sub-continent. No *ghee* or sandalwood stoked those hastily assembled bonfires. Their crackling flames were watched over, not by *mantra*-chanting mourners, but by impassive circles of British bureaucrats. It was paper those flames were devouring, four tons of documents, reports and files. Lit on the orders of Sir Conrad Corfield, that series of bonfires was converting into ashes the lurid details of some of the most tumultuous and picturesque episodes in Indian history, the chronicles of the vices and scandals of five generations of maharajas. Recorded and catalogued with meticulous care by successive representatives of the Raj, those files could have become sources of blackmail in the hands of independent Indian and Pakistan administrations, a purpose not altogether unforeseen by the British themselves when the decision was made to accumulate them.

No longer able to guarantee the future of his maharajas, Corfield had been determined to protect, at least, their past. He had secured the Attlee government's agreement to the destruction of these archives. As soon as he had returned to Delhi he ordered his Residents and political agents to begin the burning of any files in their possession dealing with the private lives of their charges.

Sir Conrad lit the first fire himself under the windows of his office, nourishing it with the documents concealed in a two-foot-high safe to which only he and one other man had the key. A hundred and fifty years of reading, a select distillation of the most juicy of princely scandals, went up in smoke in Sir Conrad's little bonfire, drifting off in ashes over the roofs and streets of Delhi. Alerted to what was happening, Nehru immediately protested at the destruction of material which was in his eyes a precious part of India's patrimony.

It was too late. In Patiala, Hyderabad, Indore, Mysore, Baroda, at Porbandar, Gandhi's home on the shores of the Gulf of Arabia, at Chitral in the Himalayas and in the sweltering rain forests of Cochin, British officials were already feeding the gossip of an era to the flames.

The accounts of the sexual eccentricities of some of India's princes were in themselves lengthy enough to keep a good fire burning for hours. An early Nawab of Rampur had made a bet with a number of neighbouring princes as to which ruler would be able to deflower the most virgins in a year. The proof of each conquest would be the thin gold ring traditionally worn by an unbedded girl in her nose. Sending out his courtiers to comb the villages of his state like beaters scaring up pheasants, the Nawab won the bet handily. By the end of the year, his collection of rings, melted down, represented several pounds of pure gold.

The bonfire consuming the archives dealing with the Maharaja of Kashmir destroyed the traces of one of the more unsavoury scandals of the world between the wars. The impetuous prince was trapped *in flagrante delicto* in London's Savoy Hotel by a man he assumed to be the husband of his ravishing bed companion. In fact, the prince had fallen into the net of a gang of blackmailers who proceeded to drain the state of Kashmir via the prince's personal bank account, of a very considerable part of its revenues. The case finally broke when the young lady's real husband, persuaded he had not been properly remunerated for the loan of his wife, went to the police. In the case which followed, the unfortunate Maharaja's identity was concealed under the pseudonym of Mr 'A'. Disillusioned for good with women as a result of his tribulations, Hari Singh returned to Kashmir where he discovered new sexual horizons in the company of the young men of his state. The accounts of his activities, had been faithfully reported to the representatives of the Crown. Now, whipped by the fresh mountain breeze of Srinagar, they disappeared into the Himalayan sky.

The Nizam of Hyderabad combined his passions for photography and pornography to amass what was believed to be the most extensive collection of pornographic photographs in India. To assemble it, the ageing Nizam had dissimulated in the walls and ceilings of his guests' quarters automatic cameras that faithfully recorded all that went on in them. He had even installed a camera behind the mirror in his palace's guest bathroom. The camera's harvest, a portrait gallery of the great and near-great of India relieving themselves on the Nizam's toilet, had pride of place in his collection.

The most recent report in the Nizam's file dealt with the British Resident's efforts to make certain that the sexual proclivities of his son and heir were those befitting a future Nizam. As tactfully as he could, the worthy gentleman alluded to certain reports reaching his ears which indicated the young prince's tastes did not encompass princesses. The Nizam summoned his son. Then he ordered into their presence a particularly attractive inmate of his harem. Over the embarrassed protest of the Resident, he instructed his son to give an immediate and public refutation of the dastardly insinuation that he might not be inclined to continue the family line.

Of all the scandals disappearing in the flames of Conrad Corfield's bonfires, none had left a trace quite as distasteful as that of the 40-year reign of the prince of a small state of 800,000 people on the edges of the Rajasthan. The Maharaja of Alwar was a man of such charm and culture that he had been able to seduce a succession of Viceroys into tolerating his activities. He happened to believe he was a reincarnation of the God Rama. As a result he constantly wore black silk gloves to protect his divine fingers from the contaminating touch of mortal flesh, even refusing to remove them to shake the hand of the King of England. He engaged a number of Hindu theologians to calculate the exact size of the turban of Rama so that he could make a copy for himself.

What with his temporal role as a prince and his conviction of his divine status, Alwar was not a man to restrain himself in the exercise of his power. One of the best shots in India, he delighted in using children as tiger bait in his hunts. Plucking them from any hut in his state, he assured their horrified parents he was certain to get a shot into the beast before it could maul their offspring. A homosexual of particularly perverse taste, he made the royal bed the military academy, qualifying young men for entry into the officer class of his army. Once there, they were expected to participate in his orgies, a number of which culminated in sadistic murders.

His abuses of authority were finally brought to a head by two incidents during the Viceroyalty of Lord Willingdon. Invited to lunch at Viceroy's House, Alwar was seated next to Lady Willingdon who admired effusively a large diamond ring on his finger. Slipping it off his hand, Alwar passed it to the Vicereine for her private contemplation.

Lady Willingdon's admiration had not been entirely disinterested. Tradition had it that a prince would offer a Viceroy or Vicereine any object he or she had admired with particular interest. Lady Willingdon, who had notably admiring eyes when it came to precious stones, had thus amassed during her stay in India a considerable collection of jewellery. She slipped Alwar's ring on to her finger, regarded it with pleasure, then passed it back to its owner.

Alwar discreetly asked a waiter to bring him a finger bowl. When it arrived, the reincarnation of Rama proceeded, before the widening eyes of his fellow guests, meticulously to wash from his ring whatever traces the Vicereine's finger might have left upon it before slipping it back on to his own hand.

The final, unpardonable crime of the depraved prince in the eyes of his British benefactors took place on a polo field. Furious at the disobedience of one of his ponies during a match, the prince had the poor beast drenched with kerosene between chukkers, then personally set a match to it. That flagrant public display of cruelty to animals weighed more heavily in the scales of justice than his more private, but equally terminal cruelty to a number of his sexual partners. Alwar was deposed and packed off into exile.

While Alwar's case was exceptional, it was not the only incident to have troubled relations between India's puritanical British rulers and their extravagant vassals. The gravest of those crises had been occasioned by a Maharaja of Baroda. Displeased that the British should have accorded their Resident in his state, an obscure, and in the Maharaja's eyes rather common, colonel, a gun salute similar to his own, the prince ordered a pair of cannon in solid gold to give his salute a resonance more regal than the colonel's. The Resident, angered by the prince's gesture, forwarded to London a distinctly unfavourable report on Baroda's morals, accusing him of enslaving the women in his harem.

Advised of what was going on, Baroda summoned his best astrologers and holy men to propose a suitable means of getting rid of the unwanted colonel and a proper conjuncture of the stars under which to do it. Their recommendation was poison by diamond dust. The prince selected one the size of an acorn, a dimension held to be suitable for a man of the colonel's rank, and his astrologers ground it into powder.

The highly indigestible result was slipped into the colonel's dinner one night, but before it could have the desired effect, the pain it produced landed the colonel in a hospital where his stomach was pumped out.

The attempted murder of a representative of the Crown became an affair of state. The Maharaja's judges were not impressed by the assurances of his Brahmin priests that they had duly performed all the rites necessary to assure the reincarnation of the colonel's soul, nor those of his jeweller who declared the value of the diamond unwillingly consumed by the Resident 'corresponded exactly to that of an English colonel'. The Maharaja was deposed and sent into exile for his failure properly to administer a state dependent upon the British Crown.

His exile was avenged by his friend and fellow ruler, the Maharaja of Patiala. When the Viceroy who'd signed the decree of exile visited his state, Patiala ordered the gunners who would fire the 31-gun salute due the representative of the King Emperor to stuff their cannon with a powder ration so small that the envoy of Imperial England would be honoured by an explosion 'not louder than a child's fire cracker'.

The destruction of those records was not the only action that followed Corfield's visit to London. From all over India, letters began to flow into New Delhi from various princes informing the central administration of their intention to cancel the agreements which allowed Indian railways, posts, telegraph and other facilities to function in their territories. It was a tactical gesture meant to underline the princes' bargaining power in the coming showdown, but the vista they opened was appalling: an India in which trains couldn't run, mail get delivered or telecommunications function properly.

The lustreless eyes of Robert Clive gazed down from the great oil painting at the seven Indian leaders filing into the Viceroy's study. Representatives of India's 400 million human beings, those millions Gandhi called 'miserable specimens of humanity with lustreless eyes', they entered Mountbatten's study on this morning of 2 June 1947, to inspect the deeds which would return to them their continent. The Viceroy himself had brought them back from London, formally approved by the British Cabinet, just 48 hours before.

One by one, they took their places at the circular table in the centre of the room: Congress, represented by Nehru, Patel and its president Acharya Kripalani; the Moslem League, by Jinnah, Liaqat Ali Khan and Rab Nishtar. Baldev Singh was present as spokesman for the 6 million people who would be more dramatically affected by the words about to be spoken than any others in India, the Sikhs.

Against the wall sat Mountbatten's two key advisers, Lord Ismay and Sir Eric Miéville. At the centre of the table, was the Viceroy. An official photographer hastily recorded the gathering for history. Then, in a silence interrupted only by the rasp of nervous throats being cleared, a secretary set before each man a manilla folder containing a copy of the plan.

For the first time since he had arrived in Delhi, Mountbatten was now being forced to abandon his tête-à-tête diplomacy for a round table conference. He had decided however, that he would do the talking. He was not going to run the risk of throwing the meeting open to a general discussion which might degenerate into an acrimonious shouting match.

He began by noting that, during the past five years he had taken part in a number of momentous meetings at which the decisions that had determined the fate of the war had been taken. He could remember no meeting, however, at which decisions had been taken whose impact upon history had been as profound as would be the impact of the decision before them.

Briefly, Mountbatten reviewed his conversations since arriving in Delhi, stressing the terrible sense of urgency they had impressed on him.

Then, for the record and for history, he formally asked Jinnah one last time if he was prepared to accept Indian unity as envisaged by the Cabinet Mission Plan. With equal formality, Jinnah replied he was not. Mountbatten moved on to the matter at hand. Briefly, he reviewed the details of his plan. The clause on dominion status which had won Winston Churchill's support was not, he stressed, a reflection of a British desire to keep a foot in the door, but was to ensure that British assistance would not be summarily withdrawn if it was still needed. He dwelt on Calcutta, on the coming agony of the Sikhs.

He would not, he said, ask them to go against their consciences and give their full approval to a plan, parts of which went against their principles. He asked only that they accept it in a peaceful spirit and vow to make it work without bloodshed.

His intention, he said, was to meet with them again the following morning. He hoped that before that, before midnight, all three parties, the Moslem League, Congress and the Sikhs, would have indicated their willingness to accept the plan as a basis for a final Indian settlement. If this was the case, then he proposed that he, Nehru, Jinnah and Baldev Singh announce their agreement jointly to the world the following evening on All India Radio. Clement Attlee would make a confirmatory announcement from London.

'Gentlemen,' he concluded, 'I should like your reaction to the plan by midnight.'

One unspoken fear had flown back to Delhi with Louis Mountbatten, marring his satisfaction with his achievements in London and his 'enormous optimism' for the future. It was that 'that unpredictable little Mahatma Gandhi' was going to go against him.

It was a prospect the Viceroy dreaded. He had already developed a genuine affection for his 'dejected little sparrow'. The idea that he, the professional warrior, the Viceroy, should have to face the apostle of non-violence in a showdown over the future of the nation which Gandhi symbolized to the world, was appalling to him.

It was, however, a very real risk. If Jinnah had been the man who had destroyed his hopes of keeping India united, Gandhi was the man who could destroy his hopes of dividing it. Since his arrival in India, Mountbatten had subtly striven to draw to him the Congress leaders, so that, in case of a showdown, he could hope to neutralize the Mahatma for a brief but vital hour.

The task had been easier than he'd expected. 'I had the most curious feeling,' Mountbatten declared, recalling that period, 'that they were all behind me, in a way, against Gandhi. They were encouraging me to challenge him, in a sense, on their behalf.'

But as Mountbatten well realized, his unpredictable sparrow had greater resources at his command than the leaders of the Party. He had the Party itself. He had the millions of four-anna members who worshipped him and he had above all, his uncommon skill at galvanizing those masses into action. If he chose to go over the heads of the politicians and appeal directly to India's masses, he could force a terrible trial of strength between the Viceroy, Nehru and Patel on one hand, and his own towering spiritual presence on the other.

Publicly, there had been every indication that he was preparing to do just that. On the day Mountbatten's York had left London, carrying the Viceroy and his plan back to India, Gandhi had told his evening prayer meeting; 'Let the whole nation be in flames: we will not concede one inch of Pakistan.'

Privately, however, the month that had elapsed since the decision of the Working Committee had been a period of anguish, turmoil and doubt for Gandhi. Every instinct, every fibre of his being told him partition was wrong. Yet not only did he sense the Congress leadership was drifting away but, for almost the first time, he was not sure the masses of India were ready to answer his call.

Walking the streets of Delhi early one morning, one of his workers said to him: 'In the hour of decision you are not in the picture. You and your ideals have been given the go-by.'

'Yes', Gandhi sighed bitterly in reply: 'Everybody is eager to garland my photos and statues. But nobody wants to follow my advice.'

A few days later, Gandhi had awakened by mistake at half past three, half an hour before his morning prayer. He had resumed his practice of sleeping with his great-niece Manu by his side. It was a practice he would continue until his death. Lying beside his straw pallet on the floor of their New Delhi sweepers' hut, Manu listened as Gandhi had agonized alone in the darkness.

'Today I find myself alone,' he said, his voice so low it was a whisper to the night. 'Even Patel and Nehru think I'm wrong and peace is sure to return if partition is agreed upon'.

'They wonder,' he said, 'if I have not deteriorated with age.' There was a long pause, then Gandhi sighed and whispered, 'Maybe all of them are right and I alone am floundering in the darkness.'

Again there was a long silence and then Manu heard a last phrase slip from his lips. 'I shall perhaps not be alive to witness it,' he said, 'but should the evil I apprehend overtake India and her independence be imperilled, let posterity know the agony this old soul went through thinking of it.'

The 'old soul' who uttered these words was to enter the Viceroy's study on 2 June, 90 minutes after the leaders, to give voice to the most awaited and most important of all the Indian reactions. His presence had hung over every minute of the earlier meeting which he had refused to attend because he was not himself an officer of Congress. Dreading the words he was about to hear, wondering if the unpredictable prompting of Gandhi's Inner Voice would set them on a collision course, Mountbatten awaited Gandhi's arrival.

Gandhi, for whom punctuality was almost a fetish, entered the room precise to the minute as the gold clock on Mountbatten's mantelpiece softly chimed 12.30.

Mountbatten rose from his desk and walked across the room to greet him, a smile and a hearty welcome on his lips. Then he stopped halfway. Gandhi's reply was to press the index of his right hand to his lips like a mother hushing a child. At that sign, a wave of relief, tinged with humour, swept over the Viceroy: 'Thank God,' he thought, 'a day of silence!'

It was Monday. The voice that might have summoned the Indian masses against Mountbatten was stilled as it had been every Monday for years in response to one of those Gandhian vows, a pledge to observe a day of total silence once a week to ease the strains on his vocal cords. Mountbatten would not have the answer he so impatiently awaited.

Gandhi settled into an armchair and drew from under the folds of his loincloth a sheaf of dirty, used envelopes and a pencil stub barely two inches long. He always refused to waste even a scrap of paper. He himself scissored up the envelopes in which his mail arrived, turning them into neat little note-pads he proceeded to cover from top to bottom with his scrawl.

When Mountbatten had finished explaining his plan, Gandhi licked the lead of his pencil stub and began to set down on the back of an old envelope the first enigmatic reaction to what were the most important and heart-breaking words he would hear during his lifetime. His writing finally covered the backs of five old envelopes and when he left Mountbatten carefully preserved them for posterity.

'I'm sorry I can't speak,' Gandhi wrote. 'When I took the decision about the Monday silence I did reserve two exceptions, i.e. about speaking to high functionaries on urgent matters or attending upon sick people. But I know you do not want me to break my silence.'

'There are one or two things I must talk about, but not today. If we meet each other again, I shall speak.'

With that, he left the Viceroy's study.

The long corridors of Viceroy's House were dark and silent. Only an occasional white-robed servant off on some errand drifted like a ghost down their carpets. In Louis Mountbatten's study, however, the lights still burned, illuminating the last meeting of his harrowing day. He stared at his visitor with uncomprehending disbelief. Congress had indicated on time their willingness to accept his plan. So, too, had the Sikhs. Now the man it was designed to satisfy, the man whose obdurate, unyielding will had forced partition on India, was temporizing. It was, in a sense, Mohammed Ali Jinnah's day of silence, too. Everything Jinnah had been striving for for years was there, waiting only his acknowledgement. For some mysterious reason, Jinnah simply could not bring himself to utter the word he'd made a career of refusing to pronounce – 'yes'.

Inhaling deeply one of the Craven A's he chain-smoked in his jade holder, Jinnah kept insisting he could not give an indication of the Moslem League's reaction to Mountbatten's plan until he had put it before the League's Council. He needed at least a week to bring its members to Delhi.

All the frustrations which dealing with Jinnah had generated in Mountbatten now welled up. It was incredible. Jinnah had got his damned Pakistan. Even the Sikhs had swallowed it. Everything he'd been playing for he'd finally got and here, at the eleventh hour, he was preparing to destroy it all, to bring the whole thing crashing down with his unfathomable inability to articulate just one word, 'yes'.

Mountbatten simply had to have his agreement. Attlee was standing by in London waiting to make his historic announcement to the Commons in less than 24 hours. He had pledged Attlee and his government that this plan would work; that there would be no more abrupt twists like that prompted by Nehru in Simla; that this time, they could be certain, they'd approved a plan the Indian leaders would all accept. He had coaxed a reluctant Congress with enormous difficulty up to the point at which, finally, they were prepared to accept partition. Even Gandhi had temporarily at least allowed himself to be bypassed. A final hesitation, the faintest hint that Jinnah was manœuvring to secure one extra concession, and the whole carefully wrought package would blow apart.

'Mr Jinnah,' Mountbatten said, 'if you think I can hold this position for a week while you summon your followers to Delhi, you must be crazy. You know this has been drawn out till we are at boiling point.'

'You've got your Pakistan, which at one time no one in the world thought you'd get. I know you call it moth-eaten, but it's Pakistan. Now all depends on your agreeing tomorrow along with everyone else. The Congress has made their acceptance dependent on your agreement. If they suspect you're holding out on them they will immediately withdraw their agreement and we will be in the most terrible mess.'

'No, no,' Jinnah protested that everything had to be done in the legally constituted way. 'I am not the Moslem League,' he said.

'Now, now Mr Jinnah, come on,' said Mountbatten, icily calm despite his growing frustration, 'don't try to tell me that. You can try and tell the world that, but please don't try to kid yourself that I don't know who's who and what's what in the Moslem League!'

No, stone-walled Jinnah, everything had to be done in the proper way.

'Mr Jinnah,' said Mountbatten, 'I'm going to tell you something. I don't intend to let you wreck your own plan. I can't allow you to throw away the solution you've worked so hard to get. I propose to accept on your behalf.

'Tomorrow at the meeting,' Mountbatten continued, 'I shall say

I have received the reply of the Congress with a few reservations that I am sure I can satisfy and they have accepted. The Sikhs have accepted.

'Then I shall say that I had a very long, very friendly conversation with Mr Jinnah last night, that we went through the plan in detail and Mr Jinnah has given me his personal assurance that he is in agreement with this plan.

'Now at that point, Mr Jinnah,' Mountbatten continued, 'I shall turn to you. I don't want you to speak. I don't want Congress to force you into the open. I want you to do only one thing. I want you to nod your head to show that you are in agreement with me.

'If you don't nod your head, Mr Jinnah,' Mountbatten concluded, 'then you're through, and there'll be nothing more I can do for you. Everything will collapse. This is not a threat. It's a prophecy. If you don't nod your head at that moment, my usefulness here will be ended, you will have lost your Pakistan, and as far as I am concerned, you can go to hell.'

The meeting which would formally record the Indian leaders' acceptance of the Mountbatten plan to divide India began exactly as Mountbatten had said it would. Once again the Viceroy condemned the leaders to an unfamiliar silence by dominating the conversation himself and, in a sense, speaking for them. As he had expected he said, all three parties had had grave reservations about his plan and he was grateful they had aired them to him. Nonetheless Congress had signified its acceptance. So, too, had the Sikhs. He had had, he said, a long and friendly conversation the previous evening with Mr Jinnah who had assured him the plan was acceptable.

As he spoke those words, Mountbatten turned to Jinnah seated at his right. At that instant Mountbatten had absolutely no idea what the Moslem leader was going to do. The captain of the *Kelly*, the supreme commander who had had an entire Army Corps encircled and cut off by the Japanese on the Imphal Plain, would always look back on that instant as 'the most hair-raising moment of my entire life'. For an endless second, he stared into Jinnah's impassive, expressionless face. Then, slowly, reluctance crying from every pore, Jinnah indicated his agreement with the faintest, most begrudging nod he could make. His chin moved barely half an inch downward, the shortest distance it could have travelled consonant with accepting Mountbatten's plan.

With that brief, almost imperceptible gesture, a nation of 45 million human beings had received its final sanction. However misshapen, however difficult the circumstances that would attend its birth, the 'impossible dream' of Pakistan would at last be realized. Mountbatten had enough agreement to go ahead. Before any of the seven men could have a chance to formulate a last reservation or doubt, he announced that his plan would henceforth constitute the basis for an Indian settlement.

While the enormity of the decision they had just taken began to sink in, Mountbatten with a pre-arranged gesture, had a 34-page, single-spaced document set before each man. Clasping the last copy himself with both hands, the Viceroy lifted it over his head and whipped it back down on to the table. At the sharp crack that followed the slap of paper on wood Mountbatten read out the imposing title on his equally imposing document: 'The Administrative Consequences of Partition'.

It was a carefully elaborated christening present from Mountbatten and his staff to the Indian leaders, a guide to the awesome task that now lay before them. Page after page, it summarized in its dull bureaucratic jargon the appalling implications of their decision. None of the seven was in even the remotest way prepared for the shocks he encountered as he began to turn the pages. Ahead lay a problem of a scope and on a scale no people had ever encountered before, a problem vast enough to beggar the most vivid imagination. They were now going to be called upon to unravel the web left behind by 30 centuries of common habitation of the sub-continent, to take to bits the product of three centuries of technology. The cash in the banks; stamps in the post offices; books in the libraries; debts; assets; the world's third largest railway; jails; prisoners; inkpots; brooms; research centres; hospitals; universities; institutions; articles staggering in number and variety, would be theirs to divide.

A stunned silence filled the study as the seven men measured for the first time what lay ahead of them. Mountbatten had carefully stage-managed the scene and their reaction was exactly what he had hoped it would be. It would, he later told his staff, have been amusing had it not been for the gravity of the hour. He had forced these seven men to grips with a problem so imposing that its resolution, he could feel certain, would leave them neither the time nor the energy for recriminations in the few weeks of cohabitation left to them.

Gandhi received the news of the decision as he was having a foot-bath after his evening walk. While one of his female disciples massaged his feet with a stone, another burst in with an account of the Viceroy's second meeting with the leaders. Sorrow seemed to spread like a stain over his pinched features as she talked. 'May God protect them and grant them all wisdom,' he sighed when she'd finished.

Shortly after seven o'clock on that evening of 3 June 1947, in the New Delhi studio of All India Radio, the four key leaders formally announced their agreement to divide the sub-continent into two separate, sovereign nations.

As befitted his office, Mountbatten spoke first. His words were confident, his speech brief, his tones understated. Nehru followed speaking in Hindi. Sadness grasped the Indian leader's face as he told his listeners, 'The great destiny of India,' was taking shape, 'with travail and suffering.' Barring his own emotions, he urged acceptance of the plan which had caused him such deep personal anguish by concluding 'it is with no joy in my heart that I commend these proposals to you'.

Jinnah was next. Nothing would ever be more illustrative of the enormous, yet wholly incongruous nature of his achievement than that speech. Mohammed Ali Jinnah was incapable of announcing to his followers in a language that they could understand the news that he had won them a state. He had to tell India's Moslems of the 'momentous decision' to create an Islamic state on the sub-continent in English, concluding with the words '*Pakistan Zindabad*'.* An announcer then read his words in Urdu.

The prophet of non-violence got his voice back the day following the leaders' acceptance of the Viceroy's plan. The brief respite accorded Mountbatten by his day of silence was over. Shortly after noon on 4 June, Mountbatten received an urgent communication: Gandhi was preparing to break with the Congress leadership and denounce the plan at his evening prayer meeting. Mountbatten immediately sent an emissary to Gandhi inviting him to come to see him.

Gandhi walked into Mountbatten's study at 6 p.m. His prayer meeting was at seven. That left Mountbatten less than an hour in which to ward off a potential disaster. His first glance at the Mahatma told Mountbatten how deeply upset he was. Crumpled up in his armchair 'like a bird with a broken wing', Gandhi kept raising and dropping one hand, lamenting in an almost inaudible voice, 'It's so awful, it's so awful.'

In that state Gandhi, Mountbatten knew, was capable of anything. A public denunciation of his plan would be disastrous. Nehru, Patel and the other leaders would be forced to break publicly with Gandhi or to break their agreement with him. Vowing to use every

* A number of his listeners failed to understand that final shift from English to Urdu and thought Jinnah had cried: 'Pakistan's in the bag!'

argument his fertile imagination could produce, Mountbatten began by telling Gandhi how he understood and shared his feelings at seeing the united India he'd worked for all his life destroyed by his plan.

Suddenly as he spoke an inspiration struck him. The newspapers had christened the plan the 'Mountbatten Plan' he said, but they should have called it the 'Gandhi Plan'. It was Gandhi, Mountbatten declared, who had suggested to him all its major ingredients. The Mahatma looked at him perplexed.

Yes, Mountbatten continued, Gandhi had told him to leave the choice to the Indian people and this the plan did. It was the provincial, popularly-elected assemblies, which could decide India's future. Each province's assembly would vote on whether it wished to join India or Pakistan. Gandhi had urged the British to quit India as soon as possible. Dominion status was going to accomplish that.

'If by some miracle the assemblies vote for unity,' Mountbatten told Gandhi, 'you have what you want. If they don't agree, I'm sure you don't want us to oppose their decision by force of arms.'

Reasoning, pleading, employing all his famous charm and magnetism on the elderly man opposite him, Mountbatten put his case, as one of Gandhi's intimates later noted, 'with a skill, persuasiveness and flair for salesmanship which the author of *How to Win Friends and Influence People* might have envied.' Gandhi was still vehemently opposed to partition, yet he was shaken by the Viceroy's vigorous plea. Approaching 78, for the first time in 30 years Gandhi was uncertain of his grip on India's masses, at odds with the leaders of his party. In his despair and uncertainty, he was still searching in his soul for an answer, still waiting for an illuminating whisper of the Inner Voice that had guided him in so many of the grave crises of his career. That June evening, however, the voice was silent and Gandhi remained assailed by doubt. Should he remain faithful to his instincts, denounce partition, even at the price of plunging India into violence and chaos? Or should he listen to the Viceroy's desperate plea?

Mountbatten had not finished presenting his case when the time came for Gandhi to leave. He excused himself because, he told Mountbatten, he never allowed himself to be late for a prayer meeting.

Less than an hour later, cross-legged on a raised platform in a dirt square in the midst of his Untouchables, Gandhi delivered his verdict. Many in the crowd before him had come, not to pray, but to hear from the lips of the prophet of non-violence a call to arms, a fiery assault on Mountbatten's plan. No such cry would come this evening from the mouth of the man who had so often promised to offer his own body for vivisection rather than accept his country's division.

It was no use blaming the Viceroy for partition, he said. Look to yourselves and in your own hearts for an explanation of what has happened. Louis Mountbatten's persuasiveness had won him the ultimate and most difficult triumph of his Viceroyalty.

As for Gandhi, many an Indian would never forgive him his silence, and the frail old man whose heart still ached for India's coming division would one day pay the price of their rancour.

Never had the handsome chamber built to shelter the debates of India's legislators seen a performance to rival it. Speaking without notes, with an authority and clarity that awed even his most virulent critics, Louis Mountbatten revealed to Indian and world opinion the details of one of the most important birth certificates in history, the complex plan which would serve as the precursor of a new assembly of the peoples of the planet, the Third World.

It was the second time in the history of Britain's Indian Empire that a Viceroy gave a press conference. It was also the last. Three hundred journalists, correspondents of the USSR, US, China and Europe, mixed with the representatives of India's press, a regional, religious and linguistic mosaic of journals, all following with extraordinary intentness the monologue of the Viceroy.

For Louis Mountbatten the press conference was the apotheosis, the final consecration of a remarkable *tour de force*. In barely two months, virtually a one man band, he had achieved the impossible, established a dialogue with India's leaders, set the basis of an agreement, persuaded his Indian interlocutors to accept it, extracted the wholehearted support of both the government and the opposition in London. He had skirted with dexterity and a little luck around the pitfalls barring his route. And as his final gesture he had entered the cage of the old lion himself, convinced Churchill to draw in his claws and left him, too, murmuring his approbation.

Mountbatten concluded his talk to a burst of applause and opened the floor to questions. He had no apprehension in doing so. 'I had been there,' he would recall later. 'I was the only one who had been through it all, who'd lived every moment of it. For the first time the press were meeting the one and only man who had the whole thing at his fingertips.'

Suddenly, when the long barrage of questions began to trickle out, the anonymous voice of an Indian newsman cut across the chamber. His was the last question awaiting an answer. It was the last square left for Mountbatten to fill in,in the puzzle he'd been assigned six months before.

'Sir,' the voice said, 'if all agree that there is most urgent need for speed between today and the Transfer of Power, surely you should have a date in mind?'

'Yes, indeed,' replied Mountbatten.

'And if you have chosen a date, Sir, what then is that date?' pressed the questioner.

A number of rapid calculations went whirring through the Viceroy's mind as he listened to those questions. He had not, in fact, picked a date. But he was convinced it had to be very soon.

'I had to force the pace,' he recalled later. 'I knew I had to force parliament to get the bill through before their summer recess to hold the thing together. We were sitting on the edge of a volcano, on a fused bomb, and we didn't know when the fuse would go off.' Like the blurred images of a horror film, the charred corpses of Kahuta flashed across Louis Mountbatten's mind. If an outburst of similar tragedies was not to drag all India into an apocalypse, he had to go fast. After 3000 years of history, 200 of *Pax Britannica*, only a few weeks remained, the Viceroy believed, between India and chaos.

He stared at the packed assembly hall. Every face in the room was turned to his. A hushed, expectant silence broken only by the whir of the wooden blades of the fans revolving overhead stilled the room. 'I was determined to show I was the master of the whole event,' he would remember.

'Yes,' he said, 'I have selected a date for the Transfer of Power.'

As he was uttering those words, the possible dates were still whizzing through his mind like the numbers on a spinning roulette wheel. Early September? Mid-September? Mid-August? Suddenly the wheel stopped with a jar and the little ball popped into a slot so overwhelmingly appropriate that Mountbatten's decision was instantaneous. It was a date linked in his memory to the most triumphant hours of his own existence, the day in which his long crusade through the jungles of Burma had ended with the unconditional surrender of the Japanese Empire. What more appropriate date for the birth of the new democratic Asia than the second anniversary of Japan's surrender?

His voice constricted with sudden emotion, the victor of the jungles of Burma about to become the liberator of India announced:

'The final Transfer of Power to Indian hands will take place on 15 August 1947.'

Louis Mountbatten's spontaneous decision to announce the date of

Indian independence on his own initiative was a bombshell. In the corridors of the House of Commons, Downing Street, Buckingham Palace, no one had suspected Mountbatten was ready to ring the curtain down so precipitously on Britain's Indian adventure. In Delhi, the Viceroy's most intimate collaborators had no inkling of what Mountbatten was going to do. Not even the Indian leaders with whom he had spent so many hours had received a hint that he would act with such decisive haste.

Nowhere, however, did his choice of the date of 15 August for India's independence cause as much surprise and consternation as it did in the ranks of a corporation which ruled the lives of millions of Hindus with a tyranny more oppressive than that of English, Congress and maharajas combined. Mountbatten had committed the unpardonable fault of announcing his choice without first having consulted representatives of the most powerful occult body in India, the *jyotishis*, the astrologers.

No people in the world were as subservient to their authority and rulings as the Indians. Nowhere did their competence extend into so many domains. Every maharaja, every temple, every village had one or two astrologers who ruled like little dictators over the community and its inhabitants. Millions of Indians wouldn't dream of setting out on a trip, receiving a guest, signing a contract, going hunting, putting on a new suit, buying a new jewel, cutting a moustache, marrying a daughter or even having their own funerals arranged, without prior consultation with an astrologer.

Discerning the divine order of things in their reading of their celestial charts, the astrologers claimed for themselves a power that made them masters of millions of lives. Children whom they proclaimed were born under an unlucky star were often abandoned by their parents. Men elected to commit suicide at the hour they announced the conjunction of the planets was particularly favourable to the act. They laid down which days of a given week would be auspicious, and which would not. Sunday was inevitably an inauspicious day; so, too, was Friday. Anybody in India could have discovered with the aid of a chart no more occult than a calendar that in 1947, 15 August happened to fall on a Friday.

As soon as the radio announced Mountbatten's date, astrologers all over India began to consult their charts. Those in the holy city of Benares and several others in the south immediately proclaimed 15 August a date so inauspicious that India 'would be better advised to tolerate the British one day longer rather than risk eternal damnation'.

In Calcutta, Swami Madananand rushed to his celestial charts as soon as he heard the date announced. He took out his *navamsh*, an enormous circular chart composed of a succession of concentric circles on which were plotted the days and months of the year, the cycles of the sun and moon, the planets, the signs of Zodiac and the positions of the 27 stars influencing the destiny of the earth. At its centre was a map of the world. He twisted the circles on his chart until they were all set for the 15th of August. Then, from a map of India in the chart's core, he began to draw a series of lines out towards the edge of his wheel. As he did so, he sat up aghast. His calculations foretold disaster. India on 15 August would lie under the Zodiacal sign of Makara, Capricorn, a sign one of whose particularities was its unrelenting hostility to all centrifugal forces, hence to partition. Far worse, that day would be passed under the influence of Saturn, a notably inauspicious planet, dominated by Rahu, scornfully labelled by astrologers 'the star with no neck', a celestial body whose manifestations were almost wholly malign. From midnight, 14 August throughout 15 August, Saturn, Jupiter and Venus would all lie in the most accursed site of the heavens, the ninth house of Karamsthan. Like thousands of his colleagues, the young astrologer looked up from his chart overcome by the magnitude of the disaster they had revealed. 'What have they done? What have they done?' he shouted to the heavens whose machinations he interpreted for man.

Despite the discipline acquired in years of yoga, meditation and Tantric studies in a temple in the hills of Assam, the astrologer lost control of himself. Seizing a piece of paper he sat down and wrote an urgent appeal to the man inadvertently responsible for this celestial catastrophe.

'For the love of God,' he wrote to Louis Mountbatten, 'do not give India her independence on 15 August. If floods, drought, famine and massacres follow, it will be because free India was born on a day cursed by the stars.'

9

The Most Complex Divorce in History

New Delhi, June 1947

Never before had anything even remotely like it been attempted. Nowhere were there any guide lines, any precedents, any revealing insights from the past to order what was going to be the biggest, the most complex divorce action in history, the break up of a family of 400 million human beings along with the assets and household property they'd acquired in centuries of living together on the same piece of earth.

There were exactly 73 days before 15 August in which to draw up the divorce papers. To keep everybody concerned working under constant, unrelenting pressure, Mountbatten had printed a rip-off day to day calendar which he ordered displayed in offices everywhere in Delhi. Like a countdown to an explosion, a large red square in the middle of each page of the calendar registered the number of days left to 15 August.

The responsibility for preparing the gigantic, unimaginably complicated property settlement accompanying the Indian divorce fell ultimately on two men, the lawyers in a sense for the contending parties. They were, appropriately, a pair of bureaucrats, superb specimens of what was, if not the finest, at least the most luxuriant flower of a century of British rule in India.

They lived in almost identical government bungalows, drove to their offices located only doors apart in pre-war American Chevrolets, earned the same salary and paid with equal fidelity their monthly contributions to the same retirement fund. One was a Hindu. The other was a Moslem.

Every day from June to August, with their despatch boxes, their neat handwritten stacks of files, each knotted firmly by its twists of red ribbon, with only the orderly thought processes and sound procedures taught by their British tutors to guide them, Chaudhuri Mohammed Ali, the Moslem, and H. M. Patel, the Hindu, laboured to divide the goods and chattels of their countrymen. As a final irony, they parcelled out the bits and pieces of India in the language of their colonizers, English. Over a hundred bureaucrats, working in a score of committees and sub-committees, submitted reports to them. Their recommendations went in turn for final approval to a Partition Council chaired by the Viceroy.

At the outset, Congress claimed the most precious asset of all, the name 'India'. Rejecting a proposal to name their new dominion 'Hindustan', Congress insisted that, since Pakistan was seceding, the name India and India's identity in groups like the UN remain theirs.

As in most divorce cases, the bitterest arguments between the two parties came over money. The most important sums were represented by the debt Britain would be leaving behind. After having been accused for decades of exploiting India, Britain was going to wind up her Indian adventure five billion dollars in debt to her supposed victims. That enormous sum had been run up during the war, part of the crippling price Britain had had to pay for the victory which had left her bankrupt and hastened the great historical process now beginning.

In addition, there were the liquid assets to be divided, the cash in the state banks, the gold ingots in the vault of the Bank of India, everything down to the few soiled rupees and the frayed postage stamps in the petty cash box of the District Commissioner in his hut among the head-hunting Naga tribes.

So intractable did that problem prove that it was not solved until H. M. Patel and Mohammed Ali were locked up in Sardar Patel's bedroom and told to stay there until they'd reached an agreement. Haggling like pedlars in the Lahore bazaar, they finally agreed that Pakistan would get 17½% of the cash in the bank and the sterling balances and in return cover 17½% of India's national debt.

The two men also recommended that the moveable assets in India's vast administrative machine should be divided up 80% to India, 20% to Pakistan. All across India, government offices began to count up their chairs, tables, brooms and typewriters. Some of the resulting tabulations were particularly poignant. They showed, for example, that the entire physical resources of the Food and Agricultural Department of the most famine-haunted country on the globe consisted of 425 clerks' tables, 85 large tables, 85 officers' chairs, 850 ordinary chairs, 50 hat-pegs, 6 hat-pegs with mirrors, 130 bookshelves, 4 iron safes, 20 table lamps, 170 typewriters, 120 fans, 120 clocks, 110 bicycles, 600 inkstands, 3 staff cars, 2 sets of sofas and 40 chamber pots.

Arguments, even fights, broke out over the division of the goods. Departmental heads tried to hide their best typewriters or to substitute their broken desks and chairs for new ones assigned to their rival community. Some offices became *souks* with dignified men, joint secretaries in linen suits whose writ ran over hundreds of thousands of people, bargaining an inkpot against a water jar, an umbrella rack for a hat-peg, 125 pin cushions for a chamber pot. The arguments over the dishes, the silverware, the portraits in state residences were ferocious. One item however, escaped discussion. Wine cellars always went to Hindu India and Moslem Pakistan received a credit for what they contained.

The meanness, the petty mindedness those divisions sometimes produced were staggering. In Lahore, Superintendent of Police Patrick Rich divided his equipment between a Moslem and a Hindu deputy. He split up everything: leggings, turbans, rifles, *lathi* staves. The last lot consisted of the instruments in the police band. Rich split them up, a flute for Pakistan, a drum for India, a trumpet for Pakistan, a pair of cymbals for India until one instrument, a trombone, was left. Before his unbelieving eyes his two deputies, who'd been comrades for years, got into a fight over which dominion would get that last trombone.

Days were spent arguing about who should pay the pensions of widows of seamen lost at sea. Would Pakistan be expected to pay all Moslem widows wherever they were? Would India pay Hindu widows in Pakistan? Pakistan would wind up with 4913 miles of India's 18,077 miles of roads and 7112 miles of her 26,421 miles of railway tracks. Should the bulldozers, wheelbarrows and shovels of the highway department and the locomotives, coaches and freight wagons of the railways be divided according to the 80/20 rule or the percentage of the track and road mileage each nation would have?

Some of the bitterest arguments came over the books in India's libraries. Sets of the *Encyclopaedia Britannica* were religiously divided up, alternate volumes to each dominion. Dictionaries were ripped in half with A to K going to India, the rest to Pakistan. Where only one copy of a book was available, the librarians were supposed to decide which dominion would have the greater natural interest in it. Some of those supposedly intelligent men actually came to blows arguing over which dominion had a greater natural interest in *Alice in Wonderland* or *Wuthering Heights*.

Certain things simply could not be divided. The Home Department noted with laconic foresight that 'the responsibilities of the existing intelligence bureau are not likely to decrease with the division of the country' and its officers stubbornly refused to yield up so much as a file or an inkpot to Pakistan.

There was only one press on the sub-continent capable of printing two of the indispensable insignias of national identity, postage stamps and currency. The Indians refused to share it with their future neighbours. As a result, thousands of Moslems had to manufacture a provisional currency for their new state by stamping huge piles of Indian rupee notes with a rubber-stamp marked 'Pakistan'.

Inevitably India's ancient ills found a reflection in the division of her assets. East Bengal, destined for Pakistan, would be short of 70,000 tons of rice and 30,000 tons of wheat in 1947. The Moslems begged the Indian government for the return of the 11,000 tons of surplus rice which their western province of Sind had already sent to Delhi. They did not get it, not because of Hindu meanness but for a reason sadly consistent with the reality of India. It had already been eaten.

Beyond the bureaucrats, there were the extremists with their claims. The Moslems wanted the Taj Mahal broken up and shipped to Pakistan because it had been built by a Moghul. Hindu *sadhus* insisted that the Indus River, flowing through the heart of Moslem India, should somehow be theirs because their sacred Vedas had been written on its banks 25 centuries before.

Neither dominion displayed the faintest reluctance to grasp after the gaudiest symbols of the imperial power which had ruled them for so long. The gold and white viceregal train whose majestic silhouette had crossed the parched plains of the Deccan went to India. The private cars of the Commander-in-Chief of the Indian Army and the Governor of the Punjab were assigned to Pakistan.

The most remarkable division of all, however, took place in the stable yards of Viceroy's House. At issue were twelve horse-drawn carriages. With their ornate, hand-wrought gold and silver designs, their glittering harnesses, their scarlet cushions, they embodied all the pretentious pomp, all the majestic disdain, that had both fascinated and infuriated the Raj's Indian subjects. Every Viceroy, every visiting sovereign, every royal dignitary passing through India in modern times had promenaded through the Raj's capital in one of them. They were the formal, viceregal carriages, six of them trimmed in gold, six semi-state carriages in silver. To break up the sets had seemed a tragedy; one dominion, it was decided, would get the gold carriages, the other would have to settle for the silver.

Mountbatten's ADC, Lt-Com. Peter Howes, proposed that the question of which dominion would get which set of those regal vehicles should be settled by a profoundly plebeian gesture, the flip of a coin. Beside him, Major Yacoub Khan, newly appointed commander of the Pakistan bodyguard, and Major Govind Singh, the commander of the Viceroy's bodyguard, watched as the silver piece went glittering up in the air.

'Heads!' shouted Govind Singh.

The coin clattered on to the stable yard. The three men stooped to look at it. A whoop escaped from the Sikh major. Luck had decided that the gold carriages of India's imperial rulers might convey the leaders of a new, socialist India through the streets of their capital.

Howes then divided up the harnesses, the whips, the coachmen's boots, wigs and uniforms that went with each set of carriages. When he reached the end of that stack of equipment a last item remained. It was the Viceroy's Post Horn, the flaring horn used by the coachman to guide his horses. In all the viceregal establishment there was only one such horn.

The young naval officer pondered a minute. Obviously, if the horn was broken in two, it would never emit another sound. He could, of course, flip a coin again. Suddenly Howes had a better idea.

He held it up to his colleagues. 'You know,' he said, 'you can't divide this. I think there's only one solution. I'll have to keep it.'

With a smile, Howes tucked the horn under his arm and sauntered out of the stable yard.*

It was not just the books, bank notes, and bureaucrats' chairs which had to be sorted out and divided up in those frantic summer weeks. So, too, did hundreds of thousands of human beings, members of the vast army of India's public employees from railroad presidents and junior ministers to sweepers, errand boys, bearers and *babus,* those infuriating, petty-minded clerks who grew like weeds through India's administration. Each was given the choice of serving India or Pakistan. Then, separated into human piles, they were shunted off to one dominion or the other.

The most painful division of all, however, involved 1·2 million Hindus, Sikhs, Moslems and Englishmen assembled in the proudest institution Britain had produced in India, the Indian Army.

Mountbatten had pleaded with Jinnah to leave the army intact for a year under a British Supreme Commander responsible to both India and Pakistan as the best guarantor of the sub-continent's peace in the troubled weeks sure to follow partition. Jinnah had refused: an army was the indispensable attribute of a nation's sovereignty. He wanted Pakistan's in being, inside its borders, by 15 August. Carved up two thirds to India, one third to Pakistan, the men of the Indian Army, along with everything else on the sub-continent, would have to be divided and a great legend laid to rest.

The Indian Army: the words alone were enough to conjure up the

* The Viceroy's Post Horn rests a quarter of a century later, on the mantelpiece of Howes' living-room. Occasionally, Howes, now a retired admiral, will recount to his guests of an evening the story of the horn and give it a playful toot for old times' sake.

old, romantic images: Gunga Din, Gentlemen Rankers off on a spree, the Road to Mandalay, the Night Runners of Bengal, White Feathers, and Gary Cooper urging his Bengal Lancers up a rocky defile. For generations of English schoolboys, stuck in unheated classrooms, their eyes looking out on some forlorn, rainswept heath, the names of its regiments, Skinner's and Hodson's and Probyn's Horse, the 'Piffers' of the Frontier Force Rifles, the First Sikhs, the Rajputana Rifles, the Guides' Cavalry, were synonymous with glory and adventure.

It had epitomized the Victorian ideal of India better than anything else: dark, plucky soldiers staunchly loyal to their distant Empress, led by doughty young Englishmen, gentlemen all, steady under the Pathan's fire, good at games, stern but devoted fathers to their men, chaps who could hold their liquor in the mess. Its deeds, the exploits of its heroes, were the stuff of the British Indian legend.

There were the *sepoys*, Indian infantry men, at the siege of Arcot offering their British officers their last rice because they knew better how to endure the agonies of starvation; the Guides, galloping down to Delhi to assault the mutineers in 1857; the 6th Gurkhas swarming up the ridge from which the Turks dominated the beaches of Gallipoli; the 11th Prince Albert Victor's own Cavalry, the 2nd Royal Lancers, and the 18th Lancers stemming the rush of Rommel's armour at Meikili in the Western Desert, spurning the Field-Marshal's call to surrender, and perhaps saving all Egypt by their stand.

The army had begun as a collection of private armies at the service of the East India Company. Its early chieftains were free-booting mercenaries who raised their private forces, then hired them out to the Company. The passage of time placed a certain aura about their names: many had, in fact, been avaricious, brutal louts principally interested in the accumulation of wealth. William Hodson, the founder of Hodson's Horse, was a hard-drinking, sadistic, personally courageous man who made his fortune by falsifying his mess accounts and borrowing large sums of money he had no intention of repaying from the wealthy Indian subalterns whom he recruited to his colours. When one of them, in the company of a young son, was foolish enough to present himself at Hodson's door to enquire about the repayment of a loan, Hodson discharged his debt with a pistol, killing both the officer and his boy. He died trying to relieve the besieged Residence at Lucknow on 11 March 1858. His awed fellows set him under a tombstone that noted: 'Here lieth all that could die of William Steven Raikes Hodson, Commandant of Hodson's Horse.'

That Mutiny changed the nature of the Army as it changed almost everything else in India. With the changes, its real saga began. For the next 75 years, the Indian Army syphoned off the best products of Sandhurst, the intense, ambitious sons of the middle and upper middle classes, determined to make a career at arms but unable to afford the good British regiments in which an officer could not keep up in the mess on his pay alone. While the pampered sons of the rich went off to the Guards to become amateur soldiers, the bright young men at the top of the class went out to India where life was cheaper, and the pay 50% higher, to become professionals.

While the British Army paraded and drilled through the long years of the *Pax Britannica*, the Indian Army fought. It fought almost incessantly along the passes and peaks of the Frontier, at Landi Kotal and up and down the Khyber. It was desolate, forbidding terrain, serrated ridges, rocky slopes, barren valleys with hardly a bush for cover, scorched by the sun in summer, swept by wild, freezing rains in winter. The enemy was cruel, Pathans like the Wazirs and Mahsouds, who finished off their wounded prisoners with their knives.

But the Pathan was a brave enemy, clever and cunning, and his British foes extended him the begrudging admiration due to the member of a 'good side'. Those Frontier wars were a kind of deadly game, fought to cruel rules but still infused with a touch of the playing fields of Eton. Its actions were small scale, an officer and a few men manning a picket, securing a hilltop. They placed a premium on courage, personal leadership, resourcefulness and initiative, and required a close, trusting relationship between officers and men.

If a young officer's life was gruelling during Frontier campaigns, back in quarters it was led with style and panache. Given the abundance of servants in India, the low cost of living, the special privileges accorded the army, it was easy for those young men to live like the gentlemen they were supposed to be. 'Pug' Ismay, Mountbatten's Chief of Staff, recalled his arrival in his regimental mess as a young subaltern exhausted by a hot and dirty trip across half India. His future brother officers 'in our magnificent mess kit of scarlet, dark blue and gold' sat around the table, a servant behind each 'in spotless white muslin with belts of the regimental colours and the regimental crest in their turbans'.

'Two or three bowls of red roses and a few pieces of superbly-cleaned silver,' reposed on the immaculate linen tablecloth, and over the mantelpiece of the fireplace was an oil of the regiment's Royal Colonel-in-Chief and, on the walls, 'the heads of tigers, leopards, markhor and ibex'.

It was an era when army officers dressed like figures from an operetta. The 'Yellowboys' of Skinner's Horse wore apricot mess kits. Others wore scarlet and gold, azure, mint green and silver. Once a month, each regiment held its 'Dining In' night, a formal, ceremonial banquet. On his first such occasion, a newly arrived officer was expected to drink himself to a stupor, then show up for morning parade at six o'clock. A trumpet call usually opened those banquets, and all gold braid and polished boots, the officers marched into their mess behind their colonel.

There in the candlelight, before a table loaded with crystal, flowers and glistening silver, they ate meals as fine as any in India. When the last dish was cleared, a decanter of port was brought out and passed clockwise around the table from the colonel. Any breach of that tradition was considered an ill-omen. Three toasts proposed by the colonel commanding invariably followed: the King Emperor, the Viceroy, the regiment. In the 7th Cavalry, the commanding officer flipped his glass over his shoulder after each toast. Behind him, stern and expressionless, eyes forward, the mess sergeant waited to crush the shards of each under his right heel as he banged his boot down to attention. The messes of the army were well stocked with whisky, claret and champagne, all accessible to an officer with his signature on a chit, and the man to avoid at all costs, one army chronicler noted, was 'a brother officer who drank water at Mess'.

Each regiment's most precious possession was its silver, an assortment of trophies which were its unwritten history. Often a new officer joining its ranks presented the mess with a piece inscribed with his name and the date of his arrival. Others marked a regiment's triumphs on the polo or cricket grounds, or celebrated its exploits on the battlefield. A tradition went with each piece. One wide cup of the 7th Cavalry received its nickname at a roisterous Dining In night in the thirties. Like drunken undergraduates, the regiment's lieutenants had clambered on to their mess table that night and gleefully urinated in unison into the cup. Unable to contain the out-pouring of their champagne-swollen bladders, it had been immediately dubbed 'the Overflow Cup'.

An officer's mornings were devoted to drill and soldiering but the rest of the day was his. There was one acceptable way to use it – at games. Whether at polo, pig-sticking, shooting, cricket, hockey or riding to the hounds, the young officer was expected to work off his youthful energies in some healthy exercise. It was a discipline akin to a Jesuit seminarian's cold baths because one pleasure was notably absent from that idyllic life, sex. The officers of the Indian Army were encouraged not to marry until their mid-thirties. Since the

Mutiny, Indian mistresses were in disfavour and while brothels were considered necessary and proper outlets for men, officers and gentlemen were not encouraged to patronize them. A hard ride on a horse was proposed instead.

Every officer got two months' leave a year, but it was easy to get far more when the Frontier was quiet. Then the army's young officers went off to hunt panther and tiger in the jungles of Central India, the snow leopard, ibex and black bear in the foothills of the Himalayas, to fish the tenacious *mahsheer* from the quick-flowing streams of Kashmir. Ismay had spent his early leaves on a houseboat in Srinagar, his polo ponies tethered on the bank nearby, flaming lotus flowers on the waters around him. When the hot weather came, he moved up to Gulmarg at 8000 feet where 'the polo ground was of real English turf and there was a club where we could all meet to settle the affairs of the world'.

They had not solved the affairs of the world, those young officers of the Indian Army. But with their rifles trained with equal aplomb on the tigers of Bengal or the rebellious tribes of India's tumultuous frontiers, with their barrack-room ballads, their burra pegs of whisky, their pugree sun helmets and their polo sticks, they had been the proud guardians of history's greatest empire.

The First World War began the Army's second great transformation. From 1918 on, ten places a year at Sandhurst were reserved for Indian cadets. In 1932, an Indian Military Academy patterned on Sandhurst was established at Dehra Dun. The young Indians those institutions produced were indistinguishable from the British officers on whom they were modelled. Above all, the British succeeded in effacing among them the communal divisions afflicting their sub-continent and infusing them with a common loyalty to army and regiment.

Expanded to 2·5 million men by 1945, the Indian Army fought with distinction in World War II in Italy, the Western Desert and Burma. Now, one more inevitable by-product of the decision to partition India, the force whose greatest pride had been its immunity to communalism, would have to be broken up on those very lines.*

* The fraternal spirit inspired by common service in the Indian Army would endure, however, through all the troubled years to come. One day, a quarter of a century later, after India and Pakistan had faced each other on the battlefield for the third time, a group of Pakistan Armoured Corps officers sought out a comparable Indian unit to whom to surrender at the end of the Bangladesh war. They finally located an Indian cavalry officer in the bar of a newly-conquered club. Before accepting their surrender, the Indian insisted on standing them a round of drinks.

A mimeographed form submitted to each Indian officer of the army early in July was the vehicle of its destruction. It requested each man to specify whether he wished to serve in the Indian or Pakistan Army. The choice raised no problem for the army's Hindu and Sikh officers; Jinnah did not want them in his army and without exception they chose to serve India.

For those Moslems whose family homes would still be located in India after partition, however, that simple sheet of paper posed an awful dilemma. Should they walk away from their lands, their ancestral homes, often their families, to serve the army of a state which claimed their allegiance simply because they were Moslem? Or should they remain behind in the land to which so many ties bound them, accepting the risk that anti-Moslem sentiment would stifle their careers?

One of those who agonized over his decision was Lt-Col Enaith Habibullah, a veteran of El Alamein. Habibullah finally took a week-end leave and went to his family home in Lucknow where his father had been vice-chancellor of the University and where his mother was a fanatical supporter of Pakistan.

After lunch, he borrowed his father's car and drove around the streets of Lucknow. He contemplated the homes of his ancestors, medieval barons in the kingdom of Oudh, the famous Residence still scarred by the shells of the 1857 Mutiny. 'For this my ancestors gave their lives,' he thought, 'this is the India I dreamt of at school in England and under the shells of the Germans on the Western Desert. This is my home, this is where I belong. I shall stay.'*

For Major Yacoub Khan, a young Moslem officer in the Viceroy's bodyguard, the decision was the most important in his life. He, too, went to ponder his decision at his family home in the princely state of Rampur where his father was Prime Minister to his uncle the Nawab.

Tense with emotion, he rediscovered his family mansion next door to his uncle's sumptuous palace. He had so many happy memories of that house: a hundred guests dining off his family's

Then, when they brought in their unit to lay down their arms, the Indians and Pakistanis who'd just finished killing each other in the rice paddies of Bengal, organized a round of hockey and football matches.

The scandalized irregulars of Sheikh Mujibur Rahman sent a vigorous protest to New Delhi. From the office of Indira Gandhi came a sharp message to the Indian commander. He was engaged, it reminded him, 'in war, not cricket.'

* Both of Habibullah's brothers, his sister and brother-in-law went to Pakistan. His mother, the fanatic Jinnahite, however, remained in India.

gold service at Christmas; their shoots; the guns heading into the jungle on the rolling backs of twenty or thirty elephants; the fabulous balls that followed them, a full orchestra playing in his uncle's palace, the long lines of Rolls-Royces drawing up to its doors, the champagne flowing. He remembered the tents lined with silk and satin cushions and exquisite oriental carpets pitched in the midst of the jungle, crammed with delicacies for their picnics. He wandered round his uncle's palace, savouring its heated swimming pool, its great banquet hall with oils of Victoria and George V. It was another life, he thought, one destined to disappear in the Socialist India that would emerge from partition. What place would that India have for someone like him, Moslem offspring of a princely family?

That evening he tried to explain his decision to his mother: he was going to leave everything behind and go to Pakistan.

'You have lived your life,' he told his mother, 'mine lies ahead of me. I do not think there will be a future for Moslems in India after partition.'

The old woman looked at him, half angry, half in disbelief. 'I do not understand all this,' she said. 'We have lived here for two centuries. "Ham hawa ki lankhön darara äye,"' she declared in Urdu, 'we descended on the plains of India on the wings of the wind. We have seen the sacking of Delhi. We've lived the Mutiny. Your forefathers fought the British for this land. Your great grandfather was executed in the Mutiny. We fought, fought and fought. And now we have found a home here. Our graves are here,' she sadly noted.

'I'm old,' she concluded, 'my days are numbered. I don't understand politics but as a mother my desires are selfish. I am afraid this will separate us.'

No, her son protested. It would be as simple as if he were stationed in Karachi instead of Delhi.

He left the next morning. It was a beautiful summer day. His mother wore a white sari, the Moslem colour of mourning, and it outlined her like a bright stain against the sombre sandstone of the house behind her. She made her son pass under the Koran which she held over his head, then take the Holy Book in his hands and kiss it. Together they recited a few of its verses as a parting prayer. When her last words had been uttered, his mother puffed her cheeks and gently blew her breath towards her son to make sure her prayer would follow him.

As he opened the door of the family Packard waiting to take him to the station, Yacoub Khan turned to wave goodbye. Erect, dignified in her sadness, the elderly woman could only nod in reply. Behind her from the windows of the mansion, a score of turbaned servants gestured their last '*Salaams*'. One of those windows gave on to the room that Yacoub Khan had used as a young man. It was still packed with his cricket pads and photograph albums, the cups he'd won at polo, all the memorabilia of his youth. There was no hurry, he thought. Once he'd settled in Pakistan he'd come back to pick it all up.

Yacoub Khan was, of course, wrong. He would never return to his family home nor would he see his mother again. In a few months time, he would be leading a battalion of the Pakistan Army up a snow-covered slope in Kashmir, assaulting a position held by men who had been his brother officers. Among the units seeking to stem his advance would be a company of the Garhwal Regiment. Its commander would be, like Yacoub Khan, a Moslem. Unlike Yacoub Khan, however, he made the other decision in July 1947. He elected to remain in the land of his birth. He, too, was from Rampur. His name, too, was Khan, Younis Khan. He was Yacoub's elder brother.

* * *

The burden of carrying out the most complex task involved in India's partition was to fall upon one lonely man labouring in June 1947 in the Dickensian gloom of his law chambers at 3 New Square, Lincoln's Inn, London. Since he had come down from Oxford with a first in Greats and an All Souls' Fellowship, an aura of brilliance had hung over Sir Cyril Radcliffe as some men are surrounded by an aura of saintliness or raffishness. The son of a wealthy sportsman, Radcliffe had followed the law with a passion comparable to that with which his father had spent his life pursuing pheasant and grouse. A slightly stout man with a deceptively benign regard, Radcliffe, it was generally acknowledged, was the most brilliant barrister in England.

Despite his encyclopaedic knowledge of a vast array of subjects, however, Radcliffe knew virtually nothing about India. He had never written about it nor become involved in any of its complex legal problems. Indeed, Radcliffe had never even set foot on the sub-continent. Paradoxically, it was for that very reason that he was summoned from his chambers to the office of the Lord Chancellor on the afternoon of 27 June 1947.

The central problem left unresolved by Mountbatten's partition plan was where the boundary lines dividing the provinces of Bengal and the Punjab were to fall. Aware that they themselves could never agree on a line, Nehru and Jinnah, the Lord Chancellor explained to Radcliffe, had decided to place the task in the hands of a boundary commission whose chairman would be a distinguished English barrister. The man needed for that job was someone without Indian experience. Anyone who knew the country was certain to be disqualified as prejudiced by one side or the other. Radcliffe's admirable legal reputation and his equally admirable ignorance of India made him, the Lord Chancellor pointed out, the ideal candidate.

Radcliffe sat back aghast. He barely knew where the Punjab and Bengal were. Trying to divide them was the last job in the world he wanted. If he was ignorant of India, he knew enough of judicial proceedings to realize it would be a thankless task. Like many Englishmen of his age and background, however, Radcliffe was a man with a deep sense of duty. England's relationship to India had been unique and if, at this critical juncture, two Indian leaders who were able to agree on virtually nothing else had concurred on the appointment of him, an Englishman, to this appalling task, then he felt he had no choice but to accept.

An hour later, for Radcliffe's benefit, the Permanent Under Secretary at the India Office unfolded a map of the sub-continent on his desk. As his finger traced the course of the Ganges and the Indus, the green stain representing the Punjab plain, the white crest lines of the Himalayas, Radcliffe discovered for the first time the outlines of the enormous provinces he'd agreed to divide: 88 million people, their homes and hovels, their rice-paddies, jute fields, orchards and pastures, railways and factories, 175,000 square miles of the earth's surface all abstracted down to a flat piece of coloured paper on a bureaucrat's desk in London.

And now, on a similar piece of paper, he was going to have to draw the line which would sever those entities as surely as a surgeon's scalpel severs the bone and muscle of a limb in an amputation.

Radcliffe's last meeting before his departure for New Delhi took place in the garden of 10 Downing Street. Clement Attlee contemplated with a certain pride the man whose work would, in a few weeks, affect the lives of more Indians than that of any Englishman in three centuries of Anglo-Indian history.

The Indian scene was menacing, Attlee acknowledged, but one thing at least gave him great satisfaction. How gratifying it was that it was an old Haileybury boy like himself who was being sent out to draw a line through the homelands of 88 million human beings.

* * *

Louis Mountbatten had barely had time to savour his triumph in wringing an agreement from India's warring politicians before another, even more complex problem was thrust upon him. This time his New Delhi interlocutors were not going to be a handful of lawyers trained at the Inns of Court but the 565 members of His Highness Yadavindrah Singh's flock of gilded peacocks, the maharajas and nawabs of India.

These unpredictable, volatile, occasionally irresponsible rulers, assembled in the Maharaja of Patiala's Chamber of Princes, forced the Viceroy to contemplate the nightmare that had haunted India for centuries. If India's politicians could divide her, her princes could destroy her. They menaced the sub-continent, not with partition but with a fatal fragmentation into a score of states. They threatened to unleash abruptly all the fissiparous tendencies of race, religion, region, and language which lurked just below the fragile surface of Indian unity. Those princes had private armies and air forces; the capacity to disrupt India's railroads, postal communications, telephones, telegraphs, even to alter the flight patterns of her commercial airlines. To respond to their pressure for independence would be to start the disintegration of the sub-continent. The remains of the Indian Empire would become a collection of warring territories certain to stir the envy of India's great neighbour, China.

Sir Conrad Corfield's secret trip to London had produced at least a limited success. The cabinet had acknowledged that in theory he was right in arguing all those ancient prerogatives the princes had once surrendered to the King Emperor should now return to them. He had opened an escape hatch for his princes and now he had no hesitation in urging the most important among them to use it.

'No one,' Mountbatten noted with a certain bitterness in a report to London, 'had given me the slightest indication that the problem of the princes was going to be as difficult, if not more difficult, than that of British India.'

Fortunately no one was better suited to deal with India's rulers than Mountbatten. He was, after all, one of their own. He had what was to those rulers the most impeccable of references, blood ties to half the royal houses of Europe and above all, to the crown that had so long sheltered them. Indeed, Mountbatten had first discovered the fabled Indian Empire in the company of many of the princes whose thrones he now proposed to liquidate. They had been his hosts all along his extraordinary odyssey with his cousin the Prince of Wales. Mountbatten had lurched through their jungles in pursuit of tigers on the backs of their royal elephants. He had drunk champagne from their silver goblets, eaten the delicacies of the Orient off their gold services, danced under the crystal chandeliers of their ballrooms with the girl who would become his wife. Among the handful of men in India, Indian or English, close enough to the Viceroy to call him in private by his familiar nickname 'Dickie', were several princely friends acquired on that trip.

For all his royal ties and his friendship with the princes, however, Mountbatten was a tough-minded realist, committed to those liberal principles which had made him acceptable to a Labour government. The princes' fathers might have been the surest friends of the Raj; in the new era opening in India, Britain would have to find her friends elsewhere, among the Socialists of Congress. Mountbatten was determined to establish those friendships, and he knew he was not going to do it by subordinating India's national interests to those of a little caste of anachronistic autocrats.

The best he could do for his friends was to try to save them from themselves, from the fantasies, the megalomaniac dreams it had been so easy to nurture in the privileged isolation of their states. Since he'd been a young man, one terrible vision had always haunted Mountbatten and could, even in 1947, bring tears to his eyes. It was a sight he'd often imagined, the grisly spectacle of the cellar of Ekaterinburg in 1918 where his uncle the Tsar and the cousins with whom he'd played, including Marie, the princess he'd secretly hoped to marry, were murdered. There were, he knew, hotheads among the princes of India irresponsible enough to launch themselves on adventures that could turn their palaces into charnel houses like the Tsar's cellar. The course his own Political Secretary, Corfield, wanted some of them to follow could lead to just that.

Many of those princes assumed Mountbatten was going to be their saviour, that he was going to perform the miracle that would preserve them and their privileged existence. He was not. He had neither the power nor the desire. Instead, he was going to try to convince his dear and lifelong friends that their only course was to go quiet and unprotesting into oblivion.

He wanted them to abandon any claims to independence and to proclaim their readiness to join either India or Pakistan before 15 August. He, in return, was prepared to use his viceregal authority with Nehru and Jinnah to secure as the price of their co-operation the best arrangements possible for their personal futures.

Mountbatten proposed his deal first to Vallabhbhai Patel, the Indian minister responsible for dealing with the states. If Congress, Mountbatten said, would agree to allow the princes to retain their titles, palaces, privy purses, immunity from arrest, right to British decorations and quasi-diplomatic status, he, in turn, would try to persuade them to sign an Act of Accession renouncing their temporal power, acceding to the Indian Union and abandoning their claim to independence.*

It was a tempting offer Patel knew there was no one in the Congress ranks who could rival Mountbatten's authority in dealing with the princes. But, he told the Viceroy, 'it's got to be everybody. If you can bring me a basket filled with every apple off the tree, I'll buy it. If it hasn't got all the apples, I won't.'

'Would you leave me a dozen?' the Viceroy asked.

'That's too many,' Patel rejoined, 'I'll let you have two.'

'Too few,' Mountbatten said.

For a few minutes, the last Viceroy and India's future Minister of States bargained like carpet merchants over those states which encompassed a population two thirds that of the USA. Finally, they agreed on a figure: six. That hardly lightened the formidable task before Mountbatten. Five hundred and sixty-five princes minus six and a few more for Pakistan, that still left Mountbatten with over 550 apples to pluck from a resistant tree in the few weeks remaining before 15 August.

The offer Jawaharlal Nehru was making was the most extraordinary an Englishman would ever receive from an Indian. It would remain unique in the annals of decolonization. In the viceregal study in which they had spent so many anxious hours together, Jawaharlal Nehru formally asked the last Viceroy, the last occupant of the throne which had symbolized the power against which so many Indians had been struggling, to become the first occupant of the most illustrious office an independent India would have to offer, that of its Governor-General.

The germ of Nehru's idea had come from his rival Jinnah. Anxious to make sure Pakistan received its fair share of the subcontinent's assets, Jinnah had suggested that Mountbatten stay on after 15 August as a kind of supreme arbiter, until their division was completed.

Despite the magnitude of the honour being offered him, Mountbatten had grave reservations about accepting it, as did his wife. He had succeeded brilliantly in his four months in India. He and his wife could now go out as they had hoped 'in a blaze of glory'. He was only too well aware that troubles loomed ahead and if he stayed on

* The terms of their accord were eventually enshrined, as a final assurance to the princes, in India's constitution. To the last Viceroy's great distress, Prime Minister Indira Gandhi, after a long series of manœuvres, finally succeeded in bypassing its provisions in 1973 and terminating the special status accorded the princes.

F.M.

they could tarnish his earlier achievements. And if he was to function properly, he felt he would have to have a similar offer from Jinnah.

The dying Moslem leader, however, could not resist the pomp, the gaudy ceremonials of the top office of the State for which he'd worked so hard. He himself, he told Mountbatten, would be Pakistan's first Governor-General.

But, Mountbatten protested, he'd picked the wrong job. Under the British constitutional process which would prevail in the two dominions, it was the Prime Minister who had all the power. The Governor-General's role was a symbolic one akin to the sovereign's with no real power attached to it.

His argument did not move Jinnah. 'In Pakistan,' he coldly replied, 'I will be Governor-General and the Prime Minister will do what I tell him to do.'

Attlee, Churchill, his cousin the King, all conscious of the greatness of the honour being paid England by Nehru's offer, urged Mountbatten to accept it. So, too, did Jinnah.

Before he could accept, however, the blessing of one man was necessary. That the man who had enunciated the doctrine of non-violence would consent to installing as independent India's first chief of state a man whose life had been devoted to the science of warfare seemed at first unthinkable. Besides, the Mahatma, in a characteristically quixotic gesture, had already given the world his ideal nominee for the post: an Untouchable sweeper girl 'of stout heart, incorruptible and crystal-like in her purity'.

For all their differences, however, a real affinity had grown up between Gandhi and the admiral thirty years his junior. Mountbatten was fascinated by Gandhi. He loved his puckish humour. From the moment he'd arrived, he had rejected all the Raj stereotypes and looked on the Mahatma and his ideas with an open mind. With each of their meetings his personal affection for Gandhi had grown.

Gandhi, an affectionate man himself, had sensed Mountbatten's warmth and responded to it. One July afternoon, the man who had spent so many years in British jails walked into the Viceroy's study. There Gandhi asked Mountbatten to accept Congress's invitation to become the first Governor-General of the nation it had taken him 35 years to wrest from his countrymen.

Gandhi's words were an immense personal tribute to Mountbatten and an equally immense tribute to the British. Looking at him, lost in his enormous armchair, Mountbatten was overwhelmed. 'We've jailed him, we've humiliated him, we've scorned him. We've ignored him,' he thought, 'and he still has the greatness of spirit to do this.' Touched almost to tears, Mountbatten thanked Gandhi for his encouragement.

Gandhi acknowledged his words with barely a nod and continued his speech. With a wave of his delicate hand, he indicated the sweep of Viceroy's House and its great Moghul gardens. All this, he said to the Viceroy who loved every regal inch of the place, who revelled in its pomp, its pageantry and glamour, who delighted in its servants, its cuisine, who savoured every one of its luxuries, all this, would have to go in an independent India. Its arrogant opulence, its associations with the past, were an affront to India's impoverished masses. Her new leaders would have to set an example. Mountbatten as their first chief of state would, he hoped, give the lead. Move out of Viceroy's House and live in a simple home without servants, he urged. Lutyens' palace could be converted into a hospital.

Mountbatten stiffened and a wry smile crossed his face. Wily Gandhi, he thought, he's all but asking me to clean out my own toilet. Attlee, the King, Nehru and Jinnah were thrusting him into a task about which he had the gravest forebodings. And now this delightful, devilish old man was trying to turn him into India's first Socialist, a symbolic leader presiding over a fifth of mankind from some spartan bungalow which he'd have to sweep out himself each morning.

The gleaming whiteness of Louis Mountbatten's study seemed to Sir Cyril Radcliffe a world away from the foreboding gloom of his own law chambers, a difference almost as great as that between the description of his task he'd received in London and the one he was getting from the Viceroy hours after his arrival in New Delhi.

In theory, Mountbatten explained, he was to be assisted by panels of four judges in each province who were supposed to submit to him joint recommendations as to where the boundary lines should run. In fact he alone would have to accept the responsibility for making all the decisions as it was most unlikely that those judges, selected by the conflicting parties to serve as advocates of their differing points of view, would ever be able to agree on anything.

He was to draw his boundary lines 'ascertaining the contiguous majority areas of Moslems and non-Moslems'. In doing so he would 'take into account other factors'. No one had any intention of spelling out for him what those other factors should be or what weight he should give them. To do so would have led Nehru and Jinnah into another of their unending arguments.

Ironically, the one specific criterion he was given was based on a totally erroneous assumption. Convinced that future relations between India and Pakistan would be friendly, the Commander-in-Chief of the Indian Army, Field-Marshal Sir Claude Auchinleck, authorized Radcliffe to ignore the elements which were usually the first concern of a nation in setting its frontiers, considerations of defence.

Those points, however, were only preliminary jolts before the real shock awaiting Radcliffe. Though his task promised to be difficult, Radcliffe had come to Delhi convinced he would at least have the time and facilities to carry it out in a deliberate, judicious manner.

Now, he heard Mountbatten explain, it was imperative his decision be ready by 15 August, a date only weeks away. Mountbatten's words meant that he would never be able even to glimpse the lands he was supposed to divide. If this awful haste was really forced on him, he warned Mountbatten, errors and mistakes, some of them perhaps grave, were bound to creep in.

Mountbatten acknowledged that he was right. But there was no time. India would just have to accept whatever anomalies crept into his decision as inevitable and necessary. He would have only one set of instructions to give Radcliffe, but they would be firm ones: finish the job by 15 August.

A stubborn, independent man, Radcliffe was not going to take the Viceroy's word as final. He called personally on both Nehru and Jinnah. To each he put the same question: was it absolutely essential to have definitive partition lines, however defective, drawn by 15 August? Both insisted it was.

Given their insistence Radcliffe had no choice but to comply. It was not, he realized, a surgeon's scalpel he was going to require to perform his vivisection of the Punjab and Bengal. What he would need was a butcher's axe.

The Punjab, July 1947

Barely a dozen miles from the windows of the Viceroy's study began the first fields of one of the two great Indian provinces destined to be severed by Cyril Radcliffe's hand, the Punjab. Never had the granary of India promised a harvest as abundant as the one ripening in those golden fields of barley, sunburnt wheat, undulating ranks of corn and sugar cane. Already, with their slow, painful shuffle, the bullocks lurched along the dusty roads, tugging the wooden-wheeled platforms on which were heaped the first fruit of the richest soil in India.

With few variations, the villages towards which they strained were identical: a water tank covered by a slick of green scum where women beat their clothes and boys, flicking switches, washed black, dung-crusted water buffaloes; a cluster of mudwalled compounds in which buffaloes, goats, cows, dogs and barefoot children churned their way through ankle-deep mud and puddles of cow urine evaporating in the sun; a humpbacked ox plodding dumbly around the eternal circle of the millstone, crushing grain to meal; a bevy of women patting steaming piles of fresh cow dung into the flat cakes that would fuel their cooking fires.

The heart of the Punjab was the city which had been the capital of the empire of a Thousand and One Nights, Lahore, the pampered princess of the Moghul emperors. Upon it they had lavished the finest flowering of their artisans' skill: Aurangzeb's great mosque, its faiences still glistening across the dust of centuries, the 99 names of God writ in marble upon its cenotaph; the sprawling enormity of Akbar's fort with its enamelled terraces and marble grilles sculpted like lace; the mausoleum of Nurjahan, the captive beauty who married her jailer and became an empress; the tomb of Anarkali, 'Pomegranate Blossom', jewel of Akbar's harem, buried alive for bestowing a smile on his son; the 300 sibilant fountains of the Shalimar Gardens.

More cosmopolitan than Delhi, more aristocratic than Bombay, older than Calcutta, the city was for many the most attractive in India. Its heart was the Mall, a wide boulevard flanked by cafés, shops, restaurants and theatres.

Lahore boasted more bars than bookshops. As many customers crowded its cabarets than faithful its temples and mosques. Its red light district was the most elegant in India and the city had long savoured the reputation of being the Paris of the Orient.

Its students, noted one observer, dressed like actors, its actors like gigolos; its society ladies like courtesans and its courtesans like London models. It was the home of the *khazanchi*, the elegant, silk tunic some Indian women wore instead of saris, its folds falling to knee length over silk trousers knotted at the ankle like those worn by the girls of the harems of its ancient emperors.

It was also here that the English had chosen to implant the best of those educational hot-houses in which they had nurtured a new generation of leaders. From the Gothic spires of their chapels to their cricket fields, their Latin- and Greek-filled curricula, their cane-swinging masters, their school caps and blazers with seals and mottoes like 'Heaven's Light our Guide' and 'Courage to Know', those schools were perfect replicas of their English models transplanted on to the hot plains of the Punjab.

In yellowing ranks the photos of their games teams, stared down from their walls, rank upon rank of dark, solemn little faces peering out from under their rugger caps or proudly clutching their hockey sticks and cricket bats. Hindu, Moslem and Sikh, those young men had stood side by side at chapel, belting out the robust old Christian hymns, had studied the works of Chaucer and Thackeray, bruised and bloodied each other on the playing-fields in pursuit of the manly virtues of the rulers from whom they had now claimed the keys to their sub-continent.

Lahore was above all, a tolerant city and communal distinctions between its 500,000 Hindus, 100,000 Sikhs, and 600,000 Moslems had traditionally mattered less than anywhere else in India. On the dance floors of the Gymkhana and Cosmopolitan Clubs, the distance between the communities was often reduced to the thickness of a sari as Sikhs, Moslems and Hindus rumbaed and did the fox-trot together. At receptions, dinners and balls, the communities mingled indiscriminately and the sumptuous villas of its wealthy suburbs were owned without distinction by Hindus, Sikhs, Moslems, Christians and Parsees.

All that had been a lovely dream and it was a dream coming rapidly to an end in July 1947. Since January, Moslem League zealots had been holding secret rallies in the areas of the Punjab where Moslems predominated. Using pictures and the skulls and bones of alleged Moslem victims of Hindu atrocities elsewhere in India, they fanned the fires of communal hatred. Occasionally, a mutilated victim himself was sent from rally to rally to display his wounds. A concerted campaign of riots and demonstrations had forced the Hindu-Moslem-Sikh coalition government that had run the province for a decade to resign. As a result the governor, Sir Evan Jenkins, had been obliged to take its administration into his own hands.

A first wave of violence had erupted early in March after a Sikh leader had hacked down a pole flying the Moslem League banner with a cry of '*Pakistan Murdabad*' – 'Death to Pakistan'. The Moslems had given his challenge a swift and bloody reply. Over 3000 people, most of them Sikhs, had died in the clashes that had followed. Flying over a series of Sikh villages devastated by Moslem vigilantes, Lt-Gen. Frank Messervy, Commander-in-Chief of the Indian Army's Northern Command, had been horrified by the rows upon rows of murdered Sikhs, 'laid out like pheasants after a shoot.'

The authorities had finally succeeded in restoring order, but since then outbursts of trouble, such as that which had destroyed the village of Kahuta which Louis Mountbatten had visited in April, had been occurring with growing frequency.

Inevitably the poison they spread seeped into the streets of Lahore. The man whose tracings on a map would determine its destiny, Sir Cyril Radcliffe, came to the city, his head full of tales he'd heard in England of the glamorous Lahore, of its dazzling Christmas season, its hunt ball, its horse shows, its glittering social life. There were few echoes of that Lahore in the city he discovered. Instead, he found 'heat and dust storms, riots and burning'.

Already, 100,000 people had fled its streets in fear. Despite the terrible heat, its inhabitants had given up an old Punjabi summer custom of sleeping outside under the stars. The danger of a stealthy hand slitting a sleeping throat had become too great. In certain parts of the city Moslem youths would lay strips of wire along the road, then jerk them taut in the path of a fast-moving cyclist. Their victims were always Sikhs because their beards and turbans gave them away.

The most troubled area in Lahore was inside a seven mile belt of stone, the ancient wall of Akbar enclosing one of the most densely populated areas of the world. There, 300,000 Moslems and 100,000 Hindus and Sikhs, 104,000 people per square mile, seethed like fermenting foam in a labyrinth of alleys, *souks*, shops, temples, mosques and dilapidated dwellings. All the odours, the shrieks, the clamours of the bazaars of Asia abounded in that turbulent mass of humanity. Every open place was a thicket of ambulatory merchants. On round tin trays, on platters balanced on their heads, on rolling carts, they displayed their wares: puffy spice balls fried in fat, pyramids of oranges, gooey mounds of *halva* and ***barfi***, oriental sweets, papayas, guavas, stacks of bananas, glutinous clumps of dates each surrounded by its black cloud of flies. Children, their eyes whitened by the granular crusts of trachoma, squeezed the syrup from stalks of sugar cane on rusty presses.

Alleys were a byzantine maze of stalls and shops, cage-like cells set two feet above the ground to protect them from sudden floods during the monsoon. Some undefined frontier grouped them into rigid little guilds, leather workers on one side, tin-smiths on another. There were the jewellers' quarter, its trays sparkled with the gold bangles that were many Hindus' traditional form of savings; the perfumers' quarter with its clusters of incense sticks and Chinese flasks with their exotic essences from which the perfumer mixed his scents to each client's whim; shoemakers' shops displaying rows of gold-embroidered slippers, their ends tapering to a point resembling a gondola's prow; craftsmen displaying cups and ornaments of vitreous enamel, silver inlaid in pewter, perforated metal work in spun gold as fine almost as cotton candy, lacquered platters and rose and sandalwood boxes inlaid with mosaics of ivory and mother of pearl.

There were shops selling arms, daggers, *kirpans*, the ritual swords of the Sikhs. There were flower merchants behind mountains of roses and garlands of jasmine strung by their children like beads on a string. There were tea merchants with a dozen varieties of tea from jet black to olive green. There were cloth merchants squatting bare-footed in their stalls, bolts of cloth in dozens of colours behind them. There were shops selling wedding turbans cascading in gold trim and embroidered vests in soft floss silk of cotton interspersed with chips of coloured glass, the emeralds, rubies and sapphires of the poor. There were barbers; ironworkers; copper, brass and tin-smiths working in a cacophony of clanging hammers; tailors; carpenters; scavengers, specializing in the sale of old tyres, bottles, rags, newspapers; all the trades and commerce of the world succeeding each other in noisy and picturesque confusion.

Moslem women, shrouded in the dark folds of their *burqas*, eyes flashing behind the gauze grilles screening their faces, slipped like nuns at vespers through the honking, jangling swirl of tongas, rick-shaws, bicycles, lumbering bullock carts. Staring down on that hubbub from behind the hand-carved wooden screen of his office windows in the Hindu neighbourhood was the richest man in Old Lahore. Almost a quarter of the farmers of the Punjab were en-meshed, some of them for life, in the golden web the ageing Bulagi Shah spread from that window. He was the most successful usurer in India.

Now murder stalked those cluttered alleys below Bulagi Shah's windows. It was senseless, wanton murder, its victims selected at random because a man wore a Sikh's turban or a Moslem's goatee. The murderers were *goondas*, thugs, of all three communities, prowl-ing the Old City in search of a member of a rival community ventur-ing into their neighbourhoods, striking, then melting off into a maze of alleyways.

Death, one British police officer remembered, 'could come like lightning. It was over in a flash. Before you could say "knife" you'd see a body dying in the streets, every door was shut, and no one was in sight.'

The killings had maintained an eerily even balance between Moslems and non-Moslems. 'The Moslems are one up today,' the

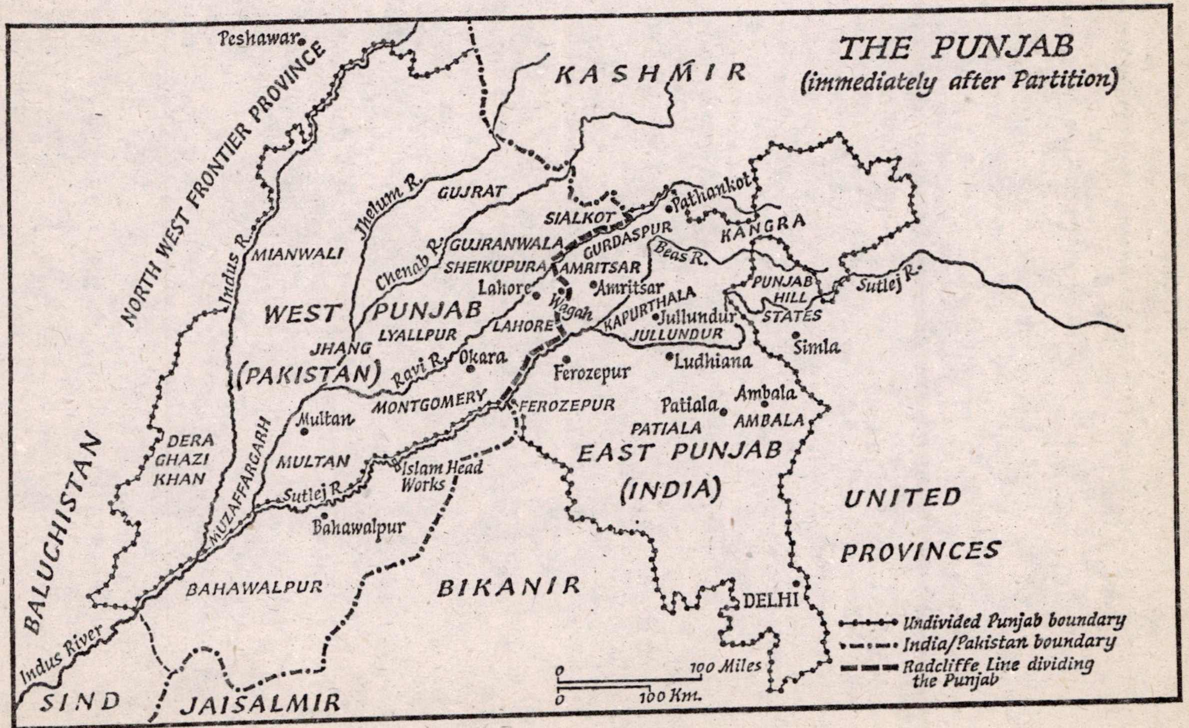

THE PUNJAB
(immediately after Partition)
KASHMIR
Peshawar
NORTH WEST FRONTIER PROVINCE
Indus R.
MIANWALI
Jhelum R.
GUJRAT
SIALKOT
Pathankot
KANGRA
GURDASPUR
Beas R.
GUJRANWALA
Chenab R.
SHEIKUPURA
AMRITSAR
Lahore
Amritsar
PUNJAB
HILL
STATES
Sutlej R.
Simla
WEST
PUNJAB
LYALLPUR
LAHORE
Wagah
KAPURTHALA
Jullundur
JULLUNDUR
JHANG
(PAKISTAN)
Ravi R.
Okara
Ferozepur
Ludhiana
Ambala
Patiala
AMBALA
PATIALA
MONTGOMERY
FEROZEPUR
Multan
MULTAN
DERA
GHAZI
KHAN
MUZAFFARGARH
EAST PUNJAB
(INDIA)
Islam Head
Works
Sutlej R.
Bahawalpur
UNITED
PROVINCES
BALUCHISTAN
BAHAWALPUR
BIKANIR
DELHI
Indus River
SIND
JAISALMIR
0
100 Miles
0
100 Km.
Undivided Punjab boundary
India/Pakistan boundary
Radcliffe Line dividing the Punjab

city's Inspector-General of Police, John Bannet, would note, 'who wants to bet the Hindus get it back tonight?'

Every Saturday, the police prepared two weekly diaries, the Weekly Crime Diary and the Weekly Confidential Political Activities Diary. Unable to decide into which category communal murders should fall, Bannet, with a fine British bureaucrat's regard for thoroughness, ordered them logged into both.

The man who would have to decide into which dominion Lahore would fall was such a controversial figure that the Punjab's governor refused to offer him the hospitality of his residence. Instead, Cyril Radcliffe stayed at Falletti's, a hotel founded in 1860 by a Neapolitan who'd fallen in love with a Lahore courtesan. With the fervour of a desperate man, he struggled to extract some minimal measure of agreement from the judges who were supposed to assist him. Mountbatten had been right. It was a useless effort.

Whenever he went out, he was assailed by the heat and by Indians desperate to influence his decision. Pathetic, terrified people, fearful of seeing a lifetime's accumulation of wealth wiped out by a stroke of his pen, they were ready to offer him anything for a boundary line favourable to their community.

At night, to avoid their importunings, he retreated to Lahore's last 'European Only' bastion, the Punjab Club, nicknamed 'the pig' by its members.

There, on its lawns, his ICS aide by his side, waiters in white robes flitting through the darkness, the man who knew nothing about India sipped his evening whisky and soda and wondered where in the hot and hatred-torn city he might find an echo of the glamorous Lahore of legend.

His Lahore would aways be the sounds and sights rising through the dark horizon surrounding the Punjab Club's lawns: an occasional shower of sparks from a burning bazaar; the wail of sirens; the piercing war cry of the city's rival factions – '*Sat Sri Akal*' for the Sikhs, and '*Allah-o-Akbar*' for the Moslems – the sinister drumbeats of the fanatic Hindu RSSS thumping like tom-toms in the hostile night.

Thirty-five miles east of Lahore lay the second great city of the Punjab, Amritsar, whose ancient alleyways enfolded Sikhism's most sacred site, the Golden Temple. Ringed by a shimmering tank of water, the white marble temple rose at the end of a marble causeway. Its dome, covered in glittering gold leaf, sheltered the original manuscript of the Sikh's Holy Book, the *Granth Sahib*, its pages wrapped in silk and covered in fresh flowers daily. So revered was the site that it was swept only with a broom made of peacock feathers.

The 6 million Sikhs to whom that temple was a spiritual lodestone practised the only major religion indigenous to the soil of God-haunted India. With their flowing beards, the hair they never cut piled under bright turbans, their often imposing size and physiques, they represented only two per cent of India's population but they made up her most vigorous, most closely knit, most martial community.

Sikhism was born of the impact of monotheistic Islam on polytheistic Hinduism along the warring frontiers of the Punjab where the two faiths had first collided. Founded by a Hindu *guru* who tried to reconcile the two faiths proclaiming, 'There is no Hindu. There is no Moslem. There is One God – the Supreme Truth,' Sikhism was favoured under the Moghuls with faith's great fertilizer, persecution. Hounded by their cruelty, the tenth and final *guru* in line of succession from Sikhism's founder converted the religion that had been born to reconcile Moslems and Hindus into a militant, fighting faith. Gathering his five closest followers, the *Panj-piaras*, the Five Beloved, Gobind Singh launched his new style Sikhism by making the five drink sugared water stirred by a double-edged dagger from a common bowl, an action which shattered their caste. Proclaiming them the founders of his new fighting fraternity, the *khalsa*, the pure, the *guru* baptized each with a name ending in Singh – 'lion'. They should, he said, stand out among the multitudes, men so instantly recognizable they could never deny their faith. They would have to develop instead the courage to defend it with their lives.

Henceforth, he ordered, Sikhs would follow the law of the five 'Ks'. They would let their beards and hair grow (*kesh*). They would fix a steel comb (*kangha*) in their uncut hair, wear shorts (*kuchcha*) to have a warrior's mobility, carry a steel bangle (*kara*) on their right wrist, and always go around with a *kirpan*, sword. They were enjoined not to smoke or drink alcohol, nor to have sexual intercourse with a Moslem woman, nor to eat meat slaughtered as Moslems slaughtered their animals, by cutting their throats.

The collapse of the Moghul empire gave the Sikhs the chance to carve out a kingdom of their own in their beloved Punjab. Britain's scarlet-coated troops had ended their brief hour of glory, but before collapsing in 1849, the proud Sikhs handed the British the worst defeat they would experience in India at the Punjabi crossroads of Chillianwala.

In July 1947, 5 of India's 6 million Sikhs still lived in the Punjab. They constituted only 13% of its population, but owned 40% of its land and produced almost two thirds of its crops. Almost a third of the members of India's armed forces were Sikhs and close to half of the Indian Army's medal winners in two World Wars had come from their ranks.*

The tragedy of the Punjab was that while Moslems and Sikhs could live under the British they could not live under each other. The Moslems' memory of Sikh rule in the Punjab was one of 'mosques defiled, women outraged, tombs razed, Moslems without regard to age or sex butchered, bayoneted, strangled, shot down, hacked to pieces, burnt alive'.

For the Sikhs, the tales of their sufferings at the hands of the Punjab's Moghul rulers were embedded into a bloody folklore preached to every Sikh child as soon as it reached the age of understanding. At the Golden Temple was a museum designed to maintain alive in the memory of each succeeding generation of Sikhs, the details of every indignity, every horror, every atrocity their people had suffered at the hands of the Moslems. In gory profusion, huge oil paintings depicted spread-eagled Sikhs being sawed in half for refusing to embrace Islam, ground to pulp between huge stone mills; crushed between meshing wheels studded with blades like gears; Sikh women at the gates of the Moghul's palace in Lahore seeing their infants speared and beheaded by the Moghul's Praetorian guard.

The failure of the Sikhs to react to the violence done in March to their community had surprised and comforted both the Moslems and the politicians in Delhi. The Sikhs had lost their old martial vigour, it was whispered, they had gone soft with prosperity.

That was a grave misjudgment of their mood. Early in June, while the Viceroy and India's leaders had been reaching agreement in Delhi on India's division, the Sikh leadership had met at a secret council in Nedou's Hotel in Lahore. Its purpose was to decide Sikh strategy in case partition was accepted. The dominant voice at the council was that of the hot-eyed fanatic who had started the March conflagration by hacking down a Moslem League banner with his *kirpan*. Tara Singh, called 'Master' by his followers because he was a third-grade schoolteacher, had lost many members of his own family in the violence he had provoked and one passion motivated him now, revenge.

'O Sikhs,' he had shouted in a speech that foretold too well the

* Endowed with some mysterious aptitude for mechanics, they had gravitated to the automotive industry. In India's cities, Sikh truck and taxi drivers were such legendary figures, it sometimes seemed no one else could -- or dared -- drive on the same road with them.

tragedy soon to overtake the Punjab, 'be ready for self-destruction like the Japanese and Nazis. Our lands are about to be over-run, our women dishonoured. Arise and once more destroy the Moghul invader. Our mother land is calling for blood! We shall sate her thirst with our blood and the blood of our enemies!'

* * *

In New Delhi, every new day thrust a score of major and minor decisions on the Viceroy and his staff. There were interminable discussions about the responsibility for paying the pensions of thousands of Britishers being prematurely retired by independence and about the condition under which hundreds of other civilians and officers, staying on at India and Pakistan's request, would labour.

His interim government composed largely of Congress and Moslem League ministers was already beginning to break down under the strains imposed by the forthcoming partition. To keep it functioning until 15 August, Mountbatten devised an ingenious arrangement. Congress was given all the ministries but each minister was assigned a Moslem League delegate to look over his shoulder and make sure he did nothing injurious to Pakistan's interest. Mountbatten assigned a British general, Sir Robert Lockhart, to supervise the referendum which would determine whether the North-west Frontier Province joined India or Pakistan. Since, at Congress's behest, he had refused Bengal the chance to opt for independence, he now refused Congress's demand to offer the Frontier a similar choice.

Most vexing problem of all was that posed by Mountbatten's impetuous selection of 15 August as the date for Indian independence. A congeries of astrologers finally advised India's politicians that, though 15 August was a wholly inauspicious day on which to begin their nation's modern history, 14 August represented a considerably more favourable conjuncture of the stars. A relieved Viceroy accepted the compromise the Indian politicians proposed to propitiate the celestial bodies: India and Pakistan would become independent dominions on the stroke of midnight, 14 August 1947.*

For 30 years, the tricolour sash of homespun cotton *khadi*, soon to

* At a staff meeting shortly after his press conference, the Viceroy had noted with a smile that there was 'a complete lack of high level advisers on astrology on his staff'. Insisting this be 'remedied forthwith', he assigned his able young press attaché, Alan Campbell Johnson, the additional responsibilities of viceregal astrologer.

replace the Union Jack on India's horizons, had flown over the meetings, marches and manifestations of a people thirsting for independence. Gandhi had designed that banner of a militant Congress himself. At the centre of its horizontal bands of saffron, white and green, he had placed his personal seal, the humble instrument he'd proposed to the masses of India as the instrument of their non-violent redemption, the spinning-wheel.

Now, with independence at hand, voices in the ranks of Congress contested the right of what they called 'Gandhiji's toy' to occupy the central place in what was about to become their nation's flag. To a growing number of party militants his spinning-wheel was a symbol of the past, a woman's thing, the hallmark of an archaic India turned inwards upon herself.

At their insistence the place of honour on the national flag was assigned to another wheel, the martial sign the conquering warriors of Ashoka, founder of the Hindu empire, had borne upon their shields. Framed by a pair of lions for force and courage, Ashoka's proud symbol of strength and authority, his *dharma chakra*, the wheel of the cosmic order, became the symbol of a new India.

Gandhi learned of his followers' decision with deep sadness. 'However artistic the design may be,' he wrote, 'I shall refuse to salute a flag which carries such a message.'

That disappointment was only the first in a harvest of sorrows awaiting the elderly leader in the nation he'd done so much to create. Not only was Gandhi's beloved India being divided, but the partitioned India soon to be born was going to bear little resemblance to the India Gandhi had dreamed of and fought for during his long crusade.

Gandhi's dream had always been to create a modern India which would offer Asia and the world a living example of his social ideals. To his critics, those ideals were a cranky old man's obsessions. To his followers, however, they constituted a lifebuoy thrown out to mankind by a sane man in a world going mad.

The Mahatma was wholly opposed to those who argued India's future lay in imitating the industrial and technological society of the West. India's salvation, he argued, lay 'in unlearning what she has learnt in the past 50 years'. He challenged almost all the Western ideals that had taken root in India. Science should not order human values, he argued, technology should not order society, and civilization was not the indefinite multiplication of human wants but their deliberate limitation so that essentials could be equitably shared by all.

The industrialization of the West admired by so many of his followers had concentrated power in the hands of the few at the expense of the many. It was a doubtful blessing to the poor in the West and a menace to the non-white races of the underdeveloped world.

Gandhi's India would be built on her 600,000 villages, those multitudinous facets of the India he knew and loved, an India unstained by technology, a haunted India marking the passage of her years with the cycle of her religious feasts, her decades with the memory of her failed crops, her centuries with the spectre of her terrible famines.

He wanted each of those villages to become self-sufficient units, able to produce its own food, cloth, milk, fruit and vegetables, to educate its young and nurse its ill. Proclaiming 'many a violent war in Asia could have been prevented by an extra bowl of rice', he had constantly sought the perfect food to nourish India's hungry peasants, experimenting with soya, peanuts, mango kernels. He attacked machine-polished rice because it removed the hard husk rich in vitamin B.

He wanted to close down India's textile mills and replace them with his spinning-wheel as part of a programme to give work to the village under-employed, to provide activities that would hold the population in those villages.

His economic manifesto was 'the traditional old implements, the plough and the spinning-wheel, have been our wisdom and welfare. We must return to the old simplicity'. When man invented a tractor that could produce milk, *ghee* and dung, he said, he would recommend it as a replacement for the cow to India's peasants.

His nightmare was a machine-dominated industrial society which would suck India's villagers from the countryside into her blighted urban slums, sever their contact with the social unit that was their natural environment, destroy their ties of family and religion, all for the faceless, miserable existence of an industrial complex spewing out goods men didn't really need.

He was not, as he was sometimes accused of doing, preaching a doctrine of poverty. Grinding poverty produced the moral degradation and the violence he loathed. But so too, he argued, did a surfeit of material goods. A people with full refrigerators, stuffed clothes cupboards, a car in every garage and a radio in every room, could be psychologically insecure and morally corrupt. Gandhi wanted man to find a just medium between debasing poverty and the heedless consumption of goods.

He also wanted him to live in a classless, egalitarian society because social and economic inequality bred violence. All labour, physical or intellectual, would carry the same reward in Gandhi's India. It was not a property qualification that would earn a man the right to vote in his state, but a labour qualification. To get it everybody would have to contribute physical labour to the state. Nobody, including saints or sages, would be exempt. The ditch digger would get his almost automatically, but the lawyer or millionaire would have to earn his with his calluses.

Most important for Gandhi was the example leaders set for their followers. He had not been indulging in idle prattle when he had stunned the elegant Viceroy by proposing he abandon Viceroy's House for a simple bungalow. The way to abolish privilege, he had always maintained, was to renounce it yourself.

Indeed, none of the other great social prophets of his century, Lenin, Stalin, Mao, had led their lives in such utter conformity to their ideals.* Gandhi had even held his daily food intake to the barest minimum he needed to stay alive so as not to abuse the resources of his famished land.

Gandhi's advocacy of his theories had been accompanied by a number of piquant contradictions. He had denounced the machine-age at prayer meetings across India with the aid of one of its most recent manifestations, a microphone, and the 50,000 rupees a year that sustained his first ashram had been the gift of an industrialist, G. D. Birla, whose textile mills represented the most splendid incarnation imaginable of the Mahatma's industrial nightmare.

Now, with independence approaching, his continuing espousal of his ideas was becoming an embarrassment to Fabian Socialists like Nehru or ardent capitalists like Patel. Their faith was in machines, industry, technology, all the apparatus the West had brought to India. They longed to build the giant factories and industrial complexes he loathed, to gird India's future in five year plans. Even Nehru, the beloved son, had written that to follow Gandhi's ideas was to step backward into the past, to submit India to the most confining autarchy imaginable, that of its villages. To their chagrin, the Mahatma insisted on proclaiming publicly the canons by which he hoped they and the other leaders of the new India would live.

Every minister, he said, should wear *khadi* exclusively and live in a simple bungalow with no servants. He should not own a car,

* Gandhi and the Marxists had little use for each other. To most Marxists, Gandhi was unscientific. He, in turn, regarded Communism with its atheistic overtones and its inherent violence as anathema. Most Socialists, he felt, were 'armchair Socialists' unwilling to alter their own life style or sacrifice any of their comforts while they waited the arrival of Socialist Nirvana.

should be free of the taint of caste, spend at least one hour a day in physical work, spinning, or growing food and vegetables to ease the food shortage. He should avoid 'foreign furniture, sofas, tables and chairs', and go around without bodyguards. Above all, Gandhi was sure 'no leader of an independent India will hesitate to give an example by cleaning out his own toilet box'.

Naïve yet unassailably wise, his words were poignantly revealing of the dilemma inherent in all of Gandhi's ideals. They were a perfect scheme cast for imperfect actors. A quarter of a century after his death, India's gravest political ill would be the corruption and venality of the very Congress ministers whom Gandhi had hoped would follow in his footsteps.

*

For all his concern about India's future, Gandhi's day to day preoccupations in July 1947, remained the communal violence which continued to plague the sub-continent. Taking Nehru with him, he insisted on seeing the first Hindu and Sikh refugees spilling out of West Punjab.

It was a staggering confrontation. Thirty-two thousand people, the survivors of a hundred Kahutas – the village whose horrors had so struck the Viceroy – had been assembled 120 miles from Delhi in the heat and the dirt of India's first refugee camp.

Shrieking their anger or wailing their grief, they engulfed Gandhi's car in a sea of misery, their hands and fingers gesticulating, beseeching; their faces contorted in anger or hate; their dark eyes begging for some solace to their despair. Buzzing swarms of flies hovered over them, alighting in black, wriggling patches on their still-open wounds. A great pall of dust stirred by their running feet invaded their nostrils and parched throats and left its powdery veil everywhere. From all sides, they pressed on Gandhi and Nehru, a smelly, sweaty, foul-breathed wall of miserable human beings.

All day Gandhi worked with them, trying to bring some order to their improvised camp. He showed them how to dig latrines, lectured them on sanitation and hygiene, organized a dispensary, nursed as many of the sick as he could.

Late in the afternoon, they started back to Delhi. His 77-year-old body worn out by strain, his spirit saddened by so much misery, Gandhi stretched out in the back seat of the car and fell asleep with his gnarled feet resting in the lap of the disciple who had turned his back on him just two months before.

Eyes straight ahead, his usually expressive face a mask, Nehru rode for a long time in silence, pondering, perhaps, what future the sights they had witnessed portended for the India he would soon be called upon to govern. Then, slowly, tenderly, as though to expiate with his fingers' gentle touch the pain he'd caused him, he began to massage the callused feet of the sleeping man to whom he'd devoted so much of his life.

At sunset, Gandhi awoke. From each side of their speeding car, the broad fields of sugar, wheat, paddy, flat as a man's hand, ran down to a horizon so distant it might seem the edge of the world. A fine haze stood above the vast plain, filtering through its screen the last roseate glow of the sinking sun. It was the cow dust hour, an hour as ancient, as unforgettable as India itself. From a thousand, tens of thousands of mudbrick huts speckling the great Punjab plain it came, the smoke of India's mealtime fires. Everywhere, squatting on their haunches, faded saris clutched to their shoulders, bangles clanking on their bare arms, the women tended those fires, fussing over the *chapatis* and *channe* they cooked, stoking them with the round flat patties of dried dung that fuelled them, the last of the many gifts of India's sacred cows. The mantle of Indian night, the smoke from those numberless cow-dung fires, drifted through the evening sky, permeating it with the distinctive pungent smell that was the body odour of Mother India.

There in the gathering darkness Gandhi stopped the car and sat down by the side of the road for his evening prayer. His stooped, shrivelled figure was at one with that vast and mournful plain, the neem and peepul trees folding over him. In the back of the car, Nehru, his eyes closed, his fingers pressed to his eyelids, listened as the high, wavering voice of a broken-hearted man beseeched the God of the *Gita* to deliver his beloved India from the fate he foresaw for her.

10

'We Will Always Remain Brothers'

London, July 1947

The solemn thumps of a black ebony stave on an antique floor had heralded the accomplishment of every great legal act in the elaboration of the British Empire. For centuries, the stave of the King's Messenger, the Gentleman Usher of the Black Rod, had summoned a delegation of the Commons down the aisles of the Houses of Parliament to the Lords, there to witness the Royal Assent, the final sanction for the edicts that had carried Britain's imperial power to the ends of the earth. The ancient ritual had not changed but this summer day the metronomic beat of the ebony stave rang out a funeral knell; a knell marking the death of the British Empire. One of the bills awaiting the Royal Assent on Friday, 18 July 1947 would sever forever the British connection with India.

At the height of Britain's imperial power, men on the benches of Westminster had been able to call the world's unruly to order by the dispatch of a gunboat or topple a foreign despot with the threat of a thin red line of British soldiers. The last European nation to embark on the imperial adventure, the British had sailed more seas, opened more lands, fought more battles, squandered more lives, drained more exchequers, administered more people more fairly than any other imperial power. Indeed, something in their island peoples' character seemed to have fitted them for that brief moment in history when it was held a self-evident moral imperative that white, Christian Europeans should 'hold dominion over palm and pine'.

The vehicle by which a new generation of men in Westminster would end all that was tucked into a wallet embellished with the Royal Arms and a gold thread. It lay in a pile of similar documents on the long table dividing the chamber in which the House of Lords sat.

The Indian Independence Bill was a model of conciseness and simplicity. To give India her freedom, members of Parliament required only twenty clauses and sixteen typewritten pages. Never had so momentous a measure been drafted and enacted with comparable speed. Barely six weeks had been required to prepare it and send it through its readings in the Houses of Parliament. The debate accompanying those readings had been marked by dignity and restraint. There had been instances in history, Clement Attlee had told the House in introducing the historic bill, 'in which a state at the point of a sword has been forced to surrender power to another people, but it was very rare for a people who had long enjoyed power over another nation to surrender it voluntarily'.

Even Winston Churchill, giving his melancholy consent to what he had labelled 'a tidy little bill', had paid a rare tribute to his rival Attlee for the wisdom he'd displayed in selecting Louis Mountbatten as his last Viceroy. Probably none of the words uttered in the course of those debates, however, had caught as accurately the mood of Britain's law-makers as a remark by Viscount Samuel.

'It may be said of the British Raj,' he noted, 'as Shakespeare said of the Thane of Cawdor: "nothing in his life became him like the leaving it".'

Now, the Prime Minister, Clement Attlee, at their head, a 30-member delegation from the House of Commons took their places behind the bar in the House of Lords to witness the final act in its passage.

Dominating one end of the chamber were twin symbols of the royal power, a pair of gilded thrones on a dais under a tapestry embroidered with the Royal Arms. Before them was the Woolsack, the upholstered seat of the Lord High Chancellor, looking upon a long table on which were piled the bills awaiting the assent of George VI.

The King's representative, the Clerk of the Crown, took his place on one side of the long table. The Clerk of Parliament took his opposite him. He reached out for the first bill in the pile, and in a solemn voice, read out its title: 'The South Metropolitan Gas Bill.'

'*Le Roi le veult*,' replied the Clerk of the Crown in the ancient Norman phrase which for centuries had signified a sovereign's pleasure at the enactment of a royal decree or act of parliament.

The Clerk of Parliament took the next bill from the stack.

'The Felixstowe Pier Bill,' he said.

'*Le Roi le veult*,' the Clerk of the Crown intoned in return.

The Clerk of Parliament reached for another bill.

'The Indian Independence Bill,' he read.

'*Le Roi le veult*,' came the reply.

Attlee flushed lightly and lowered his eyes, at those words. A hush filled the chamber as the echoes of the Clerk's voice died. It was over. In four words of archaic French, in the company of a gas works and a fishing pier, Britain's great Indian Empire had been consigned to history.

* * *

It was the last assembly of the world's most exclusive fraternity.

Sweating profusely under their brocaded tunics, their decoration-covered uniforms, their bejewelled turbans, 75 of the most important maharajas and nawabs of India and *diwans* representing 74 others, waited in the drenching humidity of a New Delhi summer day to learn from the mouth of the Viceroy the fate History held in store for them.

Mountbatten, decorations glittering on his own admiral's white uniform, entered the little hemicycle of the Chamber of Princes. The Chamber's Chancellor, the Maharaja of Patiala, escorted him to the podium from whence he gazed calmly out at that host of unhappy men arraigned before him.

The Viceroy was ready to start tossing the apples into Patel's basket. His most bitter opponent, Sir Conrad Corfield, was at that moment in a plane flying back to London and premature retirement. He had left India rather than urge on that bizarre body of rulers to whom he'd devoted his career a policy of which he did not approve.

The Viceroy was happy to see him go. Convinced his course represented the best arrangement the princes could possibly hope for, Mountbatten intended to herd them, however reluctantly, however anguished their protests, into Patel's waiting apple basket.

Speaking without notes, his tone a mixture of frankness and fervour, he urged his listeners to sign the Act of Accession which would join their states to either India or Pakistan. A resort to arms, he stressed, would produce only bloodshed and disaster. 'Look forward ten years,' he begged them, 'consider what the situation in India and the world will be then, and have the foresight to act accordingly.'

The tides of history, however, were a less impressive argument to that motley gathering than the next point the Viceroy advanced. They were on the verge of extinction, the world as they'd known it was collapsing, but the argument that moved some of them most concerned the bits of coloured enamel dangling on their chests. Sign the acts, Mountbatten urged, and he had good reason to believe Patel and Congress would allow them to continue to receive from his cousin the King those honours and titles they so cherished.

When his speech was finished, the Viceroy invited questions from the princes. Mountbatten was stunned by their absurdity. So ludicrous did some of their preoccupations appear that the Viceroy wondered if these men and their Prime Ministers really understood what was about to happen to them. The prime concern of one member of that distinguished gathering was whether he could retain the exclusive right to hunt tigers in his state if he acceded to India. The *diwan* of another prince, whose employer at this critical juncture had found nothing better to do than to go on a tour of Europe's gambling casinos and cabarets, pleaded that as his ruler was on the high seas he did not know what course of action to adopt.

Mountbatten pondered a moment, then picked up a large round glass paper-weight which rested on the rostrum before him. Twisting it in his hand like some ancient Oriental sage, he announced: 'I will look into my crystal ball for your answer.'

Furrowing his brows, he fixed the ball with the most intensely mysterious gaze of which he was capable. For ten seconds a heavy silence, broken only by the laboured breathing of some of the more corpulent rulers, stifled the chamber. The occult was after all not a matter taken lightly in India, even by maharajas.

'Ah,' Mountbatten whispered, after milking all the drama he could from the gesture, 'I see your prince. He's sitting at the captain's table. He says . . . "yes, what is it?" – he says "sign the Act of Accession".'

The following day, for the last time, a formal banquet assembled a Viceroy of India and her ruling princes. Profoundly saddened by his awareness of what was happening, Louis Mountbatten called for a final toast to the King Emperor from his oldest and most faithful allies.

'You are about to face a revolution,' he told them. 'In a very brief moment you'll lose forever your sovereignty. It is inevitable. Do not,' he pleaded, 'turn your backs on the India emerging on 15 August. That India will not have enough capable men to represent her overseas.' She was going to need doctors, lawyers, able administrators, trained officers to replace the British in her army. Many of those princes educated abroad, experienced in handling the affairs of their states, combat veterans, had skills India would need. They could become playboys on the beaches of the Riviera, or they could offer their services to the nation and find a new role for themselves and their class in Indian society. He had no doubt which course they should follow. 'Marry the new India,' he begged them.

Kashmir, July 1947

Like a canoe shooting the rapids, the station wagon twisted through the ruts and rocks of the dirt path parallel to the torrents of the Trika River. The driver's face with his pouting lips, his wary, mistrustful eyes, his chin, its outline lost under soft pouches of flesh, was an accurate reflection of his character. He was a weak, vacillating man whose perversions and orgies had given him the reputation of a Himalayan Borgia. Unfortunately, Hari Singh, the man who as 'Mr A' had titillated the readers of Britain's penny press before the war, was something else. He was the hereditary Hindu Maharaja of the most strategically situated princely state in India, the vast, sparsely-settled crossroads State of Kashmir where India, China, Tibet and Pakistan were destined to meet.

This morning, a particularly distinguished visitor occupied the seat beside Hari Singh. Louis Mountbatten had known the Hindu ruler since they had galloped side by side on the manicured grass of his polo field at Jammu during the Viceroy's tour with the Prince of Wales. Mountbatten had deliberately arranged his state visit to Hari Singh's capital Srinagar to force a decision on Kashmir's future out of its hesitant ruler.

It was not, however, into Patel's basket that Mountbatten proposed to drop the Kashmiri apple. Logic seemed to dictate that Kashmir wind up in Pakistan. Its people were Moslem. It had been one of the areas originally selected for an Islamic state by Rahmat Ali when he'd first formulated his impossible dream. The 'k' in Pakistan was for Kashmir.

The Viceroy accepted that logic. He had, he told the Maharaja, brought with him the guarantee of Patel on behalf of the future government of India that if, as seemed natural with his overwhelming Moslem population and his geographical situation, Hari Singh joined Pakistan, India would understand and raise no objection. Furthermore, he said, Jinnah had assured him that Hari Singh, even though he was a Hindu ruler, would be welcomed and given an honoured place in his new dominion.

'I don't want to accede to Pakistan on any account,' Hari Singh answered.

'Well,' Mountbatten said, 'it's up to you, but I think you should consider it very carefully since after all almost 90% of your people are Moslem. But, if you don't, then you must join India. In that case, I will see that an infantry division is sent up here to preserve the integrity of your boundaries.'

'No,' replied the Maharaja, 'I don't wish to join India either. I wish to be independent.'

Those were just the words the Viceroy did not want to hear. 'I'm sorry,' he exploded, 'you just can't be independent. You're a land-locked country. You're over-sized and under-populated. What I mind most though is that your attitude is bound to lead to strife between India and Pakistan. You're going to have two rival countries at daggers drawn for your neighbours. You'll be the cause of a tug-of-war between them. You'll end up being a battlefield. That's what'll happen. You'll lose your throne and your life, too, if you're not careful.'

The Maharaja sighed and shook his head. He kept a gloomy silence until he reached the fishing camp his peons had set up by a bend on the river for the trout fishing he was offering his distinguished visitor. For the rest of the day, Hari Singh made certain Mountbatten had no chance to corner him alone. Instead the Viceroy spent his day casting in the Trika's crystalline waters for trout. Even they were not prepared to accommodate the frustrated Viceroy. His ADC caught all the fish.

For the next two days, Mountbatten repeated the process. Finally, on the third day, he felt his old friend beginning to waver. He insisted they have a formal meeting the following morning before his departure with their staffs and the Maharaja's Prime Minister present to draw up an agreed policy statement.

'All right,' the Maharaja agreed, 'if you insist on it.'

This particular apple, however, was going to remain firmly attached to its tree. The following morning an ADC came to Mountbatten's suite. His Highness was sorry, he declared, but he was suffering from an upset stomach and his doctor would not allow him to attend their little meeting. The story, Mountbatten was sure was 'absolute baloney'. Invoking doctor's orders, however, Hari Singh refused even to see his old friend before he left. A problem which would embitter India-Pakistan relations for a quarter of a century and imperil world peace had found its genesis in that diplomatic stomach-ache.

Elsewhere, Mountbatten enjoyed considerably more success in his efforts to fill Patel's basket with apples. For some of the rulers, appending their signature to the Instrument of Accession was a cruel tragedy. One Raja of Central India collapsed and died of a heart attack seconds after signing. The Rana of Dholpur told Mountbatten with tears in his eyes: 'This breaks an alliance between my ancestors and your King's ancestors which has existed since 1765.' The Gaekwar of Baroda, one of whose forebears had fed his British Resident diamond dust, collapsed weeping like a child in the arms of V. P. Menon on signing. One ruler of a tiny state hesitated for days before appending his signature because he still believed in the divine right of kings. The eight maharajas of the Punjab signed their Instrument together during a formal ceremony in the state banquet hall at Patiala where Sir Bhupinder Singh 'the Magnificent' had once lavished the most prodigious hospitality in India on his guests. This time, one participant recalled, 'the atmosphere was so lugubrious we might have been at a cremation.'

A handful of rulers continued to resist the blandishments of Mountbatten, V. P. Menon and Patel. One of Mountbatten's closest personal friends, the Nawab of Bhopal, bitterly claimed 'the rulers were being invited like the oysters, to attend the tea party with the Walrus and the Carpenter'. Udaipur tried to form a federation with a number of fellow princes whose states adjoined his. So, too, did Gwalior, the son of the man with a mania for electric trains. At the behest of his Prime Minister, the Maharaja of Travancore, a southern state with a seaport and rich uranium reserves, clamoured for independence.

The pressures to herd these last reluctant resisters into Patel's basket became intense as 15 August drew near. Where he had local Congress organizations, Patel ordered demonstrations and street agitation to force their hands. The Maharaja of Orissa was trapped in his palace by a mob which refused to let him leave until he'd signed. Travancore's forceful Prime Minister was stabbed in the face by a Congress demonstrator. Shaken, the Maharaja cabled Delhi his accession.

None of the accessions was quite as tempestuous as that of the young Maharaja of Jodhpur. Jodhpur had just ascended his throne on his father's death. He was given to a number of expensive hobbies like flying, women and conjuring tricks; none of them, he realized, likely to stir the sympathy of Congress's Socialists. Together with his colleague, the Maharaja of Jaisalmer, he arranged a secret meeting in Delhi with Jinnah to enquire of the Moslem leader what sort of reception they might expect if they took their primarily Hindu states into his dominion.

Delighted at the thought of ripping two key princes away from his Congress rivals, Jinnah took a blank sheet of paper from his desk drawer and passed it to Jodhpur.

'Just write your conditions on this paper,' he said, 'and I'll sign it.'

The two men asked time to withdraw to their hotel to ponder them. There they found V. P. Menon waiting for them. Tipped off by one of his mysterious sources about their initiative which eventually could have drawn other states into Pakistan, Menon told Jodhpur the Viceroy wanted to see him urgently at Viceroy's House.

Seating the prince in a waiting-room, Menon set off on a frantic search for Mountbatten. Finally locating the Viceroy, who had no idea what he'd done, in his bath, Menon begged him to come down and reason with the stubborn prince.

His recently deceased father, who'd been his friend for 26 years, would have been outraged by his behaviour, the Viceroy told the young ruler. It was folly to try to take the subjects of his Hindu state into Pakistan for purely selfish reasons. In return, he promised Jodhpur that he and Menon would persuade Patel to adopt as tolerant a view as possible towards his personal quirks.

Mountbatten left Menon to get the impetuous young ruler's signature on a provisional agreement. When he'd gone, Jodhpur pulled a fountain pen made in his workshop out of his pocket. After signing the text, he unscrewed its cap and revealed a miniature ·22 pistol which he pointed at Menon's head.

'I'm not giving in to your threats!' he shouted. Mountbatten, hearing the noise, returned and confiscated the pistol.*

Three days later Menon delivered a final Instrument of Accession to the prince's palace. Glumly the prince signed. Then he decided to bury his past in a celebration with Menon as his unwilling guest. All afternoon he poured whisky down the poor civil servant's throat. After that, Menon was forced to gulp draughts of champagne while the prince ordered a full scale banquet of roast meats and game, an orchestra and a selection of dancing girls. For Menon, a prudish vegetarian, the evening was a nightmare. The worst, however, was still to come. Hurling his turban on the floor in a fit of rage because he thought the music was too loud, the drunken Jodhpur dismissed the girls and the band and announced he would fly Menon to Delhi in his private plane. He rocketed off the field, then twisted his violently ill passenger through every acrobatic stunt he could perform before landing him at Delhi airport. Green and retching, Menon half-crawled from the plane but in his shaking fingers was the document which would deliver one more apple into Patel's waiting basket.

Despite the tergiversations of a last bunch of diehards, the Viceroy would, by 15 August, be able to honour his contract with Patel. The basket of apples he would present him would be overflowing. Five princes whose states would be inside Pakistan rallied to Jinnah, Mountbatten and Menon had plucked all the rest, with just three exceptions.

The exceptions, however, were major ones. Driven by a cabal of Moslem fanatics terrified at the idea of losing their privileges in Hindu India, the ruler of the largest and most populous state in India had rejected all of Mountbatten's counsels. Ignoring every

* Years later, Mountbatten, fascinated himself by magic, performed the required conjuring trick to win election to the Magic Circle. He loaned Jodhpur's pen-pistol to the group to be displayed in the Magic Circle Museum where it still rests.

effort to bring him into an agreement with India, the Nizam of Hyderabad strove in vain to force Great Britain to recognize his state as an independent dominion. From his palace the miserly ruler had not ceased a bitter plaint at being 'abandoned by his oldest ally', and seeing 'the bonds of long devotion' linking him to the King Emperor severed. Kashmir, too, continued in his refusal to align himself with either dominion.

The reasons keeping the third and last ruler from acceding to India were of a somewhat different order. Convinced by an agent of the Moslem League that the first act of an independent India would be to poison his dogs, the Nawab of Junagadh had decided either to proclaim his independence or join Pakistan despite the fact his tiny Hindu state would share no borders with the Moslem nation.

* * *

'Gentlemen, this is Mr Savage of the Punjab CID,' Louis Mountbatten told the two startled Indian politicians in his study on 5 August. 'He has a story you should hear.'

Whatever that story was, it was certain to get the close attention of Jinnah and Liaqat Ali Khan because the body Savage represented was known as the best British intelligence organization in India. Indeed, its operatives had penetrated their own political movements at the highest levels.

The nervous Savage cleared his throat and began. The information he was about to reveal had been wrung from prisoners in an interrogation centre the CID had set up in an unused wing of the Lahore lunatic asylum. So secret was it considered that Savage had been obliged to memorize it the evening before in Lahore rather than bring it to Delhi on paper.

A group of Sikh extremists had linked hands with the most fanatical political group in India, the bigoted Hindu zealots of the Rashtriya Swayam Sewak Sangh, the RSSS. At their head, stood Master Tara Singh, the third-grade schoolteacher who had called on his followers to drench India in blood at the Sikh's secret convocation in Lahore. The two groups had agreed to pool their resources and energies in terrorist activity.

The Sikhs, with their better organization, training and knowledge of explosives, would destroy the heavily guarded 'Pakistan Specials', the trains destined to convoy from Delhi to Karachi the key men and stores assigned to the new state. Tara Singh had already installed a wireless set and an operator to pass information about the trains' departures and their route to the Sikh armed bands designated to attack them.

The responsibility for the second action, Savage said, had been assigned to the RSSS whose Hindu members, unlike the Sikhs, could easily pass themselves off as Moslems. The organization was in the process of infiltrating an unidentified number of their most fanatical supporters into the city of Karachi. Each had been given a British Army Mills hand-grenade. None of them was aware of the others' existence so that the arrest of one man would not compromise the plan.

On 14 August, those men were to station themselves along the route which would carry Mohammed Ali Jinnah in triumphant procession through the streets of Karachi from Pakistan's Constituent Assembly to the official residence of the new Governor-General. As a young Serbian had plunged Europe into the horror of World War I, so one of those zealots was to assassinate the founder of Pakistan at the height of his glory by hurling a grenade into his open carriage. The furore provoked by that grisly murder, the RSSS hoped, would launch the entire sub-continent into a savage civil war from which the numerically superior Hindus were bound to emerge as undisputed rulers.

The face of the man they wanted to murder whitened at Savage's words. Beside him, Liaqat Ali Khan excitedly demanded that Mountbatten arrest the entire Sikh leadership. Stunned, the Viceroy wondered what to do. Rounding up the Sikh chieftains, he feared, might well start the civil war the RSSS wanted.

Turning to the young CID officer, he said: 'Suppose I ask the governor to arrest the Sikh leaders?' Listening to his proposal, Savage thought, 'I'll be bloody scared if you do.' They were, he knew, isolated in Amritsar's Golden Temple. No Sikh or Hindu police would accept an order to go in after them and to send in Moslem police was unthinkable.

'Sir,' he replied, 'I am sorry to have to say there are not enough reliable police left in the Punjab to accomplish an action of that sort. I hate to say it, but I can see no way to carry out such an order.'

Mountbatten pondered a moment. Then he announced he would ask for a joint recommendation on what to do from the Punjab's Governor, Sir Evan Jenkins, and the two men designated to govern its Indian and Pakistan halves after 15 August. Liaqat Ali Khan half rose from his chair at Mountbatten's words. 'You want to murder the Quaid-i-Azzam!' he protested.

'If that's really the way you feel about it, I'll go along in the same car and get murdered with him,' Mountbatten replied, 'but I'm not going to throw the leaders of five million Sikhs into jail without the agreement of those governors.'

That night, the security-conscious Savage returned to Lahore, his briefcase stuffed with toilet paper as a decoy for the letter from Mountbatten to Jenkins he carried tucked into his underpants. He found Jenkins at a reception on the lawn of Falleti's Hotel. As the man who knew more about the Punjab than any Westerner alive read Mountbatten's letter, his shoulders sagged in despair.

'Whatever can we do?' sighed Sir Evan Jenkins. 'How can we stop them?'

Five days later, during the night of 11 to 12 August, the Sikhs of Tara Singh successfully executed the first phase of the programme they'd agreed with the RSSS. Two charges of gelignite buried along its right of way destroyed the first Pakistan Special five miles east of the Giddarbaha Railroad Station in the Ferozepore District of the Punjab.

* * *

Sequestered in a green-shuttered, stucco bungalow on the edge of Delhi's viceregal estate, sweltering in the oppressive summer heat, Sir Cyril Radcliffe began to trace out boundary lines on a Royal Engineers' map. The remorseless demand of all concerned for speed had given him no alternative but to perform his vivisection in the solitude of his bungalow. Cut off from any human contact with the great entities he was dividing, he was forced to visualize the impact of his work on areas that seethed with life, with only maps, population tables, and statistics to guide him.

Daily, he was compelled to slice away at an irrigation system embedded into the surface of the Punjab like the veins in a man's hand without being able to see on the ground the effect his line would have. Radcliffe knew water was life in the Punjab and he who controlled the water controlled life. Yet he was unable to survey the meanderings of his line down even one of those vital concrete spillways, sluice gates and reservoirs.

Never would he walk in a rice paddy or study the jute field his pencil was going to mutilate. He would not be able to visit a single one of the hundreds of villages through which his line would run, to contemplate its effect on the helpless peasants it might isolate from their fields, their wells or their roads. Not once would he be able to soften the human tragedies his boundary was certain to produce by following its trace upon the surface of the land he was dividing. Communities would be severed from the lands they tilled, factories from their freight depots, power plants from their grids, all because of the terrible haste India's leadership had imposed on Radcliffe, compelling him to demarcate, on an average 30 miles of frontier every day.

The meagre tools he possessed turned out to be hopelessly inadequate. It proved almost impossible to find an ordnance map large enough to serve as his master map. The details on the maps he did find were often inexact. The Punjab's vital five rivers, he noted, had a curious tendency to stray as much as a dozen miles from the beds assigned them by the Punjab's vaunted engineering services. The population tables which were supposed to be his primary guide were inadequate and constantly distorted by each side to support their conflicting claims.

Bengal proved the simpler task. Radcliffe hesitated for a long time over Calcutta's fate. There was, he thought, much logic in Jinnah's claim to it so there might be a unitary flow of jute from field to mill to port. In the end, however, he felt its Hindu majority population had to overrule economic considerations. Once he had resolved that question, the rest of his work in Bengal was easier. His boundary, however, was 'just a pencil line drawn on a map' with all the heartbreak that implied. Almost nowhere in that tangle of swamps, marshes and low-lying fields could he find the points of reference a boundary-maker seeks, rivers or a line of hills.

The Punjab was infinitely more difficult. Lahore's almost equally balanced populations shrieked their rival claims to the city with which all felt such a deep emotional tie. For the Sikhs, Amritsar with its Golden Temple could only be in India; yet it was wedged between Moslem areas.

Beyond them was the mosaic of communal pockets set haphazardly amongst each other. Either, Radcliffe thought, he followed population as his sole guide, creating a host of unmanageable enclaves to which access could never be assured, or he followed the dictates of geography and a more manageable boundary, and lopped the pockets off with all the tragedy that might imply for those he was condemning to live as minorities inside a hostile majority.

Above all, as the weeks of that terrible summer passed, Radcliffe suffered from the heat, the cruel, ennervating heat. The three rooms of his residence were littered with maps, documents and reports all typed out on thin, Indian rice paper. As he hunched over his desk, sleeves rolled up, those sheets of paper would stick to his sweating forearms, leaving on their damp skin when he had peeled them off a peculiar stigmata: the smudged, grey imprint of a few typed words, each representing, perhaps, the hopes, the desperate pleas of thousands of human beings.

The slowly revolving wooden blades of a fan suspended from the

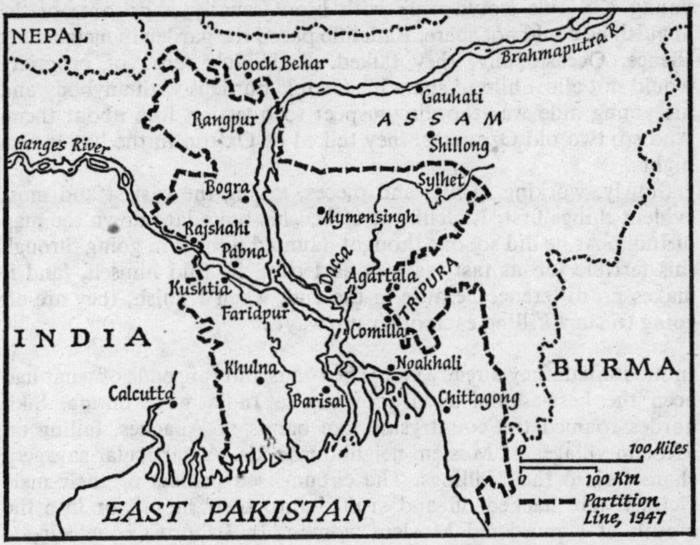

ceiling provided the only air in the bungalow. Occasionally, charged by some mysterious surge of electricity, it went berserk, filling the bungalow with great, gusty bursts of air. Like leaves in an autumn wind, dozens of Radcliffe's papers would go swirling around the room, the villages of the ill-fated Punjab driven before the storm.

From a very early hour, Radcliffe knew that no matter what he did, there would be terrible bloodshed and slaughter when his report was published. Almost every day as he laboured over his boundary, he received reports from Punjabi villages, sometimes the very communities whose fate he was deciding, in which people who had lived side by side for generations had suddenly turned on each other in a frenzy of killing.

He saw virtually no one. Every time he tried to venture out for a cocktail party or dinner, Radcliffe found himself surrounded by people pressing their claims upon him. His only recreation was walking. In the afternoon, he would stroll along the ridge on which the British had gathered their forces in 1857 to crush the mutineers in Delhi.

At midnight, weary with fatigue, he would walk in the stifling heat among the groves of eucalyptus trees in his garden. Occasionally, his young ICS aide would walk with him. Usually, a prisoner of the anguish he could not share, Radcliffe paced the garden in melancholy silence. Occasionally, they talked. Radcliffe's sense of propriety would not allow him to share his terrible burdens with anybody and his young aide was too circumspect to question him about them. And so, two old Oxonians, they talked of Oxford in the hot Indian night.

Slowly, working in bits and pieces, taking the easiest and most evident things first, Radcliffe stretched his boundary down the map of India. As he did so, one thought haunted him: 'I'm going through this terrible job as fast, as well as I can,' he told himself, 'and it makes no difference because in the end, when I finish, they are all going to start killing each other anyway!'

In the Punjab they already had. The roads and railroads of what had been the best-administered province in India were unsafe. Sikh hordes roamed the countryside like bands of Apaches, falling on Moslem villages or Moslem neighbourhoods. A particular savagery characterized their killings. The circumsised penises of their male victims were hacked off and stuffed into their mouth or into the mouth of a murdered Moslem woman. In Lahore one evening a bicyclist raced out of an alleyway past the crowded coffee shop where the city's most renowned Moslem criminal held court. He hurled an enormous, bell-bottomed brass pot used to carry milk on to its packed terrace. The pot went clanging through the coffee house, sending its occupants diving for cover. When it failed to explode, a waiter opened it. The pot contained a gift to the Moslem criminal from his Sikh rivals in crime in Amritsar. Stuffed inside instantly recognizable, was a supreme provocation: scores of circumcised penises.

In Lahore murder and arson were so senseless, so chaotic in nature, that to one British police officer it seemed 'like a city committing suicide'. The Central Post Office was flooded with thousands of postcards addressed to Hindus and Sikhs. They depicted men and women being raped and slaughtered. On the back was the message: 'This is what has been happening to our Sikh and Hindu brothers and sisters at the hands of the Moslems when they take over. Flee before those savages do this to you.' They were part of a campaign of psychological warfare being conducted by the Moslem League to create panic among Sikhs and Hindus.

Moslem residents of Lahore's good residential neighbourhoods, once the most tolerant in India, had begun to paint green Islamic crescents on their gateposts to protect their villas from Moslem mobs. On Lawrence Road, a Parsee businessman, member of a small religious sect unaffected by the communal frenzy, painted a message on his gatepost. Its words were an epitaph for Lahore's lost dream of brotherhood. 'Moslems, Sikhs and Hindus are all brothers,' it read, 'but, O my Brothers, this house belongs to a Parsee.'

As the police, largely Moslem in Lahore as elsewhere in the Punjab, began to collapse, the responsibility of stemming the tide of violence fell increasingly on a handful of British officers. 'You grew calluses on your emotions,' remarked Patrick Farmer, a policeman who had previously fired a weapon only once in fifteen years of Punjab service. 'You learned to use your tommy-gun first and ask questions later.'

Bill Rich, another British police officer, remembered riding through Lahore's darkened bazaars, the horizon rosy from the glow of distant fires, while Moslems on the rooftops above called softly to each other in the darkness. Like jackals' cries their whispered warnings flitted through the night: 'Beware, beware, beware.'

On an arms search in a wretched *mohalla*, an Old City slum, the officer who'd warned of the plot to kill Jinnah, Gerald Savage, banged open the flimsy door of a hut. Below him in a squalid, unlit room, he could see an old man dying of smallpox stretched out on a *charpoi*, his body withered, his face a mass of pus and sores. A terrible smell like a musty rag pervaded the room. Sickened by that unexpected glimpse of India's other, timeless miseries, Savage groaned and closed the door.

Devoted to India, proud of their service, imbued with a paternalistic belief in their unique capacities to police the Punjab, these men were embittered by the violence sweeping their province. They blamed their superiors, the Sikhs and the Moslem League, but above all, they blamed the proud admiral in Viceroy's House and what was, to their eyes, his damnable haste in bringing British rule in India to an end.

Even nature seemed determined to thwart them in their last hours in the Punjab, failing to provide the succour that might have saved them. Day after day, their despairing eyes scanned the sky looking for the clouds of a monsoon that refused to come. The monsoon with its lashing sheets of rain could have quelled the fires ravaging the Punjab cities, its cool air could have ended the maddening heat driving men to violent rage. It was, the police had always said, the most effective riot control weapon in India, but it was the one weapon that was not theirs to command.

In Amritsar, the situation was even worse. Murder was as routine an occurrence in its bazaars and alleyways as public defecation. The city's Hindus devised the cruel tactic of walking up to an unsuspecting Moslem and splashing his face with a vial of nitric or sulphuric acid. Arsonists were in action everywhere.

The British Army was finally called in and a 48-hour curfew proclaimed. Even the respite these measures brought was temporary. One day, after a particularly savage outburst of arson had swept the city, its despairing Superintendent of Police, Rule Dean, employed as a last resort a tactic not to be found in his riot-control manual. He ordered his police band to the central square. There, in the heart of that city dissolving in flames, struggling to force the sound of their music over the crackle of a dozen major fires, they gave a concert of Gilbert and Sullivan, as though somehow the kindly strains of *HMS Pinafore* might restore reason to a city going mad.

To keep order in the Punjab after 15 August, Mountbatten had decided to set up a special force of 55,000 men. Its members would be culled from units of the Indian Army like the Gurkhas, whose discipline or racial origins made them relatively immune to communal passions. Called the Punjab Boundary Force, the unit was placed under a Briton, Maj.-Gen. T. W. 'Pete' Rees, whose brilliant handling of his 19th Indian Division in Burma had impressed the Viceroy. The force represented double the number of men the province's governor had estimated would be required to maintain order in the Punjab in the event of partition. When the storm broke, however, it would be swept aside like coastal huts splintered by an unrolling tidal wave.

The blunt fact was no one, Nehru, Jinnah, the Punjab's knowledgeable governor, the Viceroy himself, foresaw the magnitude of the disaster. Their failure to do so would baffle historians and focus a wave of criticism on India's last Viceroy.

Tolerant, unbigoted themselves, Nehru and Jinnah each made the grave error of under-estimating the degree to which communal passions they did not share could inflame the masses of their subcontinent. Each man genuinely believed partition would cool, not provoke violence. They assumed that their people would react to events with the same reasonableness as they would. They were both grievously wrong. Swept up in the euphoria of their coming independence, however, they took their desires for reality and communicated them to the relative newcomer in their midst, the Viceroy.

Their failure to foresee events would have been mitigated had any of the vaunted administrative or intelligence services with which the

British had governed India for a century been able to predict their course. None of them did. As a result, India, apprehensive but not genuinely alarmed, headed for disaster.

Ironically, the one Indian leader who foresaw the awful dimensions of the tragedy ahead was the man who had tried so hard to prevent partition. Gandhi had so immersed himself in the lives of India's masses, sharing their sorrow and sufferings, their daily existence, that he had a unique ability to perceive the mood of his nation. He was, his followers would sometimes say, like the prophet in an ancient Indian legend sitting by a warm fire on a cold winter's night. Suddenly the prophet begins to tremble.

'Look outside,' he tells a disciple, 'somewhere, in the darkness a poor man is freezing.'

The disciple looks and indeed a man is there. Such, they maintained, was Gandhi's intuitive feel for the soul of India.

One day, while the Viceroy was constructing his Punjab Boundary Force, a Moslem woman attacked Gandhi for his opposition to partition. 'If two brothers were living together in the same house and wanted to separate and live in two different houses, would you object?' she asked.

'Ah,' said Gandhi, 'if only we could separate as two brothers. But we will not. It will be an orgy of blood. We shall tear ourselves asunder in the womb of the mother who bears us.'

Mountbatten's real nightmare was not the Punjab. It was Calcutta. Sending troops to Calcutta, he knew, would be futile. If ever trouble broke out in its foetid, pullulating slums and congested bazaars, no number of troops was going to be able to control it. In any event, the creation of his force for the Punjab had taken almost all the Indian Army units regarded as reliable in case of a religious conflict.

'If trouble had ever started in Calcutta,' Mountbatten would one day recall, 'the blood that would have flown there would have made anything that happened in the Punjab look like a bed of roses.'

He would need another tactic to maintain calm in the city. The one he finally chose was a wild gamble, but the dangers in Calcutta were so great, the resources available to meet them so limited, that only a miracle could save the situation anyway. To erect a dyke against the communal frenzy of the world's most miserable city, he planned to employ his dejected sparrow, Mahatma Gandhi.

He put his idea to Gandhi in late July. With his Boundary Force, he explained, he could hold the Punjab, but if trouble broke out in

Calcutta, he said, 'we're sunk. I can do nothing. There's a brigade down there, but I don't even propose to reinforce it; if Calcutta goes up in flames, well it just goes up in flames.'

'Yes, my friend,' Gandhi told him, 'this is the fruit of your partition plan.'

It might be, Mountbatten admitted, but neither he nor anyone else had been able to propose an alternative solution. There was, however, something he could do now. Perhaps Gandhi, through the force of his personality and his non-violent ideal, could achieve something in Calcutta which troops could not do. Perhaps his presence could guarantee the peace of Calcutta. He, Gandhi, would be the sum total of the reinforcements the Viceroy would send his beleaguered brigades. Go to Calcutta, Mountbatten urged, 'you'll be my one man boundary force.'

Despite Mountbatten's plea, Gandhi had no intention of going to Calcutta. He had already decided he would spend India's independence day praying, spinning and fasting beside the terrified Hindu minority of Noakhali to whose safety and protection he'd pledged his life on his New Year's Day Pilgrimage of Penitence. Mountbatten's, however, was not to be the only voice urging him to the terror-ridden slums of Calcutta.

The owner of the second voice was the most unlikely political ally of Mohandas Gandhi on the entire Indian sub-continent. Indeed, if one had deliberately set out to find a man who represented the very antithesis of everything the ageing Gandhi had stood for, whose lifestyle was as remote as possible from Gandhi's aesthetic existence, a more ideal figure than Shaheed Suhrawardy could not have been found.

The 47-year-old Suhrawardy was the prototype of the corrupted, venal politician Gandhi meant to condemn by his description of the ministers whom he hoped would rule a new India. His political philosophy was simple: once a man had been elected to office there was never any reason to leave. Suhrawardy had assured his continued presence in power by using public funds to maintain a private army of hoodlums who, quite literally, clubbed his political rivals into silence.

During the 1942 famine that had devastated Bengal, Suhrawardy had intercepted and sold on the black market tons of grain destined for the starving of Calcutta, an operation which had earned him millions of rupees. He dressed in tailor-made silk suits and two-tone alligator shoes. His jet black hair, dressed each morning by his personal barber, sparkled with brilliantine. Where Gandhi had spent the past four decades of his life trying to uproot the last vestiges of sexual desire, Suhrawardy had given his free run, setting himself, it seemed, the prodigious task of bedding every cabaret dancer and high-class whore in Calcutta. The fizzing glass in Gandhi's hand invariably contained water with a dash of bicarbonate of soda. Suhrawardy's usually held champagne. While the Mahatma had been nourishing himself on soya mash and curds, Suhrawardy's diet had run to filet mignon, exotic curries and pastries, leaving him enveloped by swelling rings of fat that sloped from his breasts to his groin.

Worst of all, his hands were covered with blood. By declaring a public holiday and letting his Moslem League followers know the attention of his police would be elsewhere, Suhrawardy had set the stage for the killings which had ravaged Calcutta on Jinnah's Direct Action Day in August 1946. It was fear that the Hindus of Calcutta were now preparing to wreak their vengeance for those killings, that drove Suhrawardy to call for Gandhi's help.

Rushing to the Mahatma's Sodepur Ashram, he caught him on the eve of his departure for Noakhali. He begged Gandhi to stay in Calcutta. Only he, he said, could save Calcutta's Moslems and damp the firestorm of hate threatening the city.

'After all,' he pleaded, 'the Moslems have as much a claim on you as the Hindus. You have always said you were as much of us as of the Hindus.'

One of Gandhi's unique faculties had always been discerning the best in a foe, then subtly working on it, appealing to it. He sensed a genuine concern in Suhrawardy's heart for the fate of his Moslem followers.

If he agreed to stay in Calcutta, Gandhi said, it would be on two conditions. First, Suhrawardy would have to extract from the Moslems of Noakhali a solemn pledge of the safety of the Hindus in their midst. If a single Hindu was killed, Gandhi made clear, he would have no choice but to fast to death. In typical Gandhian fashion he was thrusting on Suhrawardy the terrible moral responsibility for his own life.

When Suhrawardy brought him the pledge he wanted, Gandhi set out the second part of his bargain. He proposed the most incongruous alliance imaginable. He was prepared to stay, he said, provided Suhrawardy came to live with him day and night, side by side, unarmed and unprotected in the heart of a sordid slum in Calcutta. There, the oddest couple on the sub-continent, they would together offer their lives as the gage of the city's peace.

'I have got stuck here,' Gandhi wrote to Delhi after Suhrawardy accepted his idea, 'and am now going to undertake a grave risk. . . . The future will reveal itself. Keep close watch.'

* * *

Like the peeling leaves of an artichoke, the last pages of Mountbatten's famous calendar came flicking off. To the overworked Viceroy and his staff, those last days of British rule in India appeared 'the most hectic of any', and each disappearing page of the calendar seemed to carry its problem. The referendum in the North-west Frontier Province which gave the territory to Pakistan had to be organized, as did a second referendum in Syhllet near the great tea plantations of Assam. There were all the festivities marking independence to be arranged. The Congress leaders insisted 'there should be plenty of pomp' to mark the occasion in the old tradition of the Raj. Their grim, grey Socialism could come later.

Congress ordered slaughter houses throughout India to be closed on 15 August. Free cinema shows were to be offered in all the nations' theatres and in Delhi every school-child would receive a sweet and an independence medal. There were problems. In Lahore, a government announcement declared that 'in view of the disturbed situation, an active and colourful programme has been ruled out'. The leadership of the right-wing Hindu Mahasabha, bitter opponents of India's partition, told their followers, 'it is impossible to rejoice and participate in the celebrations on 15 August.' They urged their members instead to rededicate themselves to the forceful reunification of their 'mutilated Motherland'.

A wrangle over protocol temporarily brought plans for Pakistan's independence celebrations to a halt. The proud Jinnah wanted precedence over the Viceroy despite the fact that, technically, his dominion would not become independent until midnight. He did not get it.

There were other disappointments in store for the Moslem leader. One of the horses trained to pull the semi-state carriage he'd inherited by the flip of a coin went lame and the Viceroy had to offer him an open Rolls for his first official drive through the streets of Karachi. Jinnah drew up himself the schedule of ceremonies he wanted to mark Pakistan's birth. They had been scheduled to open with a formal state luncheon at his residence on Thursday, 13 August until, after some embarrassed discussion off stage, one of his aides delicately reminded the man who was about to become the head of the world's most important Islamic nation that Thursday, 13 August fell in the last week of the holy month of Ramadan when faithful Moslems around the world were expected to fast from sunrise to sunset.

While the Viceroy and the leaders of the two new dominions attended to those myriad details, three and a half centuries of British colonization of India was tottering to a close with the rattle of ice in a thousand glasses, the melancholy mutter of gin-inspired sentiments and the shrill, empty pledges of cocktail-party farewells. All across the sub-continent, a crushing round of parties, at homes, teas, dinners, farewell receptions, marked the passing of an era.

Most of the British in India, of course, those concerned in the commerce which had brought their forebears to her shores in the first place, were staying on. For 60,000 others, however, soldiers, ICS officers, police inspectors, railroad engineers, foresters, communications clerks, it was time to go back to that island they'd always referred to as 'out home'. For some, the transition would be painfully abrupt, an almost overnight move from a superb governor's mansion manned by scores of servants to premature retirement in a country cottage on a pension soon to be ravaged by inflation. There were few who would not miss the good life, the clubs and the polo, the servants and the hunting in the spartan climate of the Socialist Britain to which they were returning. For years it had been a standard joke among the British on the sub-continent that the best view of India was from the stern of a P & O steamer homeward bound from Bombay. Many of them in the coming weeks, however, would remember that sight as the saddest vision upon which his eyes ever rested.

In hundreds of bungalows the lace doilies, the bridal silverware, the tiger skins and the stories that went with them, the oils of moustachioed uncles lost in the 9th Bengal Lancers or Skinner's Horse, the pugree helmets, the depressing dark and solemn furniture shipped out from London 40 years before, was packed up for the trip back.

A people whose great fault in India, Winston Churchill would remark, had been their aloofness, departed in a burst of uncharacteristic conviviality. As though implicitly recognizing the new order which would follow their departure, saris, *sherwani* tunics and the folds of cotton *khadi* mixed with the business suits and dresses of the British in clubs and homes across India where they had rarely been seen before. An extraordinary air of friendliness infused those gatherings. It would be unique: a colonizing people were leaving those they had colonized in a burst of goodwill and friendship.

The bazaar of Old Delhi, Chandni Chowk, swarmed with departing

British civil servants bartering Victrolas, a refrigerator, or even a car for Persian carpets, elephant tusks, ivory, gold and silver pieces, even on occasion, the stuffed skins of the animals they'd never been able to hunt in the jungles of the sub-continent.

There were the sad legacies left behind, the monuments, the statues, those lonely cemeteries where almost 2 million Englishmen lay in Oscar Wilde's 'wandering graves' by 'Delhi's Walls' and 'Afghan lands and many where the Ganges falls through seven mouths of shifting sand'.

The foreign fields in which they lay would not be forever England, but at least their custody would remain a British preoccupation. Because 'it was unthinkable we should leave our British dead in foreign hands', the departing Raj had provided for their future administration by Britain's High Commission in India. In England, the Archbishop of Canterbury began a collection for a fund to provide for their upkeep.*

A decision was made to move the famous Well of Cawnpore into which Nana Sahib's rebels had thrown the butchered remnants of 950 men, women and children at the height of the Mutiny to the cemetery of the city's All Souls Church. Its inscription: 'Sacred to the perpetual memory of a great company of Christian people, chiefly women and children who, at this spot, were cruelly massacred by rebels of Nana Dhoomdo Pant of Bitar and cast, the dead and the dying, into the well below' – was covered on 15 August so as not to offend Indian sensibilities.

The departure was characterized by events almost touchingly British in nature. Unwilling to condemn their tough little polo ponies to finish their lives between the slots of a tonga cart, many an army officer chose to put his mounts down with his service revolver. The hundred hounds in the pack of the hunt of the Staff College at Quetta were put down on the orders of the College's last Commandant, Col. George Noel Smyth, because he was unable to find them suitable homes. The task of killing those 'delightful companions with whom we had shared so many hours of sport' was, the Colonel noted, 'one of the most painful in his career.' Even the Viceroy's Staff devoted part of one of its meetings, despite the appalling demands on its time, to debating what should be the proper future of the Indian Kennel Club in a partitioned India.

* The effort was shortlived and the harvest it produced meagre. Few sites in India a quarter of a century later are as forlorn and desolate as those British cemeteries going slowly wild for lack of maintenance funds. Screeching monkeys chase lizards across the grey cement slab over Brig. John Nicholson who led the post-mutiny assault on Delhi, and from Madras to Peshawar, the weeds and wild grass now obscure the fading inscriptions on the tombs the British left behind.

Mountbatten issued strict orders that everything was to be left behind, all the stern oil portraits of Clive and Hastings and Wellesley, all the sturdy statues of his great-grandmother Victoria, all the seals, the silverware, the banners, the uniforms, the diverse paraphernalia of the Raj were to be left to India and Pakistan for whatever use they wanted to make of them.

Britain, his Chief of Staff Lord Ismay noted, wanted India 'to look back upon our association of the past two hundred years with pride. It is true,' he admitted, 'they may not want those reminders, but it is up to them to say so.'

Despite the Viceroy's orders, not all the treasures of British rule would be left behind. On occasion, British officers in the Indian Army walked off with pieces of their regimental silver. In Bombay a pair of assistant inspectors of customs were summoned to the office of their departing superior, Victor Matthews.

'We may be liquidating the empire,' Matthews growled, 'but we're not turning this treasure over to Indian hands.' He pointed to a large metal locker behind his desk to which he had the only key.

John Ward Orr, one of his two subordinates, timidly opened the box, wondering if it would contain some priceless Hindu sculpture, some jewelled Buddha. To his surprise, he saw it was filled with neat piles of books. He picked up one and immediately understood the nature of the treasure. The trunk was a supreme accolade to the bureaucratic mind. In a land whose temple walls were covered by the most erotic sculptures ever fashioned by the fingers of man, it contained a selection of the pornography which, over the course of fifty years, Britain's zealous customs officers had adjudged too scabrous to allow on to Indian soil. Orr picked up one, an album called *The 39 Positions of Love*. The prosaic postures it recommended, he noted, bore about as much relation to the elegant and imaginative delights practised by the Hindu deities in the temples of Khajuraho as an overweight dowager's waltzing would to the pirouettes of the prima ballerina of the Ballet Russe.

Matthews solemnly extended the key of the trunk to William Witcher, the senior of his two aides. He could now, he declared, leave India secure in the knowledge that the customs' greatest treasure remained in British custody.*

* The famous trunk remained safe in British keeping for almost another decade. Witcher kept it in his own home where it was found by his wife, the daughter of an Anglican bishop. The good woman almost collapsed when one day, after her husband had inadvertently left it open, she peered inside. Witcher, in turn, passed the trunk on his departure to Orr. When it was Orr's turn to leave in 1955 there were, alas, no survivors left of the high-minded line of British

Bombay, August 1947

As always, he was alone. Shrouded in silence, Mohammed Ali Jinnah walked through the early morning sunlight towards a simple stone grave in a corner of Bombay's Moslem cemetery. There, he performed a gesture which, in the days to come, millions of other Moslems would perform because of what he had wrought. Before setting off to his promised land of Pakistan, Jinnah placed a last bouquet on the tomb he was leaving behind forever in India.

Jinnah was a remarkable man, but probably nothing in his life had been more remarkable or more seemingly out of character than the deep and passionate love which had linked the austere Moslem leader to the woman beneath that tombstone. Their love and marriage had defied almost every accepted canon of the Indian society of their day. Indeed, the woman should not even have been there in an Islamic cemetery. The wife of India's Moslem Messiah had not been born into the faith of Mohammed. Ruttenbhai Jinnah had been born a Parsee, the descendants of the Zoroastrian fire worshippers of ancient Persia who left the corpses of their dead on watchtowers to be consumed by the vultures.

Jinnah had been 41, seemingly a confirmed bachelor,* when he fell madly in love with Ruttie, the 17-year-old daughter of one of his close friends, during a vacation at the Mount Everest Hotel in Darjeeling. Ruttie had been equally mesmerized by Jinnah. Her furious father had obtained a court order forbidding his ex-friend to see his daughter, but on her eighteenth birthday, with only the sari she was wearing and a pet dog under each arm, a defiant Ruttie stalked out of her millionaire father's mansion and went off to marry Jinnah.

Their marriage lasted ten years. Ruttie Jinnah grew into a spec-

---

customs officers who'd laboured so hard to prevent Indian minds from being exposed to the scurrilous influence of such material. After first selecting two volumes, *Le Guide des Caresses* and *Les Nuits du Harem*, from the trunk for the improvement of his French, Orr decided to turn it over, at last, to Indian hands. Noting it was perhaps the last British treasure thus to pass into Indian possession, he selected as its new custodians a group of young men whose healthy appetites might make them reasonably immune to the trunk's message, the members of the Bombay Rugby Club. Orr himself returned to England. Shortly after his arrival he received in the mail an official document informing him his colleagues in the British Customs were detaining his luggage at Southampton – for the illegal possession of pornographic material.

* Jinnah had in fact, been married previously to a child bride he'd never seen, picked out for him by his family before his departure to London for his studies. She had, according to Moslem custom, been represented at their wedding by a male relative and died of illness before his return from England.

tacularly beautiful woman, a woman of legendary attractiveness in a city known around the world for its beautiful women. She loved to flaunt her lean figure in diaphanous saris and tightly cut dresses that shocked staid Bombay society. She was both a gay, vivacious socialite and an ardent and quick-tongued Indian nationalist.*

Inevitably, the differences in their ages and temperaments produced their strains. Ruttie's flamboyance and outspokenness often embarrassed Jinnah and inhibited his political career. For all his passionate love for her, the unbending Jinnah found it difficult to communicate with his mercurial, blithe-spirited wife. Jinnah's dream collapsed in 1928 when the beautiful wife he'd loved but failed to understand, walked out on him. A year later, in February 1929, she died of an overdose of the morphine which she had been taking to ease the pain of chronic colitis. Jinnah, already hurt by the public humiliation of her departure, was grief-stricken. As he threw the first fistful of dirt into the grave on which he now placed his bouquet, he had wept like a child. It was the last time anyone had ever seen a public display of emotion from the Quaid-e-Azzam. From that moment forward, lonely and embittered, he had consecrated his life to the awakening of India's Moslems.

New Delhi, August 1947

The only thing that remained of the perfect English gentleman was the monocle still clamped imperiously in his right eye. Gone were the immaculate linen suits. Mohammed Ali Jinnah was flying home to Karachi in clothes he had rarely worn since leaving the city half a century before to study law in London: a tight-fitting, knee-length *sherwani*, long coat, ankle-hugging *churidars*, trousers, and slippers.

His newly appointed naval ADC, a young officer named Syed Ahsan who had been, until the previous day, the Viceroy's ADC, followed Jinnah up the steps to the silver DC3 given him by the Viceroy for his historic flight to Karachi. As he reached the top of the steps, he turned back for a last glimpse at the distant skyline of the city in which he had waged his relentless struggle for his Islamic state. 'I suppose,' he murmured, 'this is the last time I'll be looking at Delhi.'

* At a luncheon in New Delhi in 1921, she was seated next to the Viceroy, Lord Reading, who was lamenting the fact that, in the atmosphere engendered by World War I, it was quite difficult for him to visit Germany. But why, asked Ruttie Jinnah, was it so difficult?

'Well,' explained Reading, 'the Germans don't really like us British. I can't go.

'Then,' Ruttie quietly asked, 'how is it that you British came to India?'

The house at 10 Aurangzeb Road in which he had masterminded his fight under an enormous, silver map of India, the frontiers of his impossible dream traced upon it in green, had been sold. Ironically, its new owner was a wealthy Hindu industrialist named Seth Dalmia. In a few hours time, he would hoist on to the flagstaff which for years had flown the green and white banner of the Moslem League the banner symbolizing the house's new function as headquarters of the Anti-Cow Slaughter League, 'Sacred Flag of the Cow'.

Exhausted by the effort of climbing the few steps to the plane, Jinnah, his ADC Syed Ahsan noted, 'practically collapsed' into his seat gasping for breath. He sat there staring impassively ahead while the plane's British pilot started his engines and taxied down the runway. As the DC3 lifted off the ground, Jinnah murmured to no one in particular: 'That's the end of that.'

He spent the entire flight silently exercising that curious passion of his for newspapers. One by one, he picked papers from a stack in the seat at his left, read them, then neatly refolded them and placed them in a second stack rising in the seat to his right. Not the faintest trace of emotion crossed his face as he read those laudatory accounts of his achievements. Not once during the entire trip did he speak or reveal even the slightest hint of his feelings, the meagrest indication of what this flight meant to him.

As the plane reached Karachi, Jinnah's aide suddenly saw below the aircraft 'the huge desert with its little hills becoming a white lake of people', the white of their robes accentuated by the sun's reflected glare.

Jinnah's excited sister took his hand. 'Jinn, Jinn, look!' she called. Jinnah's eyes flicked coldly to the window. His face remained immobile as he stared for an instant at the extraordinary spectacle of the masses in whose name he had laid claim to Pakistan. 'Yes,' he said, 'a lot of people.'

So exhausted was the Moslem leader by the trip that he seemed barely able to lift himself from his seat when the DC3 rolled to a stop. One of the aides offered him his arm to guide him out of the aircraft. Jinnah spurned it. The Quaid-e-Azzam was not coming home to Karachi on the arm of another man. With another effort of his indomitable will, Jinnah, stiffly erect, walked unaided down the steps and through the shrieking, almost hysterical mob to his waiting car.

All the way to Karachi the sea of people they'd seen from the plane's window spread like a shimmering white blanket along the car's route. From the dense throng, like the shrieking gusts of a desert wind came a constantly repeated chant: '*Pakistan Zindabad.*' Only once did the crowds fall silent. A Hindu neighbourhood, Jinnah observed, 'after all, they have little to be jubilant about.' Later, with the extraordinary impassivity that had marked him over the entire trip, Jinnah rode without comment or expression through the lower middle-class neighbourhood in which he'd been born in a two-storey sandstone house on Christmas Day, 1876.

Only as he walked slowly up the steps to Government House, the sombre mansion that was now his official residence as Pakistan's first Governor-General, did a faint hint of the emotions he must have felt emerge from behind Jinnah's cold façade. Pausing at the top of the stairs to catch his breath, he turned and looked at his new aide. His eyes seemed to glow and for just an instant something vaguely like a smile passed across his face.

'Do you know,' he whispered hoarsely to Syed Ahsan, 'I never expected to see Pakistan in my lifetime.'

* * *

The great moment, the moment for which Louis Mountbatten had been sent to India, was almost at hand. In barely 36 hours, the 3-century-old British experience in India would end. That experience was ending far sooner than anyone, even the last Viceroy himself, had foreseen when his York had flown out of the morning mists of Northolt Airport five months before.

Now, as the end approached, Mountbatten's actions were dominated by one concern. He wanted the Raj to go out in a final burst of glory, its recessional permeated with an air of goodwill and understanding so profound that it might create an atmosphere in which a new relationship between Britain and the nations sprung from her Indian Empire could emerge.

There was, Mountbatten knew, one thing which could sour in an instant the atmosphere he was so carefully creating. It was the boundary award Sir Cyril Radcliffe was completing in his green-shuttered bungalow. On no account did Mountbatten want the details revealed before the independence ceremonies could be held.

He knew his decision would cause grave complications. India and Pakistan would come into existence without the leaders of either nation being aware of two of the vital components of their nationhood, the number of citizens whose allegiance they commanded and the location of their most important frontiers. Thousands of people in hundreds of villages in the Punjab and Bengal would have to spend 15 August in fear and uncertainty, unable to celebrate because they would not know to which dominion they were going to belong.

There would be areas without proper administrative and police arrangements. Knowing all that, Mountbatten was still determined to keep the boundary decision a secret until after 15 August. Whatever award Radcliffe had decided upon it would, he realized, infuriate both parties. 'Let the Indians have the joy of their Independence Day,' he reasoned, 'they can face the misery of the situation after.

'I decided,' he advised London, 'that somehow we must prevent the leaders from knowing the details of the award until after the 15th of August; all our work and the hope of good Indo-British relations on the day of the Transfer of Power would risk being destroyed if we did not do this.'

Radcliffe's ICS aide delivered the report to Viceroy House in two sealed brown manilla envelopes on the morning of 13 August. On Mountbatten's orders they were locked inside one of his green leather viceregal despatch boxes. The box was set on his desk just before his midday departure for Karachi and the ceremonies marking the birth of Pakistan. For the next 72 hours, while India danced, those envelopes would lie in the Viceroy's despatch case like the evil spirits in Pandora's box, awaiting the turn of a key to deliver their sobering message to a celebrating continent.

In barracks, cantonments, along Military Lines, Hindu, Sikh and Moslem soldiers of the great army being sliced in two along with the sub-continent it had served paid a last homage to one another. In Delhi, the troopers of the Sikh and Dogra squadrons of Probyn's Horse, one of the army's legendary old cavalry regiments, offered a gigantic banquet to the men of the departing Moslem squadron. They savoured together on an open parade ground a final feast of mountains of steaming rice, chicken curry, lamb kabab and the regiment's traditional pudding, rice baked with caramel, cinnamon and almonds. When it was over, Sikh, Moslem and Hindu joined hands and danced a last *bhangra*, a wild, swirling farandole climaxing the most moving evening in their regiment's history.

The Moslem regiments in the areas which would fall to Pakistan offered similar banquets to their Sikh and Hindu comrades leaving for India. In Rawalpindi, the Second Cavalry gave an enormous *bara khana*, a 'good luck' banquet to their former comrades. Every Sikh and Hindu officer spoke, often with tears in their eyes, to bid farewell to the Moslem colonel, Mohammed Idriss, who'd led them through some of the bitterest fighting of World War II.

'Wherever you go,' said Idriss in reply, 'we shall always remain brothers because we spilled our blood together.'

Idriss then cancelled the order he'd received from the headquarters of the future Pakistan Army insisting that all departing Indian troops turn in their weapons before leaving. 'These men are soldiers,' he said, 'they came here with their arms. They will leave with them.'

The next morning those soldiers who'd served under his command owed their lives to his last intervention on their behalf. An hour out of Rawalpindi, the train bearing the Sikhs and Hindus of the 2nd Cavalry was ambushed by Moslem League National Guardsmen. Without their arms they would have been massacred.

The most touching farewell of all took place on the lawns and in the grand ballroom of an institution that once had been one of the most privileged sanctuaries of India's British rulers, the Imperial Delhi Gymkhana Club. Invitation was by engraved cards sent by 'The Officers of the Armed Forces of the Dominion of India' inviting guests to a 'Farewell to Old Comrades Reception in honour of the Officers of the Armed Forces of the Dominion of Pakistan.'

An air of 'overwhelming sadness and unreality' overlaid the evening, one Indian remembered. With their well-trimmed moustaches, their Sam Browne belts, their British uniforms and the rows of decorations they had won risking their lives in the service of India's British rulers, the men mingling under the lantern chains all seemed to have been pressed from the same mould. In the ballroom the flashing rainbow colours of their women's saris sparkled through the dim lights.

Above all, they talked and drank in the bar, telling the old stories one last time; the stories of the mess, of the desert, of the jungles of Burma, of the raids against their own countrymen on the frontier, the ordeals and pleasures of entire careers spent together in that special fraternity of the uniform and shared danger.

None of those men could envisage on that nostalgic evening the tragic role into which they would soon be cast. Instead, it was arms around each other's shoulders and boisterous cries of: 'we'll be down for pig-sticking in September', and 'don't forget the polo in Lahore', and 'we must go after that ibex we missed in Kashmir last year'.

When the time came to end the evening, Brigadier Cariappa, a Hindu of the 1st-7th Rajputs, climbed to the raised dance platform and called for silence. 'We are here to say *au revoir* and only *au revoir*, because we shall meet again in the same spirit of friendship that has always bound us together,' he said. 'We have shared a common destiny so long that our history is inseparable.' He reviewed their experience together, then concluded: 'We have been brothers. We will always remain brothers. And we shall never forget the great years we have lived together.'

When he'd finished, the Hindu brigadier stepped to the rear of the bandstand and picked up a heavy silver trophy draped with a cloth shroud. He offered it to the senior Moslem officer present, Brigadier Aga Raza, as a parting gift from the Hindu officers to their Moslem comrades in arms. Raza plucked the protective cloth from the trophy and held it up to the crowd. Fashioned by a silversmith in Old Delhi, it represented two sepoys, one Hindu, one Moslem, standing side by side, rifles at their shoulders trained upon some common foe.

After Raza on behalf of all the Moslems present had thanked Cariappa for the gift, the orchestra struck up 'Auld Lang Syne'. Instinctively, spontaneously, the officers reached for each other's hands. In seconds, arm in arm, they had formed a circle, Hindu and Moslem scattered indiscriminately along its rim, swaying in unison together, their booming voices filling the damp and sweltering Delhi night with the words of that old Scottish dirge.

A long silence followed its last chorus. Then the Indian officers went to the ballroom door and, glasses in hand, formed an aisle down its steps and out on to the lawn leading towards India's sleeping capital. One by one, their Pakistani comrades walked down the passage formed by their ranks into the night. As they did so, on either side, the Indians raised their glasses in a final, silent toast to their departing comrades.

They would, as they had promised each other, meet again, far sooner and in far more tragic circumstances than any of them might have imagined that night. It was not on the polo fields of Lahore that those former comrades in arms would have their next rendezvous but on a battlefield in Kashmir. There, the rifles represented by the pair of silver sepoys on the trophy Brigadier Raza had carried away from the Gymkhana Club would no longer be trained upon a common foe, but upon each other.

11
While the World Slept

Calcutta, 13 August 1947

Thirty-six hours before the date fixed for India's independence, Mahatma Gandhi left the restful coconut groves of Sodepur Ashram in search of a miracle. His destination was only ten miles from his ashram, but it might have been light years away. It was the closest approximation to hell on the surface of the earth, one of the blighted slums of Rudyard Kipling's *City of Dreadful Night*, Calcutta. There, in the meanness and misery of the world's most violent city, the soft-voiced archangel of non-violence hoped to perform the miracle which was beyond the powers of the Viceroy's armies. Once again the artisan of India's independence prepared to offer his life to his countrymen; this time not to free them from the British, but from the hatred poisoning their hearts.

Even in its legends and the choice of the deities it worshipped, the city waiting at the end of Gandhi's brief ride venerated violence. Its patron saint was Kali, the Hindu Goddess of Destruction, a fiery-tongued ogress garlanded with coils of writhing snakes and human skulls.* Each day, thousands of Calcutta's citizens bent in adoration before her altars. Once infants had been sacrificed in her honour in secret temples near the city and her devotees still practised animal sacrifice, drenching themselves in their victim's blood.

In August 1947, a mirage of prosperity concealed the reality of Calcutta. The lush green sweep of the Maidan, the Georgian mansions and offices of its great trading companies along Chowringhee, were only a surface veneer, a façade as false as a cinema set. Behind them, through awful mile after awful mile, stretched a human sewer packed with the densest concentration of human beings on the face of the earth. It included 400,000 beggars and unemployables, 40,000 lepers. The slums they inhabited were a foetid, stinking horror. Their streets were cluttered lanes lined with open sewers overflowing with their burden of garbage, urine, and excrement, each nourishing its hordes of rats, cockroaches, its buzzing clouds of flies and mos-

* According to Hindu lore, Kali was a suicide and her husband, Shiva, grief-stricken at her death, went on a mad rampage through creation, waving her body from a trident. Vishnu saved the world by hurling a discus at Kali's body shattering it into a thousand fragments. Each spot on earth where one of them fell was sanctified, but the holiest spot of all was Kalighat in Calcutta where the toes of her right foot came to rest.

quitoes. The water flowing from their rare pumps was usually polluted by the corpses decomposing in the Hooghly from which it was drawn. Once a week, down those lanes, the pitiless *zamindars* stalked in search of the rent for each corner in hell.

At the moment when India was about to attain her freedom, 3 million human beings in Calcutta lived in a state of chronic undernourishment, existing on a daily caloric intake inferior to that given the inmates of Hitler's death camps.

Those slums were breeding grounds for violence in all its forms. Men murdered in Calcutta for a mouthful of rice. With the savage killings of Direct Action Day in August 1946, that violence had taken on a new dimension, fed by the solid religious and racial fanaticism animating its Hindu and Moslem communities. Since then, not a single day had passed without its toll of communal murder. Organized into political gangs of *goondas* – hoodlums, armed with clubs, knives, pistols, vicious steel prongs, called tiger's claws, that could pluck out a man's eyeballs – the two communities faced each other with reciprocal fear and mistrust. While India waited to celebrate her long-sought freedom, they, the wretched of Calcutta's slums, stood poised to compound their infinite miseries in a frenzy of communal slaughter and destruction.

Shortly after three o'clock on the afternoon of 13 August, the man who wanted somehow to stop them arrived in their midst in a dilapidated pre-war Chevrolet. Cautiously, Gandhi's car crept down Beliaghata Road past a clump of tin-roofed shacks towards a low stone wall ringing number 151. There, rising over an open patch of dirt the monsoon rains had churned into a muddy slush, was a crumbling ruin, a decaying vision from a Tennessee Williams stage set.

Once the broad terraces of Hydari House with their Doric pillars and carved balustrades had represented the Palladian dream, transposed into the tropics, of some English merchant prince. Its current owner, a wealthy Moslem, had long ago abandoned it to the rats and cockroaches running rampant in its dingy corridors. Swept out, the dark dry coils of human excrement littering its grounds, blanketed with bleaching powder, the toilet, a rarity in Calcutta which had recommended the building to the Mahatma, repaired, was ready to receive Gandhi and his followers. There amidst the stench, the filth and the mud, he had now to begin his quest for a miracle.

The people upon whom he would have to work it were already waiting for him, an excited crowd in vests and *dhotis*. They were all Hindus and many of them had seen relatives butchered, wives and daughters raped by the Moslem mobs of Direct Action Day. At the approach of his car, they began to shriek Gandhi's name. For the first time in three decades, however, Indians were not cheering Mohandas Gandhi's name. They were cursing it.

Faces contorted with rage and hate, they shouted, 'Go save the Hindus in Noakhali,' 'Save Hindus, not Moslems,' and 'Traitor to the Hindus.' Then, as Gandhi's car stopped, they produced their welcome for the man half the world believed a saint. They showered the car with stones and bottles.

Slowly, one of its doors opened. The familiar figure emerged. Glasses slipping down his nose, one hand clutching his shawl, the other raised in a gesture of peace, the frail 77-year-old man walked alone into the shower of stones.

'You wish to do me ill,' Gandhi called, 'and so I am coming to you.'

At that sight, at his words, the demonstrators froze. Drawing near, the squeaky voice that had pleaded with Kings and Viceroys for India pleaded with them for reason. 'I have come here,' he said, 'to serve Hindus and Moslems alike. I am going to place myself under your protection. You are welcome to turn against me if you wish,' he continued. 'I have nearly reached the end of life's journey. I have not much further to go. But if you again go mad, I will not be a living witness to it.'

He was saving the Hindus of Noakhali by his presence on Beliaghata Road, Gandhi explained. The Moslem leaders who bore the guilt for the slaughter of so many Hindus in Noakhali had given him their word: not a single Hindu would be harmed there on 15 August. They knew he would undertake a fast unto death if they failed their promise.

In response to that pledge, he had come to Calcutta. As he had thrust on the Moslem leaders of Noakhali the moral responsibility for the safety of the Hindus in their midst, so he was now going to try to persuade the Hindus of Calcutta, like the members of the angry crowd before him, to become protectors of the city's Moslems. Implicit in his effort was the idea that, if his plea to Calcutta's Hindus failed and they went on a rampage of killing, it would be at the expense of his life. For, just as he would fast to death if the Moslems broke their word in Noakhali, so he was ready to fast to death if the Hindus ignored his message in Calcutta.

That was the essence of his non-violent strategy: a contract between the warring parties, with his life as the ultimate guarantee of its fulfilment.

'How can I, who am a Hindu by birth, a Hindu by deed, a Hindu of Hindus in my way of living, be an enemy of the Hindus?' he asked his angry countrymen.

Gandhi's reasoning, the stark simplicity of his approach, puzzled and disturbed the crowd. Promising to talk further with a delegation from their midst, he and his followers began to take over their rotting mansion.

Their respite was brief. The arrival of Suhrawardy, focus of all the mob's hatred, produced a new explosion. Howling and jeering the crowd circled the house. A stone crashed through one of its few windows, sending its shattered shards flying across the room where Gandhi sat. A barrage followed, smashing the rest of the windows and beating like gigantic hailstones against the decaying exterior of the house.

Outwardly imperturbable, Gandhi, his shoulders hunched, his head bowed, squatted cross-legged on the floor in the centre of the house, patiently answering his correspondence in longhand. Yet a terrible turning point in his life had been reached. On this sweltering August afternoon, only hours before the end of India's long march to freedom, a mob of his countrymen had turned on him for the first time since that January day in 1915 when he'd walked ashore under the arch of the Gateway of India. For Gandhi, for India, for the world, the crash of the stones against the walls of Hydari House, the hate-inflamed ravings of the mob, were the first mutterings of the chorus of a Greek tragedy.

Karachi, 13 August 1947

'Sir, the plot is on.'

Louis Mountbatten stiffened perceptibly at those words. A glimmer of apprehension flicked across his otherwise impassive features. Mountbatten followed the man who'd uttered them towards a spot under the plane's wings where no one could overhear their words.

All their intelligence reports, the CID officer said, confirmed the details of the briefing Mountbatten had been given in Delhi. At least one and probably several bombs would, they believed, be thrown at the open car scheduled to carry him and Jinnah through Karachi's streets the following morning, Thursday 14 August. Despite intensive efforts, they'd failed to apprehend any of the Hindu fanatics whom the RSSS had infiltrated into the city to carry out the assassination.

To Mountbatten's annoyance, his wife had slipped up behind them. She overheard the CID officer's last phrases. 'I'm going to drive with you,' she insisted.

'You damn well are not,' her husband replied. 'There's no reason for both of us to be blown to smithereens.'

Ignoring their exchange, the CID officer continued. 'Jinnah insists on riding in an open car,' he said. 'You'll be going very slowly. I'm afraid our means of protecting you are rather limited.' There was only one way, in the CID's judgment, of averting a catastrophe.

'Sir,' he begged, 'you must get Jinnah to cancel the procession.'

Eighteen hours after an angry mob had stoned the greatest Indian of the century, at 9.00 a.m., Thursday 14 August, 1800 miles from Beliaghata Road, Gandhi's principal political rival prepared to savour the apotheosis of his long struggle.

Mohammed Ali Jinnah had succeeded where the sorrowing leader in the ruins of Hydari House had failed. Despite Gandhi, despite the dictates of logic and reason, despite, above all, the fatal disease locked in his lungs, Jinnah had divided India. In a few moments an austere assembly hall in Karachi would witness the birth of the most populous Moslem nation in the world. Ranged in the shell-shaped hall's circling rows of seats were the representatives of the 45 million people Jinnah had led on their *Hegira* to nationhood.

They were a colourful assembly: stolid Punjabis in grey astrakhan caps and tightly buttoned *sherwanis*, white versions of a priest's cassock; glowering Pathans; Wazirs, Mahsuds, Afridis, beige and gold-flecked turbans twisted over their heads, moustaches scarring their wind-burned faces; short, dark Bengalis, representatives of a province Jinnah had never visited and whose people he mistrusted; tribal leaders from Baluchistan; women from the Indus Valley, their heads shrouded in satin *burqas*; women of the Punjab in gold-speckled *shalwars*, tunics, over bell-bottomed *culottes*.

Beside Jinnah, sat the Viceroy from whose reluctant hands the Moslem leader had prised his state. Mountbatten glowed in his white naval uniform and the decorations he so loved to wear, a splendidly fitting figure for the occasion, the first of the ceremonies which, in the course of the next 36 hours, would formally terminate Britain's overlordship of the sub-continent.

A taut smile creasing his composed features, Mountbatten rose to deliver the King's good wishes to his newest dominion. Then Mountbatten, to celebrate an occasion he had hoped would never take place, declared: 'The birth of Pakistan is an event in history. History seems sometimes to move with the infinite slowness of a glacier, and sometimes to rush forward in a torrent. Just now, in this part of the world, our united efforts have melted the ice and moved some impediments from the stream and we are carried in the full flood. There is not time to look back. There is only time to look forward.'

With those words, the Viceroy looked sideways towards Jinnah. His disdainful face, his parchment-dry skin, emitted even at this supreme instant no more trace of emotion than the features of a Pharaonic death mask.

'I would like to express my tribute to Mr Jinnah,' he declared. 'Our close personal contact and the mutual trust and understanding that has grown out of it, are, I feel, the best omens for future good relations.'

As he droned through his ritualistic phrases, Mountbatten could not help thinking that he was going to have to risk his life in a few moments because of the obdurate man to whom they were addressed. The Viceroy had had no more success in persuading Jinnah to cancel their threatened procession than he had had in trying to get him to abandon his dream of Pakistan. To cancel the ride or to rush through the streets of Karachi in a closed car would have been, Jinnah felt, an act of cowardice. He would never demean the emergence of the nation for which he'd worked so hard with a gesture like that. Come what may, Mountbatten was going to have to expose himself to an assassin's bomb in an open car, at the side of a man he disliked, to celebrate the birth of a nation to whose creation he had been vehemently opposed.

'The time has come to bid you farewell,' he concluded. 'May Pakistan prosper always . . . and may she continue in friendship with her neighbours and with all the nations of the world.'

Then it was Jinnah's turn. He looked like a pope giving an audience to the faithful with his white *sherwani* buttoned up to the base of his emaciated throat. Britain and the peoples she had colonized were parting as friends, he agreed, 'and I sincerely hope that we shall remain friends.' A 13-century-old Islamic tradition of tolerance for the beliefs of others would, he promised, 'be followed and practised by us.' Pakistan, he declared, 'would not be found wanting in friendly spirit by our neighbours and all the nations of the world.'

Then, almost before they knew it, the speeches were over, the trial at hand. Side by side, the two men, rivals in so many domains, emerged from the great teak doors of the assembly hall. Waiting before them was the black open Rolls-Royce that was to carry them through their ordeal. 'The damn thing looks like a hearse,' Mountbatten thought. For a brief second, he fixed his eyes on his wife. He had given her driver strict orders to stay well behind his car. He was certain she would find a way to thwart them.

Moving towards the waiting car, a series of grisly images forced their way across Mountbatten's mind; a vivid, mental picture screened behind his carefully arranged public façade. They had nothing to do with this procession. They were the ghosts of processions past, stirred by the pages of those genealogical charts which were Mountbatten's passion. On to one of their branches, he had meticulously placed the name of his great-uncle, the Tsar Alexander II, noting by his name, 'deceased 13 February 1881'. Alexander II had been blown into lumps of sodden flesh in Saint Petersburg – by a bomb thrown into his open carriage. Further down that same branch of his family was the name of another uncle, the Grand Duke Serge, killed in 1904 by an anarchist's bomb in an almost identical incident. On still another page, was the entry bearing the name of his cousin Ena who had gone to her wedding to Spain's Alfonso XIII, her satin wedding gown covered with the flesh and blood of the coachman killed by a bomb thrown into her carriage. Grotesque phantoms from his family's past, they seemed now to crowd into his open Rolls-Royce along with the young Viceroy.

His eyes met Jinnah's as the car started. They did not speak. He had never known Jinnah to be anything but tense, Mountbatten thought, but now the tension radiating from his being was almost palpable. A heart-stopping 31-gun viceregal salute followed them down the drive out into Karachi's streets. There, the crowds were waiting, the enormous, happy, exulting crowds, a sea of anonymous faces concealing somewhere, on some street corner, at some turning, at some window ledge or rooftop, the face of the man who wanted to kill them. The three-mile route was lined by troops but their backs were all to the crowd. They would be useless against an assassin's bomb.

To Louis Mountbatten, it would seem in later years as though that 30-minute ride had lasted 24 hours. They moved at a pace barely faster than a quick walk. The crowd lined every foot of the route, six deep on the sidewalks, clinging to lamp-posts and telephone poles, dangling from windows, lining roofs. Blissfully unaware of the drama the men in the Rolls were living, they chanted out their '*Zindabads*', for Pakistan, for Jinnah, for Mountbatten.

Trapped, the two rolled slowly down that tunnel of faces, running a kind of gauntlet from which at any second a hand grenade could come arching towards their car. Forced to respond to the rejoicing, emotionally-charged crowd, they had no choice but to act out a grotesque charade. Mountbatten would never forget having to pump his hand up and down in rhythmic waves, forcing a smile on to his face, while his eyes kept sweeping the crowd, studying those faces, looking for a sullen stare, a pair of frightened eyes, some clue to tell him 'here, this is where it's going to happen'.

It was not the first time he had been in such a situation in India. During the Prince of Wales' tour the CID had uncovered a plot to throw a bomb into the royal car as he rode through the streets of the State of Bharatpur on 8 December 1921. Young Mountbatten had been obliged to masquerade as his cousin by riding at the head of the royal procession in the car usually occupied by the Prince.

The memories of that harrowing experience flashed through his mind now as he watched that sea of faces slide past. 'Which one is it?' he kept thinking. 'Is it that one I'm waving to? Or the one beside him?' There were the silly reflections. He remembered a military secretary to a governor of Bengal who'd caught an assassin's bomb and thrown it back; but then, Mountbatten reminded himself, he'd never been able to catch a cricket ball. He kept thinking of his wife behind him, wondering if she'd succeeded in countermanding his orders. He did not dare interrupt his vigil even for a second to turn around to see. Ceaselessly, his eyes scanned the horizon above the crowd, radar beacons waiting for the first glint of a piece of metal flying towards the car.

As the cortege came into view from the balcony of his hotel on Victoria Road, a young man tightened his grip on the Colt ·45 swelling his coat pocket. While his eyes watched the faces waving from the windows of the building opposite, he slowly flicked off the safety catch of his weapon. When Mountbatten's car neared his balcony, G. D. Savage, the young officer of the Punjab CID who'd delivered word of the plot to Delhi, 'put up a prayer'. He, in fact, had no right to have that weapon. His service with the Punjab police had ended 24 hours earlier; he was on his way home to England.

In their car, Mountbatten and Jinnah continued to mask their apprehension behind their gracious smiles and waves. They were both so preoccupied with the risks they had taken that they had not said a word to each other since getting into the car. The vanity which so many of his critics considered his worst failing, was the Viceroy's greatest comfort as the strain mounted. 'These people like me,' he kept telling himself. 'After all, I have given them their independence.' He could not believe there were men in that crowd willing to kill him. His presence, he sincerely thought, might save Jinnah. 'They just won't kill him,' he insisted to himself, 'when they realize it means killing me at the same time.'

On his balcony, Savage held his breath as the car rolled under his feet. He kept his hand fixed on his weapon until the Rolls had passed beyond the range where he could offer its occupants any protection.

Then, he went into his room and poured himself four fingers of Scotch.

Ahead of the car now, the '*huzzahs*' and '*Zindabads*' gave way to a menacing silence. A Hindu neighbourhood, Mountbatten told himself, this is where it will happen. For five agonizing minutes, the cortege crept through those muted crowds along Elphinstone Street, Karachi's principal commercial thoroughfare. Almost all its shops and markets belonged to Hindus, embittered and frightened by the event their Moslem neighbours were celebrating.

Nothing happened. Suddenly, as welcome as harbour lights to a sea captain after a hurricane, the gates of Government House rose in front of the Rolls. The most harrowing drive of Louis Mountbatten's life was over.

As their car eased to a stop, for the first and only time in their intense, difficult relationship, Jinnah relaxed. His glacial façade disappeared and a warm smile illuminated his features. He clamped his bony hands on the Viceroy's knee and murmured: 'Thank God! I've brought you back alive!'

Mountbatten sat up. 'What bloody cheek!' he thought. '*You* brought *me* back alive?' he asked, incredulous. 'My God, it's *I* who brought *you* back alive!'*

Calcutta, 14 August 1947

As always, he was ready at the appointed hour. Precisely at five o'clock on the afternoon of 14 August, Gandhi's frail silhouette appeared framed in the doorway of Hydari House. Slightly stooped, his hands resting on the shoulders of the two young girls, he called his crutches, he did his quick shuffle through the crowds waiting for him in the house's courtyard.

The ceremony towards which he walked was as rigidly fixed as any of the events in the Mahatma's meticulously ordered days. As Lenin had prepared a revolution in the conspiratorial conversations of the cell, and the Fascists had fashioned theirs in the pompous glitter of their Nuremberg rallies, the regular rendezvous Gandhi had proposed India on the long march to freedom had been, appropriately, a prayer meeting.

* An intensive effort by the authors of the book to discover why the plot in Karachi was not executed revealed only one indirect testimony offered by Pritham Singh, a bicycle repairman in Jullundur. Singh was arrested by the CID in connection with the Sikh's part of the plot, the derailment of the Pakistan trains. The RSSS had indeed, he claimed, infiltrated its men into Karachi, but the leader whose grenade explosion was to be the signal to the others to hurl theirs, lost his courage when the car passed him.

In cities and villages, in London slums and British jails, neglected only on the rarest of occasions, those prayer meetings had been the favoured medium of a genius at human relations for communicating with his followers. He had discoursed at them on the nutritional values of unhusked rice, the evils of the atomic bomb, the importance of regular bowel movements, the sublime beauties of the *Gita*, the benefits of sexual continence, the iniquities of imperialism, the rationale of non-violence. Repeated from mouth to mouth, reported in the press, carried on the radio, those daily messages had been the cement binding his movement, the gospel of Mohandas Gandhi.

Now, in the open yard of his crumbling house in a city of fear and hate, he prepared for the last public prayer meeting he would address in an India under British occupation. All day, Gandhi had received delegations of Hindus to whom he had explained the non-violent contract he proposed for Calcutta, hoping that, with the constantly reiterated outlines of his doctrine, a new spirit might radiate across the city from Hydari House. The presence of almost 10,000 people at his first Calcutta prayer meeting was an indication that he was enjoying at least some success.

'From tomorrow,' he told that crowd, 'we shall be delivered from the bondage of British rule. But from midnight today,' he sadly intoned, 'India will be partitioned too. Tomorrow will be a day of rejoicing, but it will be a day of sorrow as well.'

Independence, he warned his prayer meeting, would throw a heavy burden on them all. 'If Calcutta can return to reason and brotherhood, then, perhaps, all India may be saved.' Otherwise, he asked, 'if the flames of communal strife envelope the whole country, how can our newborn freedom survive?'

The man who had won India that freedom told his audience he would not be among those rejoicing at its arrival. He asked his followers to mark India's Independence Day as he would, 'by fasting and by prayer for the salvation of all India, and by spinning as much as possible,' because it was that beloved wooden wheel that carried the message most likely to save their country from disaster.

For all the '*huzzahs*' and '*Pakistan Zindabads*', that had followed his car as it had rolled through the streets of Karachi, the birth of the nation Jinnah would one day boast he'd won 'with a clerk and a typewriter', was characterized by a puzzling coolness. The ceremonies, *The Times* noted, 'were marked by a surprising lack of popular enthusiasm' and 'a general air of apathy'. It was almost as if some instinctive prescience of the danger attendant on their nation's birth had muffled the enthusiasm of those millions Jinnah had led to their promised land.

Strangely it was in East Bengal, in those areas soon to form East Pakistan – and one day, the battlefields of the Bangladesh war – that the mood was most festive. Khwaja Nazimuddin, East Pakistan's Chief Minister-designate, left Indian soil at noon aboard a tiny steamer festooned with Moslem League banners. For hours, the steamer shunted through the monsoon-swollen waters of the Gangetic Delta *en route* to Nazimuddin's new capital at Dacca.

Every time the little steamer tooted to a stop at a cluster of huts or a ramshackle jetty stretching into the muddy delta, scores of tiny rowing-boats, canoes, and sailing boats poured out from the shore to greet it, their occupants shouting '*Pakistan Zindabad!*'

'Everybody was singing,' noted Nazimuddin's son, 'you could see the happiness in people's eyes.' One indispensable element for the proper celebration of Pakistan's birth, however, was conspicuous by its absence. Not a single Pakistani flag was on display along the steamer's route. Nazimuddin discovered why in Dacca. There were none in all of East Bengal.

In Lahore, centre of a Punjab seething with violence and the terrible uncertainty caused by its still unpublished boundary line, Bill Rich performed his final chores as the city's last British police superintendent. Outside his dingy office, Rich could hear a rhythmic sloshing as a boy threw pails of water on the *kas kas tati*, the bamboo slats screening his windows to keep down the fierce heat. He had done what he could to check Lahore's descent into chaos, he thought sadly. It had not been enough. The lovely capital of the Moghuls was submerged in a tide of fear and hate. He posted a summary of the violence he'd witnessed in the Police Order Book as a record for posterity. Then he called in his Moslem successor.

Rich took out a form used for handing over charge. It was divided into two identical halves. On his half he wrote: 'I have handed over,' and signed his name. His successor wrote 'I have taken over,' on the other and signed. Rich saluted shook hands with the few members of his staff he could find loitering about, and sadly walked away.

Thirty-five miles away in Amritsar, his colleague Rule Dean was going through a similar ceremony late in the afternoon of 14 August. Dean took from his safe the Secret Registry, the list of political informers who'd received just under 1000 rupees a month from the Amritsar police. Their number included a member of the city's Congress Committee and one of the men who prepared the *amrit*, the sugary communion paste of the Sikh's Golden Temple, but Dean had no hesitation in turning the list over to his Sikh successor. 'No gazetted officer of police,' Dean was certain, 'whatever his religion or political belief, would deliberately do down an informer.'

In Karachi, a weary Jinnah spent his afternoon prowling the rooms of the immense home which would become at midnight his official residence. Nothing escaped his enquiring eyes. Checking the house's inventory, he discovered to his consternation the croquet set was missing. He gave his young ADC his first formal order: find the missing mallets and wickets and return them to his residence.

The man who had first articulated the impossible dream of Pakistan spent the day of 14 August alone in his cottage at 3 Humberstone Road, Cambridge. There would never be any triumphant parades through Karachi's streets for Rahmat Ali, no crowds shrieking their gratitude for what he had wrought. His dream belonged to another man now, the man who scorned it when Rahmat Ali had first begged him to become its champion. On the day his great ideal was taking flesh, Rahmat Ali had been drafting a new tract, this one condemning Jinnah for accepting the partition of the Punjab. He was talking to the wind. A gratified people would vote a million dollars to the Lahore memorial that would honour Mohammed Ali Jinnah, but the man whose idea had inspired him would be buried in a numbered grave in a cemetery at Newmarket.

New Delhi, 14 August 1947

They set out at sundown. Like an ungainly crane, a player of the *nagasaram*, the Indian flute, walked alone before their car, guiding it down New Delhi's crowded streets. Every hundred yards the flautist stopped, squatted on the asphalt, and sent an eerie shaft of sound shivering through the dusk. The two holy men in the car behind him stared straight ahead with celestial indifference. They were *sanyasi*, men dwelling in the highest state of exaltation a Brahmin could attain, a state so sublime that, according to Hindu belief, it conferred on those who'd reached it more spiritual blessings in one lifetime than an ordinary man might hope to attain in ten million reincarnations.

With their bare chests and foreheads streaked with ashes, their matted, uncut hair tumbling in black strands to their shoulders, they were pilgrims from an ancient, timeless India. Beside each were the three possessions they were allowed in their life of renunciation: a seven-jointed bamboo stave, a water gourd and an antelope skin.*

* The antelope and tiger are considered by devout Hindus to be particularly clean animals and using their skins as mats is therefore not likely to defile a caste Hindu.

Each time a silhouette in a sari peered in at the windows of their 1937 Ford taxi they averted their gaze. So strict were the rules of their society that not only were they enjoined to renounce all female company; they were not even allowed to look on a woman. Condemned every morning to cover themselves with ashes, symbol of the body's transient nature, they lived on alms, never sitting down while eating the one meal they were allowed each day and drinking regular draughts of *pancha gavia*, the blessed beverage composed of equal parts of the five gifts of the Sacred Cow: milk, curds, *ghee* (clarified butter), urine and dung.

One of the two bore a massive silver platter upon which was folded a swathe of white silk streaked in gold, the *Pitambar*, the Cloth of God. The other carried a five-foot sceptre, a flask of holy water from the Tanjore River, a pouch of sacred ash and a pouch of boiled rice which had been offered at dawn at the feet of Nataraja, the dancing God, in his temple in Madras.

Their procession moved through the streets of the capital until it came to a stop in front of a simple bungalow at 17 York Road. On its doorsteps, those delegates from an India that venerated superstition and the occult had a rendezvous with the prophet of a new India of science and socialism. As once Hindu holy men had conferred upon ancient India's kings their symbols of power, so the *sanyasi* had come to York Road to bestow their antique emblems of authority on the man about to assume the leadership of a modern Indian nation.

They sprinkled Jawaharlal Nehru with holy water, smeared his forehead with sacred ash, laid their sceptre on his arms and draped him in the Cloth of God. To the man who had never ceased to proclaim the horror the word 'religion' inspired in him, their rite was a tiresome manifestation of all he deplored in his nation. Yet he submitted to it with almost cheerful humility. It was as if that proud rationalist had instinctively understood that in the awesome tasks awaiting him no possible source of aid, not even the occult he so scornfully dismissed, was to be totally ignored.

In military cantonments, at official residences, naval stations, government offices; at Fort William in Calcutta where Clive had started it all, Fort Saint George in Madras, Viceregal Lodge in Simla; in Kashmir, the Nagaland, Sikkim and the jungles of Assam, thousands of Union Jacks slid down their flagstaffs for the last time. They were not being formally struck from the Indian skyline on which, for three centuries, they had symbolized Britain's rule of the sub-continent. Mountbatten had made it clear it was his firm policy that the British flag should not be ceremonially hauled down. Nehru had agreed that 'if the lowering of the Union Jack in any way offended British susceptibilities', it should not take place.

And so, as it did every evening, the Union Jack came down those thousands of flagstaffs at sunset, 14 August, to go quiet and unprotesting into Indian history. At sunrise 15 August, its place would be taken by the banner of an independent India.

At the crest of the Khyber Pass, Capt. Kenneth Dance, adjutant of the Khyber Rifles, the only Englishman left along that storied passage, listened as seven tollings of a bell shook the still evening air. A guardroom bell to toll each passing hour had been for decades a tradition on all stations of the Indian Army, few of whose sepoys, before 1939, could afford a watch and fewer still could tell time. As the last toll sounded, Dance climbed to the quarter guard on the roof of the Landi Kotal fort. A bugler with a silver bugle stood poised to sound retreat. Below the two men, dominated by the fort's walls, the road slid its sinuous course down the pass to Jamrud and the portal through which fifty centuries of invaders had spilled on to the plains of India. Every bend along that road, every ochre outcropping, bore its cement plaque to mark a battle of the army to which Dance belonged, or to commemorate the place where some of his countrymen had died fighting for the historic defile.

The bugler stiffened and raised his instrument. Dance felt a twinge of sadness. An era was ending and the Khyber Pass with all its legends was leaving English hands forever as he lowered the flag to the bugler's melancholy call. He unclipped the flag from its halyard and folded it up, determined to bring it 'in safe custody back to England from whence it had come'. Then he presented his regiment with a brass bell he'd bought at a ship chandler's in Bombay to replace the guardroom bell. On it he'd inscribed one phrase: 'Presented to the Khyber Rifles by Capt. Kenneth Dance. 14 August 1947.'

Halfway across the sub-continent in the tower that was the repository of the Raj's most sacred memories, another informal ceremony was taking place. The Tower of the Residency, Lucknow, was the only spot in the British Empire where the Union Jack was never lowered. The tower's shell-scarred walls had been left unchanged since the day in 1857 when the 1000 survivors in the Residency greeted the column that had ended their 87-day seige. The Tower had become the shrine of Imperial India, a symbol of that doughty British ability to hold fast in adversity and, some cynics claimed, of the arrogance that got them there in the first place.

At 10.00 p.m. on the evening of 14 August, the tower's caretaker, warrant officer J. R. Ireland, had hauled that Union Jack down for the last time. Now a team of sappers stood on the floor of the tower where 'over the topmost roof our banner of England flew'. One of them took an axe and swiftly chopped the empty metal flagstaff from its base. Another hacked the base out of its masonry foundations. Then the hole was carefully cemented over. No other nation's flag was ever going to fly from Lucknow's sacred staff.

At 17 York Road, Jawaharlal Nehru had just finished washing the *sanyasi's* ashes from his face and sat down to dinner when his telephone rang. His daughter Indira and his guest Padmaja Naidu, could hear him in his study shouting to make himself heard over a bad line.

Both women gasped when he returned. He slumped ashen in his chair, clasping his head in his hands, unable to speak. Finally, he shook his head and looked at them, his eyes glistening with tears. His caller had been telephoning from Lahore. All the water in the Old City's Hindu and Sikh quarter had been cut. People were going mad from thirst in the terrible summer heat, yet women and children coming out of their *mohallas* to beg a pail of water were being butchered by Moslem mobs. Fires were already raging out of control in half a dozen parts of the city.

Stunned, his voice barely a whisper, he said: 'How am I going to talk tonight? How am I going to pretend there's joy in my heart for India's independence when I know Lahore, our beautiful Lahore is burning?'

The vision haunting Jawaharlal Nehru loomed in all its horror before the eyes of a 20-year-old British captain of the Gurkhas. Riding in his jeep over the hump-backed railway bridge leading into Lahore, Capt. Robert Atkins counted half a dozen great geysers of sparks gushing into the air above the city's darkened skyline. One image sprang to his mind; the blazing skyline of London on the night of the Great Fire Raid in 1940.

Behind Atkins rode the 200 men of his company of 2/8 Gurkhas, advance element of the column of 200 trucks and 50 jeeps bringing his entire battalion to Lahore. Part of the Punjab Boundary Force, Atkins and his exhausted troops had been rushing to Lahore since dawn. Unfortunately, while 55,000 men had been designated for the force, the Indian Army had been able to get less than 10,000 of them into position by the eve of independence.

Moving through the city towards his assigned bivouac area in the grounds of the Gymkhana Club, Atkins did not see a single human being moving. A sinister, ominous silence punctuated only by the roar of those distant fires enveloped his convoy.

That young Britisher, born in Poona in an Indian Army cantonment, was riding into the city because a single ambition had ruled his life: to emulate the career of his father, a retired colonel in the army to which Atkins now belonged.

Peering into the menacing night around him, Atkins suddenly thought of the last evening he'd spent with his father a year before. They had been playing billiards in the Madras Club discussing politics. As they'd racked their cues, his father had said: 'Yes, India's going to become independent soon and when she does, there's going to be horrible bloodshed.'

'My father,' thought young Atkins recalling his prophecy 'knows India very well.'

New Delhi, Midnight 14 August 1947

No arsonist's hand had lit the little fire burning in the New Delhi garden of Dr Rajendra Prasad, the president of India's Constituent Assembly. It was a Sacred Fire, consecrated and purified according to Vedic rite by the Brahmin priest who sat beside it rhythmically chanting his *mantras*. Together with earth, the common mother, and water, the giver of life, fire, the energizer and destroyer, composed the material *trimurti*, trinity, of Hinduism. It was the indispensible adjunct of every Hindu rite and feast, the impersonal inquisitor of the ordeal by fire, the quasi-divine agent of man's ultimate return to the ashes from which he'd sprung.

'O Fire,' intoned the Brahmin priest beside it, 'you are the countenance of all the Gods and of all learned men. Yours is the power to penetrate the innermost recesses of the human heart and discover the truth.'

As he repeated his atonal chant, the learned men and women who would shortly become the first ministers of an independent India, filed past the fire. A second Brahmin sprinkled each with a few drops of water. Then they stepped over to a woman waiting with a copper vessel, its exterior white-washed, its lip covered with palm leaves. As the ministers paused before her, she dipped her right forefinger into the vessel, then, with the liquid on her fingertip, pressed a bright vermilion dot on to their foreheads. It was the ancient Hindu symbol of the 'third-eye' which was reality behind appearances, a device to shelter its bearer from the influence of the evil eye or the malevolent designs of those who wished them ill. Thus prepared for the cruel burdens awaiting them, those men and women filed into their flag-draped Constituent Assembly Hall.

The last papers were signed, the last despatch filed. The time had come to put away forever the Viceroy's cyphers and seals, all the paraphernalia of what had been one of the world's most potent political offices. Alone in his study, Louis Mountbatten mused to himself. 'For a little while longer I am the most powerful man on earth,' he thought.

He remembered a story of H. G. Wells, *The Man Who Could Do Miracles*, the tale of a man who possessed for one day the power to perform any miracle he chose. 'I'm sitting here, living out the last minutes of this incredible office in which men really have had the power to perform miracles,' he told himself. 'I should perform a miracle. But what miracle?'

Suddenly he sat upright. 'By God,' he said out loud, 'I know. I'll make the Begum of Palanpur a Highness!' With gleeful energy he began to stab the buzzers that summoned his aides to his office.

Mountbatten and the Nawab of Palanpur had become fast friends during the Prince of Wales' tour. During a visit as Supreme Commander to the Nawab and his able, attractive, Australian wife, the Begum, in 1945, the Nawab's British Resident, Sir William Croft, came to Mountbatten. The Nawab's wife had become a Moslem, he said, she had adopted the sari and all other local customs, was performing wonderful social work, but the Nawab was heartbroken because the Viceroy would not accord her the title 'Highness' as she was not an Indian.

On returning to Delhi, Mountbatten had intervened personally with the Viceroy, Lord Wavell, but to no avail. London would not agree to a step which might start a wave of princes marrying Europeans and undermine the whole concept of the princely caste.

As soon as his aides assembled, Mountbatten announced his intentions to elevate the Begum of Palanpur to the dignity of 'Highness'.

'But,' one protested, 'you can't do that!'

'Who says I can't?' laughed Mountbatten. 'I'm the Viceroy, aren't I?' He ordered someone to go out in search of a paper scroll, then he had a secretary inscribe it with a few ringing phrases elevating the Nawab's Australian Begum 'by the grace of God', to the dignity of Highness. The result was placed on his desk at 11.58. A smile of the purest pleasure illuminating his face, Louis Mountbatten took his pen and performed the last official action to be exercised by a Viceroy of India.*

Outside, at almost the same instant, his personal standard as the Viceroy of India, a Union Jack emblazoned with the Star of India, came down the flagstaff of Viceroy's House.**

From the vast reaches of time, long before man's memory was transposed from legend to stone, the wail of the conch shell on the seacoasts of India had been the herald of the dawn. Now a man draped in *khadi* stood poised at the edge of a gallery overlooking New Delhi's packed Constituent Assembly, waiting to herald a new dawn for millions of human beings. Clutched in the crook of his arm was a spiralling shell glittering in rose and purple. He was, in a sense, a bugler, a bugler for that Congress army in white caps and flopping white shirt tails that had swarmed down the alleys and streets of India clamouring for freedom, a horde of ghosts hacking down the pillars of an empire.

Below him, on the speaker's stand, was Jawaharlal Nehru. Twisted into the button-hole of his cotton vest was the flower which, with the exception of the nine years he'd spent in British jails, had been the ever-present badge of his elegant person, a freshly plucked rose. On the walls around him, the stately oil paintings of the Viceroys of India had been replaced, their gilded frames filled this evening with green, white and orange banners.

* Mountbatten's final gesture was not without its sequel. A few days later, he received a lyrical note from the Nawab's British Resident, Croft, who said: 'I can never thank you enough. Your act was the most far-reaching and kindest gesture you could have performed for Palanpur. I am as grateful to you as the Nawab, and if ever by any chance I should be in a position to do you a service, do not hesitate to call on me.'

Three years later, in 1950, Mountbatten was Fourth Sea Lord at the Admiralty. He was, among other things, responsible for the Navy's customs' privileges, duty-free alcohol, cigarettes and other items considered vital supports for the morale of HM's seamen. Pressed by the Attlee government to find additional revenues, the Collector of Customs announced his intention of abolishing these privileges. Everyone in the naval hierarchy tried, unsuccessfully, to persuade the gentleman to change his mind. Mountbatten finally advised the Secretary of Admiralty, Sir John Lang, that he intended to try himself. Useless, Lang replied, everyone had tried, the Collector refused to budge and since it was a popular financial move, it was certain to zip through the Cabinet.

Mountbatten persisted, however, and finally found himself being ushered into the office of the Collector of Customs. To his surprise, the man who rose to greet him was Sir William Croft. 'How wonderful to see you!' exclaimed Croft. 'You know, I can never thank you enough for what you did for the Begum of Palanpur.'

'Ah,' said Mountbatten, 'but you can.' The Navy's privileges were preserved.

** It is now hung in the Norman Abbey of Romsey, the last Viceroy's parish church.

Ranged on the packed assembly benches facing Nehru, in saris and *khadi*, princely robes and dinner jackets, were the representatives of the nation to be born this night. The people they represented were an amalgam of races and religions, languages and cultures, of a diversity and contrast unmatched on the globe. Theirs was a land of supreme spiritual attainment and the most debasing misery on earth, a land whose greatest riches were its paradoxes, whose people were more fertile than its fields; a land obsessed by God and beset with natural calamities unsurpassed in cruelty and dimension; a land of past accomplishment and present concern whose future was compromised by problems more taxing than those confronting any other assembly of humans on earth. Yet, for all that, for all her ills, their India was also one of the supreme and enduring symbols protruding above the cultural horizons of mankind.

The India which those men and women represented would be a nation of 275 million Hindus, 70 million of them Untouchables; 35 million Moslems; 7 million Christians; 6 million Sikhs; 100,000 Parsees and 24,000 Jews whose forebears had fled the destruction of Solomon's Temple during the Babylonian exile.

Few of the people in the hall could talk to each other in their native language; their only common tongue was English. Their nation would harbour fifteen official languages and 845 dialects. The Urdu of the deputies of the Punjab was read from right to left; the Hindi of their neighbours in the United Provinces from left to right. The Tamil of the Madrasis was sometimes read up and down and other dialects were decoded like the symbols on a Pharaonic frieze. Even their gestures were dissimilar. When a dark-skinned Madrasi from the south nodded his head, he meant 'yes'. When a pale northerner made the same movement he meant 'no'.

India would include a leper population the size of Switzerland, as many priests as there were Belgians in Belgium, enough beggars to populate all of Holland, 11 million holy men, 20 million aborigines, some like the Nagas of Nagaland still hunting human heads. 10 million Indians were essentially nomads, exercising hereditary occupations as snake charmers, fortune tellers, gypsies, jugglers, water diviners, magicians, tight-rope walkers, herb vendors, which kept them constantly moving from village to village. 38 thousand Indians were born every day, a quarter of them to die before the age of five. 10 million other Indians died each year from malnutrition, undernourishment and diseases like smallpox eradicated in most parts of the earth.

Their great sub-continent was the most intensely spiritual area in the world; birthplace of one great religion, Buddhism; motherland of Hinduism; deeply influenced by Islam; a land whose Gods came in a bewildering array of forms and figures; whose religious practices ranged from yoga and the most intensive meditation of which the human spirit was capable, to animal sacrifice and debauched sexual orgies performed in clandestine jungle temples. The pantheon of the Hindus contained over 3 million deities, a God for every mythic manifestation and practical need imaginable. There were Gods and Goddesses for the dance, poetry, song; for death, destruction and disease; Goddesses like Markhai Devi at whose feet goats were sacrificed to check cholera epidemics, and Gods like Deva Indra who was begged to give his faithful carnal capacities akin to those displayed on India's great temple friezes. God was held manifest in banyan trees, in India's 136 million monkeys, in the heroes of her mythological epics, in her 200 million sacred cows; worshipped in her snakes, particularly cobras, who each year killed 20,000 of the humans who venerated them. India's sects included Zoroastrians, descendants of ancient Persia's fire worshippers, and Jains, a Hindu offshoot whose adherents in the land of the world's lowest life expectancy, held all existence so sacred that they refused to eat meat and most vegetables, and went about with a gauze mask over their faces so they could not inadvertently inhale and kill an insect.

The nation would embrace some of the richest men in the world and 300 million peasants living on the frontiers of existence, dispersed over what might have been one of the earth's richest surfaces and was one of its poorest. 83% of India's population was illiterate. Her per capita income averaged five cents a day and a quarter of the people in her two great cities ate, slept, defecated, fornicated, and died in their open streets. India received an average rainfall of 114 cms a year, but her skies unleashed it in an appalling inequality of time and space. Most came in the drenching downpours of the monsoon and over a third of it ran unused to the sea. 300,000 square kilometres of her land, an area the size of East and West Germany combined, got no rain at all, while other areas got so much water that the salt table was almost at the earth's surface, rendering its cultivation extremely difficult. India contained three of the great industrial families of the world, the Birlas, the Tatas and the Dalmias, but her economy was essentially feudal benefiting a handful of wealthy landowners and capitalists.

Her imperial rulers had made no effort to industrialize her. Her exports were almost exclusively commodities: jute, tea, cotton, tobacco. Most of her machinery had to be imported. India's per capita consumption of electricity was laughably low, one two hundredth that of the United States. Her soil contained at least a tenth of the world's reserves of iron ore but her steel production was barely a million tons a year. She had 3800 miles of coastline and a fishing industry so primitive she couldn't even offer her population a pound of fish per capita a year.

Indeed, to those tense, expectant men and women filling the benches of the Delhi assembly hall, it might well have seemed that problems were the only heritage being left them by their departing colonizers. No such melancholy thought, however, animated their gathering. Instead, its keynote was the good feeling with which India's former rulers were regarded, and a touching, if naïve belief that somehow their departure was going to ease the terrible burdens under which she agonized.

The man upon whom those burdens would now weigh most heavily rose to speak. After his phone call from Lahore, Jawaharlal Nehru had had neither the time nor the inclination to write a speech. His words were extemporaneous, heart-felt.

'Long years ago we made a tryst with destiny,' he declared, 'and now the time comes when we shall redeem our pledge, not wholly or in full measure, but very substantially. At the stroke of the midnight hour, while the world sleeps, India will awake to life and freedom.' One after another, the eloquent phrases fell from his lips, yet for Jawaharlal Nehru, that sublime moment of achievement had been fatally flawed. 'I was hardly aware of what I was saying,' he would later tell his sister; 'the words came welling up, but my mind could only conceive the awful picture of Lahore in flames.'

'A moment comes,' Nehru continued, 'which comes but rarely in history, when we step out from the old to the new, when an age ends, and when the soul of a nation long suppressed finds utterance.

'At the dawn of history India started on her unending quest and the trackless centuries are filled with her striving, and the grandeur of her successes and her failures. Through good and ill fortunes alike, she has never lost sight of that quest or forgotten the ideal which gave her strength. We end today a period of ill-fortune and India discovers herself again.

'This is no time for petty and destructive criticism,' he concluded, 'no time for ill-will or blaming others. We have to build the noble mansion of free India where all her children may dwell.'

At the stroke of midnight, Nehru moved, they would all rise and pledge themselves to the service of India and her people. Outside a rippling wave of thunder clattered across the midnight sky and a drenching monsoon rain spattered the thousands of ordinary Indians jamming the area around the hall. Clutching bicycles, in white Congress caps and shapeless tunics of homespun cotton, in white shirts and slacks, saris and business suits, they stood silent in the downpour, their exuberance stilled by the awesomeness of the moment approaching.

In the hall, the hands of the clock over the speaker's stand crept up to the roman numeral XII. Heads bowed, the representatives sat in meditative silence, waiting for the chimes of midnight. Not a figure stirred as those twelve heavy tolls marked the end of a day and an era.

As the echoes of the twelfth stroke fell, a toneless shriek reverberated through the hall from the figure poised in the gallery, a primitive call from across India's trackless centuries. To those Indian politicians, the conch shell's bleat heralded the birth of their nation. To the world, it played retreat for the passing of an age.

That age had begun on a soft summer day in a little Spanish port in 1492 when Christopher Columbus sailed off across the endless green seas to the edge of the world in search of India and found America by mistake. Four and a half centuries of human history bore the *imprimatur* of that discovery and its consequences: the economic, religious and physical exploitation of the non-white masses circling the globe by the white, Western, Christian masses at its core. Aztec, Inca, Swahili, Egyptian, Iraqi, Hottentot, Algerian, Burmese, Filipino, Moroccan, Vietnamese, an unending stream of peoples, nations and civilizations over 450 years had passed through the colonial experience; decimated, impoverished, educated, converted, culturally enriched or debased, economically exploited or stimulated, but finally, irrevocably altered by it.

Now the famished hordes of a continent in prayer had claimed their freedom from the architects of the greatest empire those centuries had produced, a realm that dwarfed in dimension, population and importance the domains of Rome, Babylon, Carthage and Greece. With the crown jewel of the British Empire prised away by the brown Asiatic hands to which it belonged, no other colonial empire could long endure. Their rulers might try with rhetoric and arms to check history's onrushing tide; theirs would be futile, bloody gestures condemned by this moment to failure. Irrevocably, definitively, the independence of India closed a chapter in man's experience. The conch shell's call in New Delhi's Constituent Assembly that August night marked the beginning of the post-war history of the world.

Outside the assembly hall, the rain had stopped and a jubilant mood swept over the crowd. As Nehru emerged, thousands of happy people rushed forward, threatening to engulf him and the ministers behind him in their embrace. Watching the thin screen of policemen trying to hold them back, an enormous smile animated Nehru's face.

'You know,' he said to an aide standing beside him, 'exactly ten years ago, in London, I had a fight with Linlithgow, the Viceroy. I got so mad I shouted "I'll be damned if we don't have our independence in ten years". He answered "Oh no, you won't", the Prime Minister recalled with a laugh. "India will not be free in my time Mr Nehru," he said, "nor in yours either".'

* * *

That grand and guilty edifice, the British Raj was no more. Beyond New Delhi's Constituent Assembly Hall, in the vastness of the two new states, the momentous changes portended by the conch shell's call found their echo in jubilant cheers and a thousand small gestures. In Bombay, a policeman nailed a sign bearing the word 'closed' to the gates of the citadel of white supremacy, the Bombay Yacht Club. Henceforth, those precincts in which three generations of *pukkasahibs* and *memsahibs* had sipped their whiskies undisturbed by native stares would be a mess for cadets of the Indian Navy.

In Calcutta, eager hands tore down the signs of the city's central thoroughfare. Clive Street became Subhas Road, named for an Indian nationalist who'd aligned himself with Japan against the British in World War II. In Simla, at the stroke of midnight, hundreds of Indians in saris and *dhotis* ran laughing down the Mall, the avenue on which no Indian had been allowed to appear in his native dress. In Firpo's in Calcutta, Falletti's in Lahore, the Taj in Bombay, hundreds more invaded the restaurants and dance floors that had been reserved for guests in dinner jackets and evening gowns.*

Delhi celebrated with lights. The austere, hard-working capital was ablaze with them. New Delhi's Connaught Circus, the narrow alleys of Old Delhi, were hung in green, saffron and white lights. Temples, mosques and Sikh *gurudwaras* were outlined in garlands of light bulbs. So too, was the Red Fort of the Moghul Emperors. New Delhi's newest temple, Birla Mandir, with its curlicue spires and domes hung with lights, looked to one passer-by like a hallucination of Ludwig of Bavaria. In the Bhangi sweepers' colony, among whose Untouchables Gandhi had often dwelt, independence had brought a gift many of those wretched people had never known – light. The municipality had offered them the candles and the little oil lamps flickering in the gloom of their huts to honour their new freedom. On bicycles, tonga carts, cars, even on an elephant draped in rich

* One member of the Constituent Assembly had even wanted a clause in India's constitution denying a public place the right to require the Raj's favourite apparel, the dinner jacket, for its guests.

velvet tapestry, crowds swept towards the centre of Delhi to sing, cheer and walk in a buoyant mood of self-congratulation. The restaurants and cafés of Connaught Place were thronged. Every member of that gigantic army of white-shirted bureaucrats for which Delhi was notorious, seemed to have gravitated to its pavements.

The bar of the Imperial Hotel, a sanctuary of Delhi's former rulers, swarmed with celebrating Indians. Just after midnight, one of them climbed on to the bar and asked the crowd to join him in singing their new national anthem. They gleefully accepted his invitation, but as they started through the chorus of the hymn, written by India's great national poet, Tagore, most of them made a disconcerting discovery: they didn't know the words.

At Maiden's hotel in Old Delhi, the most famous establishment in the city, a beautiful Indian girl in a sari danced from table to table, twisting a red dot, a *tilak*, for good luck on to the forehead of everyone in the place with a lipstick tube.

In the complaisant shadows of a garden near Connaught Circus, Kartar Singh, a journalist, celebrated his country's freedom with an intensely personal gesture. He used it as the pretext to kiss for the first time Aisha Ali, a pretty medical student he'd met a few days earlier. Their embrace was the first gesture of a long and marvellous love story beginning at a most inauspicious moment. Their particular passion was going to run athwart the passions about to sweep northern India. Kartar Duggal Singh was a Sikh. Aisha Ali was Moslem.

Despite the exuberance of Independence Night, the shadows of that coming storm lay already over parts of the capital. In their neighbourhoods in Old Delhi, many Moslems were whispering a new slogan put out by fanatics of the Moslem League: 'We got Pakistan by right – we'll take Hindustan by force.' That morning, a *mullah* in an Old Delhi mosque had reminded his faithful at prayers that Moslems had ruled Delhi for centuries and, '*Insha Allah* – God willing,' they would again. Meanwhile, Hindu and Sikh refugees from the Punjab, packed into makeshift refugees' camps around Delhi, threatened to turn the capital's Moslem neighbourhoods into a bonfire to celebrate independence.

V. P. Menon, the brilliant bureaucrat who had redrafted Mountbatten's partition plan and coaxed so many princes into acceding to India, passed the midnight hour in his sitting-room with his teenage daughter. When the sound of conch shells and cheering crowds drifted into their quiet parlour, Menon's daughter leaped up and cried out her delight. Her father remained fixed in his chair, no exuberance on his face.

'Now,' he sighed, 'our nightmares really start.'

For millions of others on the sub-continent, however, midnight, 14 August marked the beginning of a party 24 hours long. In the fort at Landi Kotal in the Khyber whole sheep roasted over a dozen roaring fires. The officers and men of the Khyber Rifles and the Pathan tribesmen who'd been their traditional enemies celebrated with a tribal banquet. The commanding officer offered his adjutant and guest of honour Capt. Kenneth Dance, the *pièce de résistance*, a sheep's liver wrapped in fatty yellow intestines. At midnight, the excited tribesmen grabbed their rifles and, shrieking 'the Khyber is ours, the Khyber is ours', sent a pound of lead into the night air.

At Cawnpore, a city cursed by memories of the massacres that had occurred there during the Mutiny, Englishmen and Indians embraced publicly. In Ahmedabad, the textile capital where Gandhi had founded his first Indian ashram, a young school teacher who'd been jailed for trying to hoist India's flag in 1942, was given the honour of raising it over the town hall.

In Lucknow, scores had been invited to a midnight flag-raising at the Residence. The engraved invitations had read 'National Dress: Dhotis will be suitable'. Rajeshwar Dayal, an Indian with fourteen years in the ICS, had been shocked reading it. He didn't even own a dhoti. Such a ceremony under his British employers would certainly have been in white tie and tails. The reception itself was utterly different from the stiffly formal affairs of the Raj. As soon as the gates opened, the long table loaded with sweets disappeared under a swarm of saris and struggling children. Watching India's flag take its place over the Residency, a curious thought occurred to Dayal, one which said much about the manner in which the British had ruled his country. In fourteen years service in the ICS, he thought, he had had many British colleagues. But he had never had a British friend.

In Madras, Bangalore, Patna, in thousands of cities, towns and villages, people entered temples at midnight to cast rose petals at the feet of the Gods, their poignant plea for the blessing of the cosmos on their new nation. In Benares, the leading pastry maker earned a considerable sum peddling an independence cake in India's national colours, its frosting made of oranges, pistachios and milk.

Nowhere was Independence Night celebrated with more fervour and enthusiasm than in the great port of Bombay. There, on pavements that often had been slippery with the blood spilled in *lathi* charges, in that city whose history was inextricably intertwined with India's independence struggle, whose streets had witnessed so many demonstrations, *hartals*, and strikes, an entire people went wild with joy. From the palatial apartment houses of Marine Drive to the distant slums of Parel, from the villas of Malabar Hill to the clutter of the Thieves Market, Bombay was a lake of light. 'Midnight has become midday,' wrote one newsman, 'it was a new Diwali, a new Id, a New Year's Eve – it was all the festivals of a land of festivals rolled into one – for this was the Festival of Freedom.'

Something less than outright rejoicing inaugurated that festival in a number of dinners and banquets across India. They took place in what had been her old princely states. The day of the Maharajas was over and for some of them, still unreconciled to the loss of their privileges and the end of their world of pomp and splendour, 15 August would be a day of mourning. In his brightly-lit banquet hall, the Nizam of Hyderabad offered a farewell banquet to his British administrators whose role was ending along with his own. Despite the gaiety of the Nizam's numerous progeny and the elegance of the women present, the dinner had the lugubrious air of a wake. At the end of the dinner, shortly before midnight, the old miser, dressed in a pair of torn and faded trousers, stood to propose a final toast to the King Emperor. John Peyton, an English guest, scrutinized the Nizam's mournful face. 'How sad,' he thought, 'two hundred years of history ending in one brief, pathetic gesture.'

For many Indians, the night they and their countrymen had dreamed of for years was a frightful horror. To Lt-Col J. T. Sataravala, a Parsee of the Frontier Force Rifles, it would always be associated with the most sickening sight his war-hardened eyes had ever seen. It was the gruesomely mutilated bodies of an entire Hindu family in a flaming ruin in the Baluchistan city of Quetta. Beside them, mutilated with equal savagery, were the bodies of the brave and generous Moslem family that had offered them shelter. Sushila Nayar, a beautiful young doctor assigned by Gandhi to a camp of 20,000 refugees in the western Punjab, had spent two years in jail and given most of her brief adult life to achieving the moment midnight 14 August represented. Now, it brought her no joy, no sense of fulfilment. She was conscious only of the misery of her thousands of charges most of them listening in the night for the sounds of the Moslem hordes they were certain would come to slaughter them.

Lahore, the city that should have been the gayest spot on the subcontinent, was a scene of devastation. Capt. Robert Atkins, who'd led his Gurkhas into the city at sundown, found his camp besieged by pathetic, frightened Hindus. Clutching babies, bedding, a suitcase or two, they begged to be allowed inside the protective circle of his soldiers. Almost a hundred thousand Hindus and Sikhs were trapped inside Old Lahore's walled city, their water cut, fires raging around them, mobs of Moslems stalking the alleys outside their *mohallas* waiting to pounce on anyone venturing out. One mob had set the city's most famous Sikh *gurudwara* next to the Shah Alimi Gate on fire, then shrieked with glee at the screams of the wretched Sikhs being roasted alive inside.

Calcutta, the city which should have been exploding in violence, was undergoing a bewildering metamorphosis. It had begun timidly, tentatively before sundown when a procession of Hindus and Moslems had marched through the city towards Gandhi's headquarters at Hydari House. In its wake the city's atmosphere had begun to change. In the violent jungles of Keldanga Road and around Sealdah station, Hindu and Moslem *goondas* had sheathed their daggers to join in hanging the Indian flag from balconies and lampposts. Sheikhs opened the doors of their mosques to the adherents of Kali, and they in turn invited Moslems to their temples to contemplate the grotesque image of the Goddess of Destruction.

Men who would have been prepared to cut each other's throats 24 hours earlier, now shook hands in the street. Women and children, Hindu and Moslem alike, offered sweets to members of the opposite community. The city that evening reminded Kumar Bose, a Bengali writer, of the Christmas Eve scene in *All Quiet on the Western Front*, when French and German soldiers emerged from their trenches to forget for a brief moment that they were enemies.

While India celebrated, the great house which had been the repository of Britain's imperial power in India was undergoing a revolution. From one end of the house to the other, servants rushed along the corridors, obscuring or snatching away any seal or symbol likely to offend the sensibilities of India's newly independent citizens. Mountbatten was determined that, on their Independence Day, no Indians visiting what was now Government House would be confronted with any distasteful reminders of the age just past.

One team of servants did nothing but go from room to room replacing stationery bearing the offending words 'Viceroy's House' with new ones engraved 'Government House'. Another screened off the enormous seal above Durbar Hall. One set of seals did not change however. Traditionally, the Viceroy's cypher had been his personal insignia and the cigar bands, matchboxes, soap bars and butter patties of the new Government House continued to carry Mountbatten's Viscount's coronet above his 'M of B'.

As their work was going on, a delegation of Indian leaders sent by the Constituent Assembly arrived. Rajendra Prasad, the president of the assembly, formally invited the ex-Viceroy to become India's first Governor-General. It was the second honour the admiral had received that evening. A few moments before, he had learned that his cousin George VI, in recognition of his accomplishments in India, had elevated him a rank in the peerage, from Viscount to Earl.

Mountbatten accepted Prasad's invitation, pledging to serve India as if he were himself an Indian. Then Nehru gave Mountbatten an envelope containing the list of the men who, with his approval, would constitute the first government of an independent India.

Mountbatten took out a decanter of port and personally filled his visitors' glasses. When he had done so, he raised his own and said 'To India'. After a sip, Nehru in turn raised his to Mountbatten. 'To King George VI', he said.

When they'd left, before going to bed, Mountbatten opened the envelope Nehru had handed him. As he did so, he burst into laughter. In the haste of this great evening, Nehru had not had time to set down the names of independent India's first Cabinet. It contained a blank sheet of paper.

In the dark and cavernous Lahore railroad station, a handful of Englishmen made their way towards the waiting Bombay Express. They were virtually the last minor players in an army of British administrators, policemen and soldiers who had made the Punjab the pride of British India, the repository of the best of Britain's achievements on the sub-continent. Now they were going home and leaving to other hands the canals, the highways, the railroads, the bridges, they and their forebears had built.

As they walked to the train, a group of railroad workers listlessly washed the station platform with a hose. A few hours earlier, the station had been the site of a terrible massacre of fleeing Hindus. Bill Rich, the Englishman who had handed over charge of Lahore's police a few hours earlier, noticed an appalling sight: a group of porters wheeling a luggage cart down the platform. Piled on to it, like bundles heading for the guard's van, was a stack of corpses. Rich himself had to step over a corpse lying on the platform to get his foot on to the stairs leading to his carriage. What amazed him was not the sight of that mangled body at his feet, but his own indifference to it, his sudden awareness of how hardened he'd become to the horrors of the Punjab.

Rule Dean, the Amritsar police chief who'd sent his band to play Gilbert and Sullivan in the town square, stared in melancholy gloom from the window of his compartment as the train left the city that had been his responsibility. He could see on the horizon flames devouring dozens of the villages it had been his duty to protect. Silhouetted by their roseate glow against the night sky, he caught sight of the marauding Sikh bands destroying them, dancing a kind of wild ballet around the flames. He had a feeling of 'terrible, overwhelming sadness'.

'Instead of handing over our charge in a dignified way,' he thought, 'we are leaving chaos behind us.' Then, as the express neared Delhi, a dining-car was attached to the train. Suddenly, there, among the fresh linen and polished silver, the Punjab, to the former Amritsar police chief who in three months' time would be selling plastics door to door in Welwyn Garden City, seemed a world away.

The ruin at 151 Beliaghata Road was silent. At its gate, a handful of non-violent Hindu and Moslem volunteers stood watch. Not a single lamp bulb, not even a candle flickered from the broken windows of Hydari House. Nothing, not even the events of this momentous night, had been allowed to intrude on the firmly established routine of the men and women inside. In the spacious room which served as their communal dormitory, they lay stretched out on straw pallets. On one of them, next to his neatly-aligned wooden clogs, his *Gita*, his dentures and his steel-rimmed spectacles, was the familiar, bald-headed figure. When the clocks had chimed that magic midnight and India had awakened to life and freedom, Mohandas Karamchand Ghandi had been sound asleep.

12

'Oh Lovely Dawn of Freedom'

Benares, 15 August 1947

At the first cool breath of approaching dawn, the mists began to rise from the water. As they had since time immemorial, the multitudes came with them to the banks of the great and sacred river, the Mother Ganges, the Supreme Giver of life, to search a passage to eternity in a ritual immersion in its waters. Nothing might be more appropriate than that, with the dawning of 15 August 1947, Benares, man's oldest city, should offer the unique homage of its morning rites for the birth of the world's newest nation.

Those rites were a constantly renewed expression of the ancient passion joining the Hindus and their sacred river. Their mystic union was Hinduism's expression of that instinctive human need to propitiate the inexplicable forces governing man's destiny. From an ice cave at the foot of a Himalayan snowbed 10,300 feet high, the Ganges ran 1500 miles to the grey waters of the Bay of Bengal, traversing on its way one of the most torrid, over-populated areas on the globe. It was a fickle stream, regularly savaging the lands of the peasants who adored it with floods of appalling intensity and duration. Its route was sprinkled with the ruins of deserted towns and villages, mute witnesses to the abrupt shifts its meanderings had taken over the centuries.

Yet, despite its tempestuous nature, every foot of its watercourse was considered propitious, and none more so than those along the gentle four-mile curve it made as it swung past Benares. Since the dawn of history, since the time of its contemporaries, Babylon, Nineveh and Tyre, Hindus had come there to bathe in the Ganges, to drink its water, to beseech the favour of some capricious God.

Now the silent throngs flowed across the *ghats*, the stone terraces scaling down Benares' steep river banks to the water's edge. Each pilgrim bore a bouquet of flowers and a little lamp of camphor oil, its flame the symbol of light dispersing the shadows of ignorance. In the river, thousands more, a division of the devout, were already standing waist deep in the slow-moving water, all regards turned east, each rigid, silent figure clutching his flickering lamp, so that from a distance their vacillating lights seemed to skip over the surface of the water like a horde of fireflies.

Every eye fixed on the eastern horizon, they waited for the daily ıewal of the heavens' most wondrous miracle, the appearance of a reddish disc sliding up from the entrails of the earth, the God Vishnu in his incarnation as the sun. As its edge slipped into the morning sky, an ejaculation of prayer burst from those thousands of throats. Then, in gratitude for one further renewal of God's greatest miracle, they cast their lamps and flowers upon the waters of the Ganges.

In the city, as it did every morning, the honour of being the first person to step across the threshold of the Temple of Gold, Benares' foremost shrine, belonged this morning to Pandit Bhawani Shankar. Few men in Benares felt more intensely the joy of this dawn than that ageing man of God. For years, Pandit Shankar had offered Indian nationalists fleeing from the British CID the sanctuary of his shrine.

A flask of Ganges water and a vial of sandal-wood paste in his hands, Pandit Shankar marched through his temple's gloom towards a stumpy granite outcropping. That heavy thumb rising in the darkness was the most precious Hindu relic in Benares. Shankar's forebears had earned their descendants the right to be its perpetual custodians by hiding it from the Moghul hordes of the Emperor Aurangzeb. That he should bow before it this August morning, humbly thanking the Gods for the birth of modern India, was a uniquely appropriate gesture. The cult that piece of stone represented was the oldest form of worship known to man.

It was the *lingam*, a stone phallus symbolizing the sexual organ of the God Shiva, the symbol of force and the regenerative power of nature. Benares was the centre of the cult that worshipped it. Phalli studded the city, rising from almost every one of its temples and *ghats*. At the sun's first rays, thousands of Hindus joined Shankar, expressing their gratitude at the reincarnation of their ancient nation by lovingly caressing those bulbous stone stumps with sandal-wood paste, Ganges water and cow dung, garlanding them with marigolds, offering them rose petals and the bitter leaves of Shiva's favourite tree, the *bilva.**

* The origins of the *lingam* and the cult of its worship are explained by a colourful Hindu legend. Shiva and his wife Durga, both drunk at the time, were surprised in the act of copulation by the visit of a delegation of their fellow Gods led by Vishnu. Absorbed in alcohol and their amatory athletics, the divine couple ignored their visitors. Shocked by such behaviour, their fellow Gods cursed them both and left.

When Shiva and Durga were informed of what had happened, their shame was so intense they died in the position in which they'd been surprised. 'My shame,' Shiva proclaimed, 'has killed me, but it has also given me new life and a new shape, that of the *lingam*.' Henceforth, he proclaimed, his priests were to teach men to 'embrace the worship of my *lingam*. It is white. It has three eyes and five faces. It is arrayed in a tiger's skin. It existed before the world and it is the origin

As the colours of dawn brightened the city, a parade of Untouchables, backs bent under bunches of faggots and logs, descended the steps of the most hallowed spot in Benares, the Manikarnika *ghat*. A few minutes later, four men carrying a bamboo stretcher on their shoulders appeared at the head of the steps. In front of them marched a fifth man gently stroking a gong, chanting 'Ram is Truth'. His words were a reminder to all those watching the procession that they, too, would one day come to the same end as the figure wrapped in a cotton winding-sheet on the stretcher.

For centuries, to die in Benares had been the highest blessing to which a devout Hindu could aspire. Death inside a circle 36 miles in circumference around the city liberated a soul from the ceaseless cycle of its reincarnations, and entitled it to join for eternity the wholly enlightened in the paradise of Brahma. That privilege had made Benares a city to which pilgrims came in search, not of life, but of death.

The bearers brought the remains of the first of this morning's claimants to Benares' boon to the river's edge for a last immersion in the Ganges. One of them pried open the jaws of the anonymous face on the stretcher, and sprinkled a few drops of water down the dead man's throat. Then they placed his body on a waiting pyre. The Untouchables serving the *ghat* covered the corpse with a pyramid of sandal-wood logs and poured a pail of *ghee*, clarified butter, over it.

Skull shaven, his body purified by ritual ablutions, the defunct's eldest son circled the pyre five times. Then an acolyte from the near-by temple to Ganesh, the elephant God, handed him a torch fired at the temple's eternal flame. He thrust it on to the pyre. A rush of flame burst through the log pyramid.

The mourners squatted silently around the pyre as it burned, sending an oily black column of smoke into the sky. Suddenly, a dull 'pop' came over the crackling of the flames. At the sound, a grateful prayer rose from the mourners. The defunct's skull had burst. His soul had escaped from his body. On this morning of 15 August 1947, when India was released from imperial bondage, Benares, as it did every day, had begun to offer its supreme deliverance to its dead.

The first uncertain sputtering of a candle had appeared in the windows of the house on Beliaghata Road just after 2 a.m., an hour ahead of Gandhi's usual rising time. The glorious day when his people would savour at last their freedom should have been an apotheosis for Gandhi, the culmination of a life of struggle, the final

---

and the beginning of all beings. It disperses our terrors and our fears, and grants us the object of all our desires.'

triumph of a movement which had stirred the admiration of the world. It was anything but that. There was no joy in the heart of the man in Hydari House. The victory for which Gandhi had sacrificed so much had the taste of ashes, and his triumph was indelibly tainted by the prospects of a coming tragedy.

As he had been when crossing into the turbulent marshlands of Noakhali that New Year's Day just seven months before, the gentle apostle of non-violence was assailed this morning by questioning and self-doubt. 'I am groping,' he had written to a friend the evening before. 'Have I led the country astray?'

As always in moments of doubt and pain, Gandhi had turned to the book that had so long been his infallible guide, the celestial song of the *Bhagavad Gita.* How often had its verses consoled him, permitting him to smile in those dark hours when no other ray of light appeared to soften the dark horizons.

Squatting bare-chested on his pallet, Gandhi had begun his personal day of mourning, the first day of India's independence, reading the *Gita*. With his disciples around him, the Mahatma's high, lisping voice had welcomed the dawn with the first of the *Gita*'s eighteen dialogues, the despairing plea of the warrior Arjuna to the Gods. They were eerily appropriate to this promising yet pathetic moment in Indian history.

'On the field of Dharma, on the holy field of Kuru, my men and the sons of Pandu are arrayed, burning with desire to fight. What must they do, O Sanjaya?'

It was a sound as old as man, the anguished rasp of stone on stone. In a courtyard of the village of Chatarpur, near Delhi, the figure sprawled on the ropes stretched taut between the wooden frame of a *charpoi* opened his eyes. Before him, etched in the amber glow of a twist of cord burning in a saucer of camphor oil, was the image that had marked all the dawns of his adult existence: his wife, bent over the two slabs of a millstone. Her face obscured by the folds of the shawl draping her head, she dumbly churned to powder the grains which would sustain another day in the life of an Indian peasant.

That peasant, a 52-year-old Brahmin named Ranjit Lal, murmured a brief prayer to Vishnu. Then he stepped past his wife, out of his mud hut, to join the silhouettes of his fellow villagers slipping through the half light to the nearby field which was the communal toilet for the three thousand inhabitants of Chatarpur.

The foreign rule ending in this August dawn had barely disturbed those peasants trudging dumbly through the shadows. Never in his life had Ranjit Lal addressed so much as a single word to a representative of the alien race that ruled his country. He and his fellow villagers only looked upon an Englishman once a year when a District Collector visited Chatarpur to verify the exactitude of its paltry contribution to the revenues of the Indian state. The only phrase Lal could articulate in the tongue of India's old rulers was the one he and his fellows employed to describe the act they were about to perform: 'call of nature.'

If the words used to describe it were foreign, however, it was ordered for Lal, a Brahmin, by a code of 23 strict laws uniquely Hindu in their detail and complexity. Lal carried in his left hand a brass vessel filled with water. The *dhoti* he wore was neither new nor freshly washed. The field towards which he and his fellows marched had been selected because of its distance from a river bank, a well, a crossroad, a pond, the nearest sacred Banyan tree and the village temple.

Reaching the field, Lal hung the triple cord of his Brahmin's sacred thread over his left ear, covered his head with his loincloth, and squatted as close to the ground as was physically possible. Anything less was a grave offence, as would have been performing his act from a wall or the branch of a tree. Thus ensconced, he was enjoined from looking at the sun, the moon, stars, fire, another Brahmin, the village temple or a Banyan tree. When he'd finished, he washed his hands and feet with the water in his brass vessel before heading for the village tank for his ritual ablution. Once there, he selected a handful of dirt to aid his wash. Its nature, too, was rigorously prescribed. The dirt could not come from a white ants' nest, salt earth, a potter's field, a cow pasture, a temple enclosure, or ground touched by the shade of a Banyan tree. Mixing his water with the mud, he washed his soiled parts with his left hand.*

When he'd finished, he washed his hands five times, beginning with the left; his feet five times beginning with the right; rinsed his mouth eight times taking care, at the risk of committing a terrible offence, to spit the water out each time to the left side of his body. That done, he was ready for the twenty-third and final observance of his morning bowel movement. He took three sips of water, thinking as he did so of Vishnu.

That rite accomplished, Ranjit Lal headed back to his hut past the fields from whose reluctant soils he scratched the bare ingredients of survival for himself, his wife and his seven children. Beyond them, at the crest of an almost imperceptible rise, Lal could see in the first glimmer of dawn the sweeping branches of a trio of

* To the orthodox Hindu, the navel is the body's frontier. For acts performed below it, the left hand is used; for those above, the right is generally employed.

babul trees. Like umbrellas, their branches opened over a flat piece of earth. It was the village cremation ground where for five centuries the dead of Chatarpur had been laid upon their funeral pyres. If there was one inescapable certainty in the circle of certainties that circumscribed that Indian peasant's life, it was that it would end on a bed of sticks there in that cremation ground.

Beyond, a purplish stone tower pierced the blue-grey horizon like some gigantic phallic symbol. At its left were a pair of graceful domes, ruins of the thirteenth-century metropolis of the Sultan Alauddin, founder of one of the seven cities of ancient Delhi. Barely twenty miles north, in the broad avenues of New Delhi, Ranjit Lal and his fellow villagers had an historic rendezvous this morning. For most of them, it would be the first time they'd made that brief journey. Ranjit Lal had made it only once in 52 years, to buy a gold bangle in the bazaar for the marriage of his eldest daughter.

This morning, however, for the villagers of Chatarpur as for the inhabitants of all the villages around Delhi, distance no longer existed. Tributaries of an immense and triumphant stream, they flowed with the dawn towards the centre of their rejoicing capital to celebrate in its streets the end of a colonization most of them had not even known.

New Delhi, 15 August 1947

'Oh lovely dawn of freedom that breaks in gold and purple over an ancient capital,' proclaimed India's poet laureate in benediction over the crowds swarming into New Delhi. They came from all sides. There were caravans of tongas, their bells jingling gaily. There were bullocks, harnesses and hoofs painted with orange, green and white stripes, tugging wooden-wheeled platforms crowded with people. There were trucks overflowing with people, their roofs and flanks galleries of primitive paintings of snakes, eagles, falcons, sacred cows and cool mountain landscapes. People came on donkey, horse and bicycle, walking and running, country people with turbans of every shape and colour imaginable, their women in bright, festive saris, every bauble they owned glittering on their arms, from their ears, fingers and noses.

For a brief moment in that fraternal cohort, rank, religion and caste disappeared. Brahmins, Untouchables, Hindus, Sikhs, Moslems, Parsees, Anglo-Indians laughed, cheered, and occasionally wept with emotion. Ranjit Lal rented a tonga for four annas for himself, his wife and his seven children. All around him, Lal could hear other peasants excitedly explaining to their kith and kin why they were all going to Delhi. 'The British are going,' they cried. 'Nehru is going to raise a new flag. We are free!'

The shriek of silver trumpets sundered the morning air. With a final burst of Victorian pomp the first official ceremony of this extraordinary day was beginning. It was the swearing-in of the first constitutional Governor-General of the new dominion of India.

As solemn as he had been in Karachi, Queen Victoria's great-grandson advanced towards the throne where he would receive a charge and an honour unique in the coming annals of decolonization. For Louis Mountbatten, 'the most remarkable and inspiring day in his life' was beginning, the day he would be handing over charge of the heartland of his great-grandmother's empire.

His wife walked by his side in a silver lamé gown, a diadem set in her brown hair. Determined the day 'would go off with the utmost pomp', Mountbatten had supervised every detail of India's independence ceremonies with his love of pageantry and his teutonic zest for detail. A colourful uniformed escort preceded the regal pair as they flowed towards those crimson thrones in which five months before they'd been installed as Viceroy and Vicereine.

Ranged to their right and left on the marble dais under a velvet canopy were the new masters of India, Nehru in cotton jodhpurs and a linen vest. Vallabhbhai Patel more than ever the scowling Roman emperor in his white *dhoti*, all the others in their little white Congress caps.

Taking his place, an amusing thought struck Mountbatten. The men and women ranged beside him probably had only one experience in common: they had, almost all of them, served time in a British prison. Before that array of former guests of His Majesty's government's prison administration, Louis Mountbatten raised his right hand and solemnly swore to become the humble and faithful first servant of an independent India. When he'd finished, those ministers whose names Nehru had forgotten to place in his envelope the evening before, swore their oaths at the hands of the man who'd given India her independence.

Outside, the echoes of the 21-gun salute* marking the event began to roll across India's rejoicing capital. Waiting for the Mountbattens at the foot of the red-carpeted steps leading out of Durbar Hall was the gold state carriage assembled almost half a century earlier by the craftsmen of London's Messrs Parker and Company, for the royal visit to India of George V and Queen Mary. In front of

* The old Viceregal 31-gun salute had been reduced to 21 guns for the Constitutional Governor-General.

its six matched bays, the entire Governor-General's Bodyguard was assembled in glistening black jack-boots, white riding-breeches, white tunics closed by scarlet sashes embroidered in gold.

The great procession jangled down the drive of Viceroy's House, all fluttering pennants and lances, point men and postillions, colour guards and connecting files, buglers and commanders, four squadrons of the world's finest horsemen aglitter in scarlet and gold, a portrait from an old storybook, the last parade of the British Raj.

Nodding with those stiff and graceful half-gestures with which royalty condescends to acknowledge the masses, the tautly erect Mountbattens drove down a line of saluting troops to the great wrought-iron gates of Lutyens's palace. There, outside, India waited.

It was an India such as no Englishman had seen in three centuries. This was no curious crowd come to be dazzled by the circuses of the Raj, to applaud the spectacles staged for their entertainment by their rulers. The dimensions of India had always been in her masses, and today, those masses were thronging New Delhi in numbers and a density never seen before. Jubilant, excited, gleefully unruly, they swarmed around the procession, forcing the horses of the Bodyguard down to a slow walk. All Mountbatten's protocol, all his careful arrangements calculated on the traditions of another India, collapsed, engulfed, overwhelmed by the new India born this day, a vibrant, seething mass drowning the scarlet and gold in a happy brown horde of human beings.

Caught in the crowd along the Mountbattens' route, the Sikh journalist who the night before, had greeted independence by kissing a Moslem medical student, suddenly thought 'the chains are breaking all around me'. He remembered how once, as a child, an English schoolboy had forced him off a sidewalk. 'No one could do that to me now,' he thought. In the crowd, he noted, there were no more rich or poor, Untouchables or masters, lawyers, bank clerks, coolies or pickpockets, just happy people embracing and calling to each other 'Azad Sahib – We are free, Sir!'

'It was as though an entire people had suddenly rediscovered their home,' noted one witness to that happy pandemonium. Seeing his nation's flag flying for the first time over the Delhi officers' mess, Major U.C. Dubey, an officer in the Indian Army, thought: 'in a mess where we've been stooges, now there's no one above us but our brother Indian officers.'

For many simple Indians, the magic word independence meant a new world was at hand. Ranjit Lal, the peasant from Chatharpur, assured his children that 'there will be much to eat now because

India is free'. People refused to pay bus fares, assuming they should now be free. A humble beggar walked into an enclosure reserved for foreign diplomats. A policeman asked him for his invitation.

'Invitation?' he answered, 'Why do I need an invitation? I have my independence. That's enough.'

Across India, scenes of rejoicing similar to those in the capital marked this memorable morning. In Calcutta at 8.00 a.m., a horde from the city's slums swept through the gates of the majestic governor's palace. While the last British governor, Sir Frederick Burrows, and his wife breakfasted in a corner of the house the crowd raced through the spacious salons. In Burrows' bedroom, some of those miserable creatures who'd never slept on anything softer than a patch of dirt or the ropes of a charpoi, celebrated their independence by jumping up and down like excited children on the bed in which the governor's lady had been sleeping an hour before. Elsewhere in the house, others expressed their joy at India's independence by stabbing the oil paintings of India's former rulers with the tips of their umbrellas.

Trams and trolleys ran free of charge all day. A city that had feared it would echo this day to the sound of gunfire rang with happier sounds: the explosion of fire crackers.

In Bombay, excited crowds swarmed into that citadel of imperial elegance, the Taj Mahal Hotel. All day long, in Madras, the dark south-Indian crowds streamed along the waterfront to Fort Saint George to stare with pride and rapture at their nation's flag flying at last over the first fortress of the British East India Company. At Surat, dozens of gaily-bedecked boats staged an independence regatta in the bay where Captain Hawkins had begun Britain's Indian adventure.

India's freedom brought freedom of a most tangible nature to one category of people. Jail doors opened before thousands of convicts granted pardon as an Independence Day gesture. Death sentences were commuted. Mystic India, the India of fakirs and fairy tales, joined the feast. At Thiru Kazhukunram in the south, the mysterious pair of white eagles which swooped down from the sky each noon to snatch their food from the hands of a local *sadhu*, seemed to honour the occasion with an exultant beating of their wings. In the jungles of Madura, near Madras, other holy men indulged in the outlawed spectacle of hook-swinging. Impaling the flesh of their backs on iron claws suspended from a kind of gibbet, they dangled above gawking crowds, offering their agony for India's freedom – and a particularly bountiful harvest of alms.

Everywhere, the day was characterized by the goodwill displayed towards the British and the dignity with which they participated in ceremonies which for many of them marked a sad, nostalgic moment. In Shillong, the British commanding officer of the Assam Rifles spontaneously stood down, giving his Indian deputy the honour of commanding the Independence Day parade. At the huge Chuba tea plantation near the Burmese border, Peter Bullock, the plantation manager, organized a Field Day complete with egg and spoon and sack races for his 1500 workers, most of whom didn't even know what it was they were celebrating with their unexpected holiday.

There were exceptions. In Simla, Mrs Maude Penn Montague refused to leave the home in which she had given so many grand balls and dinners. She considered herself in mourning. Born in India, of a father who'd also been born on the sub-continent, India had become her home. With the exception of five years schooling in England, her whole life had been spent there. To friends who suggested it was now time to leave, she replied: 'My Dear, whatever would I do in England? I don't even know how to boil the water for a cup of tea.' And so, while the former summer capital of the Raj celebrated, she sat at home weeping, unable to bear the sight of another nation's flag going up that pole where her beloved Union Jack had flown.

For the other great dominion born on the sub-continent, 15 August was a particularly auspicious day. It was the last Friday of the holy month of Ramadan. The festivities were almost as much a celebration of the state's founder as they were of the state itself. Jinnah's photo and name were everywhere: in windows, bazaars, stores, on enormous triumphal arches spanning city streets. The *Pakistan Times* even proclaimed that, through the voice of their caretakers, the camels, monkeys and tigers of the Lahore zoo joined in sending their wishes to the Quaid-e-Azzam and trumpeting '*Pakistan Zindabad*'. There may have been no flags of the new state in Dacca, capital of its eastern wing, but everywhere there were pictures of the leader who'd never visited its soil.

Jinnah himself celebrated the day by assuming full powers for his supposedly ceremonial office. In the year of life remaining to him, the London-trained lawyer who for years had not ceased to proclaim his faith in the constitutional process, would govern his new nation as a dictator.

He would do it without the comforting presence of his closest living relative. 500 miles from Karachi, on the balcony of a flat in Colaba, one of Bombay's most elegant suburbs, a young woman had decorated her balcony with two flags, one for India and one for Pakistan. They symbolized the terrible dilemma Independence Day had posed for her, as well as for so many others. Dina, the only child of Mohammed Ali Jinnah, had been unable to decide to which country she wished to belong, the land of her birth, or the Islamic nation created by her father.

Conscious of the terrible drama lurking behind this euphoric Independence Day, many an Indian was unable to share in the ecstasy of his celebrating countrymen. In Lucknow, Anis Kidwai would always remember the incongruous spectacle of a group of cheering, laughing people waving flags, next to others in tears because they'd just learned of the death of close relatives in the Punjab.

Khushwant Singh, a Sikh lawyer from Lahore, was totally indifferent to the gay crowds around him in New Delhi. 'I had nothing to rejoice about,' he would bitterly recall. 'For me and millions like me, this Independence Day was a tragedy. They'd mutilated the Punjab, and I had lost everything.'

The Punjab, 15 August 1947

India's joyful Independence Day was indeed a day of horror for the Punjab. The predominant colour of the dawn of freedom breaking over its ancient vistas was not purple and gold but crimson. In Amritsar, while the city's new authorities dutifully performed their independence rituals at the city's Moghul fortress, an enraged horde of Sikhs was ravaging a Moslem neighbourhood less than a mile away. They slaughtered its male inhabitants without mercy or exception. The women were stripped, repeatedly raped, then paraded shaking and terrified through the city to the Golden Temple where most had their throats cut.

In the Sikh state of Patiala, Sikh bands prowled the countryside pouncing on Moslems trying to flee across the frontier to Pakistan. Prince Balindra Singh, the Maharaja's brother, stumbled on one such band armed with huge *kirpans*. Pleading with them to return to their villages, he said: 'This is harvest time. You should be home cutting your crops.'

'There is another crop to cut first,' replied their leader slicing the air with his *kirpan*.

Amritsar's red-brick railway station had become a kind of refugee camp, a clearing house for thousands of Hindus who'd fled from Pakistan's half of the Punjab. They swarmed around its waiting room, its ticket office, its platforms, ready to scrutinize each arriving train for missing relatives and friends.

Late in the afternoon of 15 August, the station master, Chani Singh, pushed his way through their near-hysterical, weeping ranks with all the authority his little blue cap and the red flag he clutched in his hands conferred on him. Singh was prepared for the scene that would follow the arrival of the incoming Number Ten Down Express. It was the same now for every train arriving in his station. Men and women would rush to the windows and doors of the dust-yellow third-class *bogies*, carriages, desperately searching for the child they'd lost in their hasty flight, shrieking out names, trampling and shoving each other in grief and hysteria. People in tears would rush from carriage to carriage calling for a missing relative, looking for someone from their village who might bring them news. There would be the abandoned children weeping softly on a stack of luggage, the babies born in flight being nursed by their mothers in the midst of that milling mob.

At the head of the platform Singh took his place and officiously waved the incoming locomotive to a halt. As its great steel frame rolled to a stop above his head, Singh glimpsed a strange sight. Four armed soldiers were standing guard over the sullen engine driver. When the hiss of escaping steam and the shriek of the brakes had died, Singh suddenly realized something was terribly wrong.

The babbling multitudes packing the platform were petrified, frozen into an eerie silence by the sight before them. Singh stared down the line of eight carriages. All the windows of the compartments were wide open but there was not a single human being standing at any of them. Not a single door had opened. Not a single person was getting off the train. They had brought him a trainful of phantoms.

The station master strode to the first carriage, snatched open the door and stepped inside. In one horrible instant he understood why no one was getting off the Ten Down Express in Amritsar that night. It was not a trainful of phantoms they'd brought him, it was a trainful of corpses. The floor of the compartment before him was a tangled jumble of human bodies, throats cut, skulls smashed, bowels eviscerated. Arms, legs, trunks of bodies were strewn along the corridors of compartments. From somewhere in that ghastly human junk-heap at his feet, Singh heard a sound of strangled gargling. Realizing that there might be a few survivors, Singh called out: 'You are in Amritsar. We are Hindus and Sikhs here. The police are present. Do not be afraid.'

At his words a few of the dead began to stir. The stark horror of the scenes that followed would be forever a nightmare engraved upon the station master's mind. One woman picked her husband's severed head from the coagulating pool of blood by her side. She clutched it in her arms shrieking her grief. He saw weeping children clinging to the bodies of their slaughtered mothers, men in shock as they pulled the body of a mutilated child from a pile of corpses. As the crowd along the platform realized what had happened, hysteria swept their ranks.

Numb, the station master made his way down the line of bodies. In every compartment of every carriage the sight was the same. By the time he reached the last one he was ill. Reeling back on to the platform, his nostrils impregnated with the stench of death, Singh thought, 'How could God permit such a thing?'

He turned to look back at the train. As he did, he saw in great white-washed letters on the flank of the last car the assassins' calling card. 'This train is our Independence gift to Nehru and Patel,' it read.

In Calcutta, the unfathomable alchemy of that strange old man with his prayers and his spinning-wheel was somehow casting its spell over the slums in which everyone had expected an explosion to dwarf in dimension and horror the worst of the happenings in the Punjab. The promise inherent in the procession which had marched to Hydari House the evening before had been realized. All across Calcutta, on the avenues and thoroughfares which just a year before had been littered with the corpses of Direct Action Day, Moslems and Hindus had paraded and celebrated together. It was, wrote Gandhi's secretary, Pyarelal Nayar, 'as if after the black clouds of a year of madness, the sunshine of sanity and goodwill had suddenly broken through.'

The almost incredible change in Calcutta's climate had been signalled at dawn with the arrival at Hydari House of another procession, this one composed of young girls. Hindus and Moslems they'd been walking since midnight to take *darshan* from Gandhi, a kind of mystic communion engendered by being in the presence of a great spirit. They had been the first in an uninterrupted flow of pilgrims that had converged all day long on Hydari House.

Every half an hour, Gandhi had had to interrupt his meditation and spinning to appear on the porch before the crowds. Because he considered this a day of mourning, he had not prepared a formal message of congratulations for the people he'd led to freedom. That message came spontaneously and it was addressed not to India's masses but to their new rulers.

'Beware of power,' he warned a group of politicians come to seek his blessing, 'power corrupts. Do not let yourselves be entrapped by its pomp and pageantry. Remember you are in office to serve the poor in India's villages.'

That afternoon, with a bleating of conch shells, 30,000 people, three times the number that had gathered the day before, poured down Beliaghata Road for Gandhiji's prayer meeting. Gandhi addressed them from a wooden platform hastily erected in the yard outside the house. He congratulated them on what they had accomplished in Calcutta. Their noble example, he hoped, might inspire their countrymen in the Punjab.

Shaheed Suhrawardy, his features taut from the strain of a 24-hour fast, addressed the multitude when Gandhi had finished. The man who'd been the unchallenged leader of Calcutta's Moslems asked the mixed assembly to set a seal upon their reconciliation by joining him in crying '*Jai – Hind* – Victory to India'. At his shout, an answering roar burst like a clap of monsoon thunder from 30,000 throats.

After the meeting, the two men set out together on a tour of the city in Gandhi's old Chevrolet. This time, however, it was not with stones and curses that the crowd of Calcutta greeted the Mahatma's car. At every street corner they showered it with rosewater and a grateful cry: 'Gandhiji, you have saved us!'

Poona, 15 August 1947

The ceremony being held on a vacant lot in the inland city of Poona, 119 miles south-east of Bombay, was similar to thousands like it taking place all across the new dominion of India. It was a flag-raising. One thing, however, set the little ritual apart from most of the others. The flag slowly moving up a makeshift staff in the centre of a group of 500 men was not the flag of an independent India. It was an orange triangle and emblazoned upon it was the symbol which, in a slightly modified form, had terrorized Europe for a decade, the swastika.

That ancient emblem was on the orange pennant in Poona for the same reason as it had been on the banners of Hitler's Third Reich. It was an Aryan symbol. It had been brought to India at some juncture lost in the mists of time by the first waves of Aryan conquerors to subdue the sub-continent. The men gathered about it in Poona all belonged to the RSSS, the para-fascist movement, some of whose members had been assigned the task of assassinating Jinnah along with Mountbatten in Karachi 48 hours earlier. Hindu zealots, they saw themselves as the heirs to those ancient Aryans.

They shared one emotion with the bespectacled prophet on the opposite flank on the sub-continent. They, too, were desperately pained by the division of India. Their identification with Mahatma Gandhi and the things he stood for, however, ended there.

The group to which they belonged cherished an historic dream, to reconstitute a great Hindu empire from the headwaters of the Indus River to eastern Burma, from Tibet to Cape Comorin. They despised Gandhi and all his works. To them, India's national hero was the arch-enemy of Hinduism. The doctrine of non-violence with which he had led India to independence was in their eyes a coward's philosophy that had vitiated the force and character of the Hindu peoples. There was no place in their dreams for the brotherhood and tolerance of India's Moslem minority preached by Gandhi. They considered themselves, as Hindus, the sole heirs to India's Aryan conquerors and therefore the rightful proprietors of the sub-continent. The Moslems, they held, were descendants of an usurping clan, that of the Moghuls.

But, above all, there was one sin for which they could never pardon India's elderly leader. That they should even have accused him of it was the final cruel irony in the cruellest year in Mohandas Gandhi's life. They held Gandhi, the only Indian politician who had opposed it until the very end, solely responsible for India's partition.

The man standing in front of their gathering in Poona that August afternoon was a journalist. Nathuram Godse had, in that summer of 1947, just become 37, yet slight pads of baby fat still clung to his cheeks, giving him a deceptively young and innocent look. He had exceptional eyes, large, sad and compelling in their slightly crossed gaze. In repose, there was always about his regard a faint air of disapproval, a strain about the mouth and nostrils as though he had just smelled a neighbour's body odour but was too polite or too inhibited to express his distaste.

Now, however, those features were not in repose. Earlier, Nathuram Godse had made clear his sentiments on India's Independence Day on the front page of the daily paper he edited, the *Hindu Rashtra - Hindu Nation*. The spot usually filled by his daily editorial had been left blank, its white columns surrounded by a black band of mourning.

The ceremonies all around India celebrating independence were, he told his followers, 'deliberate camouflage to conceal from the people the fact that hundreds of Hindu men were being massacred and hundreds of Hindu women being kidnapped and raped.'

'The vivisection of India,' he shouted, was 'a calamity condemning millions of Indians to horrible sufferings.' It was, 'the work of the Congress Party and, above all, its leader Gandhi.'

When he had finished, Nathuram Godse led his 500 followers in the salute to their flag. Thumbs pressed against their hearts, their hands' palms down,at right angles to their chests, they vowed 'to the Motherland which gave me birth and in which I have grown that my body is ready to die for her cause'.

As he always did, Nathuram Godse felt a tremor of pride flutter across his being as he recited those words. All his life, from his school examinations through half a dozen trades, Nathuram Godse had been a failure at everything he'd undertaken. Then he'd embraced the extremist doctrines of the RSSS. Steeping himself in its lore and literature, teaching himself to write, to speak, he had made himself one of the movement's foremost polemicists. Now he saw for himself a new role. He would become a vengeful spirit, purifying India of the foes of a militant Hindu resurrection. In that role, for the first time, Nathuram Godse would not be a failure.

New Delhi, 15 August 1947

For years to come, the one great memory left by 15 August 1947 in India would be the crowds, the multitudinous hordes inundating in a human sea the event that had been designed as the high point of the new nation's independence celebrations. It was the official raising of the Indian flag at five o'clock in the afternoon in an open space near New Delhi's India Gate, a sandstone arch dedicated to the 90,000 Indians who'd died for the British Empire in World War One.

Louis Mountbatten and his advisers, drawing on those manuals which had ordered all the grandiose manifestations of the Raj, had estimated 30,000 people would attend. The figure was wrong, not by a few thousand but by well over half a million. Never before had anyone ever seen anything remotely like it in India's capital city.

Stretching out in every direction, the masses that had converged on the site engulfed the little official tribune erected next to the flagpole. To one spectator, it looked like 'a raft bobbing on a stormy sea'. Everything – every vestige of the barriers, the bandstands, the carefully prepared visitors' gallery and guide-ropes – was swept away in a dense torrent of human beings. Helpless, the police looked on as barriers were trampled, chairs snapped, like twigs under a man's foot. Lost in those masses, Ranjit Lal, the peasant who'd left his village of Chatharpur at dawn, thought the only crowds in India like it must be for the *melas*, the holy bathing festivals in the Ganges. So tightly did the throng press around him that Lal and his wife couldn't even eat the *chapatis* they'd brought with them from their village. They were unable to move their hands from their sides to their mouths.

Elizabeth Collins and Muriel Watson, Lady Mountbatten's secretaries, arrived just after five. They had come dressed for the occasion, in fresh white gloves, their best cocktail dresses and bright little feathered hats. Suddenly they found themselves caught up in the surge of that happy, sweaty, half-naked crowd. They were literally swept off their feet and thrust forward by the crowd's remorseless drive. Clutching each other for support, their hats askew, their dresses dishevelled, they struggled desperately to remain upright. For the first time in her life, Elizabeth, who'd accompanied Lady Mountbatten on all her wartime trips, was frightened. Tightening her grip on Muriel's arm, she gasped: 'We're going to be trampled to death!'

Muriel scanned the hordes hemming them in on all sides. 'Thank God,' she murmured with a sigh of relief, 'at least, they're not wearing shoes.'

Pamela Mountbatten, the 17-year-old younger daughter of the Governor-General, arrived with two of her father's staff. With enormous difficulty they worked their way towards the wooden tribune. A hundred yards away they came on an impassable barrier of people, all seated, squeezed so tightly together that there was barely a breath of air between them.

Spotting her from his place on the tribune Nehru shouted at her to cross over the people to the platform.

'How can I?' she shouted back. 'I've got high heels on.'

'Take them off,' replied Nehru.

Pamela couldn't dream of doing something as undignified on such an historic occasion. 'Oh,' she gasped, 'I couldn't do that.'

'Then leave them on,' said Nehru. 'Just walk over the people. They won't mind.'

'Oh,' replied Pamela, 'the heels will hurt them.'

'Don't be a silly girl,' snapped Nehru. 'Take them off and come across.'

With a sigh, the daughter of India's last Viceroy kicked off her shoes, picked them up and set off across the carpet of human beings separating her from the platform. Laughing gleefully, the Indians over whom she was treading helped her along, steadying her shaking legs, guiding her elbow, pointing with delight to her shiny high heels.

At the instant the bright turbans of the bodyguard escorting the Mountbattens' state carriage appeared on the horizon, the crowd thrust forward with a wave-like heave. Following her parents' slow progress from the tribune, Pamela witnessed an incredible spectacle.

In that human sea surrounding the tribune were thousands of women clutching nursing babies at their breasts. Terrified that their infants would be crushed by the mob's surge, they reacted with a desperate gesture. They hurled them up into the air like rubber balls, tossing them back up again each time they tumbled down. In an instant, the air was filled with hundreds of infants. 'My God,' thought the young girl her eyes wide with wonder, 'it's raining babies!'

From his carriage, Mountbatten instantly realized there wasn't the vaguest chance of carrying out the elaborately planned ritual he'd prepared to accompany the flag raising. He himself couldn't even get out of the carriage.

'Let's just hoist the flag,' he shouted to Nehru. 'The band's swamped. They can't play. The guards can't move.'

Over the crowd's happy din, the men on the platform heard his call. The saffron, white and green banner of a free India climbed up the flagpole while, tautly erect in his carriage, Queen Victoria's great-grandson marked its progress with a formal salute.

A roar of untrammelled happiness burst from half a million throats as the folds of the flag rose above the heads of the crowd. In the joy of that sublime second, India forgot the battle of Plassey, the vengeance of 1857, the massacre of Amritsar. Forgotten for an instant were the humiliations of martial law, the *lathi*-swinging police charges, the executions of her independence martyrs. Three difficult centuries were set aside to allow her to savour unfettered the delight of that moment.

Even the heavens seemed ready to brighten its historic impact. As India's new flag neared the peak of its flagstaff, a rainbow suddenly flashed across the sky. To a people to whom the occult was an obsession and the celestial bodies the preordinators of Man's destiny, its appearance could only be interpreted as a manifestation of the Divine. Most extraordinary of all, its green, yellow and indigo bands were eerily similar to the colours of the flag framed in its perfect arc. As it glittered there, a voice quivering with wonder rose from the faceless horde around the platform.

'When God himself gives us a sign such as this,' it called out in Hindi, 'who can stand against us?'

The most extraordinary experience of their lives now awaited Louis and Edwina Mountbatten, their ride back to Lutyens' palace. Their gilded carriage became a sort of life-raft, tossed amidst the most hysterical, happy, exuberant throng of human beings either of them had ever seen. Nehru himself was passed up into the carriage to ride with them, quite literally thrust aboard by his countrymen. The whole thing, Mountbatten thought, was 'a kind of an enormous picnic of almost a million people, all of them having more fun than they'd ever had in their lives'. He immediately understood that this spontaneous, uncontrollable, but utterly happy outburst was a far truer reflection of the meaning of this day than all the pomp and pageantry he'd planned for it.

Standing up in the middle of a forest of waving hands thrust frantically towards his, Mountbatten scanned the crowd, trying to find an outer limit to that field of human heads. He could see none. As far as his eyes could reach there was the crowd, always the crowd.

Three times, Mountbatten and his wife leaned out of the carriage and hauled aboard an exhausted woman about to tumble under its wheels. The trio took their places on the black leather seats designed to cushion the King and Queen of England. They sat there, dark eyes wide with wonder, the edges of their saris pulled across their giggling mouths, bouncing along with India's last Viceroy and Vicereine laughing happily at their sides.

Above all, for Louis and Edwina Mountbatten the memory of this glorious day would always be associated with a cry, a vibrant, interminably repeated cry. No Englishman in Indian history had been privileged to hear it shouted with the emotion and sincerity that went with it that afternoon in New Delhi. Like a series of thunderclaps it burst over and over again from the crowd, the popular sanction of Mountbatten's achievement. Standing there in his shaking carriage, he received something neither his great-grandmother nor any of her progeny had received, the homage, the real homage, of the people of India. '*Mountbatten Ki Jai!*' the crowd yelled again and again, '*Mountbatten Ki Jai* – Long Live Mountbatten!'.

Six thousand miles from the exulting crowds of New Delhi, in the heart of the Scottish Highlands, an official car entered the courtyard of the castle of Balmoral. Its sole occupant was immediately shown to the study in which George VI awaited. Bowing stiffly, the Earl of Listowel, last Secretary of State for India, solemnly informed the King that the Transfer of Power to Indian hands had been accomplished. The nature of the monarch's reign was irrevocably altered; his no longer was the designation of George VI, Rex Imperator. He had now, Listowel explained, to return to George VI's custody those ancient seals which had been the badge of the Secretary of State's office, the symbol of the links binding the Indian Empire to the British crown.

Unhappily, he continued, there were no seals. Someone years before had mislaid them. The only souvenir his last Secretary of State for India could offer to the sovereign was a ritualistic nod of his head and the symbolic extension of an empty palm.

Dusk, and the dust raised by a million feet, settled over the capital of India. Thousands continued to throng its streets, singing, cheering, embracing. In Old Delhi, by the walls of the Red Fort, thousands of celebrating people swarmed through a gigantic outdoor carnival of snake charmers, jugglers, fortune tellers, dancing bears, wrestlers, sword swallowers, fakirs piercing their cheeks with silver spikes, flautists. Other thousands trudged out of the city towards the endless plains from which they'd come. Ranjit Lal, the Brahmin peasant from Chatharpur, was among them. To Lal's distress, the tonga driver who'd asked four annas to bring him to Delhi now wanted two rupees to take him home. Vowing that was too high a price to pay for freedom, he and his family set out to walk the twenty miles back to their village.

Alone at last in the private chamber of their palace, Louis and Edwina Mountbatten fell into each other's arms. Tears of sheer happiness poured down their faces. The wheel of their lives had come full circle. In the streets of the city in which a quarter of a century before they had fallen in love, they had shared a triumph, felt an exhilaration such as is given to few people to know. For the admiral, even though he had tasted the exultant pleasure of accepting the surrender of three quarters of a million Japanese, his life would never produce another experience to rival it. It had been, Louis Mountbatten thought, like the hysterical celebration at the end of a war – only this had been 'a war both sides had won, a war without losers'.

The following morning, a visitor from New Delhi rang the bell of Number 10 Downing Street. Its occupant, Clement Attlee, had every reason to feel satisfied. India's independence had been accompanied by an outpouring of goodwill and friendship towards Britain such as no one had thought possible six months before. Comparing her actions to those of Holland in Indonesia and France in Indo-China, one distinguished Indian had declared, 'We cannot but admire the courage and political capacity of the British people.'

Louis Mountbatten, however, had sent his former Secretary, George Abell, to caution Attlee against any excessive jubilation at such declarations. The manner in which independence had been achieved, Abell told Attlee in the garden of his residence, was a great triumph both for his government and the man he had chosen as his last Viceroy. But, he warned, don't celebrate the triumph too quickly or too publicly, because the inevitable consequence of partition was going to be 'the most appalling bloodshed and confusion'.

Attlee puffed at his pipe and sadly shook his head. There would be no boastful trumpetings, no self-satisfied proclamations coming from Downing Street, he agreed. He was 'under no illusion'. What they had accomplished was important but he well knew there was now a price to be paid and that price was going to be 'terrible bloodshed in the India we have left'.

The time had come to open Pandora's box. For just a second Louis Mountbatten paused, his gaze upon the two manilla envelopes in his hand. Each contained a set of the new maps of the sub-continent and less than a dozen typewritten pages of paper. They were the last official documents Britain would bequeath India, the final links in a chain that had begun with Elizabeth I's Royal Charter to the East India Company in 1599 and continued down to that act over which, barely a month before, a clerk had muttered '*Le Roi le Veult*'. None of the documents which had preceded them, however, had produced a reaction as immediate or as brutal as these were going to. They were, inevitably, the catalysts of the tragedy predicted to Britain's Prime Minister in his Downing Street garden.

Mountbatten passed them to Nehru and Pakistan's Prime Minister, Liaqat Ali Khan, suggesting they study them in two different rooms, then return for a joint meeting in two hours' time. The fury contorting their faces on their return reassured Mountbatten on at least one point: Cyril Radcliffe had performed his thankless task with true impartiality. Both men seemed equally enraged. As soon as they sat down, they exploded in a rush of angry protests. India's independence celebrations were over.

Cyril Radcliffe had followed his instructions rigorously in applying his scalpel to the map of India. With a few minor exceptions, the lines he'd traced in the Punjab and Bengal were those imposed by the religious persuasion of the majority populations. The result was exactly what everyone had predicted: technically feasible, in practical application a disaster.

The line in the Bengal condemned both parties to economic ruin unless they could collaborate. Eighty-five per cent of the world's jute was grown in the area that had gone to Pakistan, but there was not a single mill for processing it in the new state's territory. India wound up with over a hundred jute mills, the port of Calcutta from which it was shipped to the world – and no jute.

The Punjab boundary over which Radcliffe had agonized so much, began in a trackless wood on the edge of Kashmir where the western branch of a river called the Ujh entered the Punjab. Following where possible the Ravi or Sutlej Rivers, it ran 200 miles south to the northernmost edge of the Great Indian Desert. Lahore went to Pakistan, Amritsar with its Golden Temple to India.

As it was condemned from the start to do, Radcliffe's line sliced into two parts the lands and peoples of India's most closely knit, militant community, the Sikhs. Vengeful and embittered, they were now to become the principal actors in the tragedy of the Punjab.

The major controversy produced by Radcliffe's award would come over one of his rare exceptions to his majority population principle. It involved a squalid little city called Gurdaspur near the northern extremity of the Punjab. There, Radcliffe had elected to follow the natural boundary line of the Ravi River, leaving the city and the Moslem villages around it inside India, instead of creating a Pakistani enclave protruding into Indian territory.

It was a decision for which Pakistan's millions would never pardon him. For, had Radcliffe awarded Gurdaspur to Pakistan, it was not that dirty, inconsequential city Jinnah's state would have won. With it, inevitably, would have come the enchanted vale for which the dying Moghul Emperor Jehangir had cried in despair 'Kashmir – only Kashmir'.

Without Gurdaspur, India would have no practicable land access to Kashmir and its vacillating Hindu Maharaja, Hari Singh, would have had no choice except to link Kashmir's destiny to Pakistan. Unintentionally, almost inadvertently, Radcliffe's scalpel had offered India the hope of claiming Kashmir.

The man who had been asked to serve as the artisan of India's vivisection because he had known so little about it, contemplated for the last time in his life the mournful landscapes of the country he'd divided. Cyril Radcliffe, under close security guard, was going home. The last task accomplished by the ICS officer delegated to assist him had been to comb his plane for a possible bomb. Lost in his thoughts, the British jurist watched from his aircraft's window as the Punjab's endless fields of wheat and sugarcane slipped past, their furrows indelibly altered now by the tracings of his pencil on a map.

Radcliffe knew well the grief and consternation the lines he'd produced were going to cause. There had been, alas, no lines he could have drawn that would not have brought forth their harvest of anguish and suffering. The elements inexorably propelling the Punjab to tragedy had been inherent in the situation long before Cyril Radcliffe had been summoned to India. As certain as the eternal cycle of the Punjab's seasons, the consequences of his award would, he knew, be terrible bloodshed, violence and destruction. And, just as certain, he knew it was he who would be blamed for it all.

Packed away in his luggage were Radcliffe's physical souvenirs of his stay in India, a pair of oriental carpets he'd bought in Delhi's bazaar. His real souvenirs would always be mental. On his appointment both Nehru and Jinnah had agreed to be bound by his decision and use all their authority to implement it. Now, in unseeming haste, both men rushed to condemn those parts which did not suit them, sabotaging it, almost, with their 'ill-tempered reactions'.

In a few days' time, in those law chambers from which he'd set out for India, a thoroughly disenchanted Radcliffe reacted to their outburst with the one gesture available to him. He disdainfully returned the £2000 he was to have received as his fee for preparing the most complex boundary award of modern times.

On the plains below, invisible to Radcliffe, the greatest migration in human history was already beginning. Precursors of the storm to come, a first trickle of helpless people staggered along the Punjab's canal banks, down her dirt paths, and unmarked tracks, over her great Trunk Highway, across her unharvested fields. In a few hours, the publication of Radcliffe's report would add still another dimension to the horrors enfolding that province which had been the arena of so many of mankind's dramas. Villages whose Moslem inhabitants had exulted at the birth of Pakistan would find themselves in India; in others, Sikhs barely finished celebrating what they had mistakenly thought was their hamlet's attachment to India, before they had to flee for their lives towards Radcliffe's border across the fields they'd cultivated for years.

Soon the anomalies which Radcliffe had warned haste would produce became manifest. In places, the headworks of a canal system ended up in one country, the embankments which protected them in another. Sometimes the line ran down the heart of a village, leaving a dozen huts in India, a dozen more in Pakistan. Occasionally it even bisected a home, leaving a front door opening on to India and a rear window looking into Pakistan. Almost all the Punjab's jails wound up in Pakistan. So, too, did its solitary lunatic asylum.

There, in a sudden burst of lucidity, its terrified Hindu and Sikh inmates begged their custodians to send them to India. The Moslems, they reasoned, would slaughter them if they remained in Pakistan. Their plea was rejected. Far less prescient than those lunatics for whom they were responsible, the asylum's doctors foresaw no such danger. Condescendingly they assured their patients 'their fears were imaginary'. They were anything but that.

13

'Our People Have Gone Mad'

The Punjab, August–September 1947

It would be unique, a cataclysm without precedent, unforeseen in magnitude, unordered in pattern, unreasoned in savagery. For six terrible weeks, like the ravages of a medieval plague, a mania for murder would sweep across the face of northern India. There would be no sanctuary from its scourge, no corner free from the contagion of its virus. Half as many Indians would lose their lives in that swift splurge of slaughter as Americans in four years of combat in World War II.

Everywhere the many and the strong assaulted the weak and the few. In the stately homes of New Delhi's Aurangazeb Road, the silver *souks* of Old Delhi's Chandni Chowk, the *mohallas* of Amritsar, the elegant suburbs of Lahore, the bazaar of Rawalpindi, the walled city of Peshawar; in shops, stalls, mud huts, village alleyways; in brick-kilns, factories and fields; in railway stations and tea houses; communities which had lived side by side for generations fell upon each other in an orgy of hate. It was not a war, not a civil war, not a guerrilla campaign. It was a convulsion, the sudden, shattering collapse of a society. One act provoked another, one horror fed another, each slaughter begot its successor, each rumour its imitator, each atrocity its counterpart, until, like slow-motion images of a building disintegrating under the impact of an explosion, the walls of Punjab society crumbled upon each other.

The disaster had its explanations. India and Pakistan were at the moment of their birth like a pair of Siamese twins linked by a malignant tumour, the Punjab. Cyril Radcliffe's scalpel had severed the tumour, but it had not been able to carve out the cancerous cells infecting each half. His line had left 5 million Sikhs and Hindus in Pakistan's half of the Punjab, over 5 million Moslems in India's half. Prodded by the demagoguery of Jinnah and the leaders of the Moslem League, the Punjab's exploited Moslems had convinced themselves that, somehow, in Pakistan the Land of the Pure, Hindu money-lenders, shopkeepers, *zamindars* and aggressive Sikh landlords, would disappear. Yet there they were on the aftermath of independence, still ready to collect their rents, still occupying their shops and farms. Inevitably, a simple thought swept the Moslem masses: if Pakistan is ours, so too are the shops, farms, houses and factories of the Hindus and Sikhs. Across the border the militant

Sikhs prepared to drive the Moslems from their midst so they could gather on to the abandoned lands their brothers whom Radcliffe's scalpel had left in Pakistan.

And so, in a bewildering frenzy, Hindus, Sikhs and Moslems turned on each other. India was ever a land of extravagant dimensions, and the horror of the Punjab's killings, the abundance of human anguish and suffering they would produce, did not fail that ancient tradition. Europe's peoples had slaughtered each other with bombs, shells and the calculated horrors of the gas chambers; the people of the Punjab set out to destroy themselves with bamboo staves, hockey-sticks, ice-picks, knives, clubs, swords, hammers, bricks and clawing fingers. Theirs was a spontaneous, irrational slaughter. Appalled at the emotions they had inadvertently unleashed, their desperate leaders tried to call them back to reason. It was a hopeless cry. There was no reason in that brief and cruel season when India went mad.

Capt. R. E. Atkins of the 2/8 Gurkhas gasped in horror at the sight at his feet. A figure of speech he'd often heard but had never believed had taken on reality under his eyes. The gutters of Lahore were running red with blood. The beautiful Paris of the Orient was a vista of desolation and destruction. Whole streets of Hindu homes were ablaze, while Moslem police and troops stood by watching. At night, the sounds of looters ransacking those homes seemed to Atkins like the crunch of termites boring into logs. At his headquarters at Braganza's Hotel, Atkins had been besieged by a horde of pathetic, half-hysterical Hindu businessmen ready to offer him anything, twenty-five, thirty, fifty thousand rupees, their daughters, their wives' jewellery, if only he would let them flee the hell Lahore had become in his jeep.

In nearby Amritsar, broad sections of the city, its Moslem sections, were nothing but heaps of brick and debris, twisting curls of smoke drifting above them into the sky, vultures keeping their vigil on their shattered walls, the pungent aroma of decomposing corpses permeating the ruins. Everywhere the face of the Punjab was disfigured by similar scenes. In Lyallpur the Moslem workers in a textile factory turned on the Sikhs who shared the misery of their looms and slaughtered every one of them. There, the image that had horrified Capt. Atkins was magnified to an almost unbelievable dimension: this time it was an entire irrigation canal that was incarnadined by hundreds of Sikh and Hindu corpses.

In Simla, Fay Campbell-Johnson, wife of Lord Mountbatten's press attaché, gaped in horror at the spectacle she beheld from the veranda of Cecil's Hotel where the Raj's summering rulers had sipped their tea. Sikhs on bicycles, waving their *kirpans,* were swooping down the Mall chasing fleeing Moslems like hunters a fox. They would ride up behind a gasping victim and behead him with one terrible swish of their swords. Another Englishwoman saw the head of one of their victims, a fez still fixed firmly to it, rolling along the street while the Sikh assassin furiously pursued his next victim waving his bloody sword, shrieking: 'I'll kill more! I'll kill more!'

A man's executioner could be a friend or a stranger. Every day for fifteen years, Niranjan Singh, a Sikh tea merchant in the Montgomery bazaar, had served a pot of Assam tea to the Moslem leatherworker who came rushing to his shop one August morning. He was setting the man's ration on his little brass balance when he looked up to see his customer, his face contorted in hate, pointing at him and screaming 'Kill him, kill him!'

A dozen Moslem hoodlums raced out of the alley. One severed Singh's leg at the knee with a sword. In an instant they had killed his 90-year-old father and his only son. The last sight he saw as he lost consciousness was his 18-year-old daughter, screaming in fright, being carried off on the shoulders of the man to whom he'd been serving tea for fifteen years.

There were districts in which not a single village went unharmed, not a bazaar was left standing. Everywhere the minority community was gripped by fear and terror. In Ukarna, a Moslem-dominated mill-town on the Lahore/Karachi railway, Madanlal Pahwa, a stocky 20-year-old Indian Navy veteran, cowered inside the home of his aunt. Through the windows he could see the town's jubilant Moslems dancing, singing, waving flags. chanting their newest slogan: '*Hans ke liya Pakistan, Lad ke lenge Hindustan*-We got Pakistan by laughing, we'll get India by fighting.' Madanlal hated Moslems. In his khaki uniform with the black stripe of the RSSS he had helped terrorize them. Now it was his turn to be terrorized. 'We are all frightened,' he thought, 'we are like sheep waiting for slaughter.'

Where they were dominant, the Sikhs were the best organized, most vicious killers of all. Ahmed Zafrullah was a Moslem tenant farmer in a little village near Ferozpore, assaulted one night by a Sikh *jattha.* 'We knew we were going to be killed like rats,' he recalled. 'We hid behind our *charpois,* behind our piles of cow dung. The Sikhs broke down the door with axes. I was hit by a bullet in my left arm. As I tried to stand, I saw my wife get four bullets. Blood was coming from her thigh and back. My 3-year-old son was hit in the abdomen. He did not cry. He fell down. He was dead.

'I took hold of my wife and my second son. We left the dead child and crawled out to the street. I saw Sikhs shooting down the Moslems coming from the other huts. Some were carrying away girls on their shoulders. There were shrieks and wailings and shoutings. The Sikhs jumped on me and dragged my dead wife from my arms. They killed the second boy and left me to die in the dust. I had no strength to weep or tears to drop. My eyes were as dry as the rivers of the Sind before the monsoon. I fell down unconscious.'

In Sheikhpura, a trading town north of Lahore, the entire Hindu and Sikh community was herded into an enormous 'go-down', a huge warehouse used by the town bank to store the sacks of grain held as collateral for its loans. Once inside, the helpless Hindus were machine-gunned by Moslem police and army deserters. There were no survivors.

One constant refrain sprang from the lips of the British officers who'd stayed on to serve in the Indian or Pakistan armies: 'It was far worse than anything we saw in World War II.'

Robert Trumbull, a veteran correspondent of the *New York Times*, noted: 'I have never been as shaken by anything, even by the piled-up bodies on the beach-head of Tarawa. In India today blood flows oftener than rain falls. I have seen dead by the hundreds and, worst of all, thousands of Indians without eyes, feet or hands. Death by shooting is merciful and uncommon. Men, women and children are commonly beaten to death with clubs and stones and left to die, their death agony intensified by heat and flies.'

The warring communities seemed to rival each other in savagery. One British officer of the Punjab Boundary Force discovered four Moslem babies 'roasted like piglets on spits in a village raided by Sikhs'. Another found a group of Hindu women, their breasts methodically mutilated by Moslem zealots, being headed for slaughter.

In Moslem areas, Hindus were sometimes offered the choice of converting to Islam or fleeing Pakistan. Bagh Das, a Hindu farmer in a hamlet west of Lyallpur, was marched with three hundred fellow Hindus to a mosque set by a small pond in a neighbouring village. Their feet were washed in the pond, then they were herded into the mosque and ordered to sit cross-legged on the floor. The *maulvi* read a few verses of the Koran. 'Now,' he told them, 'you have the choice of becoming Moslems and living happily or being killed.'

'We preferred the former,' acknowledged Das. Each convert was given a new Moslem name and made to recite a verse from the Koran. Then they were herded into the mosque's courtyard where a cow was roasting. One by one the Hindus were made to eat a piece of its flesh. Das, a vegetarian until that instant, 'had a vomiting sensation', but he controlled it because, he thought, 'I will be killed if I do not obey their command'.

His neighbour, a Brahmin, asked permission to take his wife and three children back to his hut to get his special wedding plates and forks in view of the importance of the moment. Flattered, his Moslem captors agreed. 'The Brahmin had a knife hidden in his house,' Das remembered. 'When he got home, he took it from its hiding-place. He cut his wife's throat, then the throats of his three children. Then he stabbed his own heart. None of them returned to eat the meat.'

A motive that had nothing to do with religious fervour was more often behind the Moslem attacks on Hindus and Sikhs in Pakistan. It was greed, a simple, often carefully orchestrated effort to grab the lands, shops and wealth of their neighbours.

Sardar Prem Singh, a Sikh, exercised the occupation the Moslems detested more than any other in a village near Sialkot. He was a money-lender. 'I belonged to a very rich family,' Prem Singh noted, 'I had a big house, double-storied with strong iron gates in front. Everyone in the village knew I was the richest. Many Moslems mortgaged their jewels with me. I kept them in a big iron safe. At some time in his life almost every Moslem in the village had pledged his ornaments with me.'

One morning just after independence, Prem Singh saw a milling mob of Moslems streaming towards his house, brandishing clubs, crowbars, knives. He recognized almost every male in the crowd. They had all at one time or another been his creditors. 'The safe, the safe,' they screamed.

'They expected to reap a rich harvest,' Prem Singh knew. His safe, however, contained something more than Moslem jewels. Locked inside was a double-barrelled shotgun and twenty-five cartridges. Singh opened the safe, grabbed the gun and rushed to the second floor. For an hour he ran from window to window defending his home from the mob trying to beat in his gate. As he did so, an appalling scene was taking place on the floor below. Certain the Moslem mob was about to break into the house, his wife summoned Prem Singh's six daughters to his office. She took a huge drum of cooking kerosene and drenched herself in its contents. After beseeching the mercy of the Sikh's *guru*, Nanak, and urging her daughters to follow her example, she set herself ablaze.

On the floor above, still fighting desperately, her husband was mystified by the sickening odour drifting up the staircase. Finally, when he had only five cartridges left, the mob withdrew and the exhausted Sikh staggered downstairs. There the horrified money-lender discovered the reason for the acrid stench that had haunted him. Stretched in front of his open safe were the charred corpses of his wife and three of his daughters who had preferred self-immolation to the risk of rape at Moslem hands.

Not all the Sikhs and Hindus driven from their homes were wealthy. Kuldip Singh was a 14-year-old boy, the son of a Sikh sharecropper, one of fifty Hindus and Sikhs in a village of six hundred Moslems north of Lahore. He shared the misery of his two-room hut with his parents, two buffaloes and a cow. One day their Moslem neighbours surrounded their quarter shouting, 'Leave Pakistan or we will kill you.'

They fled to the home of the most important Sikh in the village. 'The Moslems came with swords, knives, long iron pikes with kerosene cloths tied on them to burn us. We threw bricks and stones at them, but they were able to set fire to our house. They caught hold of one Sikh and set fire to his beard. Even though his beard was burning, he still killed one Moslem by throwing a big brick at his head. Then he fell down dead muttering the name of the Sikh *guru*.

'They dragged the men outside and killed them in the streets. I ran to the roof. The women were there watching. They knew they would be captured and raped. Some of them had babies in their arms. They made a big fire on the roof. They fed their babies their breast milk, crying of the fate overtaking them. Then they threw the babies in the fire and jumped in after them.'

'I could not bear the sight,' the Sikh youth remembered. He leapt off the roof and in the confusion and growing darkness escaped to a tree in whose branches he hid for the next six hours.

'A bad smell was coming from the house because of the burning bodies,' he recalled. 'My mother and father did not come out. I knew they had been killed or had jumped into the fire. I saw two girls being carried away. They did not cry. They were unconscious.

'When there was peace late at night, I came down from the tree. I went into the house. They were all dead. Everybody in the village except the two girls and myself had been killed.' The 14-year-old Sikh spent the night in that charnel house, too stunned even to weep. At dawn, he tried to recognize the charred forms of his parents among the blackened bodies of the friends and neighbours he'd known all his life. He couldn't. He found a blood-coated knife lying on the floor and chopped his uncut hair from his head so he could pose as a Moslem. Then he fled.

Horror had no race, and the terrible anguish of those August days in the Punjab was meted out with almost biblical balance, an eye for an eye, massacre for massacre, rape for rape, blind cruelty for blind cruelty. The only difference between Kuldip Singh and Mohammed Yaqub was their religion. Mohammed too was a 14-year-old boy. He lived in India near Amritsar. The Moslem youth was playing marbles in front of the hut in which he lived with his parents and six brothers and sisters when the Sikhs attacked. He managed to hide in the sugar cane at the edge of his village.

'The Sikhs cut the breasts of some women. The others began to run around with fear,' he remembered. 'Some of our villagers killed their own wives and daughters to prevent the Sikhs from getting them. The Sikhs speared two of my small brothers through their bodies. My father could not bear the sight. He ran amok. He was running here and there like a madman, swinging a sword. The Sikhs could not catch him in the open fields. They set the village dogs to run after him. The dogs began to bite his legs and so my father had to slow down his running. Then the Sikhs caught him. Some held him tight. They pulled him down, cut him into pieces with their swords, my father. His head, hands and legs were separated from his body. Then they allowed the dogs to eat the body.'

Fifty of the five hundred Moslems in Mohammed's village survived the massacre, saved by the intervention of a patrol of the Punjab Boundary Force. Mohammed, sole survivor of his family, was 'taken into a truck manned by Gurkha army men to travel to an unknown land which the leaders said belonged to Moslems'.

The memory of that terrible upheaval would leave an indelible scar upon millions of people. Rare were the Punjabi families which did not lose a relative in the senseless slaughter. For years to come, the Punjab would be an assemblage of memories, each recollection more poignant, more harrowing than the next; the same terrible accounts of a people suddenly uprooted from the lands to which they'd been attached for years and thrown into panic-stricken flight. A special passion attached Sant Singh, a Sikh, to the land from which he was driven. He had, in a sense, bought that land with his blood, the blood he'd shed for Britain on the beach of Gallipoli in World War I. It had taken him sixteen years to clear and plant the plot he'd been awarded, like thousands of other Sikh army veterans, in an area reclaimed by a British canal irrigation scheme between the Ravi and Sutlej rivers south-west of Lahore. He had brought his bride to the tent in which he'd lived for over a decade, raised his children on that land, built there the five-room mud brick house that was both his pride and the measure of his life's achievements. Two days before independence, one of Sant Singh's Moslem fieldworkers brought him a pamphlet being secretly passed among the Moslems of the area.

'The Sikhs and Hindus do not belong to this land any more. They should be driven out,' it said. The attack came three days later. Sant Singh and the 200 fellow Sikhs of his village decided to flee for their lives. He was assigned, with five other men under an 80-year-old ex-army sergeant, to go on a truck as an escort for the village women. Before leaving, he went to the *guru dwara*, the temple he'd helped to build. 'I came here with nothing,' he prayed. 'I leave with nothing. I ask only for your protection,' he begged the *guru* Nanak.

Just outside a village called Birwalla the *guru*'s protection ended. Sant Singh's truck ran out of petrol. He remembers: 'It was dark. We had been driving beside the railway track instead of on the road, to avoid being seen by Moslems. We had been told they had made a huge road block in Birwalla and were killing all the Hindus and Sikhs they could find. We could hear them shouting and shrieking in the darkness because the town was only a few hundred yards away.

'An elderly Moslem saw us and ran off into the night. We knew he had gone to warn them. Then we heard the voices coming for us. We were terrified. Our leader took the decision that we would shoot all our women. We did not want to permit them to be raped and defiled. We arranged them in three lines side by side sitting on the ground. We bandaged their eyes. One 2-month-old baby was feeding at the breast of its mother. We told them to recite the Sikh prayer "God is truth" over and over again.

'My wife was in the middle. My two daughters were there, my daughter-in-law and my two granddaughters. I tried not to look. I had a double-barrelled shotgun. The others had a ·303 rifle, two revolvers and one Sten gun. I quoted the scriptures to them from the fifth book of the *guru*'s Holy Book which says, "Everything is the will of God, and if your time has come you have to die". I took out a white handkerchief and told the others I would wave it three times counting to three. Then we would shoot.

'I waved it once and said "*Ek* – one!" I waved a second time and said "*do* – two!" All the time I was praying "God, don't abandon me". I raised it a third time. As I did I saw headlights in the distance. I took this as a sign in answer to my prayers. I said we must ask them for help.

' "What if the people in the car are Moslem?" said the old sergeant.

' "We must ask anyway," I said.

'It was a truck of the army. They were Moslem soldiers, but the officer was a good man, a major. He said he would save us. We kissed his feet. Then we set off again.'

Calcutta, 17 August 1947

They were almost 100,000 strong. Since five o'clock they had been waiting for him, inundating the square of Narkeldonga, lining the rooftops around it, hanging from windows, clustered on balconies. Human heads, like a dense array of ripe fruits, seemed to constitute the foliage of its few trees. Eighteen hundred miles from the plains of the Punjab, where Hindu and Moslem killed each other with such sadistic fury, that indiscriminately mixed mass of Hindus and Moslems awaited the appearance of the little man who had checked the violence of the most violent city in Asia.

When at last Gandhi's frail silhouette appeared above the crowd of heads ringing his little prayer platform, a sort of mystic current seemed to galvanize the multitude. Contemplating that heaving crowd, vibrant with joy and enthusiasm, a sudden doubt gnawed the Mahatma. It seemed too good to be true.

'Everybody is showering congratulations on me for the miracle Calcutta is witnessing,' he said. 'Let us all thank God for His abundant mercy, but let us not forget that there are isolated spots in Calcutta where all is not well.'

Above all, he asked his followers, Hindus and Moslems alike, to join him in the prayer that the 'Miracle of Calcutta' would not 'prove to be a momentary ebullition'.

What one unarmed non-violent man was accomplishing in the world's meanest city, 55,000 heavily armed professional soldiers were unable to accomplish in the Punjab. The Punjab Boundary Force, put together with such care by the Viceroy and the Commander-in-Chief of the Indian Army, was overwhelmed by events in the province it had been designed to safeguard. That it was, was understandable. Twelve of the Punjab's districts were aflame; some of those districts covered areas larger than all Palestine where 100,000 British soldiers were unable to keep order that autumn. The tanks and trucks were poorly adapted to the dirt tracks and paths that criss-crossed the Punjab. The ideal would have been cavalry, of course, but there were no cavalry units left in the army which had once gloried in the horse.

The Force's task was infinitely complicated by the administrative collapse in the province. Cables, mail and telephones suddenly stopped working. For lack of better accommodation, the Indians were forced to govern their half of the Punjab from a house with one telephone line and a radio installed in a toilet.

The situation in Pakistan was far worse. The new nation was verging on chaos. Jinnah's missing croquet set had been located, but little else. Hundreds of railway carriages crammed with material destined for the new state disappeared, were stolen, or turned up at the wrong destination. In Karachi, the desks and chairs hadn't arrived. Government employees had to squat on the sidewalks in front of their offices, pecking out on their typewriters the first official texts of the largest Moslem nation in the world. Inside, their seniors governed their new nation sitting on crates and boxes.

The economy was in a turmoil. Pakistan had warehouses bulging with hide, jute and cotton and no tanneries, factories or mills to process it. She produced a quarter of the sub-continent's tobacco but did not have a match factory in which to produce matches to light her smokers' cigarettes. The banking system was paralysed because the banks' Hindu managers and clerks had fled to India.

It was over her share of the goods of the old Indian Army, however, that Pakistan encountered Indian bad faith in a way that seemed tantamount to a deliberate effort to jeopardize her survival. Of the 170,000 tons of army stores Pakistan was allotted under the Partition Agreement, she would ultimately get 6000. Three hundred special trains had been assigned to carry her arms and ordnance. Three arrived. Opening them, a team of Pakistani officers discovered they contained 5000 pairs of shoes, 5000 unserviceable rifles, a consignment of nurses' smocks, and a number of wooden crates stuffed with bricks and prophylactics.

This trickery left bitter memories in Pakistan and a deep-seated conviction among many that their Indian neighbours were trying to strangle them in the cradle. They were not alone in that conviction. Field-Marshal Sir Claude Auchinleck, who'd been asked to stay on to supervise the division of the armies' goods, informed the British Government, 'I have no hesitation whatsoever in affirming that the present Indian Cabinet is implacably determined to do all in its power to prevent the establishment of the Dominion of Pakistan.'

It was not India's machinations, however, that were the real threat to Pakistan. The new nation, like its Indian neighbour, was about to be engulfed by the most massive migration in human history. The violence racking the Punjab was producing its inevitable result, the result sought by the desperate men behind it on both sides of the border. From one end of the Punjab to the other, taking whatever possessions they could carry, by car, bicycle, train, mule, bullock cart, and on foot, a terrified people were fleeing their homes, rushing in headlong flight towards any promise of safety. They would produce an exchange of population, an outpouring of humanity, on a scale and of an intensity never before recorded. By the time the movement reached floodtide in late September, five million human beings would clog the roads and fields of the Punjab. Ten and a half million people, enough to form, if they joined hands, a column stretching from Calcutta to New York, would be uprooted, most of them in the brief span of three months. Their unprecedented exodus would create ten times the number of refugees the creation of Israel would produce in the Middle East, three or four times the number of displaced persons who'd fled eastern Europe after the war. It began, for the wretches who composed it, in a million different ways with a million different parting gestures.

For the Moslems of the Indian town of Karnal, north of Delhi, the word was announced by a drummer marching through their neighbourhoods, thumping his drum, proclaiming in Urdu, 'For the protection of the Moslem population, trains have arrived to carry them to Pakistan.' Twenty thousand people left their homes within an hour, marching off to the railway station to the beat of the drum. A town crier informed the 2000 Moslems of the Indian town of Kasauli that they had twenty-four hours to leave. Assembled at dawn the following morning on a parade ground, all their belongings except one blanket apiece and the clothes they wore were taken from them. Then, a pathetic gaggle of people, they started to walk towards their Promised Land.

Madanlal Pahwa, the man who'd cowered in his aunt's house thinking 'We're like sheep waiting for a slaughter', left in a bus belonging to his cousin. Everything the family could move went into the bus: furniture, clothes, money, gold, pictures of Shiva. Everything except its most important member, Madanlal's father. He refused to leave because his astrologer had told him 20 August 1947 was not an auspicious day to begin a journey. Despite the fact a Moslem friend had warned him an attack on the Hindus was planned for that day, despite the murders and burning that had already occurred, he refused to budge from his home until the moment his astrologer had assured him was propitious: 23 August at 9.30 in the morning.

No one was immune. The Moslem patients at the Lady Linlithgow TB Sanatorium in Kasauli were ordered out of the clinic by their Hindu doctors. Some of them had only one lung; others were recovering from operations, but they were taken to the sanatorium's gates and told to start walking to Pakistan. In Pakistan the twenty-five *sadhus* of the Baba Lal ashram were driven out of the buildings where they had devoted their lives to prayer, meditation, yoga and Hindu study. Wrapped in their orange robes, their saint, Swami Sundar, on the ashram's miraculous white horse at their head, they marched off chanting *mantras*, while behind them a mob set their ashram ablaze.

For most refugees, the major concern at the instant of their departure was to save what few possessions they could. B. R. Adalkha, a wealthy Hindu merchant in Montgomery, wrapped 40,000 rupees in a money-belt around his waist 'for bribing the Moslems along their way not to kill us'. Many, particularly wealthy Hindus, tended to have their life-savings in jewels and gold bangles. One Hindu farmer outside Lahore carefully wrapped all his wife's gold and jewellery in packages and tossed them into his well. He planned to return one day with a diver to recover them. Mati Das, a Hindu grain merchant in Rawalpindi, packed the fruits of a life's efforts, 30,000 rupees and forty tolas of gold, into a little box. To make sure he would not lose it, he tied it to his wrist. It was a useless precaution. In a few days time a Moslem assailant would steal the box by the simple expedient of cutting off Das's arm.

The most precious possession of Renu Braunbhai, the wife of a poor Hindu peasant in the Mianwalli district, was untransportable. It was her cow. The devout Hindu had a special veneration for the ageing beast. Sure 'the Moslems would kill it to eat it', she set it free. Overcome by the beast's mournful stare, she accomplished a last action on its behalf. She took vermilion powder and pressed a red *tilak* dot on its forehead to bring it luck.

Alia Hyder, a wealthy Moslem girl from Lucknow, managed to flee by plane with her mother and sister. They were leaving for a lifetime, but like tourists setting out on a trip, they were allowed only twenty kilos of luggage. She could never forget the pathetic morning they spent in the family kitchen weighing out their most precious possessions on the balance their servants had used to weigh flour and rice. Her sister finally selected her red and gold embroidered wedding sari. Her mother picked her blue velvet prayer rug, its surface emblazoned, curiously, with the star of David. Alia took a Koran, its cover in rosewood inlaid with mother of pearl.

The concern of Baldev Raj, a wealthy Hindu farmer near Mianwali, was not to save his wealth before leaving, but to destroy it. Certain they would be attacked and robbed during their flight, Raj and his five brothers took the contents of the family safe to the roof of his home. He was not going to 'let my money fall into the hands of some lazy Moslem'. They heaped their currency into a pile. Then, weeping hysterically, they lit the most extraordinary bonfire their eyes would ever behold: their lifetime savings literally going up in flames.

Some left determined to return. Ahmed Abbas, a Moslem journalist from Panipat north of Delhi, had always opposed Pakistan, and it was not to Jinnah's Promised Land he chose to flee, but to Delhi. Going out of the house, Abbas's mother hung a sign on the door. 'This house belongs to the Abbas family which has decided not to go to Pakistan', it read. 'This family is only temporarily going to Delhi and will return.'

For Vickie Noon, the beautiful English wife of one of Pakistan's most important men, Sir Feroz Khan Noon, a harrowing flight began with the arrival of an unknown messenger on her doorstep in Kulu, her vacation home. It was in a Hindu area near Simla which had gone to India.

'They're coming to your house tonight,' he said. She had two shotguns and a revolver which belonged to her husband who was already in Lahore. She armed two trusted Moslem servants with the shotguns. Although she'd never fired a gun in her life, she kept the revolver herself. As darkness fell, she could see bursts of flames flare up in the valley leading towards her home, the houses of her Moslem neighbours being set ablaze by Hindu mobs. Slowly, that chain of fires crept towards her. The 22-year-old girl kept thinking of a line a pair of Americans she'd met in the valley had taught her. They were Buddhist converts and it was a cornerstone of their new faith: 'Everything is transitory.' Suddenly, at 11.00, a savage down-pour extinguished the fires below her. She was saved. The next morning she fled to the safety of the palace of a close friend, the Hindu Raja of Mandi. Her relief would be temporary, however. An adventure was only just beginning for the beautiful English girl.

In fear and bitterness, hatred and rancour, they thus set out, first in thousands, then hundreds of thousands, finally inundating in their wretched millions the roads and railways of the Punjab. They were going to pose a terrible problem to the two new nations struggling to survive, a menace of epidemic, famine, resettlement on a mind-numbing scale. They became, inevitably, the carriers of the terrible hysteria sweeping the Punjab, spreading its virus wherever they passed with their tales of horror, creating in turn new outbursts of violence to throw still more helpless people on to the roads. Their terrible migration would alter forever the face and character of one of the richest swathes of land on the globe. Barely a Moslem would remain at many of the sites where the Moghuls had produced one of Islam's great flowerings. Barely a thousand Sikhs and Hindus would remain behind of the 600,000 who had dwelt in Lahore. In late August, as the violence reached a crescendo, anonymous hands performed before fleeing a gesture that was an epitaph to Lahore's lost dream, a silent and bitter commentary on what freedom's first hours had meant to so many Punjabis. Someone laid a black wreath of mourning at the base of the city's famous statue of Queen Victoria.

Calcutta, August 1947

This time they were half a million waiting for him. The 'Miracle of Calcutta' still held. Five hundred thousand dark faces, Hindus and Moslems in one fraternal cohort, covered the immense sweep of Calcutta's Maidan whose green expanse had once been the preserve of the polo ponies and white-flannelled cricketers. Gandhi himself, in the charitable breadth of his vision, could not have imagined a spectacle to match it. On this August day, the day fixed by the Moslem calendar for the great Islamic festival of Id-ul-Fitr, the crowds had come to his evening prayer meeting in unprecedented numbers.

Since dawn, tens of thousands of Hindus and Moslems had flowed past the windows of the crumbling ruin in which the elderly leader had taken up residence, seeking his blessing, offering him flowers and sweets. As it was Monday, his day of silence, Gandhi spent much of the day scrawling for his visitors little notes of gratitude and good wishes. As he did so, thousands of Hindus and Moslems paraded together through the streets. They chanted slogans of unity and friendship, swapped cigarettes, sprayed each other with rosewater, exchanged cakes and candy.

When Gandhi finally reached the platform raised for his prayer meeting in the middle of the Maidan, a wild burst of enthusiasm swept the crowd. At precisely seven o'clock, visibly moved by the fabulous spectacle of so much love and brotherhood shimmering before him, Gandhi rose and joined his hands in the traditional Indian sign of greeting to the crowd. Then the ageing Hindu leader broke his pledge of silence to cry out in Urdu, the popular language of India's Moslems, '*Id Mubarak* – Happy Id'.

For hundreds of thousands of Punjabis, the first instinctive reflex in the cataclysm shaking their province was to rush towards the little brick and tile buildings that offered in each important town a re-assuring symbol of organization and order – the railway station. The names of the trains which, for generations, had rumbled past their cement platforms were elements of the Indian legend and measures as well of one of Britain's most substantial achievements on the sub-continent. The Frontier Mail, the Calcutta–Peshawar Express, the Bombay–Madras, had, like the Orient Express, the Trans-Siberian and the trains of the Union Pacific, bound up a continent and sown along their tracks the benefits of technology and progress.

Now, in the late summer of 1947, those trains would become for hundreds of thousands of Indians the best hope of fleeing the nightmares surrounding them. For tens of thousands of others they would become rolling coffins. During those terrible days the appearance of a locomotive in scores of Punjabi stations provoked the same frenzied scenes. Like a ship's prow cutting through a heavy sea, those engines rolled through the mass of scrambling humans choking the platforms, crushing to a pulp of blood and bone the hapless few inevitably shoved into their path. Sometimes their passengers would have been waiting for days, often without food and water, under the remorseless sun of a summer the monsoon refused to end. In a concert of tears and shrieks, the crowd would throw itself on the doors and windows of each wagon. They jammed their bodies and the few belongings they carried into each compartment so that the train's flanks seemed to expand under the pressure of the humans inside. Dozens more fought for a hand-hold at each door, on the steps, on the couplings, until a dense cluster of humans enfolded each car like a horde of flies swarming over a sugar cube. When there were no handholds left, hundreds more scrambled on to their rounded roofs, clinging in precarious uncertainty to the hot metal until each roof was lined by its dense wall of refugees.

Crushed under that load of misery, the odour of coal smoke overwhelmed by the stench of sweating bodies, their whistles drowned by the shouts of the wretches whom they carried, the trains rolled off, bearing their pitiful burdens to death or a Promised Land.

For Nihal Bhrannbi, a Hindu schoolteacher, his wife and six children, that voyage to safety never even began. After waiting for six hours for their train to leave the station of the little Pakistani town in which he'd taught for twenty years, Nihal and his family finally heard the shriek of the locomotive's whistle. The only departure it heralded, however, was that of the engine. As it disappeared, a howling horde of Moslems swept down on the station brandishing clubs, homemade spears and hatchets. Screaming '*Allah-o-Akbar* – God is Great', they charged into the train, lashing at every Hindu in sight. Some threw the helpless passengers out of their compartment windows to the platform where their colleagues waited like butchers to slaughter them. A few Hindus tried to run but the green-shirted Moslems pursued them, killed them and hurled them, the dead and the dying, into a well in front of the station. The schoolteacher, his wife and six children clung to each other in terror in their compartment. The Moslems battered their way inside and began to shoot.

'The bullets hit my husband and my only son,' Nihal's wife would always remember. 'My son was crying "Water, water!" I had none to give him. I cried for help. None came near me. Slowly my son stopped crying and his eyes closed. My husband was speechless. Blood was oozing out of his head. Suddenly he kicked his legs about. Then he was silent. I tried to wake them up by shaking their bodies. There was no response.

'My daughters were clinging to me and holding my sari tight. The Moslems threw us outside. They carried away my three eldest daughters. The eldest was beaten on the head. She stretched her hands to me and cried; "Ma, Ma." I could not move.

'Some time later the Moslems took my husband and son from the train and threw them into the well. It was the end of them. I turned hysterical. I shouted like a mad woman. I lost all feelings, even for the two living children. I was like a dead person.'

Only 100 of the 2000 people in her train would, like the schoolteacher's wife, survive to complete their terrible journey to the other end of the Punjab.

Kashmiri Lal, the Hindu who had waited to begin his flight on a date his astrologer had proclaimed propitious, discovered on one of those ill-fated trains that astrology is an inexact science. Fourteen miles short of the safety of the Indian frontier, a band of Moslems climbed on to his slow-moving train. They leapt on the women in the neighbouring compartment, ripping the gold bangles and rings from their ankles, wrists, arms and noses. Half a dozen men threw the younger women out the window, then leapt after them.

The rest turned to Lal's compartment. One of them all but beheaded the woman opposite Lal with a sword stroke. For a grotesque instant her head, still attached to her neck by a few tendons, hung over her shoulders like a broken doll's head, while in her lap the baby she'd been nursing grinned at her. A pair of daggers stabbed Lal. He slumped to the floor to be covered almost immediately by the bodies of his fellow passengers. Just before losing consciousness, he felt an extraordinary sensation: a Moslem looter stealing the shoes off his feet.

A few cars away, spice-seller Dhani Ram threw his wife and four children on to the floor as the first volleys struck the train. A pile of wounded fell on top of them too. As their blood flowed over him,

Ram had an idea to which he would owe, perhaps, his and his children's lives. He dipped his hands in the wounds of his dying neighbours and smeared their blood over his own and his children's face so the attackers might leave them for dead.

As the pace of the flight in both directions grew, those train-loads of wretched refugees became the prime targets of assault on both sides of the border. They were ambushed while they stood in stations or in the open country. Tracks were torn up to derail them in front of waiting hordes of assailants. Accomplices smuggled into their compartments forced them to stop at pre-chosen sites by pulling on the emergency cord. Engineers were bribed or cowed into delivering their passengers into an ambush. On both sides of the border a man's sexual organ became, in the truest sense, his staff of life. In India, Sikhs and Hindus prowled the cars of ambushed trains, slaughtering every male they found who was circumcised. In Pakistan, Moslems raced along the trains murdering every man who was not.

There were periods of four and five days at a stretch during which not a single train reached Lahore or Amritsar without its complement of dead and wounded. U.C. Dubey, the Indian Army major who'd been overwhelmed with joy on Independence Day at the sight of his country's flag flying over the mess where he'd been humbled by his British superiors, had a stark demonstration of the price of that freedom in Lahore where he was an Indian liaison officer. A train-load of dead and wounded rolled into the railroad station. As it stopped, blood seeped out from under the doors of each of its silent compartments, dripping on to the rails 'like water flowing out of a refrigerator car on a hot day'.

As in so many other areas that autumn, the Sikh *jatthas* distinguished themselves by the organization and savagery of their attacks, besmirching by their viciousness the name of a great people. Once, having ambushed a train in Amritsar, they sent a party disguised as relief workers back through the train, killing any victims they'd missed in their original slaughter. Margaret Bourke-White, *Life Magazine*'s great photographer, remembered seeing a group of those Sikhs in Amritsar station, 'venerable in their long beards and wearing the bright blue turbans of the Akali sect, sitting cross-legged along the platform'. Each 'held a long curved sabre across his knee – waiting quietly for the next train'.

Military guards were placed on the trains but all too often they failed to fire on their attackers if they were from the same community. There were heroes too. Puzzled by the unexpected slackening of the speed of his train sixty miles short of the Pakistan border, Ahmed Zahur, a railroad worker, scrambled to the locomotive.

There he spotted a pair of Sikhs handing the train's Hindu engineer a wad of rupee notes as a bribe to stop the train in Amritsar station. The terrified Zahur slipped back to warn the British lieutenant commanding their escort of what he'd seen. Leaping along the roofs of the wagons like mail-train robbers in a western, the young officer and two of his men raced to the locomotive. Revolver in hand, the Britisher ordered the engineer to speed up. His reply was to slam on the brakes. The Britisher knocked him out with his pistol butt. While his soldiers tied up the engineer, he took over the train's control. Minutes later, Zahur and his 3000 Moslem passengers were treated to an extraordinary spectacle. Whistle shrieking, the young Britisher on the footplate, their train rocketed through Amritsar station at sixty miles an hour past a stunned army of Sikhs, swords glinting, waiting to massacre them. Safely delivered to Pakistan, the train's grateful Moslem passengers hung a garland around the Englishman's neck. It was not made of the traditional marigold blooms, however, but currency notes.

No trains were immune. The train bearing hundreds of Moslem servants of the old viceregal establishment in Simla down to Delhi was stopped at the sound of an exploding fire cracker in Sonipat station. Hundreds of Sikhs rushed the train. On board, Hindus turned on the Moslems at whose sides they'd served the Empire. In their compartment, Sarah Ismay, daughter of Lord Ismay, and her fiancé, Flight-Lieutenant Wenty Beaumont, one of Lord Mountbatten's ADCs, took out a pair of pistols. Concealed under a pile of suitcases at their feet was a third occupant of the compartment, invited there because of the special circumstances. It was their Moslem bearer, Abdul Hamid.

A pair of well-dressed, well-spoken Hindus opened the door of the compartment and demanded to look for the Moslem travelling with them. At their words, the suitcases hiding the bearer shook from the frightened man's trembling.

'One step forward and you're dead,' Sarah told the Hindus, pointing her Smith and Wesson at them. Abdul Hamid would be the only Moslem on the train to reach Delhi alive.

Those trains of death, as they became known, would form a part of the grisly Punjab legend in the years to come, a compendium of ghastly tales each more chilling than the next. Richard Fisher, a representative of the American Caterpillar Tractor Company, would be haunted for the rest of his life by the one through which he lived. Halfway between Quetta and Lahore, a group of Moslems stopped his train. While one band of Moslems raced through the train, throwing any Sikh they found out of the window, another waited on the platform to beat each victim to death with strange clubs three feet long, curving at one end into a half moon. The horrified midwesterner watched as thirteen Sikhs were thrown out to die in a sickening cacophony of screams and shattering bones. Between victims, the Moslems waved their bloody clubs, shouting for more. As the train pulled out, leaving the thirteen battered Sikh corpses behind, Fisher finally learned what the instruments of their destruction had been. They were hockey sticks.

His surprises were not quite over. Another startling image awaited the American in Lahore station. Above the corpses along the station's platform, a bizarre beacon amidst its chaos, was a sign similar to those posted in all the railway stations of the Punjab. It was a reminder of those happier days when the province of the Five Rivers had been 'a model of order and prosperity'.

'A complaint book is held at the disposition of travellers in the station master's office,' it read. 'Any traveller wishing to lodge a complaint about the services encountered during his journey is invited to make use of it.'

Calcutta, August 1947

This time, they were almost a million waiting for him. Day after day, during that terrible fortnight when the Punjab had gone berserk, the size of the crowds attending Gandhi's regular evening prayer meeting grew, transforming in their steady, spectacular growth the savage metropolis into an oasis of peace and fraternity. The most miserable city-dwellers in the world had heard the message of the frail messenger of love and mastered their ancestral urge for violence and hate. The miracle of Calcutta had held; the city, as the *New York Times* noted, 'was the wonder of India'.

Gandhi, with characteristic humility, refused to take credit for it. 'We are toys in the hands of God,' he wrote in his paper, the *Harijan*. 'He makes us dance to His tune.' A letter from New Delhi, however, rendered to that humble Caesar the honour he was due. 'In the Punjab we have 55,000 soldiers and large-scale rioting on our hands,' Louis Mountbatten wrote to his 'dejected sparrow'.

'In Bengal, our force consists of one man and there is no rioting.' As a military leader and an administrator the last Viceroy humbly asked 'to be allowed to pay tribute to my One Man Boundary Force'.

The Punjab, August 1947

The two men rode side by side in an open car. Three decades of struggle against British rule should have earned the Prime Ministers of the new nations of Pakistan and India the right to ride in triumph through jubilant crowds of their admiring countrymen. Jawaharlal Nehru and Liaqat Ali Khan rode instead in depressed silence through scenes of horror and misery, the faces their countrymen turned towards them alight with every emotion but gratitude at the blessings freedom had brought them. For the second time, the two men toured the Punjab, struggling to find some formula to restore order to its chaotic landscape.

Everything had escaped their control. Their police had collapsed. Their armies remained loyal – but only just. Indifference to, sometimes even active complicity in what was going on, paralysed their civil administration. Now as their car sped past devastated village after devastated village, unharvested fields, wretched columns of refugees, Hindus and Sikhs trudging dumbly east, Moslems dumbly west, the two leaders, an aide noticed, seemed to shrink into the back seat of the car, collapsing, almost, under the burden of their misery.

At last Nehru broke the oppressive silence. 'What hell this partition has brought us,' he said to Liaqat in a half whisper. 'We never foresaw anything like this when we agreed to it. We've been brothers. How could this have happened?'

'Our people have gone mad,' Liaqat replied.

Suddenly a figure broke from a line of refugees and bolted for their car. It was a man, a Hindu, his face almost disfigured with anguish, his body convulsed with sobs. He had recognized Nehru. Nehru was a big man, a sahib from Delhi, from the government, who could do something. Tears pouring down his face to mix with the mucus flowing from his nose, his contorted fingers clawing the air in a beseeching ballet, the unknown Hindu begged Nehru to help him. Three miles up the road a band of Moslems had sprung at his refugee column from the sugar cane and snatched away his only child, a 10-year-old daughter. He loved his little girl, he cried to Nehru, he loved her very much. 'Get her back for me, please, get her back.'

Nehru tumbled back on the car seat, almost, as he would tell an aide, physically ill at this stark, direct confrontation with the miseries overwhelming so many of his countrymen. He was Prime Minister of 300 million people yet he was helpless to aid this one frantically weeping man, begging him to perform a miracle and get his little daughter back. Overcome with anguish, Nehru slumped forward clutching his head in his hands while his escort gently removed the grief-stricken father from the running board of his car.

That night, still shaken by his experience, Nehru could not sleep. For hours he paced the corridor of the house in Lahore in which he was staying, worrying and thinking. The communal cruelty of which his people had suddenly shown themselves capable was a shocking revelation to Nehru. Patel, his friendly foe, could, as he had in an earlier meeting, dismiss it with a shrug of his shoulders and the words: 'Ah, this had to happen.' Nehru could not. Every fibre of his being was repelled by the hatred sweeping the Punjab. He was not afraid to oppose it, even at the risk of losing the support of his Hindu countrymen.

The trouble was he didn't know how. The cataclysm shaking the Punjab had thrust upon him a burden for which nothing in his life had prepared him. He reacted by lashing out with his quick, impetuous temper in specific situations. That afternoon, near Amritsar, informed the Sikhs of a village were planning a massacre of their Moslem neighbours, he'd ordered the Sikh leaders to be brought to him under an enormous banyan tree.

'I hear you are planning to massacre your Moslem neighbours tonight,' he told them. 'If a hair on their heads is touched, I will have you reassembled here at dawn tomorrow and personally give my bodyguards the orders to shoot the lot of you.'

Nehru's dilemma was how to translate an effective, isolated action like that to the scale of the second largest nation in the world, a nation beset by problems no new nation had ever faced. Worried and exhausted, he woke his ADC at 2.30 and asked him to raise Delhi on the wireless for the latest report. In that litany of bad news there was one item which might console him. The ageing leader he'd forsaken on the issue of partition was still performing his miracle. Calcutta was quiet.

The signal was one sharp blast of a whistle. At its note, six Hindus glided up behind the two middle-aged men walking peacefully down the middle of the avenue. The pair started to run, but there was no escape. Shrieking 'Moslem, Moslem', the teenage Hindus pummelled them to the ground. The two terrorized men swore they were Hindus, calling out Hindu names, claiming addresses in Hindu neighbourhoods. Their assailants' 17-year-old leader, a student named Sunil Roy, wanted better proof than that. He ripped open the folds of their *dhotis*. Both bore the stigmata of the faith of Mohammed: they were circumcised.

One of their teenage captors threw a towel over their heads; another knotted their arms with a rope. Followed by a growing crowd waving clubs, knives and iron bars, the two wretched men were herded down the street, the youths young enough to have been their sons, shouting for their blood. Their Way of the Cross covered 200 yards down to the majestic bend of a river.

'In normal times,' their 17-year-old captor later declared, 'we would not have polluted the sacred water with Moslem blood. There were many religious Hindus doing *puja* on the banks of the river. Some women were taking baths.'

They pushed their victims into the water up to their waists. An iron crowbar flashed into the sky and landed with a thump on the head of the first whimpering Moslem. His skull fractured, the poor man crumpled into the river, a carmine halo forming a circle on its surface where his head had slipped beneath the waters.

The other man fought for his life. 'The same boy hit him on the head,' the chief assassin recalled. 'Children threw bricks in his face. Another stabbed him in the neck to be very sure he was dead.'

Around the site the Hindu worshippers continued their prayers, their devotions undisturbed by the murder being committed a few yards away. Roy kicked the two bodies out towards midstream where the river's current could carry them away. As they disappeared and the wake left by their blood blended with the River Hooghly's muddy water, a cry, repeated three times, rose from their killers: '*Kali Mayi Ki Jai!* – Long live the Goddess Kali!'

It was early morning, 31 August 1947. After sixteen miraculous days, the virus had finally affected the City of Dreadful Night. The Peace of Calcutta had been shattered. As elsewhere, the infection had been spread by train-loads of refugees arriving with their tales of horror from the Punjab. Its ignition was provided by the rumour, never substantiated, that a Hindu boy had been beaten to death by Moslems on a trolley car.

At ten o'clock that night a parade of young Hindu fanatics burst into the courtyard of Hydari House, demanding to see the Mahatma. Stretched on his straw pallet between his faithful Manu and another great-niece, Abha, Gandhi was asleep. Thrusting forward a dazed and bandaged youth they claimed had been beaten by Moslems, the mob began to shriek slogans and hurl rocks at the house. Manu and Abha woke up and rushed to the veranda, trying to calm the crowd. It was no use. Pushing aside Gandhi's supporters, the crowd spilled into the interior of the house. Gandhi, aroused by the fracas, got up to face them. 'What madness is this?' he asked. 'I offer myself for attack.'

This time his words were lost in the crowd's din. Two Moslems, one beaten and bloody, escaped its ranks and rushed to crouch behind the protecting outline of Gandhi's frame. From the crowd a blackjack zipped towards them, missing the Mahatma's head by inches, to crash into the wall behind him.

At that moment the police, summoned by one of Gandhi's worried followers, reached the house. A shaken Gandhi lay back down on his straw pallet, unable to sleep. 'The Miracle of Calcutta,' he noted, 'has proved to be a nine days' wonder.'

What few illusions the Mahatma may have had left about Calcutta's peace were shattered the next day. Shortly after noon a concerted burst of attacks were launched on those Moslem slums whose inhabitants, inspired by Gandhi's miracle, had returned to their homes. In most cases the attackers were led by fanatics of the RSSS, the Hindu extremist organization whose followers had saluted their orange swastika-emblazoned flag in Poona on Independence Day. On Beliaghata Road, a few hundred yards from Gandhi's residence, a pair of hand-grenades were tossed into a truck carrying frightened Moslems away from the neighbourhood.

Gandhi immediately rushed to the site. The spectacle sickened him. The two dead were poor day-labourers dressed in rags. Eyes glossy, they lay in a sticky mash of blood, hordes of flies creeping over the lips of their open wounds. A four anna piece had tumbled from the rags of one of them and sparkled on the pavement beside his body. Gandhi stood hypnotized by the cold-blooded butchery. So sickened was he by the sight that he refused his evening meal. He lapsed into moody silence. 'I am praying for light,' he said. 'I am searching deep within myself. In that, silence helps.'

That evening, after a brief stroll, he sat down on his straw pallet and began to draft a public proclamation. He had found the answer for which he'd been searching. The decision his paper announced was irrevocable. To restore sanity to Calcutta, Gandhi was going to submit his 78-year-old body to a fast unto death.

The weapon Gandhi was going to brandish to restore sanity to Calcutta was a singularly anomalous one to employ in a country in which for centuries death from hunger had been a constant and common curse. Yet it was a device as old as India. The ancient prayer of the *rishis*, Hinduism's earliest sages – 'If you do that, it is I who will die' – had never ceased to inspire a people usually deprived of any other means of coercion. In the India of 1947, peasants continued to fast on the doorsteps of money-lenders, beseeching by their suffering a suspension of their debts. Creditors too could fast to force their debtors to meet their obligations. Gandhi's genius had been to give a national dimension to what had been an individual tactic.

In the hands of that cunning little man the fast became the most potent weapon ever wielded by an unarmed and underdeveloped people. Because a fast forced on an adversary a sense of urgency that compelled him to face an issue, Gandhi resorted to it whenever he found himself confronted by an insurmountable obstacle.

His career was studded by the achievements won by his major fasts. Sixteen times, for great or minor reasons, he had publicly refused to take nourishment. Twice his fasts had covered twenty-one days, carrying him to life's outer frontiers. Whether they'd been in South Africa for racial justice, or in India for Hindu–Moslem unity, to end the scourge of Untouchability or to hasten Britain's departure, Gandhi's fasts had moved hundreds of millions of people around the globe. They were as much a part of his public image as his bamboo stave, his *dhoti* and his bald head. A nation, 83% of whose inhabitants could not read and had no access to a radio, still managed somehow to follow each of Gandhi's slow crucifixions, shuddering in rare and instinctive unity whenever he was menaced by death.

Fasting was for Gandhi, first of all, a form of prayer, the best way to allow the spirit to dominate the flesh. Like sexual continence, it was an element essential to man's spiritual progress. 'I believe,' he stressed, 'that soul force can only be increased through the increasing domination of the flesh. We forget too easily that food was not made to delight the palate, but to sustain the body as our slave.' In private, fasts offered him the perfect tool with which to fulfil his constant need for penance.

In public the self-imposed suffering of a fast made it, Gandhi held, the most effective arm in the arsenal of non-violence, and he became the world's greatest theoretician on its use. A fast, Gandhi believed, could only be undertaken under certain conditions. It was useless to fast against an enemy on whose love and affection the faster had no claim. It would have been absurd and against his theories for a Jewish inmate of Buchenwald to employ a fast against his S.S. captors or for a prisoner in a Siberian *gulag* to fast against his Stalinist guards. Had a Hitler or Stalin ruled India instead of the British, the fast, Gandhi acknowledged, would have been an ineffectual weapon.

A fast gave a problem a vital dimension of time. Its dramatic menace forced people's thoughts out of the ruts in which they were accustomed to run and made them face new concepts. To be effective, a political fast had to be accompanied by publicity. It was a weapon to be used rarely and only after careful thought because, if repeated too often, it could become an object of ridicule.

Gandhi employed two kinds of public fasts. The first and most dramatic was a fast 'unto death' in which he vowed to achieve a specific end or starve. The second was a fast for a fixed, predetermined duration. Sometimes it was a form of personal penance, sometimes a public atonement for his followers' errors, a compelling way to bring them back to the Mahatma's discipline.

A set of rigorous rules governed them. Gandhi drank only water mixed with a pinch of bicarbonate of soda. Sometimes before beginning he stipulated that his followers might add the juice of one sweet lime or a lemon to the water to make it palatable. He had an aversion, understandable in the circumstances, to its taste. In 1924, during his first twenty-one days' fast, he had allowed his doctors to administer him a glucose enema when he weakened towards the end, since he was not embarked on a fast unto death, but one of a precisely defined duration.

Now, approaching his seventy-eighth birthday, Gandhi prepared to inflict on himself once again the self-imposed suffering of a public fast. This time he was employing his weapon on a new kind of conflict. He was fasting not against the British but against his own countrymen and the irrational frenzy gripping them. To save the lives of thousands of innocents who might die in Calcutta's violence, he was preparing to risk on their behalf what life remained in his elderly body.

Aware of the terrible risks a fast at his age would mean, Gandhi's disciples sought desperately to dissuade him.

'Bapu,' questioned his old Congress ally become Bengal's first Indian governor, C. R. Rajagopalachari, 'how can one fast against *goondas*?'

'I want to touch the heart of those who are behind the *goondas*,' Gandhi replied.

'But if you die,' his old follower pleaded, 'the conflagration you are trying to end will be even worse.'

'At least,' Gandhi answered, 'I won't be a living witness to it.'

Nothing was going to move him. Late in the evening of 1 September, Gandhi woke Manu and Abha to inform them his fast had begun with the supper he'd been unable to eat after viewing the victims in front of Hydari House. He would succeed or die, he said. 'Either there will be peace in Calcutta or I will be dead.'

This time Gandhi's physical forces crumbled with dizzying speed. The emotional strain he'd been under since New Year's Day had left its trace.

The following day his doctor discovered his heart was already missing one beat in four. After a midday massage and a warm water enema, he absorbed a litre of water and bicarbonate of soda. Shortly thereafter his voice became so weak it was barely a whisper.

In a few hours the news of the challenge he'd thrown down swept across Calcutta and scores of anxious visitors thronged the streets around Hydari House. But the epidemic of violence already launched could not be checked in a day. Fires, looting, killing continued to plague the city. From his pallet Gandhi himself could hear a sinister sound betokening still more killings, a distant echo of gunfire.

As he lay in agony his followers sought out the leaders of the city's Hindu extremists. Thousands of their fellow Hindus in Noakhali survived, they pointed out, because of the pledge Gandhi had extracted from Noakhali's Moslem leaders. If the slaughter of Moslems in Calcutta continued and Gandhi died, the result, they warned, would be the massacre of tens of thousands of Hindus in Noakhali.

By the morning of the second day of his fast, a new sound had begun to mingle with the crack of gunfire, the chant of calls for peace raised by the delegations streaming in growing number towards Hydari House. Calcutta's rioters paused to ponder Gandhi's blood pressure, his heart rate, the amount of albumen in his urine. Rajagopalachari called to announce that the city's university students were launching a movement to restore peace to the city. Hindu and Moslem leaders rushed to the failing Gandhi's bedside to beg him to give up his fast. One Moslem threw himself at Gandhi's feet, crying: 'If anything happens to you, it will be the end for us Moslems.' No despairing supplications, however, were going to shake the will burning inside Gandhi's exhausted body. 'I will not stop my fast until the glorious peace of the last fifteen days has been restored,' he intoned.

At dawn on the third day, Gandhi's voice was a murmur. His pulse had weakened so rapidly that his death became an imminent possibility. As the rumour he was dying spread, a fit of anguish and remorse embraced Calcutta. Beyond the city an entire nation's attention suddenly turned to the straw pallet in Hydari House on which India's Mahatma suffered.

As life seemed to ebb from Mohandas Gandhi's spent frame, a wave of fraternity and love swept a city determined to save its saviour. Mixed processions of Hindus and Moslems invaded the slums where the worst rioting had taken place to restore order and calm. The most dramatic proof that a change of heart had really taken hold of Calcutta came at noon when a group of twenty-seven *goondas* appeared at the door of Hydari House. Heads hung, their voices vibrant with contrition, they admitted their crimes, asked Gandhi's forgiveness, and begged him to end his fast.

That evening the band of thugs responsible for the savage murders on Beliaghata Road that had so sickened Gandhi appeared. After confessing their crime, their spokesman told Gandhi: 'I and my men are ready to submit willingly to any punishment you choose if you will end your fast.' At his words, they opened the folds of their *dhotis*. A shower of knives, daggers, pistols and tiger claws, some still darkened by the blood of their victims, tumbled to the floor under the astonished gaze of Gandhi and his disciples. As they clattered to rest beside his pallet, Gandhi murmured: 'My only punishment is to ask you to go into the neighbourhoods of the Moslems you've victimized and pledge yourself to their protection.'

That evening a handwritten message from Rajagopalachari announced complete calm had returned to the city. An entire truck-load of grenades, automatic weapons, pistols and knives handed in voluntarily by *goonda* bands arrived at the gates of Hydari House. Calcutta's Hindu, Sikh and Moslem leaders framed a joint declaration solemnly promising Gandhi: 'We shall never allow communal strife in the city again and shall strive unto death to prevent it.'

Finally, at 9.15 in the evening of 4 September, seventy-three hours after he'd begun it, Gandhi ended his fast by taking a few sips from a glass of orange juice. Just before making his decision, he had addressed a warning to the Hindu, Sikh and Moslem leaders hovering over his pallet.

'Calcutta,' he said, 'holds today the key to peace in India. The least incident here can produce incalculable repercussions elsewhere. Even if the whole countryside goes up in a conflagration, you must see to it that Calcutta is kept out of the flames.'

They would. This time the Miracle of Calcutta was real and it would endure. On the tortured plains of the Punjab, in the Frontier Province, in Karachi, Lahore and Delhi, the worst was yet to come, but the City of Dreadful Night would keep faith with the old man who'd risked death to give it peace. Never again during Gandhi's lifetime would the blood of a communal riot soil the pavements of Calcutta. 'Gandhi has achieved many things,' his old friend Rajagopalachari noted, 'but there has been nothing, not even independence, which is so truly wonderful as his victory over evil in Calcutta.'

Gandhi himself was unmoved by those accolades. 'I am thinking of leaving for the Punjab tomorrow,' he announced.

New Delhi, September 1947

Gandhi would never complete his trip to the Punjab. A new outburst of violence would interrupt him in mid-journey. This time the mania erupted in the vital nerve-centre from which India was governed, the proud and artificial capital of the extinct Raj, New Delhi. The city that had witnessed so much pomp and pageantry, the sanctuary of the world's vastest bureaucracy, was not to be spared the poison afflicting the slums of Calcutta and Lahore.

Set at the limits of the Punjab, once the citadel of the Moghuls, Delhi was still in many ways a Moslem city. Most servants were Moslems. So too were most of its tonga drivers; fruit and vegetable pedlars; the artisans of its bazaars. The riots had jammed its streets with thousands of Moslems from the surrounding countryside searching for shelter and safety. Inflamed by the horror stories told by Hindu and Sikh refugees pouring into the city, angry at the sight of so many Moslems in their new nation's capital, the Sikhs of the Akali sect and the Hindu fanatics of the RSSS launched Delhi's wave of terror on the morning of 3 September, the day Gandhi ended his fast in Calcutta.

It began with the slaughter of a dozen Moslem porters at the railroad station. A few minutes later a French journalist, Max Olivier-Lacamp, emerged into Connaught Circus, the commercial heart of New Delhi, to discover a Hindu mob looting Moslem shops and butchering their owners. Above their heads he saw a familiar figure in a white Congress cap whirling a *lathi*, beating the rioters, showering them with curses, trying by his actions to arouse the dozen indifferent policemen behind him. It was Jawaharlal Nehru, the Prime Minister.

Those attacks were the signal for commandos of Akali Sikhs in their electric-blue turbans and with the RSSS white handkerchiefs around their foreheads to unleash similar attacks all across the city. Old Delhi's Green Market, with its thousands of Moslem fruit and vegetable pedlars, was set ablaze. In New Delhi's Lodi Colony, near the marble-domed mausoleum of the Emperor Humayun and the red sandstone tomb of Akbar's greatest general, Sikh bands burst into the bungalows of Moslem civil servants, slaughtering anyone they found at home.

By noon the bodies of their victims were scattered about the green expanses ringing the buildings from which England had imposed her *Pax Britannica*. Driving from Old to New Delhi for dinner that night, the Belgian Consul counted seventeen corpses along his route. Sikhs prowled the darkened alleys of the Old City flushing out their quarry by shouting '*Allah-o-Akbar*', then beheading those Moslems unfortunate enough to answer their call.

RSSS bands kidnapped a Moslem woman shrouded in her *burqa*, soaked her in petrol and set her ablaze at the gate of Nehru's York Road residence as a protest against their Prime Minister's efforts to protect India's Moslems. Later, guarded by a squad of Gurkha soldiers, a score of Moslem women took refuge in Nehru's garden.

Warned by Sikh bands that any house sheltering a Moslem would be burned, hundreds of Hindu, Sikh, Parsee and Christian families turned their faithful servants into the streets, condemning them to the Sikh swords or to a hasty flight to an improvised refugee camp.

The only beneficiaries of Delhi's wave of atrocities were the spindly horses of the city's Moslem tonga drivers who'd fled or been massacred. Turned loose, they joyously celebrated their freedom on the greensward of those immense spaces with which the British had ventilated their imperial capital beside another species of animal, the Sacred Cow.

The riots sweeping Delhi, however, threatened more than just another city. They threatened all India. A collapse of order in Delhi could menace the entire sub-continent. And that was exactly what was happening. The city's Moslem policemen, over half its force, had deserted. There were only 900 troops on hand. The administration, already reeling under the impact of events in the Punjab, was grinding to a halt. So bad had the situation become that Nehru's private secretary, H. V. R. Iyenagar, had to deliver the Prime Minister's mail himself in his own car.

Early in the evening of 4 September, with over 1000 people already dead, V. P. Menon, the man who'd prepared the final draft of Mountbatten's partition plan, called a secret meeting of a handful of key Indian civil servants.

Their conclusion was unanimous: there was no effective administration in Delhi. The capital and the country were heading for collapse.

A few hours later, in his own dramatic way, Col .M. S. Chopra, a veteran of years of skirmishing on the turbulent frontier, came to the same conclusion. Standing on the terrace of a friend's bungalow, he could hear all around him in the dark night the clatter of machine-gun and rifle fire.

'The Frontier,' Col.Chopra thought, 'has come to Delhi.'

Simla, 4 September 1947

For the first time since he'd flown into Palam airport in March, an exhausted Louis Mountbatten had been able to find time to rest. Independence had lifted a crushing burden from his shoulders when its chimes of midnight had shifted him from one of the most powerful offices in the world to a purely symbolic one. He was deeply disturbed by the violence shaking the Punjab but, as Governor-General, he no longer had the authority to do anything about it. That appalling charge lay in Indian hands now. And so, not wishing to appear to be interfering in their actions so soon after independence, he had slipped discreetly out of Delhi to that Olympian paradise of the now dead Raj, Simla. That strange and fascinating little city still remained untouched by the storm raging in the plains below. The asphodels and rhododendrons were in bloom in its handsome stands of fir trees, and the snow-tipped cones of the Himalayas glistened through the clear late summer air. The city's Gaiety Theatre was giving *Jane Steps Out*, one of Simla's amateur theatricals that had so amused Kipling in the summer capital sixty years before.

The ex-Viceroy was, in a sense, in that Kiplingesque age when the telephone rang in his library in the old viceregal Lodge at ten p.m. Thursday 4 September. He was on the distant banks of the Rhine, absorbed in climbing the branches of his family tree through the Germany of Hesse, Prussia and Saxe-Coburg, assembling the genealogical tables that were his favourite relaxation.

His caller was V. P. Menon. There was no one in India for whose advice Mountbatten had more respect.

'Your Excellency,' Menon said, 'you must return to Delhi.'

'But, V.P.,' Mountbatten protested, 'I've just come away. If my cabinet wishes me to countersign something, just send it up here and I'll countersign it.'

That was not it at all, Menon said. 'The situation has got very bad since Your Excellency left. Trouble has broken out here in Delhi. We just don't know how far it's going to go. The Prime Minister and Deputy Prime Minister are both very worried. They think it's essential for Your Excellency to come back.'

'Why?' Mountbatten asked.

'They need more than your advice now,' Menon said. 'They need your help.'

'V.P.,' Mountbatten said, 'I don't think that's what they want at all. They've just got their independence. The last thing they want is the constitutional chief of state coming back and putting his fingers in their pie. I'm not coming. Tell them.'

'Very well,' replied Menon, 'I will. But there's no sense in changing your mind later. If Your Excellency doesn't come down in twenty-four hours, don't bother to come at all. It will be too late. We'll have lost India.'

There was a long, stunned silence at the other end of the phone. Then Mountbatten said, very calmly: 'All right, V.P., you old swine, you win. I'll come down.'

New Delhi, 6 September 1947

For the next quarter of a century the results of the meeting beginning in Louis Mountbatten's study on the morning of Saturday, 6 September 1947 would be the most closely guarded secret of the last Viceroy's life. Had the decisions taken at it become known, the knowledge could have destroyed the career of the charismatic Indian statesman who would emerge in the years to come as one of the world's major figures.

Three people were present: Mountbatten, Nehru and Patel. The two Indian leaders were sombre, visibly depressed men; they looked to the Governor-General 'like a pair of chastened schoolboys'. The situation in the Punjab was out of control. The migration was exceeding their worst fears. Now violence in Delhi threatened to bring down the capital itself.

'We don't know how to hold it,' Nehru admitted.

'You have to grip it,' Mountbatten told him.

'How can we grip it?' Nehru replied. 'We have no experience. We've spent the best years of our lives in your British jails. Our experience is in the art of agitation, not administration. We can barely manage to run a well-organized government in normal circumstances. We're just not up to facing an absolute collapse of law and order.'

Nehru then made an almost unbelievable request. That he, the proud Indian who'd devoted his life to the independence struggle, could even articulate it was a measure of both his own greatness and the gravity of the situation. He had long admired Mountbatten's capacity for organization and swift decision. India, he felt, desperately needed those skills now and Nehru was too great a man to let his pride stand in the way of her having them.

'While you were exercising the highest command in war, we were in a British prison,' he said. 'You are a professional, high-level administrator. You've commanded millions of men. You have the experience and knowledge colonialism has denied us. You English can't just turn this country over to us after being here all our lives and simply walk away. We're in an emergency and we need help. Will you run the country?'

'Yes,' seconded Patel, the tough realist at Nehru's side, 'he's right. You've got to take over.'

Mountbatten was aghast. 'My God,' he said, 'I've just got through giving you the country and here you two are asking me to take it back!'

'You must understand,' Nehru said. 'You've got to take it. We'll pledge ourselves to do whatever you say.'

'But this is terrible,' Mountbatten said. 'If anyone ever finds out you've turned the country back to my hands, you'll be finished politically. The Indians keep the British Viceroy and then put him back in charge? Out of the question.'

'Well,' said Nehru, 'we'll have to find a way to disguise it, but if you don't do it, we can't manage.'

Mountbatten thought a moment. He loved a challenge and this was a formidable one. His personal esteem for Nehru, his affection for India, his sense of responsibility, left him no way of escape.

'All right,' he said, the admiral back on his bridge, 'I'll do it, and I can pull the thing together because I do know how to do it. But we must agree that nobody finds out about this. Nobody must know you've made this request. You two will ask me to set up an Emergency Committee of the Cabinet and I will agree. Will you do that?'

'Yes,' replied Nehru and Patel.

'All right,' said Mountbatten. 'You've asked me. Now, will you invite me to take the chair?'

'Yes,' replied the two Indians, already dazed by the pace at which Mountbatten was moving, 'we invite you.'

'The Emergency Committee,' Mountbatten continued, 'must consist of the people I nominate.'

'Oh,' protested Nehru, 'you can have the whole cabinet.'

'Nonsense,' said Mountbatten, 'that would be a disaster. I want the key people, the people who really do things, the Director of Civil Aviation, the Director for Railways, the head of the Indian Medical Services. My wife will take on the volunteer organizations and the Red Cross. The committee's secretary will be General Erskine-Crum, my conference secretary. The minutes will be typed in relay by British typists so they'll be ready when the meeting's over. You invite me to do all this?'

'Yes,' replied Nehru and Patel, 'we invite you.'

'At the meetings,' Mountbatten continued, 'the Prime Minister will sit on my right and the Deputy Prime Minister on my left. I'll always go through the motions of consulting you, but whatever I say you're not to argue with me. We haven't got time. I'll say: "I'm sure you'd wish me to do this," and you'll say: "Yes, please do." That's all I want. I don't want you to say anything else.'

'Well, can't we . . .' Patel began to protest.

'Not if it's going to delay things,' Mountbatten said. 'Do you want me to run the country or not?'

'Ah, all right,' growled the old politician, 'you run the country.'

In the next fifteen minutes the three men put together the list of the members of their Emergency Committee.

'Gentlemen,' Mountbatten said, 'we will hold our first meeting at five o'clock this afternoon.'

After three decades of struggle, after years of strikes, mass movements, after all the bonfires of British clothes; above all, after barely three weeks of independence, India was once again for one last moment being run by an Englishman.

14

The Greatest Migration in History

New Delhi, September 1947

It was as though some extraordinary turn of the wheel of life had delivered Louis Mountbatten back to an earlier incarnation. He was the Supreme Commander again, energetically filling the role he knew best. Within hours of receiving his invitation to head the Emergency Committee, he had the red sandstone palace Luytens had designed as a backdrop for the ceremonials of an empire running like an army headquarters in wartime.

Indeed, one of his aides noted, Nehru and Patel had barely left his study before 'all hell broke loose'. Mountbatten commandeered his old Viceroy's Executive Council Chamber for the meetings of the committee. He ordered Ismay's office next door to be converted into a map and intelligence centre. He had the best maps of the Punjab delivered by hand from army headquarters. He instructed the air force to begin dawn-to-dusk reconnaissance flights over India's half of the province. The pilots were told to radio hourly reports on every refugee column: its size, its length, its progress, its apparent route.

Railway lines were placed under aerial surveillance. With his passion for communications, Mountbatten sketched out and got into being a radio net linking Government House to the key areas in the Punjab. He got Maj.-Gen. Pete Rees, whose Punjab Boundary Force had earlier been broken down into its Pakistan and Indian halves, to take charge of the intelligence centre.* Determined everyone would make some contribution to the crisis, he assigned his 17-year-old daughter Pamela to work with Rees as his secretary.

Mountbatten opened the Emergency Committee's first session by exposing the Indian leaders to the terrifying reality on the maps and charts ringing his intelligence centre. For many it was their first

* The Boundary Force had been divided at the insistence of both the Indian and Pakistani Governments who claimed there was no possibility of restoring order in the Punjab if the armed forces operating there responded not to them, but to a third authority. Their insistence nearly precipitated a major crisis when Auchinleck threatened to resign if the force was dissolved. Auchinleck was convinced the two nations simply wished to get hold of their armed forces to turn them to communal purposes. Lord Ismay, an Indian Army veteran himself, noted that, 'If Auchinleck is going to be so completely unsympathetic to political operations of the new dominions, I really believe it would be better to force the issue and face his resignation.' Mountbatten, however, had been persuaded that it would be a disaster at that critical juncture to allow his resignation.

graphic glimpse into the magnitude of the problem confronting them. To Mountbatten's astute press attaché, Alan Campbell-Johnson, their reaction was 'one of dazed bewilderment and aimlessness before the unknown'. Nehru seemed 'inexpressibly sad and resigned'; Patel 'clearly disturbed', seething with 'deep anger and frustration'.

Mountbatten drove ahead. In the weeks to come the men around that table would discover a new face to the urbane and charming man who'd been India's last Viceroy. The dominant quality now would be toughness and a ruthless determination to get things done. His Government House typists had copics of the committee's first decisions ready for distribution when the meeting broke up; the rest would be delivered by motor cycle in an hour. The first item of business at the next meeting, he said, would be making sure the directives on them had been carried out.

A number of distinguished men in that room would in the period ahead feel the cutting edge of Mountbatten's wrath because they could not keep that pace. One day, recalled H. V. R. Iyenagar, Nehru's Principal Private Secretary, the Director of Civil Aviation failed to get an aeroplane with emergency medical supplies off to the Punjab on schedule.

'Mr Director,' Mountbatten said, 'you will leave the room. You will go immediately to the airport. You will not leave, eat or sleep until you have personally seen that plane go and reported its departure back to me.' Hurt and humiliated, the man staggered out of the room, but the plane left.

At the opening meeting the committee got a stunning glimpse of the toughness of which Mountbatten was capable. If the security guards on trains failed to open fire on their assailants, he had a solution to propose. Any time a train was successfully attacked, Mountbatten said, round up its security guards. Sort out those that were wounded. Then court-martial and shoot the rest on the spot. That, he told the meeting, would have a salutary effect on the guards' discipline.

It was the situation in Delhi, however, that most concerned Mountbatten. 'If we go down in Delhi,' he said, 'the whole country will go down with us.' The city had to have first call on resources. He ordered the army to get additional troops into the capital in forty-eight hours, assigned his own Governor-General's Bodyguard to security duties, requisitioned civilian transport, arranged to collect and burn the corpses littering the streets. Public and Sunday holidays were cancelled, steps taken to get government employees back to their offices and the telephone system working again. Above all, he ordered a programme begun to get Sikh and Hindu refugees out of the capital and to prevent more from coming in.

It would take weeks before the committee's efforts would have their impact on the cataclysm overwhelming northern India. But at last, as one Indian participant noted, at the vital centre things had shifted almost overnight 'from the pace of the bullock cart to the speed of a jet aeroplane'.

For the next two months the unparalleled tide of human misery washing across the face of the Punjab would be abstracted down to rows of little red pinheads crawling like columns of ants across the maps in Government House. Encompassed in those inanimate beads of metal was an enormity of anguish and suffering almost beyond human competence to imagine or the human spirits' capacity to endure. One of them alone represented 800,000 people, a caravan almost mind-numbing in dimension, the largest single column of refugees Man's turbulent history had ever produced. It was as though all of Glasgow, every man, woman and child in the city had been forced by some prodigious tragedy to flee on foot to Manchester.

At the outset, Jinnah, Nehru and Liaqat Ali Khan had opposed the fantastic flow, so contrary to their own ideals, by urging their terrified populations to remain in place. The amplitude of the problem, however, had overwhelmed them, forcing them to accept this massive exchange of populations as the price of their independence. On both sides of the Punjab civil authorities now sought to hasten the exchange, both to make room for the floodtide of humans sweeping towards them and to finish it before winter would add still one more horror to the nightmare enveloping their once lovely province.

Each day in that Government House Map Room, with its grim, military air of purpose and efficiency, of men and women in crisp uniforms shuttling about like officers planning a war game, the tortuous progress of each column's advance was recorded by the inching forward of another red pin.*

* Even Gandhi himself was impressed by the air of purpose and decisiveness with which Mountbatten infused Government House. When his 'One Man Boundary Force' finally reached New Delhi he came to call on the ex-Viceroy. After being shown around the new headquarters, he settled into the study in which he'd begged Mountbatten not to partition India.

'My friend,' he said, 'I'm glad you listened to the voice of God, and not the voice of Gandhi.'

'Well, Gandhiji,' Mountbatten replied, somewhat puzzled, 'his is the only voice I'd sooner listen to than yours, but in what respect did I take God's advice against yours?'

'God must have told you not to listen to old Gandhi, who's a fool, when he

And each day at dawn the reconnaissance pilots took off to pick the columns up again as they emerged from under the mantle of night to crawl a few more miles towards safety. The sight spread out below their wings on those September mornings was a spectacle such as no human eyes had ever beheld. One pilot, Flight-Lieutenant Patwant Singh, would always remember 'whole ant-like herds of human beings walking over open country spread out like cattle in the cattle drives of the westerns I'd seen, slipping in droves past the fires of the villages burning all around them'. Another remembered flying for over fifteen breathtaking minutes at 200 m.p.h. without reaching the end of one column. Sometimes, slowed by some inexplicable bottleneck, it bulged into a thick cluster of humans and carts, then became a thin trickle a few miles on only to coagulate once more into a bundle of people at the next road-block.

By day pale clouds of dust churned by the hooves of thousands of buffaloes and bullocks hung above each column, stains along the horizon plotting the refugees' advance. At night, collapsing by the side of the road, the refugees built thousands of little fires to cook their few scraps of food. From a distance, the light of their fires diffused by the dust settling above the columns merged into one dull red glow.

It was only on the ground, however, among those numb and wretched creatures, that the awfulness of what was happening became apparent. Eyes and throats raw with dust, feet bruised by stones or the searing asphalt, tortured by hunger and thirst, enrobed in a stench of urine, sweat and defecation, the refugees plodded dumbly forward. They flowed on in filthy *dhotis*, saris, baggy trousers, frayed sandals, sometimes only one shoe, often none at all. Elderly women clung to their sons, pregnant women to their husbands. Men carried invalid wives and mothers on their shoulders, women their infants. They had to endure their burden not for a mile or two but for a hundred, two hundred miles, for days on end with nothing to nourish their strength but a *chapati* and a few sips of water.

The crippled, the sick and the dying were sometimes hung in slings tied to the middle of a pole, each end of which rested on the shoulder of a son or friend. Strapped to backs collapsing under their burden were bundles surpassing a man's weight. Balanced on their women's heads were precarious piles of what a desperate people had been able to salvage from their homes: a few cooking utensils, a

---

urged you to give up this house,' the Mahatma said. 'Now I see this is the heart of India. Here is where India is governed from. This is the sanctuary in the storm. We must keep it up and all your successors must live here.'

portrait of Shiva, the *guru* Nanak, a copy of the Koran. Some men balanced long bamboo staves on their shoulders, from each of which, like the pans of a balance, hung their belongings: an infant, perhaps, in a sack at one end; the ingredients with which to begin a new life, a shovel, a wooden hoe, a sack of seed grain hanging from the other.

Bullocks, buffaloes, camels, horses, ponies, sheep, goats mixed their misery with that of the distraught owners forcing them ahead. Bullocks and buffaloes lurched forward tugging the ships of this grotesque exodus, wooden-wheeled platforms heaped with goods. There were pyramids of *charpois*, straw pallets, rakes, ploughs, pick-axes, bags of last year's harvest. Life rafts to their owners' ship-wrecked lives, they were heaped with bundles of old clothes; occasionally a wedding sari glittering in gold and silver peeping from tawdry piles; hookahs; the souvenirs of a better time, a couple's wedding presents; pots and pans, their number, if they were Hindus, always ending in 'I' because a number ending in 'O' like 'IO' was inauspicious. There were, in those columns, sledges, *tongas*, the *burqa* carts used by the Moslems to carry women in purdah, haywains, anything with wheels or runners to which the emaciated frame of a horse or bullock could be hitched.

It was not just a brief trip to another village those helpless Indians and Pakistanis were making. Theirs was the trek of the uprooted, a journey with no return across hundreds of miles, each mile menaced with exhaustion, starvation, cholera, attacks against which there was often no defence. Hindu, Moslem and Sikh, those refugees were the innocent and the unarmed, illiterate peasants whose only life had been the fields they worked, most of whom did not know what a Viceroy was, who were indifferent to the Congress Party and the Moslem League, who had never bothered with issues like partition or boundary lines or even the freedom in whose name they'd been plunged into despair.

And always, stalking them from one end of the horizon to the other was the sun, the cruel, remorseless sun compounding their miseries, forcing their haggard faces to a blazing sky to beg Allah, Shiva, the *guru* Nanak, for the relief of a monsoon that refused to come.

For Lt. Ram Sardilal, escorting a column of Moslem refugees out of India, one image would always remain of that harrowing experience: 'The Sikhs, like vultures, following the caravan line, bargaining with the unhappy refugees over the few possessions they were trying to take away, holding out as the price dropped with each passing mile until the desperate refugees were prepared to give away their possessions for a cup of water.'

Capt. R. E. Atkins and his Gurkhas spent weeks escorting refugee columns, taking Sikhs into India, then bringing a horde of Moslems back over the same route. At the beginning of a march, he remembered, the refugees would be relieved, almost happy, to be *en route*. 'Then with the heat, the thirst, the fatigue, the endless miles, they started throwing things away until, at the end, they had almost nothing left.' Occasionally a plane would appear in the merciless sky to drop food. A panicked rush would follow. Atkins's Gurkhas would have to protect the pitiful rations with fixed bayonets to insure their just distribution. Once, he was startled by the sight of a black-and-white dog running away with a *chapati* and a crowd chasing it, ready to kill the dog to get the *chapati* back.

Worst of all were those who could not make it, those who were too young or too old, too weakened by illness, exhaustion or hunger to go on. There was the pitiful sight of children whose parents no longer had the strength to carry them, left behind to die in the wake of a caravan. There were the elderly, resigned to death, tottering off into the fields in search of the shade of a tree under whose comforting branches they might await their end. Engraved in the memory of Margaret Bourke-White would be the image of a child left by the side of the road tugging the arms of its dead mother, failing to comprehend why those arms would never pick it up again.

Kuldip Singh, an Indian journalist, could never forget 'an old Sikh, flowing beard flecked with grey' thrusting his baby grandson towards his jeep, begging him to take him, 'So at least he will live to see India'. H. V. R. Iyenagar, Nehru's principal secretary, came on two Indian Army lieutenants in a station wagon riding behind a column of 100,000 refugees. Their job, they explained, was to look after the newborn and the dead. When a woman went into labour, they would put her into the back of their wagon with a midwife. They would stop just long enough to allow her to deliver. Then, when the next candidate for their improvised delivery room arrived, the mother, only hours perhaps from delivery, would have to take her newborn infant, leave the wagon, and resume her walk to India.

The human debris left behind by those columns was terrible. The forty-five miles of roadside from Lahore to Amritsar, along which so many passed, became a long, open graveyard. Before going down it, Capt. Atkins would always sprinkle a handkerchief with after-shave lotion and tie it around his face to temper the terrible smell. 'Every yard of the way,' he remembered, 'there was a body, some butchered, some dead of cholera. The vultures had become so bloated by their feasts they could no longer fly, and the wild dogs so demanding in their taste they ate only the livers of the corpses littering the road.'

Protecting those chaotic columns, spread out over miles of road and field, was a staggering problem. They were likely to be attacked almost anywhere along their march. As always, it was the Sikhs whose attacks were the most formidable and the most savage. They would rise in shrieking hordes from the sugar cane and wheat fields to strike helpless stragglers or those parts of a caravan that were most vulnerable. Lt. G. D. Lal would never forget an old Moslem in a column he was escorting tugging towards Pakistan the only possession he'd saved from his homestead, a goat. A dozen miles from the frontier of his new home, the old man's goat began a dash towards a stand of sugar cane. The old man followed in frantic pursuit. Suddenly, like a vengeful wraith, a Sikh rose from the sugar cane, beheaded the old man and ran off with his goat.

Often it fell to a handful of heroic Sikh army officers to defy the sentiments of their own people by defending helpless Moslems. Outside Ferozpore, Lt. Col. Gurbaksh Singh came on the most ghastly sight he'd ever seen: the corpses of a Moslem column waylaid by Sikhs, being devoured by vultures. He marched his two Sikh platoons to the site. He made them stand at attention in the heat and stench while he told them: 'The Sikhs who did this disgraced their people. For you to let it happen to those under your protection would be an even worse disgrace to our people.'

Marching columns of refugees often passed each other on the highways of their exodus. Occasionally their embittered occupants leapt on each other in a last spasm of hate, adding a few victims to the toll each had suffered. More rarely, a strange phenomenon would occur. Hindu or Moslem peasants would call to each other the locations of the homestead they'd fled, urging those passing in the other direction to lay claim to their lands.

Ashwini Kumar, a young police officer, would always remember the sight of two refugee columns streaming down the Great Trunk Highway between Amritsar and Jullundur. There, where the Macedonians of Alexander the Great and the hordes of the Moghuls had trod, a line of Moslems flowed towards Pakistan, a line of Hindus into India. They passed in eerie silence. They did not look at each other. They exchanged no hostile gestures, no menacing glances. Occasionally a cow escaped from one column to the other in a mooing gallop. Otherwise the creak of wooden wheels, the weary shuffling of thousands of feet, were the only sounds rising from the columns. It was as though, in the depths of their own misery, the refugees in each column had instinctively understood the misery of those passing the other way.

Whether moving east or west, those columns all eventually spilled into human pools by the riverbanks of the three of the Punjab's great rivers barring their route, the Ravi, the Sutlej, and the Beas. There, around each of the ferries, canal headworks and bridges offering a route across the waters, they waited for hours, sometimes days, to infiltrate the flow of traffic pouring over those hopelessly encumbered passages. Escape valves along the route of Cyril Radcliffe's wandering pencil, those bridges and ferries would be for ten million Indians and Pakistanis in that awful autumn an end and a beginning, a point of transition from the lives and lands they'd left behind to the uncertain destinies towards which they were fleeing.

Lost in the faceless hordes pouring across the Sutlej at Sulemanki Head one September afternoon was a stocky 20-year-old youth. He had wide, dark eyes, thick lips glazed by a sparse moustache, and a dense shock of jet-black hair. It was Madanlal Pahwa, the young man who'd fled in his cousin's bus while his father had stayed behind waiting for the auspicious date picked by his astrologer.

The Pakistani soldiers at the western end of the bridge had confiscated his bus and everything it contained: furniture, clothes, gold, currency, pictures of Shiva. As millions of others would that autumn, Madanlal was entering his new country without a coin in his pocket, with the clothes he wore as his only baggage. Stepping from the bridge into India, Madanlal felt 'naked, as if I'd been totally looted, thrown on the road'. Embittered, he vowed that the Moslems of India should flee as he had, without a suitcase or a soiled rupee note to comfort them.

His angry face was just another in an indistinguishable flow of miserable faces, each etched to a common design by common suffering. Yet Madanlal was a man picked by the stars India worshipped to be set apart from those anonymous figures shuffling over the bridge with him. One day, shortly after his birth, the astrologers had predicted his was 'a name that would be known throughout all India'. His father remembers:

'I did not notice the postman standing beside me that December day in 1928 until he shook me to give me the telegram. It was from my own father. A son had been born to me the previous night. I had become a father at the young age of 19. I gave some tips to the postman because he had brought me good news, and bought some *ladoos*, sweets, for my office colleagues. Then I hurried home.

'When I reached home I touched the feet of my father as a sign of respect. He put sugar in my mouth because it was a happy reunion. I took the child on my lap. I thought: "I will give him the best education. Let him be an engineer or a doctor so that he should bring a good name for the family."

'I called the learned pandits and astrologers to choose a name for him. They said it must begin with "M". I chose "Madanlal". The astrologers studied their charts. They prophesied Madanlal would grow up well. One day, they announced, my son's was a name that would be known throughout all India.

'Evil eyes fell on me, however. Forty days after Madanlal was born, my wife died of a chill. My son was bright and mischievous in his schooldays, but slowly he became a problem child and began to show rebellious tendencies. In 1945 he ran away from our house. I contacted all my kith and kin throughout the Punjab, but none knew his whereabouts. After some months, I received a letter. He had run away to Bombay to join the navy. When he came home, he began his political activities with the RSSS, attacking the Moslems. I was worried for him. So in July 1947 I went to Delhi to see my friend Sardar Tarlok Singh, one of the secretaries of the great Pandit Nehru. I asked him to help save my son from his evil companions. He agreed. He promised to send me a letter recommending my son for the finest position I could have asked for him, an appointment to the grade of Assistant Sub-inspector of Police.'

*

Madanlal learned from relatives shortly after reaching Indian soil that his father had been severely wounded in a train ambush. He found him in Ferozpore Military Hospital. There in that enormous ward reeking of blood and antiseptic, the sufferings of India suddenly had a face for Madanlal, that of his father 'all pale and trembling, covered over by bandages'.

By some miracle, through the chaos and confusion of the Punjab, the letter Kashmiri Lal had sought in Delhi had reached him. He pressed it on his son. Go to Delhi, he begged. Start a new life and 'join a good government service'.

Madanlal took the letter, but he had no interest in joining a good government service. The astrologers had been right. It would not be his destiny to become an anonymous policeman lost in some provincial police station. His would indeed be a name that would one day be known throughout all India.

Stepping out of that hospital, the vision of his mutilated father still before him, one emotion pervaded Madanlal, an emotion felt by thousands in India that autumn. It had nothing to do with joining the police. 'I want revenge,' Madanlal vowed.

The life of Vickie Noon, the beautiful English wife of Sir Feroz Khan Noon, depended on the contents of a small, round, tin can. It contained Kiwi mahogany shoe polish. The respite Vickie had found in the palace of the Hindu Raja of Mandi had been short-lived. The whole countryside was after her. Sikh bands had threatened to kidnap the Raja's children if he did not turn her out.

The Raja and Gautam Sahgal, a young Hindu cement-dealer her husband had sent to rescue her, bathed her in permanganate of potassium to darken her skin. Now they stained her face with the shoe polish that was going to have to convince any Sikh who encountered her in the hours ahead that she was an Indian. At sunset, the Raja's Rolls, its curtains drawn to give it a mysterious air, was sent racing out of the palace as a decoy. Vickie, wrapped in a sari, a red *tilak* mark on her forehead, a gold ring attached to her left nostril, followed a few minutes later in Gautam's 1947 Dodge. That first manœuvre was a success. As her tension eased, Vickie had to stop for a call of nature. It was pouring with rain and in the darkness the can of shoe polish suddenly tumbled from the unfamiliar folds of her sari. Listening to it rolling away on the pebbles in her roadside ditch, Vickie groaned. The lashing mountain rain was washing away her disguise. She was becoming either a zebra or an easily identifiable white woman. That can was her only hope of retreating back into the dark anonymity that could save her. Cursing, she groped in the darkness among the pebbles and brambles looking for it. Finally, with a shriek, she found it. Clutching the can as though it contained diamonds, she rushed to the car where Sahgal smeared a new coat of polish on her face.

Just short of Gurdaspur the car ran into a roadblock manned by a band of Sikhs. They surrounded the car. Sahgal spotted a cement merchant with whom he'd done business.

'What's going on?' Sahgal asked.

'The English wife of Feroz Khan Noon has escaped from the Maharaja of Mandi,' the man explained. Every Sikh in the countryside was looking for her.

Ah, said Sahgal, he'd passed the Raja's Rolls twenty miles up the road. He was going to Amritsar with his pregnant wife. The man peered into the car. As he did so, Vickie prayed for the efficacy of her shoe polish and that the Sikh wouldn't address her in Hindi. He stared at her with curious eyes. Then he pulled back and waved them through the roadblock. As their car rolled off towards Indian Army Headquarters and safety, Vickie sank back on to her seat. Absentmindedly she began to tap the lid of her shoe polish can with her fingernail. She turned to her companion.

'You know, Gautam,' she said with a smile, 'my husband will never buy me a jewel I'll treasure as much as this tin can.'

Vickie Noon's experience was unusual. She had been the target of the Sikhs' hatred, not because she was English but because she was married to a prominent Moslem. The English were rarely molested in that tempestuous autumn. During the worst weeks of August and September, Faletti's Hotel in Lahore remained an oasis in the exploding Punjab, its orchestra playing for dancing every night, Englishmen and ladies in dinner jacket and evening dress sipping cocktails on its moon-lit terrace only blocks away from the gutted ruins of a Hindu neighbourhood.

And yet, of all the hundreds of refugee columns streaking the face of the Punjab that autumn, the most incongruous was not Hindu, Sikh or Moslem, but British. Two buses guarded by a company of Gurkha soldiers carried dozens of elderly retired Britishers away from that isolated and secluded haven to which they'd retired, Simla. In charming dark-beamed little cottages called 'Trail's End', 'Safe Haven' and 'Mon Repos', their façades enlivened by rambler roses and violets, they had chosen to end their lives along that aloof ridge which had symbolized so well the Raj they'd served. Many of them had been born in India and knew no other home. They were the retired Romans of the Raj, ex-colonels of the best regiments in the Indian Army, former judges and senior officers of the ICS who'd once administered the lives of millions of Indians.

They and their wives had had little more time in which to prepare their flight than the desperate Punjabis on the plains below. When Simla's situation had deteriorated sharply the buses had been sent to bring them to Delhi and safety. They'd been given an hour to pack a suitcase, close their bungalows and board their bus.

Fay Campbell-Johnson, the wife of Mountbatten's press attaché, rode down to Delhi with them. Inevitably, most of the Englishmen on the bus were over 65. Like most men of their age, they suffered from a common affliction, weak bladders. Every two hours the buses stopped and the men tottered out. Watching those old men who had once ruled India urinating by the roadside under the impassive, bronze stares of their Gurkha guards, a strange yet hauntingly appropriate thought flashed across Fay Campbell-Johnson's mind.

'My God,' she said to herself, 'the White Man really has laid down his burden!'

* * *

For Capt. Edward Behr, a 22-year-old Brigade Intelligence officer in Peshawar where the Mountbattens had faced 100,000 Pathan tribesmen, the prospects offered by his Sunday morning were identical to those which young English officers had savoured in India for years. After his bearer had finished serving him his breakfast of papaya, coffee and eggs on the lawn of his bungalow, Behr was going to his club where he would play squash, have a swim, then enjoy a couple of gin-and-tonics before a leisurely lunch.

It was almost as though nothing had changed in the city which had been the northern gateway to the Indian Empire. Like many another adventurous young English officer in the Indian Army, Behr had volunteered to stay on after Independence, serving, in his case, Pakistan. Peshawar, despite the turbulent Pathan tribesmen at its gates, had been quiet. The events of Behr's Sunday, however, were to have little resemblance to those he'd planned. He had barely begun his papaya when his telephone rang.

'Something terrible has happened,' gasped a lieutenant at army headquarters, 'our battalions are fighting each other.'

The stupidest of accidents had provoked the conflagration. At about the time Behr was sitting down to breakfast, a Sikh in a unit that had not yet been repatriated to India had accidentally discharged a round from his rifle while cleaning it. By an incredible misfortune, the bullet had pierced the canvas of a passing truckload of Moslem soldiers newly arrived in Peshawar from the horrors of the Punjab. Convinced the Sikhs were assaulting them, the Moslems had leapt out of the truck and opened fire on their fellow soldiers.

Behr changed into uniform, took a jeep and rushed to the bungalow of his brigade commander, Brig. G. R. Morris, a bemedalled veteran of Wingate's Chindits. Morris calmly dabbed the breakfast egg from his lips and finished his coffee. Then he planted his brigadier's cap with its bright red band on his head and, without even bothering to get out of his white shirt and shorts, set off in Behr's jeep.

When the two British officers got to the cantonment they found the Moslems in a long row of brick barracks lining one side of the parade field firing across the open ground at the Sikhs in an identical set of barracks on the opposite side. Morris studied the scene an instant. Then he grasped the jeep's windscreen and stood up.

'Drive right down the middle of the parade ground,' he ordered a terrified Behr.

Erect, supremely confident, the unarmed English officer in his brigadier's cap, dressed for a game of tennis on a Sunday morning, rode straight into the middle of his men's fire, bellowing as he did 'Cease Fire'. The magic of the Indian Army remained stronger than the hatred dividing Sikh and Moslem. The firing stopped.

Peshawar was not, however, to escape so easily. Rumour was probably responsible for more deaths in India that autumn than firearms, and while Morris was restoring order the rumour that Sikh soldiers were killing their Moslem comrades swept the tribal areas. As they had for Mountbatten's visit, Pathan tribesmen swept into the city in trucks, buses, tonga carts, on horseback. This time, however, they came not to demonstrate but to murder.

And murder they did. Ten thousand lives would be lost in barely a week because of that one round of ammunition accidentally discharged by a Sikh soldier. Inevitably, in its wake similar outbursts swept the frontier province, hurling yet another wave of refugees on to the highways of India. That so minor an incident could produce so terrible a result was indicative of the volatile emotions lurking just below the surface. Bombay, Karachi, Lucknow, Hyderabad, Kashmir, all Bengal needed only a spark similar to Peshawar's stray rifle bullet to explode in their turn with a savagery equal to Peshawar's.

New Delhi, 9 September 1947

Still weak from the strain of his fast, Mahatma Gandhi arrived in Delhi from Calcutta on 9 September 1947, never to leave again. This time there would be no question of Gandhi's staying among the Untouchables of the Bhangi Sweeper's Colony. The area had been overrun with wretched, embittered refugees from the Punjab. A worried Vallabhbhai Patel insisted instead on taking Gandhi from the railroad station to another residence at 5 Albuquerque Road, a broad and handsome avenue in New Delhi's best residential area.

With its protecting wall, its rose-garden and beautiful lawns, its marble floors and teakwood doors, its army of bustling servants' Birla House stood at the opposite end of the Indian social spectrum from those miserable sweepers' huts which were Gandhi's usual Delhi residence. Yet, in still another paradox of his puzzling career, the man who rode in third-class railway carriages and had renounced possessions would, because of the pressures of Nehru and Patel, agree to move into that millionaire's mansion.

Its owner, G. D. Birla, was the patriarchal head of one of India's two great industrial families, a monetary Moghul whose array of interests included textile factories, insurance, banks, rubber, and manufacturing. Despite the fact that Gandhi had organized Indian labour's first strike in one of his mills, he had been one of Gandhi's earliest followers. He was one of the principal financial supporters of the Congress Party. Now he offered the Mahatma four rooms in one of the two wings of his palatial estate. It would be the most elegant site in which Gandhi had lived since his return to India. It would also be the last.

The capital of India beyond Gandhi's new abode continued to reel with violence. There were so many uncollected corpses littering the city that one policeman remarked it was 'no longer possible to distinguish between a dead man, a horse or a buffalo'. At the morgue, the exasperated coroner protested about the insistence of the police that he continue to fill out proper bureaucratic forms for each of the bodies pouring into his establishment. 'Why do the police make me examine each of them for "cause of death"?' he protested. 'Anybody can see what happened to them.'

Finding people to handle the corpses littering the streets was difficult because of India's caste and religious taboos. One day Edwina Mountbatten and her husband's naval aide, Lt.-Cmdr. Peter Howes, passed a bloated corpse in the centre of New Delhi. She told Howes to stop and waved a passing truck to a halt. Its Hindu driver looked at the corpse, as a caste Hindu, and refused to touch it. Unperturbed, India's last Vicereine picked it up herself with Howes's help and loaded it into the truck.

'Now,' she ordered the astonished driver, 'take him to the morgue.'

Delhi's Moslems, most of whom now wanted to flee to Pakistan, were assembled in a series of refugee camps where they could wait in relative safety for transportation to Mr Jinnah's Promised Land. Cruel irony, those Moslems were herded into two magnificent monuments of that brief era when their Moghul forebears had made Delhi the most splendid city in the world, Humayun's Tomb and the Purana Qila (old fort). Between 150,000 to 200,000 people were going to live in those relics of Islam's ancient grandeur in conditions of indescribable filth without shelter from the sun or the monsoon's cataracts. So terrified were those wretches by the thought of leaving their protective walls that they refused to venture out even to bury their dead. Instead, they threw them from the ramparts to the jackals. Initially, the Purana Qila had two water taps for 25,000 people. One visitor noted its inmates defecating and vomiting in the same pool of water in which women were washing their cooking pots.

Sanitation was by open latrine, and the constraints of India's society remained in vigour. Despite the growing filth, the refugees in Purana Qila refused to clean their latrines. At the height of Delhi's troubles the Emergency Committee had to send 100 Hindu sweepers under armed guard into the fort to perform the chores its Moslem inmates refused to carry out.*

Another of Delhi's curses, its bureaucracy, remained unmoved by the catastrophe. When the refugees in Humayun's Tomb began to dig additional latrines, a representative of the New Delhi Commissioner's Office promptly protested because 'they were spoiling the beauty of the lawns'. Inevitably, cholera broke out. Sixty people died of the dread disease in forty-eight hours at Purana Qila. The Health Department chose to give the cause of their death as 'gastro-enteritis' to cover their failure to provide serum in time. When the department's representative finally arrived, he brought 327 batches of serum and no needles or syringes.

Despite these problems, the efforts of the Emergency Committee set up by Mountbatten, Nehru and Patel began to be felt. With troop reinforcements in the city, a 24-hour curfew was proclaimed and a series of arms searches carried out. Gradually, the tide of violence began to ebb.

The ordeal of those days brought Louis Mountbatten and Jawaharlal Nehru even closer together. Nehru met with the ex-Viceroy two or three times a day; often, as Mountbatten noted at the time, 'simply and solely for company, to unburden his soul and obtain what comfort I can give him'. Sometimes Nehru would write to him, beginning: 'I don't know why I am writing this letter except that I feel I must write to someone to get my troubles off my chest.'

The Indian leader drove himself without pity during that period. In a few months he went, one of his female admirers noted, 'from

* There were other, similar incidents elsewhere. In Pakistan, the Hindus and Sikhs in a refugee camp complained bitterly to their Moslem guards that they were being forced to live in filth because there were no Untouchables to clean out their latrines. In Karachi, Jinnah's capital, the city's sanitation and street-cleaning services began to collapse because of the flight of Hindu Untouchables. To check the haemorrhage the city's Moslem administrators proclaimed the Untouchables what they always had been in Hindu society, a people apart. Instead of making them pariahs, however, they made them a privileged sect. They were allowed to distinguish themselves by wearing green and white armbands similar to those of the Moslem National Guard. The police were given rigorous instructions to protect anyone wearing those armbands.

looking like a 33-year-old Tyrone Power to a man who'd spent three years in Belsen'. His secretary, H. V. R. Iyenagar, caught him one day, his head on his chest, catching five minutes' sleep.

'I'm exhausted,' Nehru said. 'I sleep only five hours a night. God, I wish I could sleep six. How many do you sleep?' he asked.

'Seven or eight,' was his secretary's reply.

Nehru looked at him with a grimace. 'At times like this,' he said, 'six hours is essential. Seven is a luxury. Eight is a positive vice.'

For Gandhi in Birla House the dimensions of Delhi's violence were a surprise and a shock. The man who had opposed Pakistan so resolutely would now replace Jinnah as the idol of the Moslems who'd been left behind in India. As soon as Gandhi arrived in Delhi, a stream of Moslem delegations flooded Birla House, their leaders cataloguing the ills they'd suffered at Sikh and Hindu hands, begging Gandhi to remain in the capital, blindly certain his presence would guarantee their safety. Stunned, the Mahatma argeed not 'to leave Delhi for the Punjab until it has once again become its former peaceful self'.

Gandhi was never more faithful to the ideals by which he'd lived, never more wholly consistent to the message he'd preached, than in that sad twilight of his life. Confronted with the cataclysm he'd predicted, he clung to the principles that had sustained him since South Africa: love, non-violence, truth, a belief in the God of all Mankind. Their relevance to Gandhi had not changed, his faith in them remained intact. What had changed was India.

To preach love and non-violence to India's masses as a means of opposing her British rulers had been one thing: to preach love and forgiveness to men who'd witnessed the massacre of their children, the rape of their wives; to women who'd had their relatives' throats cut before their eyes; to people despairing in the totality of their loss; was something else. Gandhi desperately believed in the validity of his message as the only escape from the cycle of hatred. But it was a message for saints, and there were few saints in the refugee camps of India that autumn.

Despite his uncertain health, Gandhi went each day to those camps, trying somehow to reach their embittered inmates crying for vengeance. 'Tell us, O apostle of non-violence,' screamed the inhabitants of one, 'how are we to exist? You tell us to give up our arms, but in the Punjab the Moslems kill Hindus at sight. Do you want us to be butchered like sheep?'

'If all the Punjabis were to die to the last man without killing,' Gandhi replied, 'the Punjab would become immortal.' As he had counselled the Ethiopians, the Jews, the Czechs and the British, so he now counselled his enraged Hindu countrymen: 'Offer yourselves as non-violent, willing sacrifices.'

His answer was a chorus of outraged jeers and 'go to the Punjab and see for yourself'. His reception in the Moslem camps was often no better, despite his achievements in Calcutta. At one, a man thrust an orphaned 2-month-old baby at him. Tears in his eyes, Gandhi could only console the Moslems looking on by saying: 'Die with God's name on your lips if necessary, but do not lose heart.' Astonished, the Moslems in their turn jeered at him.

When he drove unescorted into Purana Qila camp, a mob of Moslem refugees swirled around his car, cursing him. Someone pulled open its door. Unperturbed, he stepped out of the car into their midst. His voice was so weak from the fast that someone had to repeat his words as he addressed the angry crowd.

There was no difference as far as he was concerned, he said, 'between Hindu, Moslem, Christian and Sikh. All are one to me.' The reward for that fraternal message was an outraged roar of protest from the Moslems around him.

And yet nothing would enrage many Hindus that autumn as much as his solicitude for the Moslem victims of their violence, his insistence that pain and suffering knew no religion, and a Moslem's wounds could be as grievous as a Hindu's. The Miracle of Calcutta had won the little man the gratitude of many an Indian Moslem, but it also set many a Hindu heart against him.

Gandhi was not a man to compromise with the emotions which were stirred up by his fidelity to his own beliefs. He had always mixed Christian and Hindu hymns, readings from the Koran, and the New and Old Testament with those of the *Gita* at his prayer meetings, and despite the tension he went on reading from the Koran at his meetings in Delhi.

Suddenly one afternoon a furious voice in his assembly called out: 'Our mothers and sisters were raped, our people killed to those verses.' '*Gandhi Murdabad* – Death to Gandhi,' another voice shrieked. The rest of the audience joined in the uproar. There was pandemonium. Stunned, Gandhi was unable to go on. He was shouted down. What the British and the Boers of South Africa had never been able to achieve, Gandhi's own countrymen succeeded in doing. For the first time in his life, Gandhi was unable to complete a public prayer meeting.

For Madanlal Pahwa, the young man whose name would one day be known throughout all India, the road to revenge began in a doctor's office. The office was located in the city of Gwalior, 194 miles south-east of Delhi, the capital of the state whose maharaja had been addicted to electric trains. With his bald, high-domed head and toothless smile, the homeopathist who occupied that office bore an eerie resemblance to Gandhi. Dr Dattatraya Parchure was famous throughout Gwalior for his *sita phaladi*, a nature cure of cardamom seeds, onions, bamboo sprouts, sugar and honey with which he treated bronchitis and pneumonia.

He was famous for something else as well. It was not a chest complaint that had brought Madanlal to his office. Parchure's real passion was politics. He was the leader of the Hindu extremist organization, the RSSS, in Gwalior.

An anti-Moslem fanatic, Parchure maintained a private army of 1000 followers with which, as he would later boast, he would drive 60,000 Moslems from India. Most of the six-anna fees he collected from his patients and of the political funds he raised went to purchasing clubs, knives, tiger claws and firearms for his little army. He was always on the lookout for new recruits, and this stocky refugee with his hatred of the Moslems and his experience in the RSSS seemed an ideal candidate. Parchure promised Madanlal a chance to savour the vengeance he sought. In return for allegiance, the homeopath offered Madanlal food, lodging and all the Moslems he could kill.

Madanlal accepted. For the next month he operated in one of Parchure's 'commandos', slaughtering helpless Moslems fleeing from Bhopal to Delhi exactly as Moslems had tried to slaughter his father in Pakistan. 'We waited at the station,' Madanlal would recall. 'We stopped the train. We got on board. We murdered them.'

Their activities became so blatant that they incurred Delhi's wrath. Gandhi himself denounced them at a prayer meeting. Gwalior's Hindu Maharaja finally counselled Parchure to rein in his men.

Frustrated, Madanlal left for Bombay. He was beginning to enjoy the life of a professional refugee. This time, however, he'd decided it was his turn to play the leader's role. He registered in a refugee camp and organized a band of fifty young followers. Then he moved into action.

'We would go every day to Bombay to the Moslem quarter. We would enter a hotel, the best, order a big meal, things I'd never eaten before. Then, when they asked for money, we would say we had none, we were refugees. If they didn't like it we would beat them and break things.

'Other times we would beat Moslems in the street and take their money. Or we would take the trays of Moslem vendors and sell the things on them ourselves. Every night at the camp my boys would report to me and give me what they had taken. I would divide it. It was a good life. Slowly, I was getting wealthy.'

Soon Madanlal was forced to justify his right to leadership by actions more substantial than petty theft. At the Moslem festival of Bairam he took two followers and three hand-grenades and set out for the city of Ahmednagar, 132 miles away. There they threw their grenades at a passing Moslem procession. As they exploded, Madanlal dashed down the city's unfamiliar alleyways, looking for a place to hide for a few hours. Suddenly, floating from a balcony on the first floor of a dilapidated hotel called the Deccan Guest House, he saw a familiar object, the swastika-stamped orange pennant of the RSSS. He ran inside.

'Hide me,' he said, bursting into the hotel keeper's office. 'I've just thrown a bomb at a Moslem procession!'

Seated at his desk in the office was the local leader of the RSSS, the pudgy 37-year-old owner of the Deccan Guest House, Vishnu Karkare. Karkare leapt up and threw his arms into the air in a gesture of thanksgiving. Then, opening them wide, he gathered up the young bomb-thrower in a fraternal embrace. For Madanlal, the road to revenge would no longer be a solitary one.

New Delhi, 2 October 1947

An independent India and the world along with it celebrated the seventy-eighth birthday of the greatest Indian alive. By the thousands, telegrams, letters and messages flooded Gandhi's suite at Birla House, bringing the Mahatma the affectionate homage of his people and his friends around the world. A procession of refugees and Hindu, Sikh and Moslem leaders flowed through his room, placing at his feet their offerings of flowers, fruits and sweets. Nehru, Patel, Lady Mountbatten, ministers, newsmen, diplomats, gave the day with their presence the stamp of a national holiday.

There was no holiday spirit in Gandhi's quarters, however. Each of his visitors was struck by the physical weakness of India's ageing leader, and above all by the profound melancholy dampening his usually cheerful spirit. The man who had once vowed he would live to be 125 years because that was the time needed by a soldier of non-violence to fulfil his mission, had decided to mark the passage of another year in his life by praying, fasting, and spending most of his day at his beloved spinning-wheel. He wanted his birthday celebration to be a celebration of that primitive device and the virtues it stood for, the virtues an independent India was hastening to forget in savagery and violence.

Why was everyone showering congratulations on him, he asked his evening prayer meeting. It would have been more appropriate 'to offer condolences'.

'Pray,' he told his followers, 'that the present conflagration ends or He takes me away. I do not wish another birthday to overtake me in an India in flames.'

'We had gone to him in elation,' Vallabhbhai Patel's daughter noted in her diary that day, 'we returned home with heavy hearts.'

The radio of independent India honoured his birthday that evening with a special programme. Gandhi did not even listen. He preferred instead solitude and his spinning-wheel, hearing in its whir the murmuring of 'the still, sad music of humanity'.

The Punjab, September–October 1947

The tragedies of partition would not have been complete had they not been accompanied, as every conflict since the dawn of history, by an outpouring of sexual savagery. Nearly all of the atrocities cursing the unhappy province were embellished by their orgy of rape. Tens of thousands of girls and women were seized from refugee columns, from crowded trains, from isolated villages, in the most widescale kidnapping of modern times.

If they were Sikh or Hindu, a woman's abduction was usually followed by a religious ceremony, a forced conversion to make a girl worthy of her Moslem captor's home or harem. Santosh Nandlal, a 16-year-old Hindu, the daughter of a lawyer near the Pakistan city of Mianwali, was taken after her kidnapping to the home of the village mayor.

'I was slapped a few times,' she remembered, 'then somebody arrived with a piece of beef they forced me to eat. It was atrocious. I had never eaten meat in my life. Everyone laughed. I began to cry. A *mullah* arrived and recited a few verses of the Koran which he forced me to repeat after him.'

Then he gave her a new name. Santosh became 'Allah Rakih – She whom God has saved'. The girl God had saved was offered at auction to the village males. Her purchaser was a wood-cutter. 'He was not a bad man,' she would recall with gratitude a quarter of a century after her ordeal, 'he didn't make me eat any more meat.'

The Sikhs' tenth *guru* had specifically enjoined his followers against sexual intercourse with Moslem women to prevent what happened in the Punjab. The inevitable result was a legend among the

Sikhs that Moslem women were capable of particular sexual prowess. Under the impact of events in the Punjab, the Sikhs forgot the *guru*'s admonishment and gave free rein to their fantasies. With morbid frenzy, they fell on Moslems everywhere, until a trade in kidnapped Moslem girls flourished in their parts of the Punjab.

Boota Singh, a 55-year-old Sikh veteran of Mountbatten's Burma campaign, was working his fields one September afternoon when he heard a terrified scream behind him. He turned to see a young girl, pursued by a fellow Sikh, rushing towards him. The girl threw herself at Boota Singh, begging 'Save me, save me!'

He stepped between the girl and her captor. He understood instantly what had happened. The girl was a Moslem whom the Sikh had seized from a passing refugee column. This wholly unexpected intrusion of the province's miseries upon his plot of land offered Boota Singh a providential opportunity to resolve the problem most oppressing him, his own solitude. He was a shy man who'd never married, first because of his family's inability to purchase him a wife, then because of his natural timidity.

'How much?' he asked the girl's captor.

'Fifteen hundred rupees,' was the answer.

Boota Singh did not even bargain. He went into his hut and returned with a soiled pile of rupee notes. The girl whom those banknotes purchased was 17 years old, thirty-eight years his junior. Her name was Zenib; she was the daughter of smallholders in Rajasthan. To the lonely old Sikh she became an adorable plaything, half daughter, half mistress, a wondrous presence who completely disrupted his life. The affection he'd never been able to bestow burst over Zenib in a floodtide. Every other day Boota Singh was off to the nearest bazaar to buy her some bauble: a sari, a bar of soap, a pair of embroidered slippers.

To Zenib, who'd been beaten and raped before her flight, the compassion and tenderness poured out to her by the lonely old Sikh was as overwhelming as it was unexpected. Inevitably, her response was grateful affection and she quickly became the pole around which Boota Singh's life turned. She was with him in his fields during the day, milked his water buffaloes at dawn and dusk, lay with him at night. Sixteen miles from their hut, the wretched tides of the refugees flowed up and down the Grand Trunk Highway. Boota Singh's twelve acres of land became a lump of ice cut apart from the hatred-filled floe to which it belonged.

One day that autumn, well before the dawn as Sikh tradition dictated, a strange melody of flutes advanced down the road to Boota Singh's house. Surrounded by singers and neighbours carrying sputtering torches, astride a horse harnessed in velvet and bangles, Boota Singh rode up to the doorstep of his own home to claim as his bride the little Moslem girl he'd purchased with a soiled stack of rupee notes.

A *guru* bearing the *Granth Sahib*, the Sikh Holy Book, followed him into the house where, trembling in the new sari he'd bought her, Zenib waited. Radiant with happiness, his head covered in a new scarlet turban, Boota Singh squatted beside Zenib on the floor of his house. The priest explained to them the obligations of married life. Then, while the gathering intoned his phrases after him, he read from the sacred text.

When he'd finished, Boota Singh stood up and clutched one end of an embroidered sash; Zenib clutched the other. Four times, Zenib followed him in *lawans*, four mystic circumambulations of the Holy Book. At the instant the fourth circle was joined, they were married. Outside, the sun of another day rose over their fields.

A few weeks later the season which had brought so much horror and hardship to his fellow Punjabis bestowed a last gift on Boota Singh. His wife announced she was bearing the heir he'd despaired of ever having. It was as though some special providence had singled out the elderly Sikh and the Moslem girl for its blessing. That was not the case. For that unlikely couple, a long and cruel ordeal which would one day become for millions the symbol of the evils of partition was soon to begin.

Slowly, the wriggling lines of red pins on the maps of Government House advanced towards their destination, a refugee camp. For both the Indian and Pakistan Governments, the deluge of homeless, wandering millions pouring across their borders posed problems such as few nations had been called on to face. Those suffering multitudes expected miracles. They had won the panacea of freedom and they believed that somehow it would give their leaders the power to efface their ills.

D. F. Karaka, an Indian journalist, found a dazed, elderly Sikh wandering around a camp in Jullundur clutching in his hands a sheaf of paper torn from a schoolboy's notebook. On it, a public writer had inscribed a list of all the belongings the Sikh had lost in Pakistan; his cow, his house, his cot, pots and pans. To each item the Sikh had assigned a value. The total was 4500 rupees. He was, he told Karaka, going to present his bill to the government because the government would pay him.

'Which government?' Karaka asked.

'My government,' replied the old Sikh. Then with touching ignorance he added, 'Please, Sahib, can you tell me where I can find my government?'

The rich suffered as well as the poor. One Sikh officer in Amritsar turned his garage into a private refugee camp. It was filled by half a dozen of his friends. Two months before they had been millionaires in Lahore. Now they were destitute. Another officer would recall a man weeping uncontrollably on the refugee train he was escorting towards Delhi. The man, well dressed, told him he'd been wiped out, ruined.

'You really have nothing left?' asked the officer.

'Only 500,000 rupees,' answered the man.

'But,' protested the officer, 'you're still rich!'

No, was the reply. 'I'm going to donate every *pie* of it to having Nehru and Gandhi killed.'

Handling the influx of refugees was a task of unbelievable dimensions. Millions of blankets, tents, vaccines had to be found and distributed. Providing the food to keep them alive demanded a logistical effort of staggering size. As the camps overflowed conditions became unbearable. The stench of death, decay and disease seemed to rise above each one like the morning mist off a lake.

'The stench of freedom,' bitterly complained a Sikh colonel, driving into such a camp near Amritsar. Inside another, an Indian journalist noted one young man keeping a vigil beside his dying mother – not to comfort her last hours, but to be sure it was he who would snatch away the blanket covering her body when she died.

Gandhi excepted, none of Delhi's political leaders would be as familiar to the inmates of those camps or as loved by them as a brown-haired Englishwoman in a crisply pressed St John uniform. As the weeks preceding partition had in a sense belonged to her husband, so the weeks of India's trial would be Edwina Mountbatten's. She drove herself during that autumn with a relentless fury, a self-discipline that not even her husband could surpass. It was as though in the squalor of those camps, comforting the sick and the dying, she was somehow atoning for every extravagance of her self-indulgent youth. Her compassion, backed by her innate sense of authority; her devotion enhanced by her knowledge and talent for organization, made Edwina Mountbatten an unforgettable figure to thousands of Indians.

She was at her desk every morning at 6 a.m., with barely five hours' sleep behind her. All day she moved from camp to camp, from hospital to hospital, probing, studying, criticizing, correcting. Those were not perfunctory visits. She knew how many water taps a camp should have per thousand inmates, how to make sure no one missed an inoculation, how to organize hygiene and sanitation.

H. V. R. Iyenagar, Nehru's chief secretary, remembered her arriving for an Emergency Committee at six o'clock one evening after twelve hours touring the camps under a beating sun. Her ADCs collapsed in sleep in the committee anteroom, while inside Edwina, 'cool, precise, pragmatic, perfectly groomed, set out her observations and recommendations on a whole range of problems'.

She hated to fly and was violently ill every time she was in the air. Yet she flew whenever she could to save time, putting a fresh coat of lipstick on her vomit-stained mouth before each landing. She had no hesitation in ordering RAF war heroes to take off against all safety regulations in total darkness when an urgent problem awaited her.

'The one stupid thing to tell her was, Your Excellency, I don't think it would be suitable for you to do this,' Lt. Cmdr. Howes, her husband's ADC, recalled. 'If you did, she would immediately do it.'

No sight was too gruesome, no hut too filthy, no task too demeaning, no Indian too ill for her consideration. Howes would always remember her squatting up to her ankles in mud beside men dying of cholera, one of the most frightful of deaths, calmly stroking their fevered foreheads during the last moments of their existence.

Those tragic weeks in India and Pakistan were a time of horror, but they were a time of heroes as well, most of them unknown and unthanked heroes, their deeds forgotten as soon as they were accomplished. The sentiments of many were summed up by Ashwini Kumar, a Hindu police officer in Amritsar. 'The only way to cling to one's sanity in that hell,' he noted, 'was to try to save one life a day.' It was a task to which the young policeman consecrated himself with a notable and successful ardour. There were Sikhs who hid Moslem friends for months or saved them from the mobs; Hindus, like an unknown travelling salesman who pulled Ahmed Anwar, a 22-year-old Moslem railroad clerk, from the mob trying to kill him, shouting 'He's a Christian'; Moslems, like the captain of the Frontier Force Rifles who died defending a column of Sikhs against his countrymen.

Gradually, a semblance of order began to emerge from the chaos. Discipline in both armies improved, effective tactics for protecting trains and refugee columns were devised. The Emergency Committee, which Nehru would call 'the best lesson in administration a new government ever had', began to get its grip on the Punjab. The millions of refugees staggered on, but the violence which had provoked their flight began to diminish. Its waning was signalled in one laconic line in an intelligence report submitted to the Emergency Committee.

'The practice of throwing Moslems from train windows,' it noted, 'is on the decline.'

One last malediction awaited those unfortunate multitudes. The monsoon arrived. The heavens, from which the Punjab's miserable millions had begged succour in the searing heat of August and September, finally hurled down the rains they'd hoarded with a fury such as India had not seen in half a century. It was almost as though a pantheon of the Punjab's angry gods were flinging a parting curse upon a people who had displeased them. Turned into torrents, the five rivers of the Punjab, the rivers which had given the province its name and sustained and nourished its uprooted children, were now to become the final instruments of their destruction.

Coursing off the great slopes of the Himalayas, swelling their tides with melted snow, the rains burst into the plains in walls of water the height of a house. Riverbeds which had been dried to a trickle by the summer sun became foaming torrents. Partition and the Punjab's chaos had disrupted the flood warning system installed under the British. Almost without notice those walls of water swept into the heart of the Punjab on the evening of 24 September, surging past their riverbanks, drowning in a rumble like the end of the world tens of thousands of refugees who'd collapsed there for a night's sleep.

Abdul Rahaman Ali, a Moslem smallholder, had stopped for the night with hundreds of fellow villagers by the banks of the dried-out riverbed of the Beas. A special air of joy and relief had animated their camp; Pakistan and the safety of its frontiers was only fifty miles away. For most, those frontiers would remain a dream. Barely a score among them survived the frenzied rush of the Beas that night.

Ali, his bullock cart planted on a lip of high ground at the outer ridge of the camp, was awakened by screams and the thunder of the onrushing water. He scrambled on to his cart with his family. The water leapt up to the hubs of its wheels, to its platforms, to their knees, finally to their chests before its rush abated. For two days Ali's family clung to their cart, without nourishment, trembling with cold, watching the waters carry past them in an indiscriminate tide the splintered bullock carts, bloated animals and corpses of their friends and neighbours.

Bridges that had held fast for decades were submerged or ripped from their pilings by the water's terrifying force. Major U.C. Dubey, of the Indian Army, saw the waters of the Beas inundate the railway bridge over the river outside Amritsar. Bullock carts, their bullocks, their owners were being swept along by the river, then smashed against the girders with a force that 'snapped the carts like matchboxes and killed the humans and animals'.

Life Magazine's Margaret Bourke-White had to flee the banks of the Ravi in water up to her waist, her life saved by the frantic warning of an Indian officer. When the waters finally receded, she went back to the site, a meadow between a railway ramp and the river where 4000 Moslems had halted for the night. Less than a thousand had survived. The meadow 'was like a battlefield: carts overturned, household goods and farm tools pressed into a mash of mud and wreckage'.

For Gurcharan Singh, a Sikh police officer, one image would always remain as a symbol of that final agony. He saw it in the sublime sunlight of early morning the day the waters began to go down. Festooned in the branches of a peepul tree, above the remains of the refugees he'd been assigned to protect, was the corpse of a Gurkha soldier, his remains being methodically devoured by vultures.

* * *

No one would ever know how many people lost their lives during those terrible weeks. So chaotic were the circumstances surrounding them, so complete was the province's brief administrative collapse, that it was impossible to make any accurate canvass. The number of those left to die by the roadside, thrown in wells, cremated in the flames of their homes or villages, was beyond reckoning. The most extravagant estimates would talk of one or two million deaths. The foremost Indian student of the massacres, Judge G. D. Khosla,* set the figure at 500,000. Britain's two leading historians of the period, Penderel Moon,** who was serving in Pakistan at the time, and H. V. Hodson,*** would place the deaths at between 200,000 and 250,000. Sir Chandulal Trivedi, India's first Governor of the Punjab and the official most connected with events in the province, estimated the toll at 225,000.

The number of refugees, at least, would be known. All that autumn and well into the winter they would continue to flow through Waga, across Sulemanki and Balloki Heads, 500,000 this week, 750,000 the next, until the full complement of ten and a half million had been

* *Stern Reckoning* by Gopal Das Khosla, Bombay: Jaico Books 1963.
** *Divide and Quit* by Penderel Moon, London: Chatto & Windus Ltd., 1961.
*** *The Great Divide* by H. V. Hodson, London: Hutchinson and Co., 1969.

reached. Still another million would cross the frontiers in more peaceful circumstances in Bengal. Inevitably, the horrors of the Punjab cast a wave of criticism on the last Viceroy and India's political leaders. From London, Winston Churchill, so long a foe of Indian freedom, commented with ill-concealed satisfaction on the spectacle of people who had dwelt in peace for generations under the 'broad, tolerant and impartial rule of the British Crown', throwing themselves on each other 'with the ferocity of cannibals'.

Clement Attlee asked Lord Ismay in early October if Britain 'had not taken the wrong course and rushed things too much'. His was, of course, an impossible query to answer. What had happened, had happened. What might have happened had not the conviction that speed was essential if India was to be saved from a disaster governed the last Viceroy's actions, had not. One thing was certain. India's leaders had not only endorsed Mountbatten's policy to move as quickly as possible, they had, without exception, urged that course upon him. Speed, Jinnah never ceased repeating, was the essence of the contract. Speed was the element Vallabhbhai Patel had bargained for by making it clear Congress would accept membership in the Commonwealth only if power was transferred immediately. Nehru constantly warned the Viceroy that delay in reaching a decision would confront India with the risk of civil war. Even Gandhi, despite his opposition to partition, still urged one course on Mountbatten: get out of India immediately. Mountbatten's predecessor, Lord Wavell, was equally convinced of the need for speed, even at the price of the province-by-province evacuation he had urged in his Operation Madhouse.

Lord Mountbatten himself would always remain persuaded that, given the circumstances he found on his arrival in India in 1947, following any other course would have plunged India into civil strife on an unprecedented scale, strife Britain would have had neither the resources nor the will to control.

The violence the partition agreement produced in the Punjab was far worse than anything Mountbatten or the experts counselling him had envisaged. The 55,000 men of the Punjab Boundary Force, created to maintain order in the province, were overwhelmed by the sheer dimension of a cataclysm without precedent. Yet however terrible the consequences of that upheaval were, they were still confined to one Indian province and one-tenth of India's population. The risks of any other course was that it might expose all India to the horror which partition had visited on the Punjab.

For the millions of victims of partition, the long and painful months of resettlement and reintegration still loomed ahead. They had paid the price for freedom, and that price would leave its bitter imprint for years to come. That autumn it found its extravagant expression in a cry of rage and frustration, a cry shrieked to a British officer by an embittered group of refugees starving in a Punjab camp: 'Bring back the Raj!'

15

'Kashmir – only Kashmir!'

Kashmir, 22–24 October 1947

The ceremony in the brilliantly illuminated Durbar Hall of the palace of the Maharaja of Kashmir in Srinagar was the climax of one of the most ancient feasts in the Hindu calendar. Every year at the rising of the October moon, Hindus marked the legendary nine-day struggle of the Goddess Durga, the wife of Lord Shiva, with the minotaur Mahishasura by a nine-day festival. As his ancestors had for a century, Hari Singh, Maharaja of Kashmir, closed the 1947 festival on the evening of 24 October by receiving a ritual pledge of allegiance from the assembled nobles and dignitaries of his state. One by one they advanced to the foot of his throne and pressed into his princely palm a symbolic offering of a piece of gold wrapped in a silk handkerchief.

The petulant maharaja was a fortunate man. He was one of three rulers left from that extravagant caste of princes who still sat upon their thrones. The two others were the Nawab of Junagadh, where it was better to have been born a dog than a man, and the Nizam of Hyderabad. Against every argument of geography and logic, Junagadh had tried to take his little state, locked in the heart of India, into Pakistan. His days were numbered: in barely a fortnight's time the Indian Army would walk into his state, giving the ruler just enough time to fill a plane with his wives and his favourite pets and flee to Pakistan. The Nizam's days were numbered as well. Despite a long, last-ditch struggle to force Britain and India to recognize his independence, he too would see his state forcibly integrated into an independent India not long after the last Viceroy's departure.

Hari Singh had long recovered from the diplomatic stomach-ache which had spared him the decision Louis Mountbatten had wanted him to take, making up his mind to join either India or Pakistan before 15 August. Seated under his golden umbrella, its folds shaped in the form of a lotus blossom, a diamond-encrusted turban on his head, his neck ringed by a dozen strands of pearls setting off the emerald that was the proudest possession of his dynasty, Hari Singh still clung to the dream he had articulated to his old friend by the banks of the Trika River. He wanted to stay on that throne, to secure the independence of the enchanted vale which the East India Company had sold his forebears a century before for six million rupees and an annual tribute of six shawls spun from the gossamer thin *pashmina* wool that grew on the necks of the goats pastured in Kashmir's mountain ranges. That was just a dream, however. A brutal awakening was barely forty-eight hours away.

While the nobles of Kashmir, in Hari Singh's brilliantly illuminated Durbar Hall, were performing their ritual act of obeisance to their ruler, another group of men were forcing their way into a machinery-packed room fifty miles east of Srinagar, on the banks of the Jhelum River. One of them strapped a clump of dynamite sticks to a panel cluttered with levers and dials. Shouting a warning, he fired it with a match and ran out of the building. Ten seconds later, an ear-splitting roar shook the power station of Mahura. As it did, from the borders of Pakistan to Ladakh and the mountain walls of China, the lights went out.

In one terrifying stroke, the hundreds of bulbs glittering in Hari Singh's crystal chandeliers blinked out, plunging his palace into darkness. At that same instant, power disappeared throughout his lovely capital. On their flower-bedecked houseboats moored in the glimmering waters of Lake Dal, scores of Englishmen and women pondered the meaning of the mystifying darkness. Those retired colonels and civil servants could not realize it yet, but the failing lights were an omen announcing the end of their untroubled existence in a paradise of sunshine and flowers where a man could live the dream of the Emperor Jehangir on thirty pounds sterling a month.

In his bedroom in his father's palace where an operation on his leg had confined him, Karan Singh, the Maharaja's eldest son, listened to the moaning of the wind driving down the Vale of Kashmir from the glaciers of the Himalayas. Then, like his father, his guests and thousands of other Kashmiris, the young Karan Singh heard another sound drifting along the wind's bitter currents. His blood ran cold as, lying in the darkness, he listened to it. It was the distant cry of jackals descending on the city.

A horde of jackals of another sort was also sweeping towards Srinagar and the Vale of Kashmir on that night of 24 October 1947. For the past forty-eight hours hundreds of Pathan tribesmen had been spilling into Hari Singh's state to put an end to his dream of independence. The private army he had counted on to defend him had, for the most part, either deserted to the invaders or disappeared into the hills.

The origins of that brutal and unannounced assault almost certainly lay in an innocent request made two months earlier, on Friday, 24 August, by Mohammed Ali Jinnah to his British Military Secre-

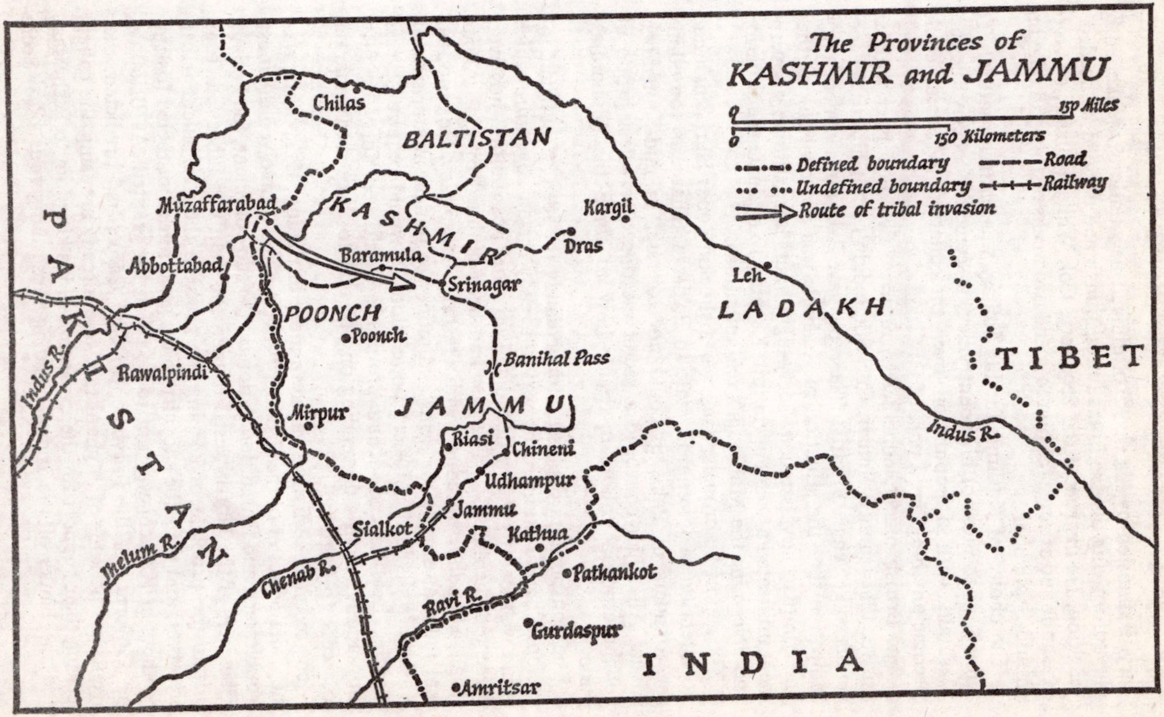
The Provinces of
KASHMIR and JAMMU
0
150 Miles
0
150 Kilometers
Defined boundary
Undefined boundary
Route of tribal invasion
Road
Railway
PAKISTAN
INDIA
TIBET
LADAKH
BALTISTAN
KASHMIR
POONCH
JAMMU
Chilas
Muzaffarabad
Abbottabad
Rawalpindi
Baramula
Srinagar
Poonch
Banihal Pass
Mirpur
Riasi
Chineni
Udhampur
Jammu
Sialkot
Kathua
Pathankot
Gurdaspur
Amritsar
Kargil
Dras
Leh
Indus R.
Jhelum R.
Chenab R.
Ravi R.

tary. Exhausted by his week of difficult negotiations, weakened by the unforgiving disease in his lungs, Jinnah had decided he needed a vacation. He instructed the Secretary, Col. William Birnie, to go to Kashmir and arrange for him to spend two weeks resting and relaxing in mid-September.

The choice of Kashmir for his holiday was entirely natural. To Jinnah, as to most of his countrymen, it seemed inconceivable that Kashmir, with a population over threequarters Moslem, could become anything but a part of Pakistan.

The British officer, nonetheless, returned five days later with an answer that stunned Jinnah. Hari Singh didn't want him to set foot on his soil, even as a tourist. The reply gave Pakistan's leaders a first indication that the situation in Kashmir was not evolving as they had complacently assumed. Forty-eight hours later, Jinnah's government infiltrated a secret agent into Kashmir to evaluate the situation and determine the Maharaja's real intentions.

The report he brought back was a shocking one: Hari Singh had no intention of joining his state to Pakistan. That was something the founders of Pakistan could not tolerate. In mid-September, Liaqat Ali Khan convened a secret meeting of a select group of collaborators in Lahore to decide how to force the Maharaja's hand.

The conspirators dismissed immediately the idea of outright invasion. The Pakistani Army was not ready for an adventure which could well lead to war with India. Two other possibilities, however, presented themselves. The first had been outlined by Col. Akbar Khan, a Sandhurst graduate with a taste for conspiracy. He proposed that Pakistan supply the arms and money to foment an uprising of Kashmir's dissident Moslem population. It would require several months, but the end, Khan promised, would see 'forty or fifty thousand Kashmiris descending on Srinagar to force the Maharaja to accede to Pakistan'.

The second alternative was even more intriguing. Its sponsor was the Chief Minister of the Frontier Province, and it involved the most troublesome and feared population on the sub-continent, the Pathan tribesmen of the North-west Frontier. Pakistan had inherited from Britain the problem of keeping the peace in their turbulent tribal preserves, and the tribe's loyalty to the government of their Moslem brothers in Karachi was not to be taken for granted. As Britain's last Governor of the Province, Sir Olaf Caroe, had predicted, the agents of the king of Afghanistan were already arousing the tribes seeking their support for the expansion of his kingdom to Peshawar and the banks of the Indus. Sending those dangerous hordes to

Srinagar had considerable appeal. It would force the swift fall of the Maharaja and the annexation of his state to Pakistan. And offering the tribesmen the opportunity to loot the bazaars of Kashmir, would keep their covetous eyes off the bazaars of Peshawar.

The gathering closed with a stern warning from the Prime Minister. The operation must be a complete secret. Finance would be provided by secret funds from his office. Neither the officers of Pakistan's army, her civil servants, nor, above all, the British officers and administrators in the service of the new state, were to be given access to the secret.

Three days later, in the cellar of a ramshackle building in Peshawar's old walled city, a group of tribal leaders met the man chosen to arouse their emotions and lead them on the march to Srinagar, Major Khurshid Anwar. Anwar, a volatile character with a penchant for getting himself up in weird disguises, seemed an unlikely choice. His conventional military career had ended when he had been cashiered from the Indian Army for appropriating mess funds to his own use. The tribal leaders around him, with their loose robes and untrimmed beards, looked like the warriors of Saul and David. Sipping their scented tea, drawing on their hookahs, they listened to Anwar's sombre assessment of the situation in Kashmir. The infidel Hindu Maharaja was about to join his state to India. If something was not done urgently, India, he warned, would soon occupy Kashmir, and millions of their Moslem brothers would fall under Hindu rule. They must assemble their tribal levies, to begin a Holy War for their brothers in Kashmir. Implicit in his invitation to join that patriotic crusade was another equally ancient but less heroic lure. It was more likely to galvanize the ardour of the Pathans than any spiritual appeal – the promise of loot.

Within hours, in the mud-walled compounds of their villages, in encampments, in Landi Kotal, along the Khyber, in the hidden grottoes where for decades they'd manufactured their rifles, in the secret depots of their smugglers' caravans, the Pathans passed the ancient call of Islam for Holy War, Jihad. From bazaar to bazaar, secret emissaries began to buy up stocks of hard tack and *gur*, a mixture of corn meal, ground chickpeas and sugar. A few mouthfuls of that mixture, taken two or three times a day with water or tea, could sustain a Pathan for days. Gradually, the men, the weapons and the supplies began to flow to the secret assembly points from which they would launch their crusade to save their Kashmiri brothers and slake their ancestral thirst for pillage.

Not only were the voices at both ends of the telephone line English but they belonged to two of the most important men in Pakistan. Sir George Cunningham was the governor of the North-West Frontier Province, and the man to whom he was telephoning from his office in Peshawar was Lt. Gen. Sir Frank Messervy, the Commander-in-Chief of the Pakistani Army.

'I say, old boy, I have the impression,' Cunningham told Messervy, 'that something strange is going on here.' For days, he said, trucks crowded with tribesmen chanting '*Allah-o-Akbar*' had been pouring through Peshawar. His own Chief Minister seemed to be the man stirring up the Pathans. Everyone in the city except him appeared aware of the destination of that enthusiastic armada.

'Are you absolutely certain,' he asked Messervy, 'that the government is still opposed to a tribal invasion of Kashmir?'

Cunningham's telephone call had caught the general in the middle of his preparations for a trip. The government of Pakistan had made certain that, when the tribal invasion began, the British Commander-in-Chief would be 6000 miles away in London trying to purchase arms to replace those India had failed to deliver.

'I can assure you I'm opposed to any such idea,' Messervy told his colleague, 'and the Prime Minister has personally given me his assurance he is too.'

'Well,' Cunningham said, 'you'd better inform him of what's going on up here.'

Messervy called on Liaqat Ali Khan a few hours later on his way to London. As serene as a Buddha on a bas-relief in the temples of Gandhara, Liaqat Ali Khan reassured the commander of his army. His fears were groundless, he said. Pakistan would never tolerate such an action. He would immediately contact the Chief Minister of the Province and order him to stop his outrageous actions. Thus reassured, Messervy flew off to London to purchase the shell and cannon to fuel the conflict that had been so carefully designed to erupt during his absence.

The Pakistani–Kashmiri Frontier, 22–24 October 1947

Its lights out, its motor cut, the pre-war Ford station-wagon slid through the glacial night to draw to a stop a hundred yards from the bridge. Behind it stretched a chain of dark shadows, a column of trucks each filled with silent men. The fracas of the torrents of the Jhelum River rushing through its rocky bed below them filled the night. In the station-wagon, Sairab Hayat Khan, a 23-year-old leader of the Moslem League's Green Shirts, nervously picked at the tips of his flaring moustache. The territory of the state of Kashmir lay at the other end of the bridge before him.

Eyes fixed to that bridge, he watched for the flare which would tell him that the Moslem troops of Hari Singh's army on the other side had mutinied, killed their Hindu officers, cut the telephone line to Srinagar and seized the guard at their end of the bridge. Suddenly he saw its roseate tail cut an arc against the black night sky. Sairab Khan started his station-wagon and lurched across the bridge. The war for Kashmir had begun.

A few minutes later his column rolled unopposed into the customs shed of the little city of Muzaffarabad. A pair of sleeping customs agents stumbled out to wave it to a halt for their inspection. Shrieking their warcries, the Pathans leapt on them. They pursued one of them back to his shed where he desperately tried to click some life into his dead telephone. There the angry Pathans tied him up with the cord of the useless instrument.

The young leader of the invasion's advance guard was jubilant. The operation could not have been more successful. The route to Srinagar lay open before the Pathans, 135 miles of paved, undefended road, a promenade without danger they could complete before daybreak. With the first light of dawn, thousands of Pathan tribesmen would sweep into the sleeping capital of Hari Singh. Sairab Hayat Khan and his advance guard would overwhelm his palace. He would, he thought, bring the Maharaja his breakfast tray and with it the news that was going to fly around the world on this 22nd of October 1947. Kashmir belonged to Pakistan.

The young man was quickly disabused of his dream. The strategists who had conceived this invasion had made one fatal miscalculation. When Sairab Hayat Khan wanted to set his force on the road to Srinagar, he discovered it had disappeared. There was not a single Pathan around his vehicles. They had faded into the night. Their crusade to deliver their Moslem brothers of Kashmir had begun with a nocturnal excursion to the Hindu bazaar of Muzaffarabad.

Because of the loot in its scores of shops, Mohammed Ali Jinnah would never again visit the Vale of Kashmir. 'It was every man for himself,' Sairab Khan recalled. 'The tribesmen shot off locks, smashed in doors and ripped out anything of value.'

Despairing, Sairab Khan and his officers tried to stop them, literally tugging at their robes in an effort to pull them away from their loot. 'What are you doing?' he kept pleading. 'We have to go to Srinagar.'

It was a concert for the deaf. Nothing could check that instinctive frenzy for loot. Srinagar was not going to belong to those Pathan tribesmen that October night. Ordering their advance to the rhythm of their pillaging, they would require 48 hours to cover the next 75 miles down to the power station whose destruction had plunged the palace of Hari Singh into darkness.

New Delhi, 24 October 1947

The first news of the tribal invasion of Kashmir reached New Delhi more than 48 hours after Sairab Hayat Khan's advance guard had seized its key bridge over the Jhelum River. The Indian Government received it, not in a despairing communication from the Maharaja, but through a channel as remarkable as it was unorthodox. Along the principal highway of the Punjab's exodus, above the road where for eight weeks the wretched millions had fled, suspended from the poles on which the bloated vultures still perched, was a telephone line linking India and Pakistan. Thanks to that line it was still possible for Rawalpindi 1704 to call a number which might have been a world away, New Delhi 3017. Those were the private numbers of the Commanders-in-Chief of the Pakistani and Indian Armies. They were British. They were close friends. They were former comrades in the old Indian Army.

Just before five o'clock on the afternoon of Friday, 24 October, Maj. Gen. Douglas Gracey, replacing General Messervy who'd been sent to London, got his first intimation of what had happened in Kashmir through a secret intelligence report. It gave the raiders' strength, armament and their location. Gracey did not hesitate. He immediately went to the private phone in Messervy's quarters and communicated that precious information to the last man Jinnah would have wanted to get it, the man who commanded the only force which could deny Kashmir to the raiders, the Commander-in-Chief of the Indian Army.

Lt. Gen. Sir Rob Lockhart, a Scot and a Sandhurst classmate of Gracey's, was stunned by his old friend's report. He in turn communicated it to two more people, both of them English: the Governor-General, Lord Mountbatten, and Field-Marshal Auchinleck.

The dialogue initiated by Gracey's telephone call that afternoon was the first in an extraordinary series of conversations. The conflict just erupting would pose for the English officers involved in it an appalling moral dilemma. As men, they were concerned with preventing the spread of the conflict, with stopping the Indians and Pakistanis who had been their comrades in arms from killing each other. As officers, the orders they would receive would frequently run directly counter to those desires.

The colloquy opened in Gracey's and Lockhart's exchange would continue, even when the armies they commanded were facing each other in the snows of Kashmir. Their attitude would earn for those unhappy Englishmen the severe disapproval of the governments they served and hasten their departure from the sub-continent. Yet, the fact that an all-out war, with all the senseless killing it would have involved, did not break out between India and Pakistan that autumn was due in no small part to the secret exchanges carried by that telephone wire linking Rawalpindi 1704 to New Delhi 3017.

Mountbatten received the news as he was dressing for a banquet in honour of Thailand's Foreign Minister. When the last guest had left, he asked Nehru to stay behind. The Prime Minister was stunned by the news. There was scarcely a piece of information that could have upset him more. He loved his ancestral home above all places, like 'a supremely beautiful woman whose beauty is almost impersonal and above desire'. He loved 'its feminine beauty of river and valley and lake and graceful trees'. Time and again during the struggle for freedom he had gone home to contemplate the 'hard mountains and precipices and snow-capped peaks and glaciers, and cruel and fierce torrents rushing down to the valleys below'.

The Governor-General was to discover another Nehru on the Kashmir issue. The cool, detached intelligence Mountbatten so admired disappeared, to be replaced by an instinctive, emotional response fuelled by passions even the Kashmiri Brahmin could not control. 'As Calais was written upon the heart of your Queen Mary,' Nehru would cry out to him one day to explain his attitude, 'so Kashmir is written upon mine.'

Still another stormy interview, this one with Field-Marshal Auchinleck, remained for Mountbatten. The Supreme Commander told the Governor-General he wanted to airlift immediately a brigade of British troops to Srinagar to protect and evacuate its hundreds of retired Britishers. If they weren't got out, he warned, they would be the victims of a frightful orgy of rape and massacre.

'I am sorry,' Mountbatten said, 'I cannot agree.' However ghastly that prospect was, he could not endorse the use of British soldiers on the soil of a sub-continent become independent. If there was going to be military intervention in Kashmir, he declared, as far as he was concerned it would have to be by Indian, not British, forces.

'Those people up there will all be murdered and their blood will be on your hands,' an angry Auchinleck protested.

'Well,' the unhappy Mountbatten replied, 'I shall just have to take that responsibility. It's the penalty of having the job. But I'm not going to answer for what will happen if British troops get involved.'

The following afternoon a DC3 of the Royal Indian Air Force put down on the abandoned dirt strip of Srinagar Airport. It carried V. P. Menon, the civil servant who had presided over so many princely accessions to India, Colonel Sam Manekshaw of the Indian Army, and an air force officer.

The decision to send the three men to Srinagar had been taken by an extraordinary meeting of the cabinet's Defence Committee that morning. The committee had been confronted with a plea for help from the beleaguered Maharaja. Worried by his conversation with Auchinleck, aware of how intense Nehru's feelings were, Mountbatten had realized military intervention was likely. Determined it should have a legal framework, he had convinced his government that India should not send her troops into Kashmir until the Maharaja had officially acceded, thus making his state legally a part of India.

He went even further. He was as attached to certain democratic notions in India's service as he had been in the service of George VI. Just as he had always believed it would be impossible for Britain to remain in India against India's will, so he believed there could be no solution in Kashmir that ran athwart the sentiments of its Moslem majority. He had no doubt what they were. 'I am convinced', he would write in a report to his cousin the King on 7 November, 'that a population containing such a high proportion of Moslems would certainly vote to join Pakistan.'

Despite Nehru's reservations, he persuaded his Prime Minister and his Cabinet to attach to Kashmir's accession a capital provision. The Maharaja's accession would be considered temporary. It would be rendered permanent only after law and order had been restored and it had been confirmed as representing the will of Kashmir's population by a plebiscite.

V. P. Menon was ordered to Srinagar to present the Cabinet's terms to the Maharaja while the officers accompanying him studied the military situation. While they flew off, the former Supreme Allied Commander South-East Asia set in motion the preparations for an historic airlift to Kashmir. He ordered all India's civil air transport to drop their passengers wherever they were and head for Delhi.

* * *

Shortly before midnight on Saturday, 26 October, yet another refugee joined the greatest exodus in history. To the ten and a half million Hindus, Sikhs and Moslems who had fled their homes that autumn was added one more figure, Hari Singh, the Maharaja of Kashmir. His bullock cart was a comfortable American station-wagon leading a caravan of trucks and cars into which his most precious belongings had been packed. No marauding bands were going to menace his flight: his well-armed bodyguard would watch over his voyage. Nor would his trip deliver the downcast Maharaja to a cholera-infested refugee camp, but to a pleasurable exile in yet another palace, his winter palace in Jammu, where he had once welcomed the Prince of Wales and his young ADC, Lord Louis Mountbatten. There, where his subjects were predominantly Hindu, he could hope to dwell in safety.

Mr 'A' and his futile hopes of independence had been engulfed by the precipitous rush of events. All Hari Singh's manœuvres had won him barely three months outside the apple basket Louis Mountbatten had tendered him. On the advice of V. P. Menon, he was leaving his menaced capital while Menon returned to Delhi to inform his colleagues that the Maharaja was ready to accept any terms they proposed in return for their aid.

He would never again set foot in the palace he was fleeing this night. In a few years, when the palace had been converted into a luxury hotel, the corridors along which he had frolicked with the officers of the army whose loyalty had proved so fragile would welcome wealthy American tourists. While his servants emptied his strongboxes of their pearls, emeralds and diamonds, Hari Singh himself sought out the two objects he treasured most, his matched Purdey shotguns with whose blue-black barrels he had blasted his way to the world's duck shooting record. A glum expression on his face, he caressed their well-oiled stocks. Then, carefully locking them into their leather case, he carried them to his waiting car himself.

After a difficult seventeen-hour trip, the Maharaja's caravan reached Jammu. The exhausted Hari Singh went immediately to his private quarters to retire. Before going to sleep, he called an ADC to issue his last order as a ruling maharaja. 'Wake me up only if V. P. Menon returns from Delhi,' he said, 'because that will mean India has decided to come to my rescue. If he doesn't come before dawn, shoot me in my sleep with my service revolver, because if he hasn't arrived, it will mean all is lost.'

As soon as they'd returned to Delhi, V. P. Menon and the two officers who'd accompanied him to Srinagar made their report to another meeting of the Cabinet's Defence Committee. Their words made sombre hearing. The Maharaja was ready at last to present Kashmir to India, but the Pathan raiders were only 35 miles from Srinagar and could at any moment seize the only airport in Kashmir on which India could land her troops.

The British commanders of India's army and air force both raised objections to military intervention. It would be a distant, dangerous operation in the midst of a population which could well prove hostile. Sensing the intensity of Indian emotion on the issue, Mountbatten overruled them. He warned that the operations they were embarking on could be long and involve far more men and resources than anyone might foresee. But with his Cabinet determined to act, Mountbatten threw the full weight of his own military experience into the balance.

He ordered an airlift to start flying troops to Srinagar at dawn the following morning. Every available transport in the country, civil and military, was to be used in the effort. The troops would have to cling at all costs to the airport and Srinagar until reinforcements in armour and artillery could reach them by land. Those reinforcements were ordered to leave immediately by the only land link joining India to Kashmir, the inadequate road Cyril Radcliffe's pencil had providentially delivered to India when he had assigned New Delhi the town of Gurdaspur with its largely Moslem population.

While the frenzied preparations for the operation were under way, Mountbatten ordered V. P. Menon to fly to Jammu. Hari Singh would not die of a bullet in the brain on the first night of his flight. V. P. Menon reached his bedside before the expiration of the ultimatum the Maharaja had given his ADC. With him, awaiting only Hari Singh's signature, was the Act of Accession which would provide a legal framework for India's action.

V. P. Menon was back in his Delhi home late on the evening of that same Sunday, 26 October. Alexander Symon, Britain's Deputy High Commissioner, joined him for a drink a few minutes after his return. Menon was jubilant. He poured them each a stiff drink. As they sat down, an enormous smile spread across his face. He raised his glass to Symon. Then he pulled a piece of paper from his jacket pocket and waved it gaily towards the Englishman.

'Here it is,' he said. 'We have Kashmir. The bastard signed the Act of Accession. And now that we've got it, we'll never let it go.'

* * *

India would be true to V. P. Menon's promise. The 329 Sikhs of the

First Sikh Regiment and eight tons of material landed by nine DC3s on a miraculously empty Srinagar airfield at dawn, Monday, 27 October, would be just the first instalment in an uninterrupted flow of men and material India would pour into Kashmir. Eventually 100,000 Indian soldiers would fight in the snowy highlands that had been paradise for so many trout fishermen and hunters of the elusive ibex.

Curiously, it was not so much to military genius or to the energy and determination of their soldiers that the Indians would owe their initial success in Kashmir, as to fourteen French, Scottish, Spanish, Italian and Portuguese nuns of the Franciscan Missionaries of Mary. By pausing to sack their convent in the little city of Baramullah only 30 miles from Srinagar, when they should have been driving on the capital of Kashmir and its vital airfield, the Pathan raiders would end Jinnah's dream of joining Jehangir's beloved vale to his nation. All day, Monday, 27 October, while the First Sikhs secured their fragile hold on Kashmir's only airport, the Pathans in Baramullah were giving vent to their ancient appetites for rape and pillage. They violated the nuns, massacred the patients in their little clinic, looted the convent chapel down to its last brass door-knob.

That evening, clutching her crucifix and praying for 'the conversion of Kashmir', the convent's Belgian Mother Superior, Sister Mary Adeltrude, died of her wounds. Her sacrifice and that of her sister nuns and patients would not shake the hold of Islam on its ancient Kashmiri stronghold at the foot of the Himalayas. But they had given the soldiers of Jawaharlal Nehru the critical hours they needed to install themselves in the Vale of Kashmir.

They would not leave again. By the time the Pathans resumed their attack it was too late. The Indians stemmed their advance, then, when their first armoured cars arrived over Radcliffe's road, routed the raiders in a pitched battle outside Srinagar. Gradually they drove them in disorder back up the Vale of Kashmir, along the valley through which they'd descended on Srinagar, towards the bridges they'd seized on a bitter October night believing all Kashmir might be theirs without firing a shot. Seething with anger, Jinnah defied the British commanders of his army by sending Pakistani units disguised as irregulars to Kashmir to stiffen the demoralized raiders. More tribal levies were raised, and for months in the hostile cold of winter the war would rage on.

Ultimately, the dispute would reach the United Nations. The lovely vale, whose name had been the last words to pass the lips of a dying Moghul, would take its place alongside Berlin, Palestine, and Korea in the gallery of the world's unsolved problems. The plebiscite to which Mountbatten had with such difficulty secured Nehru's agreement would be relegated to that vast file of forgotten good intentions. The state would remain divided along the battle lines of 1948, the Vale of Kashmir in Indian hands, the northern territories around Gilgit with Pakistan. A quarter of a century later, Kashmir's disputed possession would remain the principal subject of discord between India and Pakistan, the one seemingly insurmountable barrier to their reconciliation.

16

Two Brahmins from Poona

Poona, 1 November 1947

The young Hindu militant who had led his followers on 15 August in their salute to the swastika-stamped banner of the R contemplated with wondering eyes the whitewashed shed which was about to become the new home of his newspaper the *Hindu Rashtra*, the Hindu Nation. The shed sheltered a flat-bed press and a teletype machine of the Press Trust of India. Next to it, a lean-to stretched over the few upturned packing cases and trestle tables that constituted the paper's editorial offices.

That was hardly an installation to inspire a Rothermere or a Hearst, yet no Anglo-Saxon press lord ever exulted over his glass and steel headquarters with a purer joy than that radiating from the face of Nathuram Godse. He was dressed in the spartan wardrobe that was his uniform: a baggy white shirt, a vest of raw cotton, and a sarong-like *dhoti* carefully arranged in the traditional Maratha style, its left end hooked under his leg and the bulk of its folds gathered on his right hip. His usually dour mien was enlivened by a wide if somewhat tense smile as he moved from guest to guest, solemnly assuring each of his determination to rededicate his journal to the Hindu cause.

At the centre of the parking lot was a small table whose contents Godse had arranged himself with the fussiness of a hostess setting out tea for the visit of the local dowager. As this was an auspicious occasion, it was laden with artfully displayed piles of sweets: rich mounds of *barfi*, coils of halva, gelatinous squares of amber and emerald candies dusted with sugar. Behind them, percolating gently, was an enormous pot of coffee. Godse was noted throughout his native Poona for three things, his politics, his monk-like life style, and his addiction to coffee. He would literally walk miles to drink a cup of coffee in a café whose brew particularly pleased him.

As he passed out his coffee-cups, another figure slipped among the guests accepting their congratulations. There was nothing spartan about the wardrobe of Narayan Apte. Tonight he wore his favourite hound's tooth tweed jacket, grey flannel slacks and a soft sports shirt whose open collar was pressed neatly over the lapels of his jacket. If Godse had passed through the crowd with abrupt, almost brusque movements, Apte glided from guest to guest, his progress governed by a hint of furtiveness, a kind of understated stealth. His smile was never full, but always quick. He was Godse's partner and *alter ego*, the business manager and administrator of the *Hindu Rashtra*. His dry, black hair had already begun to retreat back across his scalp. At the back of his head, however, its coils protruded from the underside of his skull so that, in profile, Apte, with his sloping forehead and long fine nose, resembled a kind of masculine Nefertiti. His dominant facial feature was his eyes. They were soft and black and their gaze never left his interlocutor's face. Apte, one of his friends said, 'spoke with his eyes and when those eyes spoke, people listened'.

At 34 Apte was three years younger than his partner. He was as immersed in the world as Godse was detached from it. He was a doer and a mover, an organizer and a planner. Now that the guests were served, he stepped to the centre of the parking lot and clapped his hands for attention.

For a few moments the chairman of the board delivering his annual report to his stockholders reviewed the history of the *Hindu Rashtra*. Then he presented the first attraction of the evening, a speech by his partner. Tense as a tenor waiting for the first bars of his aria, Godse stepped to the centre of the parking lot and waited for silence.

As he did, imperceptible to the crowd below, a window slowly opened on the fourth floor of the building overlooking the parking lot. The silhouette surreptitiously sliding into its frame belonged to a policeman, a plain-clothes man of the Poona CID. Intently, he leant forward to listen to Godse's speech. Since 15 August, the Poona police had been keeping a discreet watch on Apte and Godse as well as the city's other Hindu extremists. Weekly reports on their activities had been forwarded to Bombay and Delhi. Each man s identified by name, profession and political persuasion in the secret files of the CID. Apte's entry bore an additional notation that Godse's did not have: 'Potentially dangerous.'

Carefully orchestrating the rising virulence and passion of his discourse, Godse worked through the subjects that had preoccupied him since Louis Mountbatten had published his partition plan:

Gandhi, Congress and India's division. 'Gandhi said India would be divided over his dead body,' he intoned. 'India is divided, but Gandhi lives. Gandhi's non-violence has left the Hindus defenceless before their enemies. Now, while Hindu refugees are starving, Gandhi defends their Moslem oppressors. Hindu women are throwing themselves into wells to save themselves from being raped, and Gandhi tells them "victory is in the victim". One of those victims could be my mother!

'The motherland has been vivisected,' he called, his voice now a strident shriek, 'the vultures are tearing her flesh, the chastity of Hindu women is being violated on the open streets while the Congress eunuchs watch this rape committed. How long, oh, how long can one bear this?'

A roar of applause followed his conclusion. That it should was not surprising. For three and a half centuries the vocation of the city of Poona, 119 miles inland from Bombay, had been extreme Hindu nationalism. It was in the hills beyond Poona that Hinduism's greatest hero, the warrior Shivaji, had been born and had opened his guerrilla campaign against the Moghul Emperor Aurangzeb. His heirs, the *peshwas*, a tight clique of Chitpawan – 'purified by fire' – Brahmins had resisted India's British rulers until 1817. From Poona's streets had come a stream of men like Bal Gangadhar Tilak, the militant chieftain of Indian nationalism before Gandhi had turned the movement to non-violence.

Poona's Hindu fanatics had a new hero now, a man they worshipped as the authentic continuation of the line of Shivaji, the *peshwas* and Tilak. He was not physically present in the parking lot of the *Hindu Rashtra*, but as his image, cast by a 16 mm movie projector, flickered on to a cement wall an expectant hush stilled the gathering. Even to the camera's jittery rhythm, with his voice distorted by the crackle of an ineffectual sound system, there was something spellbinding about Vinayak Damodar Veer 'the Brave' Savarkar.

Above all, he was a fiery, brilliant speaker revered by his followers as the Churchill of Maharashtra. In his fiefs in Poona and Bombay Savarkar could outdraw even Nehru. Like Nehru, Jinnah and Gandhi, Savarkar had completed his education in London's Inns of Court. The lessons he had drawn from his stay in that sanctuary of the law were not theirs, however.

Arrested in London in 1910 for having commanded from a distance the assassination of a British bureaucrat, he wriggled out of a porthole in Marseilles from the ship taking him back to India for trial. Eventually deported from France, he was given a double life-sentence to the penal colony of the Andaman Islands, only to be released in a post-war political amnesty.

Savarkar detested Congress with its pleas for Hindu–Moslem unity and its Gandhian non-violence. His doctrine was *Hindutva*, the doctrine of Hindu racial supremacy, and his dream was of rebuilding a great Hindu empire from the sources of the Indus to those of the Brahmaputra, from Cape Comorin to the Himalayas. He hated the Moslems. There was no place for them in the Hindu society he envisioned.

Twice he had presided over the *Hindu Mahasabha* – the Great Hindu Society – the right-wing, nation-wide Hindu political party. His real interest, however, was its Fascist para-military arm, the RSSS. Its central core was a secret society, the *Hindu Rashtra Dal*, which Savarkar had founded in Poona on 15 May 1942. Each of its members swore an oath of personal allegiance to Savarkar who was referred to as the movement's 'dictator'. Besides their almost blind allegiance to their 'dictator', another mystic, even more binding tie linked the Dal's leader and its charter members. They shared that most restrictive and meaningful of Indian bonds – caste. All came from Poona's elite of Chitpawan Brahmins, the heirs of the *peshwas*. Among them were the editor and the administrator of the *Hindu Rashtra*.

An almost worshipful silence followed the end of Savarkar's film. That brief celluloid appearance of the Hindu Messiah had been the highpoint of the evening. Arm in arm, Apte and Godse walked to their press. Fifteen thousand rupees advanced by Savarkar had launched their journal and no one doubted it was His Master's Voice in this citadel of militant Hinduism. While their guests clapped, the two young men posed for a picture. Then, with a jubilant shout, they thrust their fingers at the red button which set their flat-bed press in motion for the first time.

With the clanking press spewing forth the latest episode in the *Hindu Rashtra*'s continuing assault on the evils of Gandhi and the Congress Party, the little gathering began to break up. At his window the policeman who'd watched the proceedings was about to close his notebook when he started. In the shadows in one corner of the lot he'd spotted Apte in animated conversation. His interlocutor too was known to the police. His dossier bore the same notation as Apte's: 'Potentially dangerous.' The policeman scribbled a hasty note. Apte's name would henceforth be linked in the files of the Poona police with this visitor who'd journeyed sixty miles to attend the inauguration of a printing press. It was Vishnu Karkare, the owner of the Deccan Guest House in Ahmednagar. He was the innkeeper into whose embrace Madanlal Pahwa, the man whose name would be known throughout India, had fallen after throwing his bomb at a Moslem procession.

*

The two young men whose fingers had jointly pushed the button of the *Hindu Rashtra* press had only two things in common, their ardently held political convictions and the membership their birth conferred upon them in the elect of Indian society, the Brahmin caste.

Held by legend to have sprung from the brain of Brahma, the Brahmins in Hindu mythology descended from the Seven Penitents, the *rishis*, whose spirits shone in the heavens from the seven stars of the Great Bear. Originally penitents and philosophers living apart from the world and its temptations, they had been transformed through the centuries into a priestly and social elite. They were, in Hindu tradition, 'twice born' like the birds. As a bird was held to enjoy two births, when his egg is dropped and when his beak breaks his shell, so too was a Brahmin, at delivery and at the age of six when the double-stranded gut of the Sacred Thread officially making him a Brahmin was looped around his neck.

Nathuram Godse's life truly began when his father and a group of *mantra*-chanting Brahmin priests passed over his left shoulder those two coils of gut marking his entry into a fraternity in which only 2% of India's vast population might claim membership. They thrust young Godse to the apex of India's social pyramid and confronted him with a bewilderingly complex network of privileges and restraints that henceforth were supposed to govern his life.

The privileges the Brahmin caste carried were not necessarily economic. Godse's father was a postman earning fifteen rupees a month. But that humble civil servant brought up his sons in the strictest Hindu orthodox tradition. Once he had taken his thread, Godse was forced to learn and recite daily in Sanskrit verses of the Hindu's sacred texts, the *Rig Veda* and the *Gita*.

Like most strict Brahmins, his father was a vegetarian. He never ate with anyone who was not a Brahmin. Godse's mother was present only to serve his father. Before eating, he bathed and donned clean clothes which had been washed and dried where no impure being – a donkey, a pig, or a menstruating woman – could touch them. As a good Brahmin, he always ate with his fingers of the right hand, first sprinkling water clockwise around his plate, then pushing aside a portion for the birds or the needy. He never read while he ate: ink was impure.

Young Godse revelled in that strict Hindu upbringing and developed a taste for mysticism. To the astonishment of his household, he displayed a capacity for a rare form of worship, the *kapalik puja*. Nathuram applied fresh cow dung to one wall of the family house. Then he mixed soot with oil and spread the resulting paste over a circular lead platter which in turn was leant against the wall before a spluttering lamp. The 12-year-old Godse would squat in front of that platter in a kind of trance, seeing figures, idols, letters or scraps of verse he'd never read in the moving patterns of oil and soot. When the spell was broken, he would have no recollection of what he'd said or seen. Only he could read the signs in the soot and that, the family believed, destined him for a life of great achievement.

There was nothing in Godse's young manhood, however, to justify any such hope. He failed English on his matriculation and did not get into a university. Out of school, he drifted from one job to another, nailing up packing crates for a shipper in a freight depot, peddling fruit, retreading tyres. A group of American missionaries taught him the gestures of the only profession he really mastered, one he continued to exercise in 1947, the tailor's trade.

His real passion was politics. He became a rabid follower of Gandhi and the first visit Nathuram Godse ever made to a jail was on the Mahatma's behalf for following his call to civil disobedience. In 1937, however, Godse had abandoned Gandhi's movement to follow another political master, a man who was, as he was a Chitpawan Brahmin, Veer Savarkar.

No leader ever had a more devoted acolyte. Godse followed Savarkar across India, a faithful and indefatigable shadow ministering to his master's most modest needs. Under the master's tutelage, Godse blossomed, to realize, at last, the promise of the youth who'd read the portents in the soot. He read and studied constantly, relating everything he absorbed to Savarkar's doctrine of *Hindutva*. He turned himself into an accomplished writer and orator. Although limited by his fanatical devotion to Savarkar and his doctrines, he became an astute political thinker. By 1942, the Gods of the youth brought up in the most religious of households were no longer Brahma, Shiva and Vishnu, but a gallery of mortals, the martial leaders who had led the Hindu uprisings against the Moghuls and the British. He abandoned for ever the temples of his boyhood for a new kind of secular shrine, the headquarters of the RSSS.

It was in one of those temples that Godse met Narayan Apte for the first time. Their paper, founded at Savarkar's request in January 1944, was the most strident journal in Poona. Called at first *The Agrani*, it was closed by the Bombay provincial government for its virulent support of a 'Black Day' protesting against partition which was proclaimed by Savarkar and the *Hindu Mahasabha* for 3 July 1947. Clearly benefitting from the complicity of someone in authority, Godse and Apte had reopened the paper in ten days under its new name, the *Hindu Rashtra*.

Their roles on the paper were typical of their relationship: Apte, the fast-dealing businessman, Godse, the outraged editorialist; Apte, the chairman of the meeting, controlling its flow, Godse, the fiery orator; Apte, the formulator of their political schemes, Godse, their vocal proponent.

Godse was as rigid, as unbending in his fussy morality as Apte was supple and accommodating in his. Apte's eyes were always on the main chance. He was always ready to deal, to acquire discreetly a few rupees, to arrange and accommodate. Godse was a determined ascetic. Apart from his irrepressible fondness for coffee, he was indifferent to food. He lived in a monk's cell opposite his tailor's shop. The only piece of furniture in it was his rope-bed. He rose at five thirty every morning to his special alarm clock: his water faucet, left open so that the first gush of the municipality's morning ration would waken him.

Apte was a good-liver. He was off to Bombay to see his tailor whenever he'd accumulated a few rupees. He loved rich food, a glass of whisky, as well as most of the other pleasures life offered. Unlike Godse, who had lost interest in Hinduism as a religion since falling under Savarkar's sway, Apte, the man of the world, was forever running into some temple to jingle a bell and cast a few rose petals at the feet of a capricious god. He was fascinated by astrology and palmistry.

Despite his advocacy of violence to reawaken the Hindu people, Godse couldn't stand the sight of blood. One day, driving Apte's Model A Ford, he was hailed by a crowd to take a badly injured boy to hospital. 'Put him in the back where I can't see him,' Godse gasped. 'I'll faint if I see all that blood.'

Yet Godse had a curious fondness for Perry Mason detective stories and films of violence and adventure. Many an evening he would spend alone on a two-rupee seat in Poona's Capital Theatre savouring films like *Scarface* and *The Charge of the Light Brigade*.

While the gregarious Apte never missed a meeting or gathering, Godse, who was painfully ill at ease socially, avoided all he could. He had few friends. 'I do not wish to meet society because I wish to remain aloof with my work,' he maintained.

It was above all in their attitude to women that the two men differed most radically. No task, no matter how urgent, ever deterred Apte from a possible seduction. Married, his first child had been born deformed, which had convinced him an 'evil eye' had cast its spell on his wife. He had ceased to have sexual relations with her, but he more than made up for that elsewhere. For years he had taught mathematics at an American Mission High School in Ahmednagar. His real interest there had been introducing his female students to the erotic message of the *Kama Sutra* rather than the principles of algebra. The dark eyes with which Apte spoke talked as often to women as to his political associates and with results at least as effective.

At the age of 28, Godse had finally taken that ancient Hindu vow whose observance had so concerned and troubled Gandhi, that of the *Brahmacharya*, the voluntary renunciation of sex in all its forms. He apparently remained faithful to it for the rest of his life.

*

Three times in its turbulent history the little town of Panipat, fifty-five miles north of Delhi, had been the site of battles which had secured the road to India's capital to Moghul hordes. Now, on the orders of Mountbatten's committee, it had become a terminus welcoming a new wave of invaders, the train-loads of miserable refugees still pouring into India from Pakistan.

Their passage through the town *en route* to refugee camps had provoked a number of alarming situations, but none to compare with that confronting Panipat's terrified Hindu station master, Devi Dutta, one afternoon in late November. Victims of a savage Moslem attack in Pakistan, the Sikh refugees aboard a train arriving in his station that day stormed on to the platform shrieking for revenge. The first Moslem in their path was Dutta's assistant. A score of enraged Sikhs, brandishing their *kirpans*, grabbed the helpless man. Terrified, the Hindu station master screamed out the only words that came into his head, a phrase that reflected the instincts he'd absorbed in his lifetime as a good bureaucrat.

'Please, please,' he cried, 'no massacres on the station platform!'

The Sikhs obliged him. They carried his colleague to the rear of the station and beheaded him. Then they set out for Panipat's Moslem quarter.

Ninety minutes later a station-wagon raced up to the entrance of the station. From it descended the only force that would come to the aid of Panipat's Moslems that afternoon, Mahatma Gandhi. Panipat had had an important Moslem population since the days when its strategic location on the banks of the Jumma had made it the key to Delhi, and that population had a particular importance to the Saviour of Calcutta.

He walked unprotected into the mob of refugees milling around the station. 'Go, embrace the Moslems of this community and ask them to remain,' he said. 'Stop them from leaving for Pakistan.'

A stupefied, angry roar greeted his words. 'Is it your wife they raped?' 'Is it your child they cut to pieces?' voices cried at him.

'Yes,' replied Gandhi, 'it was my wife they raped, it was my son they killed; because your women are my women, your sons are my sons.' As he spoke, a garland of swords, knives and spears glittered in the sunlight around him. 'Those tools of violence, those tools of hatred will solve no problems,' he sighed.

Word of his presence sped through Panipat. In the station square Panipat's municipal authorities hastily erected a loudspeaker for an improvised prayer meeting. Moslems arrived from their barricaded quarters. Hindus and Sikhs followed until, like the Maidan of Calcutta, two and a half months earlier at the feast of Id-ul-Fitr, the central square of Panipat was filled with a multitude hanging on the words of an elderly man from whom it expected a new miracle. Constantly obliged to clear his throat as though his inner turmoil would not allow his voice its freedom, Gandhi turned on the crowd the only weapon in his armoury: his words. Again, he reiterated the essence of his political belief, 'that ideal which makes us all, Hindus, Sikhs, Moslems, Christians, the sons and daughters of a common Mother India'. He offered all the compassion of his soul to the sullen refugees whom the exodus had dumped on the station platform of Panipat. But he begged them not to allow cruelty and vengeance to dehumanize their hearts. Find in their sufferings, he pleaded, the seed of a more noble victory.

A timid current began to stir the crowd. Here and there an armed Sikh extended a hand to a Moslem. A Moslem offered a coat or vest to a Sikh refugee trembling in the winter wind. Other Moslems began to bring food and water from their homes for the refugees.

Welcomed by curses, the little man was able to leave two hours later to a tumultuous ovation, carried to his car in triumph. To his intense chagrin, however, his victory would prove ephemeral. His action that afternoon had saved many lives, but it had not been able to eradicate the fear in the hearts of Panipat's Moslems. Less than a month after the Mahatma's visit, the 20,000 heirs to what had been one of the oldest Moslem communities in India decided to leave their birthplace for Pakistan. 'Islam,' Gandhi sadly noted the day they left, 'has lost the fourth battle of Panipat.' So too had Gandhi.

Poona, November 1947

The *sadhu* in a soiled orange *dhoti* and unkempt black beard to whom Narayan Apte addressed an intense regard usually reserved for his female students, was not a *sadhu* at all. It was for his police record rather than his piety that Digamber Badge was best known in Bombay Province. The orange robe and spiritual air happened to be his favourite disguise for carrying out his activities as a petty arms trafficker.

In seventeen years, Badge had been arrested a record 37 times on charges from bank robbery to murder, aggravated assault and a dozen arms violations. Out of all those charges, the police had been able to make only one stick: cutting down trees in a protected forest in 1930 during one of Gandhi's civil disobedience campaigns. It had earned Badge a one-month jail sentence.

Behind the innocent façade of a bookstore, he ran an arms shop in Poona. The back room of his store was a jumble of home-made bombs, ammunition, daggers, axes, tiger claws, brass knuckles, penknives, all the crude instruments of slaughter popularized in the Punjab. Between customers, Badge and his ageing father knitted up the garment for which they were known to thugs, bootleggers and union busters around Poona, a chain-mail, bullet-proof vest bearing a startling resemblance to the armour of a medieval knight.

Apte was one of Badge's best clients. The administrator of the *Hindu Rashtra* had purchased 3000 rupees' worth of arms from him since June. Apte, as Badge knew, was forever hatching some plot or other. Once it had been to throw hand-grenades at a Delhi meeting of the Moslem League, hopefully killing Jinnah in the process. Later, Apte had determined to lead a team of assassins to Switzerland to kill Jinnah during a visit to Geneva. To Apte's distress, however, the ailing Jinnah had never left Pakistan. Most recently, he'd been organizing guerrilla actions in Hyderabad, canvassing the possibility of an attempt on the Nizam's life.

'I'm on to something,' he now hissed to Badge. 'Something very big. I'm going to need hand-grenades, gun cotton slabs, some pistols.'

Badge pondered a moment. He had none of those items at the moment in his stores, and pistols were hard to find. Badge, however, was not a man to let a deal pass him by. 'Penny-pinching meanness of mind,' a close observer would later remark, was 'his most important trait'. Wait, he counselled, he'd have the stuff by late December. Apte hesitated a moment. Then he nodded. His 'big thing' could wait a bit longer.

To Pyarelal Nayar, the faithful secretary who'd served him for years, Mahatma Gandhi appeared in the first days of December 1947 'the saddest man one could picture'. Now that they had settled into the corridors of power to which they'd so long aspired, Gandhi sensed a psychological barrier arising between him and the colleagues he'd led in the independence struggle. Increasingly Gandhi wondered if he was not becoming an anachronism in the land whose independence he'd done so much to secure, an embarrassment to his colleagues.

'If India has no further use for non-violence,' he noted, 'can she have any for me?' He would not be surprised if India's leaders said one day: 'We have had enough of this old man. Why doesn't he leave us alone?'

Until that day, however, he had no intention of giving them any respite. He bombarded Nehru and Patel with illustrations of India's growing corruption, of lavish banquets offered by their Ministers while refugees starved. He accused them of being 'hypnotized by the glamour of the scientific progress and expanding economies of the West'. He assailed Nehru's dream of a welfare state because of the centralization of power which it implied. That always led, he said, to the people 'becoming a herd of sheep, always relying on a shepherd to drive them to good pastures. The shepherd's staff soon turns to iron and the shepherds turn to wolves.'

India's town-bred intellectuals, he warned, were forming a new elite, drawing up their schemes for the nation's industrialization without regard to the interests of his beloved villagers. With a touch of Mao Tse Tung, he proposed that elite, 'with their town-bred bodies', be sent to the villages. Let them 'drink the water from the pools in which the villagers bathe, and in which their cattle wash and roll; let them bend their backs under the hot sun as they do'. Then they might begin to understand the villagers' concerns.

If India's leaders were ignoring him, however, Gandhi could ignore them too. One day, in December, he called to Birla House the Bombay cotton-broker in whose beachside hut he had recuperated in 1944 after his release from British prison. To him he confided a secret mission he instructed him not to reveal to anyone in India, not even Nehru and Patel. It was the realization of a dream Gandhi had cherished for weeks. Go to Karachi, he ordered, and make plans for a visit by Gandhi to Pakistan.

The broker gasped. The idea was madness, he told Gandhi. He was certain to be assassinated if he tried to carry it out.

'No one can shorten my life by a minute,' Gandhi replied. 'It belongs to God.'

Before setting out for Pakistan, however, Gandhi felt he had first to make another effort to get India's house in order. 'What face can I turn to the Pakistanis,' he asked, 'if the conflagration still rages here?'

Nowhere did the conflagration disturb him as much as it did in Delhi. The Moslem leaders continued to insist that their only assurance of safety lay in his presence in the capital. The police, their ranks swollen by refugee Hindus and Sikhs from the Punjab, were violently anti-Moslem. Hindu and Sikh refugees were seizing for their personal use mosques and Moslem homes, some abandoned, some not.

What distressed him most, however, was the fact that only a large contingent of troops kept the city from exploding into another orgy of violence similar to that it had endured in September. That the peace of an independent India's capital rested solely on the force of arms and not his cherished 'soul-force' haunted Gandhi. How could he hope to exercise moral authority in Pakistan if he had not been able to exercise a similar authority in India's capital? Increasingly he lapsed into those contemplative silences which always preceded a major decision on his part. As the year wound to a close, his moodiness seemed to grow.

'Stoning prophets and erecting churches to their memory afterwards had been the way of the world through the ages,' he told a group of Englishmen one night. 'Today we worship Christ, but the Christ in the flesh we crucified.'

In any event, he said, as far as he was concerned, he intended to be guided by the ancient saying of Confucius: 'To know what is right, and not to do it, is cowardice.'

Karachi, October–December 1947

The dark circles the size of ping-pong balls discovered by a physician's X-ray continued inexorably to spread their deadly stain across the lungs of Mohammed Ali Jinnah. The prognosis of his friend and doctor in Bombay was not to be denied. For a while, the intensity of Jinnah's will had seemed to impose a kind of remission on the disease's progress. Now that the realization of his long dream had eased his spirit, the disease had once again begun its advance.

On Sunday, 26 October, Jinnah had left Karachi for a brief visit to Lahore. Watching him go, his English Military Secretary, Col. William Birnie, thought he looked 60. When he returned, five weeks later, he thought he looked 80. Jinnah had spent those five weeks in bed with a cough and a debilitating fever that had left him weakened and exhausted.

As he felt his strength ebbing away, a strange melancholia gripped the Moslem leader. He became more remote than ever from his retinue and his followers. It was almost as though in the closing months of his life he could not bear to entrust his realized dream to hands other than his own. He gathered into his frail fingers almost all the strings of power in Pakistan and refused to share them. He would not delegate authority and, as he lay ill, dossiers awaiting his decision piled up unread and unacted on in his office. He became hypersensitive to criticism. He was, Birnie noted in his diary, 'like a child who by some miracle had been given the moon and won't lend it to anyone, even for a moment'.

A perplexing meanness of spirit overtook the man who'd ordered his ADC to get back his croquet set. His personal aircraft sat unused for weeks on end, its crew standing by, yet he refused to lend it to anyone, even to his own people to help evacuate refugees, because he didn't want to 'create a precedent'. He plunged his household staff into despair by picking at every detail of their administration, saving pennies with one hand and, with the other, insisting that the best

Bordeaux and the most delicious food be set upon his table nightly.

Above all, Jinnah was haunted by the idea that his old Hindu foes in Congress were determined to prevent his state from taking root and to destroy it after his death. On all sides, Junagadh, Kashmir, in the Punjab, he read indications of a vast Indian design to undo the achievement of partition. The crowning blow came in mid-December. After weeks of arduous negotiations, India and Pakistan finally reached agreement on the division of the last financial and material assets remaining to them. At Independence, India's cash reserves had totalled four billion rupees. Pakistan had been given an immediate advance of 200 million rupees. Under the agreement, she was to receive as the balance of her share an additional 550 million rupees (about 45 million pounds). Arguing that the money would be used to purchase arms to kill Indian soldiers, India refused to pay the sum until the Kashmir problem was solved.

The decision confronted Jinnah with a desperate situation. His new nation was almost bankrupt. Only 20 of the original 200 million rupees remained. Civil servants' salaries had to be cut. Finally, the proud Jinnah had to accept a crushing humiliation. A cheque issued by his government to the British Overseas Airway Corporation for aircraft chartered to carry refugees was returned – for insufficient funds.

The sojourn in the city of Ahmednagar of Madanlal Pahwa, the 20-year-old whose name the astrologers had foretold would be known throughout India, had been a particularly pleasant one. His life as a professional refugee was proving far more agreeable than a policeman's lot would have been. Under the guise of his newest mentor, Vishnu Karkare, the owner of the Deccan Guest House, Madanlal had organized the 10,000 refugees in a camp five miles from the city.

With Karkare, Madanlal decided 'to tax all business and particularly Moslem businesses for a fund for refugees'. The technique they employed to collect their tax was a classic and simple one. 'Those who wouldn't pay,' Madanlal noted, 'we burned down their shops.'

The funds they amassed were not destined solely to ease the lot of the refugees. They also embellished their own existence and nourished a dream of Karkare, a zealot of the RSSS. The cell-like rooms on the top floor of his Guest House were cluttered not with travelling salesmen but with arms. Like his friend Apte, the business manager of the *Hindu Rashtra* in Poona, Karkare cherished visions of leading a guerrilla movement against the Nizam of Hyderabad.

Karkare's ambitions of imitating the exploits of Shivaji were punctured, however, on New Year's Day 1948, when the police, searching the room of Karkare's hotel manager in connection with a murder, came on a pile of arms. The terrified manager immediately admitted they belonged to Karkare. Four days later, Karkare and Madanlal, at the head of a squad of hoodlums, broke up a meeting of the Indian Socialist Party advocating tolerance of India's Moslems. They were detained by the police, reprimanded and let off.

The following morning, leaving behind their arms cache, Karkare and Madanlal fled Ahmednagar. Their destination was a city 60 miles away, Poona. There, Karkare assured Madanlal, they would find shelter and spirits akin to theirs.

New Delhi, 12 January 1948

So much had changed since their crucial meetings in this same viceregal study in the spring of 1947. Then, Louis Mountbatten and Mahatma Gandhi had seemed to hold the destiny of 400 million people in their hands. Now events appeared to have passed both men by. The Emergency Committee with which Mountbatten had given India her rapid and secret return to English rule had been dissolved. He had become again what it was always intended he should be, a constitutional head of state whose powers were largely limited to whatever authority he could derive from his friendship with India's leaders.

His bare feet as always drawn up under the edge of his shawl, his air drawn and saddened, the elderly prophet in the armchair opposite Mountbatten seemed to bear all the misery of his nation on his countenance. His teachings rejected by many of his old followers, his doctrines contested by so many of his countrymen, he seemed a piece of driftwood cast up by a passing tide.

Yet, despite the pain India's division had caused him, Gandhi's personal esteem for the Englishman who had felt it his duty to impose it on India had never stopped growing. Gandhi felt only Mountbatten had really understood the meanings of his actions since independence. When, a few weeks earlier, the Mountbattens had flown to London for the wedding of Princess Elizabeth and their nephew Philip, whom they had brought up since childhood, Gandhi had manifested his affection for them with a touching gesture. Packed into their York MW102, along with the ivory carvings, the Moghul miniatures, the jewels, the silver plates offered the royal couple by India's former ruling princes was a wedding gift from the liberator of India to the girl who would one day wear Victoria's crown, a tea-cloth made from yarn Gandhi had spun himself.

Gandhi had implicit faith in Mountbatten's integrity and was persuaded that, as long as he was Governor-General, he would not countenance any dishonourable act by India's government. Indeed, for the last month, all Mountbatten's actions had been devoted to what was in Gandhi's eyes the most honourable of ends: preventing an all-out war between India and Pakistan over Kashmir. He had placed his friendship with Nehru under almost intolerable strain to get India to submit the issue to the United Nations. He had even suggested that Clement Attlee should fly to India to arbitrate between the two dominions. He had opposed India's decision to withhold Pakistan's 550 million rupees; an action, he feared, that might drive a desperate and bankrupt Jinnah to war. He also believed the decision had no moral basis. The money belonged to Pakistan, and refusing to pay it was almost an act of international embezzlement. His arguments, however, had failed to move Nehru and Patel. They were not going to risk inflaming an already disturbed public opinion by giving Pakistan money which would almost certainly be used to pay for arms that would fire on their own troops.

Now, in his still small voice, the elderly man in the armchair opposite him revealed to Mountbatten a decision he had not yet discussed with either of those two colleagues of his. For weeks, he said, his Moslem friends in Delhi had been begging him for advice: should they stay in India and risk death, or give up the struggle and go to Pakistan?

His advice had always been 'stay and risk death rather than run away'. He could not, he felt, go on offering that advice without himself taking a grave risk.

He hoped Mountbatten would not be angry, he told the Governor-General, but he had decided to undertake a fast unto death until there was 'a reunion of hearts of all the communities in Delhi', a reunion provoked not by 'outside pressure, but an awakened sense of duty'.

The Governor-General sank back in his armchair. Mountbatten knew full well there was no arguing with Gandhi. Besides, as he noted at the time, he admired 'the extreme courage, based on a lifetime's creed and convictions', which this decision implied.

'Why should I be angry?' he said. 'I think it's the most magnificent and fine thing anybody could do. I admire you immensely and, furthermore, I think you'll succeed where all else has failed.'

As he spoke those words, a thought suddenly occurred to Mountbatten. Gandhi's action would give him a unique moral force. During those hours or days when, on his straw pallet in Birla House, he would tiptoe towards death, he would have a power over the

Indian Government no one else could rival. What Nehru and Patel could deny to the Governor-General, they could never deny to Gandhi dying in the agony of a fast.

India's refusal to pay Pakistan her rupees was, Mountbatten told Gandhi, the only dishonourable act his government had consciously committed.

Gandhi sat upright. Yes, he agreed, it was dishonourable. When a man or government had freely and publicly entered into an agreement, as India had on this issue, there could be no turning back. Moreover, he wanted his India to set the world an example by her international behaviour, to offer a display of 'soul-force' on a world-wide scale. It was intolerable to him that so soon after her birth India should be guilty of so immoral an action.

His fast, he told Mountbatten, would have a new dimension. He would fast not just for the peace of Delhi, but for the honour of India. He would set as a condition for ending it India's respecting to the letter her international agreements by paying Pakistan her rupees. It was an honest and courageous decision. It would also prove to be a fatal one.

A mischievous smile enlivening his face, he told Mountbatten, 'They won't listen to me now.' But, he added with a chuckle, 'once my fast has started, they won't refuse me.'

17

'Let Gandhi Die!'

The Last Fast, New Delhi, 13–18 January 1948

The last fast of Mohandas Gandhi's life began at 11.55 on the morning of Tuesday, 13 January. As all his days that chilly winter had, that one had begun with a pre-dawn prayer. 'The path to God,' Gandhi had sung in the darkness of his unheated room, 'is for the brave, not cowards.'

At 10.30 he ate a final meal: two *chapatis*, an apple, sixteen ounces of goat's milk, and three grapefruit sections. When he had finished, an impromptu religious service in the garden of Birla House marked the formal beginning of his fast. Only a few close friends and the members of his community were there: Manu, whose straw pallet was still stretched out each night beside his on the floor of Birla House; Abha, another great-niece who was his second 'walking-stick'; his secretary, Pyarelal Nayar, and Nayar's sister, Sushila, the doctor who would care for Gandhi during the fast; his spiritual heir, Jawaharlal Nehru. The service ended with Sushila singing the Christian hymn whose words had never ceased to move Gandhi since he had heard them for the first time on the veldt of South Africa: 'When I survey the Wondrous Cross.'

After she had sung its last notes, Gandhi stretched out on his cot to snooze in the midday sun. A strangely contented air seemed to invade the pinched features on which so much sorrow had been reflected in the past weeks. Not since returning to Delhi in September, his secretary thought, had Gandhi appeared as 'cheerful and care-free' as he did now that his fast had begun.

The concentration of the Indian and international press in Delhi immediately gave Gandhi's new ordeal a dimension his Calcutta fast had not had. But the fast also perplexed many because, unlike Calcutta, no outburst of violence had preceded Gandhi's sudden decision to begin it. Delhi was tense, but the communal massacres in the city had stopped. Yet Gandhi, with his intuitive feeling for his people, had perhaps sensed something others did not: that another massive explosion of violence was dangerously close to eruption in India.

His countrymen greeted the news of his fast and the conditions he'd set for ending it with a mixture of confusion, consternation and even outright hostility. Conditions in Delhi were far less conducive to success than had been the case in Calcutta. The capital was overflowing with refugees crying out their hatred of the Moslems. To escape the cold and misery of the refugee camps, they had seized mosques and Moslem homes all across the city. Now their Mahatma wanted them to return those dwellings to their hated Moslem owners and go back to their wretched camps. Gandhi's decision to make the payment to Pakistan of its 550 million rupees a condition for ending his fast also infuriated a wide segment of public opinion and divided the Indian Government.

All those considerations, however, now lay behind the skinny octogenarian sleeping in the sun outside Birla House. For weeks, even months, it might have seemed to some that Gandhi was India's forgotten man, the message he had preached a conveniently discarded doctrine. No more. By turning on his own countrymen that ancient weapon of the *rishis* which he had used so dramatically against the British, Gandhi had suddenly reminded all India who he was and what he stood for. For the last time, he was forcing his countrymen to ponder the meaning of his life and the message he had sought to deliver them.

Poona, 13 January 1948

Seven hundred miles from the capital of India, in the white-washed shed in which barely ten weeks earlier they had inaugurated the new offices of their *Hindu Rashtra* newspaper, two men stood transfixed before the glass window of a teletype machine. The flow of urgent bulletins pouring from their teleprinter would alter irrevocably the destinies of Nathuram Godse and Narayan Apte. They announced the beginning of Gandhi's fast and the conditions he'd set for ending it. One of them catalysed the virulent emotions of the two Hindu zealots and thrust them on the road to a crime that would horrify the world. It was Gandhi's demand for the payment of Pakistan's 550 million rupees.

Nathuram Godse paled. It was political blackmail. The man for whom he had once gone to jail and whom he now loathed with such intensity was trying to coerce India's government into surrendering to the Moslem rapists and murderers. Like Apte, like all the other Hindu fanatics of Poona, Godse had often proclaimed it would be a blessing if Gandhi were forcibly removed from the Indian political scene. His words, as theirs, had been nothing more than the ravings of a political fanatic.

Godse turned to Apte. All his grandiose plans for guerrilla campaigns in Hyderabad, for killing Jinnah, were 'sideshows', he said.

Only one act should concern them now. They must concentrate all their energies, all their resources, on one supreme objective. 'We must kill Gandhi,' Godse declared.

The last shafts of Delhi's winter sunlight warmed the slender brown figure of Mahatma Gandhi as he advanced with steady strides across the immaculately trimmed lawn of Birla House. One hand resting lightly on Manu's shoulders, the other on Abha's, he shuffled up the four red sandstone steps to the heart of the garden, a raised lawn the size of a pair of tennis courts, its perimeter ringed by a knee-high balustrade rising above a scarlet swathe of roses. There, in the tranquil beauty of that garden, Gandhi had found the spot he preferred in Delhi for his regular rendezvous with his countrymen, his evening prayer meeting.

At the edge of the raised lawn, under the decorative arches of a sandstone pavilion lining one of its sides, Gandhi's followers had installed a wooden platform six inches high. On it were a straw pallet for the Mahatma and a microphone. Manu carefully set out beside his pallet the three articles that always accompanied him to the prayer ground: his *Gita*, his notebook with the text of his address, and his brass spittoon. Because of the extraordinary importance of this day, over 600 people crowded in front of the platform. Gandhi began the prayer by asking the crowd to join him in singing Tagore's hymn which he had sung each day a year earlier as he had strode through the marshes of Noakhali on his Penitent's Pilgrimage: 'If they answer not thy call, walk alone, walk alone.'

A hush stilled the crowd as he prepared to speak. His fast, he declared, was 'an appeal to God to purify the souls of all and make them the same. Hindus and Sikhs and Moslems must make up their mind to live in amity here as brothers.'

Listening to those words, each pronounced with such burning conviction, *Life Magazine*'s Margaret Bourke-White suddenly thought, 'This is really it. He has a religious position of his own to defend, his belief in the brotherhood of men.' Like many in the garden of Birla House that evening, she sensed 'greatness hovered over that frail little figure talking so earnestly in the deepening twilight'.

'Delhi is on trial now,' he warned. 'What I demand is that no amount of slaughter in India or Pakistan should deflect the people of Delhi from the path of duty.' Should all the Hindus and Sikhs in Pakistan be killed, 'the life of even a puny Moslem child in this country must be protected'. All communities, all Indians, should become again 'true Indians, by replacing bestiality with humanity. If they cannot do so, my living in this world is futile.'

A worried silence stilled the garden, while Manu gathered up his spittoon and his *Gita*. Then, wordlessly, the crowd parted, opening an alley through which the little man might pass back across the lawn to Birla House. Margaret Bourke-White watched him go, photographing with affectionate eyes his lean brown figure disappearing from the garden, wondering with so many others, 'whether we would ever see Gandhiji again'.

Poona, 13 January 1948

No prying eyes observed the meeting of the four men in the office of the *Hindu Rashtra* this time. The policeman who, three months earlier, had discreetly watched the inauguration of the paper's press, had been ordered to discontinue his activities. It was a tragedy, for the words spoken by Nathuram Godse that night were the most important an Indian policeman could hear. Beside him, uncharacteristically silent, was his partner Apte. Opposite him were Vishnu Karkare, the owner of the Deccan Guest House, and Madanlal Pahwa, the Punjabi refugee whom the stars had destined for notoriety.

Godse reviewed the Indian political scene for them. Then he vowed, 'We must take action.'

'We must stop Gandhi,' he declared.

His words elicited Madanlal Pahwa's immediate agreement. Before Madanlal at last was the opportunity to savour that revenge he'd sought since he'd left his father on his hospital bed in Ferozpore six months earlier. Karkare agreed as well.

From the *Hindu Rashtra*, the four men went to the home of the arms peddler who walked about Bombay Province disguised as a *sadhu*. Like a jeweller laying out his earrings and necklaces on his black velvet cloth, Digamber Badge set on to a rug on his floor the choicest items in his armoury. He had everything except the most vital tool of all – an easily concealable automatic pistol. They made a selection of hand-grenades, detonators and high explosives. Apte asked them all to meet him after dark on Wednesday, 14 January, in the office of the *Hindu Mahasabha* in Dadar, a working-class quarter of Bombay. Then they discreetly slipped off into the night.

Before leaving the city in which he'd been born and in which he'd absorbed his zealot's philosophy, Godse had a final act to perform. Like the leader he wanted to murder, Nathuram Godse was a man of few possessions. His were represented by the two slips of paper he set before a clerk in the Poona office of the Oriental Life Insurance Co. They were a pair of life insurance policies to which Godse had never stipulated a beneficiary. He made over the first, number 1166101 for 3000 rupees, to the wife of his younger brother Gopal who had agreed to join him in Delhi with a pistol. The second, number 1166102 for 2000 rupees, he assigned to the wife of his partner Apte. Like a condemned man who'd drawn up his last will and testament, Godse was now ready to die in his effort to murder the man half the world held to be a saint.

As long as his strength permitted, Gandhi insisted on carrying on with his normal routine during a fast. And so, in the cold dawn of Wednesday, he was up as usual reciting his *Gita*. A few minutes later, while he massaged his gums and the few teeth left in his mouth with his 'toothbrush', a carefully shredded stick, Manu heard him exclaim: 'Ah, I really don't feel like fasting today!'

At those words the young girl, who twice during the night had woken up to make sure her Mahatma was properly shielded from the cold, handed Gandhi his first 'meal' of the day, a glass of lukewarm water and bicarbonate of soda. Gandhi looked at it with a grimace, then gulped it down.

When he had finished, he turned to a task he had been brooding over since the day before, answering a moving appeal from his youngest son, Devadas, to renounce his fast. 'What you can achieve while living, you cannot achieve by dying,' his son had written. Calling Manu to his side, he dictated his reply.

'Only God who has ordained this fast can make me give it up,' he wrote. 'You and all the others should bear in mind that it is equally unimportant whether God ends my life or allows me to survive. I have only one prayer to offer: "O God, keep me firm during the fast lest I should hastily break it in the temptation to live." '

His chances of survival were already a concern to the young girl who was his doctor. His physical resources had diminished notably since his return to Delhi. His kidneys had still not recovered from the strain his fast in Calcutta had placed on them. His anguish at events in the Punjab had destroyed his appetite and subjected him to fits of labile blood pressure whose precipitous rises could induce spasms in his blood vessels. The only medicine Dr Sushila Nayyar could get him to take was a potion made from the bark of the Sarpagandha tree, and even that was now proscribed by the rigorous rules he'd laid down for his fast. Anyway, no medicine could mitigate his age, 78. Guiding him to what would be an agonizing daily ritual, his weighing, Sushila Nayyar admitted to herself that she did not know how much strain the system of the man beside her could stand.

The needle of her scale gave a tentative and disconcerting answer to her question. The first twenty-four hours of the fast had cost Gandhi two precious pounds. His weight that morning was 109 pounds. There was little fat to spare on his slender frame, and Sushila knew that, before long, what little Gandhi had to burn would be gone. For Gandhi, as for anyone on a fast, the critical moment would come then, when he had consumed those reserves of fat and his system began to devour its protein. That began a process which, if not stopped, would be fatal. In Gandhi's weakened condition it could begin, Sushila Nayyar knew, with brutal swiftness.

That in those crucial hours of his fast Gandhi should have confided the task of caring for him medically to a young woman instead of one of the eminent physicians in India's capital, reflected a little known but essential part of his philosophy. From the moment he had launched his first civil disobedience campaign in South Africa, women had always been in the forefront of his movement.

There could be no hope for the emancipation of India, he had never ceased to maintain, so long as India's women were not emancipated. Women were 'the suppressed half of humanity' and the roots of their servitude lay, he believed, in the narrow circle of domestic chores to which a male-dominated society condemned them. With the establishment of his first ashram in South Africa he had decreed that men and women would share equally in domestic tasks. He abolished separate family kitchens in favour of a common mess. The women, thus unburdened of their household drudgery, would be free to participate equally with men in the community's social and political activities.

And participate they did. At every stage of India's freedom struggle they had stood equally with men before the charges of the British police. They had filled the jails and led the mass movements.

Gandhi would not have been Gandhi, however, had not his efforts on behalf of India's women been accompanied by their piquant contradictions. His advice to girls menaced with rape in the Punjab had been to bite their tongue and hold their breath until they died. He had always rejected modern birth control as a solution to India's soaring population rate because he felt the devices it required were incompatible with his ideas on natural medicine. The only form of birth control he accepted was the one he himself practised – sexual continence.

Nonetheless, a society which centuries earlier had condemned its widows to leap into the blazing funeral pyre of their deceased husbands, had so evolved under Gandhi's prompting that a member of the first cabinet of an independent India was a woman.

Just before midday, the members of that cabinet gathered around the man who was becoming again the conscience of India. Headed by Nehru and Patel, they had abandoned their sumptuous office buildings to hold a cabinet meeting around the *charpoi* of the man who had opened the doors of those edifices for them. The subject that brought them to Gandhi's bedside was his demand for the payment of Pakistan's 550 million rupees.

That demand had shocked and angered most of the cabinet and particularly Vallabhbhai Patel. Nehru, then Patel, tried to justify the decision to withhold the money. Gandhi, weak and dizzy, lay on his pallet staring silently up at the ceiling as they pressed their arguments. He said nothing. Patel pressed on. Slowly, painfully, tears in his eyes, Gandhi raised himself on his elbows and looked at the man who had stood by his side during so many bitter struggles.

'You are not the Sardar I once knew,' he said in a hoarse whisper, and tumbled back on to his mattress.

All that day a stream of Moslem, Hindu and Sikh leaders filed past his bed begging Gandhi to abandon his fast. Their concern sprang from an awareness of a phenomenon of which Gandhi's entourage, wrapped in the protective shelter of Birla House, did not know. For the first time, a fast by India's leader was stirring the active resentment of a number of his countrymen. In New Delhi's commercial heart, Connaught Circus, in the crowded alleys of Old Delhi's Chandni Chawk, every conversation turned on the fast. But as a shocked Congress Party official, G. N. Sinha, discovered as he mingled with these crowds, no ardent desire to save Gandhi's life animated them. To many, the sufferings of the man on his *charpoi* in Birla House seemed a prejudiced manœuvre designed to aid the Moslems. The question Sinha heard most frequently that January afternoon in Delhi's bazaar was not, 'How can Gandhi's life be saved?' but 'When will that old man stop bothering us?' In the centre of the city an angry gang of refugees even broke up a demonstration calling for communal peace to save Gandhi's life.

Early in the evening, a faint yet familiar sound drifted towards Birla House. Hopeful and eager, Gandhi's entourage listened. They had heard that sound in Calcutta, the chanted slogans of a distressed population beseeching their Mahatma to abandon his fast. One of Gandhi's secretaries raced to the gate. In the indistinct glare of the street lights he could see the procession moving towards him down Albuquerque Road, a forest of waving banners and blurred figures.

Inside, in the darkened room where Gandhi lay, the sound drew closer. Weak and dizzy, Gandhi was stretched out in the shadows on his *charpoi* half asleep. Finally, as the demonstrators reached the gate, the rumble of their chanted slogans vibrated through the room. Gandhi beckoned his secretary Pyarelal.

'What's going on?' he asked.

'It's a crowd of refugees demonstrating,' Pyarelal replied.

'Are there many?'

'No, not many.'

'What are they doing?'

'Chanting slogans.'

For a moment, Gandhi listened, trying to understand the rumbling echo of their chant.

'What are they saying?' he asked.

Pyarelal paused, pondering his answer. Then he swallowed.

'They are chanting, "Let Gandhi die!"' he said.

Bombay, 14 January 1948

Three men who wanted Gandhi to die stood in the darkness before an iron grille barring the entrance to a tawdry two-storey building of weather-beaten cement in the northernmost suburb of Bombay. The only trace of elegance on its facade was a marble plaque sealed into one wall. It denoted in Marathi the building's function: Savarkar Sadan – Savarkar's House.

Few men in India loathed the man lying on his *charpoi* in Birla House with an intensity comparable to that animating the self-styled dictator of militant Hinduism who lived in that residence. Veer 'the Brave' Savarkar detested almost all the principles for which Gandhi stood. If Gandhi had made Birla House and every other place he'd lived temples of non-violence, Savarkar Sadan, set innocently among the palms and medlar trees of Bombay's Keluksar Road, was a shrine to violence. Nothing was more natural than that the first act on arriving in Bombay, of the men who wanted to murder Gandhi, had been to make their way to its gate.

One of the three bore under his arm a *tabla*, an Indian drum. This evening Digamber Badge had chosen to dress not as a *sadhu* but as a musician, a disguise which came naturally to a man born into the caste of wandering minstrels who had gone about early India singing and dancing. The drum under his arm concealed the selection of arms the conspirator had made at his shop in Poona.

A guard showed the trio into Savarkar's cluttered reception room. Very few people had the right to move immediately past that room up a flight of stairs to the personal quarters of the dictator of the Hindu Rashtra Dal. Nathuram Godse and Narayan Apte were among them. Digamber Badge was not and so, taking Badge's *tabla*, they went upstairs without him.

Godse, Apte and Badge were not the first of their little group to penetrate the headquarters of Veer Savarkar that January day. Earlier, Karkare had ushered Madanlal into the master's presence. Karkare had described the young Punjabi as 'a very daring worker'. Savarkar's response was to bestow one of his glacial smiles on Madanlal. Then he had caressed his bare forearm as a man might stroke a kitten's back. 'Keep up the good work,' he had urged.

Their meeting with Savarkar finished, the trio split up for the night. Badge went to the common dormitory of the *Hindu Mahasabha*. Apte and Godse, the two Chitpawan Brahmins, left for a more becoming destination, the Sea Green Hotel.

As soon as they'd reached the hotel the irrepressible Apte made a telephone call. The number he requested was the last in the world which one would have expected from the man vowed to commit India's crime of the century. It was the central switchboard of the Bombay Police Department. When the switchboard answered, Apte requested extension 305. There at the other end of the line was the welcoming voice of the girl who would share Apte's bed that evening, the daughter of the Chief Surgeon of the Bombay Police.

The critical moment Gandhi's young doctor had been watching for since he'd begun his fast arrived with a swiftness so shocking that even she had not foreseen it. Analysing his urine on the morning of Thursday, 15 January, Sushila Nayyar found in it the dread presence of acetone and acetic acid. The fatal process had begun. Gandhi's reserves of carbohydrates were gone. His body was starting to gnaw at its own entrails, to consume its life-sustaining protein. Barely forty-eight hours after he'd launched his fast, the exhausted octogenarian was already gliding into the medical danger zone.

Nor was that the only sign worrying the girl who'd given up a United Nations' fellowship in the United States to care for Gandhi. The meticulous examination of his urine had uncovered another. In the previous twenty-four hours he had absorbed sixty-eight ounces of the lukewarm water and bicarbonate of soda he so detested. Her careful tabulations showed he had eliminated only twenty-eight.

Gandhi's kidneys, damaged by his Calcutta fast, were not functioning properly. Deeply concerned, Sushila tried to explain to Gandhi the seriousness of his condition, why this time he might never recover from his ordeal. He would not listen.

'If I have acetone in my urine it is because my faith in Rama is incomplete,' he murmured.

'Rama has nothing to do with it,' Sushila replied. Patiently she explained the scientific process beginning with the appearance of those foreign bodies in his discharge. He listened in silence. When she'd finished, he fixed his eyes on her face.

'And does your science really know everything?' he asked. 'Have you forgotten the Lord Krishna's words in the tenth chapter of the *Gita* – "I bear this whole world in an infinitely small part of my being"?'

At 7.20 the following morning, while Gandhi reminded his young doctor of the limitations of her science, a well-dressed Narayan Apte walked into the office of Air India Ltd in Bombay. He asked for two tickets on the Bombay–Delhi DC3 service on the afternoon of Saturday, 17 January, for Mr D. N. Karmarkar and Mr S. Marathe. While he began to count out the fare, 308 rupees, the clerk politely enquired if he would be requiring return passages as well.

Narayan Apte looked at him and smiled. No, he said, he and his associate had no plans for their return. They only wanted one-way tickets.

Despite his sharply weakened condition, Gandhi insisted, as he would every day of his fast, on that ritual that constituted a regular part of his hygienic code, an enema. Its purging liquid purified the body, he maintained, as prayer purified the soul. The person responsible for that delicate and intimate operation was the self-effacing little Manu to whom Gandhi had declared on the eve of his fast, 'You are my sole partner in this great sacrifice.'

Hers was not an easy role. It exposed the slender girl to a surprising number of petty demands and petulant outbursts from a man whose external image was one of serenity and detachment. A few moments' delay in bringing the warm water for his enema provoked a surge of annoyance in Gandhi. Then, regretting his impatience, he fell back on his bed exhausted. 'One becomes aware of one's faults,' he whispered contritely to Manu, 'only when one faces a trial such as a fast.'

The enema left him, Manu noted, limp with exhaustion and 'white as a roll of cotton'. Seeing him crumpled up in his bed, the frightened girl, afraid he was dying, started to go for help. Sensing what she was doing, he beckoned her with a weak movement of his wrist.

'No,' he told her, 'God will keep me alive if he needs my presence here.'

Now into its third day, his fast began at last to affect the mood of India's capital. Ten thousand people came to Red Fort to hear Nehru plead that 'the loss of Mahatma Gandhi's life would mean the loss of India's soul'. It was an important gathering; yet half a million people had rallied to the same site on 15 August the year before. At Government House, Louis Mountbatten had ordered all receptions and official meals to be cancelled out of respect for the suffering of the frail man he so admired. A few processions calling for communal peace began to make their timid appearance in Delhi's streets. That was, however, hardly comparable to Calcutta where, from the first day, Gandhi's fast had provoked a dramatic shift in the city's mood. Sensing the capital's indifference, an uneasy feeling invaded Manu, the fear that Delhi might, after all, 'let Gandhi die'.

It was in Pakistan that emotions seemed strongest. A telegram from Lahore informed Gandhi, 'Here everyone asks only one thing: how can we help save Gandhi's life?' All across their new nation, leaders of the Moslem League suddenly began to praise their old adversary as 'the archangel of fraternity'. In the country's mosques sheikhs offered prayers for him. From the seclusion of their purdah, thousands of Moslem women called for Allah's mercy on the 78-year-old Hindu holding out the hand of brotherhood to India's Moslems.

No piece of news from Delhi would move Pakistan as dramatically, however, as that flashed across the sub-continent by the teletypes of its news agencies late on Thursday afternoon. Gandhi had won his first victory. The pain and hunger to which he was submitting his body had saved Mohammed Ali Jinnah's state from bankruptcy. As a gesture to restore the sub-continent's peace, and above all 'to end the physical suffering of the nation's soul', the Indian Government had announced it had ordered the immediate payment of Pakistan's 550 million rupees.

Bombay, 15 January 1948

Like a group of crapshooters, the men who had decided to kill Gandhi because of those rupees knelt in a circle on the floor of the

Hindu temple in which Badge had hidden his *tabla* full of arms the evening before. The false *sadhu* opened his drum and set its contents before them. Patiently, like a salesman demonstrating a new kitchen knife at a country fair, he showed them how to insert fuses into the slabs of high explosive, how to arm their hand-grenades.

While Badge talked, Apte contemplated with dismay the last weapon he'd drawn from his *tabla*, the weapon they needed most of all, a pistol. It was a crude, home-made arm, as likely, Apte murmured to Godse, to blow up in their hands as it was to kill Gandhi. A pistol, the simplest element of the murder they planned to commit, was proving maddeningly difficult to find. They had been able to locate enough high explosive to blow up a three-storey building, but still lacked the arm that was essential to their success. Even money had been easier to find than a pistol. A day of opportuning his extremist friends for money and a revolver had produced the wad of 1000-rupee notes in Apte's pocket, but no gun.

Watching Badge's agile fingers dance over his explosives, Apte suddenly realized that his knowledge might be indispensable in Delhi. Badge was not a part of their conspiracy. Neither Apte nor Godse entirely trusted him. His aid now seemed so essential, however, that Apte called him into the courtyard. Looping his arm over his shoulder, he whispered to Badge, 'Come to Delhi with us.' Savarkar wanted Gandhi, Nehru and Suhrawardy 'finished off', he said. He and Godse had been entrusted with the job. Then he added the phrase that convinced Badge's avaricious spirit: 'We'll pay expenses.'

The enlistment of an arms expert completed the circle of the conspirators. The time had come to start the trek across half the subcontinent to India's capital and their rendezvous with the architect of Indian independence. The arms Badge had furnished were carefully concealed in Madanlal's bedding roll. He and Karkare would begin their two-day journey that night, catching the Frontier Mail at the Victoria Terminus, the station in which so many young Englishmen had had their first introduction to the land they'd come to rule. Badge and Gopal Godse, Nathuram's younger brother, would follow by separate trains 48 hours later. Apte and Godse would travel in a more suitable manner, flying with the tickets Apte had purchased that morning. Their rendezvous would be the *Hindu Mahasabha Bhavan*, the *Hindu Mahasabha* Lodge. It was attached to Birla Temple, the rococo Hindu shrine which had been offered to Delhi by the family in whose residence the man they planned to kill was living.

Hundreds of faithful crowded the lawns behind Birla House at dusk on Thursday evening, hoping some miracle might allow the legendary figure to attend his prayer meeting. It was a doomed hope. Gandhi no longer had the strength to walk or even sit up unsupported. He offered his audience the only piece of himself he could, a few words whispered into a microphone by his bedside and delivered over a loudspeaker to the gathering on the prayer grounds. The familiar voice that had galvanized India's masses for three decades was so faint that it seemed to some on the lawn that evening that he was already addressing them from beyond the grave.

Contemplate their nation and its need for brotherhood, he urged, not his suffering. 'Do not be worried on my account. He who is born in this world cannot escape death.

'Death,' he went on, 'is a great friend to all. It is always worthy of our gratitude because it relieves us of all sorts of miseries once and for all.'

When the prayers had finished, a clamour rose from the gathering for *darshan*, for a glimpse at least of their beloved leader. Women first, then men, the audience assembled into a long column. In a poignant silence, palms pressed together in the ritual gesture of *namaste*, they began to flow past the glassed-in veranda where Gandhi slept, exhausted by the few words he'd addressed to them. He was curled up in a foetal position, a white shawl drawn over his emaciated frame, his eyes closed, his face lined yet somehow radiating an almost supernatural glow. His hands were clasped in the position of *namaste*, returning even in sleep the greeting of his sorrowing admirers.

Manu could not believe her eyes. The unpredictable old man who the evening before did not have the strength to raise his torso from his bed was now standing up, shuffling painfully across the room to take his place at morning prayers. After the prayer, Gandhi sat down to an activity as remarkable as it was curious in a man who had gone without nourishment for four days and was menaced by death. He began his daily study of Bengali, a language he'd striven to master since his tour of Noakhali. Then, with a voice that was surprisingly firm, he began to dictate the message he wished read out at his evening prayer meeting.

His apparent vigour was an illusion, however; like the periods of remission accorded a patient with terminal cancer during his descent to the abyss. A few minutes later, trying to get to the bathroom on his own, his head began to reel and he collapsed unconscious on the floor.

Sushila Nayar rushed to his side and helped carry him back to his bed. She knew what had happened. Gandhi's lean brown frame was becoming waterlogged because his damaged kidneys were unable to pass the water he was absorbing. The strain was now affecting his heart. She had foreseen it a few minutes earlier when she'd put him on her scale. Its needle had remained set on the figure it had registered for 48 hours: 107 pounds. A check of his blood pressure and pulse confirmed the young girl's diagnosis. The cardiogram of a heart specialist rushed to Birla House provided the final corroborative evidence of the deterioration in the 78-year-old Gandhi's vital organ. A sudden, fatal end to Gandhi's fast had now become a distinct possibility. Almost worse was the danger that, if the fast continued much longer, the result, even if it ended successfully, would be permanent and irreparable damage to Gandhi's vital organs.

Her own heart aching, Sushila took a pencil in hand and wrote the first of her twice-daily bulletins on the state of Gandhi's health. It was a grief-stricken cry of alarm. Unless a rapid term was set to his sufferings, she wrote, the strain his system was undergoing would leave India's beloved Mahatma an invalid for the rest of his days.

Once again, that extraordinary current which somehow linked India's millions to their Great Soul emanated from Birla House. Instinctively, even without the warning of Sushila Nayar's bulletin, India had sensed that Friday morning that Gandhi's life was in danger. As had happened so often before during his fasts, the mood of India changed with puzzling speed. The second most populous nation in the world began to hang attendant on the struggle between a man and his conscience in Birla House.

All India Radio started to broadcast hourly bulletins on Gandhi's condition direct from Albuquerque Road. Dozens of Indian and foreign newsmen gathered in a death watch at its gates. Hundreds of Maidans in every city and town suddenly swarmed with shouting crowds waving banners, crying 'Brotherhood', 'Hindu–Moslem Unity', 'Spare Gandhi'. Everywhere in India 'Save Gandhi's Life' committees sprang up, their membership carefully selected to reflect a full spectrum of political views and religious communities. Post office employees all across India cancelled millions of letters that day by writing 'Keep Communal Peace – Save Gandhi's Life' across their stamps. Thousands gathered in public prayer meetings, begging for his delivery. There was not a mosque in India that did not pray for him at Friday prayers. The Untouchables of Bombay sent a moving cable telling Gandhi 'Your life belongs to us'.

But it was above all in Delhi, Delhi the heretofore indifferent, that the change was most startling. From every neighbourhood, every bazaar, every *mohalla*, the chanting crowds now rushed forth. Shops and stores closed in acknowledgement of Gandhi's agony. Hindus, Sikhs and Moslems formed 'Peace Brigades', marching through the capital with linked arms, thrusting at passers-by petitions begging Gandhi to give up his fast. Convoys of trucks rolled through the city jammed with clapping, cheering youths crying 'Gandhiji's life is more precious than ours'. Schools and universities closed. Most moving of all, 200 women and children, widowed and orphaned by the slaughters of the Punjab, paraded to Birla House declaring that they were going to renounce their miserable refugees' rations to join a fast of sympathy with Gandhi.

It was an extraordinary, overwhelming outburst of emotion but it left the man on his cot in Birla House quite unmoved. It had taken more time than anyone had expected for Gandhi's fast to stir his countrymen but, now that it had, he was determined not to let go, to drive himself as close to the darkness as he could go so as to force the deep and meaningful change he wanted into his countrymen's hearts.

'I am in no hurry,' he told the worried crowd at his prayer meeting in a voice that, even magnified by loudspeakers, was barely a whisper. 'I do not wish things half done.' Gasping for breath with each word, he said, 'I would cease to have any interest in life if peace were not established all around us over the whole of India, the whole of Pakistan. That is the meaning of this sacrifice.'

Nehru brought a delegation of leaders to his bedside to assure him there had been a radical change in Delhi's atmosphere. Almost cheerfully he told them, 'Don't worry. I won't pop off suddenly. Whatever you do, should ring true. I want solid work.'

As they talked a telegram arrived from Karachi. Could Moslems who'd been chased from their homes in Delhi now return to re-occupy them, it asked.

'That is a test,' Gandhi murmured as soon as the text was read out to him.

Taking the telegram, Gandhi's faithful Pyarelal Nayar rushed off on a tour of the capital's refugee camps, explaining to their embittered Hindu and Sikh inmates that Gandhi's life was now in their hands. Over 1000 of them signed a declaration that night promising to welcome returning Moslems to their homes even if it meant they and their families would have to endure the winter cold in a tent or in the streets. A group of their leaders returned to Birla House to convince the Mahatma something had really changed.

'Your fast has moved hearts all over the world,' they told the shrivelled little figure on his cot. 'We shall work to make India as much a home for Moslems as it is for Hindus and Sikhs. Pray break your fast to save India from misery.'

Sushila Nayyar watched the needle's fluctuations with anguished eyes. It might seem a paradox yet, on this fifth day of Mahatma Gandhi's fast, she desperately wanted the scales to indicate her weakening patient was losing weight. They did not. The needle came to rest an almost immeasurably small distance below the figure on which it had remained fixed for the past three days, 107 pounds. Gandhi's kidneys still refused to discharge the 70 ounces of water he was absorbing regularly each day. To the strain that five days without food was placing on his heart was being added the steadily increasing burden of the superfluous body fluid his faltering kidneys could not evacuate.

All the other examinations to which she and the three physicians who had joined her put him that morning produced equally dismaying results. The excess of acetic acid in his urine was now a grave problem. Even Gandhi's breath reeked of acid. His blood pressure was 184, his pulse fast and feeble, the beat of his 78-year-old heart irregular.

The four doctors had not in fact needed their instruments to determine Gandhi's condition. Their eyes alone had been enough to tell them it was desperate. They quickly reached a common conclusion. Gandhi could not survive on his fast for more than 72 hours. Far worse, all the conditions which could lead to his death in less than 24 hours were now present. Their first bulletin that Saturday was terse and straightforward.

'It is our duty', they wrote, 'to tell the people to take immediate steps to produce the requisite conditions for ending the fast without delay.'

Poona, 17 January 1948

A shiver of nervous excitement fluttered through the stocky woman as, in a cloud of hissing steam, the Bombay Express rolled to a halt in the Poona railway station. 'I am the only one,' she thought, her eyes scanning the faces of the crowd pushing past her husband towards its third-class wagons, 'I am the only one who knows why my husband is going to Delhi.'

Gopal Godse was going to Delhi that morning to kill Mahatma Gandhi. He had been good to the word he'd pledged his brother

Nathuram. In his bedding was a ·32-calibre pistol he'd purchased for 200 rupees from a fellow worker in Poona's military stores depot. He had even tested it in the woods near his home. His wife, who shared his passionate convictions, was the only person to whom he'd revealed the use to which he intended to put that pistol. She had blessed him for it.

Now she held their 4-month-old daughter Asilata – 'Sword Blade' – up for his final embrace. 'We were in the bloom of our youth,' she would remember 25 years later, recalling that parting in a crowded railway station. 'Romance and revolution were our dreams.'

As Gopal reached the carriage door, she pulled him to her. 'Whatever happens, don't worry,' she whispered, 'I shall find a way to take care of myself and the child.' She pressed into his hands a packet of *chapatis* she had made for him to eat during the voyage. Then she drew back and watched him settle into his seat. In a cacophony of banging couplings and shouted farewells, the train began to lurch forward. Waving their daughter's chubby arm, she stood transfixed on the platform, waving goodbye, watching his proud silhouette disappear, silently wishing him 'the best of success' with all the ardour of her militant's heart.

Despite his critical state, Gandhi's mind remained crystal clear that Saturday morning. He had entered the third and final phase of a fast. The first 48 hours were always characterized by intense stomach cramps and hunger pains. Then the need for food passed, to be followed by two or three days of nausea and dizziness. When they in turn had run their course a strange tranquillity invaded him. Apart from a constant aching in his joints, which Manu and his other aide massaged with *ghee*, he no longer suffered. While Sushila and her three colleagues debated how many hours of life remained to him, he was tranquilly writing a few words in Bengali on the backs of his old envelopes.

When he'd finished he gestured to his secretary Pyarelal Nayar. His unfailing sense of timing had not abandoned him. If his fast was on the verge of achieving its goal as his followers promised him it was, then the time had come to make sure that what it secured would be permanent and not just the result of a compassionate desire to save his life. He dictated to Pyarelal a seven-point charter of the conditions he wished fulfilled if he was to end his fast. The leadership of every political organization in Delhi, including his foes of the *Hindu Mahasabha*, would have to sign it before he would consider his terms had been met. The conditions were unobjectionable in principle, yet reached out to touch almost every phase of the city's life. They ranged from returning to the Moslems the 117 mosques seized and converted into homes or temples by refugees to ending the boycott of Moslem shopkeepers in the bazaars of Old Delhi and guaranteeing the safety of Moslem voyagers.

Nayar rushed off to present his conditions to the Peace Committee established to save Gandhi's life. Delhi was wrapped in a mood of tension and excitement such as it had not seen since Independence Day. A wave of popular fervour exploded from Connaught Circus to the most remote alleyways of the city. Everywhere people marched about in chanting crowds. Delhi's commercial life simply stopped. Offices, stores, factories, bazaars, cafés, all were closed. Almost a hundred thousand people of all castes and communities assembled in a mammoth rally before Old Delhi's Juma Masjid, shouting for their leaders to accept Gandhi's demands. The Hindu fruit pedlars of Sabzimandi, one of the capital's most explosive areas, rushed to Birla House to inform Gandhi that they were ending their boycott of their Moslem colleagues.

Inside, Gandhi swung between bursts of lucidity and a comatose state. Someone suggested adding a few teaspoons of orange juice to his water. Alert, he opened his eyes and proclaimed that would be a sacrilege which would oblige him to fast for 21 days. Sushila Nayyar begged to be allowed to 'cup' his kidneys, to cover them with suction cups which might speed up their slowing rhythm. He refused.

'But Bapu', she protested, 'it's a part of the nature cure you accept'.

'Today,' he murmured weakly, 'God is my only nature cure.'

His most devoted disciple, Jawaharlal Nehru, abandoned his Prime Minister's office to sit by his pallet. The spectacle of the old man's decline was too much for the leader who'd been his favourite son over the long years of their crusade together. Unable to bear it, Nehru turned his face to a corner and wept.

Louis Mountbatten and his wife came in their turn. The ex-Viceroy was astonished to discover that, despite the torments he'd endured, Gandhi still had a 'chipmunkish glow', he was still capable of little bursts of humour.

'Ah,' Gandhi said in greeting, 'it takes a fast on my part to bring the mountain to Mahomet.'

Edwina was profoundly saddened. As they left his room, she burst into tears. 'Don't be sad,' her husband told her. He had been inspired by the sight. 'He's doing what he wants to do,' he said. 'He's a most brave little man.'

No phenomenon was as deeply rooted in the Indian psyche, nor as defiant of precise definition, as the mystic rite of *darshan*. A peasant experienced *darshan* when, after walking barefoot for hundreds of miles, he first glimpsed the waters of the Holy Mother Ganges. He knew it again when the first rivulets of that sacred water coursed down his skin. A man might have it in Hinduism's most sacred shrines, at a cremation, at a political rally, in the crowd around a great leader or, above all, in the presence of a holy man. *Darshan* produced an indefinable current, passing from giver to receiver, a blessing, a benediction, the emanation of some beneficent spiritual influence.

On the afternoon of Saturday, 17 January, that ancient and imperious Indian need for *darshan* found expression for two men separated by 700 miles, by an almost unbridgeable gulf of sentiment, yet whose names were soon to be linked by the tides of history.

The voice that reached the faithful who crowded on to the lawn of Birla House that afternoon for Gandhi's evening prayers was little more than a faint gasp. Gandhi barely had the force to speak for three minutes, and even those minutes were punctuated by long silences as he groped for the strength to go on. 'It is not within anybody's power to save my life or end it,' he said. 'It is only in God's power.'

Today he told his audience he saw 'no reason' for ending his fast. A worried groan escaped the crowd. As soon as the prayer was concluded all fell into a long column for their evening *darshan*. The sense of anguish filling those men and women was terrible. The news of how close Gandhi was to death had by now touched them all. Many a sorrowing Indian walking slowly across the lawn of Birla House in the fast-falling sunset wondered whether he was about to see India's Great Soul for the last time. For almost an hour their touching *darshan* went on, the long and silent column shuffling by, many faces wet with tears, while on the sun-porch the frail and withered little thing that was the centre of their attention tossed in fitful sleep under his white shawl.

Everything was ready now. Madanlal and Karkare were in Delhi with their hand-grenades, time bombs and the home-made pistol Badge had found them. Gopal Godse with a second pistol was *en route* to join them. Badge would leave in his turn that evening. And in barely an hour's time, Apte and Nathuram Godse would board the Air India DC3 that would set them irrevocably on the road to Birla House.

The two men were welcomed to Savarkar Sadan with the same deference they had been shown on Wednesday evening. This time their stay was brief. Savarkar accompanied them back down the stairs to the grille of his sadan. His most ardent disciples were setting out to murder a man Veer Savarkar detested with all the fury of which his zealot's soul was capable. Despite that fact, there was nothing in his rigidly composed demeanour to indicate the enormity of that moment. Hardly an emotion registered on his glacial regard, his taut, pursed lips. He laid a hand on Godse and Apte's shoulders:

'Be successful,' he whispered, '. . . and come back.'

In New Delhi an interminable flow of human beings converged on Birla House, its members beseeching Gandhi to end his fast. They poured down Albuquerque Road, a column 100,000 strong, three miles in length, waving a galaxy of coloured flags and banners, the roar of their cry 'Live Gandhi!' ten thousand times stronger than the cries of 'Let Gandhi Die' that had rung out on that same street five days earlier.

'The Association of Tonga Drivers', 'The Railway Workers' Union', 'Post and Telegraph Employees', 'The Harijans of the Bhangi Sweepers' Colony', 'Delhi's Women's League'; they bore the signs of an entire people seized by the urgent need to rush towards the pallet where the Mahatma lay dying. They flooded through the gates of Birla House, trampling its flowerbeds and rose gardens, a bobbing tide of heads crying out their slogans of brotherhood, offering their lives to save Gandhi's.

Sensing their mood, sensing perhaps that the climax of Gandhi's efforts was at hand, Nehru moved to the microphone on the prayer ground from which the Mahatma addressed his followers.

'I saw the freedom of India as a vision,' he said. 'I had charted the future of Asia on my heart.' It was Gandhi, he told the crowd, 'an odd-looking man with no art of dressing and no polish in his way of speech', who had given him that vision.

'There is something great and vital in the soil of our country which can produce a Gandhi,' he cried. 'No sacrifice was too great to save him because only he can lead us to the true goal and not the false dawn of our hopes.'

A sudden discordant note, the angry cry of protest of a refugee in the crowd milling in front of Birla House, greeted his words. It came from the lips of Madanlal Pahwa. Driven by a kind of morbid curiosity, Karkare and Madanlal had followed the crowds to Birla House, listening to them beseeching the man they had come to Delhi to kill to end his fast. Unable to control his emotion at Nehru's words, the 20-year-old Madanlal had committed the incredibly stupid blunder of shrieking out his protest.

Karkare watched in despair as two policemen took him into custody. If the hated figure inside the house survived his fast, Karkare told himself, he might now, because of Madanlal's idiotic gesture, never have to face their attempt on his life.

Karkare's fears were groundless. A few minutes later, as the crowds drifted away, Madanlal was released. Disgruntled refugees were commonplace in Delhi. The police had not even bothered to question him or take his name.

Late in the evening a man rushed into Birla House. In his hands Pyarelal Nayar bore the one message which could save Gandhi from the death his doctors feared was imminent. Gandhi's life hung on a thread that night. His pulse was weak and irregular. He had been delirious earlier in the evening. His continuing inability to pass urine seemed to foretell a general collapse of his system.

Gandhi was asleep when Pyarelal entered the room, but a funereal atmosphere pervaded his quarters. Pyarelal whispered to his beloved employer. He did not move. Finally, he shook his shoulders. Gandhi stirred and his eyes opened. Pyarelal drew a paper from his pocket, unfolded it and held it up to the Mahatma's face. It was a charter the Peace Committee had just signed, he explained, a pledge to restore 'peace, harmony and fraternity between the communities'.

Gandhi gave a sigh of satisfaction. Then he asked if all the city's leaders had signed it. Pyarelal hesitated. It still lacked two signatures, he admitted, those of the leaders of the local branches of the organizations headed by his most implacable foes, the *Hindu Mahasabha* and the RSSS.

They would sign tomorrow, Pyarelal said. The others guaranteed their signatures and their acceptance of the charter. Break his fast now, Pyarelal begged, take something to sustain him through the coming night.

Gandhi shook his head in an impatient little gesture. With difficulty he turned to his secretary.

'No,' he murmured. 'Nothing must be done in haste. I will not break my fast until the stoniest heart has melted.'

A telephone's jarring ring interrupted the meeting in the office of

Dr Rajendra Prasad, the President of the Congress Party. The call came from Birla House. Gandhi's condition had taken a sudden turn for the worse. If the resolution accepting his seven points, this time signed by all the leaders whose signatures he'd requested, was not rushed to his bedside it might well arrive too late. It was 11.00 a.m., Sunday, 18 January. For almost an hour, Gandhi had been dangerously close to slipping into a coma.

A shattered expression on his face, Prasad passed the news to the men crowding his office. They were there to put the last signatures on that critical document, the paper his secretary had shown Gandhi the evening before. Taking a few key leaders with him and telling the others to follow as fast as they could, Prasad rushed to Birla House. Gandhi was lying unconscious on his bed, the members of his entourage hovering around him like nurses around a dying patient. As he had the evening before, Pyarelal tried to call him, then to wake him by gently caressing his forehead. He did not respond. Someone brought a damp compress which was applied to his head. As its chill penetrated his being, Gandhi stirred, then opened his eyes. Seeing the gathering around him, a faint smile creased his face. He had accomplished a miracle of which only he was capable. The men standing by his bedside were divided by rivers of blood and antagonisms centuries old. There were Sikhs in the blue turbans of the militant Akali sect next to Moslems in fezzes and flowing robes; Congressmen in *dhotis*; Parsees and Christians in London-made lounge suits; Hindu Untouchables from the Bhangi Sweepers' Colony; orange-robed *sadhus*; the leaders of the extremists of the Hindu Mahasabha; and even the seldom-seen representative of that brotherhood of zealots, the RSSS, standing tranquilly alongside the High Commissioner of Pakistan.

Rajendra Prasad knelt down beside the figure crumpled up on his *charpoi*. His seven-point charter, he told Gandhi, now bore all the signatures he'd requested. It was their unanimous, deeply-felt wish that he break his fast. One by one the men around the bed confirmed Prasad's words with their own. At their recital, an air of serenity flowed across the Mahatma's countenance. He indicated that he wanted to speak.

Manu pressed her ear against his lips. She noted down each phrase in a notebook, then passed it to Pyarelal who read it to the gathering.

They had given him everything he had asked for, but he was still not quite ready to pronounce the words they so desperately wanted to hear. What they had achieved in Delhi they must now seek to achieve throughout all India, he warned. If they were pledging peace in Delhi but were going to be indifferent to violence elsewhere, their pledge was worthless and he would be making a mistake to break his fast.

Even in his feeble condition, the cunning despot of brotherhood knew he had the men around him where he wanted them, and he intended to extract the last measure of accord from them. Panting, he paused for two minutes to gather his strength before beginning again. Pyarelal, overcome by emotion, could no longer read out the scraps of paper Manu passed up from Gandhi's *charpoi*. He handed the task over to his sister Sushila.

'Nothing could be more foolish than to think India must be for Hindus alone and Pakistan for Moslems alone. It is difficult to reform the whole of India and Pakistan, but if we set our hearts on something, it must become a reality.

'If, after listening to all this, you still want me to give up my fast, I shall do so. But if India does not change for the better, what you say is a mere farce. There will be nothing left for me but to die.'

A tremor of relief rippled through the room. One by one the men present came to Gandhi's bedside to assure him they understood the full import of their covenant with him. The leader of the RSSS, the organization that claimed the allegiance of the commando which was in Delhi to murder Gandhi, added his pledge to the others. 'Yes,' he vowed, 'we swear fully to carry out your commands.'

When the last of their protestations of good faith had been uttered, Gandhi beckoned Manu back to his side. 'I will break my fast. God's will be done,' she wrote on her pad. A shriek of the purest joy burst from her lips as she read those words to the gathering.

An extraordinary air of relief and triumph swept the room, a burst of enthusiasm as exuberant as that greeting the news of a popular candidate's electoral triumph. When it had stilled, Gandhi insisted that all join him in prayer, a Buddhist *mantra*, readings from the *Gita*, the Koran, the Bible, the 'Mazdah' prayer of Zoroasterism, finally a hymn to the Sikh's great *guru*, Govind Singh, whose feast day it was. Gandhi's eyes remained closed. A radiant air of joy illuminated his pinched little face as he listened, his lips moving at each prayer.

Forcing her way through the crowd of newsmen and photographers who'd swarmed into the room at the news that Gandhi was breaking his fast, Abha brought a glass of orange juice reinforced with glucose to Gandhi's bedside. Maulana Azad, a Moslem and former president of Congress, and Jawaharlal Nehru, both trembling with emotion, took the glass in their hands and raised it to Gandhi's lips. The glare of exploding flash-bulbs filled the room with dazzling white light as Gandhi took his first sip. It was 12.45. At the age of 78, Mohandas Gandhi accepted his first nourishment after existing for 121 hours and 30 minutes on lukewarm water and bicarbonate of soda.

A roar of cheering broke out in the crowded gardens and alleyways outside as the confirmation of the news that Gandhi had at last broken his fast came from the house. Inside, all the women of Gandhi's entourage moved up to his bed carrying trays covered with orange sections. It was *prasad*, the gift of God. A feeble wave of the Mahatma's hand gave the gift his blessing. Tears of joy streaming from their eyes, the girls pushed their way through the crowds, offering their mounds of orange sections, the hosts of a gigantic and mystic communion binding those disparate and divided men.

By the time it was finished, his emotion and the energy he had consumed in addressing the gathering had left Gandhi in such an exhausted state that his doctors cleared the room. Only one man remained behind. His face transfigured by happiness, Jawaharlal Nehru squatted cross-legged by his old guru's *charpoi*. When the others had gone, he bent to place his lips close to the Mahatma's ear and whispered to him a secret he had shared with no one, not even his own daughter. Since the day before, he too had been fasting in a symbolic gesture of sympathy with his spiritual father.

His body reinvigorated by glucose as his triumph had revived his spirit, the voice that had been a whisper for the past 36 hours found again some of its old strength as Gandhi addressed his faithful on the lawn that evening.

'I can never forget all my life the kindness shown to me by all of you,' he said. 'Do not differentiate between Delhi and other places,' he begged them. Let peace return to all India and Pakistan as well. 'If we remember that all life is one, there is no reason why we should treat one another as enemies.' Let every Hindu study the Koran, let Moslems ponder the meaning of the *Gita*, and the Sikhs' Granth Sahib.

'As we respect our own religion so must we respect other peoples. What is just and right is just and right, whether it be inscribed in Sanskrit, Urdu, Persian or any other language.

'May God bestow sanity on us and the whole world,' he concluded. 'May He make us wiser and draw us closer to Him so that India and the whole world may be happy.'

His *darshan* that evening was an extraordinarily moving spectacle. Placed on a chair, wrapped in warm blankets like a new-born baby, the diminished figure was carried out to the terraces in full view of the crowd. Then his supporters hoisted him to their shoulders. Like a triumphant boxer who'd just knocked out his foe to become heavyweight champion of the world, the little man waved happily to his jubilant admirers. His ecstatic Manu could only think of the ancient Hindu legend of the Lord Ramchandra returning to his people from fourteen years in exile to hear them proclaim: 'Lord, we ask only one boon – to serve you.'

Three hours later, while a festive Delhi celebrated the end of his fast, Gandhi absorbed his first meal, eight ounces of goat's milk and four oranges. When he had finished, he called for that primitive device which had embodied his message to his people, his spinning-wheel. No pleas from his doctors or his entourage could deter him. With the first strength returning to his body, his trembling fingers set the wheel in motion.

'Bread obtained without labour is stolen bread,' he whispered. 'I have now started to take food, therefore I must labour.'

18

The Vengeance of Madanlal Pahwa

New Delhi, 19–20 January 1948

It had been years, Pyarelal Nayar thought, since he'd seen Gandhi as cheerful, as radiant with fervour and enthusiasm, as he was in the aftermath of his fast. The successful conclusion of the fast, Nayar noted, had opened before Gandhi 'boundless dreams and soaring hopes'. Not since the 1929 Salt March had one of his actions so galvanized the world.

A deluge of congratulatory cables and telegrams poured into Birla House. Newspapers around the world hailed Gandhi's exploit, 'The mystery and power of a frail 78-year-old man shakes the world and inspires it with new hope,' wrote the *News Chronicle*. Gandhi, the paper said, 'had demonstrated a power which may prove greater than the atom bomb and which the West should watch with envy and hope'. *The Times*, not always among his admirers, noted: 'Mr Gandhi's courageous idealism has never been more plainly vindicated', and the *Manchester Guardian* commented that Gandhi might 'be a politician among saints, but he is no less a saint among politicians'. In the United States, the *Washington Post* remarked that the 'wave of relief' sweeping the world because his life had been spared was 'a measure of the sainthood with which he has been invested'. Egypt hailed 'a noble son of the East dedicating his life to peace, tolerance and brotherhood', and Indonesia saw in his achievements 'the dawn of freedom for all Asia'.

The little man in Birla House was hardly indifferent to that avalanche of accolades. 19 January, as all his Mondays, was his day of silence, but the mischievous gaiety bubbling through his spirit infected everybody in his entourage. The bleak despair that had shrouded Birla House during the last days of his fast was replaced by a kind of mystic euphoria, a conviction that grand new horizons were about to open for Gandhi and his doctrine of non-violence.

The Mahatma remained weak and confined to a liquid diet of fruit juices, barley water and glucose, yet even his health seemed infected by the new spirit pervading his quarters. For his followers, the most reassuring moment came at the daily ceremony which had stirred such deepening anxiety during his fast, his weighing. That morning his weight fell one pound, to 106 pounds. It was the best news the faithful in Birla House could have had. Gandhi's waterlogged kidneys were beginning to function again. Once more,

India's resilient, indomitable Great Soul was emerging from the shadows.

At about the same time as Gandhi was mounting his scales, six men emerged into a little clearing in the dense undergrowth stretching behind New Delhi's Birla Temple. There, well out of earshot of any curious visitors, they paused. Before deciding when and how to make their attempt on Gandhi's life, Nathuram Godse and Narayan Apte wanted to test the weapons with which they planned to kill him.

Gopal Godse took out from under his jacket the ·32 calibre pistol he'd bought in Poona for 200 rupees. He loaded it, picked out a tree, backed 25 feet and pulled the trigger. Nothing happened. He shook it and pulled the trigger again. Again nothing happened.

Apte motioned to Badge to take out his pistol. While his fellow conspirators looked on tensely, Badge pointed the gun at the tree at which Gopal had been aiming. He pulled the trigger. This time there was a sharp report. The conspirators rushed to the tree to check the mark the bullet had made. There was none. It had fallen to the ground halfway to the tree. Badge fired again. This time the round fled well to the right of the tree. He fired four more times. Not a single round hit the target. As Apte had feared in Bombay, his pistol was as likely to kill them as it was to kill Gandhi.

A dismal silence settled over the conspirators. Nathuram Godse watched with silent fury as his brother began to pick at his pistol with his inexpert fingers. Everything had worked perfectly, he thought, everything except the vital element that was at the heart of the matter, a firearm that could kill a man at 25 feet. They had got themselves and their luggage to Delhi undetected. They were all committed to the deed. But now, unless his brother could fix his firearm, they would have to kill Gandhi with one pistol that didn't work and a second that couldn't hit anything.

The most important visitor to enter Birla House that day was the Bombay cotton-broker whom Gandhi had sent to Karachi to arrange his visit to Pakistan. As Gandhi had been living his ordeal, Jehangir Patel had been conducting secret negotiations with Jinnah for a trip which had appeared less and less likely ever to take place with each passing day. Jinnah's first reaction had been wary and hostile. His deep, ingrained mistrust of the man whose tactics had driven him years before from the ranks of the Congress Party remained unshaken. In addition his almost paranoiac suspicion of India's intentions prompted him to look for some ulterior motive in the proposal of the man he'd once labelled a 'cunning Hindu fox'.

India's decision to pay him the rupees he so desperately needed, and the growing realization among his own countrymen that it was, after all, for their fellow Moslems in India that Gandhi was suffering, softened Jinnah's stand. If Gandhi's fast had not opened the door to his heart, it had at least opened the doors of his new nation. On the day the fast ended, Jinnah finally agreed to welcome his old political foe to the soil of Pakistan.

The decision aroused a soaring sense of purpose and vigour in the Mahatma. A great turning-point in his life had been reached. At last he could move his doctrine of non-violence out of India. He had always refused to do so before because Indian independence was his first task. Now independence was secured and his fast had set his countrymen back on the course he'd charted for them. Where better to begin his new mission than in Pakistan? The Indian sub-continent had lost its physical unity, but he, at least, would strive to restore its spiritual unity.

Not only would he go to Pakistan, but he had a vision of how he would go. It was a dream that had been stirring within him for weeks. Jinnah wanted him to go by boat from Bombay to Karachi, but that was too banal a means of locomotion for a man with Gandhi's genius for the dramatic gesture. As he had marched across the borders of the Transvaal, as he had gone down to the sea for his fistful of salt, as he had gone to a thousand villages to preach brotherhood, non-violence and proper hygiene, so would he go to Pakistan: on foot. He would walk to Jinnah's new nation across the sore and bleeding Punjab, along the roads of the exodus on which so many of his fellows had suffered and died. Just a year before he had been walking through the marshes of Noakhali delivering with each step of his Penitent's Pilgrimage his healing message. Now he would set off again on a new pilgrimage, a pilgrimage of hope to bind up his nation's wounds and substitute a spiritual bond of brotherhood and justice for the physical bonds partition had cast away.

For the moment the feet Gandhi wanted to carry him to Pakistan could not carry him even across the lawn of Birla House. He was not, however, going to let that handicap keep him from the most regular and revered of his appointments, his daily confrontation with his countrymen at his evening prayer meeting. Despite the pleas of his entourage that he was still too weak to attend in person, Gandhi insisted on being carried to the meeting in a chair. Borne aloft on the shoulders of a pair of his followers, he rode like some Oriental potentate through the waiting crowd, his hands joined, his head bowing in the *namaste* greeting to the scores of people who waited for a new *darshan* with India's resuscitated prophet.

Every eye in the crowd followed his progress past Birla's long trellis, billowing with its orange and scarlet bougainvillaea blossoms, up the little flight of sandstone steps, across the lawn to the platform from which a week earlier he had announced his near-fatal fast. Not all the eyes scrutinizing his movements as he settled on to his straw pallet studied them with awe and reverence, however. At widely scattered intervals on the lawn, three pairs of eyes watched with an assassin's glare. Nathuram Godse, his brother Gopal, and Narayan Apte had not come to the prayer meeting to receive Gandhi's *darshan*. They were there to study the grounds of Birla House and to find a way to assassinate him.

It was the first time in his life Gopal Godse had seen Gandhi. He wasn't impressed by the wan silhouette squatting on his prayer platform. To Gopal he was 'just a shrunken little old man'. He did not feel any surge of hatred looking at him. 'Killing him,' he would one day declare, 'was an impersonal thing to me. He was a bad influence on the people.' What the wary Gopal Godse did sense was the presence in the crowd of a number of plain-clothes policemen. Leaving the prayer grounds he noticed a sub-machine-gun on the camp table of the police tent at the gate.

'We have very little chance of getting away,' he thought to himself.

Forty-five minutes later, taking precautions to see that they were not followed, the principal conspirators slipped one by one into Room 40 of the Marina Hotel in New Delhi's Connaught Circus where Apte and Godse had registered as S. and N. Deshpande. Karkare ordered whiskies for himself and Apte.

Apte announced the time had come to take a decision. His observations at Birla House had convinced him there was only one moment when they could be certain Gandhi would be exposed and vulnerable. That was when they would strike.

They would kill Gandhi, he said, at five o'clock the next afternoon, Tuesday, 20 January, during the ritual which had constituted the Mahatma's most faithfully kept appointment with his people, his prayer meeting.

Shortly after 9 a.m. on the following morning, a taxi rolled along the red brick wall screening the rear of the Birla estate up to the whitewashed wooden gate that was its service entrance. Unmolested, its two passengers walked through the gate into a little courtyard, on one side of which was a one-storey cement shed divided into cell-like rooms. It housed the estate's servants. The rear of that shed constituted the red sandstone wall of the pavilion in front of which Gandhi held his evening prayers.

The two men continued their stroll to the garden. It was silent and empty in the morning sunlight. A slick of dew still glistened on the green lawn and clung to the roses in the trench running along the little sandstone balcony which ringed the lawn's outer limit. Narayan Apte and his false *sadhu*, Digamber Badge, were reassured. There would be no one to trouble them as they accomplished their critical task: deciding exactly how they would execute the crime they planned to commit in the garden that afternoon. As he contemplated the sandstone pavilion in front of which Gandhi's prayer platform lay, Apte suddenly froze. A series of little grilles looking out on to the prayer ground were cut into its wall. Clearly, they were windows giving on to the servants' quarters behind the pavilion. One of them was directly behind the microphone from which Gandhi addressed his nightly gathering.

Apte walked over to it and made a quick calculation. The distance between that open window and the base of Gandhi's skull as he delivered his address would be barely ten feet. It was a shot so simple that even Badge's defective pistol could not miss it.

That was the revelation for which he'd come to Birla House. All he had to do was place Badge in the room behind that window. To provide a final *coup de grâce*, Apte would send Gopal Godse into the room with him. He would roll a hand-grenade through the cross-hatched iron grille screening the window at the instant Badge opened fire. Apte measured the opening in the grille with a string. It was five inches square, more than enough to allow the grenade to pass through into the midst of Gandhi and his entourage.

One last calculation remained. Apte made it as they left the prayer ground by the route through which they'd entered it. The servants' cell, the window of which lay behind the microphone, was the third from the end on the left. Satisfied, the two visitors returned to their waiting taxi. In barely eight hours, Apte assured Badge, Gandhi would be a mangled corpse lying on his prayer platform under the window they'd just spotted.

Five pairs of anxious eyes followed every movement of Badge's dextrous fingers. Squatting on the bathroom floor of Room 40 of the Hotel Marina he slowly inserted detonators into the hand-grenades they planned to employ that evening.

White-faced and unsteady, Nathuram watched from the doorway. 'Badge,' he whispered hoarsely, 'this is our only chance. Make sure they work properly.'

When Badge had finished, he cut a length of fuse with a knife and told Apte to take a watch. They had to calculate the speed at which it would burn. Badge lit the cord. It flamed up in a cloud of smoke that left the seven conspirators coughing and choking. As the acrid fumes billowed through the bathroom, they all began to puff frantically on cigarettes to cover the smoke that seemed certain to betray them.

When calm was restored, Apte assembled them in the bedroom to assign each man his task. The man whose sudden determination to kill Gandhi had brought them to Delhi took no part in the discussions. Nathuram Godse lay groaning on his bed, crippled by a migraine headache. Madanlal, Apte explained, would hide a time bomb against the outside edge of the brick wall behind Birla House near the prayer gathering. Its explosion would launch their action and set off a wave of panic to facilitate the assassination.

Badge and Gopal Godse would in the meantime have entered the servants' cell that he and Badge had reconnoitred that morning. If someone stopped them, they would explain that they were going to photograph Gandhiji from the rear as he addressed his prayer meeting. At the instant Madanlal's bomb went off, Badge would open fire on Gandhi from almost point-blank range. Gopal beside him would push a hand-grenade through the aperture.

To be absolutely certain their victim did not escape, Karkare, armed with a grenade, would be in front of Gandhi, mingling with the faithful. He too would hurl his grenade on Gandhi at the moment Madanlal's bomb went off. Nathuram and Apte would control the operation. Nathuram would signal to Apte when Karkare was in place in front of Gandhi, and Apte would give Madanlal the sign to detonate his bomb.

In their determination to exterminate Gandhi, innocent lives, Apte admitted, would be lost. That could not be helped. A few more innocent lives was the price India would have to pay for the death of the man he held responsible for the slaughter of so many hundreds of thousands of Hindus in the Punjab.

An excruciating tension settled over the room. Nathuram Godse lay sprawled on his bed moaning softly under the torture of his headache. So that there would be no visible link between them they dressed themselves as differently as possible. To accomplish the supreme gesture of his existence, Apte, the lover of well-cut tweeds, put on a *dhoti*. Karkare darkened his eyebrows and pressed a red *tilak* dot to his forehead. Madanlal donned a new blue suit he had bought in Bombay. The refugee from the Punjab was going to the rendezvous the astrologers had predicted at his birth dressed as a gentleman. For the first time in his life, Madanlal Pahwa was wearing a coat and tie.

As the hours slowly passed, the tension in Room 40 became almost unbearable. Silent, not looking at each other, the conspirators squatted on the floor counting the minutes go by. Nathuram Godse proposed they share a last ritual libation. He asked the room bearer to bring coffee for them all. When they'd finished, it was time to go. Madanlal, Karkare and Nathuram Godse went first. They left one by one at five-minute intervals to go to Birla House in separate tongas. Ten minutes later Apte and the others left to follow them by cab. Instead of getting into the first taxi he found, Apte decided to bargain over the fare to Birla House and back. For fifteen minutes he marched around Connaught Circus, going from cab to cab, haggling. Finally he settled on a green Chevrolet PBF 671 he found in front of the Regal Cinema. It was 4.15. His negotiations had succeeded in reducing the fare for their trip to the Calvary he had chosen for India's prophet from sixteen to twelve rupees.

At Birla House, Gandhi, still too weak to walk to the prayer meeting, was placed on a chair and carried across the lawn to his platform. Caught in the crowd pressing their hands together, respectfully bending forward as his tiny figure drew near, was Madanlal Pahwa. He too clasped his hands and reverently bowed his head to the man he intended to kill. His time bomb was in place, hidden under leaves and grass at the base of the wall behind him. As Gandhi passed, he raised his eyes to look at him. Hatred rushed over him as he contemplated Gandhi for the first time. 'He is my enemy,' he thought. Indeed, it was not Gandhi's diminutive image he saw bobbing along towards the prayer platform, but the image of another man, his father on his hospital bed in Ferozepore.

Almost before Gandhi had settled into position, a figure rushed from the audience to prostrate himself at Gandhi's feet, urging him to proclaim himself the incarnation of God. Gandhi detested such protestations. Still, he smiled tolerantly at the man. 'Sit down and be quiet,' he said. 'I am a mortal just like you are.'

At the rear of Birla House, Apte's green Chevrolete was drawing up at the service entrance. Apte was late for the most important rendezvous of his life because of his desire to save four rupees. Karkare told him Madanlal's bomb was primed and planted. There would be no problem getting into the servants' cell whose window looked on to the back of Gandhi's head. Karkare had given the man who lived in it ten rupees to let them use it. He pointed to him. Then the owner of the Deccan Guest House left to take up his own position in the crowd before Gandhi.

Apte beckoned Badge, indicated the man Karkare had paid, and told him to go into his room. Badge took half a dozen steps towards the door and froze. Nothing would ever make Digamber Badge go into that room. No hatred, no passion, no menace would be strong enough to drive him across its threshold. A voice had spoken to Badge. It was the voice of an India as old as its *rishis* and its rain forests, the India of signs and portents. The owner of the room, sitting basking in the sun, had one eye. There was no omen as inauspicious as that. Trembling, Badge returned to Apte. 'He has one eye,' he whispered, 'I'm not going into his room.'

Apte hesitated. On the prayer ground the hymns had finished and Gandhi was beginning to speak. His voice was so weak that Sushila Nayyar had to repeat each phrase he uttered to the crowd. Clearly, the exhausted Gandhi's speech was not going to last long. Apte realized he did not have time to argue. He told Gopal Godse to go into the room as planned and push his grenade through the window when he heard the explosion of Madanlal's bomb. He assigned the reluctant Badge a new mission. Mix with the crowd in front of Gandhi, he said. Get in as close as possible and fire at him head on when the time comes.

Gopal Godse walked to the servants' room, nodded to its one-eyed owner, and closed the door behind him. In the darkness he started to move towards the light pouring through the windows from which he would thrust his grenade towards the Mahatma's back.

On the prayer ground, Gandhi continued his address. 'He who is an enemy of Moslems is an enemy of India,' he declared. Gopal Godse could hear Sushila repeating his words as he moved through the darkness towards the grille. When he reached it, he discovered to his horror the first grave flaw in Apte's scheme. Apte had not bothered to enter the cell on his morning inspection. The grille through which Godse was supposed to push his grenade was eight feet above the ground. Apte had not understood in making his calculations that the level of the prayer ground lawn was considerably higher than the level of the courtyard in which the servants' quarters were located. Even with his arms extended full length, Gopal's fingertips barely reached the base of the grille. Desperately, he groped in the darkness for the one-eyed man's *charpoi*. Finally locating it he frantically began to pull it towards the window so that it could serve as a base on which to climb.

Outside everything was set. Nathuram Godse saw Karkare in position, prepared to throw his grenade at the man who at that instant was discussing the 'cruel treatment' of blacks in America. The time had come. Nathuram put his hand to his chin and scratched.

Apte saw him. He in turn raised his arm to Madanlal. The Punjabi was ready. The moment for which he'd been waiting since he'd walked across the bridge at Sulemanki Head that August afternoon had arrived. He was going to get his revenge. It was a chance he was not going to miss. Calmly, deliberately, he drew on his cigarette. Then he bent over and pressed its glowing tip to the fuse of the bomb at his feet.

'If we cling to the excellent decisions taken,' Sushila was repeating to the assembly, 'with God as our witness, we shall rise to a much higher moral plane . . .'

At that precise moment the roar of Madanlal's exploding time bomb burst over the prayer ground with frightening fury. A column of smoke spewed up from the bomb site. 'Oh Mother!' Sushila gasped.

'What better death could you ask,' Gandhi asked her, reproach in his faint voice, 'than to die in the act of prayer?'

In the cell just behind them, Gopal Godse was climbing on to a *charpoi* to reach the grille above him. The ropes of the *charpoi* which he'd counted on as a platform were so slack that they sagged almost to the dirt floor. His efforts had added barely three inches to his height. Balancing on its wooden frame, Gopal pulled himself up as far as he could. His eyes still did not quite reach the base of the opening. The only thing he could do was push the grenade blindly through the grille and let it fall on whoever was sitting there. He reached for the grenade. As he did so, he realized no sound of firing, no roar of Karkare's exploding grenade was coming from the prayer ground. All he could hear was the voice of Gandhi calling for order.

With all the strength of his weak frame, Gandhi was pleading to the crowd. 'Listen! Listen!' he said. 'It's nothing. It's just the army having some practice. Sit down and be calm. The prayers continue.'

Confusion had swept the garden in the wake of Madanlal's bomb. No one had been injured by the explosion, but it had provoked exactly the burst of panic the conspirators had counted on to cover the assassination. Under its cover, Karkare pushed up to within fifteen feet of Gandhi.

The weakened man was an exposed, helpless target, as defenceless as a cripple in a wheelchair.

Karkare started to pull out his grenades. As he did so he looked at the grille behind Gandhi's head for the confirming glint of a pistol barrel or the tumbling black shape of a grenade. There was nothing. Karkare froze.

Gopal Godse jumped down from the *charpoi.* He wasn't going to do it. Let the others strike, he thought. He wasn't prepared to drop his grenade with no idea whom he would kill. He hurried through the darkness to the door and grasped for its clasp. He couldn't find it. When his nervous fingers located it, they couldn't make it work. A sense of panic swept him. He was going to be trapped there in the room of the one-eyed man.

In the garden, Karkare, his fingers wrapped tight around his hand-grenade, continued to stare at the little grille, waiting for some gleam of a pistol. With each passing instant, the courage of the owner of the Deccan Guest House faded. Suddenly he saw Badge in the crowd 30 feet away. 'What's he doing here?' Karkare thought. 'Why doesn't he do something?'

Badge no longer had any intention of doing anything except flee. The man who'd had 37 arrests did not propose to get another. He was not an idealist or a political fanatic but a businessman. His business, he told himself, was selling arms, not using them. Avoiding Karkare's glare, he slipped off into the crowd.

To the rear of Birla House the mother of a 3-year-old boy playing behind the brick wall had seen Madanlal light his bomb and walk away. Now she pointed him out to an air force officer. 'It's him! It's him!' she screamed.

Gopal, solving at last the riddle of the door-clasp, emerged from his cell blinking at the sunlight. He heard her screams, then saw two men, one in a blue uniform, dragging Madanlal to the ground. He spotted Apte and his brother in the crowd. They seemed bewildered, not yet comprehending the enormity of their failure. Gopal joined them. The three Chitpawan Brahmins hesitated a second then, realizing their effort had been a total failure, headed for the green Chevrolet taxi Apte had hired. Without a thought for their fellow conspirators, they got in and told the driver to head for downtown Delhi as fast as he could.

A few seconds later Karkare saw the police bundling Madanlal along the drive at one side of the garden towards the tent they'd set up in front of the house. Whatever resolution he had left now disappeared. He relaxed his grip on his grenade. He had only one thought: how to escape.

On the platform, Gandhi had at last restored order. While the rumour that 'a crazy Punjabi refugee' had made a demonstration against him swept the crowd, he calmly announced: 'I may start for Pakistan now. If the government and doctors permit me, I can start immediately.'

Then, smiling happily, quite unaware of the miraculous escape he'd just experienced, Gandhi was lifted back into his chair and carried in triumph from his prayer meeting.

An overwhelming sense of failure assailed Apte and the Godses in their taxi heading back to town. Nathuram buried his head in his hands, the pain of his headache had become unbearable. They had no idea what their next step should be. Their confidence in Apte's scheme had been so complete that none of them had even envisaged the possibility of its failing. They were in grave danger now. Madanlal did not know their names, but he knew they came from Poona and he knew the name of their paper. With that, it would not take the police long to get them.

To the bitter draught of failure was added the pang of humiliation. They had failed the fanatics in Bombay from whom they'd taken money for their 'important mission'. Above all, they had failed the zealot at Savarkar Sadan to whom they'd sworn allegiance.

Nathuram aroused himself from his stupor and told his brother in Marathi to go back to Poona and establish an alibi. He had a family to worry about. He and Apte would decide on the next step. Apte ordered the driver to stop. Gopal got out. The taxi bearing Apte and his brother disappeared in the traffic.

At Birla House the mood was similar to that which had followed Gandhi's escape from death when he'd broken his fast two days before. Telegrams began to pour in congratulating the Mahatma. The phone rang incessantly. Nehru and Patel rushed to embrace him. Scores of visitors descended on his quarters. Among the first to arrive was Edwina Mountbatten.

'I have shown no bravery,' Gandhi gaily told the ex-Vicereine. He really had thought Madanlal's bomb was an army unit practising.

'Ah,' he sighed, 'but if someone fired at me point blank and I faced his bullet with a smile, repeating the name of Rama, then I should indeed be deserving of congratulations!'

Three messages reached the bedside of D. W. Mehra, the Deputy Inspector-General of Police for Delhi, and the man who would normally have been responsible for investigating the attempt on Gandhi's life was that evening lying in bed with the flu and a 103° fever. The first simply informed him someone had exploded a bomb at Gandhi's prayer meeting and the bomb thrower had been arrested. The second, two hours after the first, informed him the bomb thrower was resisting interrogation. Mehra authorized third-degree procedures.

It was the third and last message he received that was going to determine the course of the investigation. It came from the man who was the nominal head of the Delhi police, D. J. Sanjeevi, a political policeman whose real function was directing India's Central Intelligence Bureau. A tacit accord existed between the two men. Sanjeevi had arranged to be assigned the top job in Delhi because, as he explained to Mehra, 'before I retire I want a flag flying on my car, a jeep escort and a guard presenting arms when I get to the office'. He got that by making himself Delhi's police chief, but he had always left running the police to Mehra. Now, to Mehra's surprise, Sanjeevi bluntly informed him: 'Don't bother about the Madanlal case. I'll handle the investigation myself.'

In his cell in the Parliament Street police station, Madanlal was beginning to pay the price of his notoriety. Bruised and exhausted, he began to cave in under the pressure brought by the three policemen who had been interrogating him for two hours. Madanlal was still loyal to his fellow conspirators. Despite the fact he alone had acted, he was sure they would try again. He was determined to win them as much time as he could by refusing to talk.

Nonetheless, at the very beginning he yielded a vital piece of information. He admitted he was not a crazy Punjabi refugee acting alone, but one of a group of killers. He gave the number of people involved, seven. They had agreed to kill Gandhi, he said, because 'he was forcing the refugees to give up the mosques, was responsible for giving Pakistan her rupees and helping the Moslems every way he could'.

Then, calculating that the others had by now had time to flee, he gave a harmless account of their activities in Delhi. Suddenly, in a moment of self-assertion, he gave the police a second clue. He admitted he had been at Savarkar Sadan with his associates and boasted he had personally met the famous political figure. The police then forced him to describe each of his fellow conspirators. His descriptions were not very helpful. He gave only one name, Karkare's, and managed to give it wrong: 'Kirkree.'

His description of Godse, however, contained a third vital scrap of information. He gave his occupation. He said he was the 'editor of the *Rashtriya* or *Agrani Marhatta* language newspaper'. The name of the paper was incomplete and mis-spelled, but those words were still the most precious scrap of information the police could have had.

While the interrogation continued, police rushed off to search the *Hindu Mahasabha* and the Marina Hotel. They found no one. Badge and his servant were miles away on a train heading for Poona.

Karkare and Gopal Godse were registered under false names in a hotel in Old Delhi. Apte and Nathuram Godse had disappeared from the Marina hours before. On the desk of Room 40, however, the police found a fourth vital clue. It was a document denouncing the agreement produced by Delhi's leaders to get Gandhi to end his fast. The man whose signature it bore, Ashutosh Lahiri, an official of the *Hindu Mahasabha*, had known Apte and Godse well for eight years. He knew well they were the administrator and editor of a Savarkarite Marathi newspaper called the *Hindu Rashtra*.

At midnight the police ended their interrogation of Madanlal for the night and closed their first daily register of the case. They had every reason to be satisfied with the results of their seven hours' work. They knew they were faced with a plot. They knew how many people were involved. They knew it involved followers of Veer Savarkar whose organization had been under regular police surveillance since May. They had information which, with a little patient effort, would allow them to identify Nathuram Godse and, with him, Apte. It was an impressive performance. No reasonable policeman in Delhi that night would have given the conspirators more than a few hours before they were identified and the stage set for their arrest. Yet that inquiry, so well begun, was now to be pursued in a manner so desultory, so ineffectual that it would still, almost thirty years later, inflame controversy in India.

19

'We Must Get Gandhi Before the Police Get Us'

New Delhi and Bombay, 21–29 January 1948

Gopal Godse's half-eaten biscuit clung to the roof of a mouth suddenly gone dry at the sight before him. Handcuffed, a hood into which eye-slits had been cut over his head, a score of policemen surrounding him, a man was being marched straight towards the lunch counter at which Gopal and Karkare stood in the Old Delhi railway station. Petrified, Gopal recognized his rumpled blue suit. It was the suit Madanlal had so proudly donned the day before to kill Gandhi.

As unobtrusively as possible, he turned back to the counter trying to disappear into its dark wooden bulk. Under his stifling hood, Madanlal continued his march. For the fifth time since dawn, in their search for his co-conspirators, the police were forcing him to scrutinize the passengers boarding a train in Delhi station.

Hungry, dizzy with fatigue, he contemplated the crowds rushing towards the cars of the Bombay Express with the restricted vision imposed by the sack over his head. As his eyes fell on the familiar bulk of Karkare's back hunched over the lunch counter, he started. A policeman, sensing his movement, caught his arm. Madanlal coughed to cover his inadvertent gesture. Then he marched straight past Godse and Karkare to the waiting Bombay train. The last two conspirators left in Delhi would flee undetected.

The major preoccupation of the police in the aftermath of Madanlal's bomb explosion was assuring Gandhi's safety. If his nominal superior, Sanjeevi, had taken over responsibility for the investigation, Gandhi's protection was still the responsibility of the flu-stricken D. W. Mehra. Bundled up in an overcoat, his fever still raging, Mehra presented himself at Birla House at midday.

'Double *mubarak*,' he said, as he bowed in greeting to India's leader.

'Why this double *mubarak*?' asked Gandhi.

'Because', Mehra said, 'you successfully completed your fast and did what my police could not do. You brought peace to Delhi. Secondly, you escaped the bomb.'

'Brother,' Gandhi replied with his toothless smile, 'my life is in the hands of God.' It was precisely because he wanted the Mahatma to put it in his hands that Mehra was in the garden of Birla House.

The man who had tried to kill him, Mehra explained to Gandhi, had not acted alone. He was one of a group of seven plotters. There was a serious likelihood that the others would try again. He wanted his permission to increase the guard at Birla House, and to search suspicious characters coming to his prayer meetings.

'I will never agree,' Gandhi said in a sort of half shriek. 'Do you search people going into a temple or chapel for prayer?'

'No, Sir,' Mehra replied, 'but there is no one in them who is a target for an assassin's bullet.'

'Rama is my only protection,' Gandhi retorted. 'If he wants to end my life, nobody can save me, even if a million of your policemen were posted here to guard me. The rulers of this country have no faith in my non-violence. They think your police guard will save my life. Well, my protection is Rama, and you will not violate my prayer meetings with your police or stop people coming in. If you do, I will leave Delhi and denounce you as the reason for my leaving.'

Mehra was crestfallen. He knew Gandhi well enough to know he was not going to change his mind. He would have to find a way to protect the Mahatma in spite of himself.

'At least,' Mehra said, 'will you allow me to come to the prayer meeting every day personally?'

'Ah,' said Gandhi, 'as an individual you are always welcome.'

At ten minutes to five, despite his fever, Mehra was back at Birla House in civilian clothes. He had already increased the police contingent around the house from five to thirty-six, most of them plain-clothes men ordered to mingle with the crowd. Hidden under Mehra's coat, loaded and cocked, was a Webber and Scott 38. The veteran of the Frontier could get it off his hip and put three rounds in a bull's-eye twenty feet away in less than five seconds. As the Mahatma left his quarters for the prayer ground, Mehra took up the spot he intended to occupy every afternoon while Gandhi remained in Delhi. It was right at Gandhi's side. As long as he was there, the veteran policeman felt reasonably confident no assassin was going to kill Gandhi.

Once again, Gandhi had to be carried to his prayer platform. His first words were for the hate-filled young refugee who'd vowed to take revenge for the sufferings partition had thrust on him and his family. 'Do not hate or condemn the man who threw the bomb,' Gandhi pleaded. He urged the police to release Madanlal. 'We have no right to punish a person we think wicked,' he said.

For the man who had so unexpectedly taken over the investigation into the attempt on Gandhi's life, one thing was obvious. The conspiracy with which he was confronted had been hatched in Bombay Province. Madanlal had indicated his fellow conspirators were all Maharashtrans. He himself had come to Delhi from Bombay where he admitted having visited Savarkar's residence. Sanjeevi's first action, therefore, was to alert the Bombay police and ask them to assign someone to the case. To co-ordinate Bombay's investigation with his, Sanjeevi ordered two officers of the Delhi CID to fly to Bombay to present the Bombay police officer assigned to the case with 'all the facts' uncovered in Delhi.

Their trip would produce the first, almost incomprehensible blunder of the investigation into the attempt on Gandhi's life. The two Delhi policemen neglected to take with them a copy of the key document in the investigation, Madanlal's preliminary statement completed and typed before midnight the evening before. The only document they took was a two by four card on which a few salient facts had been jotted down by hand. They included Karkare's name, mis-spelled as 'Kirkree'. Missing was the most vital information the Delhi police possessed, the approximate identification of Apte and Godse's newspaper.

The man for whom their report was destined already had more and better information sitting on his desk than they had on their little slip of paper. At 32, Jamshid 'Jimmy' Nagarvalla was a Deputy Commissioner of Police in charge of the Bombay CID Special Branch's Sections One and Two, responsible for the gathering of local political intelligence and the surveillance of foreigners. It was not for his abilities as an investigator, however, that Nagarvalla had been assigned to the Madanlal case. The reason spoke volumes about the dilemma confronting the Indian police in selecting men for the investigation. It was his religion. To give the case to a Moslem had seemed inappropriate. To put it in the hands of a Hindu risked selecting an officer who harboured secret anti-Gandhi sentiments. Nagarvalla, fortunately, was neither. He was a Parsee.

Bombay Province's Home Minister, Morarji Desai, had given him the case along with the precious scrap of information on his desk. Desai had received this from a source to whom Madanlal had boasted of his intention to kill Gandhi the week before. Madanlal's principal associate, the source revealed, was a man named Karkare. He came from Ahmednagar.*

* By an extraordinary coincidence, Desai on 12 January had come upon the Ahmednagar police report of the discovery on 1 January of Karkare's arms cache in the room of the manager of his hotel. Desai had immediately demanded

Nagarvalla set the machinery in motion to identify him. For the young officer there seemed no question that, sooner or later, the road to the men who had tried to murder Gandhi had to pass by the quiet house among the palms and medlar trees of Keluksar Road. Nagarvalla had asked Desai for permission to arrest Savarkar on the basis of Madanlal's visit to him the week before. Desai had refused with the angry query: 'Are you mad? Do you think I want this whole province to go up in smoke?'

If Nagarvalla could not confine Savarkar to a prison cell, however, he could at least confide him to a brilliant organization created by the British that was the pride of the Bombay CID, its Watchers' Branch. The branch was composed of 150 men and women whose identities were known only to their commander. Blind men, beggars with stunted limbs, Moslem women in *burqas*, fruit pedlars, sweepers, they had kept Bombay's political agitators under their gaze for a quarter of a century. During all those years, they liked to boast, not a single figure assigned to their scrutiny had escaped them. Nagarvalla's first action in his new assignment was to fix their watchful eyes on Veer Savarkar and his Bombay residence.

Nagarvalla's investigation began with the same promising swiftness as Delhi's had. Within a few hours he had got the full identity of Vishnu Karkare, as well as his occupation and the fact that he had been missing from Ahmednagar since 6 January. Shortly thereafter, he learned from a police informer that 'one Badge of Poona', a petty arms merchant, was an associate of Karkare in his 'conspiracy to take the life of the Mahatma'.

Immediately informed of the report, the Poona police called on Badge's shop to find he was missing. They told Nagarvalla he was probably hiding 'in the jungles around the city'.

Unfortunately, the Poona police never bothered to verify the continued absence of the wanted arms pedlar. A few hours after the first enquiry, Badge returned to the city from his expedition to Delhi. For the next ten days, while the police who'd associated his name with Madanlal's bomb less than forty-eight hours after its explosion

why Karkare had not been arrested. The slow journey of his query through the channels of the Indian police provided a painful illustration of another factor destined to retard the investigation of the bomb at Birla House, the crushing burden of red tape strangling police procedures. It took seven days, until 19 January, for Desai's query to reach the Ahmednagar CID. There, it would sit for another five days before a warrant for Karkare's arrest would be issued on 24 January. Desai himself, who saw hundreds of similar papers cross his desk each day, did not remember the report at the time he received the name of Madanlal's colleagues.

were looking for him, the fake *sadhu* would be sitting in the back room of his arms shop knitting up the bullet-proof vests of which he was so proud.

Given the progress of his own investigation, Nagarvalla was not impressed by the information handed to him by the Delhi police officers. Moreover, the two men, one of whom was a Sikh, had elected to stay in a hotel whose proprietor was known to the Bombay CID as a Sikh extremist agitator. That hardly seemed to Nagarvalla a judicious action on the part of officers assigned to investigate a conspiracy to kill Gandhi.

He decided he didn't need their help. Brusquely, he ordered them to return to their hotel and stay out of sight until he sent for them. The following day, 23 January, he called them, gave them the information he had uncovered, and ordered them to return to Delhi.

On their return, the senior of the two officers submitted a police case diary covering their visit to Bombay. It contained an astonishing declaration. They had, he said, laid 'special stress' on the 'immediate apprehension' of the editor of the '*Hindu Rashtriya* or the *Agrani* newspaper'. To substantiate the report, the officer appended to his diary a document containing that information which he claimed to have shown to Nagarvalla. The Bombay policeman had never laid his eyes on it. Years later, it would be conclusively established that the document was written after the Delhi policemen had left for Bombay, and appended by them to their diary following their return to the capital.

At midday on the Friday following the attempted murder, the investigation into the conspiracy in India's capital took an enormous leap forward. Madanlal finally broke down and told his interrogators he was ready to make a full statement. The Punjabi refugee would claim his decision was the result of torture, a charge the Delhi police would always deny.* It took his interrogators almost two full days to record and type his 54-page confession. Madanlal finally re-read it and signed it in his cell at 21.30 on the evening of 24 January. It was immediately rushed in triumph to Sanjevi's desk.

* In a series of interviews with the authors of this book in the spring and autumn of 1973, Madanlal claimed blocks of ice had been suspended from his testicles by a string to get him to talk. On another occasion, he claimed sugared water was splashed on his face, and a horde of ants set upon it. Such charges are dismissed by the Delhi police as Madanlal's fantasies. Their own records of his interrogation note that on 21 and 22 January, he was repeatedly warned he was giving incorrect information and the interrogators were told to 'instruct him accordingly'.

This time, Madanlal had not held back. Everything he knew was in his statement. Although he did not identify Badge by name, he described him as the owner of the *Shastra Bhandar* of Poona. He gave Karkare's name and the details of his political activities. Above all, this time the name Madanlal gave for Godse and Apte's paper was almost letter perfect, *Hindu Rashtriya*. Most important, he gave its location, Poona. To identify its proprietor and editor was now for Sanjeevi an act of almost juvenile simplicity. He had only to send an inspector to one of two places in Delhi, the Home Department or the Information and Broadcasting Department, to examine a slim volume called the Annual Statement of Newspapers, Bombay Province. One of its pages contained the following entry:

'*Hindu Rashtra*. A Marathi daily of Poona.

Editor: N. V. Godse. Proprietor: N. D. Apte. A Savarkarite group newspaper.'

The conclusive evidence that the man they were looking for was 'N. V. Godse' had been deposited in the laps of the Delhi police the day Madanlal had begun to make his confession. It was a pile of laundry left behind by the occupants of the Marina Hotel's Room 40 in their hasty departure on 20 January. The spartan items of apparel in the bundle turned over to the police by the hotel's laundryman all contained one common laundry mark, the initials N.V.G.

From the moment he had taken on the case, a puzzling lack of zeal had characterized D. J. Sanjeevi's handling of it. He was a vain, secretive man and he had watched over the investigation with an obsessive jealousy that made him hostile to any attempt on the part of his subordinates to become involved. He had rebuffed even the efforts of his senior aide to join the investigation.

He now had in Madanlal's confession the material needed rapidly to establish the identity of at least five of the six men involved in the conspiracy. Yet no one from the Delhi police, no one from his office, ever made the rudimentary gesture of consulting the list of Bombay Province newspapers in which Godse's name was to be found. Nor did anyone question the *Hindu Mahasabha* official whose text had been found in the Marina Hotel and who had known Apte and Godse for almost a decade. He did not communicate the information contained in Madanlal's confession by urgent courier to Nagarvalla in Bombay. Even worse, he made no effort to contact the Poona police by telephone to ask the identity of the editor of the *Hindu Rashtra*. He was the author of a series of acts of such staggering incompetence, so close, finally, to being criminal in nature, that a quarter of a century later India would still be wondering how they could have happened.*

Nor was he the only police officer whose behaviour would never be satisfactorily explained. In Delhi for a conference on Sunday, 25 January was the Deputy Inspector-General of Police in charge of the Criminal Investigation Division of the Poona Police, U. H. Rana. His files in Poona contained the material that could instantly have identified Godse, Apte, Badge and Karkare. They contained photographs of Karkare and Apte which could have been given to the police at Birla House to prevent the conspirators returning to the Mahatma's prayer meetings. They contained all the reports of their Hindu extremist activities which his own officers had been making regularly for months.

Sanjeevi summoned him to his office, and for two hours went over Madanlal's confession with him page by page. Almost every line of that text should have alerted the Poona police officer. It established the fact that at least two of the men who'd tried to murder Gandhi came from his jurisdiction in Poona. It was inconceivable that the name *Hindu Rashtra* was not almost as familiar to him as that of the *Times of India*. The paper had been ordered to be closed the previous July because of its subversive tone and it was he himself who had cancelled in November the police surveillance, of which the editor and administrator had been the object. Apte had even been named as having furnished the only bomb exploded in Poona the summer before.

His reaction, when confronted by that accumulation of vital material concerning his jurisdiction, was and would always remain incomprehensible. He did not bother to telephone his subordinates in Poona with the information. He did not send back orders to begin an immediate investigation. Nor did he rush back by plane with the information to take charge himself. He did not like to fly. It made him

* A long and patient effort to investigate the circumstances surrounding Mahatma Gandhi's assassination and the failure of the police to arrest his killers after the explosion of Madanlal's bomb on 20 January 1948 was undertaken in the late 1960s by an official Commission of Inquiry. The work of the Commission, headed by Justice J. L. Kapur, a retired judge of the Indian Supreme Court, was severely handicapped by the fact many of the key police officers in the investigation, including Sanjeevi, were dead. The Commission uncovered the fraudulent entry made by the Delhi officers in their case diary on their return from Bombay, but the officer responsible was dead.

The Commission's six volume report was submitted to the Indian Government on 30 September 1969. It came to the unhappy conclusion that at no point was the investigation into the conspiracy to murder India's national hero conducted 'with that earnestness or that alacrity which an attempt on the life of Mahatma Gandhi required or deserved'.

sick. He took the train home, the long, slow train that took almost thirty-six hours to cross half the sub-continent on its route from Delhi to Bombay. He did not even take a fast train. He took instead a roundabout route that added an additional six hours to his trip.

He would claim his bizarre behaviour had been inspired by the attitude of the man in charge of the investigation. If one overwhelming certainty determined Sanjeevi's actions, it was his belief the killers would never come back. He dismissed them as a bunch of crackpots. His was the innate conviction that after the lamentable fiasco of 20 January, they would never raise the courage to strike again. He was wrong. Time was running out on Sanjeevi and the 78-year-old leader who had so narrowly escaped death at Birla House five days before. What Sanjeevi's investigation needed was the thing it lacked above all, a sense of urgency.

One emotion motivated the leader of the four men squatting in the darkness just outside the reach of the pale shafts of light falling from the last lamp-post along the platform of the little railroad station of Thana, a suburb of Bombay. It was a sense of urgency. What a high police officer in Delhi had dismissed as utterly improbable was going to happen. The killers were coming back. This time their deed would not be the work of a disorganized gang. It would follow the classic pattern of political assassination, one man, one weapon; one zealous fanatic prepared to sacrifice his life to commit murder.

Since fleeing Delhi, Nathuram Godse and Narayan Apte had lived in constant dread of arrest, sure they were the object of one of the most intensive manhunts in Indian history. They had summoned Gopal Godse and their innkeeper friend Karkare to the secret rendezvous to hear the decision Nathuram revealed in a hoarse whisper.

'We failed in Delhi,' he declared, 'because there were too many people involved.' There was only one way to kill Gandhi. 'One man must do the job whatever the risks.'

Gopal looked at the brother who had been a failure all his life, who'd never been able to hold a job. His eccentric brother, with his passion for coffee and his hysterical hatred of women, seemed transformed. Nathuram, who'd been pale and trembling in Delhi, almost unable to move because of his migraine, exuded an air of tranquillity such as Gopal had never seen in him before. Even the ebullient Apte who usually ran things seemed in awe of him.

Nathuram's voice was calm, composed. He who had read the portents in the soot had read the meaning of his own life. Nathuram

Godse was going to fill the role to which his speeches had been subconsciously beckoning him since the troubled summer of partition. India vivisected, India raped, called out for an avenging spirit. He was going to be that spirit.

'I am going to do it,' he announced. No one had imposed that decision on him. 'The sacrifice of one's life is not a decision to be imposed.'

He would kill Gandhi as soon as possible. He wanted two aides. Apte would be with him. He invited Karkare to join them. Together they would form a new *trimurti*, a trinity of vengeance like those mystic trinities of earth, water and fire, Vishnu, Brahma and Shiva, that dominated Hindu lore.

Karkare agreed. Godse told him to get to Delhi as fast as possible. Every day at noon he was to stand by the public water tap outside the Old Delhi railway station. They would meet him by that tap on the afternoon of the day they arrived in the capital.

He and Apte in the meantime would concentrate all their energies on locating an absolutely reliable, easily concealed pistol. This time there could be no margin for error.

The most important thing, Nathuram told him in a strident whisper, the element that counted above everything else, was speed. 'Now that the police have Madanlal, they are bound to get us sooner or later.'

'We must get Gandhi,' he said, 'before the police get us.'

In New Delhi a minor change was appended to the constantly repeated scenario that governed Gandhi's prayer meetings on the evening of 25 January. D. W. Mehra, the Delhi police officer who had determined to walk by Gandhi's side each night with a cocked pistol in his hip, was back in bed with the flu. He had assigned his role to another Delhi police officer, A. N. Bhatia. Though Bhatia was not as deadly a marksman as Mehra, he had the advantage of also knowing Gandhi personally. That acquaintance assured him of being able to occupy the vital position by Gandhi's side each night.

26 January 1948 was a particularly memorable day in the life of Mahatma Gandhi and his countrymen. Exactly eighteen years earlier, on 26 January 1930, in every town and city in India, in hundreds of thousands of her villages, almost everywhere a Congress Party cell existed, millions of Congress men and women had sworn for the first time to win their nation independence. Gandhi himself had written the text of the vow they had sworn that day. Since then,

26 January had become known as Independence Day to India's patriots. Like his millions of fellow Indians, Gandhi now marked another anniversary of the swearing of that vow in an India in which its words had become at last a reality.

Appropriately enough, Gandhi's principal occupation in Birla House that winter day was preparing at Nehru's request a new constitution for the Congress Party, a manifesto to define its role and purpose in the independent India to which he had guided it.

The robust nature beneath the deceptively fragile exterior was showing itself once again. That morning the octogenarian whom doctors had pronounced 24 hours from death barely a week earlier had begun to take solid food and had resumed a long and cherished habit, his morning walk. Those brisk strides across the lawn of Birla House constituted, in a sense, his first steps towards the great vision that thrilled and preoccupied him, his march to Pakistan across the ravaged Punjab.

A Moslem visitor from Pakistan had the day before conjured up a vision that had become the last great dream of Gandhi's life. He looked forward, the visitor had said, 'to witnessing a 50-mile long procession of Hindus and Sikhs returning to Pakistan with Gandhiji at its head'.

What an exalting prospect: the slender figure that had shown India the way for so long, opening the path again: marching along, bamboo stave in hand, at the head of an endless chain of the dispossessed, taking them home again along the highway of their cruel exodus. And who could know; if he succeeded, what would prevent him from marching back the other way, leading a horde of homeless Moslems back to the lands and hearths from which they'd been cast in India? What a victory for non-violence, what a triumph for his doctrines of love and brotherhood. That would be the crowning achievement of his lifetime, a 'miracle' to dwarf in significance and dimension all the 'miracles' his enraptured followers attributed to him. Even Gandhi's humble soul thrilled at such a likelihood. He could formulate no prayer more ardent than that God might grant him the faith, the strength and the time to realize it.

Returning from his walk, he called for his doctor, Sushila Nayyar. It was not for a medical consultation, however, that he beckoned her to his side, but to assign her a mission in Pakistan as part of the preparations for his trip. As he always did with himself and his entourage, the methodical Gandhi imposed on his attractive young doctor a precise time limit in which she was to carry out her assignment; three days. Sushila always walked directly in front of Gandhi on his way to evening prayers. God willing, she should be back in

Delhi in time to occupy her regular post for the prayers on the evening of Friday, 30 January.

For the second time in ten days, Nathuram Godse and Narayan Apte were flying to Delhi to murder Mahatma Gandhi. Seated side by side in the back row of their Air India Viking, they occupied themselves in pursuits perfectly illustrative of their divergent characters. Godse had his face plunged into a copy of the book that had inspired his life, Veer Savarkar's *Hindutva*. Apte was engaged in a more temporal pursuit. He could not take his eyes off the attractive stewardess gliding up and down the aisle with her breakfast trays.

Their last day in Bombay had been a most inauspicious one for the two young men. The item whose procurement had given them so much trouble before their first assassination attempt was once again proving incredibly difficult to find. All day they had gone from one fanatic friend to another, begging for money and a gun. Apte had tucked into his pocket the result of their day-long efforts, the extravagant sum of 10,000 rupees (about £1000). He did not, however, have even the promise of a pistol.

Haunted by the conviction the police were closing in on them, sure they had to strike fast, they had decided to leave Bombay without it. They would get their pistol in Delhi in one of those depots of hatred and suffering ringing the capital, the refugee camps.

For the moment Apte's mind was on other things. When she'd finished picking up the breakfast trays, he beckoned to the handsome stewardess. He was a palm-reader, he told her. She had a fascinating face which always reflected a fascinating palm. He suggested he might read her hand for her. Delighted, the girl settled on the arm of his seat and extended her hand. As she did, she saw the man plunged in his reading in the next seat draw away, virtually thrusting himself against the aircraft's window in visible distaste at their activities.

The last seduction on which Narayan Apte would embark was off to a promising start. By the time their flight reached Delhi, his recital of the girl's future had secured the immediate future Apte sought. The stewardess had agreed to meet him at Delhi's Imperial Hotel at eight o'clock that evening.

No spectacle could better justify the suffering Mahatma Gandhi endured during his fast than the one awaiting him around the Quwwat-ul-Islam – the Might of Islam – Mosque at Mehrauli, seven miles south of Delhi, at mid-morning on 27 January. That shrine, built from the ruins of 27 Hindu and Jain temples, was the oldest mosque in India. Once a year, on the anniversary of the death of its builder, the Slave King, Qutb-ud-din, Delhi's first Moslem Sultan, thousands of faithful streamed to its pastoral surroundings for a great religious festival.

One of the seven conditions Gandhi had laid down for ending his fast was that the festival should go on unimpeded, that the Moslems swarming to it could do so 'without danger to their lives'. Even he, however, could not have imagined a success as complete as the one his fast had secured.

Hindus and Sikhs who, a fortnight before, would have welcomed Moslems to Mehrauli with daggers and *kirpans*, stood at the entrance to the mosque decorating the arriving pilgrims with garlands of marigolds and rose petals. Inside, other Sikhs had set up little stalls at which they offered pilgrims free cups of tea. Mingling with that enormous, fraternal crowd of Moslems, Sikhs and Hindus, his hands on Manu and Abha's shoulders, Gandhi was moved almost to tears.

As the ultimate expression of their gratitude, the mosque's *maulvis* invited Gandhi to address the faithful from the heart of their shrine. They even waived for Manu and Abha the stern Islamic tradition banning women from a mosque's sanctuary because, they declared, they were 'Gandhiji's daughters'.

Overwhelmed, Gandhi begged all, Hindus, Sikhs and Moslems alike, to 'resolve in this holy place' to 'live as friends and brothers'. After all, he said, 'we may live separately, but we are the leaves of the same tree'.

He returned to Birla House exhausted by strain and emotion. Relaxing under his mudpack, he lapsed into a curious, brooding mood. It was a mood that had come upon him in recent days whenever he pondered the meaning of his escape from Madanlal's bomb.

His escape, he noted, 'was God's mercy'. But, he added, 'I am quite prepared to obey his order when it does come. I talk of leaving Delhi on 2 February, but I do not myself feel that I shall be able to go away from here. After all, who knows what is going to happen tomorrow?'

As Nathuram Godse had ordered him to, Karkare paced the circular garden around the water tap in front of the Old Delhi railway station most of the afternoon of 27 January. Suddenly he saw his two friends drifting towards him through the horde of refugees who were sleeping, defecating, begging, and occasionally dying on that trampled patch of ground.

They seemed completely discouraged. Their hours combing the

refugee camps of Delhi had produced nothing. Those storehouses of misery in which they had counted on finding a revolver contained only suffering and hatred. Another day had been wasted in their vain pursuit of a weapon, another day in which the police were gaining on them, another day in which the measures protecting Gandhi were being perfected. Their time had just about run out. One last place remained where they might find the pistol, a final hope of carrying out the assassination. It was 194 miles away in Gwalior. If even that failed to yield a weapon they would have to abandon their efforts and accept the humiliation of their failure before Savarkar and their supporters in Bombay.

They told Karkare to meet them there again in 24 hours. Then, discouraged, they disappeared into the station to catch the last train to Gwalior. Narayan Apte would miss his rendezvous with his beautiful Air India stewardess at the Imperial Hotel at eight o'clock that evening. He was renouncing the last seduction in his amatory career to journey to Gwalior in search of a pistol with which to kill Mahatma Gandhi. That journey would ultimately cost him his life.

•

It was just before midnight on 27 January when the urgent call of his night bell woke the Gwalior homeopath Dattaraya Parchure. He stumbled sleepily to the door of his dispensary, expecting to find a distraught mother clutching a child with pneumonia. He found instead a pair of old friends and zealots whose devotion to extreme Hinduism surpassed even his own. The doctor who, four and a half months earlier, had set Madanlal on the road that had ended in a Delhi jail cell was Nathuram Godse's last hope in his desperate quest for a pistol.

All the next day Apte and Godse sat on the spare wooden benches of Parchure's waiting-room under the primitive oil painting of the doctor's *guru*, a Hindu ascetic who had spent his life in contemplation in the tiger-infested forests of Gwalior. The two downcast, depressed young men appeared as much in need of the doctor's care as any of his unhappy patients around them, coughing up lungs inflamed by bronchitis or pneumonia. While his medical aides scoured the markets of Gwalior for the cardamom seed, onions, bamboo sprouts, and the other plants he mixed daily into his beneficent compounds, his political aides combed the city for his prescription for Godse and Apte.

The two finally left Gwalior aboard the evening express just after 10.00 p.m. on the evening of 28 January. Their long and complex odyssey was over. The search that had taken them twice across half the surface of the sub-continent, led them into refugee camps, Hindu temples, the slums of Bombay, to laundries, printing presses and Savarkar Sadan, had ended in the reek of herbs and spices in the Gwalior homeopath's office. Wrapped in an old rag in a paper bag under Godse's arm was a blunt, black Beretta automatic pistol, number 606824–P, and twenty rounds of ammunition. All Nathuram Godse needed now was the skill and determination to use it.

At about the same time Apte and Godse were boarding their train in Gwalior station, another man over 800 miles away was completing a journey. The long, slow voyage home of U. H. Rana, the Deputy Inspector-General of the CID in Poona was over at last. The officer whose files contained the information that could identify Godse and Apte and bar their entry to Birla House was back in his jurisdiction. No inspired urgency, however, drove the policeman as he stepped off his train in the Poona railroad station. He did not bother to go to his office that evening. He was tired after his long journey. He went home to bed instead.

'We've got it! Oh, Karkare, this time we've really got it!' The jubilant Nathuram Godse drew the owner of the Deccan Guest House out of the crowds ringing the water tap opposite the old Delhi railway station. Then, like a smuggler offering a fleeting glimpse of his forbidden goods, he flashed open the folds of his shabby brown coat. There, tucked into his waist-band, Karkare saw the black glint of the pistol they had despaired of ever finding.

Their murder weapon in hand at last, events were now to carry the three men forward to their inevitable conclusion with compelling swiftness. The only member of the trio to survive would recall them:

As we stood there by the water tap, Apte told us, 'this time we do not want to make a mistake. We want to be sure of the pistol's aim, that the pistol works. We have enough bullets, just see!'

At those words, he pulled open the pocket of his coat. He was right. Inside I saw many bullets. So all three of us decided to go in search of a place where we could have a trial of the shooting. But everywhere we went, we found the places full of people. The refugees were spread all over Delhi.

As we were moving from place to place, Nathuram told a little fable. That was about one of the Maratha premiers, Raja Rao Peshwa. He was waging most of the wars against the Moghul Empire at that time, and he was always in need of money. But before one war would end, another would start and he would have to borrow more money.

'Well,' said Nathuram, 'that is the position with us. We have been

begging money for this task, but nothing has been accomplished. Ours will be the terrible humiliation if we do not succeed.'

Finally we decided to go to the place where we had previously gone for shooting and that place was just behind Birla Mandir or Birla Temple. We went there. We had to imagine whether Gandhiji would be sitting when the time for the shooting came, or whether he would be in a standing position. We could not know which it would be. It was a matter of chance so we had to try things both ways.

Accordingly, Apte picked out a tree which was a babul tree set apart from the others. He sat down beside it to imagine the height Gandhiji would have been while he was sitting. Where his head was, he made some marks on the tree with a knife. 'Well,' he said to Nathuram, 'take this to be Gandhiji's head; this to be his body. Now find the target.'

Nathuram drew away to a range of about 20 to 25 feet. From there, he fired at the target. One after another he goes on firing, four times. He finds his target: he finds it O.K. Apte went up to the tree. He looked at the place where he had made the marks for Gandhiji's head. The bullets were all there.

'Well, Nathuram,' he said, 'it's perfect!'

Gandhi's great work in Delhi was almost done. He had arrived four months before in a city of the dead, its grand boulevards edged with corpses, panic and fear rampant in its neighbourhoods, its government frightened and in disarray. Now, the capital was calm. Order had been restored. The agony of his fast had dramatically altered its moral climate. It was time for him to leave.

While, in a nearby glade, a man fired four bullets at a mark on a tree-trunk representing his head, Gandhi set a tentative date for his departure from New Delhi. He chose 3 February. He would return first to his ashram outside Wardha. Then, ten days later, he would start his aged feet down the highways where so many had been massacred, hoping with the force of his love to reverse the currents of the greatest migration in human history, seeking in his pilgrimage to Pakistan the last great miracle beckoning to him like a mirage on a desert horizon.

As always, every moment of Gandhi's day was carefully planned and used. He spun. He had his mudpack and his enema. He studied Bengali. He wrote a dozen letters. He laboured on his draft of his new constitution for the Congress Party. He received a stream of visitors. He joked with Indira Gandhi and her cousin, Tara Pandit; autographed a picture for Margaret Bourke-White. As he did so, he told her America should abandon the atomic bomb. Non-violence, he said, was the only force the bomb could not destroy. In an atomic attack, he would urge his followers to stand firm, 'looking up, watching without fear, praying for the pilot'.

Suddenly, with the swiftness of a monsoon downpour, a discordant note intruded upon that busy, happy day. A group of Hindus and Sikhs from the Frontier Province, victims of a terrible massacre on the day he had announced his fast, came to call. Before Gandhi could offer them an expression of his grief, one of their embittered number snarled at him, 'You have done us enough harm. You have ruined us utterly. Leave us alone. Go retire to the Himalayas.'

His words stunned Gandhi. The little body seemed to crumple as he heard them, as though some terrible weight was crushing down on him. Going out to his prayer meeting his pace was laboured. The hands that usually rested on Manu and Abha as lightly as wisps of cotton *khadi* gripped their shoulders for support.

His voice soft and weak, a terrible sadness underlining each of his syllables, India's Mahatma began to address his countrymen for the last time. The shadows of winter twilight were already beginning to thrust their stains across the lawn as he spoke. Inevitably, he turned to the exchange with the angry refugee that had so upset him.

'Whom shall I listen to?' he asked the silent gathering before him. 'Some ask me to stay here while others ask me to go away. Some reprove and revile me, whereas others extol me. What am I to do, then?' he asked rhetorically, his voice soft and full of hurt. 'I do what God commands me to do. I seek peace amidst disorder.'

After a long and thoughtful silence, Gandhi concluded. 'My Himalayas,' he said, 'are here.'

Shortly after the conclusion of Gandhi's prayer meeting, a long-distance telephone call reached the police officer in charge of investigating the attempt on his life. Since Madanlal had broken down and given his detailed confession, Sanjeevi's enquiry had made little progress. Still governed by his unshakeable conviction that the killers would not return, he had moved it forward at the same leisurely pace that had characterized it since he had taken it under his command.

His caller too had scant progress to report. 'Jimmy' Nagarvalla's Bombay investigation had yielded little new after its first 48 hours. The Bombay Watchers' Branch continued its vigilance at the gates of Savarkar Sadan, but the Machiavellian leader inside was too clever to reveal his hand. And yet, some malignant radiation seemed to emanate from that house. Something in the constant flow of Savarkar's followers in and out of its premises spoke to Nagarvalla's policeman's instincts.

'Don't ask me why,' he told Sanjeevi, 'but I just know another attempt is coming. It's something I can feel in the atmosphere here.'

'What do you want me to do?' Sanjeevi exploded. Nehru and Patel had both urged Gandhi to allow the police to search the public coming to his prayers. Gandhi's answer, Sanjeevi explained angrily, was, 'If he sees a policeman in uniform at his prayers, he'll go on a fast to death. What can we do?'

The answer to Sanjeevi's question lay on the desk of another Indian policeman 700 miles from Delhi. U. H. Rana, the Deputy Inspector-General in charge of the CID Poona, had finally obtained the information he could have got four days earlier by the simple expedient of a telephone call. Nine days after Madanlal's first statement, five days after his full confession, a police officer was finally in possession of the identities of the vengeful trinity sworn to penetrate the precincts of Birla House.

Yet Rana did not telephone or cable a description of Apte and Godse to Delhi. He made no effort to rush their photos to the guards at Birla House Gate. Badge spent the day knitting up his bullet-proof vests in his Poona arms shop unmolested by Rana's men. The same determined belief that motivated Sanjeevi's actions in Delhi apparently governed Rana's in the capital of Hindu extremism. He seemed confident the authors of the fiasco of 20 January would never dare strike again. The most important information the Indian police possessed never left his desk.

The three men who were not supposed to come back stood in the sparsely furnished confines of Retiring Room Number Six of the Old Delhi railway station watching the bustle of tongas, carts, creaking buses, swarming by in the street below. The police of India no longer had days in which to save the life of Mahatma Gandhi. They had only hours. Godse, Apte and Karkare had just fixed in that dim railroad station room their rendezvous with history. They had chosen the hour when they would kill Mohandas Gandhi. They would assassinate him at five o'clock the following day, Friday, 30 January, in the same Birla House garden in which their first attempt on his life had failed.

Nathuram was in a good mood [Karkare recalled]. He was very cheerful. He was relaxed. At about 8.30, in a moody way, he said, 'Come. We must all have our last meal together. We must have a good meal, a feast. We may never be able to have another.'

We went down and started to walk through the station until we got to a restaurant named Brandon's run by a contractor who had a chain of such restaurants in all the stations. 'We can't go there,' Apte said, 'Karkare is a vegetarian.'

Nathuram threw his arm around my shoulder and said: 'You are right. Tonight we must all be together.' So we went in search of another place.

We asked for a sumptuous meal: rice, vegetable curries, chapatis. *The waiter said there were no sour goat curds to drink, a festive drink for a vegetarian meal. Nathuram called the headwaiter and gave him five rupees. 'Look,' he said, 'this is a party meal. We want curds brought. You go anywhere you have to go, you buy at any price, but you bring us back curds.'*

Satisfied with our meal, we walked back to the Retiring Room. We were prepared to stay and chat, but Nathuram said: 'No. Now you must let me relax. I want to be alone.'

As Apte and Karkare started to leave the room, Karkare turned back for a last glance at Godse. The man who was going to kill Gandhi was already stretched out on his bed reading one of the two books he had brought with him to Delhi. It was an Erle Stanley Gardner, Perry Mason detective story.

Mahatma Gandhi spent the final evening of his life struggling to finish what would become his last will and testament to the Indian nation, his draft of a new constitution for the Congress Party. At 9.15, the task finally completed, he rose.

'My head is reeling,' he sighed.

He stretched out on his pallet and rested his bald head on Manu's lap while she slowly massaged it with oil. For the handful of devoted disciples who shared his existence, those few moments before sleep always constituted a restful island in their crowded days, a brief quarter of an hour when their Bapu belonged to them and not to the world. Relaxed, chatting gaily, Gandhi would review the day's events, making the little jokes he loved.

This evening, however, there was no joy on his face. He could not erase from his memory the hate-constricted mouth of the refugee uttering his curse. He was silent for two or three minutes while Manu's probing fingers stretched and contracted the skin of his scalp. Then he began to discourse on a subject his draft constitution had brought to his mind, the growing signs of corruption among the men whose undisputed leader he'd once been.

'How can we look the world in the face if this goes on?' he asked. 'The honour of the whole nation hinges on those who have participated in the freedom struggle. If they too abuse their power, we are sure to lose our footing.'

He lapsed into another of his melancholy silences. Then, in a forlorn voice, he half-whispered a verse of an Urdu poet of the city of Allahabad.

'Short lived is the spring in the garden of the world,' he sighed. 'Watch the brave show while it lasts.'

After leaving Godse, Apte and Karkare were nervous. They decided to go to a cinema.

We walked around and went into the first one we saw [Karkare remembered]. It was a film based on a story of Rabindranath Tagore, the great poet. At the intermission we were standing and talking in the lobby. I was concerned because at our farewell dinner, Nathuram had said, 'It'll be all over tomorrow or the day after tomorrow.'

'Do you remember Nathuram's words?' I asked Apte.

'Yes,' he said.

'Well, why did he say so?' I asked. 'Will he really be able to do it, because it's a heavy task?'

Apte drew up close to me. 'Listen Karkare,' he said, 'I know Nathuram better than you do. I'll tell you what happened and you draw your conclusion. When we left Delhi on 20 January, we went down to Cawnpore in the first-class compartment. We were chatting for a long time and not having a good sleep. At about six in the morning, as we were nearing Cawnpore, Nathuram jumped down from his upper berth. He shook me. "Apte, are you awake?" he asked. "Listen," he said, "it's I who am going to do it, I and no one else. This must be done by one man who is ready to sacrifice himself. I will be that man. I will do it alone."'

Apte looked at me. Very fiercely, but very low so no one around us might hear, he said: 'listen Karkare, when I heard Nathuram utter those words, I saw before my eyes lying on the floor of that car, the dead body of Mahatma Gandhi. That is how much faith I have in Nathuram.'

A terrible fit of coughing engulfed the slender figure on his pallet in Birla House. The devoted girl who had shared so many of Gandhi's painful hours during the last year felt tears fill her eyes as she watched his little body quivering beside her.

Manu knew that Sushila Nayyar had left behind a package of penicillin lozenges for Gandhi's use on just such occasions as this. Life in the service of India's Mahatma, however, was not easy. Manu was afraid to suggest he take one, sure her gesture would offend him. Finally, unable to bear her Bapu's anguish any longer, she offered to bring him one.

Gandhi's reply to her solicitude was exactly what Manu had feared it would be, a reproach. She was revealing, he said, her lack of faith in his sole protector, Rama.

'If I die of disease or even a pimple,' he gasped between bursts of coughing, 'it will be your duty to shout to the world from the roof-tops that I was a false *mahatma*. Then my soul, wherever it may be, will rest in peace.'

His sad eyes fixed the girl to whom he had tried to be a mother, who had been his 'partner and helper' in so many of the struggles of the past months. 'But,' he said, 'if an explosion took place as it did last week, or somebody shot at me and I received his bullet on my bare chest without a sigh and with Rama's name on my lips, only then should you say I was a true *mahatma*. This will benefit the Indian people.'

Karkare and Apte gently eased open the door to Retiring Room Six and peered inside. Nathuram Godse was stretched out on his bed at the end of the room, sleeping soundly. He seemed to Karkare 'without a care in his head or mind'. Lying on the floor beside him was the detective story he had finished reading that evening.

20
The Second Crucifixion

New Delhi, 30 January 1948

The last day in the life of Mohandas Karamchand Gandhi began as all his days since South Africa, by his praying in the dark reaches before the dawn. Cross-legged on his pallet, his back to a cold marble wall, he and the members of his curious little company chanted together for the last time the verses of the celestial song of Hinduism, the *Bhagavad Gita*. For this Friday their morning recitation comprised the first and second of the *Gita*'s eighteen dialogues. Gandhi's high, soft voice blended with those of his followers singing out the familiar stanzas.

For certain is death for the born
and certain is birth for the dead;
Therefore over the inevitable
Thou shouldst not grieve.

When the prayer was over, Manu led Gandhi into the spare room in which he worked. He dreamed of walking to Pakistan, but he was not yet strong enough to move from one room to another unaided. Sitting down at the truncated table that served as his writing-desk, he told Manu he wanted her to chant for him throughout the day two lines of a hymn. 'Whether tired or not, O man, do not take rest!'

As they had agreed the evening before, Apte and Karkare returned to Retiring Room Number Six at the Old Delhi railroad station shortly after 7 a.m. to find Godse already awake.

For two hours we were sitting together in the room, having chats, drinking tea and coffee together. We were joking, talking, discussing. Then we started getting serious. The reasons for this seriousness was that, although Nathuram had decided to kill Gandhiji that day in the evening, we still had no idea at all how he was going to do it.

Accordingly, we had to find a plan. We imagined that after the bomb explosion of the 20th, the place around Gandhiji at Birla House would be heavily guarded and it would be difficult for us to get an entrance. Probably the people going to the prayer meeting would be searched for arms and so we knew we must find the safe, sure way to get the gun in and do the deed.

We discussed for some time and then Nathuram had this idea. We would go into the street and buy from a photographer one of those old-

style cameras on a tripod with a black hood under which the photographer works. We would conceal the pistol inside the base of the camera. Nathuram would set his camera before the microphone where Gandhi would be speaking. He would put the hood over his head, take out the pistol and while Gandhiji was talking, shoot him from under the concealment of the hood.

Accordingly, we went down into the street in search of a photographer whose camera we might buy. We found one near the station, but after we studied him for a while, Apte announced it was a bad idea. He said nobody used cameras like that any more, and anyone going to Gandhiji's prayer meeting to take his picture would use a small German or American camera.

We went back to the Retiring Room to think of some other idea. Someone suggested we take a burqa, *the garment that is generally used by Moslem women to move about in the streets. There were many Moslem women coming to Gandhiji's prayers in those times because he was their saviour. In addition, the women were usually closest to him, so that way Nathuram could get in for a close shot. We were very excited by this idea. We went to this bazaar and purchased a* burqa, *the biggest one we could find. We brought it back to the Retiring Room.*

When Nathuram put it on, he found out instantly that the idea would not work at all. The folds kept getting in the way and hindering him. 'I will never be able to take out the pistol,' he said, 'I will be caught in this woman's dress to my eternal shame without having killed Gandhiji.'

So now we had to think of some other idea. We had wasted most of our morning on bad ideas. We had only six hours left before the time of the killing and we still did not have our plan. Finally, Apte said: 'Well, Nathuram, sometimes the simplest things are the best.' He said we should dress Nathuram in a kind of greyish military suit very much used by the people at that time. It had a loose shirt which hung at the sides of the pants which would cover the bulk of the pistol on his hip. Somewhat in despair, we decided that was our best idea. Accordingly, we returned to the bazaar and purchased this outfit for Nathuram.

Then we went back to the street of the cameraman we had seen earlier in the morning, and whose camera we had contemplated buying. There we made the overwhelmingly stupid, amateurish and sentimental gesture of having a picture taken.

We returned to the room to relax and decide on our plan. Nathuram would go first to Birla House, and Apte and I would follow. When the time for the deed had come, one of us would stand on each side of Nathuram. In that way, if anyone tried to interfere with his shooting, we might stop them and Nathuram would have time to take careful aim before shooting. It was by then time to vacate the Retiring Room according to the rules of that place. Nathuram took out the pistol. He carefully put seven bullets inside. Then he placed it on his hip and we left.

We went down to the waiting-room of the railway station to pass the hours in that anonymous place until it was time to go. After we had been there for some time, Nathuram announced to us he had a desire for ground nuts, that is peanuts. It was a petty thing he was asking, and we were feeling so tender-hearted towards him we were butter in his hands. He was about to sacrifice himself. We did not want anything to disturb him or distract him. Whatever he wanted, we would do for him.

Accordingly, Apte went off to search for peanuts. After some time he came back, telling that, well, there were no peanuts available in Delhi, would cashew nuts do in place, or almonds do in place?

Nathuram said 'No. Bring me some peanuts only.'

We did not want to make him upset in view of the great task that was before him. And so, Apte set off again in search of peanuts. Finally, after some time, he came back with a large bag full of those nuts. Nathuram took it and eagerly began to gobble them up.

By the time he had finished, it was time for us to leave. We decided to go first to Birla Temple. Apte and myself particularly wanted to pray to the deities there to have darshan. *Nathuram, however, was not interested in such things. He went around to the garden behind the Temple, near the forest where we had made the practice shooting to wait for us.*

We removed our shoes at the entrance and went barefoot. At the entry we rang the brass bell hanging over our head. That is a gesture to alert the Gods to our presence. We went first to the central idol, that of Lakshmi Narayan, a deity, a couple, pious to the Hindus. Then we left that altar for the altar of Kali, the Goddess of Destruction, to have our darshan *there. First, we bowed our heads in silence with hands folded.*

We threw a few coins at the Goddess's feet. Then we gave a few more coins to the Brahmin priest who was there. In return, the Brahmin gave us some petals of flowers and some dhista, *the sacred water of the Jumna. We threw the flowers to the Goddess, asking her for success in our endeavour. Then we touched our eyes with the pious water of the Jumna.*

Outside, we found Nathuram standing in the garden. He was standing by a statue of Shivaji, the great Hindu warrior. He asked us 'did you have your darshan*?'*

We said 'yes' and Nathuram said 'well, I had my darshan, *too.'*

The *darshan* of Nathuram Godse had not been with any figure in the pantheon of Hinduism's gods inside that sanctuary redolent with jasmine and incense. His deity was that figure on the pillar above him, the wiry warrior who had driven the Moghuls from the hillsides of Poona. It was in his name, and for the dream of a militant Hindu empire that his achievements inspired in him, that Godse was prepared to commit, in just one hour's time, a murder that would horrify the world.

The three men strolled in the garden for several minutes. Finally Apte looked at his watch. It was four-thirty.

'Nathuram,' he said, 'the time has come.'

Nathuram glanced at Apte's watch. Then he looked at his two colleagues. He pressed the palms of his hands together in front of his chest and nodded to them.

'*Namaste*,' he said. 'We do not know whether and how we shall ever be together again.'

Karkare's regard followed him as he climbed down the steps of the temple and went through the crowd in search of a tonga. He found one, got in and 'without looking back proceeded towards Birla House where Gandhiji was having his prayers'.

Mahatma Gandhi had lived his Friday, 30 January in strict accordance with the injunction of the hymn he ordered Manu to repeat to him that morning: 'O Man, do not take rest!' For the first time since his fast, to the delight of his entourage, he had walked unaided. His weight indicated he had gained half a pound, proof the strength was coming back to his slender frame, evidence for Gandhi that God still had great tasks to lay before him.

After his midday rest he had gone through a dozen interviews. The most difficult was the last one, the one through which he now laboured. His interlocutor was one of his oldest and most faithful followers, the taciturn twentieth-century Moghul who had moulded Gandhi's Congress, Vallabhbhai Patel. The inevitable conflict between Patel, the tough-minded realist, and Nehru, the socialist idealist, had finally erupted. On Gandhi's little writing-desk was a copy of Patel's letter of resignation from Nehru's government. Gandhi and Lord Mountbatten had discussed the quarrel during their conversation before Gandhi's fast. The Governor-General had urged Gandhi not to allow Patel to resign.

'You can't let him go,' Mountbatten had warned, 'you can't let Nehru go either. India needs both of them, and they've got to learn to work together.'

Gandhi agreed. He convinced Patel he should withhold his resignation. The three of them, he, Patel and Nehru, would sit down together once again as they had in the old times, during the critical moments in the freedom struggle. Together, they would thrash the matter out.

While he talked, Abha brought his evening meal of goat's milk, vegetable juice and oranges. As soon as he had finished that austere repast he called for his spinning-wheel. Still carrying on his animated dialogue with Patel, he began to turn the creaking wooden device which symbolized him to millions around the world, faithful down to those closing moments of his life to one of the principles that had governed it, his dictum that 'bread taken without labour is stolen bread'.

The killers were already wandering in the gardens beyond the room where Gandhi turned his wheel. Five minutes after Nathuram, Apte and Karkare had in their turn taken a tonga to Birla House.

To our relief and surprise [Karkare remembered], *we found the entrance of Birla House posed no problem at all. The guard had been increased, but no one was searching the crowd coming in for weapons. We were relieved. We knew then Nathuram had made his entrance safely. We walked out to the garden and there we saw Nathuram mingling with the crowds. He seemed composed and good-spirited. We, of course, did not speak to one another. The crowd was scattered around the lawn. As five o'clock and the time for the prayers grew near, the people began to move together. We took our places on either side of Nathuram. We did not speak or glance at him so as not to reveal our secret. He was so much in himself, he seemed to have forgotten us, to have forgotten we were there.*

Our plan was to kill Gandhi after he had sat down on the little prayer meeting platform facing the crowd. To do it, we stationed ourselves at the outer rim of the crowd towards the right as we faced the platform. It would mean an accurate shot of about thirty-five feet. Sizing up the distance I silently wondered 'Can Nathuram do it?' He was not an experienced or particularly good shot. Will he be nervous and lose his aim, I wondered? I glanced at Nathuram. He was staring straight ahead, seemingly calm, all wrapped up in himself. I glanced at my watch. Gandhiji was coming late. I began to wonder why. I was a bit nervous.

Manu and Abha were nervous too. It was already ten minutes past five. The gentle dictator who ran their lives hated nothing so much as being late, and above all being late for his evening prayers. The tone of his talk with Patel had seemed so grave, however, that neither of them had dared interrupt to remind him of the time. Finally, Manu caught his eye and gestured at her watch.

Gandhi glanced down at his old Ingersoll, then almost leapt from his pallet. 'Oh,' he said to Patel, 'you must let me go free. It is time for me to go to God's meeting.'

As he emerged from the office into the garden the little cortege that always escorted Gandhi to the prayer grounds formed up for the last time. Two of its members were missing. Sushila Nayyar, the doctor who usually walked in front of Gandhi, was still in Pakistan. The police officer whom the bedridden D. W. Mehra had assigned to replace him at Gandhi's side was not there either. He had been summoned to an urgent meeting in downtown Delhi to discuss police arrangements for a general strike of Delhi's utilities workers scheduled for the next day.

As she did each evening, Manu gathered his spittoon, his eyeglasses, the notebook in which he'd written the text of his address. She and Abha moved up to offer him their shoulders in their familiar role as his walking sticks. Resting a hand on each girl, Gandhi set out on his last journey.

Because they were late, he decided to cut directly across the lawn to the prayer ground instead of walking under the rolls of bougainvillaea of Birla's arbour. All the way across the lawn he scolded the girls for allowing him to be late.

'You are my watches,' he said, 'why should I consult a watch? I do not like this delay at all. I cannot tolerate even one minute's delay at prayer.'

He was still chatting away when they reached the flight of four sandstone steps leading up to the prayer ground where the crowds waited. The setting sun picked out the familiar brown head with its last rays. Gandhi slid his arms from the shoulders of the two girls, clasped his palms in greeting to the crowd, and shuffled unaided up the steps. At the instant he reached the top steps, Karkare heard behind him a soft, murmuring ripple from the crowd: 'Bapuji, Bapuji.'

I turned. Nathuram, too, made a half turn to the right. Suddenly, we saw a parting in the people and coming straight towards us through that little voluntary path in the crowd was Gandhiji. Nathuram's hands were in his pockets. He took out one hand, his free hand. He kept the hand in which he had hidden his weapon in his pocket. He flicked off the safety catch of the automatic.

In a flash he had made the calculation: 'now is the time to kill him.' He knew he had been given a providential opportunity, far greater than the chance he would have had if Gandhiji had been seated on the prayer platform. He knew he needed to take only two steps to the edge of the little human corridor. Two steps. Three seconds. Then the killing would be easy, a mechanical thing. What was difficult was driving himself to the act of will to start the action, to take one step that made the killing inevitable.

Manu saw him 'a stout young man in khaki dress' taking that step. It brought him through the last ranks of people to the edge of the parting in the crowd through which their cortege was moving.

Karkare's eyes were on Nathuram. 'He took the pistol from his pocket and passed it between his palms. He had decided to make obeisance to Gandhi for whatever useful service he had rendered his country. When Gandhi was only three strides from us, Nathuram stepped into the corridor. He had the pistol concealed between his hands. He bowed slowly from the waist, and he said to him: '*Namaste* Gandhiji.'

Manu thought he wanted to kiss Gandhi's feet. Gently, she extended an arm to motion him away. 'Brother,' she murmured, 'Bapu is already ten minutes late.'

At that instant Nathuram's left arm shot out, thrusting her brutally aside. The black Beretta pistol lay exposed in his right hand. Nathuram pulled the trigger three times. Three sharp reports shattered the stillness of the prayer ground. Nathuram Godse had not failed. All three rounds tore into the chest of the slender figure advancing towards him.

Manu, groping to recover the spittoon and notebook Nathuram had knocked from her hands, heard the shots. She looked up. Hands clasped in greeting, her beloved Bapu seemed to be still moving forward, chest bare, trying to take one last step towards the prayer platform ahead. She saw the red stains spreading over the gleaming white *khadi*. Gandhi gasped, 'He Ram – O God!' Then a lifeless little bundle, he slowly sank to the ground beside her, his hands still frozen in the final gesture to which his spirit had commanded them, a greeting to his assassin. In the folds of the blood-soaked *dhoti*, Manu saw the eight-shilling Ingersoll watch whose loss had so pained Gandhi ten months before. It was seventeen minutes past five.

* * *

Louis Mountbatten received the news Gandhi had been shot as he trotted up to Government House from a ride. His first words formed a question millions would ask in the next hours: 'Who did it?'

'We don't know, sir,' the ADC who had given him the news answered. Mountbatten rushed to change. Minutes later, as he dashed out of Government House, he spotted his press attaché, Alan Campbell-Johnson. He ordered him into his waiting car.

By the time the two men reached Birla House an enormous crowd had already engulfed its grounds. As they pushed their way through the throng to Gandhi's quarters, a man, his face contorted with frenzy and hysteria, shrieked, 'It was a Moslem who did it.'

A sudden silence froze the crowd. Mountbatten turned to the man. 'You fool,' he shouted as loudly as he could, 'don't you know it was a Hindu?'

Seconds later, as they passed into the house, Campbell-Johnson turned to him. 'How can you possibly know it's a Hindu?' he asked.

'I don't,' answered Mountbatten, 'but if it really was a Moslem,

India is going to live one of the most ghastly massacres the world has ever seen.'

Mountbatten's concern was shared by thousands. The certainty that a disaster would engulf India if Gandhi's assassin turned out to be a Moslem prompted the director of All India Radio to make an extraordinary and responsible decision: instead of interrupting the radio's nationwide circuits with India's scoop of the century, he ordered programmes to continue as normal. While they did, the headquarters of the police and army, employing their emergency telephone circuits, put every major army and police command in India on emergency footing. From Birla House, the police relayed to the radio the most vital news of all: Nathuram Godse was a Hindu of the Brahmin caste. Precisely at six o'clock, in an announcement every word of which had been carefully studied, the Indian people learned of the death of the gentle man who had brought them freedom.

'Mahatma Gandhi,' the radio announced, 'was assassinated in New Delhi at twenty minutes past five this afternoon. His assassin was a Hindu.'

The slaughter had been avoided; it now remained to India to mourn.

Mahatma Gandhi's corpse was taken back into Birla House from the garden in which he had been shot and placed on the straw pallet on which he slept next to the spinning-wheel he'd turned for the last time a few minutes earlier. Abha laid a woollen wrapper over his blood-soaked *dhoti*. Someone set beside his pallet his handful of belongings: his wooden shower clogs, the sandals he'd been wearing when he was shot, his three monkeys, his *Gita*, the Ingersoll watch, his carefully polished spittoon, the tin bowl that was his souvenir of Yeravda Prison.

By the time Louis Mountbatten stepped into the room, it was already crowded with mourners. Nehru, his face ashen, was squatting on the floor, his head against the wall, tears inundating his handsome features. A few feet away, a thunderstruck Patel sat like a stone Buddha, his eyes riveted on the body of the man to whom he'd been speaking less than an hour before.

A soft flutter of sound floated through the room: the women around Gandhi's improvised bier chanting the *Gita*. The orange glow of a dozen oil-lamps wrapped the Mahatma's body in their sad and gentle aura. The aroma of incense hung on the air. Manu, soundlessly weeping, held her beloved Bapu's head in her lap. With the fingers that had massaged it with oil the evening before, she gently caressed the lifeless skull from which so many original ideas had flowed out to mankind.

Lying there on his pallet, his 'dejected sparrow' seemed to Mountbatten to be already diminished in size, a child's body barely filling his little piece of floor. Someone had removed the steel-rimmed spectacles that had become so much a part of Gandhi's features, and for an instant, looking down in the candlelight, Mountbatten did not quite recognize him. An astonishing look of repose covered his face. Never, Mountbatten thought, had he seen his features as peaceful and composed in life as they were now in death. Someone pressed a cup of rose petals into Mountbatten's hands. Sadly, he let the pink leaves tumble to the body below, the final tribute of India's last Viceroy to the man who had put an end to his great-grandmother's empire. Watching them fall, a thought struck Louis Mountbatten, a thought he would repeat in a few hours' time to a close friend.

'Mahatma Gandhi,' he told himself, 'will go down in history on a par with Buddha and Jesus Christ.'

Slipping through the throng in the mourning chamber, Mountbatten went up to Nehru and Patel. He put an arm around each man. 'You both know how much I loved Gandhiji,' he said.

'Well,' he continued, 'let me tell you something. The last time we talked he told me how worried he was that you, his two greatest friends, his greatest supporters, the people he loved and admired most in the world, were drifting apart.

'He told me "they listen to you now more than they do to me. Do your best to bring them together." That was his dying wish. If his memory means as much to you as your grief implies it does, you'll embrace and forget your differences.' Visibly moved by his words, the two grieving leaders fell into an embrace.

Mountbatten soon realized that the most useful service he could offer the nation which had asked him to be her first Governor-General would be to turn his energies to the ceremony no one in the first shock of grief and loss had yet considered, Gandhi's funeral.

With Nehru and Patel's endorsement, Mountbatten proposed embalming Gandhi's body so that a special funeral train might carry his remains across India, giving the millions he'd loved and served a chance for a last *darshan* with their Mahatma. Gandhi's timid secretary, Pyarelal Nayar, ended that idea. Gandhi, he said, had made it absolutely clear he wished his remains to be cremated within 24 hours of his death in strict accordance with Hindu custom.

'You realize,' Mountbatten told Nehru and Patel, 'that in that case we will have crowds such as India has never seen in Delhi tomorrow. There is only one organization in the country capable of organizing and conducting a funeral procession in those conditions: the military.'

The two Indian leaders looked aghast at his words. The thought that Gandhi, of all men, should be conducted to his funeral pyre by those whose profession was war, appalled them.

Gandhi admired the discipline of the services, Mountbatten assured the two leaders. He would have had no objection to their filling the role. Nehru and Patel finally nodded their reluctant agreement. The last voyage of India's prophet of non-violence through his people would be conducted as a military operation.

After Mountbatten had set the machinery in motion, he turned to Nehru. 'You know,' he said, 'you must make an address to the nation. The people will be looking to you for a lead now.'

'I can't,' Nehru gasped. 'I'm too upset. I am not prepared. I don't know what to say.'

'Don't worry,' Mountbatten replied, 'God will tell you what to say.'

Spontaneously, intuitively, India reacted to the news of Gandhi's death with the most appropriate of gestures. As Gandhi had set his people on the march to independence with a *hartal*, a nationwide day of mourning, so India now marked his passing in the sorrowing silence of a real *hartal*.

Above the vast plains, the fields, the cluttered slums and writhing jungles, the air was crystal clear. The mantle of India's night, the fine haze of the cow-dung fires burning in a hundred million hearths, had disappeared. To mourn the Mahatma, those hearths were cold.

Bombay was a ghost city. From the beautiful mansions of Malabar Hill to the slums of Parel, the people wept. Calcutta's great Maidan was almost empty. Through its streets a barefoot *sadhu*, his face smeared with ashes, walked, crying: 'The Mahatma is dead. When comes another such as he?'

In Pakistan, millions of women shattered their baubles and trinkets in a traditional gesture of grief. In Lahore, now almost entirely Moslem, newspaper offices swarmed with people clamouring for news. There were trouble spots too. Police had to protect the whitewashed shed in Poona that sheltered the press of the *Hindu Rashtra*. A thousand people tried to storm Savarkar Sadan in Bombay. Mobs attacked the headquarters of the *Hindu Mahasabha* and the RSSS in cities across the nation.

Ranjit Lal, the peasant from Chatharpur, a village outside Delhi, who had walked home from the independence celebrations because tongas had become too expensive, heard the news on a gift which freedom had brought him and his fellow villagers, a radio, provided by the Ministry of Agriculture. Instinctively, at the word of Gandhi's death, Lal and the entire village rose. Black silhouettes in the night, Chatharpur's inhabitants as well as those of scores of other villages, started to march across the hills to Delhi, returning to the avenues where they had celebrated their freedom so as to mourn its architect, harbingers of the flood of humanity Mountbatten had predicted would pour into the capital at dawn.

Buried in rose petals and jasmine blooms, Gandhi's body was carried to an open balcony on the second floor of Birla House. Four oil-lamps for the five elements, fire, water, air, earth and the light which unites them, were aligned at his head. Then, set on a wooden board, his remains were exposed to the visitors below, clamouring for a parting glance at their lost Mahatma.

They had been there for hours. As they had once braved the *lathis* of the British police in Gandhi's name, they had braved them all evening to win one swift look through the glass doors of Birla House into the room in which his body lay. Thousands of others had swarmed into the garden where Gandhi had been shot, plucking blades of grass as their personal memorials of India's liberator. Now, they flowed past the balcony in their thousands, white *khadi dhotis* and dresses shining in the glare of the searchlights, the veterans of an army of ghosts come to mourn their fallen general.

On the other side of Delhi, a heartbroken man found in the depths of his sorrow the words he'd despaired of finding. Jawaharlal Nehru's eyes were filled with tears as he stepped before the microphone of All India Radio. As they had been on Independence Eve, the words he was about to utter were spontaneous, but they glowed with unforgettable beauty.

'The light has gone out of our lives and there is darkness everywhere,' he said. 'Our beloved leader, Bapu, as we called him, the father of the nation, is no more.

'The light has gone out, I said, and yet I was wrong. For the light that shone in this country was no ordinary light.' In a thousand years, he predicted, 'that light will still be seen . . . the world will see it and it will give solace to innumerable hearts. For that light represented something more than the immediate present; it represented the living, the eternal truths, reminding us of the right path, drawing us from error, taking this ancient country to freedom.'

The light whose disappearance Nehru mourned belonged to the

rest of the world as well as to India. From every corner of a shocked globe, messages of condolence poured into New Delhi.

The news of Gandhi's death moved London as no event had since the end of the war. Londoners passed each other copies of the sold-out editions of the evening press announcing the murder of the perplexing figure who'd come to their city fifteen years earlier in a sheet, a goat by his side, to ask for the return of the crown jewel of their empire. King George VI; the Prime Minister, Clement Attlee; Gandhi's old foe, Winston Churchill; Stafford Cripps; the Archbishop of Canterbury; thousands of others sent their condolences. None were as memorable as the taut tribute from the Irish playwright Gandhi had met in London in 1931, George Bernard Shaw. His murder, Shaw said, 'shows how dangerous it is to be good'.

In Paris the Premier, Georges Bidault, remarked, 'All those who believe in the brotherhood of men will mourn Gandhi's death.' From South Africa, Gandhi's first political rival, Field-Marshal Jan Smuts, sent a simple tribute: 'A prince among us has passed,' he said. At the Vatican, Pius XII paid tribute to 'an apostle of peace and a friend of Christianity'. The Chinese, the Indonesians were shocked at the disappearance of the man who was the precursor of Asian independence. In Washington, President Harry Truman declared, 'The entire world mourns with India.'

Jawaharlal Nehru's sister, Mrs V. L. Pandit, set out a register for condolences in her newly opened Embassy in Moscow. Not a single member of Josef Stalin's Foreign Office entered his name in it.

'There can be no controversy in the face of death,' Gandhi's principal political rival, Mohammed Ali Jinnah, wrote in his message of condolence, 'He was one of the greatest men produced by the Hindu community.' When one of Jinnah's assistants, reviewing the text with him, suggested Gandhi's dimensions were greater than his own community, Jinnah demurred. Gandhi had risked his life a fortnight before for India's Moslems and to save Jinnah's state from bankruptcy, but the Quaid-e-Azzam was as inflexible as ever.

'No,' he said. 'That's what he was – a great Hindu.'

Appropriately, in that vast outpouring of tributes, it was the Indians themselves who produced the most memorable testimonial of all. It came on the editorial page of the *Hindustan Standard*. The page was left blank, ringed by a black border. At its centre was a single paragraph set in bold face type. It read:

'Gandhiji has been killed by his own people for whose redemption he lived. This second crucifixion in the history of the world has been enacted on a Friday – the same day Jesus was done to death one thousand nine hundred and fifteen years ago. Father, forgive us.'

Just after midnight, Gandhi's body was brought down from the balcony of Birla House. For a few brief hours he belonged again to the little company that had shared his austere existence: Manu and Abha, Pyarelal, his secretary, two of his sons, Devadas and Ramdas, the handful of others who had been at his side in the triumphs and heartbreak of the last year of his life.

Following the strict dictates of Hindu custom, Manu and Abha smeared fresh cow-dung over the marble floor of Birla House to prepare it to receive Gandhi's corpse. When Gandhi's sons and secretaries had given him a final bath, his body was wrapped in a winding-sheet of homespun cotton and set on the floor on a wooden plank. A Brahmin priest anointed his chest with sandalwood paste and saffron. Manu pressed a vermilion dot upon his forehead. Then she and Abha lovingly wrote '*Hé Râm*' in laurel leaves at his head and '*Om*' in rose petals at his feet. It was 3.30 a.m., the hour at which Gandhi usually awoke for prayer. Weeping softly, his companions sat down by his bier and filled the little room with a farewell hymn to the man before them.

'Cover yourself with dust,' they sang, 'because ultimately you shall be at one with the dust. Have your bath and dress in fresh garments. There shall be no return from there where you are going.'

Then, before giving the body of their beloved Bapu back to a waiting world, they performed a final gesture. They all knew how Gandhi hated the Hindu custom of garlanding the defunct with wreaths of flowers. And so Devadas knotted around his father's neck the ornament Mohandas Karamchand Gandhi would take on his voyage to eternity, a loop of homespun cotton yarn cut from the threads he'd turned that afternoon with the last revolutions of his cherished spinning-wheel.

Frozen in the still serenity of death, Mahatma Gandhi offered his visage to his people for an ultimate and pathetic *darshan*. Once again, on its raised wooden plank heavy with rose petals and jasmine, his body was exposed at sunrise to the public from the balcony of Birla House. Driven by an irresistible desire for a last vision of their Mahatma, the waves of mourners had engulfed the house with the first rays of breaking day, beating up against its whitewashed walls in a constantly renewed sea of love and despair.

Just after eleven in the morning, his disciples carried the wooden slab down from the balcony and gently set it upon the vehicle which would take Gandhi across his mourning capital to his final destination on earth, the funeral pyre waiting to receive him at the Raj Ghat, the cremation ground of the kings on the banks of the Jumna River. It was a Dodge weapons-carrier. In deference to the memory of the man who had been so determined a foe of the abuses of the machine age, the vehicle's engine would remain silent during Gandhi's last trek. It would be drawn by the force of 250 of his countrymen, sailors, soldiers and airmen, towing four ropes attached to its bumper.

Jawaharlal Nehru, his eyelids reddened from weeping, and a grief-stricken Vallabhbhai Patel joined Manu and Abha in performing a final ritual gesture. They placed across Gandhi's corpse twin strips of red and white linen, the indication the defunct had lived to the fullness of his life and his death was a joyous departure towards eternity. Then they covered his tiny figure in the most appropriate of shrouds the prophet of poverty could wear to his cremation, the saffron white and green folds of the flag of an independent India.

The man who had been responsible for organizing the funeral, Lt-Gen. Sir Roy Bucher, the British Commander of the Indian Army, gave a last look at the waiting column. By an extraordinary irony of history, this was the second funeral Roy Bucher had prepared for Mohandas Gandhi. He had also organized the funeral in Yeravda prison in 1942 which the durable little man had declined to attend during his famous 21-day fast.

At a signal from Bucher, the procession slow-marched into the human sea outside the gates of Birla House. Four armoured cars and a squadron of the Governor-General's bodyguard opened the march. Their presence in Gandhi's funeral cortege was Mountbatten's last gesture to the 'dejected sparrow' he should have scorned but had come to love. It was the first time these troops of the old Viceroy's bodyguard had so honoured an Indian.

Ministers and coolies, Maharajas, Untouchable sweepers, governors, veiled Moslem women, representatives of every caste, class, creed, race and colour in India, united by their common burden of grief, followed the procession in a fittingly unstructured flow of humanity.

The cortege's five-mile route to the Jumna was already littered with a carpet of rose petals and marigolds. Every foot along its way was dense with people in trees, hanging from windows, lining the rooftops, perched on the top of lamp-posts, clinging to telephone poles, ensconced in the arms of statues. Lost in the multitude along Kingsway, clinging to a lamp-post, was Ranjit Lal, the peasant who'd set out from his village the evening before at the news of Gandhi's assassination. As the cortege slowly slipped below his perch, Ranjit Lal saw for the first time in his life that famous face resting on its cushion of flowers. He felt the sting of tears in his eyes. One simple thought animated his grateful being as he watched Gandhi pass: 'He gave me my freedom.'

From the dome of Durbar Hall, Louis Mountbatten's press attaché Alan Campbell-Johnson watched the cortege advance with almost imperceptible movement along that imperial avenue, the vehicle at its heart locked in the embrace of vast swarms of people. There, on that boulevard designed to celebrate the triumphs of empire, Gandhi, he realized, 'was receiving in death a homage beyond the dreams of any Viceroy'.

For five hours, an hour to cover each mile of its route, that procession continued its march through the mourning throngs to the banks of the Jumna and Gandhi's funeral pyre. There at least another million people stretched out over the broad meadows beyond the waiting pyramid of logs. Contemplating that unbelievable throng, Margaret Bourke-White suddenly felt she was about to record with her Leica lens 'the largest crowd ever to gather on the face of the earth'.

In a small clearing at the heart of that mass of humanity, protected only by a thin screen of Indian airmen, were a hundred dignitaries awaiting the funeral cortege. The lean silhouette of Louis Mountbatten, his head covered by his white naval officer's cap, rose above them at the foot of the funeral pyre itself.

When at last, passed from hand to hand above the heads of the crowd, Gandhi's body began to move towards the pyre, a wave of uncontrollable hysteria thrust the multitude forward. 'There'll be quite a stir in London when they learn Mountbatten, his wife, his daughters and his staff have been cremated along with Gandhi,' Major Martin Gilliat, a member of that staff, thought.

Sensing that menace, Mountbatten patiently drove the dignitaries back twenty yards from the enormous pile of logs. Then he motioned all of them to sit down on the ground that their feet had already churned to mud. He himself, despite his immaculately clean blue naval uniform, gave the example along with his wife and daughter.

Finally, the plank bearing Gandhi's corpse reached the enclosure. His sons gently laid it upon the great round logs of sandalwood, his head pointed north, his feet pointing south according to the prescriptions of Hindu rite. It was four o'clock and it was time to hurry if, as custom demanded, the rays of the sun were to offer their final blessing to the face of the man being cremated at the instant the flames consumed his body.

Ramdas, Gandhi's second son responsible according to Hindu tradition for conducting the ceremony in the absence of his eldest brother Harilal, climbed on to the pyramid. With Devadas, his youngest brother, he soaked the pile in *ghee*, clarified butter, mixed with coconut oil, camphor and incense.

Looking at the silhouette of the man he had come to know so well in the brief span of a year, Louis Mountbatten was deeply moved. 'He looked as though he was sleeping peacefully there before our eyes,' he remembered, 'and yet in a few seconds while we looked on he was going to disappear in a flash of flames.'

Ramdas Gandhi made five mystic trips around the pyre while saffron-robed priests chanted their *mantras*. Then someone passed him a torch ignited by a glowing charcoal brought from the eternal fire of the Temple of the Dead. Ramdas raised it above his head and plunged it into his father's funeral pyre. As the first uncertain flames began to lick their way over the sandalwood logs, a quivering voice chanted the ancient Vedic prayer whose words the consuming pyre fulfilled:

> Lead me from the Unreal to the Real
> From Darkness to Light
> From Death to Immortality.

At the sight of the curls of smoke twisting up from the pyre, that vast assembly stretching down the fields to the river's edge heaved forward. Behind her, Pamela Mountbatten saw dozens of women, weeping hysterically, tear their hair and their saris, then try to thrust their way past the overwhelmed police, hoping to accomplish the ancient Indian rite of *Sati*, the traditional suicide of widows throwing themselves into their husband's funeral pyre. Only her father's foresight in forcing them all to sit on the muddy ground saved the dignitaries from being driven by the crowd's uncontrollable surge into the flames in a massive and involuntary *Sati*.

The flames, finding the volatile fuel of the *ghee*, suddenly exploded over the funeral pyre. A furious geyser of sparks boiled into the sky as the crackling wreath of flame enveloped the pyramid of sandalwood logs. The still brown figure at its heart disappeared forever behind an orange curtain of fire. The cold winter wind sweeping down the Jumna whipped the flames higher, pulling the dense, oily smoke from the pyre. As that black pillar mounted a sky incarnadined by the rays of the setting sun, a mournful cry rising from a million chests shook the plains of the Jumna: '*Mahatma Gandhi amar ho gaye!* – Mahatma Gandhi has become immortal.'

All night while the funeral pyre cooled, the mourners filed silently past the smoking remains of what had once been a great man. Lost among them, unrecognized and unremarked, was the man who should have lit those flames, a derelict ravaged by alcohol and tuberculosis, Mahatma Gandhi's eldest son Harilal.

Another man, too, his face distorted by grief, kept an all-night vigil over the glowing embers of the fire that had consumed the man he had so loved and admired. An epoch in Jawaharlal Nehru's life had ended in the blaze that had made him an orphan. At first light he laid a little bouquet of roses on the still smouldering ashes.

'Bapuji – Little Father – ' he said, 'here are flowers. Today at least I can offer them to your bones and ashes. Where will I offer them tomorrow and to whom?'

* * *

As Hindu practice dictated, the ashes of Mahatma Gandhi were immersed in a body of water flowing to the sea on the twelfth day after his cremation. The site chosen to receive the remains was one of the most sacred in Hindudom, the *sangam* at Allahabad, the spot where the muddy waters of the Eternal Mother Ganges join the clear running Jumna and the mystic Saravas. There, at the confluence of those great rivers whose names had coursed down through India's history, in the majestic tides that had carried away the ashes of so many of those faceless millions whose joys and sufferings he had made his own, Gandhi would blend with the collective soul of his people as a drop of water in an endless sea.

The copper urn containing his ashes was borne over the 393 mile journey from New Delhi to Allahabad in a train composed solely of third-class cars, passing along its route through a human corridor of millions of Indians come to offer a final homage to India's Great Soul. At the Allahabad station the urn was carried to a waiting truck which drove it through the mammoth crowds to the water's edge. There, a white, flower-banked Indian Army amphibious vehicle, a 'duck', waited to bear it to mid-stream.

Nehru, Patel, Gandhi's sons Devadas and Ramdas, Manu, Abha, his other close associates, took their places beside the urn on the duck. From the riverbank, 3 million people followed its progress across the waters.

As the sublime instant approached, a chorus of Vedic chants and tinkling bells mingled with the dissonant wail of the Indian flute rose above the crowd. Hundreds of thousands of mourners, foreheads streaked with ashes and sandalwood paste, strode into the river to join in a gigantic and mystic communion. They thrust coconut shells filled with flowers, fruit, sweets, milk, bits of hair, on to the current. Then, thrusting their cupped palms into the waters, they gulped three mouthfuls of the river's sacred broth.

When the duck reached the legendary junction of the rivers, Ramdas Gandhi filled the urn containing his father's ashes with the milk of a Sacred Cow. He gently swirled the urn's contents while the passengers on the duck chanted a last hymn: 'Holy Soul, may sun, air and fire be auspicious unto thee; may the waters of all the rivers and the oceans be helpful unto thee, and serve thee forever in thy good deeds.'

Then, as their chant concluded, he leaned over the duck's gunwales and slowly let the mixture in the urn flow on to the waters below. Caught by the river's current, the milk-grey slick speckled with dark flecks of ash, slid down the vessel's hull. Lovingly, each of its passengers bent over and sprinkled a fistful of rose petals on the stain that once had been a man.

Borne on by the river's remorseless currents, the grey film with its crown of rose petals glided from sight down to a distant horizon. The ashes of Mohandas Gandhi were off on the last pilgrimage of a devout Hindu, their long voyage to the sea and the mystic instant when the Eternal Mother, the Ganges, would deposit them in the eternity of the oceans and Gandhi's soul, 'outsoaring the shadows of the night', would become one with the *Mahat*, the Supreme, the God of his celestial *Gita*.

Epilogue

Mahatma Gandhi achieved in death what he had striven for in his last months of life. His murder ended forever the insensate communal killing of neighbour by neighbour in India's villages and cities. The antagonisms of the sub-continent would remain, but they would henceforth be transformed to the conventional plane of a conflict between nation states waged between regular armies on the battlefield. The sacrifice in the gardens of Birla House would stand as the climax of the triumph and tragedy which embraced the Indian sub-continent in 1947–8.

Its author, Nathuram Godse, was taken into custody with his pistol in his hand. He made no effort to resist arrest. The arrest of the remaining members of the conspiracy followed quickly. Narayan Apte and Vishnu Karkare were betrayed to the police by Apte's amorous appetites. On, appropriately enough, 14 February, St Valentine's Day, Apte answered a knock on the door of the Bombay hotel in which he'd been hiding for 48 hours. He expected to find his mistress on the doorstep. He found instead three Bombay policemen. The police had discovered his liaison with the daughter of their chief surgeon and had been listening to the telephone conversation in which he'd asked her a few minutes earlier to come to his hotel room.

Eight men, Apte, Nathuram and Gopal Godse, Madanlal, Karkare, Savarkar, Parchure and Digamber Badge's servant were sent to trial on 27 May 1948 for conspiracy to murder Mahatma Gandhi. From the outset, Nathuram Godse claimed sole responsibility for the murder for political purposes, and denied the others had participated with him in a conspiracy.

Digamber Badge's astonishing record of 37 arrests and only one conviction was not to be tarnished by his participation in the murder. The false *sadhu* turned state's witness and never had to stand trial for the crime. Largely on his testimony, seven of the eight accused were convicted. Veer Savarkar was acquitted for lack of evidence.

Nathuram Godse and Narayan Apte were condemned to death for the crime. Apte would pay on the gallows for the rendezvous he had missed with an Air India stewardess in New Delhi on the evening of 27 January 1948. He was sentenced to die because he had been present in Gwalior at the moment the murder weapon was procured.

The judge sentenced the five remaining men to life imprisonment. Parchure and Badge's servant, however, succeeded in reversing their convictions in Appeal Court.

Their own appeals denied, the date of Nathuram Godse's and Narayan Apte's execution was set for 15 November 1949. Two of Gandhi's sons, his close friends and associates joined in a petition for clemency to the man who had been the most devoted follower of the prophet of non-violence, Jawaharlal Nehru. The petition was denied. At dawn, 15 November 1949, as provided for by the Indian Code of Criminal Procedures, Narayan Apte and Nathuram Godse were taken from their cells to the courtyard of Ambala prison where they were 'hung by the neck until dead'.

Apte had not believed he would die for the murder of Mahatma Gandhi until a hangman's assistant opened his cell door that morning. He knew that a last minute reprieve would come because he had read it in the lines of his hand. Standing at the foot of the gallows, confronted by the terrible evidence of how fallible a science palmistry was, Narayan Apte collapsed. He had to be carried to the waiting rope.

Nathuram Godse declared in his last will and testament that the only possession he had to leave his family was his ashes. He chose to postpone his entrance into immortality until the dream for which he had committed murder had been realized. Defying the canons of Hindu custom, he asked that those ashes should not be immersed in a body of water flowing to the sea but be handed down instead, from generation to generation, until they could be sprinkled into an Indus river flowing through a sub-continent reunited under Hindu rule.

Dattaraya Parchure, after his conviction was reversed, returned to the office where he still sits under the oil painting of his *guru*, prescribing his concoctions of cardamom seeds, bamboo sprouts, onions and honey for the congested lungs of the citizens of Gwalior.

Digamber Badge, fearing for his life in Poona, moved after the trial to quarters provided for him by the police in Bombay. There he re-established himself in the profession for which he was esteemed throughout Bombay Province; knitting up his chain-mail, bullet-proof vests. Badge has prospered. His vests now sell for 1000 rupees (£55) and his order book contains a six months' backlog. He sells them throughout India, most frequently to politicians who have reason to fear an attempt of their lives.

Karkare, Madanlal and Gopal Godse, having served their sentences under the provisions of Indian law, were released from jail in the late 1960's. Karkare returned to Ahmednagar where he resumed direction of the Deccan Guest House, offering travellers the questionable comfort of one of his *charpois*, set seven to a room, for 1·25 rupees (7 pence) a night. He died of a heart-attack in April 1974. Madanlal Pahwa settled in Bombay. He manufactures toys in a loft behind his dwelling, seeking to compete in his small way with the Japanese industrial barons whose products flood the markets of India and the Far East. The proudest creation today of the man who tried to destroy Gandhi with a bomb at Birla House is a rocket powered by compressed air which shoots 100 yards into the sky, then returns to earth with its own parachute.

Gopal Godse resides on the third floor of a modest dwelling in Poona. On one wall of his terrace outlined in wrought-iron is an enormous map of the entire Indian sub-continent. Once a year, on 15 November, the anniversary of his brother's execution, Nathuram's ashes are set before that map in a silver urn. The map is outlined in glowing light bulbs. Before it, Gopal Godse assembles the most zealous of the old disciples of Veer Savarkar.

No twinge of remorse, no hint of contrition, animates their gathering. They are there to celebrate the memory of the 'martyr' Nathuram Godse and to justify his crime to posterity. Aligned before Gopal's wrought-iron map, stirred by the strumming of a *sitar*, those unrepentant zealots thrust the open palms of their right hands into the air and swear before the ashes of Nathuram Godse to reconquer 'the vivisected portion of our motherland, all Pakistan, to reunite India under Hindu rule from the banks of the Indus where the sacred verses of the Vedas were composed, to the forests beyond the Brahmaputra'.

As he had maintained he would from the moment he accepted the appointment, Louis Mountbatten laid down his charge as independent India's first Governor-General in June 1948. His final weeks in India were absorbed with an unsuccessful effort to induce the one Indian prince who still sat upon his throne, the Nizam of Hyderabad, to abandon peacefully his pretensions of independence and accede to the Dominion of India.

The last official gesture of his wife Edwina was to visit two of the great refugee camps to whose inmates she had consecrated so much of her time and energy. By the thousands, the wretched inhabitants of those camps rushed to bid her farewell, honouring her departure with the only gift their poor existence permitted, the tears of genuine sorrow filling their eyes.

On the evening before they left, Jawaharlal Nehru honoured the couple at a farewell banquet in the formal dining hall of their old viceregal palace. Raising his glass to the couple to whom he was linked by so many bonds of friendship and affection, forged during the most memorable year of his life, he called for a toast to them both.

'Wherever you have gone,' he told Edwina Mountbatten, 'you have brought solace, you have brought hope and encouragement. Is it surprising therefore that the people of India should love you and look up to you as one of themselves.

'You came here, Sir,' he said to her husband, 'with a high reputation, but many a reputation has foundered in India. You have lived through a period of great difficulty and crisis, and yet your reputation has not foundered. That is a remarkable feat.'

His rival Patel added his words to Nehru's. 'What you have achieved in the way of friendship and goodwill,' he told the Mountbattens, 'emphasizes what your predecessors missed as a result of their aloofness and their failure to take into their confidence the leaders of public opinion.'

The following morning as the Mountbattens rode away from Lutyens' palace in the same gilded carriage as had delivered them to its ceremonial grand staircase fifteen months before, one of their six-horse team jibbed. At the sight of that balking animal refusing to advance, a voice called from the crowd the final accolade of their historic and tumultuous months in New Delhi: 'It is a sign from God. You must remain in India.'

The terrible disease a Bombay doctor had discovered on Mohammed Ali Jinnah's lungs ended his life in September 1948, just eight months after the murder of his old political foe, barely three months after the expiration of the death sentence his friend and physician had pronounced on him.

With the personal courage that had characterized all his actions, Jinnah laboured to secure the future of his cherished Pakistan as long as his resources allowed him to do so. He died in Karachi, his birthplace, the provisional capital of the great Islamic nation born because of his iron will, on 11 September 1948. Even in death, Jinnah remained faithful to his uncompromising self. At ten minutes to ten that evening, his doctor bent close to the dying Quaid and whispered: 'Sir, I have given you an injection. God willing you are going to live.'

Jinnah fixed his unwavering glare on the last sight his eyes would ever see, his doctor's face.

'No, I am not,' he firmly replied. Half an hour later he was dead.

His nation survived the difficult period that followed its birth, but the democratic institutions with which it had been endowed did not. A military *coup d'etat* led by Field-Marshal Ayub Khan in 1958 ended a series of corruption-plagued civilian regimes. After a decade of authoritarian but effective rule, Khan's regime was overthrown by another military *coup*.

The traumatic experience of the 1971 Bangladesh war, which realized Louis Mountbatten's prophecy that the union between the two halves of Pakistan would not last a quarter of a century, brought civilian rule back to Pakistan under Zulfikar Ali Bhutto. Dissident tribal factions in Baluchistan and along the Frontier which the British had found so difficult to control remain a constant concern to Pakistan's leaders. Nonetheless, with the more homogeneous nation that emerged from the Bangladesh war and the possibility of economic assistance from their oil-rich Moslem neighbours, Pakistanis could contemplate their nation's future in 1975 with greater serenity than at any time since its conception.

On a Karachi hilltop a superbly proud mausoleum shelters the burial site of Pakistan's founder, a strangely appropriate tribute from his people to the last of their Moghuls.

As Mahatma Gandhi had predicted, the terrible legacy of partition would trouble the sub-continent for years to come. Twice, in 1965 and 1971, the two nations sprung from a common womb would face each other on the battlefield. Their continuing conflict imposed a staggering burden of expenditure on them both, diverting their limited resources from the development of their hungry people to the sterile instruments of war.

Both nations accomplished in barely a decade the prodigious feat of resettling and integrating into a new existence their millions of refugees. The fertile fields of the Punjab, soaked with the blood of so many innocent victims in the autumn of 1947, found again the tints of happier days, the gold of wheat and mustard fields, the white of thick stands of cotton, the green of sugar cane plantations. In India, the province, animated largely by its Sikh population, made a major contribution to the Green Revolution which, before the searing droughts of the mid-seventies and the world petroleum crisis, had brought India to the threshold of the dream of generations: self-sufficiency in the production of food grains.

A return to prosperity, however, did not efface the bitter memories left by the nightmare of exodus. On both sides of the frontier created by Cyril Radcliffe's pencil a legacy of hatred, deep and malignant, remained. One unfortunate man, Boota Singh, the Sikh farmer who had purchased a Moslem girl fleeing her abductor, came to symbolize for millions of Punjabis the tragic aftermath of their conflict as well as the hope that ultimately man's enduring aptitude for happiness might overcome the hatred separating them.

Eleven months after their marriage a daughter was born to Boota Singh and Zenib, the wife he'd purchased for 1500 rupees. Following Sikh custom, Boota Singh opened the Sikh Holy Book, the *Granth Sahib*, at random and gave his daughter a name beginning with the first letter of the word he found at the top of the page. The letter was a 'T' and he chose Tanveer – Miracle of the Sky.

Several years later, a pair of Boota Singh's nephews, furious at losing a chance to inherit his property, reported Zenib's presence to the authorities who were trying to locate women abducted during the exodus. Zenib was wrenched from Boota Singh and placed in a camp while efforts were made to locate her family in Pakistan.

Desperate, Boota Singh rushed to New Delhi and accomplished at the Grand Mosque the most difficult act a Sikh could perform. He cut his hair and became a Moslem. Re-named Jamil Ahmed, Boota Singh presented himself at the office of Pakistan's High Commissioner and demanded the return of his wife. It was a useless gesture. The two nations had agreed that implacable rules would govern the exchange of abducted women: married or not, they would be returned to the families from which they had been forcibly separated.

For six months Boota Singh visited his wife daily in the detention camp. He would sit beside her in silence, weeping for their lost dream of happiness. Finally, he learned her family had been located. The couple embraced in a tearful farewell, Zenib vowing never to forget him and to return to him and their daughter as soon as she could.

The desperate Boota Singh applied for the right as a Moslem to immigrate to Pakistan. His application was refused. He applied for a visa. That too was refused. Finally, taking with him his daughter, renamed Sultana, he crossed the frontier illegally. Leaving the girl in Lahore, he made his way to the village where Zenib's family had settled. There he received a cruel shock. His wife had been remarried with a cousin only hours after the truck bringing her back from India had deposited her in the village. The poor man, weeping 'give me back my wife', was brutally beaten by Zenib's brothers and cousins, then handed over to the police as an illegal immigrant.

Brought to trial, Boota Singh pleaded he was a Moslem and begged the judge to return his wife to him. If only, he said, he could be granted the right to see his wife, to ask her if she would return to India with him and their daughter, he would be satisfied.

Moved by his plea, the judge agreed. The confrontation took place a week later in a courtroom overflowing with spectators alerted by newspaper reports of the case. A terrified Zenib, escorted by an angry and possessive horde of her relatives, was brought into the chamber. The judge indicated Boota Singh.

'Do you know this man?' he asked.

'Yes,' replied the trembling girl, 'he's Boota Singh, my first husband.' Then Zenib identified her daughter standing by the elderly Sikh.

'Do you wish to return with them to India?' the judge asked. Boota Singh turned his pleading eyes on the young girl who had brought so much happiness to his life. Behind Zenib, other eyes fixed on her quivering figure, a battery glaring at her from the audience, the male members of her clan warning her against trying to renounce the call of her blood. An atrocious tension gripped the courtroom. His lined face alive with a desperate hope, Boota Singh watched Zenib's lips, waiting for the favourable reply he was sure would come. For an unbearably long moment the room was silent.

Zenib shook her head. 'No,' she whispered.

A gasp of anguish escaped Boota Singh. He staggered back against the railing behind him. When he'd regained his poise, he took his daughter by the hand and crossed the room.

'I cannot deprive you of your daughter, Zenib,' he said. 'I leave her to you.' He took a clump of bills from his pocket and offered them to his wife, along with their daughter. 'My life is finished now,' he said simply.

The judge asked Zenib if she wished to accept his offer of the custody of their daughter. Again, an agonizing silence filled the courtroom. From their seats Zenib's male relatives furiously shook their heads. They wanted no Sikh blood defiling their little community.

Zenib looked at her daughter with the eyes of despair. To accept her would be to condemn her to a life of misery. An awful sob shook her frame. 'No,' she gasped.

Boota Singh, his eyes overflowing with tears, stood for a long moment looking at his weeping wife, trying perhaps to fix forever in his mind the blurred image of her face. Then he tenderly picked up his daughter and, without turning back, left the courtroom.

The despairing man spent the night weeping and praying in the mausoleum of the Moslem saint Data Gang Baksh, while his daughter slept against a nearby pillar. With the dawn, he took the girl to a nearby bazaar. There, using the rupees he'd tendered to his wife the afternoon before, he bought her a new robe and a pair of sandals embroidered in gold brocade. Then, hand in hand, the old Sikh and his daughter walked to the nearby railroad station of Shahdara. Waiting on the platform for the train to arrive, the weeping Boota Singh explained to his daughter that she would not see her mother again.

In the distance a locomotive's whistle shrieked. Boota Singh tenderly picked up his daughter and kissed her. He walked to the edge of the platform. As the locomotive burst into the station the little girl felt her father's arms tighten around her. Then suddenly she was plunging forward. Boota Singh had leapt into the path of the onrushing locomotive. The girl heard again the roar of the whistle mingled this time with her own screams. Then she was in the blackness beneath the engine.

Boota Singh was killed instantly, but by a miracle his daughter survived unscathed. On the old Sikh's mutilated corpse, the police found a blood-soaked farewell note to the young wife who had rejected him.

'My dear Zenib,' it said, 'you listened to the voice of the multitude, but that voice is never sincere. Still my last wish is to be with you. Please bury me in your village and come from time to time to put a flower on my grave.'

Boota Singh's suicide stirred a wave of emotion in Pakistan and his funeral became an event of national importance. Even in death, however, the elderly Sikh remained a symbol of those terrible days when the Punjab was in flames. Zenib's family and the inhabitants of their village refused to permit Boota Singh's burial in the village cemetery. The village males, led by Zenib's second husband, barred entrance to his coffin on 22 February 1957.

Rather than provoke a riot, the authorities ordered the coffin and the thousands of Pakistanis touched by Boota Singh's drama who'd followed it to return to Lahore. There, under a mountain of flowers, Boota Singh's remains were interred.

Zenib's family, however, enraged by the honour extended to Boota Singh, sent a commando to Lahore to uproot and profane his tomb. Their savage action provoked a remarkable outburst from the city's population. Boota Singh was re-interred under another mountain of flowers. This time hundreds of Moslems volunteered to guard the grave of the Sikh convert, illustrating by their generous gesture the hope that time might eventually efface in the Punjab the bitter heritage of 1947.*

India's memorial to her lost Mahatma was a simple black stone platform set upon the site at which his funeral pyre rested at the Raj Ghat on 31 January 1948. A few words in Hindi and in English on a plaque beside it bear Mohandas Gandhi's prescription for a free India.

'I would like to see India free and strong so that she may offer herself as a willing and pure sacrifice for the betterment of the world. The individual, being pure, sacrifices himself for the family, the latter for the village, the village for the district, the district for the province, the province for the nation, the nation for all. I want Khudai Raj, the kingdom of God on earth.'

Gandhi's vision, however, was to remain the impossible dream. His countrymen proved no less susceptible to the lures of technology and industrial progress than any other people. As he had feared they would in the last year of his life, his heirs turned their backs on his message. India chose to pursue the twentieth century's criteria of power and success, the development of a strong industrial society, instead of following the course Gandhi had tried to indicate with his spinning-wheel. Central planning, growth rate, basic industry, infrastructure, the take-off point, the revolution of rising expectations, the common language of a world yearning for material progress, became the vocabulary of an independent India's first generation of leaders. The interests of her half-million villages in which Gandhi proclaimed her salvation lay were subordinated to those of her towns and cities, slowly filling with the great industrial complexes for which Gandhi's successors yearned. The Congress Party Gandhi had hoped would become a People's Service League continued in its more conventional and comfortable role, remaining India's dominant political force, increasingly prey to the malady it had demonstrated in the first months of independence – corruption.

The most paradoxical gesture of all occurred in the spring of 1974 in the Rajasthan Desert. The government of the land whose most famous citizen had urged America to abandon the atomic bomb the day before he died, employing the resources of a country barely able to feed its population, exploded a nuclear device. That event, in the most dramatic of fashions, marked the final rejection by India of the doctrine of *ahimsa*, the accession of the land of the prophet

* Boota Singh's daughter, Sultana, was adopted and raised by foster parents in Lahore. Today, the mother of three children, she lives in Libya with her engineer husband.

of non-violence to the select circle of nations possessing the ultimate weapon in the arsenal of violence, the atomic bomb.

And yet, though India had not chosen to follow in the path of Mohandas Gandhi's impossible dream, she had not forsaken all his ideals either. The simple cotton *khadi* he urged upon his countrymen is still the uniform of many an Indian minister and bureaucrat, evidence that the man under it reveres at least the memory if not the message of the man who espoused it. That most elegant of men, Jawaharlal Nehru, continued until his death to wear the simple clothes in which Gandhi had dressed him. Sensitive to Gandhi's admonishment to government leaders to employ simplicity in style and restraint in example, he crossed the capital of his country, not in a Rolls-Royce, a Mercedes Benz or a Cadillac, but in a small Indian car with, as his only escort, the driver at its wheel.

Despite the fissiparous pressures of its multiplicity of languages, cultures and people, despite the cynical suggestion of many an Englishman that those forces would shatter its unity once the bonds of British rule were removed, Gandhi's India has remained what it became on 15 August 1947, a strong, united nation. The enormous areas and disparate peoples of her old princely states were integrated into India's administrative structure in relatively painless fashion.

Not a few of Gandhi's ideas which once appeared an old man's quirks have become, almost three decades after his death, strangely relevant in a world of dwindling resources and expanding populations. Cutting up old envelopes to make notepads rather than wasting paper, consuming only the food necessary to nourish one's frame, eschewing the heedless production of unneeded goods, began to appear by the seventies not so much a set of charming eccentricities as a prescription for man's uncertain future on his exhausted planet.

In one domain, above all, however, India would keep faith with the memory of the lean brown figure with the bamboo stave who'd led her famished millions to liberty. India was born a free nation: she would remain a free nation. After all her years of travail and struggle, despite the pressures induced by the relentless growth of her population, India remains what she became on that magic stroke of midnight, 14 August 1947, the world's most populous democracy. She, almost alone of the scores of nations who in their turn broke the chains binding them to their old colonial rulers, is a free society, respectful of the rights and dignity of its inhabitants, whose citizens have the right to dissent, to protest, to express themselves freely and openly in a free press, to select their government in free, secret, honest elections. She has resisted all temptations to follow the example of her Chinese neighbour, buying progress by reducing its millions to regimented robots, or the more numerous examples of cheapjack military dictatorships with their carefully coached crowds of cheering citizens and their equally carefully concealed torture chambers.

India's is an achievement of unsurpassed magnitude, worthy of the world's respect, worthy, above all, of the great leader who had led her to the liberty she had refused to cast away.*

Fifteen days after the immersion of Mahatma Gandhi's ashes, a brief ceremony in the shadows of the Gateway of India ended the era he had begun when he marched home from South Africa through that same archway in January 1915, his copy of *Hind Swaraj* under his arm. Saluted by an honour guard of Sikhs and Gurkhas, played off by an Indian Navy band, the last British soldiers left on the soil of an independent India, the men of the Somerset Light Infantry, passed under the gateway's soaring span and slow-marched down to its concrete landing.

As their figures disappeared through that triumphant archway, an incongruous sound rose above the crowd of Indians along the Bombay waterfront watching them go. It came first from a few scattered throats, then from others, until finally it burst from a thousand faces. Sadly moving, it was the strains of 'Auld Lang Syne'. Congress veterans, some of whose skulls still bore the scars of British *lathis*, weeping women in saris, teenage students, toothless old beggars, even the men of the Indian honour guard fixed at attention in their rigid ranks, all suddenly and intensely aware of the significance of the moment, joined the chorus. While the last of the Somersets stepped into their waiting barges, the sound of that spontaneous song rang across the esplanade of the Gateway of India, a poignant recessional for the Englishmen setting out to sea.

It was also a hymn to the memory of the little figure who'd walked up that concrete ramp on a winter morning so long ago. For, if an era was ending there at the Gateway of India, another was beginning, the one Gandhi had opened for three-quarters of the inhabitants of the earth, the era of decolonization. The last of the race of the captains and the kings were departing and the freshening breezes speeding them on their homeward journey were the heralds of those winds of change which would remake the map of the world and realign the balance of its forces in the next quarter of a century.

* This book went to press in June, 1975. Consequently it does not attempt to evaluate the events of that month or to measure their possible impact on the future of Indian democracy.

Because of Mohandas Gandhi and what he had wrought in India, many a spot on the globe would witness in the years to come a ceremony similar to the one that took place in Bombay on 28 February 1948.

Not many of them, however, would be marked by the goodwill manifested that morning in the shadows of that once triumphant arch of empire. It was the final accolade to India's murdered Mahatma, and to the Indians and Englishmen who had had the wisdom to seize the inexorable logic of his message.

What They Became

VALLABHBHAI PATEL

Patel suffered terribly in the weeks following Gandhi's assassination from a whispering campaign which insinuated that, as Home Minister, he shared in the responsibility for the police's failure to apprehend the Mahatma's killers between 20 January and his murder. Some of his political foes even circulated the wholly unfounded accusation that he had been indifferent to Gandhi's fate because of his own differences with him. The strain of that campaign of innuendo coming on top of the genuine grief the murder had produced in him, led to a major heart-attack in March 1948. Patel recovered and resumed his posts as Deputy Prime Minister and Home Minister. After Lord Mountbatten's departure, he organized and directed the 'police action' against Hyderabad which forcibly integrated the last of India's old princely states. His conflict with his old rival, Nehru, temporarily shelved in the months following Gandhi's assassination, broke out again in the beginning of 1950. Patel's death of a heart-attack on 15 December 1950, however, prevented it from leading to a public parting of the ways between the two men.

JAWAHARLAL NEHRU

Until his death in New Delhi on 27 May 1964, Nehru occupied the office he'd assumed on 15 August 1947. He emerged as an internationally respected statesman, one of the most familiar figures of what became known as the third world and the principal architect of the policy of non-alignment which engaged the support of most of the Afro-Asian nations that emerged from colonial tutelage in the fifties and sixties. He travelled extensively throughout the world, visiting most of Europe's capitals, the USA, the USSR and China. Domestically, he presided over three Indian Five-Year Plans designed to provide for his nation's industrial and social development; the consolidation of India's democratic institutions; and the forcible integration of the Portuguese enclave of Goa into the Indian Republic.

His most bitter disillusionment came in October 1962 with the massive Chinese invasion of his country's frontier in Ladakh above Kashmir and in the North East Frontier Agency between Tibet and Assam. Nehru never fully recovered from his shock at that action by the nation friendship for which had been the cornerstone of his foreign policy for fifteen years. From that moment his health faltered. He fell seriously ill in January 1964, recovered, but died four months later. Among those who rushed to New Delhi to attend his cremation was Louis Mountbatten. Appropriately the parting gift to his countrymen of that most eloquent of leaders was words, the words of his last will and testament now inscribed outside the Nehru Memorial Library in the grounds of the former residence of the Commander-in-Chief of the Indian Army in New Delhi. In them, he asked that his ashes be scattered from an aircraft 'over the fields where the peasants of India toil so that they might mingle with the dust of the soil of India and become an indistinguishable part of her . . .'

THE MOUNTBATTENS

In October 1948, Rear-Admiral Louis Mountbatten returned to active naval service, taking up in Malta the command of the First Cruiser Squadron for which he had been destined when he had been appointed Viceroy of India. The man who as Viceroy had ranked second only to the King Emperor in the British Empire found himself ranked thirteenth in Malta's social order of precedence.

His rise through the senior ranks of the navy was rapid and, on 18 April 1955, he realized his lifelong ambition. He was appointed First Sea Lord, the office from which his father had been hounded by the outcry of a narrow-minded public in 1914. As First Sea Lord, he presided over the modernization of the Royal Navy which brought Britain's Senior Service her first nuclear submarine and guided missile destroyers. In 1958, as Chief of the Defence Forces, he began his last major official task, the reorganization of the British Armed Forces and their integration into a unified Defence Establishment.

Mountbatten left active service in 1965 and now divides his time between his estate, Broadlands, on the edge of Romsey, a London flat and a castle in Ireland. To the dismay of his daughters and doctors, he retains undiminished, on the eve of his seventy-fifth birthday, his consuming appetite for work. He is an active member of almost 200 organizations, their nature as diverse as the Institute of Naval Architects, the Institute of Electronic and Radio Engineers, the London Zoological Society, the Magic Circle, the Society of Genealogists, a Maltese skin-diving group, and the Royal Thames Yacht Club.

His principal activities, however, are concerned with the National Electronics Council, of which he is the Chairman, and the United

World College, which maintains over 1500 students on campuses in England, Canada and Singapore.

He maintains a close and active interest in India. In 1969 he served as Chairman of the Gandhi Centenary Year, addressing the Remembrance Service which opened it at Saint Paul's Cathedral on 30 January of that year. He helped to raise and administer the Jawaharlal Nehru Fund created to honour the memory of his old friend by sending Indian scholars to study in the United Kingdom.

Almost every day the postman delivers some plea from an Indian to his desk. These authors, perhaps, or maharajas and generals, bearers and bankers, are seeking an introduction to someone in England, or asking assistance in unravelling the complications of a pension fund or the regulations governing immigration to the UK. Diverse, touching and never-ending, that flow of letters is evidence of a strong tradition: India's last Viceroy has become, in a sense, her first Ombudsman.

Edwina Mountbatten continued to devote herself to the Red Cross and the St John Ambulance Brigade, serving both with an energy she refused to diminish even after being warned by her doctors that she was exhausting herself. Four days after the wedding of her younger daughter Pamela in February 1960 she left on a tour of the Far East in her capacity as superintendent of St John. Despite her evident exhaustion, she refused any curtailment of her busy schedule and died in Borneo after having attended a reception offered in her honour on 21 February 1960. When the news of her death was announced on the floor of the Indian Parliament, its members rose to offer her memory the spontaneous tribute of a moment of silence.

Four days after her death, as requested in her will, she was buried at sea off Spithead. Escorting the British frigate *Wakeful* which took her to her burial place was the Indian frigate *Trishul*, a poignant parting gesture from the nation she had loved to the last of the *memsahibs*.

THE POLICEMEN

Two of the principal figures in the investigation into Gandhi's murder survive: D. W. Mehra and 'Jimmy' Nagarvalla, the man who conducted the investigation in Bombay. Both are retired. Mehra is an executive with a brewery outside Delhi. Nagarvalla engages in a commerce curious for a man who devoted most of his life to pursuing fugitives. He runs a travel agency.

THE MAHARAJAS

The princes who once ruled a third of India's people have faded so totally from the scene that their days of glory now seem as distant as those of the Moghuls. Their palaces have become museums, schools, hotels, or crumbling ruins. Some have gone abroad, some into business, or government service. A few, like the Raj Matas of Gwalior and Jaipur, are active in politics. After three years of struggle, the Indian Supreme Court in the spring of 1973 upheld a constitutional amendment promoted by Indira Gandhi's government which terminated the concessions the princes had been granted in 1947 in return for their peaceful accession to the Indian Union. The flock of gilded peacocks has disappeared for ever from the Indian skyline.

Acknowledgements

As was the case with two of our previous books, *Is Paris Burning?* and *O Jerusalem!*, *Freedom at Midnight* is the result of almost three years of long and patient research. The trail over which our work took us was difficult, often physically trying, but never dull. Eventually, it brought us into contact with almost 500 people, Indians, Pakistanis, Englishmen and women, took us over 6000 miles from the Khyber Pass to Fort St George in Madras, from the *bustees* of Calcutta to quiet villages in Sussex and Kent.

Inevitably that trail began at the doorstep of the sole survivor of the quintet of great men largely responsible for the sub-continent's destinies in 1947, Admiral of the Fleet the Earl Mountbatten of Burma. Over the course of fifteen tape-recorded interviews in 1972–3, the last Viceroy of India permitted himself to be subjected to the most painstaking and exhaustive review of his Indian experiences to which he has ever been exposed. The result of those interviews alone covered almost thirty hours of tape and 600 typewritten pages; they therefore constitute in themselves a unique record of the Mountbatten viceroyalty.

The last Viceroy retains in his possession what is probably the most extensive collection of documents and papers in the world relating to his viceroyalty and the period following India's independence. By nature a very meticulous man, Lord Mountbatten has retained in those archives every paper relevant to the period, including materials as diverse as the hand-written note sent to him by his cousin the King on his departure for India and the menus and seating arrangements for his state dinners. There is, however, a series of five sets of documents which are the indispensable historical record of the period. They are:

(1) The record of Lord Mountbatten's conversations with everyone who entered his office and particularly with the key Indian leaders: Gandhi, Nehru, Jinnah and Patel. As explained on page 83, Lord Mountbatten met alone with these men, limiting his talks to 45 minutes and dictating a summary of his conversation to a secretary as soon as each man left. The summaries of these conversations are vivid, detailed, and appear today almost as fresh as at the moment they were dictated;
(2) The minutes of his almost daily meetings with his staff at which the Viceroy had the habit of unburdening himself with great frankness;
(3) The minutes of the meetings of the Emergency Committee of the Indian Cabinet over which he presided during the crisis in the Punjab;
(4) His seventeen weekly reports together with the extensive annexes to the Secretary of State during his service as Viceroy;
(5) His Monthly Report to the King during his period as Governor-General.

Lord Mountbatten was able to refer constantly to that material during the hours of our work together, as a means of refreshing his own memory and providing an authentic and historically valid guide to his activities in India. Our thanks, therefore, must go first and foremost to Lord Mountbatten.

We also owe a special debt of gratitude to two members of his personal staff; John Barratt, his Private Secretary, and Mrs Mollie Travis, the Archivist of the Broadlands Archives, both of whom were particularly generous in the time and effort they devoted to our behalf. Lord Mountbatten's two daughters, Lady Brabourne and Lady Pamela Hicks, were both kind enough to reminisce with us about their parents and, in Lady Pamela's case, about her experiences with them in India. Lord Brabourne, himself the son of a former Governor of Bombay and Bengal provinces, who was for a month Viceroy, kindly gave us his agreement as the principal trustee of the Broadlands Archives to work in those areas which concerned us.

The surviving members of Lord Mountbatten's staff in India in 1947–8 were without exception most generous with their time, submitting themselves agreeably to our long and exhaustive interviews, interviews which in many cases concerned three or four tape-recorded sessions of at least two hours each. Not only did they patiently comb through their memories of the time, but they also searched attics and country houses for diaries dating back to 1947, letters written to wives and parents recounting their experiences, all of which were immensely valuable to us in reconstituting the atmosphere of those remarkable days.

Alan Campbell-Johnson, Lord Mountbatten's press attaché in 1947–8 and the author of a remarkable, first-hand account of the period, *Mission with Mountbatten*, was particularly helpful. So too were Sir George Abell, his brilliant private secretary; Vice-Admiral Sir Ronald Brockman, personal secretary to the Viceroy; Rear-Admiral Peter Howes, Lord Mountbatten's senior ADC; Elizabeth Collins and Muriel Watson, Lady Mountbatten's secretaries whose recollections of the last Vicereine were particularly helpful; G. Vernon Moore, a member of the Viceroy's secretariat, who provided us with most helpful descriptions; Lt-Col Martin Gilliat, the Assistant Military Secretary; his ADCs Lt-Col Frederick Burnaby-Atkins, Flt-Lt the Hon. W. H. C. Wentworth Beaumont, now Lord Allendale, and Sir James Scott. All gave us valuable and informal glimpses into the workings of Viceroy's House in 1947.

We owe a very particular debt to that remarkable and extraordinary man who has left his imprimatur on so many of the key legal studies of his time, the Rt Hon. Viscount Radcliffe. Within the limitations he has always imposed in talking of his award – declining to discuss the reasoning that led him to any particular decision – he was notably frank and helpful during the course of two long interviews.

Our work on the Indian Army brought us into contact with numerous veterans of that remarkable organization: General Robert Lockhart; General Sir Roy Bucher; the late General Sir Frank Messervy, first

Commander-in-Chief of the Pakistan Army; Lt-Col John R. Platt, who commanded the Somerset Light Infantry when it became the last unit of the British Army to leave the soil of an independent India; Col E. S. Birnie, who furnished us with an account of the last months in the life of Mohammed Ali Jinnah whom he had the honour of serving as first Military Secretary.

It was also our pleasure and privilege to be able to meet and interview a number of that company which guided India's destinies for three-quarters of a century, the ICS. We are particularly grateful to Sir Olaf Caroe, the last Governor of the North-West Frontier Province, probably the West's outstanding authority on the Pathan tribesmen he loved and served so long; Sir Conrad Corfield, the last shepherd of India's Princes, and his principal deputy, Sir Herbert Thompson; Lord Trevelyan who, as Humphrey Trevelyan, was the author of a fascinating account of his life as a young ICS officer in India, *The India We Left*; Judge H. C. Beaumont, Lord Radcliffe's ICS aide; and Maurice and Taya Zinkin, who were kind enough to read us their enthralling diary written during Delhi's troubled September of 1947.

Among the many others whose assistance was invaluable were the Earl of Listowel, Britain's last Secretary of State for India; Sir Alexander Symon, Britain's first Deputy High Commissioner to an independent India; and Mr G. R. Savage, who provided a fascinating account of the plot to kill Jinnah and Mountbatten in Karachi on 14 August 1947. Gerald MacKnight kindly furnished much material on post-war London.

In France we owe a special debt of gratitude to the Baron and Baroness Geoffroy de Courcel who, as France's Ambassador and Ambassadress in London, most kindly provided the auspices for our first meeting with Lord Mountbatten. Alain and France Danet also opened for us many doors.

We are also indebted to Francis Deloche de Noyelle and Jean Badbedat of the Quai d'Orsay for their assistance, and to Max Olivier-Lacamp and Paul Guerin, both correspondents in India in 1947, for the accounts furnished of their experiences. Both are themselves authors of remarkable works of the period, *Impasse Indienne* by Olivier-Lacamp, and *Les Indes Familières* by Guerin.

In India we are first of all indebted to Prime Minister Indira Gandhi who so graciously recorded with us her recollections of her father Jawaharlal Nehru and her own experiences in 1947; and to her aunt, Mrs V. L. Pandit, Mr Nehru's sister, who provided us with an invaluable insight into her brother's character. Four of his former private secretaries: M. A. Baig, M. O. Mathai, Tarlok Singh and H. V. R. Iyenagar, also contributed important recollections of him, as did Russy K. and Aileen Karanjia.

Among the many other people whose assistance was particularly helpful was the late Krishna Menon; General and Mrs D. W. Mehra, the son and daughter-in-law of V. P. Menon; Miss Maniben Patel, daughter of Vallabhbhai Patel, whose recollections of her experiences with her father were invaluable; his late Highness the Maharaja Yadavindra Singh of

Patiala; their Highnesses the Raj Matas of Jaipur and Gwalior; Dr Karan Singh, son of the Maharaja of Kashmir; Inspector-General of Police Ashwini Kumar, who furnished us a fascinating account of his experiences as a young police officer in the Punjab in 1947; Mr Kushwant Singh, the author of a brilliant novel of the 1947 massacres, *Train to Pakistan*; Mrs Dina Wadia, the daughter of Mohammed Ali Jinnah, for her recollections of her father; and his doctor, Dr J. A. L. Patel; Mrs Sulochna Panigrahi for a particularly moving account of India's Independence Day; Acharya Kripalani, the last survivor of the principal Indian figures in the independence struggle; Miss Padmaja Naidu, who provided a number of trenchant observations; Mr M. S. Oberoi, for his recollections of life in old Simla; Rajeshwar Dayal, who offered an interesting perspective on the life of an ICS officer seen through Indian eyes; the 'Lion of Kashmir', Sheikh Abdullah, for his recollections of the tribal invasion; Sir Chandulal Trivedi, ICS, the first Indian Governor of the Punjab, for his vital account of the exodus and massacres. Naval and Simone Tata, Nari H. Dastur, Harry and Salina Nedou and Patwand Singh all sustained us with their help and friendship.

For our material on Gandhi we owe a very special debt to Mr Pyarelal Nayar, his secretary, who sat through five gruelling interviews. He is himself the author of what is beyond any doubt the most complete work on the last phase of Gandhi's life, a monumental three-volume study called *Mahatma Gandhi – The Last Phase*. We are also particularly indebted to his sister Sushila, Gandhi's physician, and his devoted aide, Brikshen Chandiwallah. An account of our dealings with the surviving members of the group of men who killed him will be found in the notes dealing with the chapter on his assassination.

We also wish to acknowledge a debt to a very special group of men, who not only helped us enormously in our work but were also delightful and stimulating companions, a number of officers of the Indian Army: General Jangu T. Sataravala, whose hospitality we shall always remember; General J. N. Chaudhuri; General M. J. Chopra, whose name is engraved at the border crossing at Waga between India and Pakistan; General Harbaksh Singh. Finally, no account of our stay in India would be complete without a special word of thanks to Ambassador and Madame Jean Daniel Jurgensen, France's charming representatives in New Delhi, who were so kind to us; to Francis Doré, France's remarkable Cultural Attaché in India's capital; to Florence Prouverelle, our old friend of other days, who is now Press Attaché at the French Embassy in New Delhi; and to René and Claude de Choiseul-Praslin and Francis and Annick Wacziarg who made our visits to Bombay so agreeable.

Among the many Pakistani personalities who made important contributions to our work and to whom we would like to address our particular thanks are Admiral Syed Ahsan, a naval ADC to both Lord Mountbatten and to Mohammed Ali Jinnah, who gave us an intimate insight into the Quaid-i-Azzam's momentous journey to his new nation; Badshah Khan, the 'Frontier Gandhi', still alert despite the burden of his years; A. I. S. Dara, who was both a charming and hospitable friend and invaluable source of information on happenings in Lahore in the summer and autumn of 1947; Ambassador Yacoub Khan, who gave us his touching and vivid account of his decision to opt for Pakistan; Ambassador Akhbar Khan and Sairab Khayat Khan, both of whom offered unique, first-hand accounts of the tribal invasion of Kashmir; Begum Feroz Khan Noon, a most gracious hostess who kindly recounted for us in detail her remarkable adventure in the Punjab in 1947; Chaudry Mohammed Ali, who together with his Indian colleague H. M. Patel with whom he had worked in India was responsible for that prodigious task of dividing the assets of the subcontinent.

These, of course, are only a few among the many without whose help, encouragement and time this book would never have been possible. Space prevents us from acknowledging the real debt that we owe to them all: English missionaries, retired army officers, businessmen, civil servants, scholars, leaders of the Congress and Moslem League, schoolteachers, journalists, hundreds of refugees from both sides who endured the agony of recounting to us in all its horror their recollections of the exodus of 1947, many dear friends, both Indian and Pakistani, who requested us not to mention their names. To all of them, wherever they are, go our thanks, and with them the assurance that their assistance has not been forgotten.

One closing word, a gesture of gratitude to four gentlemen, Messrs Thernisien and Luquet of Air France in New Delhi, Messrs Vaish and de Gironde of Air India and Pakistan International Airways, all of whom were most helpful in helping us unravel the complexities of our numerous travel arrangements, as was our friend M. Hobherg.

In the task of collating the material uncovered in our research, arranging it in systematic fashion, and writing the manuscript, it was our immense good fortune to have as comrades and associates a team of remarkably able people. Key among them was Mlle Dominique Conchon for whom *Freedom at Midnight* was the third of our books on which she has worked. As always her work was invaluable, her spirit indefatigable. She supervised the complex task of organizing our research material so that never in a year of writing did we misplace even one of the 6342 pages of research with which we had to contend.

Working with her was a charming newcomer to our team, Julia Bizieau. With unfailing good cheer, she stood by us through the long months of research and writing, a constantly engaging friend and companion, ably seconding Mlle Conchon, ready to take on any task. Among our researchers we would like to thank particularly Michel Renouard, Professor of English Literature at the University of Rennes, who devoted his summer holiday in 1972 to conducting interviews for us in Great Britain. It was for us an especially moving reunion; Michel, as a 17-year-old student, was the first researcher to become associated with us when we began work on *Is Paris Burning?*

Jeannie Nagy transcribed for us many hours of tape-recorded interviews, bringing to the task the most alert Scottish ear in the South of France. Jeanne Conchon, Michel Foucher, Jacqueline de la Cruz and Marjorie Rolt all laboured with us at one time or another in the preparation of our final manuscript.

We must acknowledge with sadness a special debt to the late Raymond Cartier of *Paris Match*. He first encouraged us on the road to *Freedom at Midnight*. Twice during the last months of his life he read the manuscript, offering on both occasions the most helpful and constructive of criticisms. It is our regret that he could not have lived long enough to read these final pages of a manuscript to which he contributed so much.

We owe, too, a special debt of gratitude to Nadia Collins who devoted long hours to translating cheerfully and ably our English text into French. Paul Andreota, Pierre Peuchmaurd, Colette Modiano, author of *Twenty Snobs in China*, now preparing a book on Queen Victoria, Pierre Amado and Francis Doré all found the time to read the French manuscript of *Freedom at Midnight*, each offering helpful comments and criticisms.

Finally to Michael Korda and Dan Green of Simon and Schuster, Robert Laffont and Daniel Marmet at Editions Laffont, Philip Ziegler and Michael Hyde at Collins, Mario Lacruz in Madrid, Donato Barbone in Milan, Andreas Hopf in Munich, Narencha Kuman in Delhi and our old friend and agent Irvine Lazer, go our thanks for their sure support through the difficult months that led to *Freedom at Midnight*.

L.C.
D.L.P.
La Biche Niche
Les Bignolles
Ramatuelle, France
3 March 1975

Bibliography

I BOOKS

ABBAS, K. Ahmad, *A Report to Gandhi*. Bombay: Hind Kitabs, 1947.
I Write as I Feel – I – The Atom Bomb
II – Lahore
ACKERLEY, J. R., *Intermède Hindou*. Paris: Gallimard, 1935.
ALI, Chaudhri Muhammad, *The Emergence of Pakistan*. New York: Columbia University Press, 1967.
ANAND, Balwant Singh, *Cruel Interlude*. Inde: Asia Publishing House, 1961.
ANARYAN, *A Group of Hindoo Stories*. London: W. H. Allen & Co., 1881.
ANWAR, Muhammed, *Jinnah Quaid-e-Azam, A Selected Biography*. Karachi: National Publishing House Limited, 1970.
ASHE, Geoffrey, *Gandhi – A Study in Revolution*. Bombay: Asia Publishing House, 1968.
ATAL, Amarnath, *The Maharajah of Jaipur – 1922–1947*. Allahabad: The Allahabad Law Journal Press.
AZAD, Maulana Abul Kalam, *India Wins Freedom*. New York: Longmans, Green & Co., 1960.
BAIG, M. R. A., *Muslim Dilemma in India*. Delhi: Vikas Publishing House PVT Ltd, 1974.
BAMM, Peter, *Alexandre le Grand*. Bruxelles: Elsevier–Sequoia, 1969.
BAREAU, André, *Bouddha*. Paris: Editions Seghers, 1962.
BARY de, Théodore, *Sources of Indian Tradition*. New York: Columbia University Press, 1968 (2 volumes).
BETTELHEIM, Charles, *L'Inde Indépendante*. Paris: Armand Cohen, 1962.
BHAITACHARYA, Sachchidananda, *A Dictionary of Indian History*. New York: George Braziller, 1967.
BIARDEAU, Madeleine, *Clefs pour la Penseé Hindoue*. Paris: Seghers, 1972.
BIRKENHEAD, Lord, *Walter Monckton – The Life of Viscount Monckton of Brenchley*. London: Weidenfeld & Nicolson, 1969.
BOLITHO, Hector, *Jinnah – The Creator of Pakistan*. London: John Murray, 1954.
BOURKE-WHITE, Margaret, *Halfway to Freedom*. New York: Simon & Schuster, 1949.
BRECHER, Michael, *Nehru – A Political Biography*. Boston: Beacon Press, 1970.
BRECKNOCK, The Countess of, *Edwina Mountbatten – Her Life in Pictures*. London: Macdonald, 1961.
CAMERON, James, *An Indian Summer*. London: Macmillan and Co. Ltd, 1973.
CAMPBELL, Alexander, *The Heart of India*. New York: Alfred A. Knopf, 1958.
CAMPBELL-JOHNSON, Alan, *Mission with Mountbatten*. London: Robert Hale Ltd, 1951.
CAROE, Olaf, *The Pathans*. London: Macmillan & Co. Ltd, 1964.
CHANDIWALA, Brijkrishna, *At the Feet of Bapu*. Ahmedabad: Navajivan Publishing House, 1954.
CHATTERJI, Usha, *La Femme dans L'Inde*. Paris: Plon, 1964.
CONNELL, Brian, *Manifest Destiny – A Study in Five Profiles of the Rise and Influence of the Mountbatten Family*. London: Cassell and Co. Ltd, 1953.
COOLIDGE, Olivia, *Gandhi*. Boston: Houghton Mifflin Co., 1971.
COOMARASWAMY, Ananda K., *The Dance of Shiva*. New York: H. Wolff, 1957.

CORBETT, Jim, *Man-Eaters of Kumaon.* London: Geoffrey Cumberlege Oxford University Press, 1946.

COUPLAND, R., *The Cripps Mission.* New York: Oxford University Press, 1942.

CROCKER, Walter, *Nehru – A Contemporary's Estimate.* New York: Oxford University Press, 1966.

DANIELOU, Alain, *Histoire de L'Inde.* Paris: Fayard, 1971.

DAS, Durga, *India from Curzon to Nehru and After.* London: Wm. Collins Sons & Co., Ltd., 1969.

DASS, Diwan Jarmani, *Maharaja – Lives and Loves and Intrigues of Indian Princes.* Allied Publishers (P) Ltd, 1970.

DASS, Diwan Jarmani and Rakesh Bhan, *Maharani – Love Adventures of Indian Maharanis and Princesses.* New Delhi: S. Chand & Co., 1972.

DORE, Francis, *L'Inde d'Aujourd'hui.* Paris: Presses Universitaires de France, 1974.

Les Régimes Politiques en Asie. Paris: Presses Universitaires de France, 1973.

DOWSON, John, *A Classical Dictionary of Hindu Mythology and Religion, Geography, History and Literature.* London: Routledge & Kegan Paul Ltd, 1968.

DRIEBERG, Trevor, *Indira Gandhi – A Profile in Courage.* New Delhi: Vikas Publishing House PVT Ltd, 1973.

DUBE, S. C., *Indian Village.* London: Routledge & Kegan Paul Ltd, 1955.

DUBOIS, J. A., *Hindu Manners, Customs and Ceremonies.* Oxford: At the Clarendon Press, 1906.

DUGGAL, Kartar Singh, *Banked Fires and Other Stories.* Bombay: Pearl Publications Private Ltd, 1969.

Death of a Song and Other Stories. New Delhi: Arnold-Heinemann, 1973.

Nails and Flesh. Bombay: Pearl Publications Private Ltd, 1969.

EDWARDES, Michael, *The Last Years of British India.* London: Cassell & Co. Ltd, 1963.

EGLAR, Zekige, *A Punjabi Village in Pakistan.* New York: Columbia University Press, 1960.

ELLIOTT, Maj. Gen. J. G., *The Frontier 1839–1947.* London: Cassell, 1968.

ERIKSON, Erik H., *Gandhi's Truth – On the Origins of Militant Non-Violence.* New York, W. W. Norton & Co. Inc., 1969.

ESCARPIT, Robert, *Rudyard Kipling.* Paris: Hachette, 1970.

FISCHER, Louis, *The Life of Mahatma Gandhi.* New York: Harper & Row, 1950.

FORBES, Rosita, *India of the Princes.* London: The Book Club, 1939.

FREDERIC, Louis, *L'Inde au Fil des Jours.* Paris: S.C.E.M.I., 1963.

GANDHI, Manuben, *Last Glimpses of Bapu.* Delhi: Shiva Lal Agarwala & Co., 1962.

GANDHI, Mohandas Karamchand, *An Autobiography* or *The Story of My Experiment with Truth.* Boston: Beacon Press, 1970.

GAUBA, K. L., *Assassination of Mahatma Gandhi.* Bombay: Jaico Publishing House, 1969.

GAVI, Philippe, *Le Triangle Indien – De Bandoeng au Bangladesh.* Paris: Le Seuil, 1972.

GHOSH, Sudhir, *Gandhi's Emissary – A Nonconformist's Inside Story of India's Past Twenty Years.* Boston: Houghton Mifflin Co, 1967.

GOLISH, Vitold de, *L'Inde Impudique des Maharajahs.* Paris: Robert Laffont, 1973.

Splendeur et Crépuscule des Maharajahs. Paris: Hachette, 1963.

GORWALA, A. D., *The Queen of Beauty and Other Tales.* Bombay: A. D. Gorwala, 1971.

GRANT, W. J. *The Spirit of India.* London: B. T. Batsford Ltd, 1938.

GRIFFITHS, Percival J., *The British Impact on India.* London: MacDonald, 1952. *The British in India.* London: Robert Hale Ltd, 1946.

GROSS, John, *Rudyard Kipling – The Man, His Work and His World.* London: Weidenfeld and Nicolson, 1972.

GUERIN, Paul, *A l'Affut de Gandhi.* Paris: (Emission de la Radiodiffusion Française du 30/01/49).

Les Indes Familières. Paris: Edition des Deux Artisans, 1950.

HODIWALA, Shapurji Kavasji, *History of Holy Iranshah (Extracts).* Bombay: Godrej M. Printing Press, 1966.

HODSON, H. V., *The Great Divide – Britain – India – Pakistan.* London: Hutchinson and Co., 1969.

HUTTON, J. H. *Caste in India – Its Nature, Function, and Origins.* Cambridge University Press, 1946.

ISMAY, Lord, *The Memoirs of General Lord Ismay.* London: Heinemann, 1960.

JAIN, J. C., *The Murder of Mahatma Gandhi – Prelude and Aftermath.* Bombay: Chetana Ltd, 1961.

JONES, Stanley, *Mahatma Gandhi – An Interpretation.* London: Hodder & Stoughton, 1948.

KAMENSKY, Anna, *La Bhagavad-Gita (Le Chant du Seigneur).* France: Editions J. B. Janin, 1947.

KARANJIA, R. K., *The Mind of Mr Nehru.* London: George Allen & Unwin Ltd, 1960.

The Philosophy of Mr Nehru. London: George Allen & Unwin Ltd, 1966.

KHAN, Akhbar, *Raiders in Kashmir – Story of the Kashmir War 1947–48.* Karachi: Pakistan Publishers Ltd, 1970.

KHOSLA, Gopal Das, *The Murder of the Mahatma and Other Cases from a Judge's Notebook.* Bombay: Jaico Books, 1963.

KINCAID, Dennis, *British Social Life in India – 1608–1937.* London and Boston: Routledge & Kegan Paul Ltd, 1973.

KIPLING, Rudyard, *Le Chat Maltais.* Paris: Mercure de France, 1927.

Le Livre de la Jungle and *Le Second Livre de la Jungle* (2 vols.). Paris: Mercure de France, 1930.

KRIPALANI, Krishna, *Gandhi, A Life.* New Delhi: Orient Longmans, 1969.

LACOMBE, O., *Gandhi ou la Force de l'Ame.* Paris: Plon, 1964.

LACY, Creighton, *The Conscience of India.* New York: Holt, Rinehart and Winston, 1965.

LAKSHMANNA, C., *Caste Dynamics in Village India.* Bombay: Nachiketa Publications Ltd, 1973.

LASSIER, Suzanne, *Gandhi et la Non-Violence.* Paris: Editions du Seuil, 1970.

LE BOURGEOIS, Jacques, *L'Inde aux Cent Couleurs.* Paris: Hachette, 1935.

LLEWELLYN, Bernard, *From the Back Streets of Bengal.* London: George Allen & Unwin Ltd, 1955.

LORD, John, *The Maharajahs.* New York: Random House, 1971.

LOTHIAN, Arthur Cunningham, *Kingdoms of Yesterday.* London: John Murray, 1951.

MAHADEVAN, T. M. P., *Outlines of Hinduism.* Bombay: Chetana Ltd, 1956.

MAJUMDAR, S. K., *Jinnah and Gandhi – Their Role in India's Quest for Freedom.* Calcutta: Firma K. L. Mukhopadhyay, 1966.

MALRAUX, André, *Antimémoires*. Paris: Gallimar NRF, 1967.
MASANI, R. P., *Britain in India*. London: Oxford University Press, 1960.
MASON, Philip, *Matter of Honour – An Account of the Indian Army – Its Officers and Men*. London: Jonathan Cape, 1974.
MASSON, Madeleine, *Edwina, The Biography of the Countess Mountbatten of Burma*. London: Robert Hale Ltd, 1958.
MAULE, Henry, *Spearhead General – The Epic Story of General Sir Frank Messervy and his Men in Eritrea, North Africa and Burma*. London: Transworld Publishers, 1961.
MEGRET, Christian, *Les Chimères Bleues de Chandernagor*. Paris: Robert Laffont, 1964.
MEHTA, Krishna, *This Happened in Kashmir*. Delhi: Publications Division, 1966. (Ministry of Information and Broadcasting Government of India.)
MEHTA, Ved, *Portrait of India*. New Delhi: Vikas Publications, 1971.
Walking the Indian Streets. New Delhi: Vikas Publications, 1972.
MENON, V. P., *The Transfer of Power in India*. Princeton: Princeton University Press, 1957.
MITRA, Asok, *Delhi Capital City*. New Delhi: Thomson Press, 1970.
MOON, Penderel, *Divide and Quit*. London: Chatto and Windus, 1961.
Gandhi and Modern India. New York: W. W. Norton & Co. Inc., 1969.
MOORHOUSE, Geoffrey, *Calcutta*. London: Weidenfeld and Nicolson, 1971.
MORRIS, James, *Pax Britannica*. London: Faber & Faber, 1968.
MOSLEY, Leonard, *The Glorious Fault*. New York: Harcourt, Brace and Company, 1960.
The Last Days of the British Raj. London: Weidenfeld & Nicolson, 1961.
NAIR, Kusum, *Blossoms in the Dust – The Human Element in Indian Development*. India: Allied Publishers Private Ltd, 1961.
NANDA, B. R., *Mahatma Gandhi – A Biography*. London: George Allen & Unwin Ltd, 1965.
NAYAR, Kuldip, *Distant Neighbours – A Tale of the Subcontinent*. Delhi: Vikas Publishing House, 1972.
India – The Critical Years. Delhi: Vikas Publications – (c) Weidenfeld & Nicolson, 1971.
NEHRU, Jawaharlal, *An Autobiography*. India: Allied Publishers Private Ltd, 1962.
The Discovery of India. New York: The John Day Company, 1946.
India's Freedom. London: Unwin Books, 1965.
Ma Vie et mes Prisons, Paris: Denoël, 1952.
Toward Freedom – The Autobiography of J. Nehru. New York: The John Day Company, 1941.
NICHOLS, Beverley, *L'Inde Secrète*. Paris: Jules Tallandier, 1946.
NOON, Feroz Khan, *From Memory*. Lahore: Editions Feroz Sons Ltd, 1969.
OLIVIER-LACAMP, Max, *Impasse Indienne*. Paris: Flammarion, 1963.
Les Deux Asies. Paris: Grasset, 1966.
PAYMASTER, Rustom Burjorji, *Early History of the Parsees in India*. Bombay: Zartoshti Dharam Sambandhi, 1954.
PRIVAT, Edmond, *Aux Indes avec Gandhi*. Paris: Denoël, 1960.
Vie de Gandhi. Gèneve: Labor et Fides, 1949.
PYARELAL, *Mahatma Gandhi – The Early Phase*. Ahmedabad: Navajivan House, 1965.
Mahatma Gandhi – The Last Phase. Ahmedabad: Navajivan House, 1965. (2 vols.)

RAI, Satya M., *Partition of the Punjab – A Study of Its Effects On the Politics and Administration of the Punjab. 1947–1956*. New Delhi: Indian School of International Studies, 1965.
RAO, Shiva B., *India's Freedom Movement*. Delhi: Orient Longman's, 1972.
ROBINSON, Donald H., *The Raj*. Greenwich (Conn.): Fawcett Publications, Inc., 1971.
ROLLAND, Romain, *Gandhi et Romain Rolland* (*Correspondence, Extraits du Journal et Textes Divers*). Paris: Albin Michel, 1960.
SAHNI, J. N., *The Lid Off*. New Delhi: Allied Publishers, 1971.
SATPREM, *Par le Corps de la Terre ou le Sannyasin*. Paris: Robert Laffont, 1974.
SAVARKAR, V. D., *Hindutva – Who Is a Hindu?* Bombay: Veer Savarkar Prakashan, 1969.
SAYEED, Khalid B., *Pakistan – The Formative Phase 1857–1948*. London: Oxford University Press, 1968.
SCHMID, Peter, *India – Mirage and Reality*. London: George G. Harrap, 1961.
SEN, L. P., *Slender Was the Thread*. Bombay: Orient Longmans, 1969.
SHEEAN, Vincent, *Lead, Kindly Light*. London: Cassell & Co., 1950.
Mahatma Gandhi – A Great Life in Brief. New York: Alfred Knopf, 1970.
SHUJAUDDIN, Muhammad, *The Life and Times of Noor Jahan*. Lahore: The Caravan Book House, 1967.
SINGH, Joginder, *Sikh Ceremonies*. Chaudigarh: Sikh Religious Book Society, 1968.
SINGH, Karan, *Contemporary Essays*. Bombay: Bharatiya Vidya Bhavan, 1971.
Prophet of Indian Nationalism. Bombay: Bharatiya Vidya Bhavan, 1970.
SINGH, Kushwant, *India – A Mirror For Its Monsters and Monstrosities*. Bombay: IBH Publishing Company, 1969.
The Sikhs Today. Bombay: Orient Longmans, 1967.
Last Train to Pakistan. London: Chatto & Windus Ltd, 1956.
SINGH, Parkash, *Guru Nanak and His Japji*. Jullundur: Swan Printing Press, 1969.
SINHA, Durganaud, *Indian Villages in Transition – A Motivational Analysis*. New Delhi: Associated Publishing House, 1969.
SPEAR, Percival, *A History of India*. London: Penguin Books, 1970.
SRINIVAS, M. N., *India's Villages*. Bombay: Asia Publishing House, 1960.
STOCQUELLER, J. H., *The Hand Book of British India*. London: W. M. H. Allen & Co, 1854.
SWINSON, Arthur, *Mountbatten* War Leader Book No. 6. New York: Ballantine Books Inc. (c) 1971, Arthur Swinson.
SYMINGTON, J. M. D., *In a Bengal Jungle – Stories of Life on the Tea Gardens of Northern India*. Chapel Hill, N.C., 1935 chez Kegan Paul, London No. 1708.
TANDON, Prakash, *Punjabi Century – The Fascinating Story of a Virile People*. Delhi: Hind Pocket Books, 1961.
TENDULKAR, D. G., *Mahatma – Life of Mohandas Karamchand Gandhi* (In 8 volumes). New Delhi: The Publications Division Ministry of Information and Broadcasting Government of India, 1963. (Volume III, 1947–1948.)
TERRAINE, John, *The Life and Times of Lord Mountbatten*. London: Arrow Books, 1970.
TINKER, Hugh, *Experiment with Freedom – India and Pakistan 1947*. London: Oxford University Press, 1967.
TOURNAIRE, Hélène, *Poivre Vert – L'Inde aux Rayons X*. Paris: Raoul Solar, 1965.
TREVELYAN, Humphrey, *The India We Left*. London: Macmillan, 1972.

TROTTER, L. J., *The Life of Hodson of Hodson's Horse*. London: Sweepman's Library, 1912.

TUKER, François, *While Memory Serves*. London: Cassell & Co. Ltd, 1950.

VASTO, Lanza del, *Le Pèlerinage aux Sources*. Paris: Denoël, 1943.

VERNE, Jules, *La Maison à Vapeur – Voyage à Travers l'Inde Septentrionale*. Paris: Hachette, 1968.

WAINWRIGHT, Mary, and C. H. Philips, *The Partition of India*. London: George Allen & Unwin Ltd, 1970.

WOODRUFF, Philip, *The Men who Ruled India*. Vol. I: *The Founders*
Vol. II: *The Guardians*
London: Jonathan Cape, 1954.

YEATS-BROWN, F., *Les Trois Lanciers du Bengale*. Paris: Hachette, 1955.

YOUNG, Desmond, *All the Best Years*. New York: Harper & Brothers, 1961.

II OFFICIAL DOCUMENTS

ACTS OF PARLIAMENT

The Government of India Act
23 December 1919.
9 & 10 Geo. V, c. 101.

The Government of India Act
2 August 1935.
Geo. V. c. 2.

The Indian Independence Act
18 July 1947.
10 & 11 Geo. VI, c. 30.

INDIAN STATUTORY COMMISSION REPORT

(Vol. 1. Survey)
H.M.'s Stationery Office. 1930.

PARLIAMENTARY PAPERS

Cmd 6835 (1946).
India: Statement by the Cabinet Mission, 25 May 1946.

Cmd 6861 (1946).
India: Statement by the Cabinet Mission.

Cmd 6862 (1946).
India (Cabinet Mission): Papers relating to:
(a) the Sikhs,
(b) the Indian States,
(c) the European Community,
May–June 1946.

Cmd 7047 (1947) Indian Policy Statement
20 February 1947.

Cmd 7136 (1947) Indian Policy Statement
3 June 1947.

TIME ONLY TO LOOK FORWARD

Speeches of the Earl Mountbatten of Burma as Viceroy of India and Governor-General of the Dominion of India 1947–1948.
by Nicholas Kaye, London, 1949.

III NEWSPAPERS AND PERIODICALS

ENGLAND

The Round Table, London.
The Times, London.
Time Magazine, London.

FRANCE

Histoire pour Tous
No. 146–147 – Juin/Juillet 1972.
Extract: 'L'Inde Déchirée'
by Patrick Turnbull and Albert Vulliez.

Histoire pour Tous
No. 150 – Octobre 1972.
Extract: 'Lord Mountbatten en Birmanie'
by Albert Vulliez.
Boulogne Billancourt, Editions Rouff, 1972.

Le Monde, Paris.

INDIA

Harijan, Ahmedabad.
Illustrated Weekly of India, Bombay.
The Times of India, Bombay.
Dawn, New Delhi.
The Hindustan Times, New Delhi.
The Hindustan Times Weekly Review, New Delhi.
The Statesman, New Delhi.

PAKISTAN

Civil and Military Gazette, Lahore.
Pakistan Times, Karachi.

UNITED STATES
The New York Times, New York.

IV SPECIAL DOCUMENTS RELATING TO GANDHI'S MURDER AND THE TRIAL OF HIS ASSASSINS MADE AVAILABLE TO AUTHORS.

CRIME REPORTS
by J. D. Nagarvalla.

From 30/01/48 to 28/05/48.
Special Branch, CID, Bombay.

GANDHI'S ASSASSINATION AND I

by Gopal Godse.
Asmita Prakashan, Poona, 1967.
(Available only in Maharathi.)

REPORT OF INVESTIGATION MURDER

Sec. 302 IPC and Articles 4 & 5.
Explosive substances Act into the Conspiracy to Murder Mahatma Gandhi.
Dossier No. 663/A.
Office of the Deputy Commissioner of Police, Special Branch, CID, Bombay.

REPORT OF THE COMMISSION OF ENQUIRY INTO CONSPIRACY TO MURDER MAHATMA GANDHI

by J. L. Kapur, Judge of the Supreme Court of India. (6 volumes.)
Government of India Press, New Delhi, 1970.

Notes

CHAPTER 1 *'A Race Destined to Govern and Subdue'*

The material on Lord Mountbatten's interview with Clement Attlee is based largely on an interview with the last Viceroy and his own notes of their conversation made at the time. Certain material on the decision to appoint Lord Mountbatten was obtained in an interview with Lord Listowel, the last Secretary of State for India. Krishna Menon in an interview in New Delhi furnished the details of his conversation with Sir Stafford Cripps at which he revealed that Nehru and Congress would react favourably to Mountbatten's appointment.

The description of London in 1947 is from contemporary newspaper accounts plus the files written from the city at the time by Raymond Cartier of *Paris Match*.

The passage on the British experience in India, the life of the British in India and of ICS and army officers is based on numerous interviews: most important, those with a series of former ICS men – Lord Trevelyan, Sir George Abell, Christopher Beaumont, Sir Olaf Caroe, Sir Conrad Corfield, Sir Herbert Thompson, Rajeshwar Dayal, S. E. Abbott, Sir John Cotton. Written sources include: *The Last Years of British India; Britain in India; British Social Life in India; The Fall of the British Empire; Pax Britannica; A Handbook to the ICS Examinations, 1892; The Handbook of British India, 1854.*

CHAPTER 2 *'Walk Alone, Walk Alone'*

The passage on Gandhi's tour of Noakhali is based largely on interviews with Pyarelal Nayar, his private secretary, and his physician Sushila Nayar, Pyarelal's sister, both of whom were present. Material was also used from interviews with other members of his entourage including Gurcharan Singh, Brikshen Chandiwallah, Padmaja Naidu and K. Rangaswamy. No other source of written material is as useful as Nayar's 2000 page epic *Mahatma Gandhi, The Last Phase*. The contemporary newspaper accounts in the *Times of India, The Hindustan Times* and *The Statesman of India* were also employed.

Mr Anwar Ali, a lawyer in Lahore who has devoted considerable time to the study of Rahmat Ali, provided us with the original text of his Pakistan manifesto from which the quotations used on pages 27–28 were taken as well as a number of insights into the career of the man who originated the idea of Pakistan.

CHAPTER 3 *'Leave India to God'*

The account of Mountbatten's conversation with his cousin George VI is from an interview with Lord Mountbatten and his notes of their talk made at the time, plus a personal letter sent to him by the King. The portrait of the last Viceroy is based on interviews with Mountbatten himself, his daughters, Lady Brabourne and Lady Pamela Hicks, his valet, Charles Smith and a number of his staff and associates including Lt-Cmdr Peter Howes, Alan Campbell-Johnson, Admiral Ronald Brockman, Capt. Sir James Scott. Written material includes Swinson's *Mountbatten*, Terraine's *Life and Times of Lord Mountbatten*, and Lord Mountbatten's personal diary of his tour of India with the Prince of Wales in 1921.

The two passages on Gandhi in Noakhali are based on interviews and written material covering the same subject as set out in the notes in Chapter 2. The biographical passages are based on interviews with: the Nayars, Brikshen Chandiwallah, Gurcharan Singh, Acharya Kripalani, Jehangir Patel, Padmaja Naidu, Mme V. L. Pandit, Wali and Badshah Khan, the 'Frontier Gandhi', Krishna Menon and Raymond Cartier. Written material: Sheean, *Lead Kindly Light* and *Gandhi: A Great Life in Brief*; Coolidge, *Gandhi*; Ashe, *Gandhi: A Study in Revolution*; Payne, *Gandhi*; Nayar, *Gandhi: The Last Phase*; Fischer, *The Life of Mahatma Gandhi*; Gandhi, *An Autobiography or The Story of My Experiment with Truth*; Kripalani, *Gandhi, A Life*; Mojumdar, *Jinnah and Gandhi*.

The passage on the House of Commons' debate is from *Hansard* and contemporary newspaper accounts. The description of the Mountbatten's departure is based on interviews with Lord Mountbatten, Admiral Brockman, Lt-Cmdr Howes and Charles Smith.

CHAPTER 4 A Last Tattoo for a Dying Raj

The passage dealing with Gandhi's relationship with his great-niece Manu is based on interviews with Pyarelal and Sushilla Nayar and Nayar's book. Certain Gandhi quotations, notably those dealing with his dream in Bombay, are from his original editorials written for his paper the *Harijan* at the time.

The account of Mountbatten's interview with Lord Wavell is from an interview with Mountbatten and his notes made at the time from their conversation. Lady Mountbatten's profile is based largely on interviews with her husband, her two daughters and her three secretaries in India, Muriel Watson, Elizabeth Ward Collins and Jaya Thadani. The quotations and reflections referring to Lord Mountbatten's 1921 visit are from his private diary.

His arrival at Viceroy's House and his swearing-in as Viceroy as well as the account of the preparations for the ceremony are based on interviews with Charles Smith, Capt. Sir James Scott, Capt. F. J. Burnaby-Atkins, Lt-Cmdr Howes, Admiral Brockman and the Viceroy himself. Written sources included contemporary newspaper accounts, Capt. Scott's diary, Campbell-Johnson's *Mission with Mountbatten* and the original programme and instruction sheets for the ceremony furnished the authors by Elizabeth Collins. The descriptions of Viceroy's House come from the Viceregal Establishment lent to the authors by Lt-Cmdr Howes.

The account of Mountbatten's first reactions to his task is based on interviews with the last Viceroy and with Alan Campbell-Johnson, Lt-Cmdr Peter Howes, Admiral Brockman and Mr Peter Scott, a member of the Viceroy's ICS staff. His conversation with Sir George Abell is based on an interview with Abell corroborated by Lord Mountbatten.

CHAPTER 5 An Old Man and his Shattered dream

As described in the Acknowledgement section, Lord Mountbatten dictated a lengthy summary of each of his meetings with the Indian leaders as soon as they had left his study. The accounts of his talks with Patel, Jinnah, Nehru and Gandhi are based on those memoranda to which Lord Mountbatten was able constantly to turn during our interviews. The direct quotations employed are from them.

The portrait of Nehru is based on interviews with his daughter Prime Minister Indira Gandhi, his sister Mrs V. L. Pandit, Lord Mountbatten, his secretaries H. V. R. Iyenagar, M. O. Matthai, Tarlok Singh and M. A. Baig. Also helpful were Padmaja Naidu, Durga Das, Acharya Kripalani, Krishna Menon, Alan Campbell-Johnson, Jaya Thadani, and R. K. Nehru, his nephew. Written sources include: Das, *India from Curzon to Nehru and After*; R. K. Karangia, *The Mind of Mr Nehru*; Nehru, *An Autobiography* and *The Discovery of India*; Sahni, *The Lid Off*.

The portrait of Patel is based primarily on interviews with his daughter Maniben, and his secretary S. Shankar. Also helpful were Durga Das, C. H. Bhabha, Gen. J. N. Chaudhuri, Sir George Abell, Sir Conrad Corfield, Acharya Kripalani, Raymond Cartier.

The most important written sources are Das's *India – From Curzon to Nehru and After* and the annotated papers of Mr Patel by the same author.

The portrait of Mr Jinnah was based primarily on interviews with his daughter Dina Wadia, his nephew Akhbar Peerboy, his first naval ADC Vice-Admiral Syed Ahsan, his physician in Bombay Dr J. A. L. Patel, Col William Birnie, his first military secretary, who made available his detailed diary of his days with the Pakistani leader. Also helpful were Yousef Burch, Syed Pinzada, Anwar Ali, M. A. Baig, members of his staff or associates and, among his friends Durga Das, J. N. Sahri, J. M. Tayeebji and Padmaja Naidu, an intimate friend of his wife.

The account of his illness was furnished by his physician and daughter. The primary written source is Hector Bolitho's *Jinnah – The Creator of Pakistan*.

The account of the Governors' Conference is based on interviews with Lord Mountbatten who retains in his possession the minutes of the Conference. Among those attending who were interviewed were Sir Olaf Caroe, Sir Chandulal Trivedi and Sir George Abell. The description of Mountbatten's visit to Peshawar and the Punjab is based on interviews with Lord Mountbatten, Sir Olaf Caroe, Abdul Rashid, Deputy Superintendent of Police in Peshawar and Col. Mohammed Khan, an organizer of the demonstrations. Gandhi's debate with his colleagues is based on interviews with Pyarelal Nayar and Acharya Kripalani.

CHAPTER 6 A Precious Little Place

The descriptions of Simla are based on interviews with M. S. Oberoi, Mrs Penn Montague, Sir Chandulal Trivedi and a delightful 1895 Guidebook to the city, plus a visit to the site itself. The account of the Viceroy's 'hunch' is based on interviews with Lord Mountbatten, Alan Campbell-Johnson, the Earl of Listowel and Admiral Brockman. The account of Nehru's reaction was furnished by Krishna Menon who accompanied him. V. P. Menon's daughter, Mrs D. Misra, provided access to his personal papers which include a detailed account of the incident.

CHAPTER 7 Palaces and Tigers; Elephants and Jewels

The account of Sir Conrad Corfield's London visit was provided by interviews with the two key people involved, Corfield and the Earl of Listowel.

The description of the Maharajas, their lives and eccentricities are based on interviews with Corfield, his deputy Sir Herbert Thompson, the Raj Matas of Gwalior and Jaipur, the Maharajas of Patiala, Faridkot, Kapurtala, Bundi, Baroda, Dewas, the Nawab of Malerkotla. Also most helpful were Lady Ruthven, the widow of the Nizam of Hyderabad's legal adviser, Sir Walter Monckton, and Sir Walter's assistant John Peyton; Gen. Ali Yavar Jung of Bombay who was on the Nizam's staff; H.E. Karan Singh, a member of the Indian government and the son of the late Maharaja of Kashmir who does not choose to employ his title; and Robin Duff. Primary written sources are Lord's *The Maharajahs*; Forbes', *India of the Princes*; and de Golish's *Splendeur et Crépuscule des Maharajas.*

CHAPTER 8 A Day Cursed by the Stars

The account of Lord Mountbatten's visit to London, his meeting with the cabinet and with Sir Winston Churchill is based on interviews with Lord Mountbatten and his notes of those meetings dictated at the time, with Sir George Abell who was also in London and with the Earl of Listowel, the Secretary of State for India, who attended the first meeting.

The passage dealing with the destruction of the archives of the Maharajas' doings and the material they contained is based on interviews with Sir Conrad Corfield and his deputy Sir Herbert Thompson. Sir Conrad also allowed one of the authors to read an unpublished manuscript covering his experiences with India's princes, their doings and his own career.

The account of Mountbatten's meeting with the Indian leaders on 2 and 3 June is based on interviews with him and the actual minutes of the meetings from his archives from which all direct quotes are taken. The account of his conversations with Jinnah and Gandhi are based on interviews with Lord Mountbatten and his notes taken of them at the time. The quotation from Gandhi at his prayer meeting is from *Harijan*. The press conference was reconstructed from the transcript of the conference and interviews with Lord Mountbatten and Alan Campbell-Johnson. The account of the astrologer's reaction is from interviews with Lord Mountbatten, M. O. Matthai and Swamin Manaran who still retains his original charts and a copy of his letter to the Viceroy.

CHAPTER 9 The Most Complex Divorce in History

The description of the manner in which India's assets were divided is based principally on interviews with the two men responsible, H. M. Patel and Chaudry Mohammed Ali. A full set of the reports submitted to them, their recommendations and the minutes of their meeting were made available to the authors. The description of the division of the viceregal carriages comes from interviews with Lt-Cmdr Howes and General Yacoub Khan. The passage treating the breaking up of the Indian Army is based on interviews with General Roy Bucher, Col Mohammed Idriss, General Enaith Habibullah, General Karbaksh Singh, Capt. Samsher Singh, General J. N. Chaudhuri, General Frank Messervy, Field-Marshal Sam Manekshaw, General D. M. Misra, General J. T. Sataravala, Maj.-Gen. A. Dubey. An excellent recent history of the Indian Army is available in Mason's, *Matter of Honour*. Much interesting material on its tactics and campaigns is to be found in Elliott's, *The Frontier 1839–1947*.

The passage on Lord Radcliffe's summons, his meetings with the Lord Chancellor and Clement Attlee is based on his own recollections as recorded in an interview, plus certain correspondence relative to his appointment exchanged between London and Viceroy's House. The account of his first meeting with Lord Mountbatten is taken from interviews with the two men. The description of Mountbatten's approach to the problem of the princes comes from interviews with Lord Mountbatten, Sir Conrad Corfield, Patel's daughter and secretary and the private papers of V. P. Menon.

Lord Mountbatten's nomination to the post of Governor-General of an independent India and the thought which preceded it – that he become a joint Governor-General of the two new dominions is treated in great length in Moon's *Divide and Quit* and Campbell-Johnson's *Mission with Mountbatten*. The account here is based on interviews with Lord Mountbatten and the records of his many discussions of it with his staff and the Indian leadership.

In describing the pre-partition troubles in the Punjab, interviews with four former officers of the Punjab police, Gerald Savage, Rule Dean, W. H. Rich and Patrick Farmer were employed. A copy of the Punjab CID's weekly summaries of events in the province was also made available to the authors. The account of Gandhi's first contact with the refugees is is from Pyarelal Nayar.

CHAPTER 10 'We Will Always Remain Brothers'

The account of the Royal Assent is based on contemporary newspaper reports. Mountbatten's final address to the Chamber of Princes, their farewell dinner and the reluctance of some of the princes to adhere to one of the new dominions is based on interviews with Lord Mountbatten and his records of the process, the private papers of V. P. Menon who was the Indian official most closely concerned, and interviews with the Raj Matas of Gwalior and Jaipur; the Maharajas of Patiala, Karpurthala and Malerkotla; Sir Conrad Corfield; Lady Monckton; Sir Herbert Thompson and John Peyton. The description of Lord Mountbatten's visit to Kashmir is based on interviews with him, his memoranda of conversations dictated at the time, the minutes of his discussions with his staff on his trip and his report on his talk to the Attlee government. The account of the attempt to assassinate Jinnah was furnished by G. R. Savage, who brought the information to Delhi, Lord Mountbatten, and certain documents which the last Viceroy found in his archives relative to the plot.

The account of Mountbatten's request to Gandhi to go to Calcutta is based on interviews with Mountbatten and his record of their conversation as well as interviews with Pyarelal Nayar, Brikshen Chandiwallah and K. Rangaswamy.

Jinnah's departure for Karachi and his flight was reconstructed from interviews with his ADCs Admiral Ahsen, Wing Commander Ata Rabani and Col William Birnie. Lord Mountbatten's decision to hold back Lord Radcliffe's award until after independence was discussed with Lord Mountbatten, Lord Radcliffe and Sir George Abell. The quotations are from the Viceroy's last report to London. The earlier passage on how Lord Radcliffe worked is based on interviews with Lord Radcliffe and his ICS aide, H. C. Beaumont.

The account of the farewell dinner at the Delhi Gymkhana Club is based on interviews with a number of those present.

CHAPTER 11 While the World Slept

The account of Gandhi's mission to Calcutta is based on interviews with Pyarelal Nayar, R. N. Bannerjee and Ram Goburbhun. Written sources include *The Last Phase*, *Harijan* and other contemporary newspaper accounts. The account of Mountbatten's ride through the streets of Karachi with Jinnah is based largely on an interview with the last Viceroy. Written sources include *Mission with Mountbatten* and contemporary newspaper accounts.

The description of Independence night at the Khyber Pass, Lahore, New Delhi, Bombay, etc., comes from a great variety of sources. They include interviews with Lord Mountbatten, Alan Campbell-Johnson, Generals

Yacoub Khan, Messervy, Lockhart, Bucher and Chauduri, Col Birnie, Brig. Mohammed Idriss, R. E. W. Atkins, Anwar Ali, Khwaja Mohiuddin, Mrs Sucheta Kripalani who sang the Indian national anthem for the Constituent Assembly, H. V. R. Iengar, Mrs V. L. Pandit, General and Mrs D. Misra, Dr Sushila Nayar, Col Mohammed Sharif Khan, Rule Dean, W. H. Rich. Among the written sources employed were the official programmes for the celebrations, contemporary newspaper accounts, special reports on the celebrations prepared by Lord and Lady Mountbatten, numerous letters and diaries made available to the authors. The story of Nehru's telephone call was recounted by Padmaja Naidu, his dinner guest that evening. The passage on the visit of the leaders to Mountbatten is based on his own recollections of the moment.

CHAPTER 12 'Oh Lovely Dawn of Freedom'

The descriptive passage on Benares and the village of Chatharpur are based on interviews and research in the two locations. The descriptions of the independence celebrations in Delhi as well as elsewhere in India on 15 August are based on interviews with Lord Allendale, Elizabeth Collins, Commodore Rusi Gandhi, Lt-Col Sir Martin Gilliat, Lt-Commander Howes, Gen. Lockart, Capt. Scott, Duggal Singh, Indira Gandhi, Lord Mountbatten, Ram Goburbhun, Kushwant Singh, Gen. Shadid Hamid, Gen. Habibullah, Padmaja Naidu, Ahmed Zahur. Written sources include the Viceroy's final report to London, the diary of Capt. Scott, letters written at the time by Elizabeth Collins, contemporary newspaper accounts and the official programmes. The account of Pamela Mountbatten's experiences is based on interviews with her and her Oral History Transcript of the incident on deposit at the Jawaharlal Nehru Library in New Delhi.

The story of the trains arriving in Amritsar was recounted by the station master Chani Singh. The description of the raising of the RSSS flag in Poona is based on the account of the ceremony in the *Hindu Rashtra* of the time and an interview with the brother of Nathuram Godse, Gopal Godse. Lord Listowel described his visit to Balmoral without the missing seals. Sir George Abell provided the account of the visit to Clement Attlee The meeting at which Lord Mountbatten presented the Radcliffe award to the Indian leaders was recreated from interviews with Lord Mountbatten and the minutes of the meeting itself. The description of Radcliffe's departure is based on interviews with Lord Radcliffe and H. C. Beaumont.

CHAPTER 13 'Our People Have Gone Mad'

CHAPTER 14 The Greatest Migration in History

The passages in these two chapters describing the intercommunal killing in the Punjab, the flight of the refugees, the train massacres, the rape and abduction of women from both communities are based primarily on particular experiences selected from those recounted by over 400 refugees from both sides interviewed in the course of the research for this book.

Wherever possible the personal experiences selected for use were those which could be authenticated or corroborated by a second source. In addition to those refugees whose names are employed in the body of the text, interviews with a number of other people were employed in constructing those passages in Chapters 13 and 14. They include Sir Chandulal Trivedi, the Governor of the Indian half of the province; Maj.-Gen. M. S. Chopra, who supervised the military escort for the refugees bound for Pakistan from the Indian side of the border; General Raza, Shahid Hamid and Akhbar Khan of Pakistan; Lt-Col Nawab Sir Malik Khazar Khan Tiwana, who also furnished a number of unpublished studies on the origins of the violence; Mr G. D. Harrington Howes; Col A. D. Iliff; R. E. W. Atkins and Edward Behr. The written sources employed included the following: contemporary newspaper accounts, G. D. Khosla's *Stern Reckoning*, the most detailed Indian study of the upheavals; the minutes and records of the Emergency Committee; a detailed report on the refugee problem prepared for the St John Ambulance Brigade by Lady Mountbatten; D. F. Karala's *Freedom Must Not Stink*; Moon's, *Divide and Quit*; Campbell-Johnson's *Mission With Mountbatten*; Hodson's *The Great Divide*; Kuldip Nayar's *Distant Neighbours*. Also available is an excellent novel of the period, Kushwant Singh's *Last Train to Pakistan*.

The account of Gandhi's Miracle in Calcutta is based on interviews with Pyarelal Nayar and his *The Last Phase*, Brikshen Chandiwallah, Nirmal Kumar Bose, Ram Goburbhun and contemporary newspaper accounts. The description of the tour of the Punjab by Nehru and Liaquat Ali Khan is based on interviews with two of the men who accompanied them, H. V. R. Iyenagar and Maj.-Gen. Dubey. The passage relating to Mountbatten's summons to Delhi from Simla is based, first, on interviews with Lord Mountbatten and a confidential memorandum he prepared at the time, and, second, papers of V. P. Menon and interviews with his daughter and with H. V. R. Iyenagar who was with him when the government's senior civil servants realized India was close to collapse.

The account of the Emergency Committee's initial session and its function is based on its minutes, Campbell-Johnson's *Mission With Mountbatten* and interviews with Lord Mountbatten, C. H. Bhabha and H. V. R. Iyenagar.

The account of the flight of Madanlal Pahwa and his subsequent encounters with Dr Parchure and Vishnu Karkare is based on interviews with the three men. The story of Boota Singh and his daughter related in this chapter and the epilogue is based on interviews with Rabia Sultan Qari who became the foster mother of his daughter and Lahore newspaper accounts published at his trial and death.

CHAPTER 15 'Kashmir – Only Kashmir!'

The account of the lights fading during the Maharaja's Diwali celebration is based on an interview with Dr Karan Singh, his son, and Mrs Florence Lodge, a British resident of Srinagar. Jinnah's efforts to spend a vacation in Kashmir were noted at the time by Col Birnie in his diary. The account of how the Pakistan government came to plan its tribal invasion of Kashmir was furnished by Gen. Akhbar Khan, now Pakistan's ambassador to Prague, who was involved in the planning from the outset. The account of the invasion itself and the physical preparations for it were furnished by Sairab Khayat Khan and Col Mohammed Sharif Khan who became physically involved at a later stage. The description of the telephone exchanges between the British officers commanding the two nations' armies was provided by Generals Messervy, Lockhart and Bucher. The Maharaja's flight was described by his son Dr Karan Singh. The account of reactions in Delhi and V. P. Menon's flight to secure the Maharaja's accession is based on interviews with Lord Mountbatten, Field-Marshal Sam Manekshaw, Sheikh Abdullah, Sir Alexander Symons, Mrs D. Misra, V. P. Menon's daughter, V. P. Menon's personal papers seen by the authors in Bangalore in 1973 and the minutes of the India Defence Committee which decided to intervene after the Maharaja's accession. Two interesting accounts of the origins of the conflict have been written by the men responsible for the military operations on each side, *Slender was the Thread* by India's General L. P. Sen and *Raiders In Kashmir* by General Akhbar Khan. General Harbaksh Singh also provided an excellent and detailed account of the early military operations around Srinagar.

CHAPTER 16 Two Brahmins from Poona

A more extensive account of the source material on Gandhi's assassins will be found in the notes for Chapter 17. The description here of the opening of the *Hindu Rashtra* is from interviews with Gopal Godse and Vishnu Karkare and the paper's own account of the event. The police watch was revealed by the Kapur Commission.

The account of Gandhi's actions in Panipat is based on interviews with Pyarelal Nayar, witnesses in the city, and *The Last Phase*. The passage on Jinnah's physical decline and his concerns in the autumn of 1947 is based on interviews with his former ADC Admiral Ahsen and his Military Secretary Col Birnie as well as the latter's diary. The descriptions of Lord Mountbatten's conversations with Gandhi which closes the chapter is based on an interview with him and his own records of it.

CHAPTER 17 'Let Gandhi Die!'

The account of Gandhi's last fast is based first of all on two long interviews with his physician Dr Sushila Nayar and her notes made at the time. Also particularly helpful were Gandhi's secretary Pyarelal Nayar, his close associate Brikshen Chandiwallah, and Gurcharan Singh who served on his Delhi staff. Others interviewed for the passage included D. W. Mehra, Padmaja Naidu, Lord Mountbatten, and G. N. Sinha. Written sources include contemporary Indian newspaper accounts, particularly *Harijan*, Gandhi's own paper and three books by his associates, Nayar's

The Last Phase, Chandiwallah's *At the Feet of Bapu*, Manu's *Last Glimpses of Bapu.*

CHAPTER 18 The Vengeance of Madanlal Pahwa
CHAPTER 19 'We Must Get Gandhi Before the Police Get Us'
CHAPTER 20 The Second Crucifixion

Two of Gandhi's assassins, Nathuram Godse and Narayan Apte, were hanged after their conviction in 1949. The other members of the conspiracy -Gopal Godse, Vishnu Karkare, Madanlal Pahwa, Digamber Badge and Dattraya Parchure – were all alive when research on this book began, the first three having served out their jail sentences. All were located and extensively interviewed. In addition, the authors brought Godse and Karkare back to Delhi for the first time since their trial. We returned with them to all of the places which they had visited while they were in the city on their two assassination attempts. The Retiring Room of the railway station, the Birla Temple, the woods where they held their target practice and finally the grounds of Birla House itself where they re-enacted their murder. They also took the authors to a number of Godse and Apte's associates in Poona, the headquarters of their paper and the other places they frequented. Gopal Godse also made available a biography he has prepared in Maharatti of his brother.

Two of the police officers involved in the investigation of the conspiracy to murder Gandhi, James Nagarvalla and D. W. Mehra, were also interviewed extensively. Nagarvalla made available the Bombay Police Diary and his own case file. An officer who chose to remain anonymous offered the authors similar material on the Delhi investigation. The directors of the Nehru Library in New Delhi kindly made available the full transcript of the trial proceedings which were restricted at the time because of N. Godse's highly emotional statement in his own defence. These constitute the sources on which the material relevant to the assassins and the police investigations in these chapters is based.

The account of Gandhi's plan to visit Pakistan is based on interviews with Jehangir Patel, Sushila and Pyarelal Nayar. His last days were described by those three as well as by Gurucharan Singh, Maniben Patel who was with her father during his last talk with Gandhi, and Abdul Gani. Written sources include *The Last Phase*, *At the Feet of Bapu* and *Last Glimpses of Bapu.*

The description of his funeral and the arrangements for it are based on interviews with Lord Mountbatten, Pyarelal Nayar, Alan Campbell-Johnson, General Sir Roy Bucher, General J. N. Chaudhuri, Elizabeth Collins, Field-Marshal Sam Manekshaw and numerous others. In addition to contemporary newspaper accounts, written sources include *The Last Phase* and *Mission with Mountbatten.*

The account of the immersion of his ashes at Allahabad is based on an interview with Padmaja Naidu. Another view of it is available in Sheean's *Lead Kindly Light.*

Index

Reminiscences of the Nehru Age 2/e *M O Mathai* Rs 12.00
A Tale Told by an Idiot *R P Noronha* Rs 9.50
Where My Caravan Has Rested *P L Bhandari* Rs 6.50
With Two Presidents 6/e *C L Datta* Rs 5.50